The Gardener's
Complete
Q&A

The Gardener's Complete

Q&A

The Editors of Storey Books

STOREY BOOKS
Schoolhouse Road
Pownal, Vermont 05261

*The mission of Storey Communications is to serve our customers
by publishing practical information that encourages personal independence
in harmony with the environment.*

———————— • ————————

Edited by **Gwen W. Steege**
Cover design by **Greg Imhoff**
Front cover photographs by **(clockwise from upper left): Madelaine Gray, A. Blake
    Gardner, Madelaine Gray, Positive Images (Jerry Howard)**
Back cover photography by **Cynthia N. McFarland**
Text design and production by **Andrea Gray**
Production assistance by **Michelle Arabia**
Chapter opening photographs: 1, A. Blake Gardner; 2, 20, 26, Positive Images (Jerry
    Howard); 3, 4, 6, Positive Images (Gary Mottau); 5, 13, 15, 16, 18, 19, 23, Maggie
    Oster; 7, 8, 9, 10, 25, 27, Ann Reilly; 11, 12, 17, Madelaine Gray; 14, Positive Images
    (Margaret Hensel); 21, Henry W. Art; 22, Ron West; 24, Positive Images (Tad Goodale)
Illustrations: Parts I & II, Alison Kolesar and Wanda Harper; Part III, Judy Eliason;
    Parts IV, VI, and VII, Alison Kolesar; Part V, Brigita Fuhrmann; insect drawings
    throughout, Judy Eliason

The material in this book was created by the Editors of Storey Books in five individual
volumes, as part of the *1001 Gardening Questions Answered* Series:
Lawns and Landscaping, © 1989 by Doubleday Book & Music Clubs, Inc.
Annuals, © 1989 by Doubleday Book & Music Clubs, Inc.
Perennials, © 1989 by Doubleday Book & Music Clubs, Inc.
Herbs, © 1990 by Doubleday Book & Music Clubs, Inc.
Fruits and Vegetables, © 1990 by Doubleday Book & Music Clubs, Inc.

The information in this book is true and complete to the best of our knowledge. All recommendations
are made without guarantee on the part of Storey Communications, Inc. The publisher disclaims any
liability in connection with the use of this information. For additional information, please contact
Storey Books, Schoolhouse Road, Pownal, Vermont 05261.

Storey Books are available for special premium and promotional uses and for customized editions.
For further information, please call the Custom Publishing Department at 1-800-793-9396.

Printed in the United States by R.R. Donnelley
10 9 8 7 6 5 4 3 2 1

Library of Congress Cataloging-in-Publication Data

The Gardener's Complete Q & A / The Editors of Storey Books
    p.   cm.
    "A Storey Book"
    Includes bibliographical references (p.   ) and index.
    ISBN 1-58017-0897
    1. Gardening — Miscellaneous. I. Title: Gardener's Complete Q & A.
    SB453.G276   1998
    635—dc20
                                                                    98-44673
                                                                        CIP

Contents

Unfortunately, most of us are not blessed with the proverbial green thumbs that automatically do everything right in the garden. Instead, we must make do with plenty of dirt under our fingernails and collect all the gardening information we can find.

As beginners we all need basic facts about plants, soil, light, and watering, and even after years of kneeling in the soil, our search for answers never ends. Each season brings new plants we want to try and the desire to propagate a few more of our favorites. We're frequently faced with unfamiliar weeds, bugs, diseases, and unusual weather. Sometimes we need to create a garden in a new location or remake an old one.

Experimentation and trial-and-error can be among the joys of gardening, but many a time we've longed to have an experienced gardener working in the yard next door who could quickly supply satisfactory answers to our questions. How should we prune our overgrown lilacs? What are the best carrots to grow? How deep should we plant the iris? When's the best time to water? How can we cope with powdery mildew?

Lacking professional advice next-door, the best friend a gardener could have is *The Gardener's Complete Q & A*. It supplies clear, concise answers to questions nearly all of us have about plants and all aspects of growing them. Whether you want to raise herbs, vegetables, annuals, perennials, berries, tree fruits, or install a landscape, construct a new lawn, or redo the old one — or perhaps all of the above — you'll find a wealth of information.

Thanks to this book's well-organized layout and easy-to-follow tips, you won't need to waste hours searching through many different encyclopedias and garden books for solutions to your growing problems. But you'll find it isn't just a collection of questions and answers. It provides inspiration and practical ideas on everything from developing a beautiful setting for your home to supplying goodies for the larder. You won't want to relegate this volume to the top shelf of your garden library, but instead keep it handy for frequent reference.

Be warned, however, that as soon as your grounds begin to display the results of your knowledge, people will believe you were born with a "green thumb," and you will become the expert your neighbors call when they need answers to their horticultural questions.

Lewis and Nancy Hill

PART I
LAWNS

1 Creating a New Lawn or Rebuilding an Old One

For all those who are fortunate enough to have some open space around the place where they live, a lawn, no matter how modest, can be a source of pleasure and pride. It can also be a challenge, evoking a thousand and one questions related to its creation and maintenance. In the pages that follow, you will find the answers to many of those questions, so that you can approach your lawnkeeping tasks with a new understanding of grass's growing habits and needs. The ideal—a healthy, lush carpet of green—is within the reach of anyone who wishes it, and with less difficulty than you might think.

Today, a "good" lawn consists of an overcrowded population of dwarf grass plants—often a thousand or more shoots to the square foot—all so very much alike as to create an unblemished surface, a carpetlike lawn. This provides a superlative backdrop for home landscaping, whether the emphasis is on flower gardens or the form and texture effects created by trees, shrubs, and the varied grasses themselves. We expect this dense, perpetually defoliated carpet to be constantly solid underfoot, so that pets and people walking over it are well out of the mud in all seasons. It must look good even when given inexpert attention, refresh the air, cool the environs in summer, insulate the ground in winter, prevent soil erosion, sometimes even serve as a playfield and a picnic ground. The grass family alone provides the qualities that meet all these requirements.

There are several approaches to acquiring this kind of lush carpet in your front and backyards, and what approach you take depends on what you have to start with, how much you are interested in doing yourself, and the amount you are willing to

◀ *A carpetlike lawn provides a superlative backdrop for home landscaping.*

3

spend to achieve the desired results. If you have just built a new home, creating a lawn from the raw earth is a big undertaking, requiring rototilling and grading to do the job right. You may decide to hire someone else to do these chores if your area is large. For small lawns, you can do the tilling yourself with a rented or purchased rotary tiller and the grading with a steel garden rake, or better still a landscaping rake. In the pages that follow you will find step-by-step instructions on how to proceed, so that even if you decide to contract out some or all of the work, you will find here valuable information on how to give your lawn a good healthy beginning, thus saving disappointment and added work in years to come.

Those who have established lawns with bare spots, weeds, drainage problems, or the host of other difficulties that plague lawnkeepers, will find suggestions on how to correct and avoid these flaws, and even information on how to rebuild the lawn completely—again a big project requiring a commitment of time and energy.

Whether your tasks are major or minor, they are doable, and the results will make you glad you made the effort. Let's begin with creating an entirely new lawn.

PREPARING THE SITE

The first and most urgent consideration when developing a lawn is to improve the soil *before* spreading the seed. There are many kinds of lawn grasses (see pages 14-15), and most are widely adaptable. They will grow in soils having a range of nutrient content (*fertility*; see pages 32-36), with wide pH dif-

Ringer Corporation

The ideal lawn consists of an over-crowded population of dwarf grass plants. This unblemished surface is constantly solid underfoot, cools and freshens the air in summer, insulates in winter, and prevents soil erosion. Here, the lawn is Kentucky bluegrass.

THE EVOLUTION OF LAWNS

Centuries ago, lawns were "mowed" by the livestock that, for their safety, grazed near their owner's homes. The advantages of having lawns were so obvious that by the Middle Ages wide swards were kept within bounds by scything.

The first mechanical lawn mower was invented in 1830 in England. About a century later, gasoline-propelled mowers were common, and soon these conveniences had changed the face of· American towns. While in years past, well-tended lawns, blemished by neither dandelion nor crabgrass, were seen only around the mansions of the rich, by World War II carefully tended lawns—lawns that were fed, weeded, mowed, and watered— became the rule. The days of merely trimming whatever vegetation volunteered were over, even for those of more modest means. Ultimately, small tractors with grass-clipping blades spinning beneath rolled onto the scene, providing country towns and suburbs alike with acres of carpetlike lawns.

ferences (*acidity*; see page 36-38), and varying from clayey to sandy (*texture;* see page 8). You will have a healthier, more carefree lawn, however, if the soil's fertility, acidity, and texture are optimal. The ideal soil for a healthy lawn is three to five inches of good *loam* (soil that is neither very sandy nor very clayey), rich in organic matter. Once a lawn is established, fertilizers and other soil treatments can be applied only at ground surface rather than around the grasses' roots where they are most beneficial. The extra efforts you make to be certain your soil is of top quality before you grade, roll, and seed your new lawn, therefore, will pay gratifying dividends in years ahead.

When should I sow my new lawn?

It depends entirely on where you live. Here are a few general rules to guide you, but you might want to check with your Extension Service agent for the best advice for your particular area. In the South, the grasses that grow most rapidly in the heat are best started in the spring, whether you decide to use grass seed or to put down sod. In the central area of the country, from Philadelphia and Washington, D.C., west to the Plains, fall seeding is recommended. In the more northern areas, seeding is possible in both spring and fall, though fall is recommended, because the cool nights and fall rains encourage grass growth and make frequent watering less necessary. Also, early frosts tend to kill weeds before they can go to seed and spread through the lawn. In the Western Plains, seeding should be done in the spring to take advantage of the period of greatest rainfall during the summer months.

What time of year is best for starting a lawn in southern California?

A lawn may be started at any time, but the best time is in the early fall—September or October. The plants will be well established before winter's heavy rains, and a good turf should be underway before summer's heat.

I'm planning to start a lawn. Any hints before I sow the grass seed?

Grade the soil so any water will drain away from the house. Don't leave any low spots that will turn into puddles after every rain. You can check for low spots by running a taut string between two stakes so that the string just touches the ground. You will be able to see immediately any areas that fall below the level of the string. Also, rake the finished soil surface so that it is one or two inches below the level of walks and driveways; this will save you hours of edging in future summers and look far neater.

A string stretched taut between two stakes reveals low areas in the seedbed that will cause puddling in the lawn if not corrected.

How much grade must be given a new lawn, and how is the grade determined?

A grade of one foot in twenty, or even thirty, feet is sufficient to give surface drainage. The grade can be established by using a line level, but in most cases simple sighting can assure you that the slope will provide adequate drainage away from the house. When you water the area, note runoff and any areas of ponding.

How would you grade the front lawn of a small house that is several feet below the highway level?

A gradual slope from the house up to the street is more pleasing than an abrupt terrace. To prevent water from draining into the house, however, the grade should first be carried down

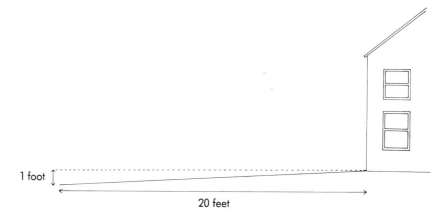

In order to prevent drainage problems, maintain a grade away from the house of 1 foot for every 20 feet.

1 foot

20 feet

STEPS IN PREPARING THE SITE FOR A NEW LAWN

- Remove all building debris and large stones from the site. Bottles, cans, bricks, and wood waste will obstruct roots, impede water movement, and sometimes cause disease. Mushrooms, not welcome in lawns, are the fruiting bodies of fungi living on rotting wood in the soil.

If you decide to add topsoil, first grade the area, to make certain drainage will be carried away from the house and to avoid small hills and valleys in the lawn that are both unsightly and a source of puddling. Use a steel garden rake or arrange for mechanical equipment if the work entails moving a lot of soil. Steep slopes should be terraced rather than graded; although grasses will grow on steep slopes, mowing will be a headache. If you plan to use a riding mower, it is particularly important to determine the slope that the mower will navigate safely. Remember, you are actually creating a subgrade on which you will be adding topsoil; keep the top of this subgrade four to eight inches below the desired finished lawn level.

This area is being graded prior to addition of topsoil, which will be trucked in. Dotted line shows finished lawn level, 4 to 6 inches above subgrade.

the subsoil using a rotary power tiller, if necessary. Chopped hay, leaves, rotted sawdust, rotted manure, compost, and peat are all effective for this purpose. A one- to three-inch-deep layer is acceptable and more is helpful. Add 50 to 100 pounds of lime and 10 to 15 pounds of superphosphate per 1,000 square feet. Mix all of this into the subsoil with a tiller or by hand.

- Add a layer of topsoil, three to five inches in depth. Figure on twelve cubic yards per 1,000 square feet of lawn. Ideally, this topsoil should be tested, using a soil-testing kit available from garden centers or by sending soil samples to your Extension Service. Chemical fertilizers should then be added and tilled in if needed.

Positive Images, Jerry Howard

After watering or heavy rains, puddled areas quickly indicate trouble spots where grading must be improved.

- Maintain the existing grade around trees. Lowering the grade may damage tree roots; raising it will change the amount of oxygen available to them from the soil. Many trees will tolerate up to eight inches of additional soil, or fill; some, such as oaks, are threatened by two or three additional inches. To avoid this threat, build a rockwell, extending out three or more feet all around the tree.
- Before adding the topsoil, mix organic matter into

When grading results in a ground level too high for existing trees, construct a retaining wall (called a rockwell) at least 3 feet from the tree trunk, so that roots maintain their original level and thus receive adequate air and moisture.

from the house slightly, to a low point from which the water can drain off to the sides before the slope up to the street begins.

Our backyard has no flat areas to use for a patio or play area. Could I terrace it?

Terracing can be very effective in such a situation. If the area is large, you may need to hire someone to do the work of pushing the earth into two or more flat levels that will be held in place by retaining walls of such materials as stone or railroad ties.

If there is much unevenness in the ground, should it be dug or plowed before being graded?

The soil, of course, will have to be loosened to move it. Although it is a lot of work, the practical thing to do is to remove all the topsoil, loosen and enrich the often more compacted and less fertile subsoil, grade the area and then finish the grade with the topsoil. This ensures an even depth of good soil over the entire area.

I know that the type of soil is important when starting a lawn, but how can I determine what kind of soil I have? Mine looks like a mixture of clay and sand—with some gravel.

Put a cup of your soil into a quart jar. Add a cup of water. Screw on the top and swirl the mixture. Let it settle, and repeat this procedure several times. Now allow the mixture to stand until the water is clear. The various-sized particles will settle out in layers with the clay on top and the larger ones—sand—below it. If the top layer is deepest, you have clay soil; if the bottom one is deepest, you have sandy soil. If the various layers are fairly equal, consider yourself lucky because you have a balanced soil.

Soils are generally broken down into three groups—*sandy soils*, *loamy soils*, and *clayey soils*.

Sandy soils range from very fine sands, with 50 percent or more of very fine sands, to coarse sands containing 35 percent or more of fine gravel and less than 50 percent finer sands. Any of these soils will form into a ball when moist, but the ball will break easily when touched.

Loamy soils have about a 50-50 mixture of sand and silt-clay. A ball of damp, loamy soil will not break when handled.

Clayey soils range from those containing 30-percent clay to those that are nearly 100-percent clay. Clay is fine-textured and sticky when wet.

The varieties of grass seed you can grow successfully and the type and amount of lawn care you must do are determined in part by the kind of soil you have.

Can thin soils and stony ground be used to start a new lawn?

These are trouble areas. If there is sufficient soil to support grass roots and the drainage is adequate, a stony soil can be

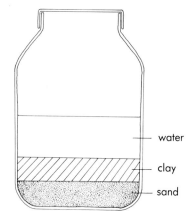

water

clay

sand

To determine what type soil you have, place 1 cup of soil in a quart jar with 1 cup of water. Shake and allow the mixture to settle several times and then note the relative size of sand and clay layers. The soil illustrated is a fairly balanced one, with clay and sand layers about equal.

made into a good lawn. Even so, any obtrusive stones that materially interfere either with the level of the land or the use of a mower should be removed. Rocky outcrops are very difficult, for they tend to hold moisture in rainy periods and to dry out quickly during dry weather. You have two choices in such instances. One is to bring in enough good soil to provide at least four inches of rooting area over the poor base. The other is to forget about a lawn and treat the area as a semirock garden with appropriate plantings (see pages 135-37).

The area where we hope to create a lawn is heavy clay. One of my neighbors tells me to add lots of sand to improve it; another one tells me to add organic matter. Which one is right?

Sand alone will not do too much to improve the soil; in fact, it may even "set up" in the clay as it does in concrete. You can add some sand, but concentrate instead on incorporating as much organic material as you can. Loosen the compacted soil at least two or three inches deep by tilling and then add six or more inches of organic material, such as compost, rotted manure, or peat moss, to help lighten the heavy soil. You can then work in it earlier in the spring. Organic material also permits better aeration around the roots and adds nutrients to the soil. Sand does none of these. Ideally, you would make this a continuing project, adding more organic material each year, but because you are seeding the area for a lawn, you must make your addition to the clay a heavy one: You will not be able to till lawn areas up regularly to work on soil texture improvement. In the worst cases, you may decide to remove some of the clay and replace it with good topsoil.

Heavy soils are not completely bad. They have the advantage of holding moisture and soil nutrients relatively well.

Why shouldn't clay be worked when wet?

Clay compacts easily, especially when wet. It then puddles and hardens, making it practically useless for at least one growing season. Clay is made up of the tiniest particles—1,000 or more of them together are the size of a single particle of sand. When damp, a handful of clay will form a very slick, pliable ball. As it dries, it becomes hard, with a baked appearance. For instance, air circulating around the surfaces of the fist-sized chunks kicked up by a tiller causes them to dry and harden quickly, leaving a garden in which it is impossible to get seeds to germinate and grow. Clay, the last of the soil to dry in the spring, should not, therefore, be worked when it is wet. If you have a clay soil, learn to judge when the soil can be worked: It is impossible when puddles can be seen. After the water slowly penetrates the soil, step on it, then look at the footprint. If it is shiny, wait before tilling. The only long-term solution for the inconvenience of having to wait to work this soil at the proper time is to add organic matter to it, year after year. This will separate that mass of tiny particles and provide space in the soil so both air and moisture can move through it.

My tract of land has a heavy, tough, red clay base, with only a light topsoil covering. What is the best treatment?

In the spring, grow a cover crop of soybeans and till them in before the beans are ripe. Follow with a crop of rye, leave it in place over the winter, and till it under the next spring.

What about planting a lawn on sandy soil?

Sandy soils have the advantage of not compacting easily and needing little cultivation. On the other hand, they do not hold moisture or fertilizer nutrients well. To offset this problem, mix in at least an inch of organic material, such as peat moss or weed-free compost (see page 111) when preparing the soil for planting. Even without special modifications, a sandy soil can be made to support grass if fertilized and watered lightly and frequently.

We are ready to build a new house on a lot and wonder if we should plan our lawn now?

You can plan it, but wait until the house is built before actually planting a lawn. The most important thing to do initially is to plan the lawn's location. Before your cellar hole is dug, have the contractor scrape away all of the topsoil where both the house and the lawn will be, and set it aside. The cellar hole earth can then be spread over the entire site and the topsoil distributed on top, saving you the expense of buying and trucking in topsoil for the lawn. Alternatively, you may prefer simply to have the cellar hole subsoil hauled away.

Is bringing in topsoil advisable when starting a new lawn?

This depends on how adequate your soil is. If the soil is very thin, topsoil may be needed. But in many instances, the residual soil can be improved sufficiently to make a good seedbed for much less than additional topsoil would cost. Moreover, topsoil is often of poor quality, not necessarily fertile, and almost invariably full of weed seeds.

If, in starting a lawn, I truck in topsoil, should I add fertilizer to it?

There is no way to know whether, or how much, to fertilize without having the soil tested (see pages 32-40). Usually, however, people want to spread the topsoil and seed it immediately. If you must do this, it's good to add ground limestone (unless you live in an area where you know soils are generally alkaline) and a complete garden fertilizer to the soil. Using a fertilizer spreader, broadcast fifty pounds of ground limestone per 1,000 square feet, using dolomitic limestone with magnesium, if it is available at your garden center. Fertilize sandy topsoils with thirty pounds of 5-10-10 or fifteen pounds of 10-20-20. Clays and loams require thirty pounds of 5-10-5 or fifteen pounds of 10-20-10. Don't use so-called special lawn fertilizers before seeding a lawn. They do not add enough phosphorus or potassium for establishment.

If you prefer using organic materials, apply limestone as above and substitute fifty pounds of rock phosphate plus 500 pounds of rotted cow manure for the commercial fertilizer.

Work both commercial and organic fertilizers into the soil with a rake or, better, by tilling.

I expect to purchase topsoil for my lawn site. How will it be dumped on my lot?

You control this. Most drivers will run the soil off the truck so that it is spread roughly where it should be. Others will spot loads where the soil is needed. Then you can complete the spreading. For this, use a steel garden rake or a landscaping rake, which is three or four feet in width, with large teeth to catch the soil. This rake simplifies the task and makes getting a good grade much easier. To prevent unnecessary compaction of the soil, do not allow trucks to drive over the ground any more than absolutely necessary.

I'm planning to improve the sandy soil around my house by adding a lot of topsoil. How much should I add?

To get the most value out of added topsoil, first work as much organic matter as you can into the soil already on the site. This can be leaves, hay, peat moss, or material from a partially decomposed compost pile. This material will help to hold moisture and prevent the topsoil you spread from being washed down through the sand. Next, add about three inches of topsoil, and till or spade it to a depth of six inches. Complete the job by working fertilizer, either commercial or decayed manure, into the soil. Your soil is now ready for a lawn (or a garden).

How high can the soil be raised around a tree without injuring it?

This varies with the kind of tree, the soil, and the effectiveness of surface drainage. In general, where the soil is light and well drained, the grade may be raised around trees eight inches without appreciable injury. If the soil is heavy and poorly drained, raising the grade as little as two or three inches may cause waterlogging and make it impossible for necessary oxygen to reach the tree roots (see also page 7).

How thoroughly should the soil be cultivated before sowing?

Seedbed cultivation has these objectives: to break up any clods; to destroy unwanted vegetation; to mix fertilizer into the

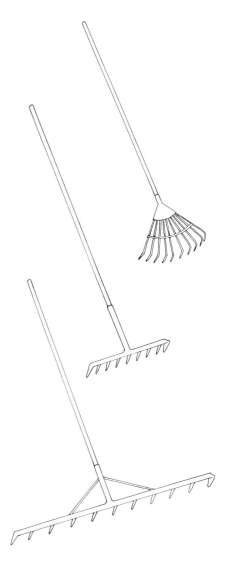

From top: leaf rake, garden rake, landscaping rake.

soil; to loosen the soil enough so that air exchange occurs well beneath the surface, permitting deeper root growth; and to create a pebbled surface that accepts seed well and allows water to penetrate. Overtilling is possible. It will pulverize the soil past the pebbled surface stage desired, eliminating the larger pieces that are so helpful for the movement of air and water into the soil.

Must the soil for a lawn be fertilized?

Most soils benefit from fertilization. To determine the fertility levels, use a soil-testing kit or send a soil sample to your Extension Service and follow the recommendations suggested by the results. If the addition of phosphorus is recommended, now is the time to add it. Phosphorus tends to stay at the level where it is applied, unlike other nutrients that leach down into the soil. Thus, if applied after the lawn is planted, it remains near the surface, out of reach of the roots.

Should I roll the lawn area before seeding it?

Yes, but do not overdo it. First, rake the area, breaking up any surface crust. It's good to rake in both directions, to get the proper grade for the lawn. Then roll the area with a lawn roller, and rake again in both directions. This gives a fairly compact surface, but with a pebbled top into which seeds will drop. The surface is good when it shows only a very shallow footprint when you walk on it. If the soil is quite sandy, don't worry about overcompacting it—you can't.

A well-prepared seedbed offers a rough, pebbled surface for seeds and is firm enough to show only a shallow footprint.

CHOOSING THE RIGHT SEED

Because of the many fine turf species for lawns, there are some for almost any geographical area and every soil, shade, or moisture condition. The number grows as new cultivars are offered each year. While most grass species are started from seed, many are propagated in other ways. Some have surface runners, called *stolons*. Others have underground spreading stems, called *rhizomes*. Stolons, *sprigs* (young shoots), or *plugs* (small cubes of sod) are often used to start lawns.

Some grasses have a greater tendency than others to create *thatch*, a layer of dead grass that builds up between the soil and the grass blades, and cuts off the flow of moisture down to the roots.

How do I know which package of seed mixture to choose?

There is, or course, no limit to the grass seed mixtures that can be offered. Study the accompanying Extension Service list, which demonstrates how mixture can be created for specific conditions.

Why are mixtures of grass seed offered?

Seed dealers package mixtures in an effort to introduce enough variability into the lawn so that not all the grass will be susceptible to the same affliction. Because of the necessary overcrowding of the grass plants that make up a lawn, individual plants are apt to be weaker than they might be if uncrowded and unmowed. If all were hereditarily alike, they would be fair game for diseases, which, if they encounter no resistance readily spread from one plant to another. When grass blends or mixtures are used, some resistant grass may confront whatever disease or other pest invades the lawn. One cultivar, or variety, may suffer in an attack by a certain disease, while another grass remains resistant.

In addition, some grasses are better suited than others to various conditions, such as sun and shade, south and north slopes, poor and good soil pockets. While a single cultivar would not adapt to all of these conditions, a mixture offers a range of possibilities. A bluegrass-fescue combination, with a bit of perennial ryegrass for quick cover, is a typical mixture. The bluegrasses are great for open areas, but the fescues will survive better in the shade and on dry, infertile soil under trees. Even when an all-bluegrass lawn is desirable, blends of cultivars are advocated to spread the risk.

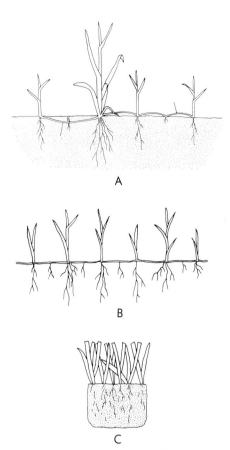

(A) Grass plants spread by surface runners, called stolons, and underground spreading stems, called rhizomes; (B) sprigs are stem fragments with young blades of grass and bits of root attached; (C) plugs are small cubes of sod, about 2 inches wide and 2 inches deep.

Seed Mixtures

SITUATION	KENTUCKY BLUEGRASS	CREEPING RED FESCUE	WINTER-HARDY RYEGRASS
General use in a diversity of situations and soils	20	40	40
Full sun, good fertility and management	50	20	30
Quick cover, but persistent	20	20	60
Clay soil, full sun, densely growing sod	100	—	—
Putting-green turf, to be mowed short	100[a]	—	—
Slope, never to be mowed	20	60	20
Temporary cover for summer	—	—	100 (annual)
Dry, sandy soils, open shade, or under trees	20[b]	80	—
Moist shade much of day, under trees, or north side of house	30[b]	40	30

a Use low-growing varieties, such as Glade and Nugget.
b Use shade-tolerant varieties, such as A-34, Nugget, Glade, and Touchdown.

●

Positive Images, Gary Mottau

Seed mixtures combine such variants as shade- and sun-loving grasses so that the lawn is adaptable to different conditions.

Do you have any comments on buying grass seed?

Just one piece of advice: Read the label. Most states now require the labeling of grass seed containers to show the species, variety, purity, weed seed content, and germination. The seed must be laboratory tested within the current year. Seeds should have at least 75- to 80-percent germination and 85- to 90-percent purity. The higher the content of pure live seeds, the less seed you need to sow. If you have some seed left over after sowing, save it. You'll find a use for it: Seeds are good for up to three years if stored in a cool, dry place. Freezing won't hurt them if they are kept dry.

There are so many new grass varieties (cultivars) now. How can I choose intelligently?

It is helpful to realize that all bluegrasses behave somewhat alike, and the same is true with other varieties. The difference between individual cultivars is mostly a matter of preferred color, texture, or growth habit. Care is less of a consideration. Seed firms provide helpful information about their own cultivars, and responsible houses will utilize quality components in their seed mixtures that you can accept on faith. The new cultivars would not have been brought to market had they not exhibited at least some superior characteristics. They are chosen for reasonable resistance to the usual lawn diseases, for comparatively low rather than tall growth, and for their attractive appearance.

SOUTHERN TURF SPECIES

Typically planted from Tennessee southward, these grasses grow best at relatively warm temperatures (above 80° F.). They experience most growth in spring and summer and should therefore receive major attention then.

BAHIA GRASS, *Paspalum notatum.* This fairly open, coarse grass has unattractive seed heads and is hard to mow. It is one of the easiest southern turf grasses to plant and to care for, however, and is sometimes used in mixtures.

BERMUDA GRASS, *Cynodon Dactylon* and hybrids. Bermuda grass has an attractive texture and deep color if well tended. Fast-growing and aggressive, it is so vigorous that it requires frequent mowing. It is a pest in flower and shrub beds and readily forms thatch. It grows in sun only, ceases growth when temperatures fall and is doubtfully hardy north of Tennessee.

CENTIPEDE GRASS, *Eremochloa ophiuroides.* This medium-textured, low-maintenance grass actually suffers if fertilized too heavily, but it does need iron. It turns yellowish unless soils are acid.

ST. AUGUSTINE GRASS, *Stenotaphrum secundatum.* St. Augustine grass is coarse but not unattractive. Its few seed heads are usually dark green. This grass is subject to chinch bug and several diseases, but resistant cultivars can be purchased. It tends to form thatch and is tolerant of shade.

ZOYSIA GRASS, *Zoysia Matrella.* Slow-growing, dense, and attractive, zoysia grass does not require a great deal of attention. It is very fibrous and tough to mow. Billbug damage can be serious.

NORTHERN TURF SPECIES

These grasses grow best when temperatures do not exceed 80° F. (at least at night). They conserve resources best in autumn, winter, and spring, are weakest in summer, and benefit most from attention in autumn.

BENT GRASS, *Agrostis*. Bent grass has small light green to blue-green leaf blades with excellent texture. Low, trailing, or semitrailing, bent grass spreads by above-ground stolons. Like other trailing stoloniferous grasses, it tends to build up a mat of vegetation on the soil surface. If this is slow to decompose, it will quickly create a layer of interfering thatch. It is a fine "show" grass for turfs that are fertilized, watered, and frequently mowed, but it is prone to diseases in muggy weather and to snow-mold under cool, damp conditions. It is used on greens at golf courses and is not commonly chosen for home lawns.

New York Turfgrass

The lower half of this illustration is a weed, an annual bluegrass in full seedhead stage. The upper half shows good Kentucky bluegrass.

KENTUCKY BLUEGRASS, *Poa pratensis*. This deep green grass has gracefully arching shoots and fine- to medium-textured, uniform foliage. Spread by rhizomes, it forms one of the thickest and most vigorous sods, well able to compete with weeds. Widely adaptable, it is one of the best all-around grasses and rather easy to care for.

FINE FESCUE, *Festuca rubra* in varieties. Also known as red fescue, this attractively fine-textured, beautifully dark green grass is rather stiff, with a windswept appearance. Best in cooler seasons, it may become patchy under hot and humid conditions. One of the finest shade grasses, it persists on poorish soils in dry locations. Because it wears well, it makes an excellent playing surface.

New York Turfgrass

Some grass species have desirable forms as well as those of lesser quality. Tall fescue is here contrasted with the more desirable fine, turf-type fescue.

TALL FESCUE, *Festuca elatior*. A tall grass, common in meadows and pastures, but four varieties, while coarser than Kentucky bluegrass, are drought-tolerant and satisfactory for lawns. Both fine and tall fescue produce rhizomes.

PERENNIAL RYEGRASS, *Lolium perenne*. The new turf types of ryegrass bred for lawns are just as attractive as bluegrass. Their shiny green leaves are quick to sprout, grow rapidly, and are tough. They adapt to a wide range of soil types, form a thick cover, and are easy to maintain. Ryegrass is reasonably hardy, although not so widely adapted to climatic extremes as Kentucky bluegrass. Because ryegrass does not spread and the seeds are larger than other grass seeds, it must be sown more densely than any other grass, about six pounds or more per 1,000 square feet.

How can I avoid confusing good lawn grasses with poor ones?

Unfortunately, some uncertainty occurs with common names, and the botanical names seldom appear on the packages, or, if they do, they are easily misunderstood by the uninitiated. As an example, "bluegrass" generally refers to the valuable Kentucky bluegrass species, *Poa pratensis*. Note, however: "Annual" bluegrass is a weed, and other bluegrasses, such as Canada or Woods, are of lesser quality. To add confusion, Kentucky-31 is a tall fescue (*Festuca elatior*) with coarse blades, and is definitely not a Kentucky bluegrass. It is easy to be misled, and it pays to acquaint yourself with lawn grasses in order to recognize their names on the required seed package list.

I don't want to make a lifetime mission out of caring for the lawn I am planning, but it is a fairly large lawn. Any ideas on what I should plant?

Look for some of the old-fashioned, self-reliant cultivars so well adapted to the casual care of yesteryear. Among the Kentucky bluegrasses are Arboretum (Missouri) and Kenblue (Kentucky) strains for the southern portions of the bluegrass belt, and Park (Minnesota) for northern and western zones. They are best mowed fairly tall, with at least a two-inch clipping height (see page 40). Some of the newer cultivars, such as Birka and Plush, are similar. Also, the better recent cultivars, such as Rugby, Parade, and Baron, while they are finest when well cared for, do reasonably well under some neglect.

What is meant by nurse grass?

This term is not common anymore, since the methods of starting a lawn have changed. In older seed mixtures, nurse grass was the grass that came up first, until the slower starting, permanent turf could take over. However, experts found that the nurse grass competed for space and nutrients, thus slowing the permanent grass, or even preventing its establishment. Annual ryegrass and redtop were much used for nurse grass, but the ryegrass was found to be overly aggressive, and redtop often carried a few unwanted species, such as timothy, with it. Sometimes as much as 25 percent or more of this nurse grass is still found in cheaper blends of grass seed. Today, fine fescue in a bluegrass blend serves as a nurse grass and has the added advantage of being useful as the lawn continues to develop.

What are the advantages and disadvantages of having white clover in the lawn?

White clover is an excellent companion of Kentucky bluegrass. The nodules on its roots trap nitrogen from the air and thus enhance soil fertility. However, clover is patchy in the lawn. It is especially disruptive when the white flower heads form and attract bees. Clover foliage is soft compared with grass,

Ann Reilly

White clover is patchy in the lawn, is likely to stain clothing, and dies back in winter.

Most seed companies offer mixtures for shade that are formulated for the needs of specific geographical areas.

so it may be slippery underfoot and likely to stain clothing more readily than would grass. Clover leaves die back in winter and do not, therefore, provide the continuous green cover of cool-season grass foliage.

What grasses are recommended for shade?

Essentially the same species are planted for shade as for sun, although the proportion of shade-tolerant types may be increased in the seed blend. Grasses perform better in the shade if helped by tall mowing and more frequent fertilization and watering. Rough bluegrass (*Poa trivialis*) adapts well to moist, shady spots. Although attractive, it is shallow-rooted and thus does not wear well. Do not sow it where there is much lawn traffic. Fine fescues are good for dry shade. All southern grasses except Bermuda stand shade reasonably well. Most seed companies now offer mixtures for shade that are formulated to meet the needs of specific geographical areas.

Are timothy and other farm grass species suitable for lawns?

Hay grasses are better left to the pasture and hay field. In the lawn they become coarse and clumpy. There's one exception to this: These sturdy grasses can be used in difficult sites where survival of the finer grasses is questionable.

Ground covers provide dependable, often evergreen, blankets of growth in areas where grass may not thrive, or where mowing is difficult or undesirable.

In Georgia, can I make a good lawn in a wooded area?

Spread a layer of manure, compost, or rotted oak leaves, together with some balanced lawn fertilizer, over the area. Spade or till this and rake level. Then in October or November, sow Italian ryegrass for a winter cover until warm weather. In the spring, plant sprigs (see page 13) of St. Augustine grass in rows about twelve inches apart. Water well, as growing grass needs a great deal of moisture.

What grasses are best for winter color?

Southern lawn grasses turn dormant and brown when the temperature nears freezing. For persistent green in winter, lawns must depend almost entirely on grasses introduced from Europe, such as the bluegrasses, fescues, bent grasses, and ryegrasses. In the South, sow ryegrass or a mixture of these cool-season species for a green lawn. In the North, the same grasses remain green much of the winter and turn brown only when exposed to drying winds or bitter cold. Lawns adequately, but not excessively, fertilized show better late color (see pages 32-36).

How much grass seed should I buy for 1,000 square feet of lawn?

Recommendations are usually printed on the containers. In general, these recommendations call for up to six pounds per 1,000 square feet for mixtures that are mostly ryegrass and red fescue, five pounds for 80-percent mixtures of these two, four pounds for 60- to 80-percent mixtures, and two to three pounds for bluegrass mixtures.

Why are there such differences in seeding rates?

There are several reasons for this, but the chief one is the size of the individual seeds. Bent grass seed runs about 8,000,000 to the pound; fescues, over 500,000; Kentucky bluegrass, 1,000,000 or more; and ryegrass, about 250,000. The more seeds to the pound, the fewer pounds needed.

Is there any grass that will stay green the year around in New Mexico?

In regions with sufficiently cool summers, yet not too extremely cold winters, Kentucky bluegrass stays green if well watered.

What grasslike ground covers other than grass can be used?

Much more on this later in the book (see pages 89-95). But for now, think of the creeping broad-leaved species, such as ivy, which make excellent ground covers. Of them, only dichondra needs seeding and mowing like lawn grass. It is pretty well confined to southern California. Creeping legumes, such as white clover, are acceptable for warm-weather cover, but are generally not favored because their blossoms and leaves add unwanted contrasting colors to the lawn.

What could we plant in April on bare ground that would be lawn enough for our fifteen-month-old son to play on by June? It needn't be a permanent lawn.

This question will make lawn lovers cringe, since the only answer is to recommend planting either of two species generally disfavored—timothy or oats. Both will cover the ground with a rough, haylike coating that can be mowed. The only other possibility is perennial ryegrass, which makes a very good temporary turf that will last a couple of years.

SPREADING THE SEEDS

Once you have chosen the type of grass seed you want, and have fed, graded, and lightly rolled the seedbed, it is time to spread the seed. Since you've put a lot of time and energy into getting the seedbed prepared, this is no time to save a few cents or a few minutes. Here are some guidelines:

- Buy high-quality seed. You may think it expensive, but you will also find that it has a large quantity of good seed in it and few weeds or cheaper seeds, such as annuals. Be sure the species of grass seed is suitable for your geographical area and your lawn conditions. Usually, garden centers carry the seeds most adapted to the area.
- Give the area a final raking, so it will be loose enough to accept seed.
- Don't skimp when spreading the seed. If the recommendation is for four pounds per 1,000 square feet, use that much. A thick growth will leave less space for weeds.
- After spreading the seed, scratch it in lightly with a steel garden rake, in an effort to cover it with no more than one-half inch of soil. Then, with a light roller, roll in two directions to assure good seed-to-soil contact.
- Sprinkle water over the area immediately after seeding, and never let the soil become dry until the grass is growing well. This may mean watering as many as three times a day. Do not water heavily enough to erode the soil or the seeds, of course, but supply enough water to keep the top inch of soil moist.
- Don't be surprised if a few weeds emerge. Weeds are annuals, and you can avoid future generations of them by mowing them before they go to seed.

I'm in a hurry to get my lawn planted. After I have prepared the soil for the lawn, is there any reason to wait before sowing?

It is best to wait a week between preparing the soil and spreading the seeds. After this period of settling, use a rake to

A shoulder-carried spinner spreader, useful for both seed and fertilizer applications.

remove low spots, debris, or clumps of vegetation you missed earlier.

Grass seed is expensive. How can I be certain that I'm spreading it evenly?

You should have two aims. One is to get the seed scattered evenly; the other is to get as many seeds as possible to germinate.

Before seeding, rake the topsoil surface again to make small furrows that will accept seeds.

If your lawn is small, you can scatter seed by hand. The seeds will be visible, so you can check for spots you missed.

For a larger lawn, use a mechanical spreader, which can be rented or purchased at a garden center. We recommend a shoulder-carried spinner spreader, which allows you to scatter the seed by turning a crank. You can use a push spinner spreader, the type often used for spreading commercial lawn fertilizers, but its wheels will leave tracks in the seedbed. To get a more even spread of the seed, mix it well with an equal quantity of some material of similar size, such as sand.

Divide the mixture into two equal amounts. Spread half the seed mixture by walking back and forth—east and west, for example—then spread the remainder walking the other way—north and south.

Scuff the seed in with a steel garden rake or a landscaping rake (see page 11). A few seeds will still be seen, but most of them should be covered in the top half-inch of soil. Roll the lawn twice, going in different directions, as in seeding. Then water, using the finest of sprays, so that the seeds are bedded down in the soil, but no soil is washed away.

A final thought on seeding: Select a windless day. It's impossible to spread grass seed consistently when even a light breeze is blowing.

Does a new grass seeding need protection?

Protection is essential only in special cases, such as steeply sloping ground or a poorly prepared seedbed that leaves the seed perched right at the surface. Most grass seed sifts into soil crevices where it is hidden, and it is too small to tempt birds. However, any seeding will benefit from a protective mulch, more to keep the seedbed moist than to protect the seed. A surface blanket of any inert material that is open enough to let sprouts emerge and permit moisture to soak into the bed makes a good mulch. Straw, a few straws deep, is widely used where it can be procured inexpensively, as well as such materials as excelsior, finely chopped twigs, grass clippings, sphagnum peat moss, and woven nettings. Mulches such as these break the force of rain and help both to prevent soil wash and to keep the seedbed moist. Seed will sprout quickly only if kept continuously damp. A mulched seeding requires less frequent watering

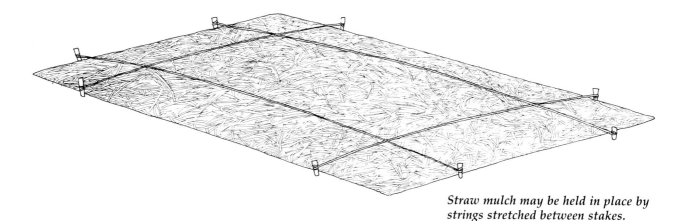

Straw mulch may be held in place by strings stretched between stakes.

than one exposed directly to air and sunshine, and thus usually makes a stand more quickly.

How do you lay the mulch down?

Mulches must be thick enough to retard evaporation of moisture but loose enough not to interfere with water penetration or seedling growth. Mulches that will not easily blow away in the wind and that decay naturally, so they do not have to be removed later, have advantages. On the whole, nothing has proved much more satisfactory than straw. Most of the time, a straw mulch stays in place if you walk on it to press it down. In especially windy spots, it can be held down with string tied between stakes. Excelsior is another excellent mulch. Hay is sometimes used, but has the serious shortcoming of containing a lot of weed seeds, which drop into the seedbed and quickly sprout and take root.

Is mulching a large area feasible?

Machines have been developed for mulching large areas, such as newly seeded roadsides. Some blow straw combined with an asphalt "tack" that binds the straw. Other hydraulic seeders pump on a mulch that is a slurry, made usually of woodpulp fibers. These machines can cover acres per hour. Many landscaping services have smaller versions, which can be engaged for custom service.

Is it all right to sow seed in the winter?

Seed will not sprout until warm spring weather. But this makes no difference. It is good to get the seed in place as soon as you can, since it may work down and become better imbedded in the soil from the freezing-thawing cycles. Old almanac advice was to sow grass seed on the "last snow of the year." One warning on this: Don't sow the seed where it might wash away; better in such areas to wait until warmer weather. And remember, use this method only if it is essential that you start your lawn in the spring. It's better to postpone the job until fall if you can.

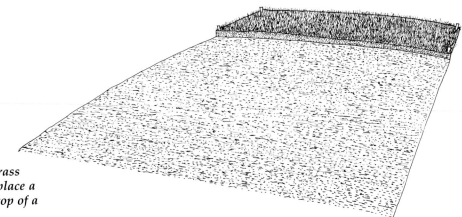

To help control erosion until grass seedlings become established, place a strip or two of sod across the top of a steep slope when seeding.

Are there any special precautions for seeding slopes with grass seed?

First, because of the obvious problem of erosion, consider sodding rather than seeding (see pages 24-27). Even a strip or two of sod across the top of the slope will help to control the soil from eroding. A seeded slope should receive protective measures, including ryegrass in the seed mixture, getting roots down quickly, and application of a good mulch. In the case of truly steep slopes, grass may not be the solution, since not only will it be difficult to get it to grow, but it will also be difficult to mow. Consider planting ground covers, such as creeping junipers, English ivy, or myrtle.

I've seeded my new lawn. What next?

You must keep it moist until the individual grass plants have pushed their roots down into the soil. This often means sprinkling three times daily, so that the soil looks moist at all times.

Both at the beginning and when the tiny plants emerge, keep pets and children off the lawn. They're the biggest lawn pests at this point.

How should a new seeding be watered?

New seedings are best watered with a fine spray, frequently applied. Forceful watering, especially on an unmulched seedbed, disperses soil, preventing water penetration. Spray lightly, frequently enough to keep the seedbed moist without surface runoff.

What about sprinkler systems for lawn seedings?

An underground system activated by a time clock set for brief waterings at frequent intervals is most convenient. Systems using plastic components that don't require plumbing skills for installation are now available. If you use conventional above-ground sprinklers, set them along the edge of the seeded area and aim them so that each will cover a section of the new lawn. Take care with heavy sprinklers: Many of them apply water more rapidly than a newly seeded area can absorb it, and thus may damage a seedbed.

How quickly does newly sowed lawn seed sprout?

This depends both upon the kind of grass and the weather. Ryegrass is fast, sprouting in just a few days. Fescues are slightly slower, and bluegrasses and bent grasses are even slower, often taking as long as two weeks. Seed must be kept moist and warm for fast sprouting, and germination is most rapid when daytime temperatures get into the seventies. Seed can lie dormant in the soil during freezing weather and will sprout only very slowly in temperatures below 50° F. Still, for spring sowings, it is best to seed the lawn as early as possible, letting the seed imbibe water and begin the sprouting process even though much action won't be seen until warmer temperatures later in the spring.

When should a lawn be mowed first?

Before being mowed, seedlings need a good root system so that the tiny plants won't be torn out of the ground; but don't let the grass grow so long that it flops over. It should be rooted deeply enough to begin mowing when the grass is almost twice the height at which it will be mowed when mature (see page 40). The soil should be allowed to dry out sufficiently to avoid footprints and mower tracks in the seedbed and to prevent damaging the tiny plants.

We seeded a new lawn early this spring and have a good stand of grass. Should it be mowed or left to grow this year?

It should be mowed, but not shorter than two inches.

The new grass on my lawn looks so frail and tender that I hate to mow it. What should I do?

If the grass is three inches tall, by all means go over it with the mower, setting the blade for a two-inch cut. Rather than hurting the grass, this will help to spread the growth laterally, thus creating a tight sod. If you are raising any of the low-growing bluegrasses, you can set the blade as low as one-half to one and one-half inches without doing any harm.

My new lawn is full of weeds. Should I till it up and start over?

Good heavens, no. If you imported topsoil, the weeds are probably from seeds in that. Keep the lawn mowed all summer so that none of those weeds get a chance to go to seed, and chances are good that most of them will be killed by the late fall frosts. Above all, don't use chemicals on the lawn to get rid of the weeds. Some chemicals that would be safe when the grass is more mature might kill seedlings.

THE INSTANT LAWN: SODDING

One day bare soil, and the next, a green lawn with a tight growth of grass and nary a weed. It seems like magic. But it's easy to create by sodding rather than seeding a new lawn, even for those not experienced in such work. There are many reasons for buying sod rather than planting seeds.

- Within two weeks you'll have what looks like a lawn of many seasons of growth.
- You'll be spared the seeding of the new lawn; and the need for watering and nursing sod is less than when you plant seeds.
- You'll have no mud tracked into the house, no fight to keep the children and pets off the new grass for many months, no worries about how—or if—the grass will grow.
- You will start with a dense lawn, free of weeds.

It isn't a perfect method, however. For one thing, it can be expensive. Figure the space you must sod, then get a price from a sod dealer (listed in your phone book) or a garden supply center that sells sod. The figure quoted should help you to make a decision. The next step is to prepare the soil. Although you buy sod much as you buy carpet for your home, it's not as simple as laying a rug.

If you've found a source of sod, know the price, and are satisfied with the quality of the sod, it's time to get to work. The area to be sodded must be prepared exactly as the seedbed for a new lawn is prepared. That means creating rich soil for the roots of the sod—it definitely isn't enough simply to rake a clay or sandy soil, then hope the sod will grow on it. You may have to bring in soil, then enrich it with lime and fertilizer. The area should be graded, one to one and one-half inches below the desired surface level, then rolled.

Have the sod delivered only after the area is prepared. Do not store cut sod for more than a day or two and never allow it to dry out.

Positive Images, Jerry Howard

Sodding produces a mature-looking lawn more quickly than seeding, but it is expensive and, like seeding, requires careful soil preparation.

Sod is usually delivered in rolls. Pre-pare the area before delivery and never allow the sod to dry out.

Sod is delivered in squares or, more often, in rolls. Lay the squares or strips parallel, with ends staggered and edges pressed close together, and no overlap. Use a knife to cut it at corners or edges, such as walks or driveways.

Check where the rolls or squares meet. If one is too low, fill under it to bring it up to level. If there is any space between strips, fill with topsoil.

Roll the lawn in two directions with a light roller, then spray the grass, enough so that the water soaks through the sod and into the soil. Keep it moist for at least two weeks, until the roots are reaching down into the soil. Also, keep people and pet traffic off the grass during those two weeks. After two weeks, treat it as an established lawn. It may be time for mowing.

Is there anything to be wary about in purchasing sod?

Buy sod from reputable sources that identify the grasses. Look for weeds or inferior grasses. Ask for assurance that there are no pests in the sod, such as crabgrass seed or harmful insects. Sod

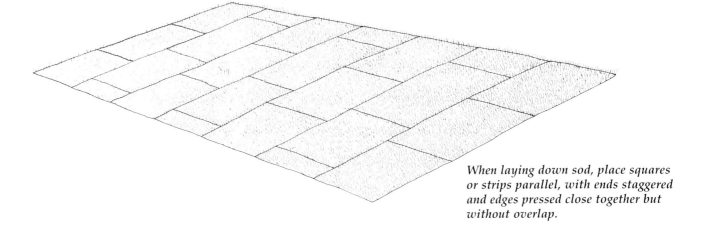

When laying down sod, place squares or strips parallel, with ends staggered and edges pressed close together but without overlap.

For best results, lay sod in early spring.

that is cut thin (one inch) roots most rapidly, but it also dries out more readily than thicker sod. Before accepting delivery, be certain that the sod is fresh and has not dried out. A yellowing sod is a sign of its drying out.

When should I lay sod for my lawn?

Early spring is the ideal time. New roots develop best during this period.

Does sodding make seedbed preparation less necessary?

Definitely not. Sod placed on poorly prepared soil will perform no better in the long haul than would a seeding given inadequate seedbed preparation. Before laying sod, add fertilizer and lime, if needed (see pages 32-38), loosen the root-zone soil, remove debris, and make sure that the site is level.

I have soil that is fairly heavy with clay. Since I plan to lay down rolls of sod, can I get away with merely leveling the surface?

No. Sod is little more than an inch thick. It must have a good layer of soil underneath it, so the roots will move down into the soil to obtain food and moisture. If it doesn't have these, the sod will, at best, not thrive, or it may eventually die.

I am going to sod a slope and will be buying rolls of sod. Should they go across or up and down the slope?

Lay them across the slope. Drive small wooden stakes into the ends of the rolls to hold them in place. Tamp or roll the sod lightly, since you want it to push roots down into the soil as quickly as possible. Then sprinkle the sodded area, enough to make certain the water gets down through the sod, but not enough to cause any erosion.

Must I take special pains with a newly sodded lawn?

Firm newly laid sod into the soil by light rolling with a lawn roller. Top-dress any depressions that are noted. It takes several weeks for the sod to reroot into the enriched soil beneath it. During this time it should be watered regularly and thoroughly enough so that not only the sod but also the soil beneath it is moistened. Care for it as you would an established lawn.

Are there less expensive alternatives to sodding?

Yes, small biscuits of sod, called *plugs*, or stem fragments, called *sprigs*, can be planted if available in your area (see page 13). Both will spread and form a tight turf within a season. Southern grasses for which no seed is available are often planted this way. Sprigs will give more coverage than an equivalent weight of plugs, but sprigs dry out quickly, so they require immediate planting. Zoysia sprigs spread a bit more quickly than do plugs.

Even so, zoysia is so slow-growing that a year or more is required to make a solid stand. On the other hand, Bermuda grass makes a stand in just a few weeks. Other southern grasses fall between these extremes.

Are sodded lawns or lawns planted from sprigs or plugs preferable to seeding?

You can get an argument on the answer to that question. The only advantage of sodding is quickness in providing mature turf. The advantage of sprigging or sodding is the perpetuation of cultivars that don't come true from seed. Sod may forestall weed appearance, but the potential for weeds is still in the soil if the sod fails. Such vegetative planting risks the introduction of pests and diseases more than does direct seeding. Some experts feel seeded grasses—rooting directly in home soil—do better than grass that is transplanted.

Can grass fragments be used to start a lawn?

Yes, this is possible with some grasses, particularly creeping bent grasses and Bermuda grasses. Sod is shredded, or stem clippings cut, to make what are called *stolons*. These are scattered over a prepared seedbed just as is grass seed. Because these stolons dry out quickly, top-dress them immediately with about a quarter-inch of soil, or press then firmly into the ground. The new stolons must be watered without fail until roots develop at the joints and new growth appears.

Must colonial bent grasses be started vegetatively (by sod, sprigs, or plugs)?

No, colonial bents such as Highland are available as pure-line seed. Colonial bents do not require the intensive care that the lower-growing creeping bent grasses do. Colonial bents are best mowed at a three-quarter to one-inch clipping height.

REBUILDING A LAWN

In the preceding sections, we emphasized the importance of doing a good job when creating a lawn. It is a lot of work, but the dividends are great: You will have a lawn of which you will be proud, and you will have far less work keeping it in excellent condition.

This section explains what you must do to rebuild an existing lawn. Those facing this job, as well as those who are getting ready to create a lawn, should understand one point: It is more work to rebuild a lawn than to do the job right the first time.

Why is this?

First, although the soil is poor, the lawn may be up to grade—that is, the lawn is at the level you want it in relation to your house, walk, and drive. Some of this earth must therefore be removed to make room for the addition of good topsoil. Second, the soil that is there is probably heavy with undesirable grasses, weeds, and weed seeds. You must get rid of these before you can rebuild your lawn.

The first step is to make a decision about the soil now in place. You must have a minimum of three to five inches of rich soil. If you have a layer of sand or clay on which you have been unable to grow grass, you may decide to bite the bullet and replace that top layer. If your lawn is average size or larger, this means arranging for mechanical equipment, such as a bulldozer or front-end loader, that can quickly scrape up and truck away the unwanted layer.

Then you must have topsoil brought in. To figure how much soil you need, estimate about one cubic yard of topsoil to spread a four-inch layer over eighty-one square feet. After this topsoil is spread, follow the instructions given earlier for a new lawn (see page 12).

In some cases, however, you may decide that even though your soil is poor, it can be improved and need not be replaced. Your first step is to test the soil with a soil-testing kit or by sending a soil sample to your Extension Service. The results of the test will indicate what types and amounts of fertilizer are needed. Phosphorus will almost certainly be recommended, since once it is in the soil, it stays at just about the same level. This is your opportunity to work it down to the level where the roots will benefit from it. You may find that your soil also needs nitrogen and potassium.

Don't wait for the test results to begin work on your lawn. First, rototill it, with the aim of destroying all vegetation, grass, and leaves that are there. Rake up all of this material—it's fine for your compost pile.

It's best to wait three weeks after tilling. During this time, bits of turf or hidden weeds will begin new growth. Rake them up. Before taking the next steps, you should be satisfied that none of the old growth will emerge.

You now have an opportunity to make soil improvements that will last for years. Add organic materials, such as chopped hay, leaves, rotted sawdust, rotted manure, compost, and peat moss, to the soil. These will help sandy soils to retain moisture and improve clay soils by enabling them to become more permeable to water and air. It is difficult to overdo this step. From one to three inches—or even more—can be added.

After spreading on organic material, add the commercial fertilizer suggested by the test results, and rototill to mix all of this into the top three to six inches of the lawn area.

At this point, follow the same procedures for preparing the seedbed as those given earlier for creating a new lawn.

A rotary power tiller.

How do you renovate an old lawn infested with "devil grass"?

You've heard that a weed is simply a plant growing in the wrong place. Here's an example of it. Devil grass is Bermuda grass, chosen for lawns in California and Florida, but the very devil to get out when it moves into gardens or lawns made up of some other grass. Even a tiny piece of root will start a new plant. Try tilling the lawn several times, raking up the root pieces carefully after each tilling, then reseeding. The care with which you remove the roots determines your success.

I plan to rebuild my lawn to get rid of a huge crop of weeds. When should I do it?

Begin preparing your soil so that you are ready to sow the seed at the same time recommended for starting new lawns. In general, seed in the spring in the South, in the fall in the area from Philadelphia and Washington, D.C., west to the Plains, and in the fall (or, less desirable, the spring), in more northern areas.

One of the reasons why I plan to rebuild my lawn is the vast number of mushrooms that pop up every summer. Can I use some pesticide to make certain I will have no more of them?

That's not necessary. You'll be rototilling your area before starting your new lawn. Mark the areas where these mushrooms grow. When you rototill, look for logs, tree stumps, or pieces of lumber scattered when your house was being built. Remove these as you till, and you will eliminate those mushrooms.

The reason that I need to rebuild my lawn is the existence of a large wet area. What should I do about it?

First, figure out why the area is wet. If it is because your soil is clay (see page 8), improve the soil by adding organic material, such as leaves and compost, to lighten the soil and permit the moisture to go down into the subsoil. If it is simply a low area in the lawn due to improper grading, you can easily build up that area when you rebuild your lawn. If it is a more serious problem, such as a high water table or chronic seepage, you will have to put in drain tiles to carry away the water.

I got rid of a lot of weeds in my vegetable garden by raising a crop of buckwheat, then tilling it in. This also improved the soil by adding organic material. Could I do the same thing on my lawn, which I'm planning to rebuild?

You could, and it would work exactly the same way (see page 46). For example, in Massachusetts, where you live, raise a cover crop in the summer and then till it under. If you till it about three weeks before you want to plant grass, it will have a chance to begin to decompose. The grass seed can then be sown on a vastly improved seedbed. There is one big question for you, however: Are you prepared to live with what would amount to an unmowed lawn for most of a summer? Perhaps equally important, are your neighbors prepared for this?

2 Basic Lawn Care

If you have built or rebuilt a lawn according to the instructions given earlier in this book, lawn care need not be a chore to be avoided if at all possible. Certain procedures are required, however, which if faithfully carried out, eliminate the much more difficult work of bringing your lawn back to first-class condition.

Lawns must be mowed—as often as weekly when the grass is determined to grow. They must be fertilized. They must be watered in dry seasons, or allowed to go dormant and brown. Finally, they must be watched, to see that none of the typical lawn problems move in. If problems do occur, action must be taken quickly, before the problem reaches unmanageable proportions.

Keep a small notebook near the mower in the garage. Enter the hours spent mowing, so you will know when your mower needs a change of motor oil. Record your lawn feeding schedule, and note when you fertilize, along with the kind and amount of fertilizer you use. When you build or rebuild your lawn, jot down the name of the seed or mixture used, so that you can later judge its worth.

Tending a lawn is a form of instruction. In northern areas, for example, you will learn that leaves left on the lawn in the fall do not disappear; instead, they are there in the spring and the grass under them is in deplorable condition. You will learn that a mower in need of sharpening will tear at the grass and leave ragged edges that brown quickly. You will learn the value of doing a job well when you are paid off with an improved lawn.

◀ *At the height of the growing season a healthy lawn needs about 1 inch of water per week, which you must provide if the rains fail.*

What makes a lawn look good?

Good looks are due mainly to density, uniformity, and rich color of the grass plants. Planting improved cultivars helps greatly, but you must also mow regularly and eliminate weeds. Proper fertilizing will help achieve a deep color and keep the grass vigorous to help you fight weeds.

Let's take an example. You have a lush lawn with five dandelions growing in the middle of it. With a deep-bladed tool, you go out and get every trace of the tap roots of these invaders. Although you have eliminated the weeds, however, you still need to fertilize the lawn, since the best defense against future growth of weeds is a healthy growth of grasses.

Do maintenance programs differ for different kinds of lawns?

Yes, indeed. Some grasses require more attention than do others, especially the heavy feeders, such as Bermuda and bent. Fast-growing types, such as Bermuda, require more of just about everything, especially mowing and fertilization, than do a "poor man's grass," such as centipede, which actually suffers if fertilization is too generous. Some grasses, such as fine fescues and zoysia, can get by with little attention, but even they look better when well cared for. Zoysia is slow-growing and can stand infrequent mowing, but looks more attractive if clipped each week or so.

Must one treat a lawn differently in the South than one would in the North?

Yes. If Bermuda grass in the South is fertilized in July, it will be better able to compete with the weeds, whereas a seeding of grass in the North at that time might help crabgrass more than it does lawn plants.

What attention can an "average" lawn be expected to need in areas where bluegrass predominates?

Mow weekly, perhaps every five days at the height of spring growth and maybe each ten days during summer slowdown. Fertilize a few times annually, particularly in autumn for bluegrass. Possibly treat against broad-leaved weeds in the spring. Finally, water during dry periods.

FERTILIZING AND LIMING
·

Can you tell me what those numbers mean on bags of fertilizer?

Let's take an example and explain it. We see a bag of 15-5-10. This means that 15 percent of the contents of the bag is nitrogen, 5 percent is phosphorus, and 10 percent is potassium. The remainder is inert filler. Nitrogen stimulates the growth of plants; it produces vigorous growth and deep green color. Phosphorus helps in the development of roots and prevents stunting. Potassium helps to produce sugars and starches, the energy foods of plants, and helps the plants to resist disease.

The temptation when spreading these fertilizers is to use a little more than the recommended rate, figuring that if a certain amount is good, more must be better. Particularly with nitrogen, it simply doesn't work that way. Too much nitrogen at one time will contribute to disease, pollution, unnecessary mowing, and even burning. This often means that several applications of fertilizer will be needed in one season. An alternative is to purchase the more expensive fertilizers that are formulated to make the nitrogen available to plant roots over a longer period.

Why are there so many combinations of fertilizers?

To meet specific needs. The following table provided by the Extension Service gives only a few of the grades of fertilizer and suggests uses for them on the lawn:

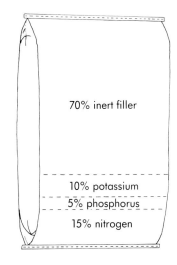

A bag of 15-5-10 fertilizer.

Choosing the Right Grade of Fertilizer

GRADE	WHEN TO USE
5-20-10	For lawns testing low in phosphorus
5-10-10	For lawns not regularly fertilized, or for preparation of a seedbed for a new lawn
10-10-10	For lawns in need of extra phosphorus and potassium, but not generally impoverished
15-10-10	For lawns fertilized regularly but in need of more phosphorus
15-8-12	For lawns fertilized regularly but high in phosphorus
20-10-5	May be used for a lawn pep-up; contains too little potassium for regular use and, because of the high percentage of nitrogen, may result in greater disease susceptibility

How much fertilizer should I use per year?

This is difficult to answer because of the many factors that must enter into the answer. For example, sandy soils require more fertilizer than clay soils, since some is lost through leaching. Also, more fertilizer is needed if you faithfully remove all grass clippings, rather than letting them gradually enrich the soil. You can cut the recommended amounts if you wish to save money, but too little means a thinner lawn—and the strong possibility that weeds will move in.

Use the accompanying table to start off, then change the amounts as you see how your lawn progresses.

A common recommendation for lawn fertilizer is a mixture with a nitrogen-phosphorus-potassium ratio of about 3-1-2. Thus, if you selected a fertilizer with 15-percent nitrogen, you would look for 15-5-10 on the bag.

Estimating the Correct Amount of Fertilizer

NITROGEN PERCENTAGE (first number on fertilizer bag)	TOTAL POUNDS PER 1,000 SQUARE FEET
30	15
20	20
15	30
10	40
8	50
5	80

When should I plan to feed my new lawn?

If you've done your preparation work well, adding both organic matter and fertilizers to the soil, you should not have to feed the lawn until the year after planting, when you should begin a program of periodic feeding.

When should I feed my established lawn with its recommended amount of fertilizer?

If you buy the bags of standard fertilizer, such as 10-10-10 or 20-10-5, you should probably divide the amount to be applied into four feedings. In most of the United States, the first feeding could be in early spring, the next two in the summer months (early June and late August in northern areas), and the last in early fall. Special lawn fertilizers have been developed that slow down the conversion of nitrogen into the nitrate form needed by the grass plants. Advertised as long-lasting or slow-release, these fertilizers are used in a single application, early in the growing season.

In the North, should I wait in the spring until my lawn is growing well before applying fertilizer?

No, it's better to spread the first feeding of fertilizer at least a week or two before the new growth begins. By doing this, the fertilizer will be available to the roots when the grass needs it most. It's best to spread the fertilizer on a dry day, then soak the lawn to wash the fertilizer off the top of the grass and down into the soil.

When should I fertilize my lawn in Florida?

Early in March apply a lawn fertilizer. Feed the lawn again when the rains start in June. In all parts of Florida except the extreme north, additional small monthly feedings in January and February help to keep the grass green through the colder months and build it up for its spurt of spring growth.

I need a fertilizer spreader. What type should I buy?

Use a grass seed spinner spreader, either shoulder-carried or push type (see page 20). Both throw fertilizer from a spinning disk. The common drop-spreader doesn't handle granulated fertilizers well, is hard to clean, rusts quickly, and is difficult to adjust for even and accurate spreading.

For fertilizing small lawns, the shoulder-carried spreader works fine. Not only is it easy to use and clean, but since it spits out fertilizer for fifteen feet, it will do a small lawn in minutes. Because the fertilizer is metered through a single large opening, it is easy to measure the amount being used. Also, there's little problem with the striping that sometimes appears on a lawn after improper use of a drop-spreader.

The push-type spreader is really a large can mounted on wheels, with the fertilizer being fed from the can onto the spinning disk. It can be used for lime as well as fertilizer.

I can't get my fertilizer spreader to measure the amount it disperses accurately. What should I do?

Mark out a square foot on your driveway. Measure one teaspoon of the fertilizer, and spread it evenly across this square foot. That is how ten pounds of fertilizer per 1,000 square feet will look. If you are spreading at twenty pounds per 1,000 square feet, measure the square foot and spread two teaspoons. Now fill your spreader and try to duplicate the density of the sample as you fertilize your lawn. When you've finished, estimate the amount of fertilizer you've used and figure how much you've used per 1,000 square feet. You can use these calculations to set your spreader for a more accurate spreading the next time you use it.

Last year I fed my lawn well, and the results were good all season, but my drop-spreader left lines of deep green where I fertilized—and much lighter areas where I missed. How can I avoid this?

I expect that you measured out exactly the amount of fertilizer needed for your lawn, loaded the drop-spreader, and then pushed it along, dropping a fairly heavy amount of fertilizer as you went. With drop-spreaders, it's best to set the amount being applied at a low figure, then apply half of it in one direction and half at right angles. If you haven't used it all up, go diagonally on a third trip.

Will lawn fertilizers help the trees?

They certainly will. A tree on a fertilized lawn will probably grow twice as fast as its unfertilized counterpart. Some gar-

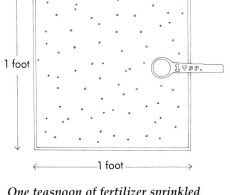

1 foot

1 foot

One teaspoon of fertilizer sprinkled over 1 square foot demonstrates the density of fertilizer necessary to apply 10 pounds of fertilizer to 1,000 square feet.

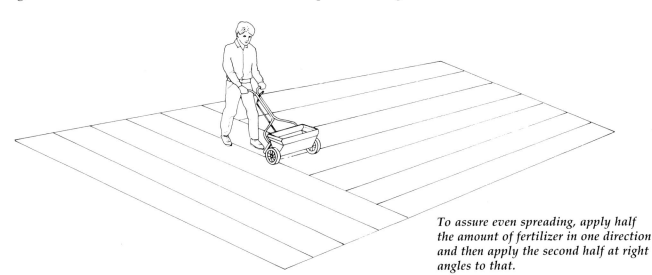

To assure even spreading, apply half the amount of fertilizer in one direction and then apply the second half at right angles to that.

deners prefer to place fertilizer more deeply in holes bored in the soil around the periphery of a tree to encourage its growth. Fertilizer compressed into spikes that can be driven into the ground with a hammer is available, eliminating the need to bore holes.

How shall I fertilize, water, and care for a lawn of centipede grass?

Centipede grass (*Eremochloa ophiuroides*) is one of the best lawn materials for the light, sandy soils of Florida. An application of a lawn fertilizer in March and another in June or July should suffice. Water the fertilizer in as soon as it is applied, and irrigate often enough to keep the grass leaves from curling and turning gray-green. Frequent mowing is necessary for a good centipede turf. During the growing season, the mower must be used at least once each week.

Why is pH so important?

pH is a scale used to measure how sweet (alkaline) or sour (acid) a soil is. It is measured on a scale of 0 to 14, with 7 being neutral. The reason that pH is so important is that even where nutrients are present in soil, plants can't absorb those nutrients if the pH is too high or too low. The pH test will not tell you, for example, if there is enough phosphorus in the soil, but it *will* indicate whether the soil conditions are too acid or too alkaline for that nutrient to be released.

Soil acidity not only directly decreases the availability of elements, but it also reduces the activity of soil bacteria: at 4.0, such activity may even cease completely. Also, some toxic elements, such as aluminum, are released at both a low pH (below 5.5) and a high one (above 8.5).

The pH scale measures how sweet (alkaline) or sour (acid) a soil is. On a scale of 0 to 14, 7 is neutral. Most lawns, flower beds, and vegetable gardens do best in a soil with a pH of 6.5 to 7.

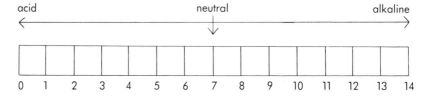

How can I know how much lime or sulfur to add to my soil to get the correct pH?

Your first step is to test the soil to determine the present pH. You can have this done by your Extension Service or do it yourself with an inexpensive kit. You must know, too, whether the soil is sandy loam or heavy clay loam (page 8). With those facts in hand, you're ready to apply lime or sulfur.

To raise the pH a full point, such as from 5.5 to 6.5, apply thirty-five pounds of ground limestone to 1,000 square feet of sandy loam, fifty pounds to medium loam, and seventy pounds to heavy clay loam.

To reduce the pH a full point, such as from 6.0 to 5.0, apply ten pounds of dusting sulfur per 1,000 square feet of light sandy loam; fifteen pounds on medium loam, and twenty pounds on heavy clay loam.

What is the ideal pH?

The homeowner with a lawn, flower beds, and a vegetable garden will do well to aim for a soil pH of 6.5 to 7. Most grass seeds will not tolerate soils with a pH below 5.5, and most garden crops need a pH above 6. Similarly, most flowers do best in soils of 6.5 to 7. A few shrubs, such as azaleas, do best in more acid soils (from 5.5 to 6.5). You can isolate such plants by growing them in raised beds and applying sulfur to lower the pH of just that one spot.

What is the action of lime on a lawn?

If the soil is heavy, lime will help to allow air and moisture to penetrate. Lawns tend to become acid in rainy climates, and most fertilizers are mildly acidifying. Lime will counteract this tendency. The importance of this is that if the soil becomes too acid (too low a pH), the plants are unable to use nutrients, even though they are available in the soil. For example, nitrogen is not available to plants below about 4.6 pH; phosphorus at 4.7, and potassium at 4.9. Thus, while lime is not a fertilizer, in acid soils it can have the effect of a fertilizer by unlocking nutrients in the soil and thus making them available to plants.

Are wood ashes good for the lawn?

Wood ashes supply lime (as well as potassium) to a lawn. It is fairly difficult to spread ashes evenly on a lawn, so many save them for the garden. Long-time burners of wood have discovered something about using wood ashes: It's very possible to overuse them if you spread them on the same soil year after year. The soil, even in the most acid of areas, simply becomes too sweet (has too high a pH), in which case you might have to reverse the action by adding sulfur to the lawn (see page 36).

I have fertilized my lawn regularly for many years, but for the past couple of years the lawn seems to have deteriorated, despite the fertilizer. What could be wrong?

Since you live in southern New York, you're in an area where the soil is acidic (has a low pH). Acid soil prevents the nutrients from being taken up and used by the grass plants. Unless lime is used on them, lawns tend to become increasingly acidic.

How do I know how much lime my lawn needs? I have never limed it, and there are signs of moss cropping up in it.

This answer applies only to areas of the country, such as the Northeast, where the soils are acid. Lawn soil becomes increasingly acid from leaching (a process in which water percolates through the soil, washing out soluble matter) and the removal of grass clippings. Sandy soils require light and frequent liming. Clay soils require heavier but less frequent liming. Pulverized, or ground, limestone, is inexpensive and easy to spread, although ground limestone is dusty and therefore messy to handle. Dolomitic limestone, if available, is good to use. Test your soil to determine whether it needs lime. Overliming can cause your grass to suffer from a tie-up of some micronutrients, such as boron, iron, manganese, and zinc, so they aren't available to the grass plants. Plan on liming the lawn every second or third year. If you haven't limed in three or more years and your soil tests acid, apply fifty to eighty pounds per 1,000 square feet.

Is it necessary to acidify alkaline lawns?

Sulfur, which acidifies, is less commonly needed than lime, which alkalizes, but it may be required in salt marshes, arid regions such as Western deserts, and areas with limestone bedrock. Depending on the degree of alkalinity, ten to fifty pounds of sulfur per 1,000 square feet may be needed. However, the problem is often one of sodium excess and not just alkalinity. Gypsum (calcium sulfate) is a better corrective for this than sulfur. Sulfur may be applied using the same techniques as one uses to spread lime.

My lawn needs both fertilizing and liming. Is there any reason why I shouldn't do them both on the same day?

There is. If you combine the two, you will cause a chemical reaction in which ammonia is lost and phosphorus becomes fixed, making it unavailable to plant life. Instead, apply the fertilizer, wait until rain or sprinkling has washed the fertilizer down into the soil, and then apply the lime.

WATERING

The water needs of a well-kept lawn do not vary greatly from species to species, although certain grasses, such as buffalo grass, are more able to endure prolonged droughts. At the height of the growing season any flourishing lawn needs about an inch of water per week. This must be provided by rainfall, irrigation, or stored moisture in the soil. Location in part determines this need. Sunny, windy spots in the deserts of the Southwest, for example, lose far more moisture than a protected lawn in the North.

Soil types, too, have an influence. The top foot of heavy soil, such as clay, can hold three inches of moisture, while a sandy soil will hold perhaps only half an inch. When watering, keep this difference in soil capacity in mind. Sprinkling a sandy soil with more than a half inch of water will be a waste, whereas clay should be watered slowly for a prolonged time until two or three inches of water have saturated the soil to the root zone. A cursory, nightly after-dinner sprinkling with the hose may relax the person sprinkling, but it does little to improve the lawn.

Why do lawn specialists criticize watering lawns every evening?

Because it does no good and, in fact, can cause harm. The roots of the grass should go down as deeply as possible in case of a drought. But if you give the lawn a light sprinkling every evening, the grass roots will stay close to the surface, where they are very vulnerable in a drought. As much as six inches of water is required to soak the soil to the depth where moisture is most needed. Check the penetration of water by cracking open the lawn surface with a shovel or a spading fork. If it is wet on only the top two inches, water enough to wet down six inches. Most of us are surprised how much water this takes—certainly much more than that twenty-minute after-dinner sprinkling.

Another potential danger with sprinkling the lawn in the evening is that the grass remains wet overnight and thus vulnerable to disease.

I'm always reading directions about how much to water my lawn. But how do I know how much water is being sprinkled onto it?

Place several coffee cans or a rain gauge in the area being sprinkled and measure the amount of water in them to get a good idea of how much is falling on the lawn. You need several cans to measure accurately, since most sprinklers tend to spread water quite unevenly. Generally speaking, you need to give about one inch of water in order to soak the lawn adequately.

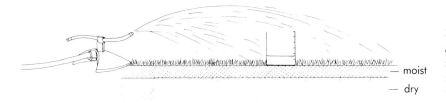

— moist

— dry

Use a coffee can to measure the amount of water you are sprinkling into your lawn. About 1 inch of water is usually necessary to soak the lawn thoroughly down into the grass roots.

I've been told the soil of my lawn is probably salty. How did it get that way and what can I do about it?

Soils become salty in arid regions where there is not enough rainfall to wash salts away from the roots of your grass. When salt is excessive, the roots are unable to take up moisture and nutrients from the soil. The salt can be from several sources, such as soil minerals breaking down, fertilizers, or irrigation water. It takes a lot of water to wash those salts down and out of the way—as much as twelve inches to move salts down a foot.

Is treated water all right for a lawn?

Any water suitable for general home use is harmless to grass, even if the water is heavily chlorinated. Muddy water from ponds is satisfactory for irrigation. In arid regions, where the soil is already quite salty, highly saline water from wells could worsen the soil structure, especially if not applied heavily enough to leach completely through the root zone.

Can a new growth of grass be overwatered?

Definitely. While the roots need moisture, waterlogged soil is unfavorable to the root growth. To avoid overwatering, watch the surface of the soil and rewater only when it begins to dry.

Would a covering of peat moss over the grass in summer help to hold moisture and do away with watering?

No. Most water loss occurs as the grass blades transpire (exude water vapor from the surface of the leaves). Soil coverings do not, therefore, help. Moreover, thatch that normally accumulates is the equivalent—free of charge—of applied peat moss. Save your peat moss for mixing into the soil.

MOWING

How close or high your grass is mowed has a strong influence on the health of the grass itself. Some grasses—bent and Bermuda grasses, for example—are better adapted to low mowing. But, in general, reasonably high mowing, not less than two inches, benefits the grass. Disease is less severe and weeds are fewer. This is most likely because more green leaf is left to make food for the plant and because the roots of tall-mowed turf tend to reach more deeply into the soil, thus tapping into a greater soil mass for more moisture and nutrients.

What kind of a mower should I buy?

Most equipment dealers today recommend small tractors. If you have a very large lawn, they are good, but buy a mower that matches your lawn size. If you have a small lawn, a hand-push unmotorized mower is perfectly adequate.

The reel-versus-rotary mower question has been pretty well settled in favor of the latter. Reel mowers have the advantage of cutting with a scissorslike action against a fixed bed knife and are highly recommended for low-mowed turfs that are well tended. These mowers are also somewhat safer than other types. Rotary mowers, on the other hand, are less expensive and easier to sharpen, adjust, and maintain than reels. They are also more versatile, able to get closer to walls and other obstructions, and because of the way grass is sucked up into the cutting chamber, especially useful for mowing tall, floppy grass.

No matter how sharp I keep the blades of my rotary mower, they seem to tear rather than clean-cut my grass (*Zoysia japonica*). The result is that the grass tips look ragged and usually turn brown soon after being mowed. A neighbor suggested that I use a reel mower. Do you agree?

Zoysia tissue is unusually fibrous. Heavy-duty mowers are recommended, and a well-adjusted reel mower would mow it more neatly than a rotary.

What is your opinion of electric mowers?

They're best for crowded neighborhoods on early Sunday mornings, since their noise will rouse only the lightest of sleepers. These mowers start easily, require little maintenance, are usually less expensive than similar size and weight gasoline-powered mowers, and are fine for small lawns with few trees or other growth around which the cord must be carried. They should not be used on wet turf.

I need specific instructions on how close to the ground to cut my lawn. The neighbor on one side tells me one thing, the neighbor on the other side tells me another.

Use the accompanying chart to determine your grass's mowing height. The length of the grass depends on the variety of grass that you have. If you have a grass mixture, as most of us do, use the recommendations for the taller grass.

To estimate when your lawn should be mowed, mow when the grass is 50 percent taller than the indicated higher mowing height. As an example, mow Bahai grass to three inches just before it gets four and one-half inches long; in other words, cut one-third off of its height to bring it to its optimal length.

What if I can't keep up with mowing, due to rain or some other cause?

If the grass gets excessively tall, cut it back a little at a time, letting several days pass between cuttings. If a lawn is scalped under such conditions, the plants will be weakened and roots will fail to grow for many weeks. This is especially damaging in the spring when stored food has been used to make fresh leaves; eliminating this growth then may even kill the plants.

I've been told to cut our grass "high." How high is that?

Leaving two or three inches is a high cut.

Does it make any difference which direction I mow?

Not too much. Purists mow parallel to the street, so that the mowing lines are not seen by passers-by. Specialists also recommend mowing in different directions in subsequent mowings,

Mowing Heights for Various Grasses

GRASS VARIETY	MOWING HEIGHT (in inches)
Bahai grass	2–3
Bent grass	⅜–¾
Bermuda grass	½–1½
Bluegrass	2–3
Centipede grass	1–2
Fine fescue	1–2½
Ryegrass	1–2½
St. Augustine	1½–3
Tall fescue	2
Zoysia	½–1½

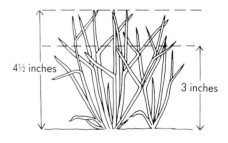

4½ inches

3 inches

Mow the grass when it is 50 percent taller than its optimal length.

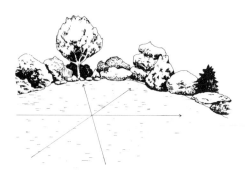

Change the direction of your mowing week by week to avoid "stripes."

saying that this will avoid a curved nap (a tendency of the grass to lean in one direction).

Should grass clippings be removed from the lawn?

This depends upon the kind of grass and how fussy you are about the looks of your lawn. Bent and Bermuda cultivars are very dense; these clippings should be removed because they won't sift down to the soil where decay is rapid. Clippings of most other grasses, if regularly mowed, are short enough to work into the soil unnoticed and even feed the lawn. If clippings are an inch or more in length and a heavy layer covers the lawn, remove them.

Are collected clippings of any value?

They certainly are. Because they are very high in nitrogen, they can be scattered in the garden or added to the compost pile. Whatever use you find for them, however, don't leave them in a heap on the lawn. If you do, they will heat up, become moldy very quickly, and much of their value will be lost. Scattered in a thin layer, they make an excellent mulch in the garden, adding nutrients and keeping down weed growth.

Thatch is building up on my lawn. What *is* thatch, and what should I do about it?

Thatch is a layer of dead material lying between the blades of grass and the soil. There are several schools of thought on what creates it: an accumulation of heavy layers of clippings left on the lawn, an overfertilization with nitrogen, or a drop in the pH that results in solid bacteria not being vigorous enough to break down grass clippings. Finally, those opposed to the use of

Ringer Corporation

Thatch is a layer of dead material lying between the blades of grass and the soil. Thatch-removal machinery can slice down through the sod, leaving the rooted grass plants in place, but removing quantities of thatch.

chemicals on a lawn believe chemicals kill off the microorganisms that would break down the thatch.

The chief problem with thatch is that it soaks up moisture. In even a fairly heavy rain, all moisture is held in this layer of dried grass as it would be in a sponge, never reaching the soil and roots where it is needed. In addition, disease organisms can grow in the thatch and cause major problems.

To get rid of thatch, first mow your lawn shorter than you usually do. If thatch is one-half inch or less in depth, try raking the lawn with a steel broom rake—the type used in raking leaves. If this doesn't remove the thatch, you can rent a machine that slices down through the sod and removes quantities of thatch. Since most of the rooted plants are left, the lawn will recuperate. This procedure is stressful on the grass plants, however, so do it before or during the period of most active growth. If it requires more than one treatment to remove the thatch, space treatments two or three weeks apart, and operate the equipment at right angles to the direction used the preceding time. An alternative to this method is to buy a lawn mower with a dethatching attachment. While this is not the best choice for removal of a heavy layer of thatch, such a mower, used regularly, will prevent any buildup.

I have just removed the thatch from my lawn. It was a big job and left the lawn looking quite messy, at least temporarily. How can I avoid having this thatch build up again?

In one respect, the presence of thatch is a healthy sign. It indicates a tight sod and hearty grass growth, both of which are good. One thing you can do to avoid excessive thatch is cut back a bit on the amount of nitrogen you spread on the lawn, so the growth will not be quite as lush. Second, and this is probably more important, remove grass clippings during the period of fastest growth. But, of course, don't throw them away. Work them into your compost pile or scatter them in your garden where they will enrich the soil.

Are there any "must" tasks for lawn care in the spring?

Spring is a time of year when both lawn-tenders and the grass have the urge to get up and get going. The first task should be to remove all winter debris—carefully. Don't use a stiff, steel garden rake; it will probably do more harm than good. Instead, use a broom-type steel or bamboo rake (see pg. 11), gathering leaves and other debris, but not trying to remove any dead grass. If you attack this job too vigorously, there's a good chance you will uproot many loose grass plants. If dead grass is really high, set your mower low and mow it before raking.

Another job to be done is to roll the lawn with a roller, smoothing out irregularities and making mowing that much easier all summer. Don't overdo the rolling. It can compact the

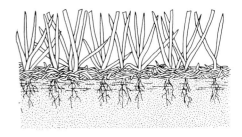

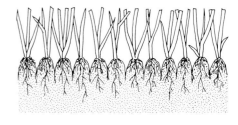

The turf above has thatch; that below is free of thatch.

OFF-SEASON CARE
—————— • ——————

soil and result in poor growth. In particular, avoid rolling heavy clay soils when they are wet.

If your lawn has any irregularities, this is a good time to fill in depressions by spreading a layer of sandy topsoil in the area. Don't use a layer more than one-half-inch thick. If more is needed, apply several thin layers, a week or two apart, so that you don't smother the grass underneath. Wait until the grass is up through one layer before adding another.

My lawn borders directly on the street. During the winter, the city salts the street during icy periods and plows after snowstorms. Result: snow and salt are tossed up on a broad belt of the lawn beside the street. Sometimes the grass revives, although slowly, but in one area it is dead. What should I do?

Usually, this doesn't require the addition of a fresh soil, since the salt should leach out during spring rains. In the spot where the grass hasn't revived, try working the soil down to a depth of at least one inch with a steel rake, removing the dead grass and exposing fresh soil. Seed this as you would a new lawn, roll or tamp it, and keep it watered until the new growth is firmly established.

Are there things that should be done to put the lawn to bed in the fall?

Only a few. Remove all leaves as soon as they come down and before snow falls. Raking is the usual method; push sweepers do the job more quickly. Rotary mowers with leaf mulching attachments are now common and efficient, chewing up the leaves

In the fall, all leaves should be removed from the lawn and the lawn should be mown until grass growth ceases.

Positive Images, Jerry Howard

into tiny pieces that can be left on the lawn if there aren't too many. If there are a lot of leaves, however, remove them, and add them to the compost pile or spread them across the garden.

Continue to mow the grass until growth ceases. Your aim is to leave the grass short during the winter. This makes raking easier in the spring. It may also help to avoid snowmold, which appears as dead patches all over the lawn in spring. When the rest of the lawn begins to turn green, these spots remain black and dead. It is particularly common on bent grass or where the homeowner has failed to cut the grass close in the fall. Snowmold looks much like the spots caused when a pile of leaves kills the grass beneath it, but the causes are different. Although fungicides can be applied to the lawn in early winter, try going into the winter with a clean, short-clipped lawn, and thus avoid the use of these chemicals.

Last fall one of my neighbors dumped several loads of manure on his lawn and scattered it around. His theory is that the manure will feed nutrients down into the soil all winter. Is it a good idea?

I don't think so. All of the manure won't work down into the soil during the winter, which means he'll have a lot of manure removal to do come spring. In addition, the manure almost certainly contains weed seeds that will come up in the spring. Finally, it is almost impossible to spread manure evenly across a surface. This means that tiny sections of the lawn will be overfed with nitrogen, while other areas will receive little or none. Stick to commercial fertilizers from your garden store.

When winter comes, can I forget about my lawn?

Pretty much so, if you've given it a final good raking and mowing (and have carefully taken every last drop of gasoline out of the mower).

There are some things, however, that you should *not* do to your lawn during the winter. Avoid running paths across it even if it is covered with snow. If you have to shovel paths across the lawn, don't shovel all the way down to the grass; leave a blanket of snow for protection. Don't use salt to melt the ice off your walks or driveway; some of it will get out onto the grass, causing brown patches and thus extra work in the spring.

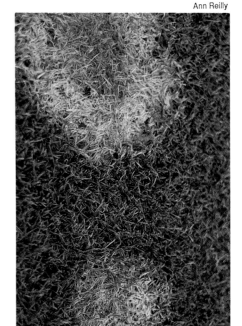

Grass left too long over winter may be invaded by a fungus disease called snowmold.

THE ORGANIC LAWN

Organic vegetable gardening has become increasingly common. Organic gardeners shun harsh chemicals or poisons to halt crop-destroying weeds, insects, or diseases because they know those chemicals may damage the very structure of the soil, with its thousands of microorganisms. Instead, they opt for naturally occurring materials, including compost (see page 111) and animal manures that will enhance the microbiological activity in their garden soil.

Blake Gardner

Organic lawn care entails conscientious maintenance; the best defense against weeds and disease is a healthy lawn.

Let's run through the steps of starting a new lawn organically, pointing out any differences from the conventional method.

Your greatest emphasis will be on preparing the area. If the lawn is to be at the site of a new home, avoid burying any trash in the soil and carefully remove any remaining on the surface.

Next, you must enrich the soil and at the same time improve its texture by adding organic materials in large amounts. These can be processed sewage sludge (a great source of nitrogen), bone meal (for phosphorus), and cottonseed meal, granite dust, or sheep manure (all good sources of potassium)—in short, any organic materials that are available in your area. If your soil is acid (see page 36), add enough lime to bring the pH up to a barely acid 6.5. Till all of this material into the top six inches of soil.

The next step—and one unique to organic gardening—is to raise a cover crop. Crimson clover and hairy vetch are common in the South; rye, winter rye, buckwheat, and field peas are just a few of the many that are popular in the North. All of these are called *green manures*. Start these in the spring, till them under when they're a foot or so high, and then wait four to six weeks for them to decompose before seeding your lawn. This process puts a large volume of rich organic matter back into the soil, often discourages weeds, and creates a fine seedbed that will be ready in the fall at exactly the right time for sowing a lawn in many areas.

Grading the topsoil, preparing it for sowing, and sowing the seed are the same for preparing organically managed lawns as for nonorganic lawns.

If you are committed to a nonchemical lawn, watch carefully for any signs of trouble—weeds, bare spots, yellowing or browning grass. Feed your lawn with organic topdressings, such as sifted compost. Mow it frequently, cutting only one-third or less of the grass blade length; in this way, clippings are short and can be left on the lawn to feed their rich nitrogen back to the grass roots. All of these good maintenance procedures keep grass healthy—the best defense against weeds and disease.

Is it better to grow a green manure crop in gray clay soil over the winter, or dig it under in the fall?

Fertilize the soil, grow a winter cover crop, and till it under in the spring. The area is then ready for grass seeding.

With commercial fertilizers, the contents' measurements are precise; you know, for example, exactly what you're getting in a bag of 5-10-5. Can organic fertilizing be that exact?

Usually not, and there's no reason why it should be. Organic gardeners—and lawnkeepers—aim instead to provide such an abundance of natural materials—including animal manures and green manures, composts and rock powders—that those major nutrients, N-P-K (nitrogen, phosphorus, and potassium) are always available, along with trace minerals and large amounts of organic material to lighten the soil.

Those not comfortable with this method, and particularly those accustomed to working with set amounts of commercial fertilizers, can work out similar fertilizer mixtures by using a chart indicating the percentage composition of common organic materials such as the following:

Nutrient Content of Common Organic Materials

	N	P	K
Alfalfa hay	2.45	.5	2.1
Wood ashes	0	1.5	7
Dried blood	12	3	0
Hair	12	0	0

I live near the ocean, so I can get seaweed by the truckload with very little effort. Should I use it, and if so, how?

Seaweed has been recognized as an excellent fertilizer for centuries, with generous amounts of nitrogen, phosphorus, and potassium. The exact amounts of these nutrients depend on the season and the variety of seaweed. It has the further benefit of being free of weed seed and plant diseases. Seaweed can be made the chief ingredient of your compost pile by mixing it with other materials, such as chopped leaves. Such a mixture, turned several times during the composting, will turn to a fine, black compost in as few as six weeks. Use it as a topdressing for your lawn by spreading it a half-inch thick, then working it under the grass blades with a steel rake. You can also spread it around shrubs or trees, or work it into the soil in a vegetable garden.

I have several large compost piles. I would like to use the compost as a topdressing on my lawn and add it to my garden soil as well, but will I be planting weeds in my lawn, since I compost all of the weeds out of my garden?

No. A compost pile built with some materials high in nitrogen will heat up to nearly 150°F. and will reach nearly this temperature even if you turn it to get the material on the outer layer into the center. This process kills weed seeds (see page 111).

Should topsoil be brought in if the soil is particularly bad?

Organic specialists usually say no to this for two reasons: You may be importing weed seeds, and you may be buying soil that is not much better than what you already have. Instead, enrich the soil that is there with organic materials, even adding bulky materials, such as leaves, that will greatly increase the percentage of organic material in the soil.

How do natural organic materials help the soil?

As the thousands of living microorganisms in the soil feed on the glucose that is released when organic material decomposes (breaks down), humus forms and enhances the soil for better plant growth.

Do I need to water my organic lawn as frequently as I would if it were nonorganic?

Because organic lawns tend to grow more slowly and to be hardier and more succulent, they may actually need less water.

Will I get thatch if I maintain my lawn organically?

Because organically managed lawns grow more slowly and there is increased microorganic activity in the soil, thatch is less likely to occur. Decomposition is able to keep pace with the dying parts of the grass plants that cause thatch build-up.

What kinds of natural controls can I use against insect pests?

Encourage birds into your yard by providing places for them to feed, bathe, and nest (see page 140). In addition, just as birds consume insect pests, so, too, do toads, snakes, and predatory insects such as lady bugs and spiders. Japanese beetles can be picked off your prize roses and dropped in a can of kerosene, and slugs can be lured away from your tender lettuce and peppers by placing saucers of beer in the garden.

INSECT PESTS AND DISEASES
•

It's amazing how many pests can eye your beautiful lawn with the worst of intentions. They range from the dogs and children in your neighborhood to the tiniest of growths—the molds.

First, however, a word of encouragement: No lawn anywhere has ever had all of these pests. In the next few years you probably will run up against two or three of them—not more. Furthermore, well-kept lawns do avoid most of the problems. For example, a thick growth of grass means there's no room for weeds. Crabgrass, particularly, loves to move in where it can find room, but will never be seen where the grass is thick. Keeping a lawn beautiful is much more satisfying than running down to the garden supply store each weekend for some chemical to solve the latest problem.

Pesticides are controlled by the provisions of the Federal Insecticide, Fungicide, and Rodenticide Act administered by the Environmental Protection Agency. Regulations change as to the legal use of specific pesticides. For this reason, we recommend that you check with a garden supply store to see what pesticide is available for a specific problem. Or, if you are in doubt about use of a specific chemical, call your local Extension Service agents. They are up on the latest EPA recommendations and can suggest what to try for specific problems.

The approach to these problems has changed in recent years. In the past, the recommendation was to find which chemical could be used to solve a particular problem. Today, the first approach is to see how the problem can be avoided, or if it appears, how it can be solved through nonchemical ways.

An example of this is the snowmold commonly found on many lawns in the North in the spring. This occurs when snow falls on unfrozen ground where drainage is poor and where grass remains under snow cover for a long time. It can be minimized by improving lawn drainage; by selecting grass seed that has proven to be hardy against threat of snowmold; by avoiding late, heavy nitrogen fertilization; and by cutting the grass in the late fall to prevent a mat of grass from developing. If none of these works, there are fungicides recommended by the U.S. Department of Agriculture that you can select.

When you do decide to use a pesticide, follow the precautions on the accompanying chart.

DO'S AND DON'TS
WHEN USING PESTICIDES

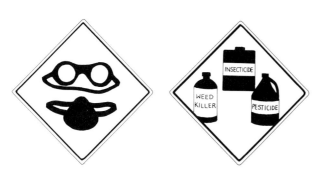

- Carefully read and follow the directions for mixing and use.
- Pour liquid pesticides at a level well below your face in order to avoid splashing them onto your face or eyes.
- Be fully clothed when you apply pesticides. If the directions recommend them, wear goggles and a respirator.
- If you spill pesticide on your clothing or skin, remove your clothing immediately and wash your skin thoroughly.
- Don't use the same sprayers for insecticides and fungicides that you use for a herbicide.

- Don't use pesticides where there is danger of drift to other areas, such as vegetable gardens or patios.
- Avoid inhalation of the spray or dust.
- Don't apply pesticides on a lawn where people or animals are present.
- Don't permit children or pets on the lawn until the pesticide has been washed off by rain or sprinkling, and the lawn has dried completely.
- In case of contracted pupils, blurred vision, nausea, severe headache, or dizziness, stop using the pesticide and contact a physician.
- After using a pesticide, bathe and change your clothing. Don't eat, drink, or smoke until you have done this.

Lawn Pests and What Insecticides to Use Against Them
(as recommended by the U.S. Department of Agriculture)

LAWN PESTS[1]	DIAZINON	CARBARYL	CHLOR-PYRIFOS	TRICHLOROFON
Ants[2]	X	X	X	X
Armyworms	X	X	X	X
Billbugs	X	X		
Chiggers	X		X	
Chinch bugs	X	X	X	
Cicada killer wasps	X			
Cutworms[3]	X	X	X	X
Earwigs	X	X	X	
Fleas	X	X	X	
Fruit flies	X			
Grasshoppers			X	
Grubs[4]	X	X	X	X
Leafhoppers	X	X		
Millipedes	X	X		
Mites, clover	X		X	
Sod webworms	X	X	X	X
Ticks	X		X	

[1] Several insects are not listed because no control measures are necessary or chemicals for their control are not registered at this time. The active ingredients shown here are present in varying concentrations in many different commercial products.

[2] If only a few ant nests are present, treat them individually. Wash the insecticide into the nests or drench the mounds with it. For control of fire and harvester ants, consult your city or county Extension Service agent.

[3] To control cutworms, apply the insecticide in late afternoon.

[4] In hot, dry areas, use lower dosages to avoid burning the grass. Consult your city or county Extension Service agent.

●

My neighbor has a dog that is allowed to run loose over nearby yards, relieving itself at will. What can I do to get my lawn back in shape?

Dogs can be one of the greatest pests on lawns. Their feces are foul, unsightly, and disease-carrying. The urine of dogs is such a concentrated source of urea, ammonia, and potassium that it produces a toxicity similar to fertilizer burn. Female dogs are the worst offenders here, because they deposit urine on the lawn, producing a spot that will remain dead for most of a growing season. Cut out the dead spot with a shovel to a depth of six inches and replace with live sod from some less conspicuous area of your lawn. Press the sod firmly into place by stepping on it, then water well.

Moles are making a mess of my lawn. What can I do?

Moles, as you may have found out, like to dine on the bulbs in your garden. They also feed on grubs in your lawn. Use a pesticide to get rid of the grubs, and often the moles will move on to more productive hunting grounds. A second approach (if the laws of your community allow it) is to set mole traps, available in areas where moles are common. Moles live in burrows six to eight inches underground. When they burrow, they raise ridges on the surface of the lawn. To determine where to set the traps, roll or tamp these ridges. The following day, any new ridges are active ones—and good locations for traps.

My neighbor says mice are causing the winter damage to my lawn. In spots, it is bare down to the soil, and there is quite a bit of loose, dead grass scattered around. Is she right?

Probably. Mice live on the stems and leaves of grass as well as weed seeds in the winter, and may even girdle shrubs and small trees. Usually lawn grass will come back, so the only task is to rake up that dead grass in the spring. An ambitious cat is very helpful in this situation. Traps are useful but less effective.

Webworms are ruining my lawn. What can I do?

Webworms live in burrows deep in the sod, usually in the hottest, driest regions, and are seldom seen because they feed at night. They chew off the grass near soil level, leaving bits of grass and chaff, and saucer-shaped patches of brown in the lawn. Webworms are the larvae of lawn moths, which are frequently seen flitting over the lawn about dusk. At that time they are dropping eggs into the lawn. The cycle from egg to moth is about one month in warm weather, so that drenching the lawn with an insecticide about ten days after lawn moths are abundant should catch the larvae (the webworms). Webworms are seldom prevalent enough in the first generation to be a bother, but become damaging as populations build up during the summer. For this reason, plan on treating the lawn every two months, beginning in the late spring.

THOSE PESTY TERMS

Pesticide is a general term referring to a wide variety of agents used to kill or control plants, animals, or insects. Some of the more specific terms include:

Acaricide	mites and ticks
Avicide	birds
Fungicide	fungi
Herbicide	plants (more popularly known as weedkillers)
Insecticide	insects
Molluscicide	mollusks, especially snails
Nematodicide	nematodes
Ovicide	eggs, particularly insects in the egg stage
Rodenticide	rodents

How do I check chinch bugs?

These little fellows can do damage in impressive amounts. When they feast on grass, it turns off-color and eventually browns in irregular patches. Chinch bugs suck the sap from grass stems, debilitating and eventually killing the above-ground parts. The active insects will be found in adjacent green grass. Shake a handful of grass over white paper and look for white and black insects, some with red spots, not much bigger than a pinhead. Spray the undamaged turf well with insecticide.

Earthworms tend to leave castings on the lawn: should I try to get rid of them?

You can get rid of them through the use of insecticides that make the soil unattractive to these worms. They do leave castings, most noticeable on low-clipped turf such as bent grass. But before you declare all-out war on these fellows, consider their value. As they constantly work up and down, they improve the flow of moisture and air in the soil, enrich the soil with their castings, and consume thatch. On most lawns, they earn their keep, and their occasional castings should be forgiven or looked upon as topdressing. A quick brush with a broom rake will scatter these castings and enrich the surrounding soil.

The Japanese beetles are driving me crazy. They eat my raspberry bushes in the summer. Furthermore, their grubs attract skunks that dig up the lawn to feed on them. I want to eliminate them. How?

Eliminating Japanese beetles is almost impossible. It helps to understand the life cycle of this pest. The beetles deposit eggs in the sod during the summer. The young that hatch are small white grubs that grow strong as they feast on the roots of your grass. Those grubs go below the frost line during the winter, but return to the roots in the spring, then transform into pupae and adult beetles, which emerge to complete the cycle.

For the best long-term treatment, use a bacterial disease called milky spore, which can be purchased as a dust. Because introducing this disease into the soil of your lawn helps eliminate only the grubs, their wormlike larvae, and not the beetles that fly in, it is most effective when spread in large areas by community authorities. This disease is harmless to humans and other warm-blooded animals and to plants. It becomes more effective after several years, when it has spread through the soil.

One-time grub-proofing of lawns can be done with a diazinon-based pesticide available at your garden supply store. Don't use this together with milky spore disease, since the disease spreads faster if there is an abundance of grubs.

Traps are also available, which attract but do not eliminate the beetles. Picking the beetles, too, will help only to reduce the population. Spraying with carbaryl is also recommended.

It's a rare lawn that doesn't have a few weeds in it. The best defense against them is a lawn grown on rich soil, fed on a regular basis, and watered adequately, but not overwatered, so that the grass makes a heavy turf. It isn't necessary to run to the store for poisons to get rid of a few weeds. For example, dandelions can be dug up, if you're careful to go deep enough to get all of that lengthy taproot.

If weeds are beginning to move into your lawn, look for the reason. If your response is "yes" to any of the following questions, you have found your answer.

- To save mowing so frequently, have you "scalped" your lawn by mowing far too close to the soil?
- Have you failed to feed the lawn, so that the grass is getting patchy, leaving space for weeds to grow?
- Have you let your lawn grow too high, so that some weeds could go to seed?
- Did you plant your lawn with inexpensive grass seed containing a lot of weed seed?
- Do you have areas of the lawn that are always damp?
- Have you overwatered the lawn so much that the grass looks unhealthy?

I use weedkiller on my lawn and the beds around it, but every time I spray, I also kill or damage desirable plants. What am I doing wrong?

Follow these four rules to avoid that unwanted damage:

- Spray only on windless days.
- Get as close as possible to the unwanted weeds with the sprayer.
- Place a shield—either cardboard or plywood—in front of the plants you wish to protect, before you begin spraying.
- Use low pressure on your sprayer in order to keep the spray in a small area.

I have found an herbicide to use on the broad-leaved weeds that have found their way into my lawn. I hate to use this over all the lawn just to remove the weeds. Any suggestions?

It would be good if all homeowners had your reluctance to use pesticides on a broad scale. Reducing the amount of weedkiller used would also cut damage to other plants due to spray drift. For limited herbicide applications, attach a small cellulose sponge or a small (one-inch) paintbrush to a dowel or broom handle with a nail, tape, or rubber band. Pour the liquid weedkiller into a can, dip the brush or sponge into it, squeeze out the excess against the side of the can, then paint or sponge the weed. A single touch will do the trick.

LAWN WEEDS

•

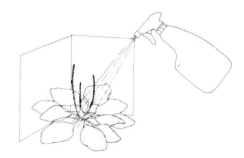

Place a protective cardboard shield behind plants you are spraying with an herbicide, get as close to the unwanted plant as possible, use a low pressure on the sprayer, and spray only on windless days.

To assure application of weedkillers on only the plant you wish to get rid of, dab the solution on with a small brush tied to a dowel.

COMMON LAWN WEEDS

Annual broad-leaved weeds include pigweed, mustard, ragweed, and lamb's-quarter. Although they make their debut in new lawns, they are usually not seen the next season, because in order to propagate, they must reseed. By mowing regularly, you interrupt this cycle. Don't bother to use chemicals on these; you may damage that crop of new grass.

Large, easy-to-kill broad-leaved perennials include some old "favorites," among them dandelion, chicory, dock, peppergrass, broad-leaved plantain, thistles, paintbrush, and sorrel. These plants form a low-growing rosette the first year, and thus duck under the threatening blade of your mower. Chemical control is necessary although digging may work if the population is small.

Ann Reilly

Broad-leaved plantain.

Small, creeping broad-leaved weeds offer a challenge—they're hard to defeat. You know them by the names of smooth chickweed, mouse-ear chickweed, knotweed, ground ivy, and clovers. They're perennial and will force their way into the best of lawns. Removing them by digging or pulling is almost impossible. Lime and fertilizer simply encourage them, and they can be cut shorter than grass without harm. Spot application of herbicides is the best treatment, but take care: The chemicals recommended for their control may injure lawn grasses as well as shrubs and trees with roots in the treated area. Repeat applications are necessary every year.

Annual grasses—goosegrass, foxtails, annual bluegrass, and worst of all, crabgrass—reproduce by casting seeds each summer and fall. The seeds overwinter in the soil and germinate in the spring. Discourage their growth by maintaining a vigorous, tight turf and keeping the lawn cut as tall as possible, so that the weeds are shaded out by the taller grass even if they manage to germinate.

Positive Images, Jerry Howard

Crabgrass.

Individual crabgrass plants may be removed by digging or pulling, but this is backbreaking when you are coping with crabgrass over a large area. Seedlings can be killed chemically, but a better approach is to use a preemergence herbicide (see page 55) early in the spring—before lilacs bloom. These chemicals work *only* on germinating seeds and will not kill crabgrass seedlings.

Perennial grasses include timothy, redtop, tall fescue, and other hay-type grasses. Maintaining a thickly growing sod will drive these out, but it won't trouble the most persistent of this family—quack grass. Some experts concede there is no control for this weed. Others suggest such drastic moves as covering the infected area with black plastic for a year. Quack grass, however, is known for longevity: Its seeds will lie in the soil four or more years and still germinate—and any pieces of rhizome quickly grow to hardy plants, with even more plants produced at each joint. In this way, the plant can quickly blanket and threaten all living things in a given area. Only persistent spading up of the plants, plus tilling in the fall, will help to keep quack grass under control.

Ann Reilly

Goosegrass.

I need some overall approach to weed control, to add some degree of sanity to my helter-skelter attempts to stamp them out. Any ideas?

Yes. It may help to consider all lawn weeds as falling into the five categories on page 54.

I've heard about preemergence herbicides. What are they?

There are two types of herbicides. *Preemergence herbicides* kill the tiny plants as the seeds germinate, but have no effect on living weeds. *Postemergence herbicides* kill only living weeds.

What are the most frequent lawn weed pests?

They vary from region to region. They are more diverse in the South, but individual species are more abundant in the North. Several broad-leaved weeds, particularly dandelion, plantain, chickweed, knotweed, and clover, are widespread in lawns, but can be chemically controlled. Annual grasses, such as crabgrass and foxtail, are abundant, too, and are best controlled with both preemergence and postemergence sprays. The perennial grasses, such as tall fescues and other forage species, are perhaps not as prevalent, but are really the worst lawn weeds because they are so difficult to control selectively. Ordinarily, to stop perennial grasses, a general herbicide that kills back all vegetation must be used, followed by replanting.

Can you dig weeds instead of using an herbicide?

Certainly—and congratulations for your ambition. When no selective herbicidal control is available, hand-digging works just fine, if there are only a few weeds.

I'm going to try to raise a lawn where there is nothing but quack grass. Any ideas?

Quack grass is a cool-season perennial that spreads by long, white underground stems as well as by seeds. If you try to till your area, you will only chop up those roots, and every one of them will form a new weed.

Author-gardener Dick Raymond suggests a way to get rid of this weed, but it takes a full season. His method recognizes that each of those pieces of root has only so much growing energy stored in it, and if this energy can be used up, the root will die and the quack grass will be eliminated. First, till the soil and then plant a heavy crop of buckwheat—three to four pounds per 1,000 square feet. As this quickly grows up, its leaves blanket the soil, discouraging the quack grass. When the buckwheat blossoms, till it in, and then plant another crop of buckwheat. When that blossoms, till it in; then plant a crop of annual ryegrass. This, too, blankets the soil, again preventing the quack grass from growing. The ryegrass will be killed by the frost and will blanket the soil during the winter. In the spring, till it in, prepare the soil for planting grass seed, and look forward to a lawn without a bit of quack grass and with soil enriched by those three crops you have tilled into it.

What can I do to prevent the spread of crabgrass?

A number of very effective crabgrass preventives are on the market. They are applied in spring before crabgrass seeds germinate, and affect only sprouting seeds. The materials, usually siduron or DCPA (dimethyl ester of tetrachloro terephthalic acid), must be used exactly as directed and spread uniformly to blanket the soil. Overapplication sometimes retards rooting of the permanent grass, so be judicious about repeated applications. Visit your local garden supply store for chemicals recommended for your area. You may also find controls for crabgrass that has sprouted, usually in spray form intended for two or three applications a week or ten days apart.

The surest way to avoid crabgrass is to leave no room in your sod for it to move in. In a one-on-one situation, a healthy grass plant can win over crabgrass.

I live in Oklahoma. Will you tell me how to get rid of Bermuda grass?

Grasses are extremely difficult to eradicate. An airtight covering of heavy building paper or old linoleum is effective. Also try persistent hoeing of the grass blades as they appear. Consult your county Extension Service agent concerning the use of herbicides.

A LIST OF DO'S AND DON'TS TO AVOID WEEDS IN THE LAWN

- Avoid weedy topsoil when starting or rebuilding a lawn. Some weed seeds are almost inevitable, but a check of where the soil comes from may help you to lessen this problem.
- Use good-quality grass seed. Inexpensive seed is likely to contain weed seeds and annual grass seeds. The annual grass will grow for one year, but won't come up the second year, and thus will leave lots of space for weeds.
- Sow grass thickly, according to instructions on the container.
- In the North, begin lawns in the fall for best results.
- Don't "scalp" a lawn by cutting it far too short. What is "short" depends on the grass you're growing (see page 38). Bent grass can be kept at putting-green height with no harm, and some of the new varieties of bluegrass and ryegrass will tolerate closer cutting than the older varieties. In general, frequent cutting is better than close cutting. The worst thing you can do is to let the grass get four to six inches in height and then cut it as short as possible. A rule of thumb is to cut one-third the length of the grass. For example, let it grow to three inches, then cut off one inch.

- After the lawn is established, water only when the ground is dry, then soak it thoroughly. Frequent, light watering is a relaxing evening pastime, but it encourages shallow grass roots and the growth of crabgrass.
- Keep grass cut so that weeds don't have a chance to go to seed.
- Enrich the topsoil when creating the lawn, and feed the lawn on a regular basis (see pages 32-36).

Are there any natural controls for weeds?

There certainly are. Much weed management is based on an understanding of weed growth. For instance, many weeds grow in infertile soil, too acid or too alkaline soil, or poorly drained or hardpan soil. Rid your lawn of these weeds by improving the soil. Let us stress again that the surest way to avoid weeds is to create a good lawn from the beginning. Close-growing grass will crowd out most weeds. Organic gardeners thus have a rule for weed control in lawns: If weeds threaten, add fertilizer. They also warn against mowing too closely and excessive watering.

The summer night is hot. The lawn needs mowing—badly. Humidity is high, and for some unknown reason, someone has watered the lawn. Conditions are perfect—for a severe case of summer grass disease. The best treatment for these diseases is to avoid them by not overwatering or overfeeding the lawn in midsummer and by sowing more disease-resistant seeds.

Such diseases as brown patch and powdery mildew are much more common today with "improved" varieties of lawn grasses than they were in the days of unimproved bluegrasses. Bent grass is very susceptible and looks dead after an attack. It usually revives, since the roots have not been touched, but such an attack does open your lawn to an invasion by crabgrass and other fast-growing weeds.

Powdery mildew occurs in the fall as white powdery fungus on the outside of the leaf blade. This fungus sucks the nutrients out of the plants. Sunlight will stop it. Plant resistant cultivars, such as fescues and many cultivars of Kentucky bluegrass.

Red thread strikes lawns lacking fertilizer, appearing as tan to reddish irregular dead patches. Treat by feeding the lawn.

Melting-out, or *helminthosporium leafspot*, is caused by a fungus, and starts as reddish-brown or purplish-black spots on the leaves. Large areas of lawn are thinned out or killed as the grass crowns and roots die. It is most common on closely cropped lawns. Excessive nitrogen fertilizer, especially in early spring, will also increase the damage. The best attack is to plant a resistant variety of grass.

Pink snowmold and *gray snowmold* appear as irregular patches in the lawn in the spring. Snowmolds are caused by late fall fertilizing, a heavy mat of grass left on the lawn over the winter, snow falling on an unfrozen lawn, poor drainage, and long periods of snow cover.

Brown patch is a fungus disease that leaves brown, water-soaked areas during periods of high humidity. High nitrogen levels increase the severity of the disease, as does overwatering. Remove clippings from infected areas.

Pythium blight is another fungus disease caused by high moisture conditions. The infected area may feel greasy or have a

GRASS DISEASES
•

Ann Reilly

Ann Reilly

Some common lawn diseases: (top) powdery mildew; (bottom) fusarium blight.

fish odor; the grass is matted and lies flat. Do not overwater or feed too much nitrogen; remove thatch.

Fusarium blight is severe during hot, dry periods after early wetness. There may be light brown dead spots on the grass, or, if the crown of the plant is infected, the grass will turn straw color. Dead areas may have a spot of healthy grass in the center. Don't mow too closely, and, most important, don't let thatch accumulate.

Dollar spot appears as light tan dead spots on individual grass blades, followed by bleached out blades as the infected areas enlarge. Remove grass clippings and thatch, as the fungus that causes this disease can live on them for long periods.

There are pesticides to control these diseases. Unfortunately, most of them are preventive and thus must be applied before the disease appears and several times throughout the season. They call for extremely exact spraying. Because of the complexity of this treatment, seek advice from specialists such as Extension Services or lawn and garden centers.

What is a fairy ring?

The fairy ring is a circle of fungi—toadstools and mushrooms—that appears in the late summer or fall. The grass in this circle is greener than the surrounding turf because the fungi fix nitrogen from the air and the lawn grasses benefit from this. These rings develop from pieces of wood, perhaps a stump or a piece of discarded building lumber buried underground. The easiest way to get rid of a fairy ring is to find the wood—it will be in the center of the ring—and remove it.

Does disease enter through the sheared tips of grass blades?

Some diseases are thought to. In most instances, however, if conditions are right for a disease, it will find ways of infecting grass, mowed or not. But unmowed (and tall-mowed) grass has some advantage in resisting disease, probably mostly due to the extra food-making power of additional green leaves.

Will tree leaves injure a lawn?

Anything that obstructs light from the lawn will reduce the grass plants' food-making abilities. Tree roots, too, may reduce growth by competing strongly for fertilizer and moisture. But no toxicants occur in tree leaves that will appreciably inhibit the growth of familiar lawn grasses. Thus, the problem is mainly a mechanical one, not a chemical one. Small leaves, or larger ones shredded by a mower, should cause no difficulty in the typical lawn of bluegrass-fescue or other open-textured turf, if not more than an inch or two thick. The leaf fragments will settle into the grass foliage, which will soon overgrow them. When fallen leaves are so abundant as to smother the grass, they should be gathered for the compost pile or for mulching around shrubs.

Ann Reilly

Fairy ring—a circle of dark green grass caused by an infusion of nutrients in the soil where fungus is breaking down organic matter—can be disguised by fertilizing other grass in the area so as to deepen its color to match the ring.

Common Lawn Problems and Their Solutions

PROBLEM	SYMPTOM	SOLUTION
Ant hills	Small mounds of sand or dirt on the lawn that can spread over and kill the grass.	Use diazinon, following directions.
Broad-leaved weeds	See descriptions on page 54.	Apply general herbicides, as well as herbicides for specific weeds, such as dandelions. Follow directions exactly to get rid of these weeds.
Crabgrass	See page 54.	To prevent the appearance of crabgrass, use DCPA or siduron two weeks before the last expected frost. These are preemergence weed killers; postemergent herbicides are also available.
Drought damage	Many grasses, such as fescues, Bahia, Bermuda, and zoysia, turn brown, but live through all but the worst of droughts.	To protect plants during droughts, don't cut the grass closely and don't spread inorganic fertilizers such as 5-10-10. When you water, do so until water has reached to the deepest roots.
Fairy ring	As fungus in the soil breaks down organic matter, it releases nutrients and turns a circle of grass dark green.	Fairy ring doesn't harm a lawn, but you may wish to disguise its appearance by fertilizing well so that all the grass is the same color.
Fusarium blight	Patches of grass turn light green, then straw color, often with a patch of green in the center.	Rake out dead grass and reseed with resistant varieties, such as bluegrass. To prevent fusarium blight, treat the lawn with a fungicide containing benomyl or iprodione in late May.
Fusarium patch	Pale yellow areas, with pink along the edge, appearing in late winter and early spring.	At first sight of this fungus disease, treat with a fungicide containing benomyl or iprodione. Repeat after ten to fourteen days. Treat again in fall, during the rainy season when temperatures are below 60°F. Make two applications, two days apart. Keep the lawn mowed, to avoid matting.
Snowmold	See page 45.	Apply fungicides containing sulfur compounds such as maneb, ferbam, or zineb. These are most effective as preventives, but if infection is rampant, use them to help keep it from spreading further.
Grubs	In late summer, grass turns brown in irregular patches, and sod lifts up easily.	Grubs are the larvae of many beetles, such as Japanese beetles, which feed on grass roots. Use diazinon when you notice damage, then water well. Retreatment is often necessary. It may take up to a month to kill grubs.
Mole tunnels	Uneven, heaved up ridges in the lawn.	Moles feed on grubs. If you get rid of the grubs, you will no longer have moles. You can also try traps in active tunnels (those that reappear a day or so after being tamped down). Avoid using poison; it's too dangerous to have around children and pets.
Scalped spots	Caused by cutting grass too closely, shaving the tops of bumps in your lawn, or cutting the grass too closely after not mowing for an extended period.	Level high spots, set the mower higher, and mow more frequently.
Shade damage	Blades of grass are thin and dark green. Moss may be seen.	Prune overhanging trees and shrubs. Select shade-tolerant grass, such as fescues and some bluegrass varieties (Glade or Nugget) in the North, and St. Augustine grass in the South. Seed in fall and rake grass frequently to keep it free of leaves. If necessary, plant a ground cover such as English ivy, pachysandra, or periwinkle instead of grass.
White or gray cast to lawn	Caused by dull lawn mower blades, which chew into grass, tearing it instead of clipping it.	Sharpen rotary mowers after every two or three mowings.

PART II
LANDSCAPING

3 Planning and Planting Your Shrubs, Trees, and Ground Covers

North American gardens and yards are products of a melting pot. Just as natives of dozens of countries have contributed to the growth and strength of both the United States and Canada, so too have they contributed their ideas—and the plants and seeds they brought with them—to the developing concepts of how to use the space around their homes, concepts molded to suit the various climates and needs of the continent. Constantly evolving over time, the gardens of today are quite different from those of earlier generations.

When you travel in England, you both expect and find, if not the actual gardens designed by Gertrude Jekyll and Edwin Lutyens, surely the formality and careful color blending that marked the work of that pair. Visit Japan, and you see the deceptively simple gardens that reflect a centuries-old art form and that demonstrate how much beauty can be created in the smallest of areas. In North America, however, there is no single garden type to be discovered. Here are carefully planned herb gardens, bountiful vegetable gardens, vast expanses of lawn, collections of plants such as daylilies or roses, fortresslike hedges, and even overgrown "foundation" plantings that threaten to shadow second-story windows—a magnificent variety of landscaping and gardening schemes all reflecting the interests, ambitions, capabilities, even ancestral backgrounds of gardeners.

◀ *Well-planned and carefully tended plantings enhance the value of any property.*

HOW TO BEGIN PLANNING YOUR OWN LANDSCAPING

Let's take a moment to mention some of the factors worth considering when we make basic landscape planning decisions.

Most of us want the growing space around our homes to be a place for family living, as well as entertaining and cooking evening and weekend meals. These purposes are well served by a patio surrounded by plantings, with areas for socializing and space for containers filled with shrubs, vegetables, and even small fruit trees. For small children, the yard is a haven, a place to enjoy and learn about the outdoors. As the children grow, it can become a gathering place for them and their friends.

Most of us, too, want a home garden that is easily maintained. We're willing—usually, if reminded—to mow a lawn weekly. In the spring, it seems as though some chemical change in our body impels us to get out there with shovel, rake, mower, and hoe, to scatter seed and fertilizer, to plant bulbs and perennials, and to prune vigorously. And for the rest of the year? Please, nothing too vigorous, and particularly nothing that has to be done daily. Remember, too, that we go away on vacation for several weeks in the summer, and, like it or not, the gardens and the lawn must take care of themselves during that time.

There are, of course, exceptions to this: the truly devoted, to whom the doing is as much a pleasure as the result. But most of us want it simple. Life has challenges enough; we have no desire to plant our own.

This attitude, perhaps surprisingly, has had a welcome effect on our gardening. In recent years, for example, we've tended away from choosing a predictable selection of foundation plantings favored by all landscapers and moved toward selecting shrubs and trees native to our own areas that fare well with little

A patio provides an outdoor space for living and entertaining.

Positive Images, Tad Goodale

help from us. This has added a refreshing divergency to our landscaping throughout the continent.

Finally, we want to be proud of our gardens and lawn. There's a purely financial reason for this. A well-planned and carefully tended garden can add thousands of dollars to the price of the house when we sell it. But this is rarely a concern unless we must move. Far more simply, we enjoy having visitors exclaim about what we have created. Perhaps even more important, we enjoy walking out of the house in the morning, or coming home to it in the evening, and smiling in satisfaction at what we see.

Our family is young and growing. How do I begin planning our yard for both beauty and function?

Whether you are designing a new landscape or improving an existing one, your first step is to define exactly what you want to accomplish. This does not mean selecting shrubs or patio furniture. Rather, you must begin by making decisions about what you want to create. Try writing down your needs and goals. Here's an example:

- Front yard should reflect the friendliness and warmth of our home, inviting our friends and neighbors to come in and join us.
- Area on right side of house should be screened in some way to eliminate eyesores in the service area, where we have tool storage and trash cans; would shrubs be better than a fence?
- Left side should be an open expanse of lawn.
- Shrubs (or beds of annual flowers?) will serve to suggest a division of the left side lawn from the rear area.
- Backyard should be an extension of our life inside the house: a place for entertaining and for evening family meals; a playing area for the children and their friends, including a sandbox now and perhaps a pool when we can afford it; space for frisbee playing and volleyball; flower and vegetable gardens—fit in as many activities as possible without having the area look crowded or allowing activities to encroach upon each other.

An open backyard with a dense growth of grass plants is ideal for games such as croquet.

Your list of goals may be far different from this example. You may want a formal public area in front of the house and a quiet place for reading and meditation in the rear. Whatever you want, get it down on paper. Listing your goals will help as you make specific decisions on such things as placement of new shrubs and trees.

How much privacy should I attempt to provide?

This really depends upon your location and the degree of privacy that you desire. You will want to wall out the noise and traffic of a busy highway; on the other hand, you may enjoy making a quiet street with beautiful residences part of your landscape. In general, unless there is a real need for privacy, it is better to share landscapes with neighbors by avoiding high hedges and fences that delineate property lines. You and your neighbors thus benefit equally from the sense of spaciousness that is created. In this way, an effort to improve landscaping at any house tends to upgrade the neighborhood and stimulates others to attempt improvements.

How can I distinguish the various areas around the house according to their uses?

First is the public area in front of your house, the area that tells people about you and your house. You can vary, of course, from these generalizations, but often the best choice for front yards is conservative—a spacious area of lawn, evergreen or deciduous shrubs to soften the foundation line, a tree or two to frame the house and provide some shade.

The service area, containing such items as vegetable garden, compost piles, and a shed for storage, can be downplayed or disguised by well-placed shrubs.

Finally, the outdoor living area should be an extension of the activities of the family in the home. A patio is often the feature point, easily accessible from the house, and placed, if possible, so it has the morning sun but is shaded in the afternoon. Too often, patios are larger than necessary. A patio should be about the same size as the rooms in your house, overly spacious only if you do a lot of large-group entertaining.

Locate other activities so they don't interfere with activities on the patio. Play areas for children should be close enough so the youngsters can be watched, either from the patio or inside the house. Remember, too, that children grow fast, and their interests change at a comparable speed. They'll soon outgrow the sandbox and the slide, so plan for these changes.

DIAGRAMMING YOUR LANDSCAPE

Whether you are landscaping your present property or studying a possible site for a new home, you need a landscape plan on paper. This takes time to draw, but it can be one of the most important moves you make. Just drawing it forces you to take a close look at your lot, and working with it enables you to make mistakes and change your mind before you plant without any cost—or, equally undesirable, the need to live with your mistakes.

What *is* a landscape plan?

It is a map of your land, showing property lines, all buildings, walks, drives, utility poles and lines, and fences or walls. It should indicate all existing trees and shrubs—including variety, height, and width—gardens, and play areas. It should also include some things that are not on your property, such as neighboring trees that shade your property and outlooks toward eyesores *or* beautiful views. If your plan is to be used to help decide the site of a house, it will need additional information, such as rock outcroppings that would complicate the placement of the foundation and any soil conditions that would influence the location for a septic system.

What is the first step toward drawing a map of my land?

To prepare for making a scale drawing, make a rough sketch of the features of your property on a sheet of paper on which you can jot down measurements later as you make them. Draw in the boundary lines first. Position the house as exactly as possi-

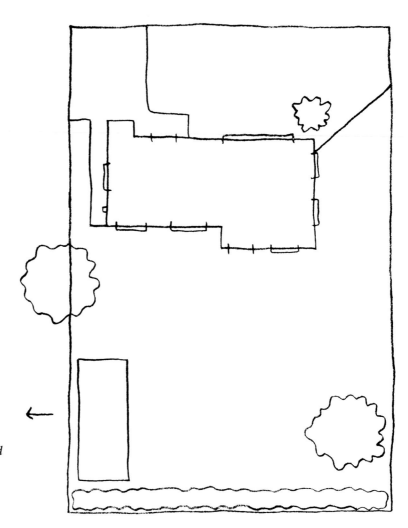

A rough sketch of your property should indicate such features as property lines, buildings, walks, drives, utility poles and lines, fences, trees and shrubs, gardens, and play areas.

ble, locating all windows, doors, and patios. Indicate the position of all objects on the property—both man-made and natural.

How do I go about making an actual scale drawing?

Depending on the size of your paper and the size of your lot, choose graph paper and establish a scale. For example, for a three-by-three-foot sheet of paper and a 100-by-100-foot lot, a scale of one-quarter inch equals one foot is good. Although a smaller sheet can be photocopied easily, thus enabling you to try out several plans on paper for comparison, it may be difficult to get adequate detail on too small a plan.

Next, take your rough drawing outdoors and make all of the measurements necessary to translate that drawing to scale on your graph paper.

When you have completed your drawing, add a North arrow and a date, then begin "planting" on it. If the permanent objects on your plan are outlined in black ink, you can make your "proposals" lightly in pencil right on the map, or you can lay a piece of tracing paper over the map and try out several different schemes.

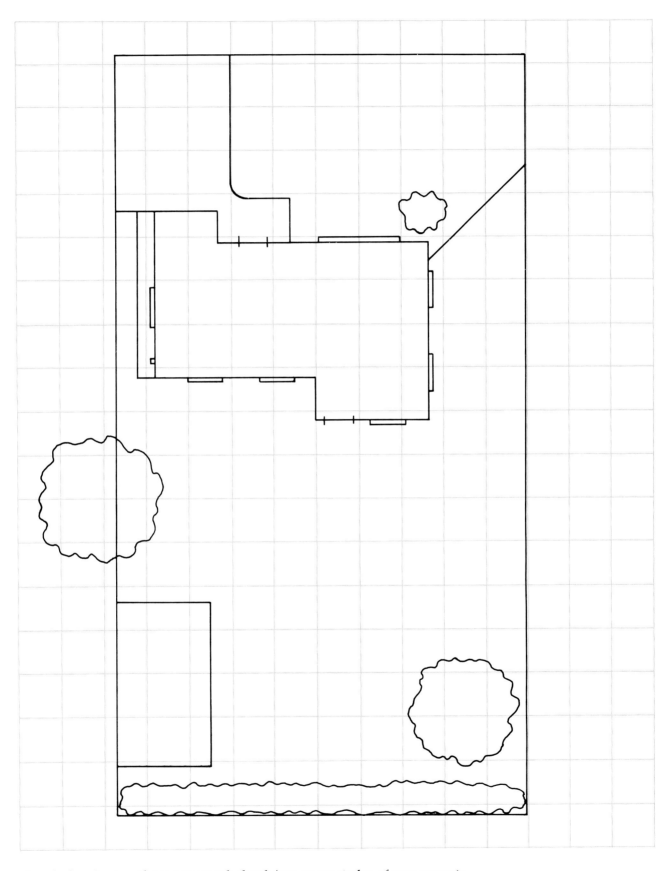

A scale drawing translates your rough sketch into an exact plan of your property.

USING YOUR LANDSCAPING PLAN

Here are some very basic thoughts to consider as you try out various arrangements on your landscaping plan:

- An unbroken lawn, bordered with shrubs and flowers, gives a good appearance. Have a valid reason before you plunk something in the center of it.
- A scattering of shrubs of various kinds looks unplanned and messy. Several of the same variety grouped together in a bed gives a unified appearance and a much stronger effect than a single shrub. If planting three or more, avoid planting them in a row.
- Foundation plantings (deciduous and evergreen shrubs planted near the house foundation) keep a home from appearing naked. There is nothing in the law that says plantings must all be small evergreens. Native plants, in particular, often make good foundation plantings. They blend in particularly well with similar plants elsewhere on the property and require very little care.
- In most cases, foundation plantings look best when taller plants are used to soften corner lines

and smaller plants are used near the main entrance door to the house.

- For plants under windows, select those that will grow no higher than the bottom of the window. Taller growing varieties may be chosen, of course, but then you should plan on annual, naturalistic pruning.
- For every shrub that you plant, have a reason, such as breaking the blankness of a wall, providing background for flower beds, suggesting divisions between various areas, or screening work or play areas.
- A tree directly in front of a house is usually a mistake. Rather, plant the tree at one side to help frame the house.
- When deciding on the location of a tree, the common error is to be guided by its size at the time it is planted, rather than by its mature size. As a result, we often see trees planted so close to a house that their branches brush against it, trees overpowering the front of a house, or large trees out of scale beside small houses.
- The first rule of planting trees is to be guided by where you do or do not want shading.

In advance of building on a lot, is there anything that can be done that would improve the land or save time later on?

Clear out undesirable trees and thick wild growth. Identify with the builder any native shrub masses that you wish to leave untouched. When the cellar hole is dug, have the topsoil saved and the soil beneath it either carried away or spread where it will not interfere with your plans. If this subsoil is dumped where you wish to plant, it will bury the valuable topsoil and make it more difficult to plant there (see pages 10-11).

We have a new home and a flat, bare lot to landscape completely, with very little money to put into it. What do you advise for first plantings to take away the bare, new look?

Shade trees come first. Bare-root trees (packaged with sphagnum moss rather than with the soil in which they grew; see page 83) are most economical, but should be planted in the early spring. Next, buy foundation plantings for the front, beginning with small, and therefore less expensive, plants. Add other shrubs and plantings as you can afford them. Not only does this spread your costs out, but if you plan carefully and buy slowly, you have a chance to evaluate and modify your plan as you see how things are coming along, and thus you may be much more satisfied with your results than if you bought and planted everything at one time.

I plan to build on a lot that's only one-hundred by fifty feet. What can I do about landscaping?

It may surprise you, but landscaping is probably more important on your lot than a larger one, simply because it's often easier to create beauty on a larger lot. You have specific and challenging conditions—little land, lack of privacy, and a need to enrich the space you have—all of which can be addressed by thoughtful landscaping. First, much can be done with the proper design and placement of the house to assure views of your lawn area that can be enjoyed from inside the house and to use as little space as possible for drives and service areas. Plan a lawn area unbroken by decorations, shrubs, or trees; it will thus appear more spacious. Don't crowd the remaining space with too many activities, such as vegetable gardens, eating areas, or flower beds. Select and concentrate on one, keeping it near the edge, rather than in the center of your lot. Finally, avoid plantings, such as hedges, on all the boundary lines of your lot. They will make the lot seem much smaller.

Will you suggest economical landscaping for a small temporary home?

Maintain extreme simplicity. Use the minimum of planting on the front and sides of the house. In the rear, if possible, plant a compact vegetable garden bordered with annual and perennial flowers.

I recently bought a 157-year-old house with overgrown shrubbery and beds, and trees shading a mossy lawn. Should I clear it all away and start fresh?

You have a challenge. In addition to buying a house, you bought the landscaping decisions, many of them poorly thought out, of generations of owners of that house. Move slowly as you improve the grounds. A tree once felled is gone forever. Shrubs, as well as trees, are expensive to buy, and many of yours probably can be salvaged by removing dead or damaged growth, then pruning them to the size you wish. And, of course, they can be moved. A thorough knowledge of the shrubs—their names, growth, and flowering habits—is essential before you make decisions on whether to retain or remove them.

Approach your challenge by drawing three plans. On one, show the lot as it is, complete with house and garage, walks and driveway, and all of that vegetation you mentioned. The second plan should show the same permanent fixtures and what you want to salvage of the natural features. You must either cut enough of those trees to introduce sunshine to your lawn and

Positive Images, Jerry Howard

Plan landscaping so that views can be enjoyed from the inside as well as outside.

An older home with many large plantings offers a different kind of challenge.

foundation beds, or select shade-tolerant plants. Consider the age, position (good or bad), size, and beauty of trees as you make decisions. The final plan should show how you want your landscaping to be when you've finished.

As you go out on your grounds to work, remove trees first, work with your shrubs next, and leave your lawn until last. Much as builders leave laying the carpet until last, you should work on your lawn after you have removed trees, possibly dug up old flower beds and some shrubs, and made all decisions on your layout. Have the soil tested by your Extension Service or do it yourself with a soil-testing kit available at garden centers (that moss makes me think it may be very acid; see pages 36-38), then follow the directions in the lawn section for rebuilding a lawn (pages 27-29).

My colonial house has a very plain doorway. How can I plant near it to make it seem more important?

When the doorway is formal but very plain, interest may be created through the planting. Use identical groups on either side, but select the plants carefully, striving for variety of form, texture, and color. Evergreens give great dignity and are less likely to get too large in a short time. Mass taller plants to accent the lines of the doorway, with spreading plants around them for the most effective arrangement.

We have large trees (oak, gray birch, maple, and ironwood) on our lawn. What should be planted near the house? The yard slopes toward the south and the house is new, so we are starting from scratch.

Let the trees be the principal landscape feature. Use a minimum of planting near the house. Try ground covers (see pages 89-95) along the foundation, plus a few shade-loving shrubs at the corners or at either side of the entrance.

What is the best method of foundation planting for a house with the front door off-center?

An unbalanced, or asymmetrical, composition for a foundation planting can be extremely attractive, and an off-center door will make it even more interesting. Use a variety of shrubs, both deciduous and evergreen, of different heights, colors, and textures, and be sure to include some flowering shrubs.

How shall I landscape the front of our Cape Cod home? Built about 1810, the main house features a front door in the center with an ell and a long shed-garage combination. What treatment along the front would you suggest?

Planting for a Cape Cod house should be very simple. A formal fountain, for example, would attract attention because of its inappropriateness. Consider a boxwood, privet (pruned to a

rounded form), or Japanese holly on each side of the door, and clumps of lilacs at each corner of the house. Many old homes traditionally have two shade trees in the front lawn, one on each side of the door. A small dooryard garden enclosed by a low picket fence would also be charming.

The central doorway of my house is a reproduction of an old colonial door, with leaded side lights and a fanlight. How should I plant around this so as to enhance rather than detract from its beauty?

For an elaborate doorway, complicated planting is unnecessary. Possibly the most effective thing would be to plant a large lilac on either side of the door. For a more formal effect, plant an Irish or cone-shaped yew on either side.

What sort of foundation planting is appropriate for a French chateau-type house?

French architecture calls for a formal style of planting. Hold the plantings to a minimum, using evergreens, such as yew, boxwood, euonymus, and holly, clipped into formal shapes.

I live on the ground floor of a small apartment house and thus have the use of a small (sixteen-by-sixteen-foot) walled-in area behind the house that I would like to use. What can I do? The area gets sunshine all afternoon, but the soil looks worthless.

You can create an outside room in that area that will give you space to garden and to entertain, and possibly provide a pleas-

Here an asymmetrical garden by the front door provides an understated and effective foundation planting.

Symmetrical and simple plantings are most suitable for a plain but formal entrance door.

73

For a new house, concentrate on placing suitable trees; use low-growing ground covers near the foundation.

ant scene from inside your apartment as well. Along the sides of your area, in both shaded and sunny spots, create a few raised beds framed by lumber or bricks and filled with three or four inches of good soil. Pave most of the rest of the area with bricks or flagstones on which to place a few lawn chairs and a table. Choose furniture of a muted color so it doesn't dominate your space. Paint the walls either a light shade or white; the reflected light will improve lighting in the area. Consider growing flowers, vegetables, and even fruits in large pots or other containers.

Choose your plants carefully. Many kinds of flowers will flourish in the sun, of course, but there are quite a few varieties, such as impatiens and begonias, that will do well in shady spots. Also consider planting ground covers, such as ground ivy or periwinkle.

Vines, either annual or perennial (see pages 125-126), will do well under the conditions you have described, and if trained on trellises or other structures, will add interest to your wall areas. You can provide more privacy for your outdoor room by erecting an overhead trellis to support the vines.

Your trees and shrubs are the backbone of your landscaping plan. They frame the house, provide an appealing background for flowers and other focal points, screen objectionable views, and provide shade, protection from the wind, and privacy. If selected and placed intelligently, they create a beautiful setting that is of colorful interest every month of the year, guaranteeing a home landscape that will provide you and others great pleasure.

For an inexperienced gardener like myself, the increasingly varied selection of specimens available at nurseries makes choices difficult. I know I want to plant a crab apple tree, but which of the hundreds available should I select? I like lilacs, mock-oranges, and other plants, too, and they offer the same bewildering number of choices.

Begin by identifying where you need plants. Then study the conditions for their growth and look for the best plants to fit your needs. If there is any buying trend today, it's toward smaller trees and shrubs—the ten-foot crab apple, for example, instead of the 100-foot oak. Consumers are learning to select with future needs in mind. If your home and grounds are small, instead of choosing a tiny lilac and finding yourself with a fifteen- or twenty-foot tall shrub years later, select a Dwarf Snowflake or some other lilac that reaches three feet in height—and remains there. Select trees and shrubs that grow well in your local conditions so that you won't have to fuss with something that will never acclimatize to your area.

Would it be better to select a landscape architect to design our property?

You may decide to hire a landscape architect or designer to advise you in plant selection. This person can make all of the decisions for you, based on your description of hoped-for results. He or she may even purchase and plant your shrubs and trees, and start to revive a lawn. This, of course, can be expensive, sometimes leaving you with little more satisfaction than writing a check.

I have never gardened before and my first trip to my local nursery was rather overwhelming. How do I know where to begin?

Neophytes are often made most clearly aware of their own ignorance about gardening on their first expedition to a nursery or garden center. Where others see handsome arrays of annual and perennial plants begging to be bought and carried home, new gardeners see only questions. Is my soil right for that one? Will that one grow in the shade? And this tree—how high will it grow, and how wide? If beginners walk away in dismay, or make a purchase just to have something to plant, they're miss-

CHOOSING YOUR PLANTINGS

— • —

ing out on one of the biggest bargains around: free information from nursery personnel. They want you, not merely as a customer, but as a satisfied customer, returning year after year as you improve the landscaping at your home. They know from bitter experience that if they sell you the healthiest of plants and it dies under the less than tender—although possibly very loving—care you provide, they've lost a customer, since you inevitably perceive the failure to be theirs and not yours.

Perhaps I would be better off saving money at a discount store?

You can, of course, save money by going to a discount store for your plants and supplies, but this can be dangerous unless you're knowledgeable. The plants shipped to these stores may not be the best for your geographical area, and they may not have received the best of care since being put out for sale. Further, you are unlikely to get informed advice on the planting and care of what you buy.

What are the advantages of depending on a garden center for my needs?

In most cases, a good nursery or garden center is the best source for beginners, in particular. They've carefully selected the best plants for your area, they've treated them like the babes some of them are, and they will charge you nothing for the information they dispense with every sale. They have one thing in common, however: In return for picking their brains, you're expected to buy at their shops.

How do I set up an effective relationship with a good garden center?

Garden centers have two methods for giving information to customers with numerous questions. Some will visit your home, talk with you, and then submit a plan showing their recommendations for purchases and where those purchases should be placed. More commonly, nursery personnel expect you to map your lot, then discuss it with them at the nursery. The advantage of this method is that they can show you the recommended plants. However they work, nursery personnel recognize that in most cases money for landscaping is limited, so they will suggest a planting schedule that extends over several years.

Get the most out of free assistance by some thoughtful preparation. First, schedule a convenient time to visit your garden center, preferably in advance of the season. Don't drop in on a spring Saturday morning when nurseries do the largest volume of their year's business. Understandably, those weekends are times for nurseries to take in cash and move to the next customer. Instead, call long before the season opens and set a time that's mutually convenient. Give them a hint of what help you want.

Next, before your meeting, make a sketch of your lot and take a few color photos of your house from different viewpoints. Be prepared to answer some basic questions about your property. Any rocky areas? Wet areas? Steep banks or hills? Is the soil sandy, clay, or good loam? You might take along a soil sample. It's often easier to show than to tell.

Expect to tell something about yourself. The person helping you will probably grasp quickly the depth of your gardening knowledge but will want to know if you're willing to do a lot of work or prefer landscaping that is nearly maintenance-free. You must also give a hint of how much you are willing to spend. Much can be done to move costs up and down, through suggestions of specific plants, as well as selection of younger and thus less expensive plants.

Given all this information, most nursery personnel will not only recommend purchases to you, but tell you where they will do best, when and how they should be planted, and how you should care for them. This can be the start of a profitable relationship for both of you.

One of the first questions I faced at my garden center was whether I was interested in deciduous or evergreen trees and shrubs. What is the difference?

Deciduous plants lose most or all of their leaves yearly; evergreen plants have foliage that stays green and functional through more than one growing season.

What do you consider some of the most handsome and functional shrubs for home landscapes, and what are their basic traits?

Endless information about specific varieties is available in books, arboretums and botanical gardens, nurseries and garden centers. The list of shrubs on page 79 provides a solid beginning catalogue of fine shrubs, but you will soon find that there are thousands of plants available to today's landscaper.

How could a rather steep, partly wooded hillside be planted to make it more attractive?

A wooded hillside can be underplanted with native shrubs, such as mountain laurel, azaleas, and rhododendrons, along with ferns and woodland wildflowers. A system of trails leading through the area would add to its interest.

What is best for planting around a small house on a small acreage? Everyone has evergreens. Can't we be different?

Deciduous shrubs can be just as interesting throughout much of the year, although evergreens are more apt to lend interest and color in the winter. An all-deciduous planting, however,

SHRUBS

•

Positive Images, Jerry Howard

Native shrubs, ground covers, and a handsome stone walkway invite browsers to explore this wooded hillside.

Azaleas and rhododendrons usher in spring with floods of color.

can certainly work well. Another possibility is to use deciduous shrubs with a few evergreens as a background.

What sort of shrubbery would you plant in front of a new house with a thirty-foot frontage?

Avoid too much planting. If the house foundation is low enough, leave some spaces bare to show the house standing solidly on the ground. Both deciduous and evergreen plantings are suitable, and a variety of colors and textures is most effective. Cypress, yews, azaleas, rhododendrons, and boxwood are only some of the many popular choices.

What plants should be used around a modern ranch-type house in front of a large rock outcrop?

By all means, make use of the natural rock, planting rock plants and creeping junipers around it. Low yews and azaleas might be in the foundation planting, with a dogwood or crab apples at the corners or off to the side.

Will you suggest some shrubs for the rocky bank in front of our house?

Junipers are always good, both bush form and trailing types for over the rocks. Memorial rose, *Crispa stephanandra*, and Arnold Dwarf forsythia all root wherever their branches touch the soil, and they are ideal for such situations. If vines would qualify, try climbing hydrangea, English ivy, or Virginia creeper.

SELECTED SHRUBS

AUTUMN SAGE, *Salvia Greggii*. Popular in the Southwest, this woody perennial grows three feet high, is drought-resistant, and has clusters of red to purple flowers in fall.

AZALEA, *Rhododendron*. There are many kinds of azalea, both deciduous and evergreen, so that in almost every part of North America you should be able to grow this popular shrub. Most common varieties grow three to six feet high and are among the most brilliant of the flowering shrubs. Many bloom before the leaves are formed. They grow both in shade and filtered sunlight and require ample moisture.

BLUE SPIREA, *Caryopteris incana* (zone 7 south*). These low plants are useful for borders. They have showy blue flowers in fall.

BOXWOOD, *Buxus sempervirens* (zone 6 south). Boxwood does particularly well in Maryland and Virginia. Boxwoods range from dwarfs to twenty-five-foot-tall trees, often pruned to formal shapes. They need acid soil and ample moisture.

CAMELLIA, *Camellia japonica* (zone 8). Particularly popular in the South Atlantic states, this shrub is sometimes seen as a tree up to twenty-five feet tall. The many varieties are all prized for their showy blooms. Most require acid soil and good drainage.

CORAL ARDISIA, *Ardisia crispa* (zones 9 and 10). This foot-high evergreen has white flowers in the spring and red berries in the fall and winter.

CRAPE MYRTLE, *Lagerstroemia indica* (zone 7 south). This shrub can grow to a twenty-foot tree. Its pink blossoms are a late summer attraction. Although it can be grown from seed, its flowers aren't always true to the color of the plant from which the seed was taken; it may also be propagated by cuttings.

FORSYTHIA, *Forsythia intermedia* (zones 5 to 8). Forsythia grows six to eight feet high and is noted for its brilliant yellow flowers early in the spring.

HONEYSUCKLE, *Lonicera tatarica* (zones 3 to 9). Bush (common) honeysuckle grows up to ten feet tall and, depending on the variety, has white to pink blossoms in spring.

HYDRANGEA, *Hydrangea macrophylla* (zones 5 to 9). This shrub usually grows three to four feet tall, though it can reach twelve feet. It has beautiful blue or pink flower clusters in midsummer.

LILAC, *Syringa*. A variety of lilac can be found for every zone except 10. One of the most popular

*Zone map appears on page 711.

shrubs, lilacs originally were always purple, but now colors range from white, pink, and blue to deep purple.

MOCK ORANGE, *Philadelphus coronarius* (zones 4 to 9). Mock orange grows about seven feet tall. This well-loved, old-fashioned shrub bears fragrant white flowers in late spring.

MOUNTAIN LAUREL, *Kalmia latifolia* (zones 4 to 9). This handsome shrub has large rose and white flower clusters in early summer. It grows well in shady areas with acid soil. It should be massed for greatest effect.

Blue-flowering hydrangea is an old-fashioned and dependable favorite.

OREGON GRAPE HOLLY, *Mahonia Aquifolium* (zones 5 to 8). Oregon grape holly does well in shade. It has fragrant yellow flowers in spring, interesting blue fruit in summer, and is particularly beautiful in fall, when its foliage turns red.

RHODODENDRON, *Rhododendron* (zones 5 to 8). Most rhododendrons today are evergreen hybrid shrubs with white, pink, red, or purple blooms. They require rich, acid soil, ample moisture, and some shade.

ROSE OF SHARON, *Hibiscus syriacus* (zones 5 to 9). Rose of Sharon grows six to eight feet high and is noted for its brilliant yellow flowers early in the spring.

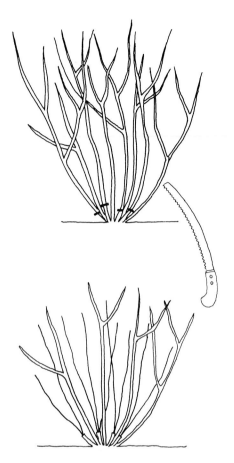

(Top) with a small saw, cut the largest stems down at ground level; (bottom) new growth will spring from the pruned branches to create a fuller shrub.

Please name a few evergreen shrubs that do well in light shade.

Abelia, barberry, mahonia, mountain laurel, leucothoe, privet, andromeda (*Pieris*), rhododendron, evergreen azalea, yew, arborvitae, and certain viburnums.

Can shrubs and small trees be used in a flower garden?

Yes, an occasional compact-growing tree or shrub in the garden relieves the monotony of perennial and annual plantings. The tree rose is especially suitable.

We plan to landscape a three-acre tract. Will you name some plants that give a succession of color throughout the year?

For spring, use azalea, forsythia, rhododendron, or spicebush viburnum. For summer, use honeysuckle, hydrangea, buddleia, roses, heather, or rose of Sharon. For fall flowers use abelia or witch hazel. For fall foliage color use *Euonymus alatus*, dogwood, enkianthus, viburnum, Japanese barberry, sumac, spicebush, and blueberry.

We have a huge, overgrown lilac. Although it is beautiful in the spring when it is covered with blossoms, it is far too large for its location. What can we do?

Using a small saw, so you won't injure the other stems, cut down at ground level the largest stems until those remaining are the height you want. This will not damage the plant. When doing this, however, don't prune the branches you wish to keep, as you might with other shrubs, or you may cut away next season's blossoms.

Maggie Oster

A variety of colors and textures of deciduous trees and shrubs, ground covers, and vines makes this an attractive nook, even without flowers.

What are some considerations to keep in mind when choosing trees?

Select trees based on their usage: shade, wind protection, ornament, or food production. In a setting near a home, the height of the mature tree is important. Many fine shade trees reach a height of 100 feet or more, excellent in a roomy setting, but far too large for smaller lots. Our list of trees contains many that are of moderate mature height and are thus suitable for the smaller home lot. Equally important, be certain the trees you choose grow well in your area. Since there are several hundred varieties of trees, our list (pages 81-82) is only a representative selection.

I have an area where I would like to have some shade as soon as possible. I know that poplars grow quickly. Would they be a good choice?

Think of poplars as a last resort if nothing else will grow in the area. The small branches that continuously fall from poplars make them messy trees. Furthermore, their spreading roots often plug drains or other pipes. Their virtues, on the other hand, are that they will grow in damp areas and they do reach full growth in a few years. A better choice, nevertheless, is one of the faster-growing maples, which will add beauty as well as shade to your area, without the disadvantages of poplars.

How do I provide shade for the patio?

Plant a dogwood, crab apple, magnolia, or some other small tree. Dogwood, in particular, is ideal because its horizontal branching habit allows one to sit under it.

TREES
•

Positive Images, Jerry Howard

This maple shows its early spring color.

SELECTED SHADE TREES

GINKGO, *Ginkgo biloba* (zone 5 south*). Ginkgo is also known as the maidenhair tree. Because female trees have a foul-smelling fruit, plant only the male trees. Young trees have irregular branches, but they eventually fill out. They can grow to more than 100 feet in height. Because of their hardiness, they are excellent for the stressful conditions along streets.

MOUNTAIN ASH, *Sorbus aucuparia* (zones 3 to 9). Mountain ash grows to about thirty feet high. It will tolerate some shade and dry soil. Its natural beauty is enhanced by white flower clusters in the spring, followed by bunches of orange-scarlet berries. This showy tree is a good selection when you want to feature a tree as a focal point.

PIN OAK, *Quercus palustris* (zones 5 to 8). Pin oak

will reach seventy-five feet in height. Its leaves turn red in fall. It is an excellent choice for a large lawn. There are some 200 other species of oaks, most of which grow to be large trees. Many of them, native to specific areas, are excellent choices for roomy grounds.

SUGAR MAPLE, *Acer saccharum* (zones 4 to 8). This slow-growing tree will reach 100 or more feet when it is mature. Along with many of the other maples it is an excellent shade tree and suitable for street plantings. Smaller maples, such as *A. ginnala*, *A. palmatum*, and *A. tataricum*, grow only twenty to thirty feet high, so they bring the easy grace of the maple to smaller home grounds without dominating the landscape.

*Zone map appears on page 711.

SELECTED ORNAMENTAL TREES

FLOWERING CRAB APPLE, *Malus* (all zones except the deep South*). There are many varieties and hybrids of flowering crab apple. All are early bloomers, and many grow only fifteen feet, with few more than thirty feet high. Many have showy fruit in the fall and winter.

FLOWERING AND KOUSA DOGWOODS, *Cornus florida* and *C. Kousa* (zones 5 to 9). This is one of the most popular of the flowering trees, with white, pink, or red flowers in early spring; the foliage is scarlet in fall. Dogwood's maximum height is thirty feet.

FLOWERING CHERRY, *Prunus serrulata, P. Subhirtella*, and *P. yedoensis* (zones 5 to 9). Flowering cherry grows from twelve to thirty feet tall. To show these trees off the best, plant them about twenty-five feet apart. They need sun, good drainage, and rich soil to achieve their peak blooms during early spring.

The famous cherry trees in Washington, D.C., usually bloom in early April.

MAGNOLIA, *Magnolia* (best in zones 5 to 9). Some magnolias produce their handsome flowers before the foliage; some come into bloom and put out leaves at the same time. Magnolia is available in shrubs as well as trees, some reaching thirty feet in height.

WEEPING BIRCH, *Betula pendula laciniata* (zones 3 to 8). The finely cut leaves of this white-barked birch turn yellow in the fall. It grows to about thirty feet in height. Consider as well, other white-barked birches, such as clump birch, with several trunks growing together to a height of about twenty-five feet; the large (up to ninety feet) canoe, or paper, birch; and European white birch, which is smaller than canoe birch.

Positive Images, Jerry Howard

Positive Images, Jerry Howard

Flowering crab apple is heavily laden with deep pink flowers in early spring.
*Zone map appears on page 711.

Flowering white dogwood with its horizontal branches is an ideal tree to use near houses.

FRUIT TREES

I've always wanted to grow fruit trees, but I have neither much space nor much knowledge. Have you any advice?

One of the finest advances for amateur gardeners who wish to grow fruit trees has been the development of dwarf trees. This, combined with the development of easy-to-follow programs of disease and insect control, now makes it possible to have a productive family orchard, complete with fruit trees, berry bushes, and grape vines, in a space as small as fifty by fifty feet.

What must I consider before I plant fruit trees?

• First consult your family about their likes and dislikes.

Positive Images, Jerry Howard

The pleasures of growing fruit trees are possible even on properties with limited space.

- Understand the pollination habits of each tree. Some fruit trees, such as peaches and apricots, are self-compatible, which means they can make use of their own pollen in order to bear fruit. Others, such as many apples, sweet cherries, and pears, require another variety of the same fruit to be blossoming nearby at the same time.
- Ascertain the area required for each tree, so you can plan your orchard properly. Available trees range from standard (with thirty-five feet between trees) to semidwarf (twelve to eighteen feet between trees), dwarf (ten to twelve feet between trees), and even extra-dwarf, which grow only seven feet tall and can be planted as closely together as six feet.
- Lay your orchard out in a sunny, well-drained area with rich soil.
- Carry out a program of pruning and spraying at the recommended times.

I have an area where I wish to plant several fruit trees. It is extremely sandy. Will it help if I place a layer of topsoil over the area?

The topsoil, tilled in, would aid you in establishing a grass crop around the trees. But to help the trees, it's necessary to get the better soil down around the root areas.

Dig large holes, taking out at least a bushel of sand from each one. Make a mix of half topsoil and half compost or other organic matter. Put enough of this in the hole so that when the tree is planted it will be at the level it was growing previously. Put the

A standard apple tree is eminently suitable for home landscapes.

Protective plastic wrapping discourages small animals from nibbling the bark of young trees.

tree in the hole, hold it straight, and cover the roots with several inches of soil mix. Fill the hole with water and wait until the water has drained away. Then fill the hole with the mix and firm the soil well in around the root area.

What is the best way to prepare heavy clay for fruit trees?

The greatest danger you face is that drainage may be poor and thus water will stand around the tree roots, requiring installation of a drainage system. If you decide this is not necessary, try to improve the soil by working in a quantity of organic material. Instead of returning the clay soil to the hole when planting the tree, substitute topsoil.

When should I prune my fruit trees?

Any time between harvest and the beginning of spring growth—in other words, late fall to late winter, the dormant, or resting period. Preventive spraying is also beneficial at this time.

I've just lost another fruit tree to mice girdling it. What can I do? It seems to happen every winter.

Just a few mice can cause an impressive amount of damage around a house. They not only injure trees but feed on bulbs as well. Trees can be protected two ways. One is to wind the lower part of the trunk with a plastic wrapping sold expressly for this purpose; or place a strip of quarter-inch metal mesh around the tree, wide enough so it extends firmly down into the soil and at least a foot up the trunk. In the fall, remove any leaf or hay mulches, which are probably living quarters for the mice. A hungry cat provides the best long-term protection.

Tape wrapping will also keep the sun and winds from drying out and cracking the bark.

It seems so simple: Buy a tree or shrub, take it home, dig a hole, and plant it. While it can be that easy, the beginner should know that one error in the process can mean that the plant may take as many as three years to return to health, or it may not even survive the transplanting. The process of transplanting begins with selection of the plant and doesn't end until that plant is in the ground and, if necessary, held in place with stakes.

PLANTING SHRUBS AND TREES
———————— • ————————

When is the best time to plant trees?

For most trees and shrubs, the planting time isn't that critical. While spring and fall are best for most plants, many of them, especially balled-and-burlapped or container-grown stock (see definitions below) can be planted during most of the growing season, since their roots will not be disturbed during planting. Bare-root plants, however, should go into the ground in the very early spring while they are still dormant.

What are bare-root plants? Are there special techniques involved in planting them?

Mail-order nurseries usually ship plants *bare-root,* with the roots covered with damp sphagnum moss or some similar material. If this covering is dry when the plants are received, the roots should be soaked in water for a few minutes. Don't leave them in water if you must delay planting them for several days; that's far too much of a good thing. Bare-root plants are the easiest to damage. Extreme care must be taken, particularly when placing them in a hole, because leaving their bare roots exposed to the sun for only a few minutes can spell their end. Plant them in the spring, before any new shoots are more than three inches long, or in the autumn, after their leaves have fallen.

Please explain what *balled-and-burlapped* means.

Balled-and-burlapped trees and shrubs have been dug carefully, with the soil around their roots maintained, wrapped in burlap, and tied. A plant with a one-inch stem should have a root ball at least a foot in diameter. The most important care for balled-and-burlapped plants is to keep the root ball moist. Handled properly, the roots should be undisturbed from the time they are wrapped until they are back in the ground.

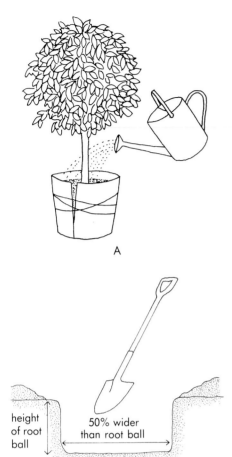

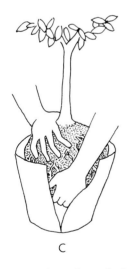

(A) Water container plants before planting; (B) dig a hole at least half again as wide as, but only slightly deeper than, the root ball; (C) cut the container if possible and remove the plant carefully, disturbing the root ball as little as necessary.

What does the term *balled-in-peat* mean?

This is a less common method, which involves digging up the plants bare-root and storing them in the late fall. In late winter or early spring, peat or other materials are placed around the roots, which are then wrapped in burlap.

What does the term *dug-and-potted* mean?

Dug-and-potted plants have been dug, bare-root, out of their nursery beds, then put into containers only a few weeks before going on sale. Thus, they've undergone stress and will undergo more when they are planted.

What are *container-grown plants?*

Container-grown plants have been grown in containers for all or most of their lives. They have the most complete and undisturbed root system.

Which packaging method offers the best chance for successful transplanting?

Container-grown or balled-and-burlapped plants.

What should I look for at the nursery when I am selecting plants?

Check for signs of mistreatment, such as broken branches, scarred or torn bark, and dry or discolored leaves. Don't buy such plants. And don't mistreat those you buy. As you carry them home, avoid slamming the stems or trunks against the side of your vehicle, ripping the root ball, or subjecting the leaves to a windy ride that will dry them out. A station wagon, rather than a pickup truck, is preferable for this trip.

Now that I have my plant home, what do I do next?

Put your tree or shrub in the shade while you dig the hole.

There are many rules for equating a plant with the size hole that's needed for it, but our recommendation is to make it wide, but not too deep. When you place the plant in the hole it should stand only slightly lower than the height at which it was originally growing. Older methods of planting suggested digging six or eight inches deeper than this so that soil enrichments could be placed in the bottom of the hole before setting the plant, but this often resulted in the plant's settling in too low after a period of time. If you have a bare-root plant, dig the hole wide enough so the roots can be spread out without crowding them. For a balled or container plant, make the hole at least half again as wide as the root ball to allow ample space at the sides to provide the plant with a rich soil mixture.

As you dig, save the topsoil and take away the subsoil. Mix enough soil enrichment to the topsoil to fill the hole. One popular mixture is half topsoil and half organic matter, such as peat moss, leaf mold, or well-rotted manure. Add a half-cup of superphosphate and, if the topsoil is acid, a half-cup of lime per bushel of the topsoil-organic material mix.

Work some of this material down into the subsoil at the bottom of the hole. Then shovel in enough so the plant will be at its former growing level. Be sure to pack it firmly, adding more if necessary.

How do I treat a bare-root plant?

Heap some soil mixture in the center of the hole, so the roots will spread out and down, the way they grew. Again, be sure it is firmly packed so that there will be soil contact all around the roots and a minimum risk of settling.

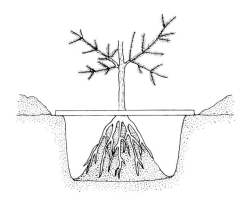

Carefully arrange the roots of bare-root plants over a mound of enriched soil; be sure plant will stand at the height it was originally planted.

What do I do with balled-and-burlapped or balled-in-peat plants? My garden center advises that I don't need to take the burlap off when I plant the shrubs. Is this right?

It is. The important thing in planting balled-and-burlapped shrubs is to avoid breaking or damaging the root ball. After you've dug a hole for a shrub, firm back into the hole enough enriched soil so the plant will stand at exactly its original height. Set the shrub in the hole, burlap and all, and add soil to about half the depth of the root ball. Then cut and remove the cord holding the burlap up to the stem. Pull the burlap away from the stem, being careful not to break the root ball. Complete filling the hole with the soil mixture. The burlap will rot away very quickly. The plastic part of plastic-reinforced burlap will not rot away, so cut away and remove it, being careful not to damage the root ball.

Unwrap about the top third of a balled-and-burlapped tree or shrub after placing it in the ground.

May plants be left in containers and planted?

Take plants out of containers before planting, even if the directions say they can be planted without doing this. These containers often restrict root penetration, which slows the growth of the plant. Take care in removing them, trying not to break the soil around the roots.

What are the final steps?

After placing the plant at the proper height, fill around it with the soil mix, making certain it doesn't settle to a lower level than it grew. The soil should be packed gently but very firmly.

With some of the remaining soil, build a small dam around the plant, out at the edges of the hole. Then water well. From five to fifteen gallons are needed to wet the soil mixture and settle it to remove air pockets. Water again a half hour later. Weekly waterings for the rest of the season are recommended; water more frequently in dry seasons.

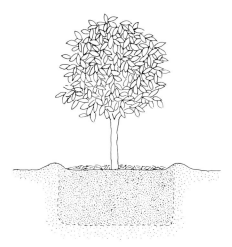

All shrubs and trees should be planted at the same depth as they originally grew. A light mulch keeps weeds down and moisture in.

I've heard I should prune trees and shrubs when I plant them. Is this true?

Pruning at planting time is no longer recommended. There are two exceptions: bare-root plants and plants you dig yourself to move to another spot. In these cases you may wish to prune in order to reduce the water requirements during the first season when roots, and particularly damaged roots, may not yet be able to furnish enough. Aim at removing from one-fourth to one-third of the leaves. First, cut away unsightly or damaged branches (but not the leader, the primary shoot), then cut back other selected branches to a lateral branch or bud. Alternatively, if you want to avoid pruning, be sure to keep the plant well watered throughout the first season, and feed it with a liquid fertilizer at half strength once a week.

Do you recommend bark mulches for newly planted trees and shrubs?

Yes, a four- to six-inch-deep layer of bark mulch is easy to apply, gives a natural, woodsy appearance, will last for several years, discourages weeds, conserves moisture, helps prevent severe freezing of roots in winter, and is easy to mow around. Begin six inches from the stem or trunk and extend the mulch to beyond the edge of the hole.

Many types of bark mulch are now available, and they have multiple uses around the yard. You'll find nuggets (three-quarters to one and one-half inches in size), larger chunks (one and one-half to three and one-half inches), shreds (stringy pieces about the size of the chunks), or chips (one-quarter- to three-quarter-inch pieces). You can also buy soil conditioner, which is dark brown and very fine in texture. It is used as a topdressing for lawns and for soil improvement in gardens and flower beds. It often has fertilizers added.

Are there materials other than bark chips that are suitable mulches?

Wood chips or pine needles are some of the materials you can use.

Do newly planted trees and shrubs require staking?

Most shrubs and small evergreen trees don't require staking, but small trees usually do, and all plants will benefit if they are apt to face high winds. The reason for staking small trees is not to prevent them from blowing over; rather, the constant force of a wind may rock the tree and loosen the small feeding roots, thus preventing the tree from becoming established.

For trees up to five feet in height, two stakes may be used. They should be hammered eighteen inches into the soil (be sure to avoid the root ball) and placed so the tree is between them. The stakes should stand high enough so that a wire can be

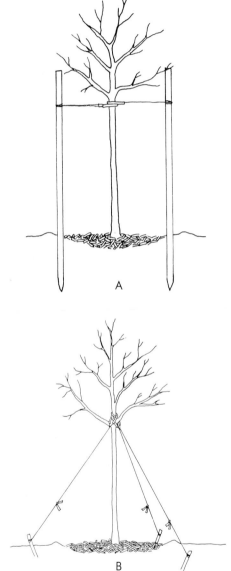

(A) Support small trees (up to 5 feet) with two wires two-thirds of the way up the tree, stretched between two stakes driven about 18 inches into the ground; (B) larger trees should be supported by 3 guy wires extending from about two-thirds of the way up the tree out to stakes about 18 inches from the tree trunk.

stretched level and reach two-thirds of the way up the tree. Cover the wire, where it touches the tree, with a section of hose. The wire should be firm, but not so tight that it pulls hard on the tree. Remove this support after a year.

To steady larger trees, use three guy wires reaching about two-thirds of the way up the tree and extending down to stakes set in the ground about eighteen inches from the trunk. Again, use sections of hose to protect the trunk. Remove the guy wires after a year.

Ground covers are low-growing plants that can be used in the following ways:

- To cover areas that are difficult to mow.
- To cover bare areas, where grass and many plants simply won't grow.
- To protect slopes where erosion is a problem.
- To add interest to lawn and garden areas.
- To guide foot traffic if used as edging along paths.

Because of the many different kinds of ground covers, one can certainly be found that is ideal for your need and that will grow well in the climate in your particular part of the country, but the variety of desirable ground covers is so great that making a final decision can prove difficult.

As a guide, consider your answers to the following questions. Is your area sunny or shady? Level or sloped? Is your soil acid or alkaline? Sand or clay? Fairly dry or usually damp? What is your plant hardiness zone? Do you want a large or small ground cover? One that is green year-round? Should it serve some additional purpose, such as providing food for birds? Your answers to these questions will determine your final choices.

What are some of your favorite ground covers?

Our list (pages 90-91) is a representative selection of ground covers suggested by the U.S. Department of Agriculture. These are among those most commonly grown. The list should be considered only as a source of suggestions, not as a limiting factor when you make your choices. All are perennials. Study also the listings for shrubs (page 79) and perennials (page 99), which often can be used with the smaller ground covers.

When should I plant ground covers?

The best time to plant in most areas is early spring; this gives the plants a chance to become well established before winter. In all cases, the soil should be prepared as for lawns by adding fertilizer and organic matter such as compost, tilling the soil, then raking it.

GROUND COVERS

Positive Images, Gary Mottau

Several varieties of thyme produce pleasing color and texture contrasts.

SELECTED GROUND COVERS

BEARBERRY, *Arctostaphylos Uva-ursi* (zones 2 to 9*). This fine-textured, broad-leaved evergreen grows six to ten inches high, with trailing stems, lustrous, dark foliage that turns bronze in winter, and bright red fruit. The stem may reach five to six feet in length and roots at the joints to form large clumps. It is excellent for stony, sandy, or acid soils, growing fairly well in sandy banks. It is difficult to transplant, so should be obtained as a sod or as a pot-grown plant. Some people transplant bearberry by digging up frozen clumps, then placing those in a prepared bed of sandy, acid soil.

BUGLEWEED, *Ajuga reptans* (zones 5 to 9). This creeping perennial is four to eight inches tall. It thrives in either sun or shade, grows rapidly, and tolerates most soils. It has purple leaves and dark blue flowers. Bugleweed can escape from cultivated beds and show its strength by crowding out other plants. It is, in fact, a good candidate for places where little else will grow. Propagate by seed or division.

CAPEWEED, *Lippia nodiflora* (zones 9 and 10). Also called phyla, capeweed is a creeping perennial, two to four inches in height, often used as a grass substitute. It spreads rapidly and grows in sun or shade. It can be walked on and mowed, and is more drought-resistant than many lawn grasses. Plants can be set about two feet apart. Propagate by planting sod pieces or making stem cuttings.

COTONEASTER, *Cotoneaster adpressus*, and *C. apiculatus* (zones 5 to 9), *C. Dammeri* and *C. horizontalis* (zones 6 to 10), and *C. microphyllus* (zones 7 to 10). There are more than fifty species of cotoneasters. These five are flat, horizontal-growing plants, six to thirty inches high, with bright red berries. They make excellent ground covers, particularly on banks and in rough areas. While they can't be walked on, they do seem to thrive despite neglect. *C. apiculatus* is the hardiest of this group. All do best in full sun and are attractive as accent plants with other ground covers. Cotoneasters are self-seeding, or propagate them by making cuttings.

COWBERRY, *Vaccinium Vitis-idaea* (zones 5 to 9). Also called red whortleberry, foxberry, lingonberry, and mountain cranberry, this evergreen shrub grows twelve inches high and makes an excellent ground cover in acid soils in regions with cool, moist weather in summer. Cowberry grows slowly. Propagate by dividing, making cuttings, or layering (rooting a branch by burying it in the soil, with only the tip protruding).

CREEPING LILY TURF, *Liriope spicata* (zones 5 to 10). This grasslike, evergreen perennial grows to twelve

*Zone map appears on page 711.

inches tall, and does well in hot, dry conditions, sun, or deep shade. The leaves are dark green, and the flowers range from white to purple. It can stand exposure to salt spray without injury. Once established, it forms dense growth from which small divisions can be removed for propagation.

CREEPING THYME, *Thymus Serpyllum* (zones 5 to 10). This is an evergreen species of thyme that bears purplish flowers, has pleasingly aromatic foliage, is often used as an edging or between stepping stones, and is popular in rock gardens. It rarely grows more than three inches in height, tolerates dry soils and full sun, and is a good substitute for grass in small areas. Propagate by dividing.

Periwinkle.

CROWN VETCH, *Coronilla varia* (zones 3 to 7). This is used frequently to cover dry, steep slopes. It grows one to two feet tall, and has small, pink flowers. Crown vetch spreads by underground stems, and a single plant can cover up to six feet in all directions. It prefers neutral soil but will tolerate slightly acid conditions. Propagate with cuttings. For large areas, sow seed at the rate of twenty pounds per acre. Seed should have been *scarified* (the seed coat filed or cut) to improve germination and inoculated to introduce bacteria for nitrogen fixation.

DICHONDRA, *Dichondra repens* (zones 9 and 10). This plant has runnerlike stems that spread rapidly. It seldom grows more than one or two inches tall and rarely needs clipping, so it is a favorite for lawns in the desert areas of California and other arid regions. Its enemies are winter cold and poor drainage. Propagate by replanting small clumps.

DWARF LILY TURF, *Ophiopogon japonicus* (zones 7 to 10). Also known as mondo and mondo grass, dwarf lily turf forms clumps of growth ten inches tall. It does best in moist, shaded areas.

ENGLISH IVY, *Hedera Helix* (zones 5 to 9). This popular ivy grows six to eight inches tall and forms a dense cover. Although it grows in both sun and shade, it does best in shade. Often it is planted so that it spreads across the ground, then climbs a wall. Propagate by pulling vines free and allowing them to root in a new site. Cuttings also can be started in sandy soil, then transplanted.

GERMANDER, *Teucrium Chamaedrys* (zones 6 to 10). Also known as wall germander, this woody perennial grows to ten inches tall and makes a fine border for walks. It grows well in sun or partial shade. A winter mulch may be needed where the ground freezes. Propagate by dividing or making cuttings.

GOLDMOSS STONECROP, *Sedum acre* (zones 4 to 10). This low evergreen is a good ground cover for dry areas. It grows about four inches tall, spreads by creeping, and forms mats of tiny foliage. It is fine for between stepping stones and in rocky places. Propagate by dividing or making cuttings.

GROUND IVY, *Nepeta hederacea* (zones 3 to 9). A weed when found in lawns, this creeping perennial grows to three inches tall, forming a low mat that does well in both sun and shade. Propagate by dividing.

HONEYSUCKLE, *Lonicera japonica* (zones 5 to 9). This climbing, twisting, fragrant vine grows well in sun or partial shade and is excellent for getting fast growth on banks and other areas subject to erosion. It can become a pest, since it tends to cover and kill shrubs and even trees. It should be pruned each year: Be sure to clear away the cuttings, or they may take root. Propagate by dividing or making cuttings.

JAPANESE SPURGE, *Pachysandra terminalis* (zones 5 to 8). This evergreen grows six to twelve inches high and spreads by underground stems. It covers an area quickly and does well under trees and in other semishade. Propagate by dividing or making cuttings.

MEMORIAL ROSE, *Rose Wichuraiana* (zones 5 to 9). A low-growing, trailing plant with semi-evergreen foliage, memorial rose has fragrant two-inch, white flowers. It grows well on banks and sand dunes and is highly tolerant to salt spray. Propagate by planting seed or making cuttings.

PERIWINKLE, *Vinca minor* and *V. major* (zones 5 to 10). This popular evergreen, trailing plant has dark green foliage and small purple, blue, or white flowers. *V. minor* grows six inches tall and has small leaves; *V. major* grows eight inches tall and has larger leaves. Both grow well in full sun or partial shade. Propagate by dividing or making root cuttings.

ST. JOHN'S-WORT, *Hypericum calycinum* (zones 6 to 10). Also called Aaron's beard, this semi-evergreen shrub does well in semishade and sandy soil, growing nine to twelve inches tall. Its bright yellow flowers are seen from midsummer to frost, when the foliage turns red. Propagate by planting seed, dividing, or making cuttings.

SOUTH AFRICAN DAISY, *Gazania rigens* (zones 9 and 10). This orange-flowered plant grows six to nine inches tall, with light green foliage. It blooms throughout the spring and summer, and once established, will thrive with little water. Propagate by planting seed.

STRAWBERRY GERANIUM, *Saxifraga sarmentosa* (zones 7 to 9). This perennial grows to fifteen inches tall and spreads by runners. It is best in partial shade and is useful around the base of other plants, in rock gardens, and in areas of heavy clay. Propagate by making cuttings.

WANDERING JEW, *Zebrina pendula* (zone 10). Commonly found in greenhouses farther north, this perennial grows six to nine inches high, roots readily, and grows easily in the shade. Propagate by dividing or by making cuttings.

WEEPING LANTANA, *Lantana montevidensis* (zones 8 to 10). This trailing shrub has hairy branches up to three feet long. It grows best in sun and is highly salt tolerant. Propagate by cuttings or seed.

WINTER CREEPER, *Euonymus Fortunei* (zones 5 to 7). This evergreen ground cover, native to the eastern United States, does well in acid soils and moist, shady areas. It grows about four inches tall. Propagate by dividing.

SWEET WOODRUFF, *Galium odoratum*. Sweet woodruff is a spreading perennial, up to twelve inches in height. In early spring it bears delicate, bright green leaves, profusely scattered with tiny white starlike flowers. Freshly cut sprigs are often added to white wine to make traditional May wine. Sweet woodruff grows well in average soils, in both sun and shade, and spreads quickly and freely. Propagate by seeds or division.

Sweet woodruff.

Where can I find more information about ground covers to help me decide what would be good for my needs? I would especially like to see some examples.

As you drive around, look for the ground covers that do best in your area. You'll find them around houses, as well as in parks and other public places. Some of the best are along our highways, thanks to Mrs. Lyndon Johnson's promotion of programs for their development along federal highways. Sources of information include Extension Service specialists, garden centers, and state or city highway engineers.

I have purchased some junipers and cotoneasters to use as ground covers. How should I plant them?

The method of planting ground covers depends, of course, on the size of the plants selected. Large ones, such as junipers and cotoneasters, should be handled as described in the section on trees and shrubs (see pages 85-89).

What steps should I take to plant small ground covers?

- Mark places to dig planting holes, spacing them so the plants will cover the area when they reach maturity, and staggering every other row to avoid straight lines in any direction.
- Dig planting holes four to six inches wider and an inch or two deeper than the plant root ball. Place a mixture of peat moss and organic matter in the bottom of the hole.
- Set the plant in the hole, making certain it is set at the same height, in relation to ground level, that it was growing.
- Fill the hole with more peat moss-organic matter mixture, or with compost, packing it firmly around the plant, but leaving a slight indentation at the top to hold water.
- Water thoroughly.
- Pull any weeds that emerge.

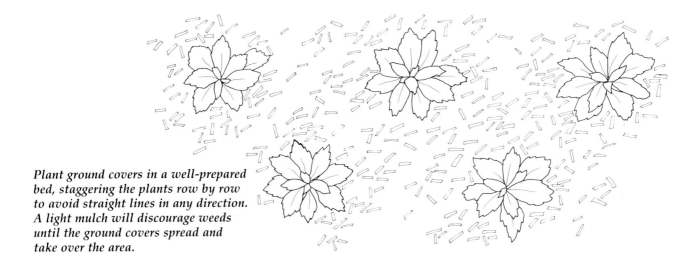

Plant ground covers in a well-prepared bed, staggering the plants row by row to avoid straight lines in any direction. A light mulch will discourage weeds until the ground covers spread and take over the area.

What can I do to beautify a large slope and manage erosion in my yard?

If your slope is steep, consider building a retaining wall (see pages 128-129). This may not only enhance your property visually, but it will also lessen the problem of erosion.

If you decide to use plantings, large plants such as creeping juniper, with roots that reach deep into the soil and spread in all directions, are best for steep slopes. Planting through sheets of plastic mulch will enable these plants to get established before being subjected to the threat of erosion.

In addition to erosion, moisture causes other problems on slopes. Because water flows off them so quickly, they often cannot build up the moisture reserve found in level areas. Thus, plants on them may be suffering from a lack of moisture when those in your garden have an ample supply. Remember to water plantings on slopes first.

Do ground covers require a lot of care?

Ground covers have the same needs for fertilizer and water as any other plants. Because of their spacing, however, young plants can be even more threatened by weeds than other new plants. Keep the weeds from taking over by light mulching, and pull up any weeds that break through the mulch as soon as possible. Avoid hoeing. Not only may you accidentally cut the roots of your plants but you may even promote the germination of more weed seeds.

Should I give my ground covers any winter protection?

In winter, evergreen plants, particularly, are often damaged by the sun. Waterproofing sprays, available at your garden center and applied in the fall, will greatly reduce the damage. The plants, too, can be protected with tree boughs or burlap laid over them.

How can I get my ground covers to move into new areas even more rapidly?

Once you have your ground cover established, you can enlarge it by propagation, either by cuttings or division.

Making tip cuttings is very easy. Get enough peat pots for the number of cuttings you want to make. Fill them with a potting mix of two parts sand and one part each of good soil and peat moss. Cut a three- to six-inch piece off the top of each plant. Strip the foliage from the lower section of each cutting where it will be below the soil line after planting. Treat each base with a root stimulant (available from a garden center). Insert each cutting into a peat pot; water thoroughly.

Place trays of these cuttings in the shade, cover them lightly with clear plastic, and continue to water regularly. Cuttings

4 to 6 inches from tip

A

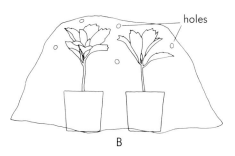

holes

B

(A) For tip cuttings, cut a 3- to 6-inch piece off the top of each plant; (B) treat cuttings with a root stimulant, place them in peat pots, cover them lightly with clear plastic, and keep them moist; when they begin to root, cut holes in the plastic to increase the air supply.

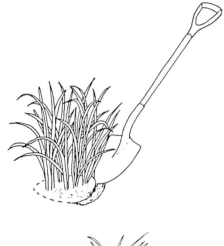

To propagate by division, dig out a clump of the plants including the roots, cut or pull them apart to form smaller plants, and replant them in enriched soil.

should begin to root in ten to thirty days. Pull one gently. If there is some resistance, it's a sign that the roots are forming. When this occurs, cut holes in the plastic to increase the air supply. Gradually increase the size of the holes so the cuttings will harden (become stronger). Finally, remove the cover. Ten days later, pinch back the tip of each cutting to promote branching.

If the tips are started in the spring, they can be transplanted to permanent sites in midsummer.

What does "propagation by division" mean?

Many plants, such as daylilies, can be propagated by division. To divide, dig up the mature plant, then cut or break off vigorous side shoots. Keep the clumps fairly large so they will provide cover the first year after being replanted. The best time to divide plants is in the late summer or fall in southern areas and in spring in northern areas.

What can be done with a narrow front lawn between an old-fashioned house with a high porch and the street, which is lined with large, old maples?

Instead of grass, which will not thrive in shade, especially under maples, try to establish a ground cover such as myrtle or pachysandra. Hide the porch foundation with a low hedge or an informal grouping of yews or Japanese holly.

I live in Southern California. How can I grow a dichondra lawn?

Dichondra is a creeping vine of the morning-glory family used for lawns in many desert areas where grasses will not grow well.

Positive Images, Jerry Howard

Daylilies are easily propagated by division.

Buy flats of the plants, and plant them about a foot apart. If well watered, they will spread rapidly. Such a lawn requires mowing three or four times a year, frequent feeding with a balanced commercial fertilizer, and plenty of water if it is to remain green and dense.

I have seen a ground cover used on highway banks. It has white and pink flowers in the late spring and seems to cover the bank with a thick coat. What is it?

My guess is that what you're seeing is crown vetch, *Coronilla varia*, which is a favorite of highway crews because it halts erosion, requires no maintenance, and will grow in most soils and climates in the United States. Don't think of this solely as a plant for highway banks. It's useful for home landscapes to cover problem areas. You can buy crowns of this plant or plant seed.

4 *Flower Gardens in the Landscape*

I f you think of shrubs and trees as the frame for your landscaping, you can then make it come alive with the many colors, sizes, and shapes of bright perennials. Perennials are plants that have a life cycle of three or more seasons, in contrast to annuals and biennials, whose life cycles are one and two years, respectively. In the careful structuring of your yard or garden, perennials are the jewels to be shown off and admired. As they flourish and demand to be thinned or divided, they make splendid gifts. Gardeners who may not know the botanical names of their perennials can—and will—recite in detail the circumstances of receiving them. From alyssum and aster to yarrow and yucca, their values are many:

- If you find you've planted one in a poor location, it's only a few minutes' work to move it, and most move without damage to the plant.
- They are among the less expensive offerings at your garden center. They are also often easy to propagate yourself: many can be grown from seed, and single plants can often be multiplied by division or other forms of propagation (see pages 93-94).
- Many are disease-resistant and easy to maintain, requiring no more than good soil, sunshine, and moisture.
- Perhaps their greatest asset, after their beauty and hardiness, is their versatility. Need a row of plants to line a walk? Something to fill that shaded spot in the corner of a lot? A bright addition to a clump of drab shrubs? A bed of cutting

◄ *Low-growing moss pink, or moss phlox, brings splendid color to a sunny slope.*

Landscaping comes alive with the many colors, shapes, and sizes of bright annuals and perennials.

flowers? Look at the perennials for any such needs. (A bed of perennials along a fence, walk, or patio is often called a flower *border*.)

I had always imagined that creating a perennial garden took quite a lot of special knowledge and care. Isn't that true?

Perennials *can* be challenging, and even the best gardeners admit they still have much to learn about such things as the lighting preferences of their many daylilies. Each perennial has its particular fascination, however, and your own favorites, some of which are quite easy to grow, will soon give you confidence.

What perennials are good for beginning gardeners?

Many of the ground covers and shrubs discussed in other sections of this book are true perennials—particularly those that flower, such as barrenwort, bugleweed, creeping lily turf, thyme, crown vetch, bergenia, sandwort, and gazania. In addition, our perennial list gives a small sampling of some all-time favorite perennial flowers. All fare well in zones 4 to 8.

I have read that a garden should not compete with a view. Why?

The intimate detail of a garden suffers by comparison with a wide view into the surrounding landscape. It is usually wiser to enclose the garden, shutting out the wide view and leaving an opening framed by trees or evergreen shrubs, so the view becomes a focal point seen from the house or patio.

Is there a rule for good proportion in the size of a garden?

No, but there are guidelines. Oblong areas are more pleasing when they are about one and a half times as long as they are wide. An oblong is better than a square, and an oval is more effective than a circle.

What's the difference between a formal and a naturalistic garden?

Formal designs use straight lines and circular curves or arcs. A formal garden thus is a composition in geometric lines—squares, oblongs, circles, or parts of these. It need not be large, nor must it be filled with architectural embellishment. Formality emphasizes lines; informality emphasizes space and uses long, free-flowing curves.

In landscaping, what is a focal point?

It's the point of highest interest in the development of the design. For example, it might be a garden fountain or a group of particularly striking plants. Planners often start with a focal point, then build the rest of the design around it.

SELECTED PERENNIALS

ASTER, *Aster*. Most of the many varieties grow one to four feet tall and blossom with a wide range of colors, particularly lavender and purple, in late summer and fall. The spectacular blossoms of new hybrids are available in even more colors. Propagate asters by dividing.

BEE BALM, *Monarda didyma*. Bee balm grows three or more feet tall with scarlet blossoms in the summer that attract bees and hummingbirds. It is easy to cover an area with these flowers, since they spread rapidly. Propagate by division.

CANTERBURY BELLS, *Campanula Medium*. Two to four feet high, with violet flowers throughout summer, Canterbury Bells are actually biennial. Many species of *Campanula*, however, from small rock garden plants to much larger ones, are perennials. Start *Campanula* from seed. Perennial varieties may be divided.

CHINESE LANTERNS, *Physalis alkekengi*. Chinese lanterns grow two feet high, with white flowers that become small red berries enclosed in large orange "lanterns," popular for dried flower arrangements. Propagate this plant by seed or division.

Ann Reilly

Canterbury bells.

DAYLILY, *Hemerocallis*. There are hundreds of hybrid daylilies, some growing up to five feet tall, but most two to three feet. New varieties appear yearly. They thrive in sunshine as well as in partial shade, and offer a long-lasting display of blossoms of many hues. These are an excellent choice for specimen plants, for both the beginner and the specialist. Propagate daylilies by division.

MONKSHOOD, *Aconitum Napellus*. Monkshood grows three to four feet tall, with blue to purple flowers in summer. It thrives as a sunny border. Some varieties are shorter and are available in a variety of colors. Propagate monkshood by division.

Positive Images, Jerry Howard

Phlox.

PEONY, *Paeonia*. The many species and hybrids of peonies offer diversity in your garden. Most are three to five feet tall, with either simple, single flowers or mammoth showy blooms in spring, ranging from white, pink, and yellow to red. Propagate peonies by dividing the root clump.

PHLOX, *Phlox paniculata*. Phlox grows about four feet tall, with spreading clusters of vividly colored flowers. It likes full sun and rich soil, and is good for borders. Propagate by dividing roots.

TICKSEED, *Coreopsis*. Some 100 species, most of them one to three feet in height, have large yellow (some white and pink) blossoms throughout summer. Propagate by dividing, or from seed.

YARROW, *Achillea filipendulina*. Yarrow may reach up to four feet, with yellow flowers in summer. It should be grown in sun, and makes a good border. Propagate by division.

How do you determine the size of a garden?

The best rule is to decide how well you enjoy garden work, and then plan as much as you can care for easily. You should keep the design of the entire lot in mind, but the details can be simple. Instead of lawns, you might design areas of ground cover (low-growing plants that cover the ground instead of lawn grass) interspersed with sections of gravel and paving for patios and walks. Accent with shrubs that stay in scale as they mature. Make flower beds only as large as you can manage to keep tended.

Should a garden have a lawn space in the middle?

Not all gardens should be designed this way, but there are many advantages to this type of layout. A grass panel serves as a foreground to the floral displays, as well as a space for chairs and tables. In addition, a continuous border garden is easier to maintain than one made up of many individual beds.

Must a garden be level?

Definitely not. A sloping garden, perhaps with a retaining wall, a walk, or even a small stream, offers many more possibilities than a flat area. A naturalistic garden should have a natural grade, rather than being level or smoothly sloping.

What sort of a garden would you plant on a plot thirty by sixty feet?

If this is a flat area, it can be effectively developed by creating an open grass or gravel panel down the center, with flower

Positive Images, Jerry Howard

A slope provides an ideal setting for, and is itself enhanced by, a naturalistic garden.

A flower bed full of old-fashioned varieties serves well as the foundation planting against an old colonial house.

borders along the sides backed by shrub borders or hedges, all leading to a strong focal point, such as a lily pool or patio.

Which is better for a small place, a formal or an informal garden?

Topography, more than size, controls the design. On flat ground near buildings, a rectangular, formal type of design is easier to adapt. On rough land—particularly on slopes and in wooded areas—greater informality is desirable.

Can I plant flowers along the foundation of our house?

Of course you can, but in most cases, shrubs and ground covers with flowers planted in front of them give a better effect than flowers alone, which are apt to look too small and inadequate near a house foundation.

What perennials will grow in a sunny, dry area? I prefer showy flowers.

Try the bright gold gloriosa daisy with its prominent dark brown center, the gay orange Oriental poppy, the red, gold, and yellow, daisylike blanketflower, and the many colorful varieties of daylilies. Many of the perennial asters will do well in sunny, dry spots as well.

How can I make my flower border more interesting?

Plantings made up of only one kind of plant, or even a few similar varieties, are monotonous and uninteresting. Use occasional plants of different varieties, sizes, and colors to provide accents. For example, clumps of tall blue delphinium blossoms add drama to a border of daisies and bee balm.

What plants (tall, medium, and low) may I use in a garden shaded by oak trees? What soil improvements should be made to overcome acidity from oaks?

You won't need to improve the soil if you select native wildflowers, such as cypripedium, fern, mayapple, and jack-in-the-pulpit. For taller plants, you have a wide choice in such shrubs as holly, mountain laurel, azalea, blueberry, and rhododendron. A combination of these would be especially attractive.

What would grow well along the north-facing wall of our house, which gets little sun?

Many perennials and wildflowers do well in such settings, including columbine, lady's slipper, hepatica, epimedium, bleeding heart, foxglove, fern rue, Virginia bluebells, anemone, primrose, blue langwort, monkshood, shooting star, rue, and some daylilies.

Which flowering plants will grow in an area that receives only two or three hours of strong sun daily?

Daylily, bleeding heart with its intriguing and distinctive, dropping blossoms, primrose in a variety of colors from pinks and blues to yellows and white, and hosta with its tall, nodding blue, violet, or white spiky blooms.

Positive Images, Jerry Howard

Bleeding heart thrives in partial shade.

What plants will grow in dense shade around the base of a large tree? Must I put them in pots because of the tree roots?

Few plants will subsist on what's left in the soil after the roots of a large tree have filled the surface and used all available food. Try digging out pockets in the ground, filling them with good loam, and planting one of the following: violets, creeping mahonia, periwinkle, English ivy, or pachysandra. If these fail, you would be better off to spread bark mulch over the area and leave it bare of plants. Potted plants, although of only temporary value, can add welcome spots of color in such a setting; use such shade plants as impatiens and begonia.

Would a garden plot laid out on the edge of a lake be satisfactory?

Why not? Have the soil tested by your Extension Service or do it yourself with a soil-testing kit, since the humus content at such a location may be low. The only special consideration you may need to be aware of is that the presence of the lake may influence frost conditions at your garden site. If it is near a large lake, the water may give off heat during the fall and protect your area from early frosts. If you are near a small body of water in a valley, you may experience exactly the opposite effect, since the cold air of early frosts tends to pour down hills and make your area colder than those higher on the hills.

Is garden lighting costly to maintain?

No. The lights are turned on for such a short time that the cost of electricity is negligible. Initially, the installation of weatherproof lights, wiring, and sockets might seem expensive, but by illuminating parts of the garden and its paths at night you gain new opportunities to appreciate the garden. Solar-powered garden lights are also readily available and not terribly expensive.

Positive Images, Gary Mottau

A variety of heights, colors, and textures make this garden stunningly successful.

SPRING BULBS

— • —

When you plant bulbs, you plant a hope in tomorrow. Triggered into motion by time or temperature, bulbs are one of the most reliable of plants, welcoming spring when most needed, long before color is contributed to the garden by any other plant.

Spring bulbs are winter hardy: they are planted in fall, grow and bloom in spring, and then lie dormant for a year. They do not need to be dug out of the ground except when they are divided. Both true bulbs (daffodils, hyacinths, glory of the snow, and others) and corms (crocus) are classified as bulbs because of their unique food-storing capabilities and their growth habits. Both are planted while dormant and then grow, bloom, and store food before going dormant again.

True bulbs are actually complete plants within a tiny package. Slice into a bulb and you will see the future roots, stems, leaves,

Maggie Oster

Daffodils are an excellent bulb to naturalize, but they must be left undisturbed until their foliage dies back.

and flowers. Fleshy scales surrounding this future growth contain all the necessary food for the bulb to grow. After the bulb has bloomed, food for the next season is manufactured in the leaves and transferred to the underground portion to start the chain again the following year.

Corms are modified stems filled with food storage tissue. They are usually short and squat and covered with a meshlike material. After a corm blooms, the original corm disappears and a new one forms for next year's growth.

When should bulbs be planted?

You can plant spring-flowering bulbs any time in fall until the soil freezes; if you can't plant them all at once, start with the smaller, earlier flowering bulbs such as crocus, squill, glory-of-the-snow, winter aconite, and other tiny bulbs, and then plant tulips and daffodils.

Where can I plant bulbs?

When you plant spring bulbs, set early charmers where you and passers-by will notice them the most. Besides growing *in* the lawn, they will do well around the base of trees near the house, or in small clumps near the front door. Line the path to the door. Squeeze them into the corner of the rock garden or use them as a border in front of foundation plantings.

Our yard is rather shady. Does this mean I can't grow bulbs?

Many bulbs like full sun, but since most spring bulbs bloom before the trees leaf out, shade from trees is usually not troublesome. However, if many hours of shade are cast from the side of the house, that will be a problem and you should look for another place to plant. You will find that those bulbs planted in a shaded spot will bloom a little later, will have a more intense color, and will last somewhat longer.

How should I prepare the soil for bulbs?

Good soil preparation is critical to a successful bulb garden, as it is to other gardens. Because bulb roots reach deep, you'll need to spade and prepare the bed to a depth of twelve inches. Look for soil with good drainage so that bulbs and roots won't rot. Provide good aeration as well as nutrients by adding organic matter, such as peat moss, compost, or leaf mold, equal to twenty-five percent of the soil volume. To encourage root growth, add phosphorus-rich bonemeal to the bottom of each planting hole as well.

How do I actually go about setting the bulbs in the ground?

You can prepare holes by one of two methods: you can either dig individual holes for each bulb, or you can dig out an entire area, put the bulbs in place and restore the soil. The latter is the better idea if you are planting a large number of bulbs.

How deep should bulbs be planted?

Consult the chart on pages 106-07 for advice, or plant a bulb to a depth approximately three times its width.

Do bulb plantings need mulching?

It's an especially good idea to mulch bulbs, as mulch can help to keep the smaller bulbs from heaving out of the ground during the winter. Use an organic mulch such as leaf mold, compost, bean hulls, wood chips, or pine needles to enrich the soil as the mulch breaks down.

Do established bulbs need to be fertilized?

Even though you properly prepared your bulb bed at planting time, you will need to add extra fertilizer each year to keep the bulbs healthy and flowering at their peak. When bulb foliage begins to emerge in spring, sprinkle fertilizer on the ground and water it in. For maximum results, feed again as the foliage starts to yellow. Use an all-purpose fertilizer such as 5-10-5 (see pages 32-36) or a specially prepared bulb food.

Do bulbs need extra water?

Once bulbs start to poke their way through the ground in spring, they will need a lot of moisture, so water deeply if the spring is a dry one. Proper flowering and growth depend on sufficient water reaching deep into the root zone.

I've seen many tulips planted so that they stand like soldiers in a row. How can I avoid this unappealing arrangement?

Almost without exception, bulbs look better when planted in clumps of at least three. The smaller the bulb, the more flowers you need in the clump. For example, plant four clumps with three tulips in each clump across a nine-foot section of the foundation planting, rather than planting the tulips single file, nine inches apart in an empty-looking line.

Bulbs can also be naturalized into an informal look, particularly appropriate in woodland settings. Left to multiply on their own, their colony will increase. Select a spot for your naturalistic planting that will not have to be disturbed until after the flowers and foliage have faded away.

When planting, toss bulbs randomly onto the planting bed, and then plant them where they fall. Even if you have to adjust them slightly to maintain correct spacing, you will still be able to achieve a less contrived effect than if you had tried to arrange them.

SELECTED SPRING BULBS

ANEMONE, GRECIAN WINDFLOWER, *Anemone blanda.* Anemones are small and daisylike with two- to three-inch flowers in shades of blue, pink, or white with bright yellow centers. They bloom in early to mid-spring. Foliage is starburstlike and grows close to the ground. Plant two inches deep, four to six inches apart, in well-drained soil in full sun or light shade.

CAMASSIA, *Camassia.* One of the last blooming of the spring bulbs, camassia have loose spikes of pale blue, star-shaped flowers on three-inch stems over large clumps of strap-shaped foliage. Plant four inches deep, four to six inches apart, in moist soil in part sun.

CROCUS, *Crocus.* Although not the first bulbs to bloom, crocus are regarded by many as the first sign of spring. Hybrid crocus bear white, purple, lavender, or yellow blossoms. Long, narrow foliage is deep green, often with a stripe. These are very hardy bulbs. Plant three to four inches deep, three inches apart, in rich, well-drained soil in full or part sun.

CROWN IMPERIAL, *Fritillaria imperialis.* On top of a thirty- to forty-eight-inch stem, yellow, red, or orange flowers hang in a tuft under a crown of foliage. Leaves clothe the stalk up to the flower. Fragrance can be very heavy. Plant five inches deep, eighteen inches apart, in average soil in part sun.

DAFFODILS AND JONQUILS, *Narcissus.* A welcome sight of midspring, daffodils and jonquils bloom atop six- to twelve-inch stems in a variety of flower shapes, including trumpets, doubles, and large and small cups. Some have a number of tiny blooms along the stem. The flowers are white, yellow, or a combination of both, or pale pink. Many are fragrant. Perfect for naturalizing, but their foliage hangs on until early summer; be sure to plant them where they can be left undisturbed. Plant six inches deep, six to twelve inches apart, in well-drained, rich soil in full sun or part shade.

DOGTOOTH VIOLET, TROUT LILY, *Erythronium.* For a wildflower look in the garden, the dogtooth violet's bloom is lilylike and white, rose, violet, or yellow, nodding on a six- to twelve-inch stem. Two strap-shaped leaves are often mottled. Its names come from the facts that the corm resembles a tooth, the leaves are mottled like a trout's back, and the flower blooms at trout season. Plant three inches deep, four inches apart, in moist, rich soil in shade.

GLORY OF THE SNOW, *Chionodoxa luciliae.* One of the earliest to bloom, glory of the snow's six-petalled, starlike flowers are mostly blue with a light center, although there are white and pink forms.

Spikes of blooms are four to five inches high from the center of straplike leaves. Easy to grow, it never needs dividing. Leave undisturbed after blooming to form colonies. Extremely hardy. Plant four inches deep, three inches apart, in dry soil in full sun or part shade.

GRAPE HYACINTH, *Muscari.* Cone-shaped clusters of drooping flowers are bright blue to purple in mid-spring. Foliage appears again in fall and can be untidy looking. Plant three inches deep, four inches apart, in average soil in full to part sun.

GUINEA HEN FLOWER, *Fritillaria meleagris.* Six-petalled, two-inch, purple and white checkered flowers resembling a lampshade or an upside-down tulip appear in mid-spring on stems six to twelve inches high. Leaves are thin and grasslike. Plant four inches deep, five inches apart, in average soil in full sun to part shade.

HYACINTH, *Hyacinthus hybrids.* The tall, rounded, fragrant clusters of small, star-shaped flowers bloom in shades of red, white, pink, blue, purple, or yellow. The six- to eight-inch blooms grow from the center of straplike leaves. They will lose some of their compactness after several years and will need to be replaced. Plant six inches deep, six inches apart, in rich, well-drained soil in full to part sun.

IRIS, *Iris.* There are two irises grown from bulbs; the others, grown from rhizomes, are categorized as perennials. Reticulatas bloom in early spring and grow four to eight inches high. Foliage is grassy. Dutch iris, orchidlike and a good cut flower, bloom in late spring with stems up to twenty-four inches high. Flowers of both are purple, blue, yellow, or white. Plant four inches deep, three to four inches apart, in well-drained soil in full sun.

PUSCHKINIA, *Puschkinia.* Small, star-shaped flowers of white or pale blue with a blue stripe are among the first bulbs to bloom. Do not disturb them, and they will quickly colonize. Plant three inches deep, three inches apart, in average soil in full to part sun.

SIBERIAN SQUILL, *scilla sibirica.* Early blooming, the deep blue to purple flowers grow four to six inches high and are surrounded by broad leaves. Bloom spikes are made up of individual pendant flowers. Do not disturb after planting. Plant two to three inches deep, three inches apart, in average soil in full to part sun.

SNOWDROPS, *Galanthus nivalis.* Another gem among early blooming bulbs, snowdrops can appear while snow is still on the ground. Perfect for a woodland setting, three-part flowers drop from a thin stem about four to six inches tall. Blooms are

Anemones, grape hyacinths, daffodils, and tulips welcome spring with a dependability and ease of maintenance that all gardeners appreciate.

white with waxy green tips on the inside that are seen as the petals open in the sun. Four- to six-inch high foliage is greenish gray and grasslike. Plant four inches deep, two inches apart, in average soil in full sun or part shade.

STAR OF BETHLEHEM, *Ornithogalum umbellatum.* Star of Bethlehem, named for the six-petalled, star-shaped flowers that bloom in clusters on stems six inches high, will thrive under the poorest conditions. Each white flower is about one inch wide, with a thin green stripe on the outside of each petal, a black center, and yellow stamens. Foliage is very dense and grassy. A good cut flower. Plant four inches deep, three to four inches apart, in average to poor soil in full to part sun.

SUMMER SNOWFLAKE, *Leucojum aestivum.* The summer snowflake blooms in mid-spring, but is so named to distinguish it from the earlier blooming spring snowflake. It has a cluster of five or six white bell-shaped flowers hanging from atop a nine- to twelve-inch stem, and resembles a large lily-of-the-valley. Plant four inches deep, four inches apart, in average soil in part shade.

TULIP, *Tulipa.* For a tall, stately, formal look, tulips are the spring favorite for massed beds of red, white, blue, purple, yellow, pink, coral, or even black color. Flowers range from classic cottage or Darwin tulips, to fringed parrot, pointed lily, and starburst miniatures. Many of the hybrids grow to thirty inches. Plant six inches deep, four to six inches apart, in rich, fast-draining soil in full sun.

WINTER ACONITE, *Eranthis hyemalis.* This early-to-bloom plant often appears when there is still snow on the ground. Six-petalled, waxy, sunny yellow, sweetly scented blooms are about two inches across and resemble buttercups. The shiny, thick, deep green foliage rays out from underneath the flower in a starlike pattern. The tuber must not be allowed to dry out, so plant it right away. Plant two inches deep, three to four inches apart, in rich, moist soil in full or part sun.

WOOD HYACINTH, *Scilla hispanica.* Loose clusters of pink or blue, bell-shaped flowers resemble informal hyacinths. Blooming in late spring, it grows to eighteen inches. Plant three inches deep, six inches apart, in average, moist soil in part shade.

Is there anything I should do after the bulbs have bloomed?

When tulips, daffodils, hyacinths, and other large bulbs have finished blooming, cut off the flowers (called "deadheading") to prevent seed formation and to direct energy to the bulb. Smaller bulbs can be left to go to seed, which will scatter and increase the colony.

Never remove the leaves until they have completely browned and pull away from the plant easily. As the foliage matures it is manufacturing the food for next year's growth. If you remove the leaves too soon, the bulb will not bloom the following spring. Where bulbs are planted in the lawn, do not mow the grass until the foliage has browned.

To achieve a neater look, you can braid the foliage of larger bulbs or twirl it into a circle until the foliage ripens.

Spring bulbs are beautiful while they are blooming, but what about the empty spaces after they have died away?

If you interplant bulbs with a ground cover, you will not have to worry. In flower beds, add annuals as soon as they can be planted in the spring; no harm is done to bulb plantings to overplant them this way. Perennials also make excellent companions to bulbs, for they come into bloom about the time the bulbs fade. If possible, divide and replant both the bulbs and the perennials in the spring when you can see the location of both to avoid accidental injury to bulbs and roots.

Will I have to dig up my bulbs once they are planted?

Many small bulbs, such as quill, can be forgotten once planted. Daffodils and crocus, on the other hand, need to be dug and divided every five or six years when the clumps get too large, and bloom size and number begin to decline. Tulips and hyacinths do not multiply in the climate found in most parts of this continent, and so diminish in size and need to be replaced every several years.

The best time to divide and replant bulbs is in spring right after the foliage starts to yellow: It's easier to locate and avoid damaging or cutting the bulbs when you can still see the leaves. Also, when you replant bulbs in the spring, you'll know where gaps are in the garden and you won't plant them on top of each other.

When moving bulbs, dig them carefully so as not to disturb the roots and replant them immediately using the same techniques as you do when planting new bulbs in the fall. Leave the foliage in place after planting and let it mature as though the bulb had not been moved.

Do bulbs have many disease and insect problems?

If a bulb shows sign of disease in the form of a misshapen or discolored flower, it's best to dig it out and prevent the problem from spreading. Few insects bother bulbs.

Whatever you are planting—lawns, trees, shrubs, flowers, or vegetables—you must know the soil on your property. You will soon discover one area is just fine and another is quite poor, perhaps because dirt was dumped there while excavating for the house foundation. Further, you must understand what you can do about these conditions.

The first possibility is to select plants that will survive in the available soil. There are plants that will thrive even in conditions as bad as the nearly pure sand of seaside gardens. A better approach is, first, to change the texture and fertility of your soil by adding organic material to the soil in large quantities (see page 9). This material is attacked by the billions of microorganisms in the soil in order to break it down into a form that the plants can use. Second, you should test the pH, or acidity, of your soil to determine whether it is in the 6.0 to 7.0 range that is best for growing most plants. This can be done by sending soil samples to your Extension Service or by obtaining a soil-testing kit at your garden center. Whether you are growing flowers or vegetables, constant soil improvement is essential, and there are many ways to do this.

YOUR GARDEN SOIL
•

A successful perennial garden is dependent upon thorough soil preparation before planting.

Positive Images, Jerry Howard

I've heard of soil nutrients. What are they, and why are they important to plants?

The "big three" in nutrient elements for plants are nitrogen, phosphorus, and potassium, listed in that order on bags of fertilizer. Thus, a bag marked 5-10-5 has 5 per cent nitrogen, 10 percent phosphorus, and 5 percent potassium. One criticism often made of chemical fertilizers is that they burn foliage. While it is true that these fertilizer salts can suck water out of leaves and roots, you can avoid this by carefully using recommended rates and watering them in as soon as you apply them.

Organic fertilizers have the same elements as chemical fertilizers, but often in a highly complex form. They are thus unavailable to plants until they have been digested or broken down into simpler forms by soil organisms. Because these organisms are partially dormant at temperatures below 60° F., they are not effective in early spring for hardy crops. On the plus side, in addition to their nutrient value, organic fertilizers add a great deal of organic matter to the soil, which pure chemical or mineral fertilizers do not.

All of the elements in fertilizers play roles in the growing of plants.

Nitrogen is vital to the formation of all proteins. It is an essential element of chlorophyll, the green chemical that permits plants to manufacture starches and sugars. Many of the compounds in plants, such as amino acids, and aromatic compounds, must have nitrogen. It is the "grow" element, and overuse of it results in soft, lush growth. Stunted growth and pale yellow foliage, on the other hand, are signs of a nitrogen deficiency.

In place of commercial fertilizers, organic gardeners often use cottonseed meal (about 3-to-5-2-1), blood meal (12.5-1.3-.7), or fish meal (10.5-6-0). The latter is also a good source of phosphorus. (See also pages 46-48.)

Phosphorus is needed for good root and stem development. The usual commercial source is superphosphate; organic gardeners turn to bone meal, phosphate rock, or soft phosphate. Signs of a phosphorus deficiency are stunted growth and purple coloring of leaves and stems.

In Victorian days, bone meal was one of the few good fertilizers available. Thus, many gardeners had bone grinders in their potting sheds to grind up fresh, raw bone with scraps of meat still clinging to it. It was a rich addition to the soil.

Potassium, in the form of potash, is abundant in most American soils, but may be soilbound and thus not available to plants. For healthy plants, it may be essential to add potassium to the soil. Bronzing of leaves, slow growth, and unusually high incidence of disease are all signs of a deficiency of this element. Sulphate of potash and muriate of potash are available as commercial products. Organic gardeners turn to kelp meal, wood ashes, crushed granite, and greensand.

If wood ashes are used, they should be applied before planting and thoroughly mixed with the soil. The reason for this is that until the potassium they contain has been dissolved and absorbed by the soil, a free lye solution is present that can damage roots for two to three days after application. Ashes, too, act to sweeten (raise the pH of) the soil, and overuse of them, by spreading ashes from a woodstove or fireplace in the same area year after year, can result in a soil that has too high a pH.

How can I improve the nutrient content of my soil?

One of the easiest ways is to make compost. This process is often made to sound so scientific that beginners avoid trying it, but it can be done very easily.

Start by enclosing an area about four by four feet with chicken wire or boards spaced to permit air to circulate. Then pile up the organic refuse from your home, lawn, and gardens—vegetable scraps, grass clippings and leaves, garden refuse. Occasionally toss on a shovelful or two of soil, and keep the pile moist—not drenched, just moist.

The compost process will be speeded if you turn the pile over once or twice during the season, forking it from one enclosure to another. But this isn't necessary if you can wait a year to use the compost.

Some materials compost much faster than others. Leaves and hay compost very slowly. The process is speeded if the leaves are ground up. Grass cuttings are just the opposite. They get so hot in a matter of hours that their value is lost. So, instead of dumping baskets of grass clippings on the top of the pile, mix them with leaves or hay.

A simple compost bin made from a cylinder of sturdy wire mesh.

Don't compost piles attract dogs?

Avoid adding meat scraps and bones to the pile, and you shouldn't have a problem.

I worry that compost piles might give off offensive odors. Is this so?

It is very unlikely. If you smell anything at all, the odor will remind you of the woods. If there *is* an objectionable smell, add dried leaves, hay, or straw to the pile and work it in. Too much moisture is occasionally responsible for unpleasant aromas.

Aren't compost piles eyesores?

Compost piles have a reputation for being unsightly, and therefore are tucked back in the far reaches of a lot. Often this means the pile is far from both the source of materials that go into it and the place where it will be spread. Better to have it near both, where experienced gardeners will see and admire it. If you wish, plant a shrub or two to hide it from the eyes of those less knowledgeable in the ways of gardening.

What is the quickest way to bring an old, used garden spot back into quick production?

Spade in organic matter in the fall or plant a green manure (see page 46) crop. In the spring, apply superphosphate, hoe, rake, and plant. Add a complete fertilizer just before planting and again during the summer.

My flowers grow very poorly and usually die before their time. What causes this?

The chances are that your soil lacks fertility, moisture-holding capacity, and aeration. Additions of fertilizers and compost should correct these conditions.

My annuals and perennials grow tall and spindly. Could this be due to overfertilization, lack of sun, or lack of some fertilizer element? The garden site receives sunlight half the day.

The spindly growth may be due to lack of sunlight, poor drainage or compacted soil, improper fertilization, or any combination of these. If you have been gardening in the same area

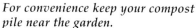

For convenience keep your compost pile near the garden.

Walter Chandoha

for several years, it is quite probable that the amount of sunlight the plants receive has decreased, due to growth of nearby trees. Try to alter this. Improve the drainage and aeration of the soil (see pgs. 6-10), and choose a fertilizer with high proportions of phosphorus and potassium in relation to nitrogen, perhaps for a few years (see pages 32-33).

I have been raising flowers on the same ground for some time. What can I use to keep it in shape?

Incorporate organic matter, such as leaves or peat moss, in the soil between the plants during the spring or summer. Apply a good complete fertilizer, such as 5-10-5, in the spring.

Is it advisable to apply lime and commercial fertilizer on the snow during the winter for absorption when the snow melts?

For some flowers (and vegetables), lime and commercial fertilizers can be applied in the fall or winter, but in most cases it is more efficient to apply them in the spring. Chemical fertilizers, particularly, will leach out and be lost over a winter.

I hear people talking about the sandy soil or the clay soil on their property. How do they know which is which?

Most of them probably guess—and some of them guess wrong. If you want to be sure, follow the suggestions on page 6 to determine what type soil you have. Different soil types require different approaches to gardening and soil treatment, whether you are growing lawns, trees and shrubs, or flowers and vegetables.

How can I use my compost?

Compost can be used in many ways, especially to be dug into the soil to improve both its texture and fertility. If you have a lot of compost, screen it and use it as a lawn topdressing, or spread it around flowers, shrubs, and vegetables to stimulate their growth.

What can I put into my compost pile?

This page isn't large enough to give you a complete answer. In general, add about anything that is organic, except for meat scraps (which encourage animal pests). From your garden and house, heap on weeds, grass clippings, leaves, table scraps, wood shavings and sawdust (though these are slow to compost), and even the contents of the vacuum cleaner. If you have them, add animal manures, peat moss, ground corn cobs, and commercial fertilizer. The fall is an excellent time to get a compost pile going, since there is a lot of material available from lawns and gardens.

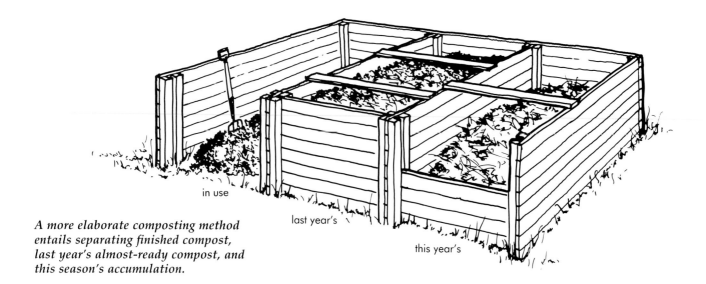

in use

last year's

this year's

A more elaborate composting method entails separating finished compost, last year's almost-ready compost, and this season's accumulation.

I was poking a stick into my compost pile to permit air to get into it, and touched the end of the stick when I pulled it out. To my surprise, it was more than warm—it was hot. I put a thermometer into the pile, and it rose to nearly 150°F. Should the pile be that hot?

That's a good sign that you've created a pile with an excellent blend of materials, and you'll have compost to use in a few weeks. To further encourage the process, wait until the pile cools a bit, then turn it over, working the outer layer into the center. This time the pile probably will not become as hot.

Are wood ashes better than coal ashes for a garden?

Wood ashes and coal ashes serve two distinct purposes. The former adds potassium to the soil, the latter improves the soil texture.

The soil in my front yard is extremely sandy. What flowers can I plant there?

You should first try to improve the soil by adding topsoil plus organic matter, such as peat moss, manure, or compost, and then working in fertilizer. If after trying these improvements, you find the soil is still quite sandy, fertilize the plants several times during the growing season, since many of the nutrients you apply will readily wash away. Flowers you might select for such soil include portulaca, California poppy, annual phlox, calliopsis, cockscomb, morning glory, anthemis, aster, baby's-breath, liatris, or yucca.

Can coal ashes be used to loosen clay soil?

Only if they have been exposed to weather to leach out harmful substances, such as toxic quantities of sulfur. You should also break up any pieces more than a quarter-inch in diameter. Prepared this way, a two-inch layer can be tilled into the clay.

My flower bed is heavy clay soil that is difficult to work up. Would well-rotted manure and wood ashes be a benefit?

Yes. You could add as much as ten pounds of ashes per 100 square feet, plus a six-inch layer of the manure. Fine cinders, too, would be beneficial. Till all of this well into the clay.

My ground gets hard and dry on the surface, so that it is difficult for young shoots to break through. It is soft enough beneath the surface. What can I do?

Incorporate well-rotted compost, peat moss, or a one-half-inch thick layer of vermiculite into the upper surface to prevent crusting.

What soil is best for a mixed flower border?

A slightly acid (pH 6.5), sandy loam, with manure, compost, and/or peat moss worked in. It's difficult to overdo the organic material when preparing a perennial garden, as once you plant you won't be able to get in easily to work soil amendments down around the plant roots.

Are earthworms harmful or beneficial in the garden? I find that they eat all the humus in the soil.

Earthworms are a nuisance in the green house or in potted plants, and they tend to leave unsightly piles of dirt on lawns. But in gardens, their constant working through the soil—eating, digesting, and eliminating waste—aerates the soil, a far greater benefit than any possible trouble they cause. Furthermore, their very presence is a sign of good soil, filled with the nutrients on which they—and your plants—thrive.

What is vermiculite?

It is a form of mica, heated so that it explodes, much like popcorn. It is sterile, holds moisture, and if not overwatered, allows air to reach the roots of plants. It is excellent for rooting cuttings and starting seeds. Use a planting flat with a window-screen wire bottom, for if overwatered, it will get soggy.

I've heard of "Cornell mix." What is it and when is it used?

This is an old favorite artificial soil mix used by gardeners for many years to start seedlings. To make a peck of the mix, combine the following:

    4 quarts vermiculite
    4 quarts shredded peat moss
    1 teaspoon 20-percent superphosphate
    1 tablespoon ground dolomitic limestone

5 *Structures in the Landscape*

Now that your healthy green lawn is well underway and many of your trees, shrubs, and flowers are in place, you may wish to turn to ways of making movement around your yard pleasant and of defining your property or parts of it: paths, patios, and walls or fences. Your prime criterion should be to make these structures enhance but not intrude on your plantings. They should look as though they belong there naturally, even though you have constructed them.

A concrete walk may be the best answer for the entrance to your house, but for other areas, alternative materials are preferable. Your choice depends largely on the style of your house, the size and style of the area around the house, and the expected traffic on the path. Garden paths can be made of grass, wood chips and bark, wood sections, gravel, flagstone and slate, or bricks.

WALKS AND PATHS

What materials do you suggest for paths, and how do you determine which materials are best in specific situations?

A *grass* walk between flower beds is attractive and a good choice if the traffic will not be too heavy. Such a walk requires no extra care other than feeding the grass often enough to encourage its growth. For better wear, yet still a natural-looking path, set twelve-inch *stepping stones* into the lawn about twelve inches apart (a comfortable stride). Cut out sod, and set the stones low enough that they won't interfere with mowing.

Wood chips or bark make very satisfactory paths, particularly in woody areas or in gardens where the same material is used as a

◀ *Lay a flagstone walk flush with ground level to make mowing grass easy.*

117

mulch around trees and shrubs. There are some disadvantages: They tend to look messy, they must be rebuilt every two or three years, and they can't be used where the path must be cleared for snow. While wood chips or bark may be expensive at a gardening center, they are often available for little or no money from sawmills or utility companies.

For a *gravel* path, select a local source of supply, since a large volume will be needed. Plan a path two feet wide for single-file traffic and four and a half feet wide for two-abreast traffic. Remove enough topsoil in the path area so that a layer of gravel at least four inches deep can be laid. A layer of cinder can be put down first. A sheet of plastic under the gravel will help to discourage weeds, but because it may also interfere with drainage, it is not recommended.

A gravel walk requires care—removing any weeds, raking smooth several times a year, and at least an annual edging to keep the boundaries straight and specific. Some see the gravel walk as too stiff and formal, but it is excellent for heavy traffic. It is not a good choice for a path that must be kept free of snow.

For the person with an idle chain saw, a tree trunk, and an urge to work, the choice of four- to six-inch *sections of a tree trunk* to be used as stepping stones, is a logical one, but there are reasons to avoid the choice. The sections will need to be treated with a wood preservative (see page 129), they are difficult to place in the ground because of their size and depth, they will be extremely difficult to replace, their appearance tends to deteriorate after a season or two, and they become very slippery, particularly in shaded areas.

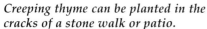

Creeping thyme can be planted in the cracks of a stone walk or patio.

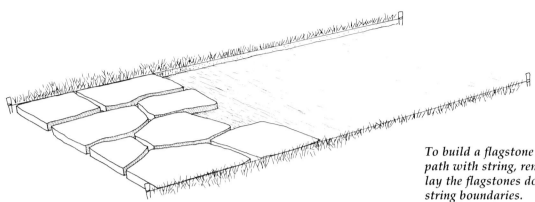

To build a flagstone path, outline the path with string, remove the sod, and lay the flagstones down within the string boundaries.

Flagstone and slate are used in paths in two ways. One way is to set them in concrete, making them the top layer of a concrete walk. The other method, not as good for heavy traffic but far more desirable in every other way, is to place them in the ground, with grass or other plants growing around them.

To build such a path, first outline the path's width with string. Next, remove the sod (use what you remove to renew bare spots in your lawn), and lay down the flagstones within the boundaries of the string. Finally, pack topsoil around the flagstones, and plant grass or plants such as creeping thyme around them. Be sure the stones aren't higher than the lawn level, otherwise they will be a nuisance when they are mowed. Step on each stone to make certain it is solidly planted, so that it won't wiggle when it is walked on.

While grass is perfectly satisfactory around the flagstones, even better is thyme, chamomile, bugleweed, or one of the sedums, all of which grow very well among the stones, adding interest, and sometimes fragrance, to your walk.

Flagstones may be set in a layer of sand three or four inches deep. Be sure this appeals to you before you try it. To some, it has the appearance of islands of stone in a sea of sand.

Bricks laid in sand rather than concrete, are an excellent choice for many situations where a path is needed. They are neat, can be laid in place even by the inexperienced, and require little maintenance. (See pages 120-22 on building a brick walk.)

While new bricks are not inexpensive, often a source of used bricks can be found. They may be less expensive, and at the same time have acquired through age a mottled tone that has a far more pleasing appearance than the sameness of new bricks.

What materials do you prefer for garden paths?

For an average flower garden, grass paths are usually best for two reasons in particular: They present a green foreground for the garden picture, and they need no maintenance other than what the lawn receives. Gravel or flagstone paths in the flower garden are likely to be a nuisance to take care of. Where a path must be dry, or at least passable in all sorts of weather, brick and flagstones are quite serviceable. Often it is possible to make a

The color and texture of a walk made of used bricks adds warmth to this garden, and such a walk is not difficult to construct or maintain.

Maggie Oster

Even as simple a material as pine needles can serve as a garden walk.

grass path more practical and hard-wearing by laying a line of stepping stones down its middle or along one side.

Would you recommend brick or stone edging for a driveway or path?

For a driveway, brick edging is somewhat too fragile unless the bricks are set in a heavy foundation of concrete, which can be unsightly. Try the new plastic driveway edging. It doesn't show, is strong, and is easy to install. For pathways, brick is an ideal edging. Small rounded stones are useless for both driveways and paths, and are not aesthetically pleasing.

I'm planning to lay a brick walk. How do I start?

Begin by determining the answers to the following questions:

- What are the dimensions of your planned walk? First, measure the length. The width should be eighteen to twenty-four inches for one person to walk easily along the path, and four and one-half to five feet for two persons.
- What brick pattern will you use? This is a matter of personal preference. Some patterns, such as herringbone, require cutting the bricks, which means more bricks to buy and lots of brick to be cut. If you have a source of used bricks, they're beautiful for walks.
- What size bricks will you use? You'll find bricks in two sizes, 7 ½-by-3 ½-by-2 ¼ and 8-by-4-by-2 ¾. If you buy bricks, get SW (severe weather) bricks, in the 8-by-4 size.
- How many bricks will you need? If you use 8-by-4 bricks, you'll need four and one-half bricks for each square foot of walk. Plan to edge the walks with bricks set on end horizontally. You will need three per foot, doubled to provide for both sides of the walk.
- How much sand will you need? You will need a two-inch layer of sand under the bricks. Divide the square footage of your walk by six to determine the number of cubic feet of sand you need. Order several buckets extra to fill in the space between bricks.
- Do you have the proper tools? You should have a cart or wheelbarrow, hose, shovel, lawn edger, trowel or some narrow digging tool, tamp, rake, broom, string, hammer, level, and a waste piece of board.

Now that I have my tools, bricks, and sand on the site, what do I do next?

- Your walk should be three-fourths of an inch above the lawn level. The first step is to mark accurately the path boundaries with string. Then remove a six-inch-deep layer of sod and soil within the strings. Use the edger so the edge of your excavation will be straight. (Don't dig out less than this in order to

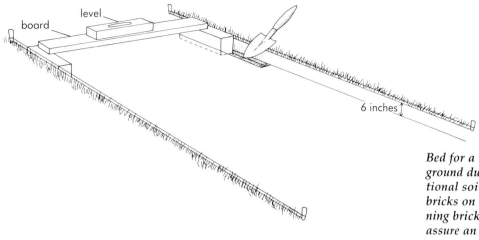

Bed for a new brick walk shows ground dug out 6 inches, with additional soil dug away to lay border bricks on end. A board and level spanning bricks from border to border helps assure an even walk.

avoid using the sand. Without sand, it will be difficult to create a level walk, and drainage on the walk will be poor.)

- Using a trowel, dig out additional space for the upright bricks on each side of the walk, for about three feet of walk. Put the upright bricks in position so that they will be at the level of the walk's surface. Next, use a board and level to span the two lines of bricks, in order to make certain that the lines of bricks are level with each other.
- Shovel a two-inch layer of sand into the walk space, level it, dampen it, and tamp it down. Use a brick to check the depth of the sand layer. Laid flat on the sand, the brick should be the same height as the upright bricks. Taking time to get the sand layer level and the proper depth will make the next steps much easier.
- Set the bricks in position, following your pattern and placing them snugly together for the three-foot section you have edged.
- Make certain all the bricks are level and all are at the same height. Any one that is too high can be lowered by placing a board on it, then hammering the board.
- Continue building short sections, making certain each section is level before moving ahead.
- When all the bricks are in place, scatter sand across the walk, and use a broom to work the sand into the cracks. Hose the walk with a very fine spray, then repeat this step several times to fill all the cracks. After several weeks, and any time you notice space between the bricks, repeat this step.
- As you use the walk, pull up any weeds that push up through the cracks so that they will not have a chance to develop roots that could push the bricks out of position.

I have access to a huge number of bricks from a building that is being demolished, but most of them have mortar clinging to them. Can I get it off?

You're lucky to have that supply of bricks; and yes, the mortar will come off. If they're fairly old, it may come off when you hit

VIEW FROM ABOVE

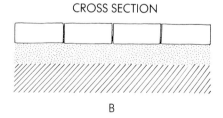

A

CROSS SECTION

B

(A) Bricks can be laid in many different patterns; the staggered one shown here is quite common, and easy to build; (B) assure adequate drainage by spreading a 2-inch layer of sand over the soil before laying the bricks.

it, gently and at an angle, with a hammer. If this causes you to break a lot of bricks, try soaking them first. Fill a couple of buckets with water and bricks, soak them for a few minutes, and then hammer them again. Be sure to wear safety glasses for this chore; bits of mortar and brick will be flying in all directions.

Used bricks are useful for many purposes, from walks and driveways to construction inside your house. Put aside a good supply of them if you get the chance; you'll be sure to find a use for them.

To build a brick walk with the pattern I like, I must cut some of the bricks. How do I do it?

You'll need a hammer (a heavy bricklayer's hammer is best) and a bricklayer's four-inch chisel.

Tap two bricks together. If each rings, use both. If one gives off a dull sound, it will probably not break true, so don't try to cut it.

Place a brick on a flat, solid surface. With the chisel edge on the line where you want to cut, tip the handle just a bit toward the end of the brick that must be discarded, and hit the brick solidly with the hammer. It should snap through with the first blow. Don't be discouraged if you waste a few bricks before getting the knack. Masons cut bricks so easily that it sometimes discourages the rest of us.

I have a fairly steep path in my yard where I would like to construct steps. Any suggestions?

Do you use the path when pushing a mower or cart or any other heavy equipment? If so, steps can be a real headache and certainly make you sympathize with persons in wheelchairs, who so often find their travels halted by steps and curbs.

Steps can be very effective if the risers (the vertical sections) are no more than eight inches in height and the tread (the horizontal area) is as much as three feet in depth.

A possible combination for this is a railroad tie or some similar timber for the riser, and one of the earlier suggestions for paths

Terraced steps created with railroad-tie risers make an effective and easy-to-maintain walkway on slopes.

for the tread. For example, several flagstones embedded in plantings of thyme would be particularly effective. The sides of these steps offer splendid locations for a collection of shrubs, giving the stroller an excuse to move slowly and enjoy the appearance of both the steps and the shrubs.

Outdoor relaxing and entertaining is infinitely easier and more pleasant if you define a space for such activities. Whether this space takes the form of a patio, terrace, or deck, plan and construct it with care, add comfortable furniture and beautiful plantings, including hanging and other container plants, and your efforts will be rewarded with hours of pleasure.

What is the difference between a patio and a terrace?

In popular thinking, not much, and the terms are used interchangeably. Technically, a terrace is a raised area supported by a wall or bank, while a patio is any paved outdoor living area.

Where should the patio be located?

Immediately outside the living or dining room or the kitchen, where it is easily accessible and can be seen from indoors. Be sure to plan the patio and its plantings so that it is attractive from indoors. The use of sliding glass, French, or patio doors increases the feeling of a connection between inside and outside.

PATIOS

•

A brick patio, framed by flower beds and furnished with heavy yet airy looking tables and chairs, is an invitation to outdoor living.

Positive Images, Gary Mottau

What is the best material for paving a patio?

You have many choices, depending on your likes and dislikes. The material should go well with the house, particularly with its masonry, such as the foundation and the chimney. Tile, gravel, paving stones, bricks, even redwood planks are all possibilities.

I've been thinking of putting a sandbox for the children on the patio. What do you think?

It's a good idea. Place it at one corner, in the shade, if possible. It provides an excellent place for children to play, and if you place it near a window, you can keep an eye on them while you're in the house. Incorporate it into your design, and after they've outgrown it use it as a planter.

Is there any special furniture that is best for the patio?

It certainly should be weatherproof. Metal chairs and tables that are heavy enough not to be blown around are ideal. Lounging chairs should be of a style that complements the architecture of both the house and the patio.

I would like to have some flower beds on my patio. Do they belong?

They certainly do. You might consider building raised beds using sides of brick or stone to make the planting surface about two feet above the ground. Herbs planted in such beds are more readily smelled and touched, and weeding is not as backbreaking as in ground-level beds.

FENCES AND WALLS, NATURAL AND MANMADE

Consider these two rules before building fences.

- Decide exactly why you need the fence, then select a fence that will harmonize with the surroundings and be the least obtrusive, yet still do the job.
- Make certain you have a legal right to erect a fence. Do you know the exact location of your property boundary? You can be in trouble if you erect a fence slightly over that line. Does your community have zoning laws on fences? Some towns prohibit tall fences; others have different restrictions. Does your deed prohibit the erection of any types of fences? Some do, and were written in to protect the open look of a neighborhood that has no fences.

Your choice of fencing materials is vast. There are a great many plants that are probably better than building materials for most home use. Here are some of them:

Trees are particularly good for blocking views and acting as wind breaks. Be sure to consider the mature size of a tree before selecting it. Some trees, such as spruce and hemlock, can be

Artfully placed evergreen shrubs interplanted with deciduous flowering shrubs and trees form a screen to disguise the lattice fence along the property line in this yard. The foreground is further enhanced by a stone retaining wall and ground covers.

planted in a row to form a high hedge that is virtually impregnable, is easy to care for, and offers a beauty and grace not found in a carefully clipped hedge.

Shrubs can be used to form either deciduous or evergreen hedges up to fifteen feet high. Formally clip them or allow them to reach their natural form guided only by occasional prunings.

Among the broad-leaved evergreens useful for hedges are crape myrtle, boxwood, privet, pyrocantha, and rhododendron. Juniper, yew, and blue spruce are only three of the many coniferous shrubs that will provide both beauty and a barrier.

Deciduous shrubs such as quince, forsythia, lilac, elderberry, and hydrangea often grow thickly enough so that a hedge of them makes a formidable barrier even when they have shed their leaves. Many of these are excellent if you need only to suggest a wall, such as near a patio. For such use, give them enough space so each plant reaches its full size and beauty.

Vines have the advantage of providing a barrier without using a great deal of space. Trees and shrubs use a band of space six or more feet in width, while a vine growing on a fence will thrive in a space only a foot wide. At the same time, it will easily reach as high as a two-story building, if that is wanted. Vines, too, are invaluable for hiding the fortresslike features of walls and

Drooping wisteria blossoms soften the harshness of a high brick wall.

heavy-duty fences, if allowed to cover heavily enough to appear to be a hedge.

Vines are extremely versatile. Some make excellent ground covers, some cling to walls, some have thorns to emphasize their roles as walls to halt traffic, and many of them are fragrant. Some vines, including clematis and English ivy, are fine for covering and hiding walls or even rock outcroppings. Wisteria, climbing hydrangea, and Virginia creeper will cling to walls. The climbing rose, jasmine, and clematis all offer beautiful blossoms. Select vines that will grow in your climate and that are fitted for the job you want done.

Screens, available in many colors, sizes, and materials, are excellent for temporary walls. They are easy to put up and to store.

Fences range from electric and barbed wire (neither of which should be used where there is human—and particularly juvenile—traffic) to solid sections of wood. They serve many functions, blocking views, supporting vines, protecting areas from unwelcome winds, and keeping animals in or out.

Fencing must be selected to fit with your landscaping and the style of your house. Think for a moment about where a picket or post-and-rail fence would look best, and you will understand the need for a careful choice. The split-rail fence is excellent around many gardens and will support vines. It looks particularly good under a healthy growth of climbing roses in country settings. The wood hurdle fence is another choice for that setting. Woven-paling fences can be chosen for complete privacy or as a background for a garden.

Vertical board fences, too, can offer complete privacy. They're built with six- or eight-inch boards nailed to two two-by-four rails that are supported with posts. Louvered fences are similar in construction, but the boards are set at an angle so they do not interfere with the flow of air.

Wire fences range from chain-link fences to lighter wires. They are utilitarian and are best if disguised by a heavy vine.

I want to grow a high hedge around three sides of our lot. My husband opposes this. What do you think?

In "Mending Wall," poet Robert Frost answered this best. Frost said that before he built a wall (and your high hedge would be a wall) he would like to know what he was walling in or walling out. The hedge you suggest could be valuable for blocking a view of some eyesore, such as a used car lot. It might serve as a background for flower beds, and it can be a good windbreak in winter. But remember that it will make a narrow lot look narrower, and a small lot appear smaller. In addition, it will destroy your views on three sides. No longer can you and your neighbors share a sense of spaciousness, allowing all of you to share your lawns and trees visually.

Would a mixture of plants with variously colored leaves or blossoms be satisfactory for informal screening to enclose a yard?

Yes, if you plant them in groups of five, seven, or nine, depending on the length of the border. Accent the groups of shrubs at intervals with taller evergreens or flowering trees. This type of border takes up more room than hedges.

What is the best fence for use along the road in front of a modified colonial house where something elaborate would be inappropriate?

A simple post-and-rail fence has long proved very satisfactory in such situations. It can be painted white, or, if made of cypress or redwood, left unpainted to weather. If it is meant to keep out (or in) small animals, chicken wire can be attached to the inside at the bottom and disguised by plants.

Is a wattle fence appropriate for the home garden?

Yes, it is excellent for screening a small garden utility area, and it provides privacy. Wattle fences are made of thin split saplings and are quite durable.

Do you recommend wire gates for gardens?

Wire gates are suitable for vegetable areas or dog runs, but for other purposes, something more decorative, such as a wooden or iron gate, should be chosen.

The profusion of blooms of a climbing rose makes it the ideal companion for a split-rail fence.

Positive Images, Jerry Howard

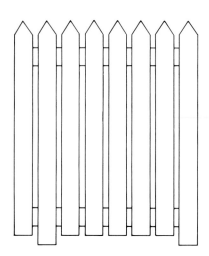

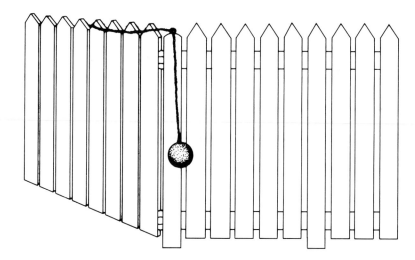

A colonial gate fixture is a practical way to be certain gates are closed, even today. The heavy ball drops down and pulls the gate closed.

We have a picket fence gate that visitors invariably leave open. How do you construct one that is self-closing?

The method used in colonial times still works well. Attach a heavy ball to a chain. On the hinged side of the gate, put a post to the side so the gate opens away from it. Attach one end of the chain to the top of the post, the other to the top of the gate, and have enough slack in the chain so that it is tight only when the gate is fully open. In this way, the weight of the ball will close the open gate.

I'd like to build a stone retaining wall. Do you think this is too difficult for an amateur to undertake?

On a sloping lot, a retaining wall can both serve many functions as well as add beauty to the property. A wall built as explained below will be stable to a height of four feet. For higher walls, you may wish to employ a contractor. Check your local ordinances; sometimes building permits are required for retaining walls. Here are some rules that will make construction easier:

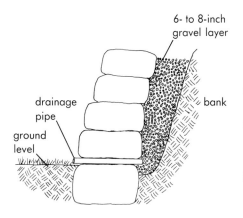

6- to 8-inch gravel layer

drainage pipe

bank

ground level

Cross-section of a stone retaining wall, showing large foundation stone below ground level, drainage pipe through wall just above ground level, 6- to 8-inch wide layer of gravel behind entire wall, wall leaning toward bank, and stones laid flat with largest stones at the bottom.

- Dig out a space so the first tier of stones will be below ground level and provide a firm foundation for the wall.
- Just above ground level, place several one-inch diameter pipes (one every six to eight feet) through the wall; they should be as long as the width of the wall.
- Place a six- to eight-inch-wide layer of gravel or crushed stone behind the entire wall, adding the gravel as you add layers of stones to the wall. This layer plus the pipes will prevent a buildup of water behind the wall.
- Keep the wall leaning slightly toward the bank, about three inches per foot height of the wall. Lay the individual stones flat; do not lean them against the bank.
- Place each stone so that it is resting on two or more below it.
- If long stones are available, place them so they anchor the wall into the bank.

- Place the largest stones at the bottom of the wall.
- If flat stones are available, save them to use as a cap for the wall.

Some of my fencing is not pressure-treated; should I apply a preservative?

As you landscape your property, you'll want to use wood preservatives in order to protect wood used for fence posts or in the construction of lawn steps, terraces, and furniture. Following a few rules will make this a safer venture.

- Avoid the use of creosote. It's highly poisonous and will kill any plants that come in contact with it. Most railroad ties have been creosoted. Old ties that have weathered for years, however, are safe to use in most conditions.
- In situations where wood will be buried, such as fence posts, buy pressure-treated wood. It will last years longer than wood you treat yourself.
- When buying a preservative, read the label first. It will tell you what fungicide is used, whether it protects against termites, whether it can be painted over, and whether it should be used where the wood will be in contact with the soil.

Are wood preservatives dangerous to handle?

Today a growing number of wood preservatives are being developed that offer long-lasting protection against rotting and that are at the same time not dangerous to use and not harmful to persons or plant life. Some of the less dangerous preservatives contain copper naphthenate, copper-8-quinolinolate, polyphase, or TBTO. Even though these preservatives are much safer to use than some of the older ones that are no longer manufactured, they should still be handled with care. Wear goggles, long sleeves, gloves, and a dust mask while applying, and don't handle the wood while it is still damp with preservatives. Here are a few guidelines:

- Work in the shade. That way the preservative will penetrate the wood before drying.
- Work on clean wood. If it's dirty, scrub it, then allow it to dry. This can take several days.
- Don't try to treat painted wood. It will do no good.
- If possible, dip the wood into the preservative, rather than painting it on. This permits the preservative to get into small cracks in the wood that a brush will skim over.
- Keep an eye on the wood after you have treated it. If it is constantly damp after treatment because of poor drainage, it will rot much more quickly. If you see mildew on it, scrub it with a mixture of bleach and water, and let the wood dry for several days; then treat it with preservative again. Plan on applying preservative again to all wood after two or three days.

A stone retaining wall of substantial flat rocks is a handsome and serviceable addition to this property.

6 *Special Gardens*

T his final chapter is a selection of garden types, some or all of which you may wish to incorporate into your landscape design. In each case, we give you only an introduction, with the hope that your appetite will be whetted for more adventures into the fascinating worlds of growing vegetables and herbs, planning specialty gardens such as rock gardens or gardens for the handicapped and elderly, and sharing your delight in gardening with children and even the birds that will find your landscape an inviting and secure haven for feeding and nesting. Happy gardening!

Vegetable gardens intended simply to supply a single family's table with fresh, crisp, and succulent vegetables are often referred to as kitchen gardens. And who says such a garden can look only functional? Carefully planned and tended, it can be an important decorative feature of your landscape at the same time it provides you food. For the beginner, a vegetable garden no more than ten by ten feet is a good starting size. Follow the principles described on pages 109-15 for soil preparation.

Decorative kitchen gardens demand that you first put aside outmoded ideas of what a vegetable garden should look like: Rather than lining crops up in single file, plant them in beds a foot or more wide. For example, start lettuce plants no more than two inches apart on all sides. Then, as the lettuce grows, keep thinning (and eating) it, so that it will have ample room even when it is full grown. Carrots, too, can be grown this way,

KITCHEN GARDENS
•

◀ The hollowed center of the large rock forms a perfect bird bath in the midst of this herb and flower garden.

Vegetable gardens need not be merely utilitarian. A creative design using raised beds makes this one a centerpiece of the landscape. Paths are mulched with salt marsh hay.

about two inches apart, and their feathery foliage will make a delightful blanket.

What vegetables, in addition to lettuce and carrots, are good for beginning gardeners with limited space?

Include a few of the smaller tomato plants, such as Pixie or the even smaller bush cherry tomatoes. Nothing is more decorative than pepper plants, with their shiny green foliage, and their heavy harvest provides an added incentive to grow them. Cucumbers take up space, running their vines here and there, but if you must be miserly with space, grow these on a fence or on trellis netting. Alternatively, select the bush varieties and get ample rewards even from small spaces. Broccoli has recently been widely promoted for its health benefits and deserves a space in the smallest gardens. Each plant bears one large head, followed after the main harvest by bite-sized sprouts all summer. Only such space-eaters as corn and potatoes must be excluded from the small garden.

How can I get the most out of my limited space?

Keep the soil producing: For example, have at least six plantings of various kinds of lettuce, starting one crop in a flat as another is reaching maturity. Don't waste an inch of space. If you have a small empty spot, plant another crop of radishes or a few onions that can be harvested at any time for salads.

I keep reading about growing lettuce all summer long. I try it, and it becomes so bitter it is not worth eating. Any suggestions?

Try varieties such as Oak Leaf, Salad Bowl, and Buttercrunch to find the one that does best in the summer weather in your region. Try growing lettuce in the shade: for example, on the north side of tall plants such as tomatoes, or under something that will give partial shade, such as several layers of cheesecloth. Finally, keep it moist at all times.

If none of these suggestions succeeds, don't give up. In midsummer during the hottest days, start a flat of lettuce indoors. It will be up and ready to be transplanted into the garden in mid-August for a fine fall crop.

I've tried planting beets in beds and find they are too crowded before reaching maturity. Am I planting them too closely together?

No, but you are missing one of the best ways to eat beets. When the plants begin to get crowded, thin them to give those remaining the space they need. Cook the thinnings, roots and all, as greens. Many people grow beets just for this, preferring the greens to the mature beets.

What vegetables can be grown in beds?

Just about any of them: It's simply a matter of leaving enough space between plants so they will thrive. For instance, beets, carrots, leaf lettuce, onions, and radishes should be planted only two to three inches apart; cabbages, cauliflower, and peppers should be a foot apart; and tomatoes should be two to three feet apart. Pole beans are one crop that does best in a single row. For best pollination, corn should be in several rows, rather than one long, single row.

I want to make several raised beds by framing them with six-by-six timbers. The wood won't last long unless it is treated. What do you suggest?

Your best choice is factory pressure-treated wood, which will last for many years. If you wish to try to do it yourself, select a copper naphthenate preservative. Cuprinol green #10 is one of these, and there are others. Treatment should make the wood last several years. It will last even longer if you take the trouble to pull up the timbers, brush the soil off them each fall, and treat them with preservative again every two or three years. This preservative will not harm the plants in your beds. (See page 129 for precautions to take in handling wood preservatives.)

HERB GARDENS

An herb garden can be as modest as a clump or two of chives beside the kitchen door, or as extravagant as the English knot gardens that entwine many herbs in beguiling patterns. It can be purely decorative—as those English gardens certainly are—or it can be grown for culinary purposes or even for medicinal use. It can be a garden for those herbs you use daily—parsley, mint, dill, and basil, perhaps—or it can be a place to try new herbs, such as chervil or hyssop, borage or lovage. An herb garden can be exactly what you want it to be. Keep it close by your kitchen door, as has been custom since prehistoric days when it was discovered easier to grow these cherished plants close to the cave entrance, rather than to seek them out when the need arose.

I'd like to grow herbs, but I don't know where to begin.

Before herbs grow best for us, as with other plants we must understand their likes and dislikes about sunlight and shade, moisture, and richness of soil. Some are annuals, some are the most persistent of perennials, and a few, like caraway and parsley, are biennials.

If you wish to try growing herbs but hesitate, fearing failure, begin with a very small area. Spade up a square, three-feet-by-three-feet, in a sunny spot with reasonably good soil. Or make a raised bed by nailing together a three-foot-by-three-foot square of two-by-six-inch boards, then filling it with soil.

What herbs grow most successfully?

Plant those herbs you now use and like. Chives are perennials, easy to start, and hard to discourage. They demand only that you clip them occasionally (clip the entire stem when you harvest them). Parsley is slow to start, but very prolific when it's underway. Dill is excellent, particularly if you pickle cucumbers. Mint is an old standby, but be ready for it to try to take over your garden. Basil is wonderful in tomato dishes. Try as well a few herbs with which you are not as familiar. Tall lovage is useful in many dishes. Borage has a taste much like cucumbers. In your small bed, you can try as many as nine herbs, allotting a square foot to each one.

A year or two with this tiny garden and you will be ready for more ambitious undertakings. Medicinal plants? An intertwining of herbs that will astonish your visitors? Herbs for tea? The choice is yours.

I've raised parsley and know it is a biennial plant, yet I have never had it reappear in the spring. Why not?

You're right, parsley is a biennial, which means it produces its seeds the second year. It does not mean that it is winter hardy. People raising parsley in cold climates should harvest the leaves the first year and plant another crop the next year.

Neat and formal, this herb garden thrives in the sandy soil and bright sun of the seashore.

Positive Images, Jerry Howard

I would like to put herb plants around the spokes of an old wagon wheel. How would you suggest doing this?

It can be made into the central feature of a small, formal herb garden. Select a level, sunny spot in the garden, and prepare the soil as you would for any garden. Put the wheel down, then plant a different variety of herbs between each set of spokes. So that the spokes won't be hidden, we would suggest using fairly small plants such as thyme, chives, sage, parsley, mint, French tarragon, winter savory, sweet basil, and chervil.

When should herbs be harvested?

By all means, harvest them as you need them. Select a few each evening for the dinner salad, and marvel at the difference. Try them in cooking. If you wish to save them for winter use, however, harvest them before they flower. Cut them early in the morning, wash them, then dry them with circulating air, not heat. When they are thoroughly dry, strip the leaves off the twigs and store the leaves in airtight containers.

ROCK GARDENS

There are rock gardens—and there are piles of rocks with plants growing among them. The difference is that the developers of the *gardens* studied and pondered, viewed and compared before making a move.

The sites of rock gardens vary widely. Often they are on problem slopes where grass would not grow well. Converted to a rock garden, such a place becomes a plus in the landscaping. Rock gardens can also be level areas, with added soil and rocks creating a setting for a collection of plants. They can even be rocky outcroppings, where the natural setting is changed only by the addition of plants.

Often they are shaded, but some are in sunny areas, and some of the best combine shaded and sunny areas, providing a variety of conditions for a variety of plants.

Can you give some general guidelines for a successful rock garden?

- Feature large plants only if the garden is large. Some of the most effective gardens are small, with everything in them— rocks and all plants—small and thus not dominating the space.
- Rock gardens are not rock collections. Use only one type of stone, usually native stone, which is cheaper and more suitable for the area. Quarried rock, such as blocks of marble, should be avoided as it detracts from the natural look of the garden.
- Place rocks naturally, partially buried, so that they look as if they belonged there and were not just placed there. Avoid round stones, particularly those sitting on top of the ground.

Gaily flowering, low-growing plants are perfect foils for the rough, light colored stones. Shrubs such as the cotoneaster spreading over the large rock on the left further soften the setting.

- Place plants so that you can easily reach them when you garden. This is not a garden you can plant and forget. Although the best gardens have a natural look, as if they somehow created themselves, this appearance is deceptive. Like any other gardens, these must be cared for—weeded, divided, cut back, fertilized, and sometimes watered.
- Feature plants indigenous to the area. In years past, many rock gardens featured the small alpine plants that flourish in cool, rocky areas. But while these plants are still popular in northern areas, you are not limited to them. Beautiful rock gardens can be found in desert areas, as well as in the warm and humid conditions of the Deep South, each with plants appropriate to the climate and topography.
- Most rock gardens feature perennials that grow close to the ground, and particularly those that grow over and cling to the rocks.
- Start small. Create a small gem of a garden, and then gradually enlarge it.
- Some rock gardens have the added beauty of running water, a tiny falls, perhaps, or water running across rocks and into a pool. Any such use of water will enhance the beauty of the garden and attract birds to the site. If there is no natural water on the site, a falls or stream can be created, using a recirculating pump.

Where can I get more information about rock gardens?

Visit the gardens of friends (or even strangers, who usually are happy to display their gardens, if asked politely), or visit the rockeries of botanical gardens, where the plants usually are identified with small signs. This provides an opportunity to identify and select plants you wish for your own garden.

The list of plants ideal for a rock garden is long. Most garden centers stock plants that are suitable for rock gardens in their area. In general, these are low-growing plants, modest when blossoming, some with green or silver foliage, some evergreen. In most gardens, it is most effective to plant in groups, rather than scatter various plants across the garden.

Are there plants I should avoid putting in my rock garden?

There are some plants that do not belong in a rock garden because they tend to overwhelm its subtle beauty. The bold blooms of zinnias and marigolds, for example, tend to over-shadow smaller plants. Some evergreens blend well in a rock garden, but those commonly found around house foundations will look overdressed and out of place. Large plants can be used, but very carefully. They are possibly best as background for the smaller plants.

How much of a rock garden should be covered with rocks?

There is no rule for this. In general, on flat areas or gentle slopes, allow broad spaces between rocks. On steeper slopes, many more rocks look very natural. In any case, large rocks look better than small.

I have access to a lot of big stone blocks that will split much like slate. Is this appropriate for a rock garden?

I am assuming these are rough blocks, not square-cut in a quarry. If so, they are excellent. But use them carefully. Thin pieces, such as slates, will look out of place. And when you position those blocks, their layers of stratification (the lines along which you could split them) should all run the same way, slightly off from horizontal.

How deep should rock plants be set in the ground?

Most form a spreading top that either roots as it spreads or grows directly from a central root system. The crown of the plant must not be covered. Dig a hole with a trowel and gather the loose tops in your hand. Holding the plant at the side of the hole with the crown resting on the surface and the roots extending into the hole, firm the soil around the roots. When the hole is filled, the crown should rest on the surface. Give it a good watering to establish it.

My rock garden site is a natural one, with lots of outcroppings and little topsoil. Any suggestions?

You have a good setting for a rock garden. For best results, look for places where you can dig out pockets among the stones to fill with topsoil to give your plants a better chance for success. If your site is sunny, these plants may require watering during dry spells, long before you think of watering your lawn or flower beds.

When is the best time to plant a rock garden?

If pot-grown plants are available, planting may be done almost any time from spring to early autumn. Although spring is good everywhere, September and October work well in moderately cold climates, such as lower New York State.

A GARDEN FOR THE ELDERLY OR HANDICAPPED

This raised garden in a housing project for the elderly offers easy access for gardeners in wheelchairs or those for whom kneeling is difficult.

Positive Images, Jerry Howard

For elderly and handicapped people, life often becomes a saddening sequence of giving up beloved activities. Gardening need not be among these, and the stronger gardeners among us can make certain that it isn't. The degree of assistance required depends on the person involved.

I know an elderly couple both of whom have always loved to garden, but who now feel they must give it up because they can no longer operate their 100-by-100-foot garden. Bending over, weeding and harvesting—it's just too much. Any suggestions?

If a volunteer gardener creates a raised bed for them, narrow enough so they can reach to the center of it, long enough to grow their needs, they can continue gardening. There's less bending with the raised bed, making wide rows of lettuce, carrots, or beans easy to care for and harvest.

How can more handicapped persons, perhaps even those confined to wheelchairs, be enabled to garden?

A garden on legs offers dramatic possibilities for raising flowers or vegetables. This can be a table-like creation, on sturdy legs and with wooden sides to hold six inches of soil.

Can container gardening be done successfully by those unable to manage larger-scale gardens?

Container gardening can indeed bring to elderly and severely handicapped persons the deep satisfaction that more ambitious gardening offers. Container gardening can mean many things: a window box on a patio, easily cultivated from a chair and offering as much as six square feet of gardening space, or just a few clay pots with favorite geraniums in them.

Pot up a Pixie tomato plant in a large pot and present it to a person who thinks his or her gardening days are over. Place the plant in a sunny spot, handy for the person who will tend it, stake it up with a light stick, and provide a liquid fertilizer for occasional use. That tomato plant will receive the tenderest of TLC, bring interest to what may be a drab life, and contribute a golfball-size tomato or more per day all summer long. See this happen once and you'll be convinced of the therapeutic value of raising plants.

My father suffers from arthritis so that holding a tool such as a hoe is painful. Any suggestions?

For some people, the pain results from closing the hands tightly enough to hold the tool. Try padding the handle with several layers of cloth so his hands do not have to close tightly to hold the tool. This is particularly useful for many persons attempting to handle small tools such as trowels.

CHILDREN'S GARDENS

Once upon a time, there were two children. The first child was introduced to gardening at the age of eight. His father and mother planted the garden, and then when weeds began to compete with lettuce, carrots, and *their* interest in gardening, the weeding was assigned to him. And he did it for five years, weeding, weeding, weeding—and grumbling, grumbling,

Quick-growing lettuce is a good choice for young gardeners.

Positive Images, Jerry Howard

Positive Images, Gary Mottau

It's never too soon to introduce children to the wonder of watching tiny seeds spring into showy flowers or tasty vegetables.

grumbling. He hasn't gardened since, nor, thankfully has he passed the work on to his next generation.

The second child began gardening at the age of six. She saw her parents in the garden, thought it looked like fun, asked for a garden of her own, and was assigned her own small space. She even got to choose her crops—pansies and radishes. She learned much that summer: how pansies can be picked and picked and still keep producing; how radishes, if planted every week, will be ready to pick every night for dinner, even when parents suggest saving some for dinner the following night. The next summer she learned how far pumpkin vines will run. And the next—was it the year of the six varieties of tomatoes, or the one of the giant sunflowers that nodded in friendly fashion to all who entered the garden?

The moral of the story is not difficult to understand. Gardening should be fun, not a chore, for youngsters. They should raise what they want to, even if raising twelve corn plants seems unproductive. Their achievements should be applauded, their failures handled constructively as lessons in horticulture—or even ignored. And if the six-year-old's interest in gardening cools in the heat of early July, that should not be recalled when he or she wants to try again the next spring.

What are good plants for children to begin with?

Children like things to happen quickly and plainly. For this reason, radishes, which seem to pop out of the soil in a matter of days, are a good choice. The growth of pole beans running up a pole can be tracked daily. A mixture of annual flowers adds a mystery to the garden: What's that, a weed or a flower?

A GARDEN FOR BIRDS

It's possible, and quite simple, to create a haven for birds as you landscape your yard. On large properties, this can mean providing food, water, cover, and places for nesting. If your land area is more modest, it can mean a few dogwoods or other shrubs that provide food that birds especially love.

How can I encourage birds to come to our yard?

Remember that birds like a variety of conditions, such as open lawn areas, the cover of shrubs and trees, small flowering trees, and pools or bird baths in which to bathe. They also love conditions that aren't too tidy, such as thick growths of brambles, brush piles, heavy growths around fences, and fallen trees.

Birdhouses, too, will encourage birds to your property. Consult a chart that shows sizes of homes and entrance sizes and heights of homes for various birds. Don't bother with perches at the entrance. They aren't needed, and provide roosts for other birds to heckle the inhabitants.

How can I protect birds from cats?

Cats are the worst enemy of birds. Remember this as you plan your bird garden, and put baths and feeding stations away from shrubs, so cats can't sneak up on the birds.

Can I choose specific plants that birds enjoy in order to make our yard more inviting?

Berry bushes, Virginia creeper, and dogwoods will all attract birds during the summer. Several attractive shrubs have the added virtue of carrying their fruits into the winter, and thus providing food for the birds. These include barberries, cotoneasters, hawthorns, holly, mountain ash, roses, snowberries, and viburnum. Add to what is offered naturally by providing food such as suet, wheat, hemp, sunflower seeds, millet, and raisins.

PART III
ANNUALS

7 Designing with Annuals

Your landscape may seem complete: tall trees providing a strong and stately framework; attractive foundation plantings enhancing the areas near the house; a comfortable patio or deck; ground covers and a lush, green lawn. Yet, something is lacking—and the crucial, missing element is *color*. Although flowering trees and shrubs and perennial flowers enliven the home landscape, there is no simpler, quicker, or more dependable source of color than those most versatile of plants, the annuals.

Whether you desire a subdued atmosphere or an exciting one, you will find annuals to suit your purposes. Throughout the growing season, no matter what the climate, there are annuals that will thrive: from forget-me-nots and pansies in the cool moistness of spring and early summer to verbenas and zinnias in the hot sun of midsummer. The smallest of properties, even balconies high over city streets, can benefit from the colors of container-grown geraniums, nasturtiums, and lantana. Annuals can be used to define areas or to add accents to them, to fill in large spaces, and to make the garden appear larger or smaller. One of the nicest things about them is that as your tastes or needs change, so too can your garden design and color scheme: go wild this year with brilliant gaillardia and California poppies; be subdued the next with gentle sweet peas, stock, and lobelia.

Designing with annuals involves determining the size and shape of planting beds or borders, locating them to their best advantage, using them in combination with other plants, selecting colors, and choosing plant sizes and shapes. Although

◀ *A sunny display of bright-colored zinnias and marigolds enlivens the home landscape quickly, inexpensively, and dependably.*

gardening with annuals can be easy and pleasurable, you will find that the more avidly you garden, the more questions you may have. We hope that in the pages that follow you will find both the questions you raise and the answers to meet them.

UNDERSTANDING THE BASIC TERMINOLOGY

What is an annual?

An annual is a plant that is sown, flowers, sets seed, and dies all within one season.

Why should I include annuals in my garden design?

Annuals are the best way to achieve summer color for long periods of time. Whereas most trees and shrubs blossom in spring, and even summer-blooming perennials last only three to four weeks, annuals produce color all summer. Creating a festive mood and thus enhancing the beauty of your home, they offer one of the easiest and most effective means of enlivening a landscape. Best of all, the color scheme can be altered from year to year as your tastes change.

In California I have seen plants such as geraniums, snapdragons, and begonias that are perennials, yet in Pennsylvania they are called annuals. What is the difference?

The term "annual" is often applied to plants that are perennials in warm areas but cannot survive cold winters. These tender perennials are not technically annuals because they do not die after they set seeds. In cold climates, however, they must be treated as annuals in the garden.

What is meant by a hardy annual? A half-hardy annual? A tender annual?

Hardy annuals are those whose seeds can be planted in the fall or in very early spring, because they are not injured by frosts. *Half-hardy annuals* are cold-resistant and seeds of these can be planted early in the spring. The seeds are frost hardy, but the plants are not. Although they will not survive heavy frost, they do not mind cool temperatures. *Tender annuals* are easily injured by frost and must be planted only after the ground has warmed up and all danger of frost is past.

What is a hybrid?

A hybrid is a new plant created by the successful cross-pollination of two plants with different genetic traits. Many of today's better flowering annuals are hybrids.

Why should I grow hybrids?

Hybrids are improvements over nonhybrids, including both of their parents. They may possess one or more desirable characteristics, such as improved disease resistance, increased flowering, or higher heat tolerance.

Can I collect seeds from hybrid plants to grow the next year?

No, seeds from a hybrid will not produce a new plant like its parent and you are likely to be disappointed in the results.

Why are seeds of hybrids more expensive?

Many hybrids are created by hand in greenhouses, and so are very expensive to produce. Others are grown outdoors, but in controlled conditions, and they, too, are therefore more expensive to produce. The results, however, are worth it.

Should I look for annuals by variety name, or is it enough to know that the plant is a marigold, an impatiens, or a petunia, for example?

By all means, shop for annuals by variety name. Knowing the variety can tell you something about the height, flower size, and disease- and heat-resistance of the plant. When you find a variety that does well for you, note what it is so that you can buy it again the following year.

What is the difference between a "variety" and a "cultivar"? I have seen both listed in seed catalogs.

A variety is a plant that is different from the true species occurring in nature. A cultivar is short for "cultivated variety." It is a variety developed by a plant breeder by crossing two different plants. However, the terms are often (incorrectly) interchanged.

What is a series?

The word "series" has been given to those annual varieties in which the same type of plant is available in a range of different flower colors. Series are very common in impatiens, begonias, petunias, marigolds, geraniums, and several other popular garden flowers.

What is the advantage of growing plants from the same series?

If you wish to grow a mixed garden of impatiens, for example, select plants from the same series to get plants of the same height and growth habit and flowers of the same size.

Is it better to buy seeds from a local store or from mail-order catalogs?

Mail-order catalogs usually have a larger selection and a more complete description of the individual varieties. They may also be available earlier, an important factor if you are beginning seeds indoors. Racks at the garden center are good for last-minute purchases. If you plan to start seeds indoors, be sure to order or buy early, especially such annuals as petunias, begonias, impatiens, and geraniums that require twelve to sixteen weeks of growing inside before being transplanted outdoors. Ordering early also saves you the disappointment of finding a variety sold out.

In mid-spring, I noticed small seedlings that I did not plant growing in my flower garden. Where did they come from?

Some annuals freely reseed, especially where winters are not severe and soil is porous. These include sweet alyssum, browallia, lobelia, four-o'clock, morning-glory, moonflower, ageratum, nicotiana, nasturtium, petunia, scabiosa, spider flower, hollyhock, salvia, and impatiens. What you see are seedlings growing from seeds that dropped the year before. They are sometimes called *volunteers*.

Is it a good idea to leave volunteers in the flower bed?

Not necessarily, for at least two reasons. If the seedlings grew from hybrids, they will not come true and you will probably be disappointed. Except in areas with long summers, volunteers may not grow large enough to produce a good flower display. If you want to be certain to have the flowers of any of these, it is best not to rely on the happy chance of volunteers but to sow seeds each spring.

If such seeds as petunia, impatiens, salvia, and phlox are permitted to self-seed, is there a true-to-original-color reproduction?

Not usually. Many annuals grown today are hybrids, and the seeds will not produce plants that are the same as the parents.

CREATING A GARDEN DESIGN

What is the difference between a bed and a border?

Flower beds are plantings, such as those in the middle of your lawn, that are accessible from all sides and intended to be viewed from all sides. *Borders* are at the edge of an area and are approached and viewed from only one side in such locations as along a fence, driveway, or foundation or in front of shrubs or a hedge.

How large should beds be?

This depends on the size of the surroundings. Keep them in scale with the rest of the property. Any bed that takes up more than one-third of the area in which it is placed is likely to look out of proportion.

What shape should beds be?

This depends on your taste and the style of your home. Formal beds are square or rectangular. Informal beds are round, oval, kidney-shaped, or free-form. Do not make the curves too sharp: the bed will appear too busy, and it will be difficult to mow the grass bordering it.

How large should borders be?

There are two considerations. First, as with flower beds, borders should be in proportion to their surroundings. A very wide border would not look good next to a very short walkway. A good rule of thumb is to make a border no wider than one-third its length. Second, because borders can be worked from one side only, they should be no wider than five feet, no matter how long they are, or maintenance will be too difficult.

Flower beds are accessible from all sides.

Ann Reilly

Where can I locate beds and borders?

Anywhere: along the driveway, in front of the foundation planting, along the patio, under the mailbox, at the base of the flagpole, in raised beds, by the driveway, along a fence, at the edge of the pool, accenting statuary, by the front door, next to garden benches. When deciding where to put your beds and borders, consider the points from which they will be viewed. If you want to see them from the dining room, locate them near those windows. If you want to see them from the patio, place them around it or in viewing line of it. Create beds or borders in the front of the house if you want people driving or walking by to share in the enjoyment of your flowers.

What else should I consider when deciding where to locate my beds and borders?

You should look at existing permanent features, such as the house, large trees, and fences, and if feasible, blend these into the flower planting. For example, carve out a circular or oval area under a stately tree, and fill the bed with shade-loving plants like impatiens or begonias, or turn a fence into an asset of the garden by highlighting it with a flower border. If you are planting flowers near the house, be sure the flower colors complement the house.

I want to have a large garden, but I have a small piece of property. What should I do?

In this case, design a free-standing garden with pathways in it, perhaps encircled by a decorative fence with a gate. You will be creating a flower garden that is more than a bed or border, one that needs no surrounding lawn.

I don't have the time for a large garden. What would be the best place for a single flower bed or border?

Select a spot where either you or your neighbors can enjoy the garden most, perhaps somewhere near the way in and out of the house or in view of a favorite indoor or outdoor sitting area.

I'm not sure how large a flower bed to create. I have never gardened before. What do you suggest?

If this is your first time, start small; you can always increase the size of the garden next year. The amount of space you devote to your garden is determined by how much space there is on your property, as well as how much time and energy you have for the garden. Particularly if you have a full-time job, and can garden only on weekends, start small—perhaps about seventy-five to one hundred square feet. If you have no trouble maintaining that, increase the size or add another bed next year. On the other hand, if even that sounds too ambitious, plant annuals in containers along the walkway or driveway, or in front of shrubs in the foundation planting.

Ann Reilly

A fence becomes a highlight of the garden and provides a decorative background for tall foxglove and a wide border of pansies.

I'd like to grow annuals in my garden this summer, but don't know where to start. What advice can you give me?

There are two things to consider before anything else in deciding which plants you want to grow: which annuals it is *possible* to grow in your garden, and which ones you would *like* to grow. First, match the plants to your growing conditions. Is your garden sunny or shady? Is your climate hot or cool? Is there a water shortage where you live? After you have determined that, you can make a list of plants that will grow well in your garden. From that list, choose those you like for their appearance or for how they will fit into your plan. Perhaps you want a particular color, or group of colors. Maybe you want only short plants, or a variety of heights. Many choices are available, but using these criteria you will soon have an interesting and varied list of annuals that you will want to try. Visit gardens in your area and study which do best there and which you like the most.

What are the differences to be considered in designing a formal garden versus an informal one?

Formal gardens are usually created with straight lines in symmetrical arrangements, quite often on flat areas with no large trees or shrubs. Formal gardens look best with more formal homes.

An informal garden is the natural choice for a cottage-style home, where the ground is hilly, where there is a stream or

Formal gardens are created with straight lines and geometric shapes in symmetrical arrangements.

Ann Reilly

brook, or many trees and shrubs. In such situations, create an informal garden with curving lines around the trees or shrubs.

On a trip to Europe, I saw formal gardens in *fleur-de-lis* patterns, as well as other designs, and liked the effect. How do I recreate this?

Draw a plan on paper to scale, then transfer your design to the garden bed, using strings or cord to lay it out before you plant (see page 177).

What types of annuals do best in these formal types of designs?

Choose plants of contrasting colors with tidy and trim growing habits. Spreading annuals such as sweet alyssum and lobelia are not good choices. For flowering plants, use begonia, candytuft, phlox, and ageratum plants; for foliage plants, alternanthera, iresine, and dusty miller.

Should beds and borders have plants of the same height or varying heights?

That depends on the size of the bed or border. In small beds, choose plants of the same or only slightly varying heights; tall plants would be out of place. In large borders, use a variety of heights to make the planting more interesting. Place tall plants in the background, with intermediate-sized plants in the middle, and low-growing annuals in the front.

A large flower border with tall foxglove in the background, medium-sized dahlias in the middle, and low-growing nasturtiums along the edge.

Ann Reilly

Should I vary the heights of annuals I select for planting on a hillside?

Since the hill itself gives height to the planting, a hillside looks best with plants of approximately the same height.

My property is flat and uninteresting. How can I use flower beds to make it more attractive?

Use tall plants in the center of a bed, with lower plants in the front. You might also consider creating a *berm*—a rounded mound of earth—to vary the topography.

How many gradients of height should I use?

It is good to work in threes. Use three different plants, or different varieties of the same plant in different heights—marigolds and zinnias have nice selections of the latter.

Please give me a list of tall annuals to use as the background in a border or as the center plant for a free-standing bed.

Hollyhock, spider flower, sunflower, Mexican sunflower, tall snapdragon, and tall zinnia are all excellent choices.

What plants are suitable for the middle of the border?

In addition to the marigolds or geraniums already mentioned, grow anchusa, amaranthus, calendula, China aster, clarkia, dahlia, California poppy, globe amaranth, snow-on-the-mountain, strawflower, impatiens, four-o'clock, petunia, Gloriosa daisy, medium-height zinnias, and African marigold.

What are good plants for edging the flower bed or border or a shrub planting?

Good low-growing plants are ageratum, dwarf snapdragon, begonia, dwarf China aster, dwarf celosia, ornamental pepper, China pink, candytuft, dwarf impatiens, lobelia, linaria, phlox, French marigold, pansy, periwinkle, nemesia, cupflower, baby-blue-eyes, portulaca, verbena, and dwarf zinnia.

Should plant shapes be varied in a bed or border?

Yes, within size limits. There are basically three different plant shapes: tall or spiked, rounded, and ground-hugging. A combination of all three is most attractive.

What are examples of plants I can use to vary plant shapes?

In the background, use spikes of tall snapdragons or salvia. In the middle, use a rounded marigold or geranium. In the foreground, finish the planting off with lobelia or petunias. Or for a more informal look, mix plumes of celosia, globes of gaillardia or African daisy, trumpet-shaped petunias or salpiglossis, flat and single begonias or impatiens, daisy-shaped dahlias, and wispy spider flowers.

The three basic shapes of flowers add variety to beds as well as to fresh bouquets: for example, tall, spiked snapdragons, rounded marigolds, and open, cascading petunias.

A brilliant display of annuals forms a border for the vegetable and herb garden.

If space is limited, try growing a vertical garden along a fence or wall. Here, begonias, impatiens, lobelia, and coleus provide a colorful display in a planter made of vertical boards and hardware cloth.

Which annuals are good where spiked shapes are desired?

These are hollyhock, snapdragon, Canterbury bells, celosia, larkspur, stock, bells-of-Ireland, nicotiana, mignonette, and salvia.

Some annuals don't seem to fall into these categories. What do I do when designing with these?

Some annuals have an upright but loose, open form. These include Swan River daisy, bachelor's-button, calliopsis, cosmos, love-in-a-mist, mignonette, salpiglossis, pincushion flower, and blue lace flower. They are best mixed into the border with other plants.

Must I combine different flowers to achieve an attractive effect?

No, the choice is up to you. A planting of the same type of annual, known as a *massed planting*, has a sleek, modern appearance that is very attractive. Good plants for massing are periwinkle, impatiens, geraniums, and multiflora petunias.

What other plants can I combine with annuals?

Almost anything. Combine spring bulbs with early annuals such as pansy or forget-me-not (see pages 284-86). For a mixed flower bed or border, plant annuals among perennials or tender bulbs. Annuals look beautiful as a border or ground cover in a rose bed, or with any shrubs.

Can I use annuals in my herb garden, or herbs in my annual garden?

Yes, they mix together quite nicely. Some herbs, such as parsley, basil, lavender, chives, rosemary, thyme, sage, and chamomile, are particularly well suited.

Can I combine annuals and vegetables?

Most definitely. A border of annuals in a vegetable garden is most attractive. Some annuals, such as marigolds, even help to repel insects. Conversely, small vegetables, such as red-leaved lettuce, make a nice border to a flower garden. If you enjoy the unusual, use eggplant and peppers, both of which develop into attractive plants with shiny, colorful vegetables, or Swiss chard for its attractive foliage.

My backyard is very small. How can I increase the space for an annual garden?

Plant a vertical garden. There are several ways to do this. Look for special pots that are flat on one side and hang them on the fence. Or construct a vertical planter with chicken wire, line it with sphagnum moss, fill it with potting medium, and plant it with flowers.

Are there qualities of foliage that I should think about other than color?

Yes, strive for a variety of kinds and textures as well. For example, Gloriosa daisies and zinnias have large, coarse foliage compared with annual chrysanthemum and cosmos, which have finely cut, lacy foliage. The foliage of periwinkle is quite glossy, while that of petunia is fuzzy and dull.

Will you give me a list of annuals requiring the least care in home gardens?

Marigolds, verbena, gaillardia, cosmos, spider flower, calliopsis, salvia, scabiosa, annual phlox, sweet alyssum, impatiens, begonia, nicotiana, periwinkle, and coleus.

I planted a large flower garden last year, but it was disappointing: it looked like a patchwork quilt. How can I avoid this next year?

Your problem was most likely in not dealing with color properly. Color is the most critical aspect of flower bed design. When planning a flower bed or border, avoid the busy "patchwork" look by choosing a color scheme. Allow your color choices to reflect your personality. If done with care, a color scheme will make your planting look more professional.

How do I choose a color scheme?

That depends on you, your home, and the look you want to achieve. Warm tones are happy, active, cheerful. Cool tones are relaxing.

After I have selected the main color I want to use, how do I select the others?

Use a color wheel to select several possible color schemes or *harmonies*. Say, for example, you choose yellow as your primary color. Directly across the wheel from yellow is violet. This is called *complementary harmony*. Another complementary harmony is orange and blue. One caution: complementary harmony is a strong harmony and may be too overpowering for a small garden.

Split complementary harmony is another possibility. In this case, you choose a primary color, say yellow, and work with the color on either side of its opposite (violet). With yellow, you would thus use blue or red. Red with blue or orange with violet are other split complementary combinations.

A third type of color harmony is *analogous harmony*. This harmony uses three colors in a row on the wheel, such as yellow, gold, and orange; or orange, russet, and red; or differing tones of violet and blue together.

USING COLOR FOR MAXIMUM EFFECT

•

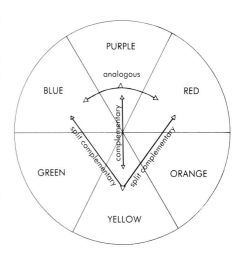

A color wheel can help suggest possible color schemes, or color harmonies.

An analogous harmony, such as this one composed of red, red-purple, and purple cineraria, consists of hues that appear in a row on the color wheel.

What are examples of plant combinations using complementary harmony?

Use yellow with violet pansies, orange marigolds or Mexican sunflower with blue lobelia, or orange calendula with blue ageratum.

What are examples of split complementary harmony?

Try red zinnias with blue ageratum, yellow marigolds with red sweet alyssum, red and blue salvia together.

What are examples of analogous harmony?

Plant yellow, gold, and orange marigolds or calendula, orange and red zinnias, or violet pansies with blue forget-me-nots.

What is monochromatic harmony?

Monochromatic harmony is a garden of only one color, such as all pink, all yellow, or all blue. To avoid monotony, use several different kinds of plants, or different varieties of the same plant, so that you have different shades of the same color. For example, plant pink geraniums, pink zinnias, and pink petunias together, or try a bed of impatiens using varieties with pale, rose, and bright pink flowers.

How many colors can I use in the garden and yet avoid a "busy" look?

Select one primary color and add one or at the most two other colors. You can use plants such as tall Mexican sunflowers, cosmos, or spider flowers across the back of the border and a mixture of colors in front of the unifying background. Even better is to use different colors of the same plant, such as mixed zinnias, celosia, or dahlias.

When I choose a color scheme, must I use the same one all around the property?

No, you can have different color schemes in front, side, and backyard as well as in different beds or borders.

Should I plant mixed beds, or beds of all one color?

That depends on your personal preferences, as well as on the style of your home. Sleek, one-variety beds and borders may be more appropriate for a contemporary setting. Massed plantings in many colors are well-suited to a traditional home, such as a New England colonial.

I want to attract attention to a lovely statue I just bought for the garden. What color annuals should I plant around it?

The eye immediately goes to red and bright orange, so these are the best colors to draw attention to your new statue. For the same reason, do not use bright colors where you are planting to hide something. Choose pastels or blues and violets for these areas.

My garden is quite large and I want to give the impression that it is smaller. What annuals should I plant?

Warm tones of red, maroon, gold, orange, and yellow will make a garden look smaller than it is. Dark-colored foliage, such as bronze-leaved begonias, dark coleus, iresine, or red alternanthera, will help, too.

I'd like a bright yellow and gold garden. What would be good choices?

Try calendula, California poppy, Cape marigold, Iceland poppy, pansy, celosia, sunflower, monkey flower, portulaca, marigold, nasturtium, snapdragon, and zinnia.

What orange flowers combine well with yellow ones in the garden?

Select different varieties of snapdragon, calendula, poppy, pansy, celosia, gaillardia, strawflower, impatiens, portulaca, marigolds, nasturtium, zinnia, and Cape marigold.

What do you think of an all-red garden?

All-red gardens are very attention-getting, so they are best if small and discreet. They make an especially nice effect against a white wall or fence. Use salvia, geranium, petunia, snapdragon, dianthus, poppy, pansy, amaranthus, China aster, celosia, gaillardia, strawflower, impatiens, begonia, nicotiana, portulaca, nasturtium, verbena, or zinnia.

Where does pink fit into the color wheel?

Pink is actually a *tone* of red, created by mixing red and white together. Pink may thus be used in the color scheme the same way as red. Excellent blends are made with pink and blue for a split complementary harmony and pink with clear red for a monochromatic harmony.

What annuals do you suggest I use for a pink garden?

Pink gardens tend to be delicate and feminine. Use begonia, impatiens, geranium, candytuft, sweet alyssum, stock, ageratum, China aster, cosmos, spider flower, baby's-breath, petunia, phlox, portulaca, zinnia, snapdragon, dianthus, or sweet pea.

My garden is quite small. How can I make it look more spacious?

Use blue and violet flowers, such as ageratum, lobelia, and blue salvia.

Complementary harmonies are strong, but can be extremely effective, as in this garden of yellow marigolds and purple ageratum.

I have created a small garden with a bench where I would like to spend summer afternoons reading. What colored annuals should I plant?

Use blues and violets, as well as white. These colors are cooling, soothing, and restful, and therefore perfect for a small garden or sitting area.

What colors should I choose for a garden that will usually be viewed at night?

Dark colors will blend into the background and not be visible, so use colors that will be seen at night, such as white or pale pink. Light-colored flowers also add a safety feature at night if planted along walkways; use garden lighting as well, to increase visibility.

What can I use in a blue or violet garden?

Many flowers come in shades of blue or violet. Although any one of them used alone makes a nice effect, the shaded combinations of two or more can be stunning. Select from bachelor's-button, larkspur, sweet pea, sweet alyssum, stock, forget-me-not, baby-blue-eyes, love-in-a-mist, browallia, China aster, morning-glory, lobelia, petunia, phlox, salvia, scabiosa, verbena, and pansy.

I have heard that white is a good buffer between strong-colored plants. I tried this last year, but it looked spotty. What did I do wrong?

White is a good buffer color, but if you use only one plant here and there to break up other colors, you will get a spotty effect. Instead, plant a large mass of white between bright colors, or, better yet, use white plants along the front of the border.

I'd like to plant an all-white garden. What could I use?

There are white flowers of certain varieties of ageratum, China aster, cosmos, baby's-breath, impatiens, begonia, lobelia, nicotiana, snapdragon, dianthus, sweet alyssum, stock, pansy, candytuft, petunia, phlox, portulaca, scabiosa, geranium, verbena, and zinnia.

My garden is on the south side of the house, and the house is a light gold in color. Should I use yellow, orange, and red annuals to complement the gold?

This would probably not give the best effect, even though the colors blend well. On a hot summer day, a garden of all warm colors against a warm-colored house may actually make you feel more uncomfortable in the heat. Use blue, violet, and white annuals instead: it won't be any cooler in your garden, but it may give the impression that it is.

Ann Reilly

Plants with white flowers or foliage, such as the dusty miller, impatiens, and zinnias shown here, are most effective if used in masses.

Ann Reilly

Coleus and other foliage plants can make a very colorful display.

Are there any rules about using color in relation to the size of the garden?

Yes, because warm colors make a garden look smaller, use them for dramatic displays. Conversely, because cool colors make the garden look larger, they are best for plantings that will be viewed close at hand. When cool colors are used in the distance, they become almost invisible.

Are there any other plants I can grow for their foliage only?

Yes, try amaranthus, flowering cabbage and kale, snow-on-the-mountain, kochia, and iresine.

How do I design with plants with colored foliage?

Treat them as though they were colored flowers. Use red-leaved coleus and alternanthera as you would use red zinnias. Use yellow-leaved forms of these same plants as you would yellow marigolds, and dusty miller, with its silver or gray foliage, as you would white-flowered begonias.

8 The Basics of Growing Annuals

The first step toward success with anything is equipping yourself with knowledge about how to do it properly. The same holds true for annual flower gardening. While some annuals naturally require less maintenance than others, there are a few basic rules to follow that will make the difference between a good garden and an outstanding one.

The annual garden starts with the seed or the plant. Depending on your time constraints and your preferences, you may enjoy the creative aspects and greater flexibility of growing your garden from seeds, or you may opt for the convenience of purchasing bedding plants. Either way, your garden will be no better than the soil in which it is planted. Although maintenance is not difficult, you should learn and follow a few basic rules regarding soil, fertilizer, water, and "housekeeping" to keep your garden at its prime.

Why should I start plants from seed? Purchased bedding plants are so much easier.

Yes, they are, but there are a number of reasons to start your own seeds. Each year, there are new varieties that you may want to try, but garden centers may not carry what you want. Old favorites are often equally difficult to find. Growing plants from seed is also more economical, which is a serious consideration if you have a large garden. Plus, starting plants from seeds can be fun!

INDOOR PROPAGATION

◀ *Gardeners will be most successful with some annuals, such as pansies, if seeds are sown indoors before outdoor planting times.*

Why do I need to start seeds indoors? Can't I sow seeds into the garden in spring?

Some seeds can be sown directly into the garden, but for several reasons, others can't. Some have a long growing season and will not have time to germinate, mature, and flower if you wait until the outdoor weather is mild enough to start them in the ground. Others may not require a long period of growth before bloom but *will* flower much earlier if they are begun indoors. Plants with fine seeds should be started indoors both because they can easily wash away in the rain outside and because they will have a difficult time competing with weeds when they are young.

What are the annuals that I should start inside?

Unless you start them indoors, or buy bedding plants (see pgs. 179-80), you will not have success with begonia, coleus, geranium, impatiens, lobelia, African marigold, petunia, salpiglossis, salvia, browallia, ornamental pepper, periwinkle, gerbera, lobelia, monkey flower, nierembergia, poor-man's orchid, wishbone flower, pansy, or verbena.

What are the basic requirements for starting seeds indoors?

A sterile sowing medium (see page 164), steady moisture (see page 169), good air circulation, suitable temperature (see pages 169-70), and adequate sunlight or fluorescent lights (see pages 171-72).

What is the proper time to plant indoors the seeds of pansy, petunia, and other annuals that should be started early but not too soon? We often have frost in New Hampshire in May.

Pansies can be sown inside in January, but the best plants for spring display come from seed sown in July or August and overwintered in the garden or a cold frame. The pansy can stand some frost. March is a good time to sow petunias for good plants that can be set out as soon as the weather is warm enough. For

A variety of containers may be useful for starting seedlings, from flats, divided flats, and peat pots that are manufactured for this purpose to recycled cartons and cans. Use containers that are not too shallow, and be sure to provide drainage holes.

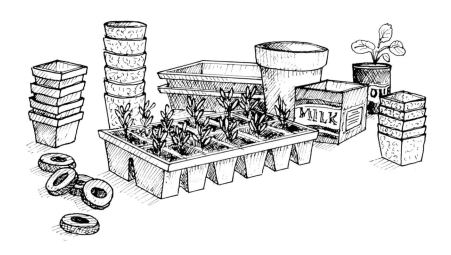

advice about when to start other annuals, see the chart on pages 284-86.

How can I start seedlings indoors so as to prevent too-rapid growth and decline?

Too-high temperatures and too early a start often account for the conditions described.

What is a flat?

A shallow, topless box (usually about three inches deep) with slits or holes in the bottom to allow for drainage of water from the soil. It is used for sowing seeds, inserting cuttings (see page 35), and transplanting young seedlings. Avoid shallow flats without drainage holes; the soil in such flats is easily over-watered. Flats that are too shallow dry out quite quickly. Various discarded kitchen containers, such as aluminum foil pans in which bottom drainage holes can easily be punched, make good flats.

Is there any rule about the dimensions of flats?

There is great variety in flat sizes. Usually they should be not less than two and one-half inches or more than four inches deep. If more than fourteen by twenty inches, they are likely to be too heavy to carry easily.

Can I purchase flats?

Specially designed units sold for the purpose help simplify the process, and are especially good for beginners. All are really just modifications of the traditional system. One such unit consists of a small plastic tray filled with a sterile planting medium (usually peat moss and vermiculite with nutrients) plus seeds that adhere to the plastic cover. To activate the tray, all one does is to punch holes in special indentations in the cover to release the seeds and then add the specified quantity of water. Such a unit eliminates the handling of seeds, provides a sterile starting medium, spaces the seeds a reasonable distance apart, and helps to avoid the danger of over- or underwatering.

Another system involves trays containing six or more compressed blocks of a special peat-based growing mixture in which one or two seeds per block are either presown or sown by the gardener. The unit is then watered.

Still another popular variant is the Jiffy-7, which when dry is a flat peat-moss wafer, but when moistened expands to form a small, filled pot in which a seed or seeds are sown. The wafers are usually placed side by side in a flat or other container. Large seeds can be sown one to a wafer and then left to grow until the plants are ready to be transplanted outdoors. Small seeds are usually sown several to a pot or seed tray and transplanted once before being set outdoors.

TIPS FOR STARTING SEEDS INDOORS

• Use a porous growing medium such as a mixture of equal parts of loam, peat moss, and sand, or a purchased soilless mix. A sterile growing medium prevents such soil-borne diseases as damping off, which can kill your seedlings.

• Keep the growing medium just moist but not sodden.

• Don't cover the seeds too deeply: fine seeds should be left uncovered, and larger seeds should be sown no deeper than twice their diameter.

Are there advantages to using flats made of compressed fiber?

Yes, they are very porous, which ensures good aeration and lessens the chance of overwatering. However, they dry out very quickly and so you must watch carefully to keep the soil moist. Do not reuse these flats as they are not sterile after their first use.

Are there any special techniques necessary when using fiber or peat flats or pots?

Yes, make sure these containers are completely soaked in water before you fill them with planting medium and sow your seeds. Otherwise, the container will act as a wick and pull moisture from the medium.

What are the reasons for sowing seeds into individual pots or Jiffy-7's?

Use these containers for seedlings that do not transplant well, because it's fairly easy to transplant from them without disturbing fragile plant roots. Some plants that do particularly well include California poppy, lavatera, love-in-a-mist, poppy, phlox, blue lace flower, larkspur, nolana, sweet pea, and creeping zinnia.

Can seed flats be reused from year to year?

Yes, but only if they are of a material such as plastic or foil that can be thoroughly cleaned to prevent transmission of disease. Those made of compressed peat or fiber should not be reused as they cannot be cleaned properly.

How should I clean flats before reusing them?

Wash them thoroughly with soap and water and rinse them in a bleach solution (1 ounce, or one-eighth cup, of bleach per gallon of water). This disinfectant is important in order to prevent damping off and other diseases.

What sowing medium is preferable for seeds sown indoors?

Use a soilless mix such as half sand, perlite, or vermiculite and half peat moss; or pure fine sand, vermiculite, or sphagnum moss watered with nutrient solution. The most convenient material is a prepared mix sold for this purpose and containing sufficient nutrients to carry seedlings through until transplanting time.

Why do seedlings begun in the house grow to about an inch, bend over, and die?

This is due to a fungus disease called *damping off*. Damping off can be virtually eliminated if you use the sterile soilless mixes. You can also help prevent it by treating the sowing medium with

Damping off, a fungus disease that frequently kills young seedlings, can be prevented by using only sterile soilless mixes for seed germination.

a fungicide containing benomyl, thinning seedlings properly, not overwatering, and giving seedlings fresh air without drafts.

How should I apply benomyl?

After you have filled the flats with growing medium, but before you sow the seeds, drench the flat with a solution of benomyl, mixed at the rate of one-half tablespoon per gallon water. Allow the flat to drain for about two hours, and then proceed with sowing.

What is the procedure for raising seedlings in sand with the aid of nutrient solutions?

Take a flat three to four inches deep, with drainage holes, and fill it with clean sand. Soak the sand with water, then with the nutrient solution (liquid fertilizer) mixed at one-quarter the strength recommended on the label. Sow seeds thinly; cover with sand unless the seeds require light to germinate; pat them in firmly with your hands or a small board. Keep the sand moist with the dilute nutrient solution. Once the seedlings have produced *true leaves* (those that appear after the seed leaves, or *cotyledons*, that spring from the plant embryo), gradually increase the strength of the nutrient solution to full strength.

How much sowing medium will I need?

About four cups of medium will be needed for each 5½-by-7½-inch flat.

I filled my flats with sowing medium and then watered the medium prior to sowing, but all the perlite floated to the top, and the medium didn't moisten evenly. What went wrong?

The medium must be moistened *before* it is placed into the flats. Put it in a large bowl or plastic bag, and use about one and one-half cups of warm water for every four cups of medium. Stir thoroughly.

Can I reuse sowing medium?

No, you should not reuse sowing medium for seeds, as it will no longer be sterile. You can reuse it, however, for transplanting seedlings from flats into intermediate pots before they are set into the ground, for container plants, and for your houseplants.

Should I use a seed disinfectant?

For most dependable germination and growth, instead of garden soil, use a sterile sowing medium, which can be purchased ready to use. If, however, you sow seeds indoors in untreated garden soil that may contain such fungus diseases as *damping off* (see pg. 164), you should use a soil disinfectant. This is available in powdered form. Place a small amount of the

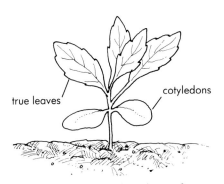

true leaves / cotyledons

True leaves appear after the seed leaves, or cotyledons.

powder in a paper or plastic bag, add the seeds, shake lightly with the bag tightly closed, and then plant the seeds immediately.

I have heard that some seeds should be soaked before sowing. Why is this?

Some seeds have a very hard seed coat that must be softened before the seed will germinate. Soaking these seeds in water prior to sowing softens the seed coat and hastens germination.

How hot should the water be for soaking seeds?

Use hot (190° F.), but not boiling, water, and cover the seeds two to three times their size in a shallow dish or container.

How long should seeds be soaked before they are sown?

Most seed coats will be soft enough after twenty-four hours of soaking. Change the water several times, and sow the seeds immediately after soaking so that they do not dry out.

Which seeds should be soaked?

Morning glory, hibiscus, and sweet peas are the primary annuals that benefit from soaking.

Is there any way other than soaking to treat seeds with a hard seed coat?

You can also try *scarification*, which entails nicking or breaking the seed coat slightly with a file or small scissors prior to sowing. Be careful not to cut too deeply into the seed coat, or you may damage the interior and prevent germination.

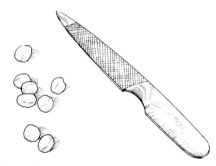

Scarification entails nicking the seed coat slightly with a small file prior to sowing.

What is pelleted seed?

Some seed companies pellet, or coat, seeds that are very fine to make them easier to handle and to increase germination. Pelleted seeds should not be covered when germinating, unless otherwise instructed on the packet. Merely press them into the surface of the sowing medium with a tamper.

What is a tamper?

An oblong piece of board with a handle attached (similar to a mason's float), used for tamping soil firmly in flats. The base of a tumbler or flowerpot can be used when sowing seeds into pots or bulb pans.

What other accessories will I need to germinate seeds indoors?

So that you don't have to rely on your memory, use labels to record the type and variety of plant and the sowing date. Keep a record book as well to help you decide next year which annual seeds to buy, how long it took for the seeds to germinate, whether you started too early or too late, and whether you grew too few or too many of a particular plant.

I have had problems germinating pansy and phlox seeds indoors. What might be the cause?

Seeds of some annuals, including pansy, phlox, blue daisy, bells-of-Ireland, verbena, and ornamental cabbage, require chilling before they are sown. This process is known as *stratification*. Seeds must also be moist during the chilling, so do not chill them in the seed packet. Mix the seeds with two to three times their volume in moistened sowing medium and place in the refrigerator for the necessary time period (see the specific plant listings in Chapter 11).

Can seeds be stratified outdoors?

Yes, you can prechill your seeds outdoors provided the temperature is constantly below 40° F. for the necessary chilling period. You may wish to sow right into their flats and place them outdoors for the necessary time.

Stratification involves mixing seeds with growing medium in an amount equal to two to three times their volume, and then chilling them in the refrigerator.

How do I go about sowing seeds of annuals indoors in a flat?

If the drainage holes in the flat are large, cover them with moss or pieces of broken flowerpot. Fill the flat to within one-quarter inch of the top with moistened sowing medium that has been rubbed through one-quarter-inch screening. Level and gently firm the surface with a flat board or tamper, and sow the seeds.

How deep should seeds be planted in flats and pots indoors? How deep in rows outdoors?

Indoors, very small seeds are merely firmly pressed into the sowing medium with a tamper, or covered with a dusting of the medium, sand, or vermiculite; medium-sized seeds are covered one-eighth to one-quarter inch; and large seeds, about two to three times their diameter. Outdoors, seeds are customarily covered a little deeper.

Are there any rules about which types of seeds to sow together? I want to grow several types of seedlings in the same flat.

Yes, combine those seeds that have the same requirements, such as temperature, the amount of light (or dark) required for germination, and the length of time needed for germination.

Is it better to scatter the seeds or to sow them in rows?

When flats are used, it is preferable to sow in rows. You can judge the rate of germination better, cultivate lightly without danger of harming seedlings, and transplant with more ease. When pots are used, seeds are generally scattered evenly and thinly. Further, when sowing very fine seeds, it is often difficult to sow them in rows and broadcasting may be easier.

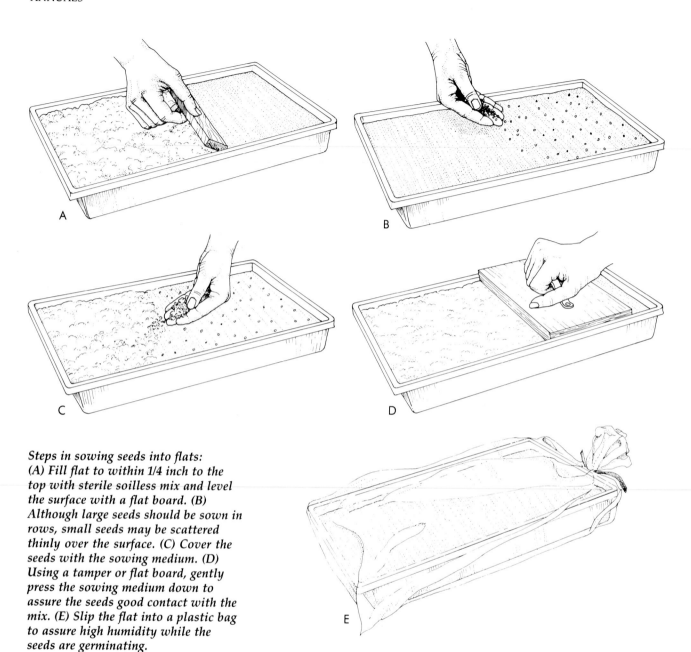

*Steps in sowing seeds into flats:
(A) Fill flat to within 1/4 inch to the
top with sterile soilless mix and level
the surface with a flat board. (B)
Although large seeds should be sown in
rows, small seeds may be scattered
thinly over the surface. (C) Cover the
seeds with the sowing medium. (D)
Using a tamper or flat board, gently
press the sowing medium down to
assure the seeds good contact with the
mix. (E) Slip the flat into a plastic bag
to assure high humidity while the
seeds are germinating.*

How can very small seeds be sown evenly?

Seeds that are too small to handle may be mixed thoroughly with sand before sowing.

How do I plant larger seeds?

First, tear a piece off the corner of the seed packet. Then, holding it between your thumb and forefinger, tap it gently with your forefinger to distribute the seed.

Should I sow more seeds than I need?

Definitely! Not all of the seeds will germinate, and some will be lost in transplanting. If you have extra plants, you can share them with your neighbors and friends.

Is it a good idea to sow all of my seeds?

No, save a few, just in case something goes wrong and you have to start over.

After I sow my seeds, how should I treat the flats?

It is important to keep humidity high around a seed flat so seeds will germinate properly. The best way to do this is to slip your flats into a clear plastic bag or cover them with a pane of glass until germination occurs. Once the seeds have germinated, remove the plastic or glass. This technique also eliminates the need for watering and the possibility of dislodging the seeds during the germination period.

I placed my flats in plastic bags, and then noticed a great deal of condensation inside. Is this a problem?

When this happens it is best to remove the flats from the bag for a few hours to let the medium dry out. Although condensation can be caused by a change in room temperature, it may also be a sign that the flats are too wet. In this case, allow the flat to dry out a little by removing the bag.

How should seed flats be watered after the seed is sown?

Water thoroughly after seeding with a fine overhead spray from a watering can or a bulb-type or mist sprinkler (see pg. 170) until the soil is saturated. Subsequently, water when the surface soil shows signs of dryness. It is important neither to overwater nor to permit the flat to dry out.

Can seed flats be watered by standing them in a container of water?

Yes, if more convenient, but do not leave the flat in water any longer than necessary for moisture to show on the surface. Place the flat in water about one inch deep. If you submerge the flat, water will wash in and displace the seeds. Many growers prefer this method to watering the surface, as it lessens the danger of washing out fine seeds.

What temperatures do seeds need to germinate properly indoors?

Most seeds require a temperature of 70° F. within the medium. (See next questions.)

Do some seeds require a cool room for germination?

Yes, some seeds require a temperature of about 55° to 60° F. These include California poppy, sweet pea, bells-of-Ireland, baby-blue-eyes, penstemon, blue daisy, linaria, forget-me-not, and annual phlox. An unheated sun room, attic, or basement might be the perfect place.

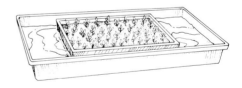

Two watering methods: (above) by sprinkling with a fine overhead spray, or (below) by placing the flat in a larger pan containing about 1 inch of water.

I have had trouble germinating seeds of double petunias indoors. Any suggestions?

Double petunias, as well as hybrid petunias, lobelia, and geraniums require temperatures that are higher than normal household temperatures to germinate properly.

I keep my house very cool in winter. What can I do to give my seeds the warmth they need to germinate?

Give the seedling flats bottom heat during the germination period. Garden centers offer heating cables or trays to place under the flats for warmth. Some have a thermostat that automatically keeps the flats at the proper temperature. In lieu of a thermostat, use a soil thermometer to check the temperature. If you don't have heating cables, the outside top of your refrigerator is often warm enough to germinate seeds.

Once the seeds have germinated, move them into good light so they will grow properly.

Are heating cables needed during the summer to germinate seeds?

No, probably not, unless your house is air conditioned.

What is the best germinating temperature for annual nicotiana and annual gaillardia? I have planted both late in the spring with dubious results. Must they have a cooler temperature to start?

Indoors in the spring, a night temperature between 50 and 55° F. is suitable. The fine seeds should be barely covered and, in fact, need light for adequate germination. Annual gaillardia germinates well outside in late spring. Self-sown nicotiana often germinates in early June, but this is a bit late for best effect in most northern regions.

I sowed snapdragon and begonia seeds last year, and did not cover them with a growing medium as they were very fine in size. However, germination was poor. What did I do wrong?

Fine seeds must be in contact with the moistened medium to germinate. Those that failed to germinate may have been caught in small air pockets. After sowing fine seeds, gently press them onto the medium, or water them with a very fine spray of water to ensure that they are touching the medium. A rubber bulb sprinkler will ensure a fine spray of water that will not dislodge the seeds.

I saved seeds from last year. Is there any way to tell if they are still good before I sow them?

Yes, take ten seeds and place them in a moistened paper towel. Place the paper towel in a plastic bag. Set it in a warm spot (unless it is an annual that likes cool temperatures to germinate).

A bulb-type sprinkler ensures a fine spray of water that will not dislodge even very tiny seeds.

Consult the chart on pages 284-86 to see how many days are normally required for germination. After that time, start checking the seeds. If eight or more have germinated, the seeds are fine. If five to seven have germinated, sow more seed than you normally would. Fewer than five, and you won't have good results. Fewer than two, don't use these seeds at all.

How much light is needed during germination?

That depends on the type of seed you are sowing. Since many seeds are covered with sowing medium during germination, they do not need to receive any special light until after they have germinated, when they must be moved into a sunny windowsill or under fluorescent lights. Yet there are some seeds that do specifically need light to germinate, and others that require darkness. See the accompanying list for advice.

How do I ensure that seeds requiring darkness do not get any light?

If you cover the seeds with sowing medium, this is all the darkness they require. Because very fine seeds such as salpiglossis, poor-man's orchid, and ice plant should not be covered with medium, their flats must be covered with black plastic during germination. Check the flats every day and remove the cover as soon as the seeds have germinated.

When starting seeds in the house in the winter, what do you put in the soil so that plants will be short and stocky, not tall and spindly?

No soil treatment will prevent this. Good light, moderate temperature, and uncrowded conditions are the preventives. Rotate the pots daily to keep the plants from turning to the light. If your windows supply insufficient light, use fluorescent lights.

What unit is best for starting seeds under fluorescent lights?

The most commonly sold unit consists of two 40-watt fluorescent tubes four feet long. Most seedlings will grow satisfactorily under such lights until they reach a sufficient size for planting outdoors. However, for superior results (or to force many annuals and houseplants to flower indoors), use a larger unit, such as one with four 40-watt fluorescent tubes four feet long. The light unit should be adjustable so that it can be raised or lowered according to the needs of the plants. When the plants are small, the lights are set about three inches above them and then gradually raised as the plants grow.

How can I tell if my seedlings are receiving the proper amount of light?

If the plants show signs of burning (foliage darkens and curls), the lights should be raised. If seedlings are growing tall and

SEEDS THAT REQUIRE LIGHT TO GERMINATE

ageratum
begonia
bellflower
bells-of-Ireland
browallia
coleus
creeping zinnia
flowering cabbage and kale
gerbera
impatiens
Mexican sunflower
nicotiana
ornamental pepper
petunia
red-flowered salvia
snapdragon
stock
strawflower
sweet alyssum

SEEDS THAT NEED DARKNESS TO GERMINATE

bachelor's-button
calendula
forget-me-not
gazania
ice plant
larkspur
nasturtium
nemesia
pansy
penstemon
periwinkle
phlox
poor-man's orchid
poppy
sweet pea
verbena

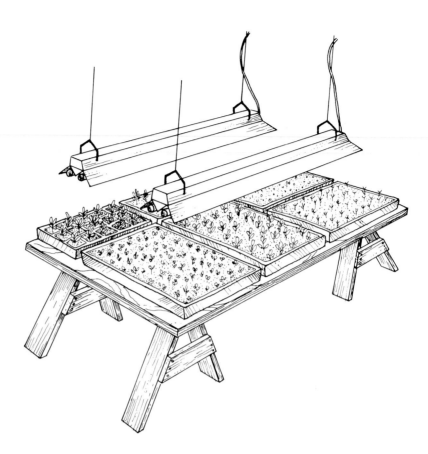

Two 4-foot-long fluorescent light units provide enough light for a substantial number of seedlings.

spindly, they are not receiving enough light, and the lights should be lowered. See the list of suggested readings in the Appendix for more information on raising both indoor and outdoor plants under lights.

Are fluorescent lights left on constantly or should plants have a dark period?

The lights are generally left on around the clock until the seeds germinate. After that, leave them on from fourteen to sixteen hours per day, during the daytime. An automatic timer is a great convenience for this purpose.

What are the advantages of growing seedlings under fluorescent light as compared to growing them in a sunny window?

Fluorescent bulbs give a steady supply of light at all seasons, whereas if you depend on natural light, cloudy days and the low intensity and short duration of light in winter can cause disappointing results.

When should I start to fertilize my seedlings?

Begin fertilizing when the first set of *true leaves* have developed (the first growth you will see are *cotyledons*, which are food storage cells, and not leaves). Use a soluble plant food at one-quarter label strength at first, gradually increasing to full strength as the plants mature.

Can I transfer my seedlings to the garden from the flat in which they were sown?

This is generally not a good practice, unless the seeds were sown into individual pots or into flats divided into cells. Once two sets of true leaves (see pg. 165) have developed, it is best to transplant seedlings into individual cells or pots so their roots can develop properly and thus not be subject to transplanting shock later on.

What is the best mixture for transplanting seedlings from flats to pots?

Four parts garden soil (two parts sand, if the soil is heavy clay), two parts peat moss, and one and one-half parts dried manure or compost. Add one-half cup of 5-10-5 fertilizer to each peck of mixture, and mix all ingredients well. Even better, use soilless mix, and apply a fertilizer according to the recommendations on the container.

What is the proper method of transplanting seedlings into pots from flats?

First, water the seedlings well. Next, prepare the cells or pots and fill them with moistened growing medium, making a hole in the center into which the seedlings will be placed. Gently lift the seedling from the flat using a spoon handle or similar tool. To avoid breaking the stem, always handle the seedlings by their leaves and never by the stem. Lower the seedling's roots into the hole and gently press the medium around the roots.

After I transplanted my seedlings, they wilted. What went wrong?

Wilting is normal after transplanting. Place newly transplanted seedlings in good light, but not full sun, for a few days before returning them to full light. If transplants wilt severely, place them in a plastic bag or mist them regularly until they recover.

Do seedlings need to be pinched after being transplanted?

Some, especially snapdragon, lisianthus, dahlia, and any other seedlings that are growing too tall, benefit from pinching at this point to keep them from becoming too leggy. Simply reach into the center of the plant with your fingers and pinch out the growing tip.

How do you make new plants blossom early in the spring?

Unless plants are begun in a greenhouse where they can be forced (pushed to earlier development than would occur at that time of the year if they were growing outdoors), there is not much that can be done to make them bloom early; most have to reach a certain age before they will flower.

Steps in transplanting seedlings into divided flats:

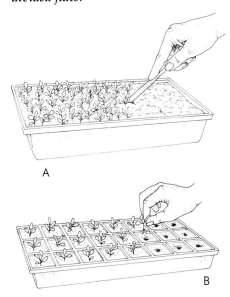

A

B

(A) After watering seedlings well, gently lift them from the flat using a spoon handle or similar tool. (B) Holding the plant by a leaf, gently place the seedling into a preformed hole in the flat.

To encourage bushy growth, pinch out the growing tip of such plants as snapdragons, lisianthus, and dahlias.

OUTDOOR PROPAGATION

I have very little room in my house to start seedlings indoors. Which annuals can be started directly in the garden?

These include African daisy, amaranthus, China aster, calendula, California poppy, candytuft, Cape marigold, celosia, spider flower, calliopsis, cornflower, cosmos, dahlia, dusty miller, gaillardia, kochia, larkspur, French marigold, nasturtium, nemesia, cupflower, love-in-a-mist, four-o'clock, phlox, portulaca, scabiosa, stock, sweet alyssum, sweet pea, Mexican sunflower, zinnia, lavatera, mignonette, sunflower, and clarkia.

Which flower seeds should be sown where they are to grow because of difficulty in transplanting?

Poppy, larkspur, California poppy, nasturtium, portulaca, mignonette, lavatera, love-in-a-mist, phlox, blue lace flower, nolana, sweet pea, and creeping zinnia.

How can I tell when my soil is ready to be worked?

To test soil for readiness, take a handful of it and squeeze it. If it stays together in a ball, it is too wet and cannot be worked or its structure will be ruined. Wait a few days and try again. If it crumbles, however, it is ready.

What should the temperature be before planting annuals in the garden in New York?

There can be no set temperature figure. Hardy annuals can be seeded as soon as the ground is ready to work; half-hardy annuals, about four weeks later. For tender annuals, wait until all danger of frost is past for the region; in and around New York State, this is usually during the second week of May.

I understand some annuals can be planted in the fall for bloom the following summer. Which annual seeds are suitable for autumn planting in the north?

Larkspur, annual poppy, California poppy, sweet pea, portulaca, nicotiana, salvia, celosia, spider flower, sweet alyssum, cornflower, calliopsis, kochia, spurge, balsam, cosmos, candytuft. Sow them sufficiently late so that they will not germinate before freezing weather, and plant them slightly deeper than you would with spring sowing.

Which annual seeds are suitable for autumn planting in the south?

You can plant the same type of plants that are recommended for the north, but they should be planted early enough so that they germinate in the fall. In the fall, mulch the plants with leaves, straw, or pine needles if freezing temperatures will occur over the winter, and remove the mulch in early spring.

Is it advisable to sow seeds of cosmos, zinnias, and marigolds in late autumn, so that they can germinate the first warm days of spring?

They won't germinate until the soil is warm—considerably later than the "first warm days of spring," so early planting won't give you any earlier germination and growth with these particular annuals.

How late is "late" when we are told to plant seed in late autumn?

Usually about the average time of killing frost. Some seeds (sweet peas and other hardy annuals) can be sown after the frost, provided the ground is not frozen.

Is it necessary to prepare the soil for seed planted in the fall?

For best results, yes. However, for an informal garden, seeds can be scattered on lightly raked-over soil.

I have purchased a self-ventilating cold frame. When can I sow annual seeds in it?

These solar-powered frames usually open automatically when the temperature reaches around 70° F. and close when it drops to 68° F. In most northern areas, hardy annuals can be sown into it in March, half-hardy annuals in early April, and tender annuals a few weeks later.

How should I prepare my outdoor seed beds? I am creating a new flower garden.

Remove the grass and any stones or debris that are in the soil. Soil must be dug to a depth of eight to ten inches. If you have a rotary power tiller, this will make the job easier. If not, use a spade or fork to turn the soil over.

How deep should the soil be prepared for annuals?

Nine inches for good results. Some growers go twice this depth to assure maximum growth.

Do annuals have decided preferences for acid or alkaline soil?

Most popular garden flowers like a soil that is slightly acid to neutral. Those annuals that like alkaline soils are China aster, dianthus, salpiglossis, scabiosa, strawflower, and sweet pea.

How do I know whether my soil is acid or alkaline?

You should test the soil to determine its pH, or acidity/alkalinity level. You can do this yourself with a soil test kit available at your local garden center, or have it tested by your local Extension Service. Most annuals like a pH of 6.5 to 7.0. If

Cosmos seeds may be planted in fall for bloom the following spring.

the pH needs to be raised, use lime; if it needs to be lowered, use sulfur. If the pH needs adjustment, do not add fertilizer to the bed for two weeks after the adjustment.

I have heard there are different types of lime. Which is best for the garden?

To avoid burning, apply hydrated lime, which is quick acting, several weeks prior to planting and water it in well. For less risk of burning, use crushed limestone, which is much slower acting and longer lasting, but requires a heavier application than hydrated lime. Dolomitic limestone is particularly good as it contains the essential trace element magnesium.

What sort of amendments should I add to the soil?

Prepare the seedbed by adding organic matter such as peat moss, compost, leaf mold, or well-rotted manure. If drainage is poor, also add perlite, vermiculite, gypsum, or coarse sand. A complete fertilizer such as 5-10-5 should also be added at this time, unless the pH needs adjustment (see above). Work the material into the soil and rake it smooth and level.

How much organic matter should I add to the soil?

After you have removed the grass, stones, and any debris, add a layer of organic matter, at least two inches thick, on top of the soil and then work it in. If a flower bed has been in the same area and improved each year for several years, less organic matter will be needed.

Why is it important to add organic matter to the soil?

Organic matter not only increases the soil's fertility because of the nutrients it contains, but it also improves the soil's texture. Organic matter makes clay-like soils more friable (more readily crumbled) and it aids sandy soils in retaining moisture.

What is meant when soils are termed "heavy" or "light"?

A heavy soil is one that is very clay-like and sticky, especially when wet. A light soil is dry and sandy. The ideal soil, often called loam, is something between the two.

How do I go about planting an annual garden from seed sown directly into the ground? The garden is about four feet wide and fifteen feet long and receives sun all day. What annuals would be the most reliable to sow?

After raking the soil as smooth as possible, use lime or string to outline the various sections where the seeds are to be planted—as though you were making a giant plan on paper. If you first draw your garden plan on graph paper, you can transfer the design quite simply in this manner.

The easiest annuals to sow directly in place are sweet alyssum as an edging, nasturtium and several varieties of French marigolds and zinnias for medium height, and spider flower and tall zinnias for background. Most seeds can be *broadcast*—scattered freely over the seedbed and then covered with the designated amount of soil. Once the seeds germinate, you can transplant or thin your plants; but in a display of this sort, a certain amount of crowding is permissible and even desirable. If one kind of seed doesn't germinate, you can spread out those from other sections to fill in its space.

Should the seed bed be wet before seeds are sown?

Definitely. Water the beds first to ensure they are evenly moist before sowing. After sowing, water again.

How deep should I plant my seeds?

Instructions are usually given on seed packets, but a good rule of thumb is to plant them to a depth equal to their thickness.

I have trouble planting my seeds at the proper depth. Any ideas?

Make a furrow in the soil at the proper depth with the side of a trowel or a yardstick. After sowing, pinch the soil together with your fingers and firm it well. Seeds will not germinate unless they are in contact with moist soil.

How close together should I plant my seeds?

Although instructions are usually given on the seed packet, a rule of thumb applies: sow them twice as close as the final recommended planting distance.

How does one sow seeds of annuals in patches outdoors?

Fork over the soil, then rake the surface to break lumps and remove large stones. If the seeds are small (sweet alyssum or portulaca, for example), scatter them evenly and pat down the soil. For medium-sized seeds, rake the soil lightly again after sowing and pat it down. For seeds that have to be covered one-quarter inch or more, scrape off the soil to the required depth, sow the seeds, and return the soil that was removed or cover the area with fine vermiculite.

I have seen seed tapes in a seed catalog. What are these?

Some seed companies implant their seeds, especially fine seeds, into tapes. Merely cut the tapes to the desired length and place them on the ground. The tapes will dissolve as the seeds grow. Their advantages are that the seeds have been properly spaced in advance, you do not have to handle fine seeds, and there is no chance that they will wash away.

Steps in making a garden plan:

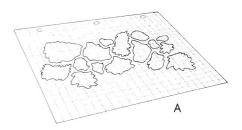

(A) Draw your garden design on graph paper. (B) Following your graph paper plan, transfer your design to the prepared bed by outlining each area with string; broadcast seed in the designated areas.

English sparrows take dust baths in my newly planted seed patches. How can I prevent this?

Lay pieces of burlap or fine brush over the seeded areas. Keep the seedbed constantly moist. When the seeds have germinated, remove the protective covering.

What is the best method of ensuring germination of small flower seeds in a heavy clay soil that consists mostly of subsoil excavated when the house was built? It grows plants very well once they get started.

First, work in a generous amount of peat moss, sifted compost, or rotted manure to improve the general texture of the soil. Then hoe out rows two inches wide and deep, fill the hollows with good screened compost, and sow the seeds into that.

How often should I water my seedbeds?

Until the seeds germinate, the bed should never be allowed to dry out; water every day if it doesn't rain. When seeds first germinate, they will still need daily watering. After a week, reduce the watering gradually until you are watering once a week. This encourages deep roots and plants better able to withstand heat and drought when summer comes.

What other care do I need to give my flower beds at this time?

Keep the beds well weeded, as weeds compete with annuals for light, water, and nutrients. Weeds also cause crowding and the possibility of disease. Remove them carefully so that the annuals are not disturbed, and water after weeding. Watch for signs of insects and disease. Slugs and snails are very damaging to young seedlings, especially marigolds and petunias. Trap them with slug bait after every watering or rain.

When should I thin my seedlings?

After seedlings are two to three inches high, or have developed two or three sets of true leaves, it is time to thin them.

What is the best way to thin seedlings?

Water the ground first to make it easier to remove unwanted seedlings. Choose cloudy weather and spread the operation over two to three weeks or as necessary as the plants develop. Pull up the weakest seedlings before they crowd each other, leaving two to six inches between those remaining, according to their ultimate size. Pull them carefully so that the ones that remain are not disturbed. When those left begin to touch, again remove the weakest, leaving the remainder standing at the required distance apart. You can use the seedlings that you remove in another part of the garden or share them with friends and neighbors.

For a bountiful display of geraniums, take cuttings from mature plants and root them.

Ann Reilly

In addition to plants begun by sowing seeds, either indoors or out, you may also begin some annuals by taking cuttings from mature plants.

How are plants like snapdragon, petunia, verbena, coleus, impatiens, geraniums, and other annuals started as cuttings from the original plant?

Root short side or tip shoots, three to four inches long, by placing them in sand in a closed container in July and August. If the shoots have flower buds, these should be pinched off. Alternatively, the cuttings—called *slips*—can be taken in the fall or through the winter if you pot up plants from the garden and bring them indoors.

Why does coleus wilt so badly when I try to start new cuttings in soil?

The air around the cuttings may be too dry. Cover them with a preserving jar or polyethylene bag until they have formed roots. Trim large leaves back one half. A soilless medium is better than garden soil for rooting.

How are geranium cuttings rooted?

Geranium cuttings may be rooted in sand or in a peat pot almost any time of year indoors and in late summer outdoors. Take a four-inch cutting one-quarter inch below a leaf attachment. Remove lower leaves and stipules. Insert about one-third of the stem into the growing medium. Keep the medium moist, but not soggy.

What is the best method of handling lantana cuttings? Our cuttings this year rooted well and seemed to be off to a good start. Soon after potting, however, they wilted and died. We kept them shaded and did not overwater them.

After potting them, water them thoroughly and keep them in a closed, shaded propagating case for a week or two. Then gradually admit more air and remove the shade.

CUTTINGS

To take geranium cuttings, cut a four-inch piece one-quarter inch below a leaf attachment, remove lower leaves, and insert about one-third of the stem in soilless growing medium.

It is now that time in spring when new life is showing everywhere: trees are leafing out, flowering trees and shrubs are in bloom, bulbs are at their peak, your hardy annuals that you began outdoors are off to a healthy start, frost danger is past. You have prepared your beds as for seeding, and it is time to plant the seedlings you began indoors as well as the bedding plants you purchased.

When should flat-raised seedlings be transplanted?

You may wish to transplant seedlings into larger flats indoors when they form their first true leaves in order to give them better

TRANSPLANTING ANNUALS INTO THEIR PERMANENT LOCATIONS

spacing. Alternatively, you may simply thin them and allow the remaining plants to grow in the original tray or flat until they are ready to go outdoors. Many plants benefit from a second transplant to individual pots when they are two or three inches high, before they are moved outdoors. In either case they may need a light feeding before being set in the garden.

When should annual seedlings be moved outdoors?

Most seedlings require six to eight weeks of growth time indoors before being transplanted into the garden. The timing is the same whether the seedlings are grown under fluorescent light or on a windowsill, provided the window supplies enough light. Plant hardy annuals outdoors as soon as they are large enough and the soil can be worked. Tender annuals must wait until all danger of frost is past.

Do any seedlings require more than six to eight weeks indoors?

Wax begonia, dianthus, geranium, impatiens, lobelia, pansy, petunia, salvia, wishbone flower, and snapdragon require ten to twelve weeks indoors before being transplanted into the garden.

Is there anything I need to do to get my annuals ready to be moved outside?

Yes, you must put them through a progress called hardening off. One week before transplanting plants into the garden, move them outdoors and place them in a shady, protected spot or a cold frame. Bring them back inside at night. Each day, increase the amount of light and time outdoors, and toward the end of the week leave the plants out all night.

Nurseries often advertise "bedding plants." What does this term mean?

Bedding plants are those raised indoors specifically for the purpose of planting in open-air beds.

If I purchase my bedding plants, when should I set them?

Wait until proper planting time, and then purchase them as close to the time that you are going to plant them as possible. If you can't get them in the ground right away, be sure to water them daily.

I like to buy my bedding plants in bloom so I know what color they are. Is this a good idea?

No. Plants do not need to be in bloom; in fact, most annuals grow better and bloom earlier if they are not in bud or bloom when planted. An exception to this is the African marigold, which must be planted in bud or bloom (see page 250).

What should I look for when buying bedding plants?

Look for healthy, dark green plants that show no sign of insects or disease and that are not too tall or spindly.

I have difficulty removing annuals from flats without ruining their root systems. Any pointers?

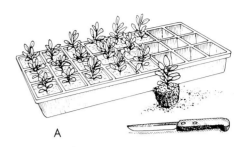

Water your annuals thoroughly before transplanting. This makes it easier to remove the plants without disturbing their root systems. Most purchased bedding plants today are grown in individual cells. Removal is easy; if the plants don't fall out easily, they can be pushed up from the bottom. If your plants are not in individual cells, with an old knife or a small mason's trowel, cut the soil into squares, each with a plant in the center. The plants can easily be removed with their root systems almost intact.

Annuals that have been grown individually in peat pots can be left in the pots when being planted, but it is advisable to break the pots in a few places to help the roots penetrate into the soil more readily. Be sure to set the top edge of the pot *below* the soil level or it will draw water from the soil like a sponge; the water will then evaporate, instead of nourishing the plant.

What is the right technique in setting out (planting) annual plants?

Water the ground, then stab the trowel in the soil and pull the earth toward you. Set the plant in the hole, remove the trowel, and push the soil around the roots. Press the soil down firmly, leaving a slight depression around the stem to trap water.

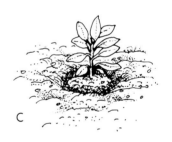

How much space should be given annuals when thinning them or setting them out?

The distance varies according to the variety and growth habit of the plant. A rough rule is to set them a distance equal to one-half their mature height. Look for directions on the seed packet, or follow the guidelines on the chart on pages 281-83.

Steps in transplanting seedlings: (A) Water plants thoroughly, then push them up out of divided flats. (B) Water the ground where the plant will be set, pull the earth toward you with a trowel, and set the plant in place, pushing the soil in around the roots. (C) Firm the soil around the plant, leaving a slight depression around the stem to trap water.

What is the best time of day to transplant annuals?

To reduce transplanting shock, do your planting late in the afternoon, or on a cloudy day. The one exception to this rule is multiflora petunias, which do not mind being transplanted in full sun during midday.

How should I care for my transplants?

Water well after transplanting and again daily for about a week until the transplants are well established and show signs of growth. Gradually reduce watering until about once per week, which should be sufficient for the remainder of the summer unless it becomes quite hot. Keep the beds well weeded and watch for signs of insects and diseases, especially slugs and snails. Some transplants may wilt at first, but daily misting and/or shading will help them to revive quickly.

After I transplanted my seedlings, we had an unexpected late frost, and I lost all of my seedlings. Is there anything I could have done?

Yes. If frost is predicted, place hot caps or styrofoam cups over the seedlings in the evening, and remove them in the morning.

GENERAL CULTURE

-------- • --------

Is it wrong to plant the same kind of annuals in the same space year after year?

As long as the soil is well dug each year and the humus content is maintained, there is nothing wrong with the practice. However, China asters, snapdragons, and marigolds are susceptible to some soil-borne disease problems, and thus should not be planted in the same spot in consecutive years.

What type of soil and what fertilizing programs are best for annuals?

Most annual flowers do best in a well-drained, rather light (as opposed to clayey) soil in full sun. Unless the soil is really run-down and deficient in plant nutrients, or you are starting a new bed, only a light annual application of rotted manure, peat moss, and/or compost, plus some standard commercial fertilizer, is advisable. (See also pgs. 175-76.)

What do the numbers on a fertilizer label mean?

The numbers indicate the percentage of nitrogen, phosphorus, and potassium (the chemical symbols N,P,K) present. For flowering annuals, it is important that the second number, or the phosphorus percentage, be higher than, or equal to, the nitrogen percentage. If it is not, you will have a lot of growth but few flowers. For this reason, lawn fertilizer, which is high in nitrogen, should not be used on your flower beds.

Nitrogen is necessary for foliage and stem growth and for the dark green leaf color. Phosphorus is necessary for root development and flower production. Potassium (sometimes referred to as potash) is necessary for plant metabolism and the production of food.

How much fertilizer should I use?

That depends on the type of fertilizer. Read the label, which will give you detailed instructions. As a general rule, use one to two pounds of 5-10-5 per one hundred square feet on a new bed and one pound per one hundred square feet on an established bed.

What is the best fertilizer for annual and perennial flower beds?

For most annuals and perennials, a 4-12-4 or 5-10-5 fertilizer is satisfactory. It should be worked into the beds before planting. Those annuals that like to be fed during the growing season as well can be fertilized very effectively with a soluble fertilizer such as 20-20-20. Check individual plant entries in Chapt. 11 to determine which annuals like additional feedings during the summer.

What is slow-release fertilizer? Can it be used on annuals?

Slow-release fertilizer is a special type that is inactive until released by water or temperature. It works very well on annuals as long as you buy the three- or six-month formulation. Apply it in early to mid-spring; no additional feedings will be necessary.

I like to apply liquid fertilizer to my annuals, but I have a big flower bed, and mixing large amounts of solution is very time-consuming. Is there another method?

Yes. You can purchase a device called a proportioner. One end of the proportioner is inserted into a container of concentrated fertilizer solution and the other end is fastened to the garden hose. As you water, the proportioner automatically dilutes the solution to the proper level.

Which annuals should not be fertilized?

There are some annuals that must be grown in infertile soil, or they will not bloom. These include nasturtium, spider flower, portulaca, amaranthus, cosmos, gazania, and salpiglossis.

How often should I water my annual flower beds?

Under normal circumstances, apply one inch of water once a week. If it becomes very hot during the summer, or if your garden is in a windy spot, or if your soil is very sandy, you may need to water more often.

How can I determine whether my soil is receiving one inch of water?

Place an empty coffee can halfway between the sprinkler and the furthest point it reaches. Time how long it takes for one inch of water to accumulate in the can. Presuming the water pressure remains constant, run your sprinklers for the amount of time it took for one inch of water to collect in the can.

Why do I need to water my flower beds only once a week? Couldn't I sprinkle them lightly every day?

This is the worst thing you could do. Light, frequent watering encourages shallow roots. When it becomes hot or if you go

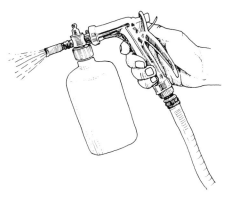

A proportioner, which is attached to your garden hose, automatically dilutes fertilizer solution to the proper level as you water.

Nasturtiums do best in infertile soil and should thus not be fertilized.

Ann Reilly

away for a few days, shallow-rooted annuals will not survive. Deep watering encourages the roots to grow down deep rather than along the soil surface.

Is it a good idea to water my flower bed with an overhead sprinkler?

Overhead watering is perfectly acceptable in most instances, and actually cools off the plants and washes dirt off the foliage. For plants such as zinnia, calendula, grandiflora petunia (see page 260), and stock that are susceptible to disease, however, water in the morning so the foliage is not wet during the night. In addition, you might not want to water your cutting garden overhead as the water could damage the flowers. In this case, soaker hoses laid on the ground are the best method.

My community has imposed severe watering restrictions. What can I do to have a flower garden in spite of this?

Prepare the soil well with abundant organic matter and use an organic mulch (pg. 176), both of which will help keep the soil moist. Plant drought-resistant annuals like portulaca, celosia, cosmos, sunflower, amaranthus, candytuft, dusty miller, gazania, spider flower, sweet alyssum, or periwinkle.

How shall I top annuals to make them bushy?

Pinch out no more than the growing point with your thumbnail and index finger. This technique, aptly called *pinching back* (see pg. 173), induces branching.

Which annuals, and at what stage, should be pinched back for better growth and more flowers?

These annuals can be pinched to advantage when they are from two to four inches high: ageratum, snapdragon, cosmos, nemesia, petunia, phlox, salvia, poor-man's orchid, marigold, and verbena. Straggly plants of sweet alyssum can be sheared back in midsummer for better growth and to induce flowering later in the season.

Is it true that if flowers are picked off they bloom better?

On plants that continue to make flowering growth, it is best to pick off flowers as soon as they fade. Known as *deadheading*, this prevents the formation of seed, which is a drain on the plant's energy.

What would cause annuals to grow well but come into bud so late in the summer that they are of little use? The seed was planted late in April.

Most annuals bloom at midsummer from April-sown seed, but lobelia, scarlet sage, wishbone flower, and Mexican sunflower are examples that should be sown indoors in March for a

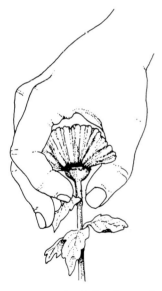

To prevent seed production and a consequent drain on plant strength, remove the faded flowers from annuals that continue to produce bloom.

head start. The late, older varieties of cosmos usually do not have time to flower in the North, even if sown early indoors. There may be another problem, as well. Did you fertilize heavily? This could cause strong leaf growth at the expense of flowering.

Why do I have to stake so many plants—zinnia, marigold, and other common plants? They grow well and bloom generously, yet if not tied, they do not stay erect.

It could be insufficient phosphorus in the soil or inadequate sun. Perhaps they are exposed to too much wind, or heavy rains could have beaten them down.

What type of material can I use as a stake?

Almost anything that will hold the plants up, such as bamboo sticks or metal poles. Tie the plants loosely to the stakes with a twist tie or a string so the stems of the annuals will not be pinched or damaged. Or place three or four stakes around a clump of plants and circle them with string high enough up to support the stems and form a kind of fence around them.

What is meant by succession planting?

Some annuals have a short blooming time. To have a continual supply of color, plant several batches of these one to two weeks apart from spring planting time through early to midsummer.

Most of our annuals cease blooming about August, leaving few flowers for fall. Is there any way we can renew our plantings so that flowers are available until late in the season?

There are numerous annuals which, sown in the summer, will provide bloom right up until the frost. These are browallia, calendula, celosia, marigold, sweet alyssum, wishbone flower, verbena, and all types of zinnias. (The following dates for sowing apply to the New York City area and are thus applicable to a large portion of the United States. Use the average date of the first killing frost in fall as a guide in more northerly sections.) With care, many seeds can be sown outdoors and seedlings can be transplanted directly to their flowering quarters. Plants such as torenia and browallia do better when transplanted into temporary pots until their permanent location is ready. Sow these the first week in June and then transplant them to three-inch pots. At the same time sow celosia, nicotiana, dwarf scabiosa, and tall marigolds. The third week in June sow candytuft, phlox, and marigold; this is the time, too, to sow California poppy, either where it is to bloom or in pots. None of these will grow to the size of spring-sown plants. The last week in June to the first week in July sow calendula, sweet alyssum, and zinnias of all types. Sweet alyssum, calendula, and verbena will survive light fall frosts.

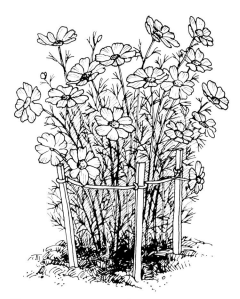

To support a group of tall annuals such as cosmos, place three or four stakes around the plants and circle them with string placed high enough to support the stems and form a fence around them.

Individual plants such as larkspur can be supported by tying stems loosely to a stake with string or a twist tie.

Ann Reilly

Gazania, neatly mulched with bark chips.

How can I save the seed from annual flowers?

Select healthy plants of the best type and allow the seeds to mature on the plant. Gather them before they are shed, then dry them in a dry, airy place that is safe from mice. (See p. 147.)

Will seed from hybrid annuals flower the following year?

Seeds of annual hybrids saved one year should give flowers the next. Some may come close to true (resemble their parents), but it is more likely that there will be wide variation. (See page 147.)

When different shades of the same flower are planted together, which ones may I save seeds from and have them come true to their parent?

You don't have much chance of getting seed that will come true from any of them.

I realize that it is important to keep weeds out of flower beds because weeds harbor insects and disease and compete with the flowers for light, water, and nutrients—but it is hard work. Any suggestions?

Weeding is a chore nobody likes to do. Since many weeds are spread by seeds, it is important to pull weeds before they flower and the seeds fall and sprout. In addition to hand-pulling, you can weed around mature plantings with a hoe, use a pre-emergent herbicide to prevent seeds from germinating, and apply mulches to discourage weeds.

I have read about using black plastic as a mulch. Does this prevent weeds?

Yes, it does, and quite well. Be sure to punch holes in the plastic, though, so water can penetrate to the plants' roots. Porous fabric mulches are now available that are better than plastic. If you don't like the looks of black plastic, cover it with a mulch of leaf mold, bark chips, pine needles, or other unobtrusive material.

What is a preemergent herbicide?

This is a granular herbicide that is applied to the soil and watered in. It prevents weed seeds from germinating and is thus effective against annual weeds. Several on the market (Dacthal and Treflan, for example) are safe for most annuals. When using such a product for the first time, try it in a test plot before using it widely in your garden.

Can I apply liquid weed killer to the flowers in my garden?

We do not recommend this practice as liquid weed killer is likely to do as much harm to the flowers as to the weeds.

What are the other advantages of mulch in addition to controlling weeds?

As well as adding a decorative finish to the flower beds, mulch keeps the soil cool and moist and thus reduces the need for watering.

What materials make good mulches?

Use an organic material, such as shredded leaves, bark chips, pine needles, or hulls of some kind. Each spring, before adding new mulch, mix the old mulch in with the soil to enrich it.

Can I use grass clippings as mulch?

Yes, provided you dry them first. As they decompose, grass clippings give off a great deal of heat, which could damage annuals' roots. Grass clippings contain some nitrogen and so are beneficial to the soil.

I read that mulches rob the soil of nitrogen as they decompose. Is this true?

Yes, it is. When adding fresh mulch, add additional nitrogen in a readily available form, such as ammonium nitrate, at the rate of one to two pounds per one hundred square feet.

9 Gardening with a Purpose

Annual gardens must be suited to the growing conditions of the area in which they are planted; yet, equally important, they can be made to serve a variety of purposes within the home landscape. To be a successful gardener, you need to learn to deal with sun and shade, with too much water or a lack of it, with very hot or very cool climates. Once you have met the inherent needs of your own garden, however, you can go on to reap the ultimate enjoyment of creating unique gardens for specific purposes.

My garden is very shady. Even if I plant annuals recommended for shade, they don't do as well as I wish. What can I do?

If the shade is from trees, remove some of the lower branches or thin out some of the upper ones to allow more light through. As a last resort you may even choose to have some of the trees removed. Add a mulch of white marble chips around the flower beds to increase reflected light. If the flower border is against a dark wall, paint the wall white, to gain light reflection.

What annual flower would you recommend for planting in a completely shaded area?

There are no annual flowers that will grow well in total shade. A perennial ground cover such as pachysandra, bugleweed, or periwinkle would be more suitable for such conditions. Your best choices, if you want to try annuals in *partial* shade, are

◀ *When designing a new garden, consider the style of the surroundings; an old-fashioned garden such as the one on the left would be especially suitable for a country home.*

cleome, lobelia, nicotiana, wishbone flower, impatiens, begonia, browallia, fuschia, monkey flower, and coleus.

Are there any special care tips for planting in the shade?

Plants that receive less light require less fertilizer and less water, so be very careful not to overfertilize or overwater annuals growing in the shade, unless they are competing with trees and shrubs for nutrients and moisture. Some gardeners mistakenly think that heavy feeding will compensate for lack of light. This is simply not true.

My flower beds receive only half a day of full sun. What plants should I use in them?

Any of the plants suitable for heavy shade would also do well in this partial shade condition. In addition, ageratum, China aster, balsam, black-eyed Susan vine, dianthus, dusty miller, forget-me-not, lobelia, nicotiana, ornamental pepper, pansy, periwinkle, salvia, and sweet alyssum will do well in partial shade.

I am considering adding a new flower bed. Of the two possible locations for it, both are in partial shade. One is on the east side of the house, and one on the northwest side. Which one would be better?

The one on the east side. Wherever possible, locate beds in morning sun. This will allow foliage that became moist during the night from rain or dew to dry out sooner, thus lessening the chance of disease. Plants also generally prefer the cooler morning sun to the hot afternoon sun.

We have very little rain and watering restrictions during the summer. Can I still have a flower garden?

Yes, there are many annuals that actually prefer dry conditions. Plant African daisy, amaranthus, celosia, dusty miller, globe amaranth, kochia, petunia, portulaca, spider flower, statice, zinnia, or strawflower.

My three-year-old garden is on a slight slope and has sun all day. The first year, cosmos and pinks did fine. Now everything dwindles and dies. Even petunias won't grow. What can I do?

Dig deeply and add a three-inch layer of well-rotted manure, compost, or peat moss. Set the plants as early as you can, depending upon your conditions. A sloping site, particularly a hot sunny one, dries out very quickly and thus many plants in that situation will be starved for moisture. Keep moisture down around the roots of the plants by placing a heavy mulch of partly decayed leaves, grass clippings, or other material over the soil in the summer.

Is there anything I can do to help my garden along? It is very dry where I live.

There are several things you can do. Prepare the soil well, adding extra organic matter, which will retain moisture. Because plants set into the garden need less water than seeds germinated outside, buy bedding plants or grow your own seeds indoors. Space plants very close together so there is no exposed soil. The foliage will shade the ground and keep it moister since water won't evaporate so quickly. Mulch well around plants to conserve soil moisture and keep roots cooler. When you water, water deeply to encourage deep roots. Collect rain water in barrels, and save rinse water from the laundry and kitchen (as long as there is no bleach or other potentially harmful chemicals in it) to water the garden.

We have a lot of rain during the summer. Which annuals like these wet conditions?

There are many plants that do well in moist areas. These include China aster, balsam, tuberous begonia, black-eyed Susan vine, browallia, calendula, flowering cabbage and kale, forget-me-not, fuchsia, gerbera, impatiens, lobelia, monkey flower, nicotiana, ornamental pepper, pansy, phlox, salpiglossis, stock, and wishbone flower.

What annuals will do best in my very hot, sunny garden?

Plant amaranthus, anchusa, balsam, celosia, coleus, creeping zinnia, Dahlberg daisy, dusty miller, gaillardia, gazania, gloriosa daisy, globe amaranth, kochia, triploid marigolds (see page 249), nicotiana, ornamental pepper, periwinkle, petunia, portulaca, salvia, spider flower, statice, strawflower, verbena, or zinnia.

Many annuals, such as strawflower, actually prefer dry conditions.

Ann Reilly

Is there anything I can do to make my plants grow better in the heat of summer?

Yes. Start your own seedlings indoors before the planting season or purchase bedding plants so they are well established before the summer's heat. Select flowers that are heat-tolerant. Prepare the soil well, and mulch to keep the roots moist and cool. When you water, water deeply. If possible, grow the flowers in morning sun rather than afternoon sun. If your beds are in afternoon sun, some sort of a shade, such as a trellis, will help them grow better. If you also have drying winds in summer, plant a hedge or put in a fence to shelter the flower beds from the wind.

The desert soil of Arizona is quite alkaline. What should I do to have a nice garden there?

Incorporate extra organic matter into the soil; this will lower the pH. For even better results, have the pH tested and lower it further, if necessary, with sulfur (see pages 175-76 for further information about pH). Plant annuals, such as dianthus, salpiglossis, scabiosa, strawflower, and sweet pea, that will tolerate alkaline soil.

Be aware, however, that because it is also hot and dry where you live, all of these flowers except strawflower will need to be watered regularly. Plant them only if you have the capability of doing this. Dianthus, salpiglossis, and sweet pea do not like heat, so you will be able to grow them only as winter flowers.

I live in Maine, and summers are cool. What should I grow in my garden?

Try African daisy, tuberous begonias, browallia, calendula, clarkia, dianthus, flowering cabbage and kale, forget-me-not, lobelia, monkey flower, pansy, phlox, salpiglossis, snapdragon, stock, sweet pea, and wishbone flower.

My soil is very heavy and clayey and retains a lot of water for a long time. What should I do?

Plant one of the flowers listed under the previous question that will tolerate moist soils. At the same time, improve your soil's drainage by incorporating perlite, coarse sand, or gypsum (see pg. 176 for more information about soil texture). In extreme cases, you may have to install drainage tiles, or you could try growing your plants in raised beds.

Raised beds allow the gardener to provide a deep, enriched soil, even in areas where soil is poor.

Positive Images, Jerry Howard

193

GARDENING WITH A PURPOSE

What are the advantages of raised beds?

Raised beds are easily made with railroad ties or wood from the lumberyard. Fill in the raised area with a soilless mix or improved soil with extra organic matter, perlite, coarse sand, or gypsum. By creating this deep bed of improved and enriched soil, you are providing the plants' roots a better medium in which to grow. In addition, raised beds are often easier to take care of, as you don't need to bend over as far to weed or pick off faded flowers; this is of particular benefit to elderly or handicapped gardeners.

How deep should raised beds be?

At least eight inches is best.

I'd like to have some color in my garden earlier than mid-June, which is when my bedding plants first have good color. What do you recommend?

Plant some hardy annuals, which can be combined with spring bulbs and flowering trees and shrubs to give color in spring until the tender annuals take over. Plant hardy annuals as soon as the soil can be worked in spring. Choose from among African daisy, calendula, clarkia, cornflower, forget-me-not, lavatera, pansy, phlox, snapdragon, stock, sweet alyssum, and sweet pea.

When planting a garden for spring color, can I grow the garden from seeds sown outdoors?

You can, but you will have a more attractive and earlier blooming garden if you start the garden with plants.

Can I use these same hardy annuals for a fall garden, when summer flowers have ceased to look their best?

Yes, but again, you'll have better success with plants. If you start your own seeds outdoors, grow them in a cool spot and keep them shaded from the hot summer sun. Add ornamental cabbage and kale to your list of annuals for a fall garden.

We use our patio at night a great deal. What types of flowers are best for around this area?

Choose white, pale pink, or yellow flowers so that they can be easily seen at night. The silver foliage of dusty miller is also effective. In addition, recessed lighting in the flower beds shows blossoms up more effectively and increases the safety of walking around outdoors at night as well.

CHOOSING ANNUALS FOR SPECIFIC GARDENING PURPOSES

A stone wall attractively planted with ageratum, geranium, marigold, and trailing periwinkle.

I have an area in the backyard where our propane tanks and trash cans are stored. It is an eyesore, and we want to hide it, yet still have it accessible. What should we do?

Purchase or make a trellis and enclose the area on three sides. Grow an annual vine such as morning-glory on the trellis to hide the eyesore and at the same time beautify the area.

What other types of vining annuals can I choose?

There are many. The quickest growing, in addition to morning-glory, are cardinal climber, moonflower, sweet pea, scarlet runner bean, and vining nasturtium. Black-eyed Susan vine is charming but smaller in size and slower in growth rate.

I have a retaining wall at one side of my property and want to make it more attractive. What can I do?

Along the top of the wall, plant annuals that will cascade down over it. These include ivy geranium, sweet alyssum, lobelia, nasturtium, black-eyed Susan vine, petunia, and candytuft.

My living room window looks out over a sloped area down to the street below. What type of annuals should I use there?

When looking down on a sloped area, choose low-growing types so your view will not be obstructed. This would be an excellent place to create a rock garden.

My property is flat and open. What can I do to gain a more private feeling?

To create a homey, intimate look, place flower borders around the property. Use tall plants at the back to define the area but still allow you to view what is beyond. Warm tones of red, orange, gold, and yellow will make the area seem smaller.

What annuals make good ground covers?

Select from periwinkle, portulaca, petunia, and sweet alyssum if your climate is hot, or phlox and lobelia if your climate is cool.

My home is a large ranch-style house. What type of flower beds should I use?

A modern ranch home looks best with a formal, straight-lined bed with a sleek appearance.

What type of design would look best at my Cape Cod house?

A tightly packed, cottage-style garden is particularly appropriate for country, or farm-style, houses. Mix a variety of colorful, old-fashioned annuals, such as bachelor's-button, calendula, calliopsis, campanula, cosmos, dianthus, English daisy, gaillardia, geranium, hollyhock, larkspur, marigold, mignonette, nasturtium, pansy, petunia, phlox, poppy, snapdragon, stock, sweet pea, verbena, zinnia.

Which annual flowers are best for flower borders along sidewalks and along the side of a house?

Ageratum, wax begonia, dusty miller, lobelia, French marigold, petunia, and sweet alyssum.

What annuals would you suggest that I plant in the borders around my terrace? The area is partially shaded.

Impatiens should do very well. They are available in a wide color range and in heights from six inches to one and one-half feet. Furthermore, you can count on the plants' remaining in good condition all summer. Wax begonia varieties should also do well.

I would like some fragrant flowers in our garden so that we can enjoy their aroma when we sit on our patio. What are good plants for this?

Choose from dianthus, scabiosa, snapdragon, spider flower, blue petunias, four-o'clock, stock, and sweet alyssum. These are also nice to plant under windows that will be open in the summer so you can enjoy the fragrance indoors.

Ageratum makes a tidy, colorful edging for a bed along a walkway.

Which are the easiest annuals to grow in a sunken garden? I prefer fragrant kinds.

If low-growing varieties are needed, use ageratum, sweet alyssum, calendula, bachelor's-button, dianthus, four-o'clock, candytuft, lobelia, dwarf marigold, nasturtium, nicotiana, petunia, phlox, portulaca, stock, wishbone flower, pansy, or dwarf zinnia. If height is unimportant any variety of annual is appropriate.

Will you give me the names of a few unusual annuals, their heights, and uses?

Bells-of-Ireland is a green, twenty-four-inch-tall flower, popular for arrangements. Nemesia is available in almost any color except blue; eighteen inches tall, it is often used in edging and bedding. Cupflower is a lavender-blue, twelve-inch-tall plant frequently used in window boxes and for edging. Blue, pink, or white love-in-a-mist grows twelve inches high and is used in bedding. Both summer poinsettia and Joseph's coat have colorful foliage. They grow two to four feet tall and make nice background plants.

I would like some quick-to-flower annuals that I can sow directly into my terrace garden. Any suggestions?

Sweet alyssum, California poppy, certain dwarf marigolds (such as Lemondrop, Yellow Boy, or Golden Boy), annual phlox,

Ann Reilly

portulaca, or annual baby's-breath. The phlox and baby's-breath may not last the summer; sweet alyssum will need some shearing back to stimulate new flowering growth; and California poppy seeds must be sown early for best germination.

I just planted some new shrubs, which are quite small. The ground between them is quite bare. What could I do to make the area look more attractive?

You could lay a bark-chip mulch, but an annual ground cover would make a more colorful filler. Replant annuals every year until the shrubs fill in enough that the ground cover is not needed. Good choices are sweet alyssum, lobelia, portulaca, creeping zinnia, forget-me-not, ivy geranium, nasturtium, and periwinkle. These same kinds of flowers may be used as a border in front of the mature shrubs.

I work and don't have too much time for the garden. Which annuals require the least amount of time to care for?

Choose those annuals whose flowers fall naturally and cleanly from the plant after bloom so that you don't have to spend time removing faded flowers. These include begonia, impatiens,

Easy-to-care-for impatiens blooms freely and vividly throughout the season, with no need for spent flowers to be removed.

Ann Reilly

ageratum, sweet alyssum, salvia, nicotiana, lobelia, periwinkle, and spider flower.

My children constantly cut across the lawn instead of using the path to the front door, and the lawn is wearing thin. Is there anything I can do to stop them from doing this other than putting up a fence?

Create a living fence of tall annuals, such as zinnia, marigold, spider flower, or cosmos.

I'd like to get my children interested in gardening and want to start them with something easy to grow. What should I buy?

If they will be growing their own plants from seed, children especially enjoy sunflower, nasturtium, four-o'clock, and zinnias, as they grow quickly and bear showy flowers. Any of the low-maintenance plants listed in the previous question will also do very well. If you want to teach them garden maintenance, add marigolds and geraniums as well.

For something different this year, I thought I'd try an all-foliage garden. Will this work?

Yes, it will. You can use coleus, dusty miller, alternanthera, iresine, kochia, or basil. Even without flowers, the bright colors of the foliage will result in a garden that is colorful, varied, and attractive.

I saw a newspaper article about letting your flower garden do double duty by growing edible plants in it. What is this all about?

Some flower favorites are also edible. The leaves, buds, and seeds of nasturtium are often used in salads. Calendula petals are most attractive when used as a garnish for fruit salads and hors d'oeuvres. Flowers of impatiens and pansies can be used as a garnish for soup. Sunflower seeds have long been a favorite snack. Parsley and basil, especially the purple-leaved varieties of basil, make excellent edgings to the flower garden. If you're going to eat flowers from your garden, be sure to spray only with pesticides safe for vegetables.

I'd like to achieve a "wildflower" look in my garden. What plants should I use?

Although most wildflower gardens are perennial gardens, many annuals can also be used. American natives such as California poppy, gaillardia, sunflower, baby-blue-eyes, blue salvia, and phlox are particularly suitable. Other favorites are calendula, clarkia, cornflower, cosmos, four-o'clock, and gloriosa daisy.

A wildflower meadow, including poppies and bachelor's-buttons.

What is the best way to plant a wildflower garden?

To make it look the most natural, mix the various kinds of seeds together and scatter them about the area.

Will I have to replant my wildflower garden every year?

Some of the suggested plants will reseed themselves, so it may not be necessary. After a few years, however, you may find that not all of the plants are coming back every year. At that time, remove some of the more aggressive plants and resow.

I love cut flowers in the house, and would like to grow my own. What do you suggest?

For a cutting garden, grow ageratum, China aster, calendula, cornflower, cosmos, dahlia, gerbera, marigold, salvia, snapdragon, spider flower, stock, African marigold, or zinnia.

I don't have room for a cutting garden, but would still like to have flowers for the house.

It isn't necessary to create a separate cutting garden, for all of the flowers mentioned above also look beautiful in flower beds and borders.

I have read that the best flower arrangements have a variety of flower shapes within them. Could you explain this?

Make use of the three basic flower shapes as you do when planning your garden. Elongated, or spiked, flowers give a feeling of movement, develop the structure of the arrangement, and give the arrangement its line. They include bells-of-Ireland, celosia, larkspur, snapdragon, stock, and salvia. Round flowers naturally become the focal points of the arrangement by joining lines, stopping your eye, and getting your attention. They include China aster, dahlia, geranium, gerbera, marigold, zinnia, calendula, gazania, and scabiosa. Filler, or transition, material softens the arrangement and gives it fullness. These are the feathery or airy flowers such as baby's-breath, spider flower, ageratum, bachelor's-button, cosmos, and coleus flowers.

How do you cut flowers for maximum life indoors? Is there anything I can do to make my cut flowers last longer?

Flowers should be picked as the buds are opening, either early in the morning or late in the afternoon when moisture and sugar content are high. Cut the stems at an angle with a sharp knife or scissors and place them immediately into warm water. Bring the flowers into the house and recut the stems under water to bring maximum moisture to the petals. Remove any foliage that will be under the water and "harden off" the flowers by placing them in a cool, dark area for several hours or overnight before arranging the flowers.

To help cut flowers last the longest possible time, do not place them in full sun or in the draft of an air conditioner. Change the water every day and add a floral preservative to the water. This prevents the buildup of bacteria in the water, which will cause the flowers to deteriorate quickly.

PRESERVING ANNUALS FOR DRIED ARRANGEMENTS

I'd like to grow some flowers for dried wreaths and arrangements. Which annuals are good for this?

The easiest to dry are the "everlastings," such as cockscomb, globe amaranth, baby's-breath, strawflower, everlasting, statice, money plant, bells-of-Ireland, love-in-a-mist, and immortelle.

What type of growing conditions do everlastings like?

Most everlastings like full sun and dry, sandy soil. Although the seeds can be started directly in the garden where the plants are to grow, it is better to sow them indoors or to buy bedding plants. Fertilize monthly with soluble fertilizer.

Strawflower is a favorite and dependable everlasting.

These statice, with their blooms fully open, are ready to be cut and dried.

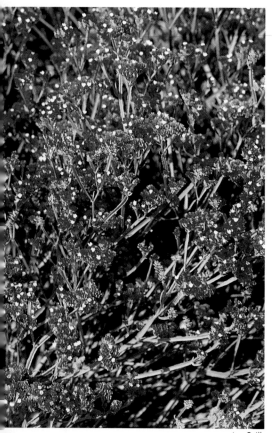

Ann Reilly

At what point should I cut flowers for drying?

That depends on the flower. Cut celosia when seeds begin to form in the flowers at the bottom of the plume. Cut globe amaranth when it matures in late summer. Cut statice when blooms are fully open. Cut money plant when the plants start to brown, but before seeds drop; rub off the outer petals to expose the central translucent disks before drying. Cut bells-of-Ireland when the flower spikes are mature and open; remove leaves and spines before drying. Cut love-in-a-mist when seedpods are mature but before they burst open. Cut immortelle when flowers are fully open. Cut strawflower just before the central petals open. Cut everlasting as soon as the buds show color; the flowers open during drying.

Which flowers can I air dry? How do I do this?

Any of the above varieties air dry. When cutting flowers for drying, make sure they are not wet with dew or rain. Strip the leaves and tie the flowers in small bunches. Hang them upside down in a dark, ventilated attic, basement, or other out-of-the-way place and let them dry for two or three weeks. Wrap fine wire around the stems of strawflower and everlastings before drying, so they will be strong enough later on. Store them away from dampness.

I have seen flower drying kits. How do these work?

Flower drying kits contain a dessicant called silica gel. Flowers such as zinnias, marigolds, dahlias, snapdragons, as well as strawflower and love-in-a-mist, can be effectively dried with desiccant. As blooms do not change during drying, pick them at the stage you want them to be after they are dried.

Place two inches of silica gel in the bottom of a cake tin, cookie container, or some other glass or metal sealable can, and lay the flowers on it face up. Do not let the flowers touch each other. Then sprinkle additional silica gel over the flowers until they are completely covered. Cover the container tightly and seal shut with tape for two to six days. When the flowers are ready, they will feel crisp or papery to the touch. When finished, blow or brush away any extra silica gel.

I have heard about drying flowers in borax or fine sand. Is this possible?

Drying with borax or sand works in a similar manner to silica gel drying. It takes at least twice as long as drying with silica gel, and the color is not as vivid.

Can I dry flowers in the microwave?

Yes. Place a few flowers at a time in a small microwaveable dish. Place the dish in the microwave with a cup of water and use fifty-percent power for from thirty seconds to three minutes, depending on the thickness of the flower and the wattage of your microwave. You will have to experiment somewhat with timing because conditions are so variable. Flowers can also be placed in silica gel during the microwaving.

My dried flowers do not stay crisp. What should I do?

Some dried flowers pick up moisture from the air when it is very humid during the summer. Although they can be redried, you can prevent this problem by storing them in a closed jar along with some silica gel and use them in arrangements only in winter. Protect pressed flower pictures with a pane of glass.

Can silica gel be reused?

Yes, but first reactivate it by baking it in a 250° F. oven for an hour. Some silica gel sold for drying flowers is mixed with blue crystals that turn pink, indicating that it needs to be oven-dried.

To dry flowers in silica gel, place flowers face up on a bed of silica gel, then sprinkle with additional silica gel until the flowers are completely covered.

I live in a small townhouse, but I would very much enjoy gardening. Can I grow annuals in containers?

Yes. Almost any annual except the taller types will do very well in pots, planters, hanging baskets, and window boxes.

What specific annuals should I select for containers?

When selecting, make sure the container is in proportion to the plant. Place a spiked plant, such as salvia, or a mounded plant, such as zinnia, marigold, or geranium in the center. At the edges, plant something that will cascade over the edges, such as sweet alyssum, lobelia, or petunia.

What shade-loving plants grow well in containers?

Begonia, coleus, impatiens, and browallia are always nice. The last two are especially good for hanging baskets.

Where can I place containers?

Containers can be used anywhere—on patios, porches, decks, balconies, along a walkway, at the front door. Put them in reach of the garden hose to make care easier for yourself.

What should the containers be made of?

Containers are available in wood, clay, plastic, ceramic, and metal. Make sure they have drainage holes. Wood and es-

CONTAINER GARDENING

•

pecially clay containers dry out the fastest, so are least desirable in very hot areas or where daily watering is a problem. Metal containers heat up very fast and are therefore an asset in cool climates.

My grandmother left me a large, copper urn into which I would like to plant annuals. Can I use this as a container?

Containers should have drainage holes. Unless you are willing to punch holes in the bottom of your urn, add a thick layer of gravel to the bottom so that the roots won't become waterlogged.

What type of soil should I use in containers? Is it all right to dig soil from the garden?

No, garden soil should not be used. It is too heavy, and root growth will not be good. It also often contains insects and diseases. Use a soilless mix of peat moss with perlite and/or vermiculite.

How often should my containers be watered?

That depends on the size of the container. Small ones will need to be watered more often than large ones. Check every day to be sure. When it is very hot or if it is windy, you may need to water daily, or sometimes even twice a day. It will be convenient to have a water source nearby if you have a large number of containers.

How much and how often should I fertilize my container plants?

Containers, because they are watered more frequently, will *leach out* fertilizer very quickly; that is, as the water percolates down through the soil, it washes out the nutrients. Therefore, feed lightly but more often than you would fertilize the same annuals in the ground.

The annuals in my containers did not grow evenly. What should I do this summer?

They probably were growing toward the light. Rotate containers regularly so this does not happen. If the container is large and heavy, place it on a dolly so it can be turned more easily.

Can I bring my containers inside for the winter?

If they are small enough, and if you have a room with enough sun. Chances are, however, that you will do better if you begin new plants next spring. Coleus will continue to flourish if you keep the growing tips pinched to keep it compact, and if you pinch off the flower heads as they form, but few other annuals

PLANT COMBINATIONS FOR HANGING BASKETS

- begonias, sweet alyssum, and vinca
- verbena and geranium
- begonias and browallia
- marigolds, alyssum, and lobelia
- petunias, geraniums, and lobelia
- impatiens and browallia
- ivy geranium and sweet alyssum
- coleus and sweet alyssum

will live successfully from one year to another. Geraniums may, but after a short time they become woody and do not bloom as well.

My patio has an overhang and I would like to add some hanging baskets for extra color. What are good plants for this?

The best plants for hanging baskets are begonias (including tuberous begonias), black-eyed Susan vine, browallia, coleus, creeping zinnia, fuchsia, impatiens, ivy geranium, lobelia, periwinkle, petunia, portulaca, sweet alyssum, verbena, nasturtium, and lantana.

How do I plant a wire hanging basket?

For a striking flower-ball of color, purchase a wire hanging basket and line the inside with moistened sphagnum moss. Fill the center of the basket with commercial soilless mix or a homemade one of peat moss and perlite. Poke holes into the moss all the way around the sides and bottom of the basket, and insert plants. Set plants into the medium in the top as well. Water well when finished.

Do hanging baskets require any different care than the same plants in the ground?

Yes. Because root space is limited and the container surfaces are exposed to the drying effects of air, they will need to be watered more often, and because they are watered more often, they will need to be fertilized more often.

What should I use to suspend my baskets?

Anything that is strong and durable, including heavy wire, chain, or strong ropes, as well as heavy fishing line, which, because it is invisible from a distance, gives the illusion that your plants are floating.

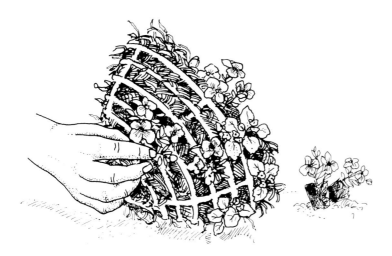

Line a wire basket with sphagnum moss, fill it with soilless mix, and insert plants from the outside all around the basket as well as in the top.

Can I use coarse sand in my potting medium for hanging baskets?

This is not recommended. Sand is very heavy, and a hanging basket should be as light as possible.

Can coarse sand be used in other containers?

Sand is a particularly good idea in small containers as its weight will keep them from falling over in the wind.

I'd like to plant a container garden using something unusual as a novelty. What do you suggest?

Anything that can hold medium can be used, from the bird cage and an unused barbecue, to drainage tiles or a wheelbarrow. You can also make forms with chicken wire, line them with sphagnum moss, fill them with soilless medium, and plant them. Let your imagination go wild!

I have a strawberry jar I'd like to plant with annuals. How should I do this?

Don't use plants that will grow too large or you'll hide the pretty jar. Good plants are candytuft, ageratum, lobelia, periwinkle, portulaca, pansy, marigold, begonia, or sweet alyssum. Choose colors such as white or blue that will complement the color of the jar.

Provide a growing medium that drains well so the plants at the top don't dry out while the bottom ones are still wet, and place a layer of gravel in the bottom of the jar to help drainage further. Fill the jar with medium, and plant the jar from the bottom up. When you place plants into the holes, be sure the roots are pointed downward, not sideways, so the plants will be secure.

Annuals such as alyssum and lobelia are especially effective planted in a strawberry jar.

I'd like to make some window boxes to brighten up the outside of the house. What type of wood should I use?

Use a high-quality grade of lumber such as redwood, cedar, or pressure-treated pine that will be resistant to water and weather.

How large should the window boxes be?

The boxes should be at least eight inches wide and eight inches deep. The length depends on the length of the window. Several smaller boxes are easier to handle than one large one. Wood should be about one inch thick to insulate the potting medium and keep it cool and moist.

What type of plants should I use in a window box?

Choose with care plants that are compact and have a long season of bloom. Place taller flowers such as geraniums, salvia,

Martha Storey

Container plantings of begonia, geranium, and pansy, in both hanging baskets and sturdy pots, enhance a deck.

marigolds, or zinnias in the back. Petunias, ageratum, and nasturtium can fill out the center, and ivy geranium, lobelia, or sweet alyssum can cascade over the front. Be sure to plant so that your window boxes look attractive from the inside of the house as well as from the outside.

Should I plant flowers directly into the wooden flower box?

As long as the box has drainage holes, you can, or you can plant the flowers in a metal liner available at garden centers. For small boxes, place individual flowerpots in the box. Then if one of the plants should fail, it is easy to replace.

How do I plant my window box?

Be sure there are drainage holes in the box, and cover the holes with window screening, pieces of broken crock, or gravel. Fill the box to within one inch of the top with soilless growing medium. Space plants somewhat closer together than you would if they were in the ground; strive for a full effect. Water well and place the box in the shade for a few days until the roots have a chance to become established.

10 Common Problems and How to Solve Them

Unfortunately, there are some pests and diseases that enjoy our gardens as much as we do. Keeping a beautiful garden entails a combination of recognizing these problems and learning how to avoid or solve them. Fortunately, in spite of many potential problems, it is unlikely that you will have to deal with more than a few of them in any one growing season. By learning to recognize the possibilities and symptoms of problems, you equip yourself to deal with them properly. Preventive or curative sprays, the avoidance of certain types of annuals, and preventive maintenance are all ways of combatting problems in your garden.

Certain annuals are particularly susceptible to attack by specific pests and diseases, and those are discussed under individual plant entries in Chapt. 11. But those same pests and diseases may at times afflict other plants as well, and the techniques for combatting them are similar. The following problems are especially common to a variety of plants.

What are the tiny green, yellow, black, brown, or red semi-transparent insects that appear along stems and flower buds? The plants are distorted and withered, and their leaves are curled and have black, sooty substance on them.

The insects are aphids, also called plant lice. They suck juices from plants. Wash them off with a stream of water, or use insecticide or insecticidal soap.

◀ Healthy gardens are the result of good preventive maintenance.

RECOGNIZING TROUBLE

•

TIPS FOR SAFE USE OF PESTICIDES

- Follow container instructions carefully.
- Protect your skin, particularly your face and eyes, from contact with pesticides; pour liquids at a level well below your face and wear goggles and a respirator, if recommended.
- If you spill pesticide on yourself, wash your skin immediately and thoroughly.
- If you must mix the pesticide for use as a spray, maintain a separate sprayer for each different product.
- Avoid inhaling the pesticide.
- Avoid using pesticides where they may drift to other areas, particularly outdoor living areas or vegetable gardens.
- Do not apply pesticides where people and animals are present, and keep children and pets away from treated areas until after rain or watering has washed pesticides off plants.
- Do not eat, drink, or smoke after using a pesticide until you have washed yourself thoroughly and changed your clothing.
- In case of contracted pupils, blurred vision, nausea, severe headache, or dizziness, stop using the pesticide and contact a physician.

Holes are being chewed in the leaves and flowers of some of my annuals. I can see small, hard-shelled insects on the plants.

There are a number of beetles that attack annuals. If they are few in number, they can be hand-picked. Traps sometimes work, but they often attract beetles from a neighbor's garden as well. Spray with Sevin or Orthene, or treat the ground with a grub-proofing insecticide to kill the grubs.

I see small, light green, triangular-shaped insects on my plants, which are becoming stunted and losing color. What are these?

These are leafhoppers, which suck plant juices and also carry disease. They can be controlled with chemical insecticides and organic pyrethrin.

The foliage of some of my annuals have serpentine, colorless markings on them. What can I do about this?

Leafminers tunnel into leaves and create "mines," the trails you observe. Remove and destroy infested leaves and keep the area weed-free so the insects have nowhere to lay their eggs.

Some of my plants wilted and lost their color. When I dug them up, I noticed swellings on the roots. Is this what caused their demise?

Yes, this was no doubt nematode damage, but only a soil test determines this for sure. Avoid this problem by not planting the same kind of plant in the same space for three to four years. Plant marigolds in infested areas to kill nematodes.

After I planted my bedding plants, something ate them at night. What is this?

If the plants were cut off at the soil surface and left lying on the ground, cutworms were at work. Prevent them from doing damage by inserting a plastic or cardboard collar around the plants when you plant them. If the foliage is being eaten and you see silvery streaks nearby, there are slugs or snails present. Use slug bait or small saucers of beer to lure and trap them.

I see webbing between the leaves of my annuals. The leaves also have black specks on the bottom, and have turned a dull color. What can I do?

You have spider mites, and if you can see webbing, the infestation is very advanced. Spray with a miticide every three days until no new symptoms appear. Keep the plants well watered, and syringe the undersides of the leaves every few days.

Some of my flower buds do not open; those that do, produce flowers with brown edges or blotches. The foliage is also distorted and discolored. What is the problem?

You have thrips, which are tiny insects that bore into plants at the base of the flower buds. Remove and discard all buds and damaged growing tips. Treat with insecticidal soap or a chemical insecticide.

When I brush against some plants in the garden, a cloud of tiny white insects appears. What are they?

These are whiteflies, which damage plants by sucking juices from them. They can be controlled with insecticidal soap, pyrethrin, or a chemical insecticide. They also like the color yellow, and you can purchase sticky yellow traps to attract them.

Place a cardboard collar around seedlings when you plant them as a defense against cutworm damage.

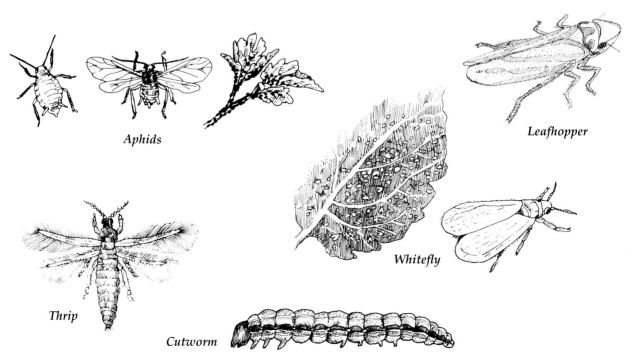

Aphids

Leafhopper

Whitefly

Thrip

Cutworm

Tarnished plant bug

Mealybug

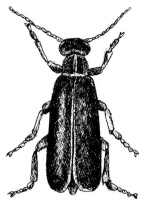

Black blister beetle

What triangular, brown or gray spotted insect stings the tops of marigolds before buds appear so that they are flat and empty?

This is the tarnished plant bug, which "stings" the buds of many flowers. It is a sucking insect and can be subdued by sabadilla, malathion, or carbaryl (Sevin). Remove all nearby weeds.

What is the scale-like insect that appears on the leaves and stems of plants?

Mealybugs are a common garden pest. As they suck sap from leaves and stems, plants often wilt, and if the insects are allowed to increase unchecked, plants may die. Spray with malathion, followed an hour later by a strong spray of water to rinse the plant and thus prevent damage from the insecticide.

What is the black beetle that is so destructive to the petals of many of my annuals?

The black blister beetle is a common pest of asters and zinnias, particularly, as well as of other flowers. Unfortunately, it does prefer the petals to the leaves. Kill the beetles with stomach poisons or contact insecticides or by brushing them into cans of kerosene. Avoid touching the insects, as their secretions can cause a blister.

I have found caterpillars boring inside and damaging the stems of some annuals. What are these?

Both corn borers and common stalk borers attack annual plants as well as vegetables. Often, individual insects can be discovered and disposed of. The best prevention is to clean up and dispose of the stalks of all herbaceous plants in the fall. Spray or dust stalks with malathion or *Bacillus thuringiensis*.

I sowed seeds in flats this spring. The seedlings germinated, started to grow, and suddenly fell over and died. What did I do wrong?

This is the damping-off fungus, which can be lethal to seedlings grown in flats. Use only sterile medium that has not been used before. Drench sowing flats with benomyl before sowing (see pg. 165). Do not overwater and provide good air circulation.

Some of my annuals lost their color and stopped growing. When I removed them, I found the roots were dark in color and appeared slimy. What happened?

This is root rot, caused by a number of fungi. Improve the drainage, and drench the soil with a fungicide before you replace the plants.

My annual flower leaves have developed an orange powder on the undersides. What is this?

This is a fungus called disease rust. Remove all infected leaves, and water only in the morning. Sulfur and a number of fungicides will control it.

What is the white powder that develops on foliage in early fall?

Powdery mildew is a fungus disease that is most prevalent when days are warm and nights are cool. Cut off infected plant parts and water only in the morning. Do not crowd plants too close together. Spray with benomyl, Funginex, or sulfur.

There is a grayish brown powder on the flowers and flower buds in my garden. How do I stop this?

This is botrytis blight, which usually occurs when it is cool or cloudy. Cut off infected plant parts. Spray your plants with fungicide.

Spots have developed on the foliage of some of my annuals. What should I do?

Remove the spotted leaves from the plant and the ground. Water plants only in the morning. Sulfur and several fungicides control leaf spot.

11 *Favorite Annuals*

One of the steps in good garden design is selecting the right plant for the right place. Before making any final planting decisions, you must consider plant height, plant shape, flower color, flower shape, bloom time, climatic restrictions, and soil requirements. As with all endeavors, there are tricks to the trade. If you grew a plant in the past and it didn't perform well for you, maybe you weren't aware of a planting or maintenance need that would turn your success around. Study this list of favorite annuals to become informed about plant selection and care.

African Daisy *(Arctotis stoechadifolia)*

I would appreciate instructions for success with African daisies. Mine achieve the bud state but then fall off and never blossom. Can it be too much water, or are they perhaps pot-bound?

Dropping of buds can be caused by extremes, such as too much moisture around the roots or extended periods of drying out. African daisies do not like warm, humid conditions, *or* a sudden chill. Use superphosphate instead of high nitrogen fertilizer. Cultivate the soil and be sure it is well-drained. African daisies prefer being pot-bound, so don't plant them in very large pots. Give them full sun.

Can I sow seeds of Africa daisy directly outdoors?

It is better to start them indoors but you can seed them outdoors in early spring as soon as the soil can be worked.

◀ *From A to Z — from ageratum to zinnia — there is an annual for every taste and garden.*

213

Ageratum *(Ageratum Houstonianum)*

How is ageratum started for outdoor planting?

Although seeds can be sown outdoors in early May when the danger of frost is past, it is best to sow them indoors in March. Sow them in either seed pans or small pots filled with sterile soilless mix available at garden centers. Do not cover the seeds with the growing medium as they need light to germinate. Set the pan in water until moisture is drawn up through the drainage holes and shows on the surface. Cover the pan with glass or polyethylene, and remove the covering when the seeds have germinated. Transplant the seedlings two inches apart or into separate pots when the first true leaves show (see pg. 165), and grow them under fluorescent lights or in a sunny window.

How can I achieve success with ageratum in the flower garden?

Although ageratum is not fussy about soil, it does best if the soil is rich, moist, and well-drained. Water when the ground starts to dry out, and fertilize monthly with a water-soluble plant food. If plants become leggy, they can be cut back, but no other maintenance should be necessary.

My ageratum do not do well during Florida summers. What could be the problem?

Ageratum does not like high heat or humidity and will not bloom well in areas where summers have these climatic conditions. Use them as a fall or spring plant in these locations.

Are all ageratum blue? I saw a plant I thought was ageratum, but it was white.

Most ageratum are blue, but there are also pink and white varieties. Summer Snow is one of the best whites; Pink Powderpuffs is a good pink. Popular among blue varieties are Blue Blazer, Blue Danube (also called Blue Puffs), Madison, North Sea, which is the darkest blue ageratum, and Royal Delft.

How can I keep woolly aphids, or milk cows, from my blue ageratum? I lose plants each year.

Ants feed on the milky honeydew that aphids excrete. They even herd the aphids together for efficiency. To fight aphids, make a shallow depression around each plant and pour in malathion solution.

Alternanthera *(Alternanthera ficoidea)*

What varicolored foliage plants can be used in garden designs?

Try alternanthera, which has foliage that is green, red with orange markings, yellow, yellow with red markings, rose, pur-

In areas where summers are very dry, grow drought-resistant annuals such as amaranthus.

Ann Reilly

ple with copper markings, and blood red. Because the plants grow very neat and trim, they are perfect for creating designs, as well as for edgings to formal plantings.

How do I grow alternanthera from seed?

Alternanthera cannot be grown from seed, but instead must be propagated from cuttings (see pg. 179). Purchase plants the first year, take cuttings from them at the end of the summer, overwinter them in the house, greenhouse, or cold frame, and plant them out the following spring after all danger of frost has passed.

What growing conditions does alternanthera like?

Plant in full sun in a warm location with average garden soil.

Amaranthus, Joseph's coat, Love-lies-bleeding,Summer poinsettia (*Amaranthus* species)

My amaranthus do not have the brightly colored foliage for which the plant is famous. What is wrong?

Amaranthus foliage will lose much of its color if the soil is too fertile, so apply little or no fertilizer in early spring. Amaranthus also does best when soil is dry and temperatures are high.

Anchusa, Summer forget-me-not (*Anchusa Capensis*)

I like to grow anchusa as a summer ground cover, but by mid-summer it has stopped blooming. What can I do to encourage it to bloom all summer?

Plant anchusa in a poor soil and do not fertilize it or it will produce many leaves but no flowers. Water only when the soil has started to dry out. After the first heavy bloom, cut plants back to encourage continued bloom throughout the rest of the summer.

Aster, China. See China aster.

Baby-blue-eyes (*Nemophila Menziesii*)

Can I start seeds of baby-blue-eyes indoors?

Yes, provided you have a cool (55° F.) room. They grow quickly outdoors, and in early spring as soon as the soil can be worked they can be sown where the plants are to grow.

The pretty blue flowers and nice fragrance of baby-blue-eyes are very appealing. How do I grow them?

Plant baby-blue-eyes in full sun or light shade in a light, sandy, well-drained soil. Fertilize them every other month

Ann Reilly

Bugloss: Plant this annual in infertile soil and cut down plants after their first bloom to encourage flowering through the summer.

during the growing season. In mild areas, they self-sow readily and act as a perennial.

Baby's-breath *(Gypsophila elegans)*

I thought baby's-breath was a perennial. Isn't this the case?

Baby's-breath has both perennial and annual forms. The most well-known annual varieties are Covent Garden, the largest flowered white annual baby's-breath; Rosea, with deep pink flowers; and Shell Pink, with light pink flowers. Baby's-breath is often grown in the cutting garden, but is also useful as a bedding plant or in a border.

I grew baby's-breath last summer, but it bloomed for only a short period. What do you suggest?

Make successive sowings or plantings of baby's-breath every two weeks for a continuous supply of flowers. Start seeds indoors four to six weeks before outdoor planting, or sow directly into the garden.

What type of soil does baby's-breath like?

Soil must be loose, alkaline, and kept on the dry side. Add fertilizer before planting and feed the plants again monthly during the growing season.

How do I dry baby's-breath for indoor arrangements?

Pick long stems before the flowers are fully open, and hang them upside down in a cool, dark, dry area.

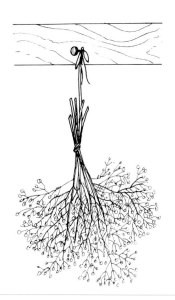

Pick long stems of baby's-breath before the flowers are fully open, and hang them upside down in a cool, dark, dry area.

Bachelor's-button. See Cornflower.

Balsam *(Impatiens Balsamina)*

What type of soil do I need to grow balsam?

Soil should be rich and heavily fertilized. It grows well in partial shade and in hot areas. Water well for best results.

Can I sow balsam seeds directly into the garden?

Yes, you can, and balsam also freely reseeds. For early bloom, use bedding plants or start your own plants indoors six to eight weeks before the last spring frost.

Basil *(Ocimum Basilicum)*

What is the best way to grow basil?

Most herbs like soil that is dry and not too rich or over-fertilized; basil is no exception. Give it full sun.

I recently saw a flower bed that was edged with a plant with purple leaves. I was surprised to discover this was basil. Is this the same basil that is grown as an herb?

Yes, it is, and both the purple and green-leaved varieties are quite attractive in flower beds. Although they do have small spikes of flowers in late summer, they are mainly grown for their leaves.

Beard tongue. See Penstemon.

Begonia, wax *(Begonia x semperflorens-cultorum)*

Can I sow seeds of wax begonia directly into the garden?

No, wax (also called fibrous) begonias have very small seeds and need a long time to develop into flowering plants, so you must start with purchased plants or start seeds indoors twelve to sixteen weeks before they are to be planted outdoors.

Why are begonias so popular as garden plants?

Wax begonias are neat, mounded plants with white, pink, or red flowers that bloom all summer with little care. They are one of the easiest flowers to grow. Although excellent for shade, they may also be grown in full sun if summer temperatures do not exceed 90° F. and if they are kept well watered.

What is the common name of the begonia with white-marbelled, green leaves?

This is calla-lily begonia, a wax begonia so called because as the young leaves emerge, they resemble miniature white calla-lilies. They are less hardy and more difficult to grow than other begonia cultivars.

I have a calla begonia that was healthy a month ago, but recently the leaves have withered and the tops of new branches are falling off. Why?

This is probably due to unfavorable environmental conditions rather than any specific organism. The calla-lily begonia is conceded to be difficult to grow. It needs cool, moist air, and fairly dry soil. Water the soil only, not the leaves. Allow the soil to dry out between waterings.

What makes the leaves of begonia turn brown on the edge and get lifeless?

This could be caused either by unfavorable environment or by injury from leaf nematodes, which cause irregular brown blotches that enlarge until the leaf curls up and drops. Prune off and discard infested portions; do not let the leaves of two plants touch; water from below instead of wetting the foliage.

Will begonias do well in the hot climate of California?

Yes. Where summers are extremely hot, use varieties with bronze leaves rather than those with green leaves. Soil should be rich in organic matter and kept well watered.

Dry spots form on the leaves of my begonias until they are almost eaten up. What is the cause?

There are three possibilities: sunscald, the leaf nematode just discussed, or lack of humidity.

Begonia, tuberous *(Begonia x tuberhybrida)*

How do I start begonia tubers?

Plant tuberous begonia plants that you have purchased or started yourself indoors eight weeks before setting them outside. Grow tubers in shallow flats of peat moss and perlite, planted round side down. Keep them in bright light, and do not overwater. When all danger of frost has passed, move them into the garden.

Is it true that tuberous begonias must be grown where summers are cool?

While they will not tolerate as high a temperature as wax begonias, newer varieties are more heat-resistant than former ones. For success, plant them in partial to full shade in a moist, rich, heavily mulched soil. Keep them well watered, and on hot days, mist the foliage to cool it off. An excellent, adaptable new series called non-stop can be started from seed and bloom all season.

Begonia: Masses of wax begonia bloom continuously over many weeks of the season.

Ann Reilly

How do I store begonia tubers over the winter?

Tuberous begonias must be dug from the soil after the first fall frost as they will not survive the winter in the ground. After digging them, remove all soil, allow them to dry, and store them over the winter in a cool but frost-free, dark, dry spot such as the basement.

When my tuberous begonia was budded to bloom, the leaves and then the stalk turned brown and dropped. What was the trouble?

It is hard to be sure without personal inspection, but it sounds like a soil fungus called pythium, which causes stem rot and may produce a soft rot and collapse of the crown and stalk. Avoid crowding the plants. Do not replant in infected soil without first sterilizing it.

A tuberous begonia rotted after a promising start. It wasn't overwatered. What could we have done wrong?

Tuberous begonias are sometimes attacked by larvae of the black vine weevil, which destroy the roots, so that the plants wilt and die. If white grubs are found in the soil and if a good root system exists, knock the soil off the roots and replant in a new spot. No insecticide is listed for this pest.

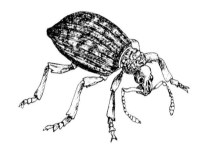

Black vine weevil

What blight or insect attacks tuberous begonias, keeping them from developing properly?

Insufficient light may be responsible even though these are shade-tolerant plants. The cyclamen mite or possibly thrips may cause deformation. Frequent spraying with Kelthane before blooming may be of some benefit.

What is the tiny white or transparent worm that gets in the stalks and roots of begonias?

It is probably only a scavenger worm feeding on tissues rotting from some other cause, possibly a fungus stem rot. If the plant is this far decayed, you should start over with a healthy plant in fresh soil.

What causes a sticky sediment on my begonia?

It is honeydew, secreted by sucking insects such as aphids, mealybugs, or whiteflies.

Bellflower, Campanula, Canterbury-bells (*Campanula Medium*)

How do I grow Canterbury-bells in the garden?

Plant in full sun or light shade in a moist, rich, well-drained soil. Feed monthly during the blooming period.

Are annual Canterbury-bells easy to raise from seed?

Yes, annual types bloom in less than three months from seed, but you must start them early indoors to get a good display in the North. Do not cover the fine seed during germination. In the South, seed may be sown outdoors in fall for growth and flowering the following spring and summer.

Why don't I have success with campanula in a dry soil? They rot away.

There are two soil fungi that may cause crown or stem rot under moist conditions, but your trouble may be physiological and due to insufficient water. Try another location and improve the soil with organic matter, such as leaf mold or peat moss.

Bells-of-Ireland (*Moluccella laevis*)

How are the seeds of bells-of-Ireland germinated? When I planted them last year they failed to come up.

Sow in a carefully prepared cold frame in May when the soil has warmed up. Do not cover the seed; it needs light to germinate. Keep the seedbed constantly moist until germination. Transplant seedlings to garden beds in late June. Seeds may be started indoors, but they require refrigeration for five days before sowing (see stratification, page 167).

How can I get my bells-of-Ireland to look like the ones in the flower-shop arrangement?

Groom flowering stems by removing all the foliage when you cut them, leaving only the bell-like bracts with the little flower "clappers" in the center of each. If you plan to dry the flowers, stake the plants during summer to produce long, straight stems.

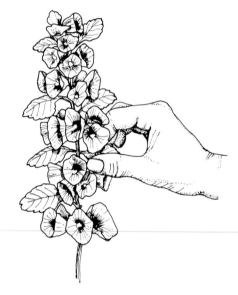

Remove the foliage from bells-of-Ireland when you pick them for drying.

Black-eyed Susan vine (*Thunbergia alata*)

How should I use black-eyed Susan vine in the garden?

Black-eyed Susan vine is a neat plant that grows five to six feet tall. It is excellent on a trellis or lamppost, or in a hanging basket. The plants like a long growing season but will not grow well where it is excessively hot.

Blanket flower. See Gaillardia.

Blue daisy (*Felicia amelloides*), Kingfisher daisy (*Felicia Bergerama*)

I would like to grow an all-blue garden this summer. Would blue daisy or Kingfisher daisy do well in Maine?

Yes, both of these annuals actually prefer cool gardens.

I've seen *Felicia* in two different sizes. Are these different kinds of plants?

There are two different *Felicia* species grown in the annual garden that are quite different in growth habit. *F. amelloides*, the blue daisy, grows three feet high and three feet wide. *F. Bergerana*, the kingfisher daisy, is a compact, bushy plant growing only six to eight inches tall. Both have blue, daisy-like flowers with yellow centers.

Can I sow seeds of blue daisy or Kingfisher daisy outdoors?

Yes, as soon as the soil can be worked in the spring, sow seeds outside where plants are to grow.

How do I start seeds indoors?

Seeds should be started indoors ten to twelve weeks before planting seedlings outdoors. Chill the seeds of blue daisy in the refrigerator for three weeks before sowing (see stratification, pg. 167), and germinate them at 55° F. Sow kingfisher daisy at room temperature. Both take thirty days to germinate.

What type of growing conditions does *Felicia* require?

Plant *Felicia* in full sun in a dry, sandy, well-drained soil. Water and fertilize sparingly.

Blue lace flower *(Trachymene coerulea)*

I've seen a plant similar to Queen Anne's lace, but blue. What is this plant?

What you saw was blue lace flower. Its lacy, sky-blue flowers have a sweet scent and make good cut flowers, too. The foliage is also quite airy and attractive.

How do I start blue lace flower from seeds?

Blue lace flower does not like to be transplanted, so seeds should be grown in individual pots if started indoors. Be sure to cover them completely as they need darkness to germinate. Seeds will also grow quite well if sown into the garden several weeks before the last spring frost.

When I grew blue lace flower in my cutting garden, I found that the stems were quite weak and the plants had to be staked. Is there anything I can do to eliminate this chore?

Blue lace flower does not mind being crowded, so they are self-supporting if planted close together. Give them full sun and a rich, sandy soil. They prefer cool weather and should be mulched to keep the ground cool and moist.

Ann Reilly

Black-eyed Susan vine: Excellent on a lamppost, black-eyed Susan vine prefers areas where summers are not excessively hot.

Calendula, or pot marigold: This hardy annual thrives in sunny, well-fertilized spots; its petals are edible.

Ann Reilly

Browallia *(Browallia speciosa)*

When should browallia be sown for outdoor flowers, and which varieties do you suggest?

For early flowering, sow in late March indoors, or in a cold frame outdoors after mid-April. Outdoor sowing can be done about mid-May. These dates apply in the vicinity of New York City; farther north, plant seven to twelve days later and as much as seven to twelve days earlier farther south. Do not cover the seeds; they need light to germinate. Good varieties include Blue Bells Improved, Jingle Bells, and Silver Bells, a white variant.

How do I grow browallia outdoors?

Browallia prefers partial shade and a rich, moist, well-drained soil. Mulch the soil to keep it cool.

How do you treat the black spotty disease that infects the foliage of browallia?

It is possible that the plants are infected with smut, a common problem for browallia. The treatment is simply to remove the smutted leaves. However, the problem may also be a sooty mold growing in insect honeydew, in which case use contact sprays for the insects.

Calendula, Pot marigold *(Calendula officinalis)*

How did calendula get the name "pot marigold"?

Calendula was referred to in poetry in the 1600s as "Mary's Gold," which was contracted to "marigold." Because it was used extensively in cooking, it came to be known as pot marigold.

Can you tell me why my calendula, or pot marigold, plants are so feeble? I sow them outdoors at the same time I sow marigold and zinnia seeds, which do very well for me.

Try sowing the calendula seeds earlier so that their roots become established during the cool weather. They will withstand light spring frosts. Also, select varieties bred for heat resistance, such as Bon Bon and any of the Pacific Beauty strain.

What kind of care does calendula need?

Calendula likes full sun but will grow in light shade in soil rich in organic matter. Keep calendula well watered. Cut off flowers as they fade.

I have heard that calendula flowers are edible. Is this true?

Yes, the petals are edible and make a colorful garnish for

soups, salads, and hors d'oeuvres. If you need to use pesticides, be sure to use one recommended for vegetables, and follow directions carefully regarding the required length of time between pesticide application and harvest.

California poppy *(Eschscholzia californica)*

Do California poppies reseed themselves?

Yes, usually, but if you cultivate the soil where reseeding took place you may bury the seed so deeply that it does not germinate.

When is the best time to plant California poppies?

As soon as the soil can be worked, sow seeds outdoors in early spring where plants are to grow. They can also be started indoors, but transplanting is difficult and not recommended.

What is the best way to achieve a long season of color with California poppies?

Plant in full sun in a light, sandy soil. Keep flowers picked off as they fade. Soil should be poor in nutrients; do not fertilize, or there will be few flowers. California poppy will withstand heat and drought, but it also does well in cool climates.

Calliopsis *(Coreopsis tinctoria)*

How does calliopsis resemble the perennial coreopsis?

Both are members of the same genus, and both have daisy-like flowers. Calliopsis, however, is available in red-, yellow-, pink-, or purple-flowered varieties, while perennial coreopsis flowers are golden yellow. Calliopsis, like the perennial coreopsis, blooms atop slender and wiry stems.

I'd like to have the earliest possible bloom from calliopsis. How can I achieve this?

Start with purchased bedding plants, or start your own seeds indoors six to eight weeks before the outdoor planting date, which is several weeks before the last expected frost. Seeds can be sown outdoors, but the plants will not bloom as early.

What type of growing conditions does calliopsis like?

Grow in full sun in a light, sandy soil with excellent drainage and low fertility. Water sparingly.

Campanula. See Bellflower.

Calliopsis: This cheerful annual prefers full sun and a sandy, well-drained but infertile soil.

Ann Reilly

Candytuft: This flower comes quickly from seed in spring and fall.

Candytuft (*Iberis* species)

My annual candytuft bloomed only a short time, then died. Why?

Annual candytuft blooms very quickly from seed but only for a short time. Cutting back after the first bloom fades may encourage a second bloom. Plant seeds at two- or three-week intervals for constant bloom during cool spring and fall weather. Annual candytuft does not do well in the heat of summer.

What are the different types of annual candytuft?

The rocket candytuft, *I. amara*, has large, upright, cone-shaped spikes of fragrant, glistening white flowers that look somewhat like a hyacinth. This is excellent as a cut flower. The globe candytuft, *I. umbellata*, is lower growing than the rocket candytuft and is dome-shaped. Fairy Mixed is the best known variety.

What is the cause of candytuft turning white and dying? The whiteness looks like mildew.

A white rust is common on candytuft and other members of the crucifer family. White pustules appear on the underside of the leaves, which turn pale. Destroy diseased plants or plant parts, and be sure to weed out such cruciferous weeds as wild mustard. Spraying with bordeaux mixture may help. Bordeaux mixture is a fungicide consisting of copper sulfate, lime, and water.

Canterbury-bells. See Bellflower.

Cape marigold (*Dimorphotheca* species)

How long can cape marigold be expected to stay in bloom? The plants I had last summer bloomed from about June 1 to July 15 and then died.

Six weeks of bloom is about all you can expect, although the time might be lengthened somewhat by snipping off all withered blossoms to prevent seed formation. To provide blooming plants for the second half of the summer, make a second sowing of seed four to six weeks after the first sowing.

What are the growing requirements for cape marigold? I have had trouble getting it to germinate, though I buy good seed.

Sow the seed outdoors in the spring when the ground has warmed up, or indoors four to six weeks earlier. Give the plants light, well-drained, but not specially enriched, soil. Be sure they get plenty of sun and not too much moisture.

Cardinal climber. See Morning-glory.

Castor bean *(Ricinus communis)*

Can you tell me about cultivation of the castor bean?

Castor bean plants grow best in full sun and a rich, well-drained soil. They prefer hot, humid weather, and they like to be heavily watered. Plant seeds in spring after frost danger has passed, where they are to grow, or start them earlier indoors and then set them out later.

Is there anything poisonous about the castor bean plant?

The seeds contain a poison called rincin. Plant them where children or pets cannot be tempted to eat the beans. Fatalities have been reported from eating as few as three seeds.

Celosia, Cockscomb *(Celosia cristata)*

Can you explain the difference between the two types of celosia?

Celosia is one of the most bizarre garden flowers, both in color and shape. The plumed type has long, feathery flower stalks. The crested or cockscomb type has round flower heads that are ridged and resemble the comb of the rooster.

I planted celosia plants last spring, but they quickly died. What might have happened?

Celosia plants should be set into the garden after all danger of frost has passed. If planted too early, they will flower prematurely, set seed, and die. For greatest success, plant celosia before they are in bloom.

How do I grow celosia?

Celosia likes full sun, a rich and well-drained soil, and very little fertilizer. It is very tolerant of heat and drought. Choose colors carefully as they are very bright and can be clashing.

What are the different celosia varieties I can buy for my garden?

Some excellent varieties among the plumed types are the tall Apricot Brandy and the Century series or the dwarf Geisha series and Kewpie series. Forest Fire is also very attractive, with red flowers and maroon foliage. Jewel Box is the shortest of the combed types; Fireglow grows eighteen inches tall; Red Velvet, Tango, and Toreador grow two feet tall.

China aster *(Callistephus chinensis)*

How should I choose asters?

Be sure to select wilt-resistant varieties. Once asters have bloomed, they will not rebloom, so look for "early," "mid-

Ann Reilly

Celosia: For best results, plant celosia, as well as marigold, directly in the outdoor bed where it will remain.

season," and "late" varieties in order to achieve continuous flowering. Consider, as well, their height. Tall (twenty-four to thirty-six inches) varieties include Super Giants and Totem Poles; medium (eighteen to twenty-four inches) varieties include Crego, Early Charm, Fluffy Ruffles, Powderpuff (also called Bouquet and Rainbow); dwarf (six to eighteen inches) varieties include Color Carpet, Dwarf Queen, and Minilady.

How do I start aster seeds outdoors?

Grow China asters in full sun. Prepare the seedbed by forking over the soil and working in well-rotted manure, peat moss, or leaf mold. Make drills (planting furrows) two to three inches apart and one-quarter inch deep; sow seeds, six or eight per inch, about mid-May. If you want cut flowers, set asters in rows eighteen inches apart, with the plants six to fifteen inches apart in the rows, depending on their size. Cover with a half-soil, half-sand mixture, and water with a fine spray. Apply light covering of hay or strips of burlap to help retain moisture just until germination, then remove this mulch immediately. Keep the seedlings well watered, and transplant them when they have formed their first true leaves (see pg. 165). Soak the soil for a few hours before transplanting; then lift the seedlings, taking care to disturb the roots as little as possible. Set the seedlings in the soil so that the bottom leaves are resting on the surface. Keep the transplants moist. When flowers show, feed with liquid fertilizer weekly.

For the choicest blooms, remove side shoots from China asters, retaining the main bud only.

What is the best method for growing asters?

Grow China asters in full sun. Before planting, enrich the soil with well-rotted manure, compost, or leaf mold. Start seeds indoors or outdoors, or purchase plants. If you want cut flowers, set asters in rows eighteen inches apart, with the plants six to fifteen inches apart in the rows depending on their size. Set the seedlings in the soil so that the bottom leaves are resting on the surface. Water well, and keep the soil cultivated or apply a mulch. When flowers show, feed with liquid fertilizer weekly.

We enjoy growing China asters in New York. Do they reseed themselves?

Yes, occasionally, especially the single-flowered kinds. However, it is better to raise new plants under controlled conditions annually.

What is the best procedure for disbudding asters? Should the tops be pinched out when they are young to make them branch?

Asters usually produce a number of branches naturally and do not need pinching. Each branch bears a terminal flower, together with numerous other buds on small side shoots. For choicest bloom, remove all side shoots and retain the main bud only.

Will paper collars adequately protect transplanted seedlings of China aster from grubworms?

Collars protect against cutworms (fat caterpillars that cut off plant stems near the surface), but they offer no protection against the white grubs, larvae of June beetles, which stay in the soil and feed on roots of garden plants. (See pg. 209.)

After reaching full growth and flowering size, my China asters dried up and died. What was the cause?

You are most likely dealing with aster wilt. This disease is caused by soil fungus, a species of fusarium, which grows into the roots and affects the vascular or water-conducting system of the plant. Young plants may be infected and not show symptoms until flowering, as in the case you describe. Plant wilt-resistant seed, many varieties of which are now on the market. No one knows exactly how long the fusarium wilt fungus lives in the soil, but it is best to wait several years before putting more China asters in a place where they have succumbed to this disease.

What can I do to prevent root rot in my China aster bed? I planted wilt-resistant seed, disinfected with Semesan, but I did not receive the desired results.

Certain soils are so infected with the wilt fungus that a percentage of even wilt-resistant plants will succumb; the situation is worse in wet seasons. Try sterilizing the soil in the seed bed. For a small area, spade the soil, and then saturate it with a solution of one gallon of commercial Formalin diluted with fifty gallons of water. Use a proportioner for this process; see page 183. Apply one-half to one gallon per square foot of soil, cover with paper or canvas for twenty-four hours, and then air out for two weeks before planting.

What causes some China aster flowers to open greenish-white instead of coloring?

This is a virus disease called aster yellows and transmitted from diseased to healthy plants by leafhoppers. The leaves lose their chlorophyll and turn yellow, while the blossoms turn green. Plants are usually stunted. This is the most serious aster disease and occurs throughout the United States.

How can I prevent China aster yellows?

Only by preventing insect transmission. Remove diseased plants immediately, so there will be no source of infection. Spray frequently with contact insecticides to kill leafhoppers. Commercial growers protect China asters by growing them in cloth houses made of cheesecloth or tobacco cloth with twenty-two meshes to the inch.

Ann Reilly

China aster: Grow these plants in full sun, and fertilize them regularly once flowering begins.

How can I get rid of the small root lice that suck life out of China asters and other annuals?

Make a shallow depression around each plant and pour in the same malathion solution used for spraying above-ground aphids.

How can I control the common black beetle on China asters?

You probably mean the long, slim blister beetle, which is very destructive to these asters. Dust or spray with carbaryl (Sevin).

China pink. See Dianthus.

Chrysanthemum (*Chrysanthemum* species)

I thought chrysanthemums were perennial plants that bloomed in the fall. But I have seen listings in seed catalogs for annual chrysanthemums. What are they?

A number of chrysanthemums are true annuals. These include the species *C. carinatum*, *C. coronarium*, *C. multicaule*, and *C. paludosum*. Most have single or double, daisylike flowers on tall plants; some have finely cut foliage. All bloom throughout the summer rather than in the fall as the perennial chrysanthemums do.

How do I grow annual chrysanthemums?

They can be grown from seeds or plants. Start seeds indoors eight to ten weeks before the last spring frost, or sow them directly into the garden where the plants are to grow. Give them full sun and an average soil. Fertilize monthly during the growing season, and keep faded flowers picked to ensure continuous bloom. Annual chrysanthemums do best where summers are mild and moist, although they will tolerate a moderate amount of heat and drought.

Cineraria (*Senecio x hybridus*)

When I visited a garden in Vancouver, British Columbia, last summer, I saw cineraria being grown as a bedding plant. Isn't cineraria a houseplant?

It is, but it can be grown as a bedding plant in climates such as Vancouver's, where summers are cool. Because they take six months to reach blooming size, it is best to start with purchased plants.

Besides cool temperatures, what other growing conditions do cineraria require?

Cineraria can be planted into the garden several weeks before the last expected frost. Soil should be rich, moist, and well-drained. Mulch to keep the soil cool and moist. Water heavily and fertilize every other month during the growing season. Remove flowers as they fade to keep the plants neat and to extend blooming.

Clarkia, Godetia (*Clarkia* species)

Can I start clarkia seeds indoors to get a head start on the season?

No, clarkia seedlings very rarely transplant well, so after all danger of frost has passed, sow seeds where plants are to grow. In warm areas, sow in the fall for growth and flowering the following spring.

I planted clarkia seeds last summer, but they did not grow well. What did I do wrong?

Clarkia prefers cool temperatures, especially at night. In areas where summers are hot, grow it as a spring wildflower. Choose a location with full sun or light shade and a light, sandy soil with excellent drainage. Do not fertilize or there will be no flowers.

Cockscomb. See Celosia.

Clarkia: Sow seeds in the spot where plants are to grow, as clarkia does not transplant well.

Ann Reilly

Coleus *(Coleus x hybridus)*

Is it possible to raise coleus from seeds?

Coleus are easily started from seeds sown any time indoors. Germination is rapid (about one week), and plants are ready for transplanting in another two weeks. Do not cover seeds; they need light to germinate.

Can coleus be rooted from cuttings? I have a favorite pink-leaved variety that I would like to increase.

Coleus roots very readily. Stem cuttings two to three inches long can be rooted in water, sand, vermiculite, or a regular rooting mixture.

How do I grow coleus outdoors?

Coleus likes partial to full shade and a rich, moist soil. If planted in full sun, the bright colors of the foliage will fade.

Do I need to remove the flowers of coleus as they appear in late summer?

That is up to you. Some people feel the flowers detract from the colorful foliage. If you remove them, the foliage will remain more colorful into the fall.

What are the differences between varieties of coleus?

Carefree has very small, deeply lobed leaves and forms a bushy plant that is excellent for small spaces and containers. Dragon has large plants with large leaves. Fiji has large plants and fringed, lacy leaves. With its pendulous branches and large leaves, Poncho is perfect for hanging baskets. Rainbow, with its large, heart-shaped leaves, was the original modern coleus. Saber has narrow, sword-like leaves. Wizard is similar in shape to Rainbow. All coleus are available in a multitude of foliage colors, with combinations of green, red, white, gold, bronze, scarlet, orange, salmon, yellow, pink, and purple.

Are mealybugs on coleus caused by too much or too little watering? They appear as a soft white, fuzzy scale.

Mealybugs, like most sucking insects, thrive in a dry atmosphere, but too little water cannot "cause" them. Also, if the plants are unhealthy from a waterlogged soil, they may succumb more readily to mealybug injury. Spray at the first sign of bugs with insecticidal soap, malathion, or Orthene.

What can I do to stop a white moldy rot on coleus, kept as a houseplant?

If this is not a mealybug infestation, it may be a black rot called "black leg" because it rots the base of the stalks. Destroy infected plants and pot new ones with fresh soil.

Cornflower, Bachelor's-button *(Centaurea Cyanus)*

Why do our bachelor's-buttons, or cornflowers, show retarded growth and weak flower stalks?

They may have been too crowded or sown too late in the spring. Sow the seeds in a finely prepared soil in the fall or as soon as you can work the soil in spring. Sow thinly; cover seeds about one-quarter inch deep as they must have darkness to germinate. When they are large enough, thin out the seedlings to nine inches apart. Yours may have been too crowded or sown too late in the spring.

What treatment do you prescribe for bachelor's-buttons to be assured of large blossoms and a long period of bloom?

You should get good results by giving them a moderately rich, well-drained soil, and extra watering during hot, dry weather; do not overwater, however. Plant in full sun. Sow seeds every two weeks throughout spring and summer. Keep faded flowers picked off.

Cornflower: For continuing bloom, keep the faded flowers picked off cornflower.

Cosmos *(Cosmos* species)

I understand there are two different types of cosmos. Can you explain the difference?

The Sensation type, *C. bipinnatus*, is tall, with lacy foliage and daisy-like single flowers of pink, lavender, or white. The Klondyke type, *C. sulphureus*, is shorter, with broad foliage and semidouble flowers of gold, yellow, or orange.

When should cosmos be started from seeds?

Sow seeds indoors five to seven weeks before the date of the last frost in your region, or use a cold frame. After all danger of frost has passed, sow seeds into the garden where plants are to grow.

Are cosmos easy to grow?

Yes. Give them full sun and a warm spot. They like a dry, infertile soil; soil too rich will produce lush foliage but no flowers. Do not overwater or overfertilize. To prolong bloom, cut off faded flowers. Tall varieties should be planted out of the wind, but should not need to be staked.

What is the cause of cosmos turning brown and dying?

It may be a bacterial wilt, but more likely it is a fungus stem blight. A grayish lesion girdles the stem and all parts above die. Spraying is of little value. Remove infected plants when they are noticed, and pull and destroy all tops after the plants bloom.

Creeping zinnia (*Sanvitalia procumbens*)

Is the creeping zinnia truly a zinnia?

No, it is not a zinnia. It is a low-growing, wide-spreading plant that makes an excellent annual ground cover, edging, or hanging container plant.

Can I start seeds of creeping zinnia indoors?

Yes, start them indoors four to six weeks before the outdoor planting date, but treat them carefully as they do not like transplanting. For best results, sow seeds directly into the garden where they are to grow.

How do I care for creeping zinnia?

Creeping zinnia is easy to grow. Because the flowers fall cleanly from the plant as they fade, maintenance is minimal. Plant them in full sun and a light, well-drained soil. They will tolerate drought and should be watered when the soil starts to dry out.

Cupflower. See Nierembergia.

Dahlberg daisy (*Dyssodia tenuiloba*)

What is the best way to propagate dahlberg daisy?

Begin seeds indoors six to eight weeks before date of expected last frost. Move seedlings outdoors when danger of frost is past.

Dahlberg daisy: This plant grows best in cool climates, but it does tolerate heat and drought.

Ann Reilly

Will dahlberg daisy grow in my garden in Kansas?

Yes, dahlberg daisy will tolerate heat and drought, although it will grow better in cooler climates. It likes full sun, and average garden soil that is watered and fertilized very sparingly.

Dahlia *(Dahlia* hybrids)

Is it true that dahlias can be grown from seed?

Yes, especially the dwarf bedding dahlias like the All-American winner Redskin, as well as Sunny, Dahl Face, Figaro, and Rigoletto. Start seeds indoors four to six weeks before the last frost, when they should be moved outside. Except for Sunny, the flower color of dahlias grown from seed cannot be predicted in advance.

How do I grow dahlias from tubers?

Tubers may be started indoors four to six weeks before the last frost, or planted directly into the garden after all danger of frost has passed. If you are growing tall varieties that will need to be staked, place the stake in the ground at planting time so you do not damage the tuber later on.

What care do dahlias require?

Dahlias like full sun, although they also do well in light shade. Soil should be light, rich, and fertilized monthly during the growing season. Water heavily, never allowing the ground to fully dry out, and mulch to keep the soil moist. Remove flowers as they fade. Bedding dahlias require little additional work. Those grown for large, cut flowers should be *disbudded*: remove all buds but the one on the central stem, so that the strength of the plants goes entirely to the remaining flower.

How do I store dahlia tubers over the winter?

After frost has blackened the tops of dahlias, dig them, allow them to dry slightly, and store them in a cool, dry, dark place that is frost-free. A particularly good storage is a plastic bag filled with dry peat moss. Check them during the winter to make sure they are not drying out; a sign of this is shrinking. If they show new growth, they are receiving too much light or heat.

What causes dahlia roots to rot?

Any one of several fungus or bacterial diseases. Verticillium wilt causes the lower leaves gradually to lose their color, the roots to decay, and the stem to show black streaks when cut across. Stem rot and soft bacterial rot causes rather sudden wilting. A heavy, wet soil encourages stem rot and bacterial wilt, but the organisms are already present. Improving drainage and lightening the soil with sand or coal ashes will help.

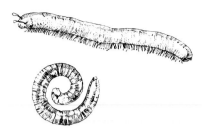

Millipede

What is the little brown worm about one-half-inch long that eats my dahlia roots?

The worms you describe are probably millipedes. They look brown to some, grayish to others. They are hard, with many legs, usually coiled into a circle, and almost always scavengers feeding on rotting tissue. The most effective treatment is to apply systemic granules around the base of the plant and water them in thoroughly.

My dahlia tubers are drying up in storage and some show rot all the way through. How do you prevent this?

Botrytis, fusarium, and other fungi and bacteria may cause storage rots. Use care to avoid wounds when digging them up. Store only well-matured tubers, avoid any frost damage, and keep at 40° F. in sand that is only very slightly moist. Too much moisture will increase rotting. Dusting tubers with captan before storage may help.

Some dahlia leaves have bright yellow mottling; is that mosaic, and what can be done?

The mottling is a typical symptom of mosaic, a virus disease carried from one plant to another by aphids. Dwarfed or stunted plants is also a common symptom of this disease. Control aphids with contact sprays, and remove and burn infected plants.

What are the chief causes of dahlia "stunt"?

Either mosaic or the feeding of sucking insects, often leafhoppers, but sometimes thrips or plant bugs. Stunted dahlias are short and bushy with an excessive number of side branches. Leafhoppers cause the margins of the leaves to turn yellow, then brown and brittle — a condition known as hopper burn. Spray once a week with malathion or pyrethrum, beginning early in the season and wetting the underside of leaves thoroughly. If the stunting was due to leafhoppers and the tubers appear sound, the plants may be used the following year. But if the stunting was due to mosaic, a virus disease, the tubers should be destroyed.

My miniature dahlia is full of buds, but they rot. What is the matter?

It may be gold-gray mold, the same type of botrytis blight that affects peony buds. Remove all diseased buds and spray with captan. Burn all plant tops in the fall.

If dahlias mildew badly at the end of the season in California, will the tubers be injured?

Probably not, but mildew is a serious disease on the West Coast, and dahlias should be sprayed or dusted with one of the above fungicides.

Is the borer that attacks dahlia stalks the corn borer?

Yes, if the borers are flesh-colored when young and later turn smoky or reddish. If the caterpillar is brown, striped with white, it is the common stalk borer, also a pest of corn. Clean up stalks of all herbaceous plants in the fall. Include the weeds, for many of these harbor borers during the winter. Spray or dust stalks with malathion or *Bacillus thuringiensis,* if this has been a severe problem.

This year, grasshoppers ate our dahlia blooms. Is there any way to prevent this?

Spray or dust the flowers with diazinon. Keep down weeds.

Delphinium. See Larkspur.

Dianthus, China pink *(Dianthus chinensis)*

Are China pinks so named because they are pink? I think I have seen white and red varieties.

You have — China pinks are red, white, pink, or lilac in color. They are called pinks because of the ruffled edges on the petals that look like they were cut with pinking shears.

Stalk borer

China pink: This tapestry-like display vividly demonstrates the variety of colors in which China pinks are available.

Ann Reilly

What are the best annual pinks?

Look for varieties such as China Doll, an All-American winner with double flowers in mixed colors; Magic Charms, with large blooms on a dwarf plant; Princess, most reliable for compactness, neatness, and all-summer flowering; Snowfire, with white blooms that have red centers and good heat resistance; and Telstar, which is also heat-resistant.

What type of climate does dianthus prefer?

All dianthus are frost-tolerant and may act as perennials where winter temperatures do not drop below 0° F. The new varieties are more heat-tolerant than older dianthus, although they still prefer a cool to moderate temperature and high humidity.

What type of growing conditions do I need for dianthus?

Dianthus likes full sun or light shade, and a rich, well-drained soil that is alkaline. If necessary, adjust the soil pH by adding lime (see pgs. 175-76). Feed monthly with soluble plant food, and cut back plants after they have flowered, to encourage a second bloom.

Dusty miller, several different genera

I'm confused about dusty miller: I have seen several different plants, each called by the same name. What are they?

Dusty miller is a common name given to several plants that have white, silver, or gray foliage and no significant flowers. They may be members of the *Senecio*, *Centaurea*, or *Chrysanthemum* genera.

How do I grow dusty miller? I planted seeds in the garden last year but the plants did not grow well.

Dusty miller must be set into the garden as plants that you have purchased, or started indoors yourself from seeds. They like full sun or partial shade, light dry soil, and little fertilizer. If the plants become leggy, they can be cut back.

I saw a dusty miller with very fine foliage and would like to buy it for my garden. What was it?

It was probably Silver Lace, which has extremely lacy, finely-cut leaves. For an interesting contrast, plant the broader-leaved Silverdust or Cirrus along with the airy Silver Lace.

English daisy (Bellis perennis)

What growing conditions do English daisies like?

Plant them in full sun or light shade in a light, rich soil. Keep them well watered, and fertilize them monthly during the blooming period. English daisy grows as a summer annual only in cool climates. Remove all flowers as they fade; English daisy can become weedy if seeds drop into the lawn.

I thought that English daisy was a biennial, but I have read that it can be grown as an annual. Is this true?

Yes. When grown as a biennial, English daisy blooms in the spring. When used as an annual, plants bloom during the summer.

How do I grow English daisy as an annual?

Start seeds indoors eight to ten weeks before planting the seedlings outdoors. The seedlings can be moved into the garden several weeks before the last expected frost.

Flowering cabbage and kale *(Brassica oleracea)*

On a visit to Mystic Seaport in Connecticut last fall, I was impressed by a display of chrysanthemums and brightly colored foliage plants I was told were flowering cabbages. Can I grow them?

Most seed catalogs offer the seed of flowering cabbage and flowering kale, which can be sown in early summer so that the plants reach maturity in the fall when the foliage color is most brilliant. The plants need the cold temperatures of fall to develop their intense white, pink, or purple coloration.

Flowering cabbage: The cool temperatures of fall bring out the subtle, rich foliage color of these unusual plants.

Ann Reilly

How do I grow flowering cabbage or kale?

Seeds must be started indoors. Flowering cabbage seeds should be chilled in the refrigerator for three days prior to sowing (see stratification, pg. 167); they need light to germinate. Their culture is the same as for regular cabbage, and both ornamental cabbage and kale are edible, although bitter. Plant outdoors in early fall in full sun in a moist, rich, fertile soil. Plants will last for several months, and even all winter where temperatures do not drop below 20° F.

Flowering tobacco. See Nicotiana.

Forget-me-not *(Myosotis sylvatica)*

I tried to grow forget-me-not last summer, but had no success. What did I do wrong?

Forget-me-not is a cool-temperature plant. Seeds should be sown outdoors in fall for growth and bloom the following spring. Be sure to cover the seeds completely as they need darkness to germinate. Seeds can also be started indoors in winter for spring transplanting, but this is not as easy a method, because they need cool temperatures for germination.

When hot temperatures arrive, all of my forget-me-nots die. Is this to be expected?

Unfortunately, yes, but forget-me-nots readily self-seed, so plants will appear every year once the bed is established.

Forget-me-not: Sow the seeds of forget-me-not in the fall for bloom the next spring.

The stems of my forget-me-nots turned black from the soil toward their tips. What caused this?

A wilt due to a fungus, probably sclerotinia, in the soil. All you can do is remove the infected plants, digging out all surrounding soil and filling the hole with fresh soil from another location.

Four-o'clock *(Mirabilis Jalapa)*

How and where should I grow four-o'clock?

Four-o'clock likes full sun and a light, well-drained soil. It tolerates poor soil and summer heat, although it will also do well where summers are cool. The plant itself is not attractive although its flowers are, so use it behind other plants.

I have been told that you get larger bushes and a greater number of flowers from four-o'clock roots the second season. In Missouri, can I leave them in the ground, or is it better to dig them up and dry them like certain bulbs?

Four-o'clocks are mostly used as annuals; the roots would be very unlikely to live through the winter outdoors in your region.

The large, tuberous roots can be lifted before hard frost and stored indoors for the winter, like dahlias. They will flower earlier and produce better blooms. Four-o'clock is so easy to grow from seeds, however, that this method is not necessary.

Fuchsia *(Fuchsia x hybrida)*

I have seen spectacular hanging baskets of fuchsia and would like to grow some this year. What do I need to do for success?

Grow fuchsia in partial or full shade in a rich soil with excellent drainage. Keep it well watered, and keep the humidity high by frequent misting. Fertilize every other week with a soluble plant food.

Is it possible to grow my own plants from seed or cuttings?

Yes. Seeds need to be started indoors six months before the desired blooming time. Do not cover them during germination, as they require light. Tip cuttings may be taken at any time and rooted in sand or a peat moss-vermiculite mixture (see pg. 179).

Black spots appear on the undersides of my fuchsia leaves, which turn yellow. What is causing this, and what is the remedy?

A rust disease causes brown spots on the underside of leaves. Yellowing of leaves, however, is probably due to sucking by whiteflies, and the black spots may be from parasitized whitefly nymphs or whitefly pupae. Control with an insecticide that combats whitefly.

Gaillardia, Blanket flower *(Gaillardia pulchella)*

I have enjoyed gaillardia in my perennial border for many years. Is there an annual form?

Yes, there is an annual gaillardia, but the flowers are ball-shaped rather than daisy-like. Lollipops is a favorite variety and very descriptive of the flower shape.

How do I grow annual gaillardia?

You can start with purchased plants or grow your own plants from seed. Gaillardia likes hot sun and dry soil. Fertilize it very little, if any, as it prefers infertile soil.

How can I keep grubs out of the stems of gaillardias?

Your grubs may be larvae of the common stalk borer. The best control depends on cleaning up all weeds and woody stems in autumn. Frequent spraying with malathion or bacillus thuringiensis may partly repel borers. (See also Dahlia, pg. 235.)

Gaillardia: This bright flower thrives in hot sun and dry, infertile soil.

Gazania *(Gazania rigens)*

I enjoy the daisy flowers of gazania in my garden all summer. Is it possible to grow it indoors as well?

Yes, dig some plants out of the garden in late summer, pot them up, and bring them inside for several months of color. Give them full sun and little water.

Can I grow gazania in my garden in Oklahoma?

Yes. Gazania prefers high temperatures and dry soil. Plant it in full sun in a light, sandy soil.

Geranium *(Pelargonium x hortortum)*

What growing conditions will be best for zonal geraniums?

Garden geraniums like full sun; rich, acid, well-drained soil; heavy fertilizing; and heavy watering. If possible, apply water to the ground and not to the foliage and flowers. Dead flowers should be removed immediately to keep the plants in full bloom. Geraniums grown in containers prefer to be pot-bound.

I have seen Martha Washington geraniums in the local botanic garden and admire their attractive flowers with the dark markings on the petals. Can I grow these at my home in Oregon? I have not seen them in seed catalogs.

Your climate is perfect for Martha Washington geraniums (*P. x domesticum*), for they prefer cool summers. They benefit from dappled sunlight, but are otherwise grown the same way as zonal geraniums. They can only be propagated from cuttings, so you will not find them in seed catalogs.

I see signs in the garden center for "cutting geraniums" and "seed geraniums." What is the difference?

Originally, all geraniums were propagated by cuttings, and many still are. Since the 1960s, there have also been hybrid geraniums that can be grown from seeds. Those grown from cuttings are best planted in containers and where they will be seen close at hand, whereas those grown from seeds are better for massed beds. Seed geraniums are also more tolerant of heat, high humidity, and diseases.

How do I grow geraniums from seed? Can I sow them directly into the garden?

Seed geraniums must be started indoors twelve to sixteen weeks before the last frost. The seeds are very fine and should barely be covered. Some of the best varieties to try from seed are the Diamond, Hollywood, Orbit, Pinto, Ringo, and Sprinter series, all of which are available in a large variety of colors.

Ann Reilly

Geranium: This familiar and colorful annual is an excellent container plant, here potted together with lantana.

How can I increase my geraniums by cuttings?

Take tip cuttings at any time, and allow the ends to dry out slightly before rooting them in coarse sand kept on the dry side to prevent disease (see pg. 179). At the end of the summer, cuttings can be taken from outdoor plants to grow inside over the winter. This method is more favorable than digging plants and bringing them indoors.

I would like to use geraniums in a hanging basket. What are the best types to use?

The ivy geranium, *P. peltatum,* is the best for use in hanging baskets because the stems naturally cascade over the sides of a container. They like dappled sunlight and moderate temperatures, and they can be propagated from either cuttings or seeds.

Is there any way to prevent geranium stalk rot? Some of mine rot each winter, but I do not think they are too wet.

Stem rot is usually associated with poor drainage or excessive watering. Start with cuttings from healthy plants placed in fresh or sterilized sand or a growing medium.

About a third of my geranium cuttings have shrivelled at the ground, turned black, and died. What is the cause?

Either a fungus or a bacteria stem rot. Take cuttings from healthy plants and place them in clean new sand. Keep them on the dry side.

After I prune geraniums at a 45° angle, the stems turn black and rot back four or five inches. What can be done?

Try frequent pinching back instead of occasional heavy pruning. When you prune, do it close to a node and disinfect your knife between cuts in 5-percent solution of Formalin or denatured alcohol.

Gerbera *(Gerbera Jamesonii)*

I have seen gerbera at the florist shop and very much like the pretty, daisylike flowers in their wide range of pastel colors. Can I grow them in my annual flower garden?

Yes. Gerbera grows easily in the garden and will last up to two weeks as a cut flower. The florist may also have potted plants that you can purchase, or you can grow your own plants from seed, provided you start them indoors ten weeks before the last frost. Seed is not long-lived and should be sown immediately. Do not cover seeds as they need light to germinate. Grow gerbera in full sun in a moist, very rich soil. Keep faded flowers removed.

Last year I planted gerbera plants that I purchased at a garden center, but they did not grow. What did I do wrong?

If you followed the instructions just given and still had problems, it's possible that you set the plants too deep. Be sure the *crown* (the point where the stem and root merge) is not planted below the soil level.

Globe amaranth *(Gomphrena globosa)*

I have seen small, cloverlike dried flowers of purple, lavender, white, orange, pink, and yellow in an arts & crafts store. Is it possible to grow these?

These are probably globe amaranth, an annual that dries well. Give them full sun and light, sandy soil; they like heat and drought.

Gloriosa daisy *(Rudbeckia hirta)*

Is gloriosa daisy sometimes a perennial?

There are both annual and perennial forms of gloriosa daisy; the perennial forms are often not long-lived and may also be grown as annuals. Both will reseed freely and act as perennials if you desire. Gloriosa daisy is easy to grow in full sun or light shade and will tolerate poor soil and drought.

Godetia. See Clarkia.

Hibiscus *(Hibiscus* species)

What makes the leaves on Chinese hibiscus dry up and fall off?

There are several possibilities. Fungus blight, stem rot, or leaf spot might cause such symptoms, but your trouble is more likely soil that is either waterlogged or too dry.

The buds on my hibiscus formed, but before blossoming they turned brown and dropped off. Why?

If you had a spell of rainy weather, it might have been botrytis blight, or gray mold, which possibly might have been prevented by spraying with captan.

I have admired hibiscus in southern gardens. Can I grow them in Minnesota?

Yes, there are several annual or perennial forms of hibiscus that bloom the first year and can be grown as annuals. To grow the perennial types as annuals, start seeds indoors three months

Hibiscus: The seeds of this dramatic flower must be nicked before being planted to assure good germination.

Ann Reilly

before the last spring frost. Start annual types eight weeks before planting date. The seed coat is very hard and must be clipped or soaked in water before sowing (see pg. 166). The perennial types will not survive your winters, however.

Hollyhock *(Alcea rosea)*

I always thought hollyhocks were biennials or perennials, yet I see annual hollyhocks listed in catalogs. Which are they?

Some hollyhocks are truly biennials or perennials, but there are some annual varieties. These include Majorette, Powder Puffs, and Summer Carnival.

How do I grow hollyhocks from seed?

Hollyhock seeds must be started indoors or they may not bloom during the summer. Sow seeds indoors six to eight weeks before the last spring frost. Barely cover the seed, for it needs light to germinate. Transplant outdoors after frost danger has passed.

How do I treat hollyhocks in the garden?

Plant hollyhocks in full sun or very light shade in rich, well-drained soil. Water hollyhocks heavily and fertilize monthly. Taller varieties will need to be staked.

Are all hollyhocks tall, stately plants?

No, some of the newer varieties are dwarf. Majorette grows only two feet tall and has large, double flowers in many colors.

Ice plant *(Mesembryanthemum crystallinum)*

When I was in California last year, I noticed a beautiful and colorful ground cover along the freeway and in many gardens. Can I grow this in Michigan?

Ice plant is a perennial in southern California, but can be grown as an annual if conditions are right. The plants must have full sun and a very dry soil. Fertilize every other month during the growing season.

I have not seen ice plant in my garden center, but would like to try some. How do I grow them from seed?

Seeds must be started indoors ten to twelve weeks before the last spring frost. Ice plant seeds are very fine, and therefore should not be covered. However, they need darkness to germinate, so cover the seed flats with black plastic until germination has occurred.

Ann Reilly

Hollyhock: The seed of annual hollyhocks should be begun indoors in order to assure summer bloom.

Immortelle: An excellent plant to be grown for drying, sow immortelle outdoors where the plants will remain.

Immortelle *(Xeranthemum annuum)*

The double flowers of immortelle dry so well, but I have had trouble growing the plants from seed. What am I doing wrong?

Immortelle does not like to be transplanted. After all danger of frost has passed, sow seed outdoors where plants are to grow. If you wish to start immortelle indoors, you must start it in individual pots.

My immortelle need to be staked each year. What am I doing wrong?

Probably nothing. It is normal to stake these plants. Give them full sun, lots of water, monthly feeding, and a light soil.

Impatiens *(Impatiens Wallerana)*

How much shade will impatiens endure?

Quite a bit. In fact, it is probably more shade-tolerant than any other annual. Bright light, with a few hours of direct sun, are needed for the best flowers, though.

Can impatiens seed be sown directly into the garden?

No. Although seed will germinate, it will not have enough time to grow into flowering plants in most sections of the country. Start seeds indoors ten to fourteen weeks before the last spring frost, or start with purchased bedding plants.

The foliage of my impatiens wilts during the day, and yet I water my plants well. What is wrong?

Nothing is wrong. Impatiens likes moist soil, and even when well-watered it often wilts during the day when it is very hot. Overwatering can cause impatiens to grow poorly. If the foliage perks up after the sun goes down, there is no need to water. Wilting can be reduced by using a mulch to retain moisture in the soil and to keep it cool.

My impatiens grew very tall and lush but did not flower well. I fertilized them again but it did not help. What do you suggest?

You have probably overfertilized your impatiens. Fertilize lightly before planting, but do not fertilize again during the growing season.

I saw a plant marked impatiens, but it did not look like the impatiens I am familiar with. There were few flowers, but the foliage was very colorful and brightly variegated. What was this plant?

It sounds as though you are describing a New Guinea impatiens, discovered in the 1970s by a team of plant explorers in New

Guinea. They are grown primarily for the brightly colored foliage that you describe. They require more sun than garden impatiens. Some varieties do have large, colorful flowers.

Why do my impatiens plants get a sticky substance on them? They have something like grains of sugar all over them.

These grains of sugar may be honeydew secreted either by scale insects or aphids, but they are more likely drops of exudate unrelated to insects.

Iresine *(Iresine Herbstii)*

I thought iresine was a houseplant, but I saw some growing in a flower bed in a public garden. Which is it?

Iresine is a houseplant, but its bright, deep red leaves make it a perfect plant for the annual bed or border. The red leaves are striking and should be used in any area where a red-flowered annual is called for.

Can I grow iresine from seeds?

No, you cannot. Buy a houseplant, and root cuttings from it in late winter (see pg. 179). After danger of frost has passed in spring, move the rooted cuttings to a sunny spot in the garden.

I have a small border along a stream in the back of my house. Can I grow iresine there?

As long as it receives full sun, yes. Iresine particularly likes moist soil.

Ivy geranium. See Geranium.

Joseph's coat. See Amaranthus.

Kingfisher daisy. See Blue daisy.

Kochia *(Kochia scoparia var. tricophylla)*

I have heard of a hedgelike annual that may be used instead of shrubs. What is it?

Burning bush or kochia. The rounded plants, which look much like sheared evergreens, grow three feet tall. During hot weather, the foliage is light green, but in autumn it turns a rich red. Plant in full sun in a dry soil. Kochia does best in areas where summers are hot. Acapulco Silver has white leaf tips and was an All-American award winner.

Lantana *(Lantana Camara)*

I recently saw a very neat plant with round flowers of pink, yellow, and orange on the same plant. What is it?

The very attractive multicolored plant you describe must be lantana, a particularly striking container plant. It is sometimes trained as a *standard*. This involves selecting the strongest stem, pruning away other stems and all lower foliage as the plant grows, and allowing the plant to fill out and bloom only at the top, like a small tree.

Can I grow lantana from seed?

Yes, but because seeds take six weeks to germinate, they must be started indoors three months before the last spring frost. You will find it easier to start with plants rooted from cuttings taken from your plants in the fall and grown indoors over the winter for use the following summer.

Larkspur, Annual delphinium *(Consolida* species)

Are there any tips for germinating larkspur seed? I have had little success in the past.

Start with fresh seeds every year, as larkspur seeds are short-lived. Be sure the seeds are completely covered in the seedbed; they need darkness to germinate. Because they transplant very poorly, sow the seeds where the plants will flower, and thin out the seedlings to nine inches apart.

What is the secret for successful larkspur? Ours start well but fade before flowering.

The secret is an early start in spring — about the time you sow peas. Larkspur grows best in cool weather, so in southern parts of the country it should be grown only as a spring plant. Grow plants in well-drained, moderately fertile, alkaline soil, in full sun or light shade.

Why do my annual larkspur plants turn yellow and die just before or after the first blooms appear?

This may be crown rot. The fungus starts working in warm, humid weather, which may coincide with the blooming time of larkspur. Remove infected plants.

Lavatera, Tree mallow *(Lavatera trimestris)*

I started lavatera seeds indoors last year, but had little success with them after I transplanted them into the garden. Any suggestions?

Lavatera seedlings do not transplant well, so seeds should be sown outdoors where the plants are to grow. Because lavatera is

Larkspur: Begin larkspur as early in spring as possible for most success.

Ann Reilly

be sown as soon as the ground
the South they may be sown
ation and growth the following
regions where nights are cool. It
sun.

roccana)

vers of linaria, but they do not
n. How should I grow them?

s, so in your area it may grow best
make an excellent complement to

tly into the garden in Oregon?

ination and bloom in the following
is soon as the soil can be worked.
ever, and may wash away in heavy
start seeds indoors four to six weeks
ng date, if you can give them a cool
(60° F.) room.

In addition to cool temperatures, what growing conditions does linaria like?

Plant them in full sun or light shade in a moist soil, and mulch them to keep the soil moist and cool. Fertilize every other month during the growing season.

Lisianthus *(Eustoma grandiflorum)*

What type of care does lisianthus require in the garden?

Plant them in full sun in average (neither clayey nor sandy) soil with excellent drainage. Soil must be fertile, so incorporate fertilizer before planting and feed again every other month during the growing season. Lisianthus is tolerant of heat, drought, and rain and prefers to be grown where summers are warm.

How do I grow lisianthus from seed?

With great patience. It takes seven months for seeds to reach blooming size, so it is better to start with purchased plants. If you do want to try growing your own plants from seed, give them a warm spot indoors and barely cover them as the seeds are very fine.

Are there both double- and single-flowered forms of lisianthus?

Yes, there are. Lion is a double-flowered series with blooms of blue, white, or pink. Yodel has single blooms in these colors as well as lavender.

Ann Reilly

Lavatera: Like larkspur, lavatera should be started very early in spring.

Ann Reilly

Lisianthus: Long-lasting as a cut flower, lisianthus should be pinched back at least twice, early in its development, in order to produce strong, compact plants.

I tried lisianthus in my cutting garden last summer, but the stems were weak and the plant flopped over. What should I do?

Lisianthus seedlings should be pinched as soon as they are transplanted, and again when two to three inches of growth have developed, to keep the plants compact and the stems strong. If this is not done, the plant will need to be staked.

How long does lisianthus last as a cut flower?

Lisianthus will last up to fourteen days.

Lobelia *(Lobelia Erinus)*

Will lobelia grow in partial shade?

Yes, the low-growing varieties are ideal for window and porch boxes or hanging baskets, as well as for partly shaded edgings around terraces. Choose trailing varieties for boxes and dwarf varieties for edgings. In hot areas, lobelia benefits from being planted in the shade; where summers are cool, it can be grown in full sun.

I have had problems germinating lobelia seed directly in the garden. Any suggestions?

Lobelia seed must be started indoors ten to twelve weeks before the last spring frost. The seeds should not be covered with potting medium; they require a warm (75° F.) place in the home for successful germination.

My lobelia plants become very leggy by midsummer. What can I do?

If it becomes leggy, lobelia can be sheared back to encourage compactness and heavier bloom. Keep plants well watered. Do not overfertilize, because this encourages growth at the expense of flowering.

What color are lobelia flowers?

Blue Moon has bright blue flowers and green foliage; Crystal Palace has bright, dark blue flowers and bronze foliage. Cascade, the best lobelia for containers and hanging baskets, is available in blue, red, white, purple, and lilac. White Lady is sparkling white.

Love-in-a-mist *(Nigella damascena)*

How did this plant get its name?

The pink, white, blue, or purple flowers of love-in-a-mist bloom within misty, delicate foliage. They make good cut flowers.

I would like to use the round, fragrant seed pods of love-in-a-mist in dried arrangements as their red markings on a green background are very attractive. How do I dry them?

Leave the flowers on the plant until the seed pods form, but cut them before they are fully mature. If left on the plant too long, the seed pods will burst. (If allowed to mature, love-in-a-mist freely self-seeds.)

I started seeds of love-in-a-mist indoors, but they did not grow well after I transplanted them into the garden. What do you suggest?

Because this plant resents transplanting, sow seeds in individual pots if you want to start seeds indoors. There is much less root disturbance to plants transplanted from pots than to those cut out of flats. Love-in-a-mist seeds grow well when sown directly into the garden; in mild areas, you can sow seeds in the fall for spring bloom. This plant likes full sun, fertile and moist soil, and cool temperatures.

Love-in-a-mist: Both the fresh flowers and the round, fragrant seed pods of love-in-the-mist are decorative in flower arrangements.

Love-lies-bleeding. See Amaranthus.

Marigold *(Tagetes* species)

What types of marigolds do you suggest for an all-marigold garden?

African marigolds (*T. erecta*) are tall plants for the back of the garden, with double flowers including carnation-flowered, chrysanthemum-flowered, dahlia-flowered, and peony-flowered types. Use French marigolds (*T. patula*) at the front of the border; these have either single, crested, anemone, carnation, or double flowers. A third type of marigold is known as a triploid and is a cross between the African and the French (*T. patula x erecta*); these are low- to medium-growing types that produce flowers all summer even in the hottest part of the country when other marigolds may lose their free-flowering habit. Because they do not set seed, the dead flowers fall cleanly from the plant, and they are easier to maintain.

I would like to try some of the triploid marigolds for their non-stop bloom. What are some of the varieties available?

The best known are the Nugget series, which includes Red Seven Star, and the single-flowered, orange and yellow Mighty Marietta.

What large-flowered, tall marigolds shall I grow for variety in color?

There are a number of African marigold series (see p. 147) that contain varieties in yellow, gold, and orange. You could choose one of these series and plant all three colors for variety in the flower bed. These include Climax, Crush, Discovery, Galore, Inca, Lady, Perfection, and Voyager varieties. All but the Crush series are hybrids.

Which French marigolds should I select for variety in color?

Again, there are a number of series of French marigolds with variety in color; in addition to the yellow, orange, and gold colors available in the African marigolds, many French marigolds are red, mahogany, or bi-colored as well. Recommended series include Bonanza, Boy, Janie, and Queen. Red Marietta is a red single, edged in gold. There are no hybrid French marigolds.

Can marigold seeds be planted directly into the garden?

Seeds of French marigolds can be sown in the garden and will germinate and grow quickly, but seeds of African and triploid marigolds must be started indoors four to six weeks before the last spring frost.

Would you tell me why my marigolds didn't blossom well last summer? Could it be the fault of the soil?

It may have been any of a number of reasons: too late sowing; too much rain; too heavy or too rich soil; pest and disease attacks; insufficient sun; overfeeding; overwatering; or failure to remove faded flowers. Also, some varieties (not triploid) of marigolds simply stop flowering in excessively hot weather.

My African marigolds did not bloom until late summer. What is the reason?

African marigolds are light sensitive, which means they bloom only when days are short and nights are long. Indoors, you can manipulate the amount of light your seedlings receive, so that they get proportionately more dark than light hours. Once they begin to bud under these conditions, they will continue to develop and bloom throughout the summer. If they receive more light hours than dark before budding, however, they will not produce blooms until late summer when nights get longer. For this reason, it is best not to plant African marigold seeds directly into the garden.

Do African marigolds need to be staked?

The new African marigold varieties are compact and should not need staking.

What is the benefit of planting marigolds in the vegetable garden?

Marigolds repel certain beetles and nematodes that afflict some vegetables.

African marigolds are one of the few plants that should be in bud when transplanted into the garden.

Ann Reilly

Why do my dwarf marigolds turn brown and dry up after blossoming well for a month? It is not lack of water.

Perhaps you cultivate too close to them and damage their roots with your gardening tools. A fungus stem, collar rot, or wilt may also be present. If the latter, you must remove diseased plants and either sterilize the soil or use another location for your next planting.

Mexican sunflower *(Tithonia rotundifolia)*

My Mexican sunflower plants never bloom. Can you tell me why?

The Mexican sunflower, with its handsome, single, brilliant orange or yellow blooms, must be started early indoors to give generous bloom in late summer and fall before frost arrives. Torch, a variety that grows only four feet tall, blooms earlier than the original species, which reaches six feet. Use it at the back of the border or as a screen plant. Goldfinger is smaller still (three feet tall) and has a longer blooming season than the species.

What growing conditions does Mexican sunflower need?

Plant Mexican sunflower in full sun in a dry soil, and do not overwater. Feed lightly each month with a soluble fertilizer.

I want to grow Mexican sunflower in my cutting garden. Any tips?

For the longest lasting cut flowers for the home, cut Mexican sunflower when it is still in the tight bud stage.

Mignonette *(Reseda odorata)*

Where in the garden should I plant mignonette?

The wonderful fragrance of mignonette calls for its being planted where its aroma can be enjoyed, such as on decks and patios or under windows. Because it is not an attractive plant, plant a lower growing annual in front of it to hide it somewhat.

Can I start seeds of mignonette indoors?

You can, but sow them into individual pots, as seedlings resent being transplanted. Do not cover the seeds; they need light to germinate. They grow very quickly outside, so not much is gained by starting them indoors.

Can I grow mignonette with spring bulbs in Alabama?

Yes. In your climate, they would not grow well in summer, as they like cool weather, but they would be perfect with spring bulbs. Plant in full sun or light shade in a soil that is kept moist and cool with watering and mulch.

Mignonette: Plant this wonderfully fragrant plant near decks or under windows where its aroma can be enjoyed.

Money plant (*Lunaria annua*)

I like to grow a few money plants for their dried branches, but the plants have sprung up all over the yard and are quite a nuisance. What should I do to prevent this?

Money plant reseeds very freely, so cut the seed pods off before they have a chance to fall onto the ground.

How do I dry money plant?

When seed pods are mature, but before the seeds fall, cut the branches, rub the covering off the seed pod, and hang the branches upside down, in a cool, airy place to dry.

How is money plant grown?

Start seeds indoors six weeks before planting outdoors, or sow seeds outdoors in mid-spring. Give them full sun or light shade in average garden soil. Little if any fertilizer is needed. Water plants when dry.

Monkey flower (*Mimulus x hybridus*)

I planted monkey flower last spring where I live in South Carolina, but when summer came, they seemed to almost disappear in front of my eyes. What happened?

Monkey flower must be grown where the climate is cool and humidity is high. Grow it in partial or full shade in a moist, well-drained soil. Mulching will help to prolong the life of monkey flower in the garden.

I tried to start monkey flower from seeds, but did not have success. How should I do it in the future?

Do not cover seeds when sowing, as they need light to germinate. Seedlings also require thirteen hours of light per day to grow, so if they are begun indoors, they must be grown under fluorescent light. Set transplants into the garden as soon as the soil can be worked; monkey flower is quite tolerant of frost.

Moonflower. See Morning-glory.

Morning-glory, Cardinal climber, Moonflower (*Ipomoea* species)

How do you start morning-glory seeds?

Because morning-glory seeds grow quickly, they can be sown where the plants are to grow after all danger of frost has passed. If you want, you can start them indoors four to six weeks before

Morning-glory: For best results, plant morning-glory seeds directly in the place they will remain, in full sun, in poor rather than fertile soil.

Ann Reilly

the last frost. They resent being transplanted, however, so handle their roots very carefully or sow them in individual pots. Morning-glory seeds have a very hard coat, so soak them in water for twenty-four hours before sowing, or nick or file the seed coat in order to help moisture get inside.

My morning-glories did not bloom well last summer, although they grew quite large. What was wrong?

Your soil was probably too fertile. Do not incorporate organic matter into the soil, and do not fertilize morning-glories, or you will have all vine and leaves and no flowers. Also, do not overwater, as dry soil is preferred. They do best in full sun, so if you tried to grow them in partial or full shade this may be another reason why they did not produce many flowers.

Nasturtium *(Tropaeolum majus)*

What nasturtiums shall I grow to produce seeds for pickles and salads?

The old-fashioned singles, either dwarf or tall, are best for seed production, whereas the much more beautiful and attractive, sweet-scented doubles produce few seeds.

I have heard that all parts of the nasturtium are edible. Is this true?

Yes, all parts — seeds, leaves, flowers, and buds — are often used in salads; flower buds and seeds can be pickled.

What shall I do to keep my nasturtiums free of little black bugs?

Spray young plants with malathion or insecticidal soap to kill aphids, but be sure to follow package instructions for application on vegetables if you are planning on eating your nasturtiums.

What is the benefit of planting nasturtiums in a vegetable garden?

Nasturtiums repel squash bugs and some beetles.

Should I start nasturtium seeds indoors?

No, nasturtium does not transplant well. Seeds grow quickly and should be sown outdoors where plants are to grow after all danger of frost has passed. Plant in full sun or light shade.

My nasturtium did not bloom well last year. What is the reason?

You probably overfertilized. Nasturtiums require a poor soil and should not be fertilized at all. In very warm climates, the bush-type nasturtiums will bloom better than the vining types.

All parts of nasturtium are edible, but be sure to use only pesticides suitable for vegetable crops if you are planning to use them as food.

Nemesia *(Nemesia strumosa)*

Nemesia does not do well for me. It grows tall and lanky and does not flower well. What is wrong?

There could be several reasons. Nemesia must have a cool, dry climate rather than a hot, highly humid one. Pinch it back at planting time to encourage bushiness. Give it full sun or light shade and a rich, moist soil that is mulched to keep it cool. Fertilize nemesia heavily.

How do I grow nemesia from seeds?

For best results, start seeds indoors four to six weeks before planting outside. Cover the seeds completely, as they need darkness to germinate.

New Guinea impatiens. See Impatiens.

Nicotiana: Flowering tobacco, or nicotiana, does well in either sun or partial shade and prefers high humidity.

Ann Reilly

Nicotiana, flowering tobacco *(Nicotiana alata)*

I have seen flowering tobacco in mixed colors. What variety is this?

There are several varieties of flowering tobacco in mixed colors. Nicki grows eighteen inches tall and is available in pink, red, rose, white, yellow, or lime green. Domino is a more compact plant, with flowers of purple, red, pink, lime green, crimson, and white.

How do I germinate seeds of flowering tobacco?

Seeds may be sown directly into the garden after all danger of frost has passed, but for best results, start seeds indoors six to eight weeks before planting outdoors. Do not cover the seeds; they need light to germinate.

I live in Florida and tried to grow flowering tobacco in my garden last winter, but the plants did not bloom well. What went wrong?

Nicotiana needs long days to bloom, so is not a good choice for a winter garden in the south.

Can I grow flowering tobacco in the shade?

Nicotiana grows well in partial shade or full sun. It tolerates summer heat as long as it is kept well watered and the humidity is high. Soil should be rich and well drained. Flowering tobacco is resistant to the disease botrytis and is often used as a substitute for petunias where humidity is high, as petunias are prone to this disease.

Nierembergia, Cupflower *(Nierembergia hippomanica)*

How shall I grow nierembergia from seed?

Start indoors in February or early March for early bloom, as seeds need ten to twelve weeks to mature into flowering plants.

How do I grow nierembergia in the garden?

Plant in full sun or light shade in a light, moist soil. Fertilize monthly with a soluble plant food.

Nolana *(Nolana napiformis)*

I saw a dwarf, spreading plant that had blue flowers that looked like a morning-glory. Is this a dwarf form of morning-glory?

What you saw was probably nolana, also known as blue bird. It doesn't grow over six inches tall and is useful as an edging or an annual ground cover.

How do I start nolana from seed?

Seeds germinate and grow quickly, so that after all danger of frost has passed, they can be sown outdoors where the plants are to grow. Transplant carefully into the garden, as the roots do not like to be disturbed. Nolana is one plant that benefits from being planted when it is in bloom: this keeps it from growing too vigorously.

What growing conditions should I give to nolana?

Plant nolana in full sun or light shade in an average garden soil. Water when dry, and fertilize little, if any. It will not grow well where heat is excessive.

Ornamental pepper *(Capsicum annuum)*

Is it true that there is an attractive pepper plant that can be grown in the flower garden?

Yes, the ornamental pepper is edible, but be careful, as most of them are very hot! Compact plants are covered with round, tapered, or cone-shaped fruit that changes color from white to cream, chartreuse, and then purple, red, or orange as they mature.

Can I start seeds of ornamental pepper in the garden?

No, ornamental pepper seeds must be started indoors six to eight weeks before the last spring frost, or start your garden with purchased plants. Don't cover the seeds; they need light to germinate.

Ann Reilly

Nierembergia: Known also as cupflower, because of its dainty cuplike blossoms, nierembergia prefers full sun or light shade.

Ornamental pepper: These unusual plants thrive in long, hot, humid summers.

What are the varieties of ornamental pepper that I should look for?

Fireworks has cone-shaped fruit; Holiday Cheer has round fruit; Holiday Flame has slim fruit; Holiday Time has cone-shaped fruit; Masquerade has long, thin fruit; and Red Missile has tapered fruit.

Will ornamental peppers do well in my garden in Texas?

Yes, ornamental peppers prefer a long, hot, humid summer and are very heat- and drought-resistant. Plant them in full sun or very light shade.

My ornamental peppers did not produce a heavy crop of peppers. What was wrong?

You most likely overfertilized. Feed the plants lightly at planting time and do not fertilize again during the summer. Soil should be watered more if fruits are not setting.

Painted-tongue. See Salpiglossis.

Pansy *(Viola x wittrockiana)*

When should I plant pansies in the garden?

Pansies prefer cool weather, especially cool nights, and should be set into the garden as early in spring as the soil can be worked. Where winter temperatures do not drop below 20° F., pansies can be planted and mulched in the fall for bloom early the following spring until the weather becomes hot. In colder climates, pansies can be overwintered in a cold frame for early planting the following spring.

What type of pansy should I plant for the longest possible bloom time in the spring?

The new hybrid pansies are more heat-resistant than the older types and should be selected for the earliest and longest blooming period. Pansies will do well where the days are hot and the nights are cool, such as along the coast. Bloom time will also be extended if pansies are heavily watered and mulched, and the flowers removed as they fade.

Can you suggest some pansy varieties of different colors, shapes, and hardiness?

There are a number of series of pansies, all of which are available in a large number of colors including red, white, blue, pink, bronze, yellow, purple, lavender, or orange. All of the following are hybrid pansies: Crystal Bowl is a multiflora resistant to heat and rain; Majestic Giant is a grandiflora; Mammoth Giant is a grandiflora that is not heat-resistant; Roc is extremely cold-tolerant and a good choice for fall planting; Spring Magic is a multiflora; Springtime is a multiflora and among the most heat-tolerant; and Universal is a multiflora type that is very winter hardy.

I have heard that there are two different classifications of pansies. What are they?

The two types of pansies are known as *grandiflora* and *multiflora*. Grandifloras have larger flowers, while multifloras have smaller flowers, but a greater number of them. The multifloras also bloom earlier then the grandifloras.

How do I start pansies from seed?

Start seeds indoors fourteen weeks before the outdoor planting date. They will benefit from being placed in the refrigerator in moistened growing medium for several days before sowing. Be sure to cover the seeds completely; they need darkness to germinate.

What type of care do pansies need?

Grow pansies in full sun or partial shade in a rich, moist soil. Fertilize them at planting time and again every month during the growing season. If plants start to become leggy, pinch them back to keep them compact.

What is the white moth, similar to the cabbage moth, that lays its eggs on pansies? These hatch into small black hairless caterpillars that eat foliage and stems. During the day they lie on the ground, and then climb up the plants at night.

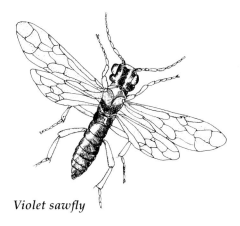

Violet sawfly

You have described the sluglike larva of the violet sawfly, the adult of which is a four-winged black fly, so the moth you mention must be something else. Spray with carbaryl (Sevin) or *Bacillus thuringiensis* for false slugs or sawfly larvae.

What is it that eats leaves and flowers of pansies? I have found one mahogany-colored worm with short hairs.

The woolly-bear caterpillar comes close to your description. It has a brown body, black at each end, and clipped hairs. It eats all kinds of garden plants. Spray or dust with *Bacillus thuringiensis* if large numbers occur, but woolly bears are seldom numerous enough to warrant spraying.

Woolly-bear caterpillar

Parsley (*Petroselinum crispum*)

I've seen parsley grown as a border to a flower garden, and thought it most attractive. I tried growing some from seed, but had no success. Any ideas?

Parsley seeds should be soaked in warm water for twenty-four hours before sowing. They do not like to be transplanted, so

Penstemon: Also known as beard tongue, penstemon prefers cool climates and light, rich, moist soil.

they should be started inside in their own individual pots, or sown where they are to grow outdoors. Cover the seeds well, as they need darkness to germinate.

Penstemon, Beard tongue (*Penstemon gloxinioides*)

I tried to grow penstemon seeds indoors, but had no success. What was wrong?

Penstemon must have a cool (55° F.) room to germinate indoors. If you don't have these conditions, sow seeds outdoors in early spring or, where winters are mild, in late fall. Outdoors, penstemon does best in cool climates in light, rich, moist soil.

Why didn't my penstemon bloom? The tips of the branches blighted and turned black instead of forming buds.

Crown rot, caused by *Sclerotium rolfsii*, a fungus infection, is common on penstemon and would blight the buds; but generally the whole plant wilts and dies. Penstemon likes a well-drained but not dry soil, and dies out in a year or two if not kept in full sun.

The tips of penstemon buds are webbed together and a small worm bores down the center of the stalks. What shall I do to prevent this?

The tobacco bud worm reported on some garden plants is probably the pest you have. Spray thoroughly with carbaryl (Sevin) or *Bacillus thuringiensis* as the buds form.

Periwinkle (*Catharanthus roseus*)

How and when should I plant the annual periwinkle (sometimes called vinca)?

Vinca is a native of the tropics and practically everblooming. Sow seeds indoors twelve weeks before the last frost. Be sure to cover the seeds completely; they need darkness to germinate. The seeds are sometimes difficult to germinate, and at first the seedlings are slow-growing. Transfer plants to the garden after all danger of frost has passed. Do not sow seeds directly into the garden as they will not reach blooming size during the summer.

What kind of growing conditions does periwinkle need?

Plant in full sun or partial shade in any well-drained soil. Although periwinkle prefers to be kept moist, it will tolerate drought and heat. Incorporate fertilizer into the soil before planting, and do not fertilize again.

Will periwinkle do well in my garden? I live near a freeway and exhaust fumes from the cars have damaged some of my plants.

Yes, periwinkle is one of the most pollution-tolerant annuals that you can grow.

I purchased periwinkle last year to grow as an annual ground cover, but the plants grew upright. Did I do something wrong?

You simply selected the wrong variety. Periwinkle, or vinca, comes in both upright and spreading forms. Carpet and Polka Dot are ground-hugging varieties. The Little series of Little Blanche, Little Bright Eye, Little Delicata, Little Pinkie, Little Rosie, and Little Linda are upright forms.

Petunia *(Petunia x hybrida)*

Can petunias be grown successfully with only four hours of afternoon sun?

Yes, provided other conditions are suitable.

How can I prepare a garden bed for petunias?

Plant in well-drained, moderately rich, and very thoroughly cultivated soil: its texture should be fine and light.

How do I start petunia seeds indoors?

Petunia seeds must be started indoors ten to twelve weeks before being planted outdoors. Because seeds are very fine and need light to germinate, they should not be covered. Seeds of hybrids and double-flowered petunias will need warm indoor growing conditions.

Can I sow petunia seeds outdoors?

Petunia seeds do not do well when directly sown into the garden. First, the seeds are very fine and can easily be washed away. Second, the seedlings take a long time to grow and thus rarely have time to develop into flowering plants during the summer even if they do germinate.

Can I take a chance and set my petunia plants into the garden before the last frost date? I'd like them to get a head start.

Petunias are slightly frost-resistant, so you could safely plant them two weeks before the last frost date.

How long does it take petunia seeds to germinate, and when should one transplant them?

Viable petunia seeds sown on soilless medium, not covered, and kept at 70 to 75° F., should germinate in eight to twelve days.

Transplant them when the first true leaves appear. (The leaves that show at germination are only seed leaves; see pg. 165). This might be approximately ten to fourteen days after germination.

Is it advisable to plant petunias when they are in bloom?

It is better to plant petunias before they flower. They will grow better and come into full bloom more quickly.

At what time of day should I transplant petunias?

Most annuals prefer being planted on cloudy days or late in the afternoon when the sun is less intense. Multiflora petunias, however, will fully tolerate being planted in the sun and will not suffer transplanting shock.

Why can't I raise petunias? They are the only plants with which I am not successful. I buy good seeds but the plants that grow just get tall (leggy), with very small blooms.

There are several possible reasons for your problems. The plants may be too crowded, the soil may be too heavy or too shaded, or you may have planted them too close together. Finally, select compact-growing kinds and be sure to pinch back young plants.

What kind of growing requirements do petunias have?

They need soil that is not too heavy, claylike, or wet. A light (even sandy and dry) well-drained soil is best, and it should be only moderately rich. They also like full sun and high temperatures.

Why do petunia plants grow large but have no blooms?

The soil may be too rich, thereby forcing excessive stem and leaf growth at the expense of blooms. Try them in another place where the soil is poorer. Don't overwater.

I understand there are two different classes of petunias. Can you explain the difference?

The grandiflora class of petunias has very large flowers; the multiflora class has small flowers, but a greater number of blooms. The grandifloras are best for containers, and other plantings that will be viewed at close range. The multifloras are best for massed plantings. Multifloras are more disease-resistant and their flowers recover more quickly after a rain or watering. Both classes contain single and double varieties.

Which kind of petunias shall I get to grow against a small white fence? I prefer something bushy rather than tall.

Choose your favorite colors in the hybrid multiflora and grandiflora classes of petunias.

Petunia: Pink petunias are particularly tolerant of poor soil and other adverse conditions.

What type of petunia is best for all-summer beauty?

Select hybrids within the multiflora and grandiflora types.

I have at times noticed a delightful fragrance when I walked by a bed of petunias. Which varieties are the ones that are the most fragrant?

Any of the blue-flowered varieties are the most fragrant petunias.

My soil is especially poor and my growing conditions are not ideal. Can I still grow petunias?

Yes, especially if you choose pink varieties, which are most tolerant of adverse conditions.

What are the outstanding grandiflora petunia single varieties?

All of the grandiflora single-variety series come in a wide range of colors. The best of them are the Cascade and Super-cascade, the improvements to the Cascade series, which are ideal for containers; Cloud, which have ruffled petals and are also excellent for containers and baskets; Daddy, with petals that are ruffled and deeply veined; Falcon, which will germinate better than others at low temperatures; Flash, which is one of the best grandifloras for weather resistance; Frost, which have white edges on the petals; Magic and Supermagic, best for bedding; Sails, with ruffled flowers; and Ultra, with a large number of blooms.

What are the best grandiflora petunia doubles?

Blue Danube has heavily fringed flowers. Purple Pirouette is the first double picotee (solid color with white petal edges); it has good heat resistance.

What should I grow if I want to grow multiflora petunia singles?

The Carpet series is low-growing and weather-resistant. Comanche is a brilliant crimson that does not fade in the heat. Joy is a series with early flowering characteristics. Madness is one of the best multifloras, with a wide variety of colors and ever-blooming characteristics. The Pearls are exquisite and tiny-flowered. All of these flowers have a white throat. The Plum series has veined flowers. Resisto was developed to resist cool, wet summers. Summer Sun is the best yellow petunia.

What would you recommend for multiflora petunia doubles?

The Tart series is early blooming, and excellent in containers.

What makes petunia plants turn yellow, especially if grown two years in succession in the same soil?

Petunias are subject to several virus diseases that discolor the leaves. The condition may also be due to a highly alkaline soil. Dig in peat moss or leaf mold, change the location, and prepare the soil well by digging it deeply.

The petunias in my flower boxes dry up and don't bloom well near the end of the season. What is the trouble?

It may be purely cultural difficulties — not enough water or poor soil conditions in the crowded box — but it may also be due to one or two fungi causing basal or root rots. Next time, be sure to use fresh soil, and continue to feed and water well throughout the season.

By the end of June, insects start to eat petunia leaves in my window boxes. What kind of spray should I use, and how often?

Spray with carbaryl (Sevin) or insecticidal soap often enough to keep the new growth covered. Look for hairless caterpillars feeding after dark. These may be climbing cutworms, which can be controlled with *Bacillus thuringiensis*.

Phlox *(Phlox Drummondii)*

When do I plant annual phlox into the garden?

As phlox is slightly resistant to frost, seeds may be sown outdoors where plants are to grow; sow them in early spring as soon as the soil can be worked. Bedding plants can also be planted at that time. When transplanting seedlings, select some of the weaker-looking ones, as these will produce more interesting colors. Select a spot in full sun.

How do I start phlox seeds indoors?

Sow seeds inside ten weeks before the outdoor planting date. A cool room is critical for germination. Cover the seeds completely, for they need darkness to germinate. Be careful not to overwater the seedlings; they are very prone to damping-off disease. Phlox resents being transplanted; it is best, therefore, to sow seeds into individual pots.

How do I keep phlox growing well in the garden?

Fertilize monthly with a soluble plant food. Keep it well watered, but try to water only in the morning to reduce disease incidence. Keep faded flowers removed; cutting the plants back will encourage compactness and further bloom. Phlox is fairly heat-tolerant, although some decline may be seen in mid-summer.

Pincushion flower *(Scabiosa* species)

I thought pincushion flower was a perennial. Is this true?

There are both annual and perennial pincushion flowers. *S. atropurpurea* looks most like the perennial form, having dark, silvery-gray filaments extending from blue, pink, purple, rose, or white flowers. These blooms are fragrant and make excellent cut flowers. Dwarf Double and Imperial Giants are widely available varieties. *S. stellata* is grown for its dried flower heads. Light brown balls of little florets with dark maroon, starlike centers remain atop stiff stems after the flowers are dried. Ping Pong is a well-known variety.

What is the best method of culture for *Scabiosa?*

Sow seeds indoors four to five weeks before the last frost, after which they may be transplanted outdoors. Sow them outdoors after all danger of frost has passed. Give the plants a sunny position where the soil is rather light in texture, moderately rich, and alkaline. Fertilize monthly with a soluble plant food. Water when dry, but do not overwater. Because scabiosa can be prone to diseases, water them in the morning so that the foliage will dry before night.

Pincushion flower: This striking plant adds an interesting shape and texture to the flower border.

The stems of my pincushion flower did not grow straight and so were not very useful in flower arrangements. What can I do?

Tall pincushion flowers need to be staked. Plant them in masses so that the stakes will not be visible.

I had disease problems with pincushion flower. What can I do?

Although they should be watered when the soil becomes dry, be careful not to overwater. Water them in the morning, and if possible, don't get the foliage wet. Plant in full sun.

Poor-man's orchid, Butterfly flower (*Schizanthus x wisetonensis*)

The exotic look of poor-man's orchid is most attractive. How can I grow it in my window box?

Poor-man's orchid likes full sun or light shade and a rich, moist potting medium with excellent drainage. Temperatures must be cool for it to thrive. In a window box or other container, it does best if it is pot-bound. Pinch the plants when they are set out (planted in the garden), and feed them every other month during the growing season.

I tried to grow poor-man's orchid from seed, but had little success. What do you suggest?

Seeds are very fine and should not be covered with growing medium during germination. However, they need darkness to germinate, so cover the seed flats with black plastic until germination occurs.

Poppy (*Papaver* species)

I have grown perennial poppies in my garden. Does this plant also have an annual form?

Yes: Iceland poppy (*p. nudicaule*) and Shirley poppy (*P. Rhoeas*). Both resemble the perennial poppy, with paperlike flowers of red, purple, white, pink, salmon, or orange with large, black centers. The Iceland poppy is actually a perennial that can be grown as an annual if it is started early in areas where there is a long growing season.

When is the best time to plant poppies? Can they be successfully planted on top of the snow? I live in Kansas.

If in your region the poppy usually reseeds itself and plants come voluntarily the following spring, you can very well sow on the snow. Otherwise, sow the seed just as early as you can work the soil. Seeds may also be sown outdoors in late fall for germination and growth the following spring. Be sure to cover the seeds completely as they need darkness to germinate. Seeds cannot be started successfully indoors as they require cool temperatures to germinate and, furthermore, do not like to be transplanted.

I tried to grow Shirley poppies last year, but the bloom was disappointing. What happened?

Shirley poppies do not have a long blooming period. Sow seeds every two weeks during spring and early summer for continual flowering. They will not do well if temperatures are high. Be sure not to overwater.

Portulaca, Rose moss *(Portulaca grandiflora)*

How can I make portulaca germinate and grow?

Portulaca is usually easy to grow from seed sown outdoors after all danger of frost has passed. It should have a well-drained, dry, light, but not rich soil, in full sun. Water very lightly.

Does portulaca self-sow? Someone told me to let my portulaca go to seed and I'd have plenty of plants next year.

They self-sow readily, but seedlings generally don't appear until fairly late in the spring after the soil has warmed. If they are crowded, they should be thinned or transplanted.

Pot marigold. See Calendula.

Rose moss. See Portulaca.

Salpiglossis, Painted-tongue *(Salpiglossis sinuata)*

How can I grow large, healthy salpiglossis plants?

For earlier bloom and a greater chance of success, start seeds indoors eight weeks before the outdoor planting date. Both seeds and plants may be set into the garden in mid-spring, several weeks before the last expected frost. The larger the plants are when they are set out, the better they will grow and bloom.

Seeds are very fine and should not be covered with growing medium. Since they need darkness to germinate, however, cover the seed flats with black plastic until germination occurs. Plant seedlings in full sun and a rich, moist, cool, alkaline soil.

I have heard that salpiglossis makes a good substitute for petunias under certain conditions. Why is this?

Petunias prefer hot, dry weather; salpiglossis prefers cool, moist weather. Since they are similar in appearance, salpiglossis can be used where petunias won't grow.

Ann Reilly

Portulaca: Easily grown from seed outdoors, volunteer portulaca seedlings may spring up in areas where planted the previous year.

Ann Reilly

Salvia: An excellent, stocky variety of salvia is Carabiniere.

Salvia, Scarlet sage *(Salvia* species)

I am familiar with the red salvia known as scarlet sage, but recently have seen a blue-flowered plant, also called salvia, that has a different appearance. The flower stalks are blue or purple, long and thin.

The red salvia is *S. splendens;* it also has forms in blue, purple, white, and salmon. The second plant you refer to is *S. farinacea.* It grows as a perennial in mild climates; in other areas it has become a popular annual.

How do you start red salvia seeds?

All red salvia seeds must be started indoors eight to ten weeks before the last frost, and those of *S. farinacea* must be started even earlier: twelve weeks before outdoor planting. Seeds of red-flowered varieties need light to germinate; the others do not. Salvia should be planted into the garden before it is in bloom for best results, so don't start seeds or buy plants too early.

What growing requirements do salvia have?

Salvia like full sun or partial shade and a rich, well-drained soil. Although they will tolerate dry soils, they do better if kept evenly watered. Salvia is very sensitive to fertilizer burn, so feed often, but very lightly, throughout the summer.

I have noticed that my salvia often reseed. Can I leave the seedlings in the garden beds?

Salvia does reseed under certain conditions, but the plants rarely grow large enough to bloom during the summer.

What are good varieties of salvia to shop for?

Look for tall Bonfire; stocky Carabiniere; early-blooming and heat-resistant Hotline; compact Red Hot Sally; and dwarf St. John's Fire. Good varieties of *S. farinacea* are Victoria and Rhea; there is also a white form.

Scarlet runner bean *(Phaseolus coccineus)*

Is the scarlet runner bean truly a bean?

Yes, it is. It is closely related to the snap bean, and the beans are edible. It is an excellent, and somewhat unusual, choice as a quick-growing annual vine to cover a trellis.

How do I grow scarlet runner bean?

After all frost danger has passed, plant the seeds outdoors where the plants are to grow. Choose a site with full sun and rich, moist, well-drained soil. Fertilize at planting time and again each month with an all-purpose fertilizer.

I grew scarlet runner bean last year, but after midsummer it produced no more flowers. What did I do wrong?

If you provided it with the sun and soil conditions it needs, it might have been that you did not remove the beans. Keep the beans picked as soon as they form to encourage the plant to continue producing its red flowers.

Scarlet sage. See Salvia.

Scabiosa. See Pincushion flower.

Snapdragon *(Antirrhinum majus)*

When should I plant snapdragons?

Seeds should be started and grown under fluorescent tubes indoors six to eight weeks before planting outdoors. Do not cover the seeds as light is needed for germination. Set the young plants out in the spring when the ground has begun to warm up.

Why can't I grow snapdragons from seed outdoors? They never come up.

Choose a well-drained place where the soil is light and only moderately rich. In mid-spring, rake the soil until it is finely textured and free of stones and lumps. Sow the seed and cover it with sand not more than one-eighth inch deep; do not pack the sand hard. Cover the seedbed with burlap. As soon as the seed germinates, remove the protective burlap. Water regularly in dry weather.

What conditions do snapdragons require?

They should have full sun and a light, well-drained soil that is only moderately enriched. Early planting is advised for best bloom.

What is the best fertilizer and what is the preferred pH for snapdragons?

Incorporate peat moss or rotted or dehydrated manure when preparing the soil, which should be neutral or slightly alkaline. Add lime to correct the pH, if necessary. Feed the plants with liquid fertilizer when they come into flower, or apply a complete chemical fertilizer such as 5-10-5 around the plants.

Must snapdragons be supported by stakes at the time of planting? Mine were all in curlicues and staking them after they were eight or ten inches tall didn't help at all.

Put in stakes at the same time you set the young plants out, and then start tying them as soon as signs of flopping begin. You can also insert sturdy, branched twigs among the plants to provide support as they grow. In an open situation, in properly

Ann Reilly

Scarlet runner bean: This is an excellent, and somewhat unusual, quick-growing annual vine; its beans are edible.

Sturdy, branched twigs make excellent supports for snapdragons.

Snapdragon: Colorful and abundant, snapdragons will benefit from being pinched back when the seedlings are young.

Ann Reilly

prepared soil, they should not need much support. Some varieties are low-growing and base-branching and do not require staking.

Can you tell me how to grow snapdragons in Mississippi? I buy plants and they bloom for a little while, then die.

It may be too warm or shady or perhaps your soil is too rich, too heavy and claylike, or poorly drained. Snapdragons like an open situation, light soil, and not too much feeding. They dislike heat and bloom best in cool weather, although some of the newer hybrids are more heat-resistant. Do not overcrowd snapdragons as this encourages disease.

How can I encourage snapdragons to send up more stems so I will have more blooms?

When you plant snapdragons, pinch them to induce branching. After the flower spikes have faded on the first bloom, remove them immediately to encourage a second bloom.

What are the best snapdragons for the garden? I haven't had good luck with "snaps" recently.

By all means get rust-resistant kinds. Good dwarf varieties are Floral Carpet and Kilibri, both growing six to eight inches tall. Little Darling grows a bit taller, twelve to fifteen inches high. Bright Butterflies and Madame Butterfly grow twenty-four to thirty inches tall, and Rocket is the tallest at thirty to thirty-six inches; it is also the most heat-resistant. Coronet is a medium-sized plant that is rust-resistant and weather-tolerant.

I live in Texas. What causes snapdragons to wilt and die?

Southern blight, cotton root rot, verticillium wilt, stem rot, and some other diseases. Remove diseased plants. Try new plants in a different location.

Spider flower *(Cleome Hasslerana)*

I have seen lovely pink and white spider plants. Are they something special?

Rose Queen is a fine variety that won a silver medal for excellence. Helen Campbell and White Queen are both a pure white.

I don't like the purplish-red spider flowers that self-seed into my beds and borders. How can I avoid them?

Take care to pull up all unwanted colors before they go to seed.

Will spider flowers grow in the hot, dry climate of Arizona?

In fact, spider flowers like these growing conditions. Give them full sun and fertilize little, if any.

Do spider flowers need to be staked?

No. Although they grow quite tall — three to six feet — they have strong stems and do not need to be staked. They are quite attractive when allowed to sway in gentle breezes.

Spurge *(Euphorbia* species)

I thought euphorbias were houseplants, but I have heard there are some that are good garden plants. What are these?

There are several euphorbias that grow well in the annual garden. They do not flower, but are grown for their highly colored bracts, some of which actually resemble flowers. The annual poinsettia, *E. cyathophora*, has red bracts like the holiday plant. Snow-on-the-mountain, *E. marginata*, is another euphorbia, with bracts of white or green edged with white.

How do I grow euphorbia?

For best results, start seeds indoors six to eight weeks before the last spring frost, or buy bedding plants. They need only average soil, and, in fact, will grow well even in poor soils, but they need full sun. Water them very lightly, and do not fertilize. All varieties tolerate high heat and humidity.

I have heard that these plants are poisonous. Is this true?

The plants are not lethal, but their sap can be irritating to the skin.

Statice *(Limonium* species)

I thought statice was a perennial, yet I see it listed as an annual. Which is it?

There are both annual and perennial forms of statice. In areas too cold for the perennial types, those, too, can be grown as annuals if started indoors eight to ten weeks before planting outside. Give all statice full sun and light soil.

Can I grow statice at my beach house?

Yes, statice tolerates full sun, heat, dry soil, and even salt spray.

Stock *(Matthiola incana)*

What causes stock to mature without blooming?

It may have been common stock, a biennial that does not flower until the second year. Look for varieties that are classified as seven-week or ten-week stock, which is the amount of time after germination it takes for the plant to bloom. These include Trysomic Seven Week blend, Giant Imperial, Midget, Dwarf Ten Week, and Beauty of Nice, which are types that branch freely,

Ann Reilly

Spider flower: Although striking spider flowers grow quite tall, their stems are sturdy and usually do not need staking.

and Giant Excelsior, which grows in a columnar form. All of these should be started in early spring, for they require cool growing weather.

Of one hundred ten-week stock plants in our garden, only the twenty smallest and frailest bloomed. The other eighty grew beautiful foliage from early summer until a hard freeze came, but they bloomed. Why?

Ten-week stock usually fails to bloom if subjected to constantly high temperatures of 60° F. and over. Yours must have been grown under borderline conditions, enabling a few individuals to bloom. Next time, try the Trysomic seven-week stock, which is more heat-tolerant.

How can I make stocks bloom? I live in New Jersey.

Buy Trysomic seven-week stock seed and start it indoors in March in order to set plants outside late in April. This enables them to make their growth before hot weather comes.

How do I start stock seed indoors?

Start seeds indoors six to eight weeks before the outdoor planting date. Do not cover the seed; it needs light to germinate.

Can stock seed be started outdoors?

Yes, but success will be limited. If you live in a climate with mild winters, you can sow stock outdoors in the fall with generally good luck.

What growing conditions do stocks like?

Plant them in full sun and a light, rich, well-drained soil. Fertilize prior to planting and again every month during the growing period. Keep them well watered. To prolong the blooming period, keep flowers picked as they fade.

What is the best place in the garden to plant stocks?

Plant stock where its lovely fragrance will be enjoyed, such as along the patio or under windows. A close relative of stock is the evening-scented stock, *M. longipetala*, which does not have as pretty a flower, but has an overwhelmingly sweet fragrance.

Why can't I raise good-looking stocks in California? Mine are always spindly and buggy. Even when I spray them, they are small and sickly.

Stocks in California suffer from several diseases. Young seedlings get a bacterial wilt, which can be prevented by immersing seed in hot water held at 130° F. for ten minutes and planting in a different location from past plantings. A fungus crown rot appears on overwatered, poorly drained soil; mosaic stunts the plants. Remove the infected plants and spray to control aphids with malathion or insecticidal soap.

What can be done to control stem rot on stock?

Stem and root rot are caused by a soil fungus that yellows the lower leaves, girdles the stem, causing wilting, and rots the roots. Since the fungus spreads for several feet through the soil away from the plant, it is not removed by taking up diseased plants and surrounding soil. Plant in a new location.

Strawflower *(Helichrysum bracteatum)*

I'd like to grow some strawflowers for drying. What advice can you give me?

If you grow them from seeds, do not cover the seeds: They need light to germinate. You will have the greatest success if you live where there are long, hot, sunny summers.

Summer forget-me-not. See Anchusa.

Summer poinsettia. See Amaranthus.

Sunflower *(Helianthus annuus)*

I would like to grow sunflowers in the garden, but do not have the room for the tall sunflowers I have seen in the Midwest.

The tall sunflower *H. giganteus*, reaching twelve feet in height, is a perennial that is often grown as an annual. For a lower-

Sunflower: Even in places where there is no room for the traditional tall annual, a cheery sunflower can be enjoyed in dwarf varieties such as this Pygmy Dwarf.

Ann Reilly

growing sunflower, choose *H. annuus*. Many of these grow four to six feet tall, but there are some varieties that are quite dwarf. The taller varieties include Italian White and Sunburst Mixed; lower-growing varieties are Sunbright and Teddy Bear.

Should I start sunflower seeds indoors?

Because sunflower germinates and grows quite quickly, it is not necessary to begin it indoors. Sow seeds outdoors where the plants are to grow after all danger of frost has passed.

My sunflowers did not bloom well last year. What was wrong?

You may have overfertilized, or the summer may have been too cool; they prefer high temperatures. Do not fertilize sunflowers, and do not give them too much water.

Swan River daisy *(Brachycome iberidifolia)*

I planted Swan River daisy last year, but the blooms lasted only a few weeks and the plant did not rebloom. Were the growing conditions unsuitable?

Maybe not. Swan River daisy is not a long-blooming plant. Add plants or seeds to the garden every three weeks to ensure continuous bloom all summer.

How do I grow Swan River daisy?

If you start your own seeds indoors, sow them four to six weeks before the last expected frost. Set plants into the garden or sow seeds after all danger of frost has passed.

Will Swan River daisy grow well in my garden in Georgia in summer?

No, your area is too hot, but it can be used in the spring where you live. Plant Swan River daisy in full sun in a warm soil, rich in organic matter. Keep it well watered and mulch to keep the soil moist and cool.

Sweet alyssum *(Lobularia maritima)*

Why does white sweet alyssum come up year after year, but purple varieties don't?

The white alyssum reseeds itself prolifically, but the seeds of the purple varieties are not as vigorous and are of more complex parentage.

What are the best varieties of sweet alyssum for the garden?

White Carpet of Snow is excellent, and Snow Cloth is similar but more compact and earlier to bloom. Rose-pink Rosie O'Day

Swan River daisy: For continuous bloom throughout the summer, make successive plantings of Swan River daisy at three week intervals.

is more heat-resistant than the others. Royal Carpet has deep violet flowers and grows taller than most.

How are sweet alyssum seeds germinated?

Start seeds indoors four to six weeks before the last spring frost, or where plants are to grow several weeks before the last spring frost. Do not cover the seeds; they need light toerminate. Sweet alyssum is very prone to damping-off disease, so be careful not to overwater or overcrowd the seedlings.

What is the best way to grow sweet alyssum?

Plant in full sun or partial shade in average soil, and do not overfertilize. It should be kept moist, although it will tolerate drought. It does best where nights are cool. Although it will grow successfully in hot areas, it may not flower as much.

By midsummer, my sweet alyssum always starts to get leggy. What can I do?

Cut it back: The plants will stay more compact and flower more freely.

Where should I plant sweet alyssum in the garden?

Sweet alyssum is very fragrant, so plant it along the patio or by the front door where you will enjoy its scent. Sweet alyssum is excellent as a border plant or cascading over the sides of a container.

Sweet pea (*Lathyrus odoratus*)

How should I go about planting sweet peas?

Cool temperatures, about 50° F., are needed for germination and good growth of sweet peas. Sow seeds in a cold greenhouse or cold frame a month or more ahead of the time when the frost can be expected to be out of the ground. For best results, use individual peat pots or Jiffy-7 pots, planting one seed per pot. Place them in a cool, sunny window or, after germination, under fluorescent tubes. You may also sow seeds where plants are to grow, as early as the ground can be worked in the spring.

Sweet pea: The seeds of sweet peas need cool temperatures for germination.

Can I plant sweet peas in the fall?

If you have a frost-free cold frame, you can sow the seed in September or October in a flat or in small pots placed in the cold frame; in March, transplant the seedlings to their permanent location. Or, if you have a cool porch or window (temperature not above 45° to 50° F.), you can sow seeds in February and shift them into pots after they have germinated. Harden the plants (see pg. 180), and set them in the garden in late March. If neither of these techniques is possible, sow them where they are to flower as early in March as you can. You can get a head start by preparing the ground the preceding fall.

Can sweet peas be planted in very early spring if the ground softens to a depth of two inches?

No; the soil will be too muddy to work. Wait until all the frost is out of the ground.

What is the planting date for sweet peas in Oklahoma?

Sow in November and give protection during the coldest part of winter; or sow in late winter, as soon as it is possible to work the soil.

I have had trouble germinating sweet pea seeds. Do you have any suggestions?

Sweet pea seeds have a very hard seed coat. Soak seed in water for twenty-four hours before sowing, or nick the seed coats with a small file. Be sure the seeds are completely covered, as they need darkness to germinate.

How shall I prepare the ground for sweet peas for cut flowers?

Dig a trench one and one-half feet wide and equally deep. Mix with the soil a three- to four-inch layer of compost and rotted manure or peat moss; and bone meal or superphosphate at the rate of one pound for every ten to fifteen linear feet. If possible, do this in the fall so the seeds can be planted without delay early in the spring.

I want sweet peas in clumps in a flower border. How do I go about it?

Prepare the soil as described above except that instead of a long trench, you should make circular planting stations two to three feet in diameter. Support the peas on brushwood or a cylinder of chicken-wire netting held up by four or five stakes. Or use a dwarf variety such as Little Sweetheart.

How deep should sweet pea seeds be planted, and how far apart should the plants be left?

Sweet peas are usually sown about two inches deep. You may also sow them in a six-inch-deep trench and cover them at first with two inches of soil. As the plants increase in stature, gradually fill in the trench. This technique works well in sandy soils. Thin the plants to stand about four inches apart.

How early must I place the supports for sweet pea vines?

When they are about four inches high. If left until they topple over, they never seem to grow as well as they do when staked early. Twiggy branches stuck in on both sides of the row, or in among the plants if they are grown in clumps, make good supports, but chicken-wire netting or strings supported by a frame will do.

Can you give me some general-care instructions for sweet peas?

Full, or nearly full, sun is best; some shade is tolerated. The soil should be deep, well-drained, rich, and well-supplied with humus. Be sure the soil is neutral or somewhat alkaline — never acid. Keep weeded and cultivated; water regularly; feed weekly with liquid fertilizer after the buds begin to show.

Should I use commercial fertilizer on sweet peas?

Apply commercial fertilizers, according to the manufacturer's directions, along the sides of the row after the plants are four inches high.

I have very healthy-looking sweet pea vines but no blossoms. Why?

The soil may be deficient in phosphorus, or the vines may have been planted too late for buds to open before the hot weather blasted them.

How can the blooming season of outdoor sweet peas be prolonged?

Pick the flowers as fast as they mature and shade plants from the hot sun with cheesecloth or similar material. Water them regularly and abundantly. Hot weather usually limits the season.

Sweet peas that are planted in November in Virginia often make some winter growth or early-spring growth. Is it advisable to cut this top growth and let the base of the plant start new and tender growth?

Yes, pinch the growth back to where the stem shows signs of sprouting at the base. This later growth produces better flowers.

Is there any way to keep birds from eating my sweet peas as they come up?

Because birds are afraid of snakes, lay a few pieces of snake-like garden hose or rope, or a rubber snake, alongside the rows to frighten them away. You can also try covering the plants with cheesecloth, or running strings hung with strips of white rags along the bed.

Which varieties of sweet peas are the best for our hot, dry Kansas climate? What is the best method of planting?

Sweet peas rarely succeed outdoors in a hot, dry climate unless sown very early. Your best chance is to plant in early

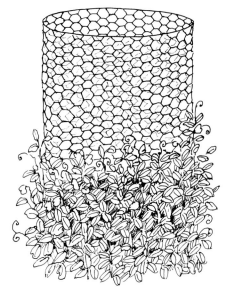

Provide support such as this chicken-wire cylinder for sweet peas.

spring, keep plants well watered, and shade them from direct sun with cheesecloth. There are, as far as is known, no varieties especially adapted to your conditions. The giant heat-resistant and spring-flowering types are effective, but need abundant moisture.

I have never been successful in Oklahoma with sweet peas, my favorite flower. I get about three bouquets and then the plants die. Can you help me? I have used a number of methods with no success.

Maybe the summer sun is too much for them; try shading the plants with cheesecloth as soon as really hot, dry weather sets in. Water thoroughly and regularly. Try preparing the soil and sowing in November or December (see page 273). Select heat-resistant strains from catalogs.

I understand there are two different types of sweet peas. What are they?

Sweet peas come in two forms: the annual vines can climb to six feet, whereas bush types grow twenty-four to thirty inches tall. Royal Family is a heat-resistant vining type; Bijou and Supersnoop are compact plants that grow about two feet high.

Will treating the soil prevent the blighting of sweet peas?

Soaking the soil with a benomyl solution before planting will help in the control of various root rot diseases that cause wilting or blighting of the plants.

What causes sweet peas to wilt just below the flower buds? The whole plant then turns greenish white and dies.

A fungus disease called anthracnose, common on outdoor sweet peas, has this effect. The fungus also causes a disease of apples. It lives during the winter in cankered limbs and mummied apples, as well as on sweet pea pods and seed and soil debris. Spray with benomyl biweekly during the growing season. Clean up all plant refuse in the fall. Plant only those seeds that appear sound and plump.

Why do my sweet peas develop a curled and puckered appearance? I plant on new ground each year, treat seeds with fungicide, and give plenty of moisture.

This is probably mosaic, carried from plant to plant by aphids. Virus diseases are common in the Northwest in particular, and there is nothing you can do except try to control aphids by sprays and remove infected plants promptly.

Tahoka daisy *(Machaeranthera tanacetifolia)*

My Tahoka daisy seeds did not germinate. What could the problem have been?

Tahoka daisy needs cold treatment to germinate, so sow seeds outdoors in early spring as soon as the soil can be worked, or chill seeds in the refrigerator for two weeks before sowing (see stratification, pg. 167). In mild areas, sow seeds in fall for spring germination and bloom.

Is it true that Tahoka daisy must have a cool climate?

Yes, and a dry one, too. Water and fertilize sparingly. Plant in full sun.

Toadflax. See Linaria.

Tree mallow. See Lavatera.

Tuberous begonia. See Begonia, tuberous.

Verbena *(Verbena x hybrida)*

How can I raise verbenas? I have not had much luck with them in Kansas.

Verbenas are not easy to raise unless you have adequate facilities, and the seed is variable in its germination. Because verbena requires a long season, sow seeds ten to twelve weeks before planting outside. Verbena seeds also benefit from being chilled in the refrigerator for seven days prior to sowing (see stratification, pg. 167). Verbena is very prone to damping-off disease, so be sure to use sterile sowing medium. Do not overcrowd seedlings and do not overwater. During germination and early growth, keep them at a temperature of 60° F. at night and 70 to 75° F. during the day. After the first true leaves appear (see pg. 165), transplant seedlings into flats containing a commercial soilless mix or equal parts of sterile loam, sand, leaf mold, and rotted or dehydrated manure or compost. When plants are established (about ten days), harden off the plants in a cold frame before planting them outside. Set them out in the ground when the danger of frost is past.

Which verbena varieties will do best in my garden?

Some verbenas grow upright whereas other varieties form a spreading ground cover. Ideal Florist, a vigorous older variety, is available in a good mixture of many colors. Romance has spreading plants that do not stretch, a breakthrough for verbenas. Showtime is also a spreading type, and one of the most heat-tolerant, with better germination than most verbenas. Sparkle is a mixture of bright colors, but has poor germination.

Verbena: These colorful annuals thrive in hot weather, even in infertile soil.

Ann Reilly

Springtime has a spreading habit, flowers early, and has a high germination rate. Trinidad, a dazzling pink, grows upright.

What type of growing conditions do verbenas like in the garden?

Grow in full sun in a light, rich, well-drained soil. Verbena is one of the best annuals to grow where it is hot and where the soil is infertile. Fertilize monthly with a soluble fertilizer.

Wax begonia. See Begonia, wax.

Wishbone flower *(Torenia Fournieri)*

What does wishbone flower look like?

It is an attractive little plant that is very bushy and has purple, lavender, and gold flowers similar to miniature snapdragons. Its foliage turns plum-colored in late autumn.

How do I grow wishbone flower from seed?

Seeds should be started indoors ten to twelve weeks before the last spring frost, when seedlings should be transferred to the garden.

Can I grow wishbone flower in the sun?

Only in cool climates, where night temperatures are below 65° F. Otherwise, grow it in partial or full shade, in a rich, moist, well-drained soil. Feed lightly.

Zinnia *(Zinnia elegans)*

How should zinnias be used in the flower garden?

Zinnias come in such diverse sizes and flower forms that they have many uses in the garden. Lower-growing varieties are excellent as borders or edgings. Taller types can be used at the back of the border, as tall hedges, or in the cutting garden. Zinnias also grow well in containers.

What are the best zinnia varieties to plant?

Border Beauty is a medium-sized plant with semi-double or double flowers. Cut & Come Again is a tall type, excellent as cut flowers. Dasher and Peter Pan are short, compact plants with large, double flowers. Pulcino, with semi-double flowers, is one of the most disease-resistant zinnias. Rose Pinwheel, with daisylike flowers, is very disease-resistant. Ruffles is a cutting type with ball-shaped flowers with ruffled petals. Small World has beehive-shaped flowers. State Fair has large flowers on tall plants; it is also disease-resistant. Thumbelina, with semi-double and double flowers, is one of the smallest zinnias.

Wishbone flower: The foliage of this bushy little plant turns plum color in late autumn.

Zinnia: One of a wide variety of sizes, colors, and shapes of zinnias, this Rose Pinwheel, a daisylike zinnia, is quite disease-resistant.

I have seen zinnias that are predominantly red-, yellow-, and mahogany-flowered. They are unlike other garden zinnias. What are they?

This is the Mexican zinnia, *A. Haageana.* Good varieties are Old Mexico and Persian Carpet.

What soil is best for zinnias?

Zinnias appreciate a fairly heavy, rich loam. Additions of rotted or dried manure, compost, or peat moss, plus commercial fertilizer, will produce sturdy plants. They prefer a neutral soil (pH 6 or higher).

What type of growing conditions do zinnias like?

Plant zinnias in full sun. Although they like hot, dry climates, they should be watered when the soil starts to dry out. Prevent mildew by watering in the morning and not getting foliage wet.

Is the middle of April too early to plant zinnia and marigold seeds outdoors in central Pennsylvania?

Yes, it is a few weeks too early — after danger of frost has passed, May 1 to May 15, would be better.

Should zinnias be transplanted?

Zinnias are very easily transplanted, but they can be sown, if desired, where they are to grow, and then be thinned out.

How should I grow zinnias for the cutting garden?

When you first plant them, pinch them back in order to encourage more growing stems. Even if you don't cut them for indoor use, keep flowers cut as they fade; this will keep the plants producing more blooms.

At the end of the summer, my zinnia leaves have a white, powdery covering on them and they sometimes develop black markings. What is the problem?

Zinnias are prone to mildew and leaf spot diseases. To reduce this problem, choose disease-resistant varieties, keep water off the foliage, and increase air circulation by giving the plants adequate space.

This year my zinnias have been badly infested with stem borers, but there were no marks or sawdust visible on the outside. I cannot find material telling their life cycle or control. Can you supply me with information?

These probably are the common stalk borers, although they are listed as general only east of the Rockies. They winter as eggs on weeds and old stalks, so that the chief control measure is getting rid of these.

Annuals Selection Guide

NAME	PLANTING DISTANCE	MAINTENANCE LEVEL	HEIGHT	LIGHT	MOISTURE	TEMPERATURE	HARDINESS
African daisy	8-10″	medium	10-12″	S	d	c	H
Ageratum	5-7″	low	4-6″	S,PSh	a-m	a	HH
Alternanthera	8-10″	low	4-6″	S	a	a	T
Amaranthus	15-18″	medium	18-36″	S	d	a-h	HH
Anchusa	8-10″	medium	8-10″	S	d-a	a-h	HH
Aster, China	6-18″	high	6-30″	S,PSh	m	a	HH
Baby-blue-eyes	8-12″	low	6-8″	S,LSh	a	c	HH
Baby's-breath	16-18″	medium	15-18″	S	d-a	a	HH
Balsam	10-15″	low	12-36″	S,PSh	m	h	T
Basil	6-8″	low	12-15″	S	a	a	T
Begonia, fibrous	7-9″	low	6-8″	S,PSh,Sh	a	a	HH
Begonia, tuberous	8-10″	low	8-10″	PSh,Sh	m	c-a	T
Bells-of-Ireland	10-12″	medium	24-36″	S,LSh	a	a	HH
Black-eyed Susan vine	12-15″	medium	3-6′	S,PSh	m	a	HH
Blue daisy	15-18″	medium	30-36″	S	d	c	HH
Blue lace flower	8-10″	medium	24-30″	S	a	c	HH
Browallia	8-10″	low	10-15″	PSh,Sh	m	c	HH
Calendula	8-10″	high	10-12″	S,LSh	m	c-a	H
California poppy	6-8″	low	12-24″	S	d-a	any	VH
Calliopsis	4-12″	medium	8-36″	S	d	a	HH
Campanula	12-15″	medium	18-36″	S,LSh	a-m	a	VH
Candytuft	7-9″	low	8-10″	S	d-a	any	HH
Cape marigold	4-6″	low	4-16″	S	d	c-a	HH
Castor bean	4-5′	low	5-8′	S	m	h	T
Celosia	6-8″	low	6-15″	S	d	a-h	HH
Chrysanthemum	4-18″	medium	4-36″	S	a-m	c-a	T
Cineraria	10-12″	high	12-18″	PSh,S	m	c	HH
Clarkia	8-10″	high	18-24″	S,LSh	d-a	c	H
Coleus	8-10″	low	10-24″	PSh,Sh	a-m	a-h	T
Cornflower	6-12″	medium	12-36″	S	d-a	a	VH
Cosmos	9-18″	medium	18-30″	S	d-a	a	HH

Maintenance level: a rough indication of the amount of care that will be required
Light: S = Full sun
      LSh = Light shade
      PSh = Part Shade
      Sh = Full shade
Moisture: d = dry
        a = average
        m = moist
Temperature: c = cool (below 70° F.)
           a = average
           h = hot (above 85° F.)
Hardiness: VH = very hardy, will withstand heavy frost
        H = hardy, will withstand light frost
        HH = half hardy, will withstand cool weather, but not frost
        T = tender, will do poorly in cool weather, will not withstand frost

NAME	PLANTING DISTANCE	MAINTENANCE LEVEL	HEIGHT	LIGHT	MOISTURE	TEMPERATURE	HARDINESS
Creeping zinnia	5-7″	medium	5-6″	S	d-a	a-h	HH
Dahlberg daisy	4-6″	low	4-8″	S	d-a	a-h	HH
Dahlia	8-10″	high	8-15″	S,LSh	a-m	a	T
Dianthus	7-9″	low	6-10″	S,PSh	a	c-a	HH
Dusty miller	6-8″	low	8-10″	S,PSh	d-a	a-h	HH
English daisy	6-8″	medium	4-6″	S,LSh	m	c	VH
Flowering cabbage/kale	15-18″	low	15-18″	S	m	c	VH
Forget-me-not	8-12″	low	6-12″	PSh	m	c	H
Four-o'clock	12-18″	low	18-36	S	d-a	any	T
Fuchsia	8-10″	high	12-24″	PSh,Sh	m	a	T
Gaillardia	8-15″	medium	10-18″	S,LSh	d-a	a-h	HH
Gazania	8-10″	high	6-10″	S	d-a	a-h	HH
Geranium	10-12″	high	10-15″	S	a-m	a	T
Gerbera	12-15″	medium	12-18″	S	m	a	HH
Globe amaranth	10-15″	medium	24-30″	S	d	h	T
Gloriosa daisy	12-18″	low	18-36″	S,LSh	a	a-h	HH
Hibiscus	24-30″	medium	48-60″	S,LSh	m	a	H
Hollyhock	18-24″	medium	2-8′	S,LSh	m	a	H
Ice plant	8-12″	low	6-8″	S	d	a-h	T
Immortelle	9-12″	medium	18-24″	S	a	a-m	T
Impatiens	8-10″	low	6-18″	PSh,Sh	m	a	T
Iresine	12-15″	low	6-8″	S	a	a	T
Ivy geranium	10-12″	medium	24-36″	S	a	a	T
Kingfisher daisy	3-4″	medium	6-8″	S	d	c	HH
Kochia	18-24″	low	24-36″	S	d	a-h	HH
Lantana	8-10″	medium	10-12″	S	a	a	T
Larkspur	12-36″	high	12-60″	S	m	c	HH
Lavatera	12-15″	medium	18-30″	S	d-a	a	H
Linaria	6-8″	low	8-12″	S,LSh	m	c	VH
Lisianthus	12-14″	high	24-30″	S	a	a-h	HH
Lobelia	8-10″	low	3-5″	S,PSh	m	c-a	HH
Love-in-a-mist	8-10″	medium	12-24″	S	a-m	c	VH
Marigold, African	12-15″	high	18-30″	S	a	a	HH
Marigold, French	3-6″	high	5-10″	S	a	a	HH
Mexican sunflower	24-30″	medium	48-60″	S	d	a-h	T
Mignonette	10-12″	medium	12-18″	S,LSh	m	c	VH
Money plant	12-15″	medium	30-36″	S,LSh	a	a	VH
Monkey flower	5-7″	low	6-8″	PSh,Sh	m	c	HH
Morning-glory	12-18″	medium	3-30′	S	d	a	T
Nasturtium	8-12″	low	12-24″	S,LSh	d	c-a	T
Nemesia	5-6″	high	8-18″	S,LSh	m	c	HH
New Guinea impatiens	10-12″	low	10-12″	S,LSh	m	a	T

NAME	PLANTING DISTANCE	MAINTENANCE LEVEL	HEIGHT	LIGHT	MOISTURE	TEMPERATURE	HARDINESS
Nicotiana	8-10″	low	12-15″	S,PSh	m	a-h	HH
Nierembergia	6-9″	low	4-6″	S,LSh	m	a	T
Nolana	12-15″	medium	5-6″	S,LSh	a	a	T
Ornamental pepper	5-7″	low	4-8″	S,PSh	m	a-h	HH
Pansy	6-8″	medium	4-8″	S,PSh	m	c	VH
Parsley	6-8″	low	12-18″	S,LSh	a	a	VH
Penstemon	12-18″	medium	24-30″	S	a	c	VH
Periwinkle	6-10″	low	4-12″	S,PSh	any	a-h	HH
Petunia	10-12″	medium	6-12″	S	d	a-h	HH
Phlox	7-9″	low	6-10″	S	m	c-a	H
Pincushion flower	10-15″	high	18-36″	S	a	a	T
Poor-man's orchid	10-12″	medium	12-24″	S,LSh	m	c	HH
Poppy	9-12″	high	12-36″	S	d	c-a	VH
Portulaca	6-8″	low	4-6″	S	d	h	T
Salpiglossis	10-12″	medium	18-24″	S	m	c	HH
Salvia	6-8″	low	12-24″	S,PSh	a-m	a-h	HH
Scarlet runner bean	2-4″	medium	8′	S	m	a	T
Snapdragon	6-8″	medium	6-15″	S	a	c-a	VH
Spider flower	12-15″	low	30-48″	S	d	a-h	HH
Spurge	10-12″	low	24-36″	S	d	a-h	T
Statice	12-24″	medium	12-36″	S	d	a-h	HH
Stock	10-12″	high	12-24″	S	m	c	H
Strawflower	7-9″	medium	15-24″	S	d	a-h	HH
Sunflower (dwarf)	12-24″	high	15-48″	S	d	h	T
Swan River daisy	5-6″	medium	12-18″	S	m	c	T
Sweet alyssum	10-12″	low	3-5″	S,PSh	a-m	a	H
Sweet pea	6-15″	medium	24-60″	S	m	c-a	H
Tahoka daisy	9-12″	medium	12-24″	S	d	c	VH
Verbena	5-7″	medium	6-8″	S	d-a	h	T
Wishbone flower	6-8″	low	8-12″	PSh,Sh	m	c	HH
Zinnia	4-18″	high	4-36″	S	d-a	a-h	T

Maintenance level: a rough indication of the amount of care that will be required
Light: S = Full sun
    LSh = Light shade
    PSh = Part Shade
    Sh = Full shade
Moisture: d = dry
    a = average
    m = moist
Temperature: c = cool (below 70° F.)
    a = average
    h = hot (above 85° F.)
Hardiness: VH = very hardy, will withstand heavy frost
    H = hardy, will withstand light frost
    HH = half hardy, will withstand cool weather, but not frost
    T = tender, will do poorly in cool weather, will not withstand frost

Annuals From Seed

ANNUAL	DAYS TO GERMINATE	BEGIN SEED INDOORS BEFORE PLANTING SEEDLINGS OUTDOORS (# OF WEEKS)	BEGIN SEED OUTDOORS BEFORE LAST FROST (# OF WEEKS)	MOVE SEEDLINGS OUTDOORS BEFORE LAST FROST (# OF WEEKS)
African daisy	21-35	6-8	4	4
Ageratum	5-10	6-8	last frost	last frost
Alternanthera	—	—	—	last frost
Amaranthus	10-15	3-4	last frost	last frost
Anchusa	14-21	6-8	last frost	last frost
Aster, China	10-14	6-8	last frost	last frost
Baby-blue-eyes	7-12	—	6-8	—
Baby's-breath	10-15	4-6	6	4
Balsam	8-14	6-8	last frost	last frost
Basil	7-10	6-8	last frost	last frost
Begonia, fibrous	15-20	10-12	—	last frost
Begonia, tuberous	15-20	12-16	—	last frost
Bells-of-Ireland	25-35	—	6-8	—
Black-eyed Susan vine	10-15	6-8	last frost	last frost
Blue daisy	25-35	10-12	6	4
Blue lace flower	15-20	6-8	last frost	last frost
Browallia	14-21	6-8	—	last frost
Calendula	10-14	4-6	6	4
California poppy	10-12	—	4-6	—
Calliopsis	5-10	6-8	last frost	last frost
Campanula	10-14	6-8	4	4
Candytuft	10-15	6-8	last frost	last frost
Cape marigold	10-15	4-5	last frost	last frost
Castor bean	15-20	6-8	last frost	last frost
Celosia	10-15	4-6	last frost	last frost
Chrysanthemum	10-18	8-10	last frost	last frost
Cineraria	10-15	24-26	—	4
Clarkia	5-10	—	last frost	—
Coleus	10-15	6-8	—	last frost
Cornflower	7-14	4-6	6	4
Cosmos	5-10	5-7	last frost	last frost
Creeping zinnia	10-15	—	last frost	—
Dahlberg daisy	10-15	6-8	—	last frost
Dahlia	5-10	4-6	last frost	last frost
Dianthus	5-10	8-10	last frost	last frost
Dusty miller	10-15	8-10	—	last frost
English daisy	10-15	6-8	6	4
Flowering cabbage and kale	10-18	6-8	—	last frost
Forget-me-not	8-14	6-8	6	4
Four-o'clock	7-10	4-6	last frost	last frost

ANNUAL	DAYS TO GERMINATE	BEGIN SEED INDOORS BEFORE PLANTING SEEDLINGS OUTDOORS (# OF WEEKS)	BEGIN SEED OUTDOORS BEFORE LAST FROST (# OF WEEKS)	MOVE SEEDLINGS OUTDOORS BEFORE LAST FROST (# OF WEEKS)
Fuchsia	21-26	24-26	—	last frost
Gaillardia	15-20	4-6	last frost	last frost
Gazania	8-14	4-6	last frost	last frost
Geranium	5-15	12-15	—	last frost
Gerbera	15-25	8-10	—	last frost
Globe amaranth	15-20	6-8	last frost	last frost
Gloriosa daisy	5-10	6-8	2	2
Hibiscus	15-20	6-8	last frost	last frost
Hollyhock	10-14	6-8	—	last frost
Ice plant	15-20	10-12	—	last frost
Immortelle	10-15	6-8	last frost	last frost
Impatiens	15-20	10-12	—	last frost
Iresine	—	—	—	last frost
Ivy geranium	5-15	12-16	—	last frost
Kingfisher daisy	25-35	10-12	6	4
Kochia	10-15	4-6	last frost	last frost
Lantana	40-45	12-14	—	last frost
Larkspur	8-15	6-8	4-6	4-6
Lavatera	15-20	—	4-6	—
Linaria	10-15	4-6	6	6
Lisianthus	15-20	28-32	—	last frost
Lobelia	15-20	10-12	—	last frost
Love-in-a-mist	10-15	4-6	6	4
Marigold, African	5-7	4-6	—	last frost
Marigold, French	5-7	4-6	last frost	last frost
Mexican sunflower	5-10	6-8	last frost	last frost
Mignonette	5-10	—	4-6	—
Money plant	10-14	6-8	4	2
Monkey flower	8-12	10-12	—	2
Morning-glory	5-7	4-6	last frost	last frost
Nasturtium	7-12	—	last frost	—
Nemesia	7-14	4-6	last frost	last frost
New Guinea impatiens	14-28	10-12	—	last frost
Nicotiana	10-20	6-8	last frost	last frost
Nierembergia	15-20	10-12	—	last frost
Nolana	7-10	4-6	last frost	last frost
Ornamental pepper	21-25	6-8	—	last frost
Pansy	10-20	6-8	—	4-6
Parsley	14-21	6-8	2-4	last frost
Penstemon	10-15	6-8	6-8	4

ANNUAL	DAYS TO GERMINATE	BEGIN SEED INDOORS BEFORE PLANTING SEEDLINGS OUTDOORS (# OF WEEKS)	BEGIN SEED OUTDOORS BEFORE LAST FROST (# OF WEEKS)	MOVE SEEDLINGS OUTDOORS BEFORE LAST FROST (# OF WEEKS)
Petunia	10-12	10-12	—	last frost
Phlox	10-15	—	6-8	—
Pincushion flower	10-15	4-5	last frost	last frost
Poor-man's orchid	20-25	10-12	—	last frost
Poppy	10-15	—	6-8	—
Portulaca	10-15	4-6	last frost	last frost
Salpiglossis	15-20	6-8	—	last frost
Salvia	12-15	6-8	—	last frost
Scarlet runner bean	6-10	—	last frost	—
Snapdragon	10-14	6-8	2	last frost
Spider flower	10-14	4-6	last frost	last frost
Spurge	10-15	6-8	last frost	last frost
Statice	15-20	8-10	last frost	last frost
Stock	7-10	6-8	last frost	last frost
Strawflower	7-10	4-6	last frost	last frost
Sunflower	10-14	—	last frost	—
Swan River daisy	10-18	4-6	—	last frost
Sweet alyssum	8-15	4-6	4	2
Sweet pea	20-30	—	6-8	—
Tahoka daisy	25-30	6-8	4-6	4-6
Verbena	20-25	12-14	—	last frost
Wishbone flower	15-20	10-12	—	last frost
Zinnia	5-7	4-6	last frost	last frost

PART IV
PERENNIALS

12 *Planning the Perennial Garden*

For the gardener who enjoys combining colors and textures to weave living tapestry, there is no better group of plants to work with than perennials. Favorite perennials—such as chrysanthemum, daylily, iris, and peony—which by definition, bloom in one season, die back in the winter, and then renew from the same roots each spring for at least several years, offer varying degrees of challenge and limitless possibilities. Their cost is reasonable, and results are fairly soon achieved. Garden designs can be changed frequently and relatively easily. Unlike the 100-foot long, eight- to ten-foot-wide perennial borders of the past, today's perennial gardens are greatly simplified, so care is minimal, yet the impact on the landscape is still maximized. For the smallest garden, where just a few species are used for accent, to the most ambitious, where massed plantings display dozens of varieties, perennials offer longevity as well as a beauty that is hard to achieve with annuals, shrubs, or bulbs alone.

ASSESSING YOUR SITE

Before trying to plan and plant perennials, you must first consider the growing environment that is available in your region and in your yard. The key factors are soil, moisture, light, and temperature. To garden successfully, you must have an understanding of the basics of each of these factors and their role in plant growth. To some extent, these factors can be modified,

◀ *Weave a living tapestry with the massed colors and textures of perennial flowers such as chrysanthemums.*

289

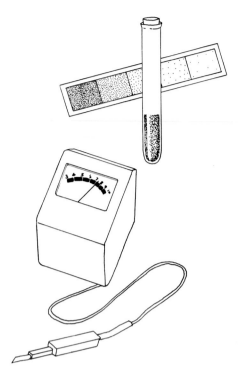

Determine the nutrient content and pH levels of your soil by testing your soil with readily available testing kits.

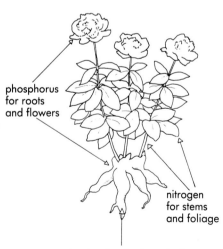

phosphorus for roots and flowers

nitrogen for stems and foliage

potassium for food production

Balanced garden fertilizers provide nitrogen (N) for foliage and stem growth, phosphorus (P) for root development and flower production, and potassium (K) for plant metabolism and food production.

but it makes sense to make the most of what you have and to select plants that will readily adapt to what is already there. Ways to modify each of the factors will be discussed in Chapter 14,"Planting and Caring for Perennials." First, let's take a look at the role of each of these factors and at which plants adapt best to various conditions.

Soil

How do I find out what kind of soil I have?

The simplest, most precise way is to have your soil tested by a commercial soil-testing laboratory or by the Cooperative Extension Service in your county. This agency is the educational arm of the U.S. Department of Agriculture. There is a branch in every county in the country, often affiliated with the State University. For information on taking the samples and where to send them, call your county's Cooperative Extension Service office. The results should tell you the type of soil you have, such as sandy or clay loam, the pH, and the status of the major nutrients, or levels of nitrogen, phosphorus, and potassium.

What type of soil do most perennials need?

Most perennials grow best in humus-rich soil that has a relatively even balance of clay, sand, and silt particles. This "perfect" soil is called loam. It will hold moisture for a reasonable length of time, yet drains quickly enough so that it does not remain soggy for very long after rain or watering.

What nutrient elements are essential for perennials?

The three elements essential to plant growth are nitrogen, phosphorus, and potassium, often referred to by their chemical symbols, N,P,K.

Nitrogen is part of the structure of protoplasm, chlorophyll, and various plant foods, and is needed for both the vegetative and reproductive stages of growth. *Phosphorus* is essential to cell division and for the formation of nucleoproteins; it aids root development, hastens maturity, stiffens tissues, and stimulates flower and seed production. *Potassium* (in the form of potash) is necessary for the manufacture and movement of starches and sugar; it is a general conditioner, overcoming succulence and brittleness, hastening maturity and seed production, and aiding in root development.

In layman's terms, what do each of the nutrients do for perennials?

Nitrogen is necessary for foliage and stem growth and for dark green leaf color. Phosphorus is necessary for root development and flower production. Potassium is necessary for plant metabolism and the production of food. For perennials, it is important that the second element, phosphorus, be higher than or equal to nitrogen. If it is not, you will have a lot of growth but few flowers.

What are trace elements?

Trace elements such as boron, chlorine, copper, iron, magnesium, manganese, molybdenum, and zinc are present in most soils and are needed in very small amounts for plant nutrition. When decaying organic matter is used freely and when pH is held between 6.0 and 6.9, you can be fairly certain these elements will be present.

What perennials tolerate relatively infertile soils?

The same plants that are tolerant of light, sandy soils listed below.

What is humus?

For practical purposes, humus may be defined as the resultant brown substance that develops following the breakdown of organic materials by various soil organisms.

In what forms is potential humus available to the average home gardener?

Well-rotted manure, peat moss, decomposed kitchen waste, seaweed, sawdust, wood chips, pine needles, leaf mold, straw, or hay. The compost pile is probably the best of all sources of humus for the home gardener, but look around your area—there may be more possibilities than you realize.

Maggie Oster

Yucca and Autumn Joy stonecrop are two easy-to-grow perennials that tolerate light, sandy soils.

PERENNIALS THAT TOLERATE LIGHT, SANDY SOILS

baby's-breath	globe thistle	sea holly
basket-of-gold	golden marguerite	spider wort
blackberry lily	goldenrod	spurge
blanket flower	hardy aster	sundrops
blue stars	hardy pinks	sunrose
butterfly flower	hen-and-chickens	stonecrop
candytuft	hollyhock mallow	thrift
Carolina lupine	lamb's ears	tickseed
catmint	Maltese cross	torch lily
coneflower	purple rockcress	wormwood
daylily	Russian sage	yarrow
false indigo	sage	yucca
gay-feather		

PERENNIALS THAT TOLERATE HEAVY, CLAY SOILS

bear's-breech	Greek valerian	ragwort
bee balm	hardy aster	saxifrage
bugleweed	lady's-mantle	self-heal
coneflower	leopard's-bane	sneezeweed
daylily	loosestrife	Solomon's-seal
foxglove	meadow rue	spotted dead nettle
goatsbeard	mist flower	windflower
goldenrod	purple loosestrife	

•

What is the function of humus in the soil?

Humus affects granulation of the soil, thereby improving drainage and soil aeration; increases the soil's water-holding capacity; increases bacterial activity in the soil; increases the percentage of such essential elements as nitrogen and sulfur; and helps to make nonavailable, essential elements available to plants.

What is pH?

The term pH refers to the measurement of the concentration of the hydrogen ion in a given substance on a scale from 0 to 14. The midpoint, of pH 7, is considered neutral, while those numbers less than seven are considered in the range of acidity and the numbers above seven in the range of alkalinity. The small pH test kits sold in garden centers are adequate and usually give a reading within a tenth of a point or so.

Why is pH important?

First, certain nutrients can be absorbed by plants only within specific pH ranges. Second, the activity of soil microorganisms is affected by pH, ceasing entirely at pH 4.0 and below. Another effect of pH is the release of toxic elements, such as aluminum, at both a low pH and a high pH value. The prevalence of certain diseases is also affected by pH.

What pH is best for most plants?

The point at which all elements are available to plants except those that require highly acid soil is pH 6.5. At neutral (7.0), acidity and alkalinity balance each other out. Thus, somewhere between 6.0 and 7.0 is perhaps the best point to strive for when you alter soil acidity.

Anemone may be grown in heavy, clay soils.

What are some perennials that grow well on acid soils of fair to good fertility (pH 5.0 to 5.5)?

Butterfly flower, gentian, *Iris ensata,* lupine, Virginia blue-bells, primrose, and violet.

What are some perennials that do not grow well on strongly acid soils, but prefer slightly acid to neutral soils (pH 6.5 to 7.0)?

Baby's-breath, basket-of-gold, bear's-breech, bellflower, betony, blue plumbago, campion, candytuft, catmint, chrysanthemum, cupid's-dart, daylily, delphinium, desert-candle, flax, foxglove, gas plant, globe thistle, golden marguerite, hardy aster, hardy pinks, hen-and-chickens, iris, lavender cotton, lobelia, Oriental poppy, ornamental onion, pearly everlasting, perennial cornflower, perennial sunflower, perennial sweet pea, phlox, purple rockcress, red valerian, Russian sage, sage, saxifrage, sea holly, snow-in-summer, stonecrop, sunrose, thrift, tickseed, toadflax, torch lily, yarrow.

Moisture

What is the role of water in plant growth?

Water is vital to healthy growth, as plants are ninety percent water; water is also necessary for absorption of nutrients.

Why is excess water a problem?

Roots are incapable of absorbing water and nutrients unless oxygen is also present in the soil. A plant top can actually wilt for lack of water while its roots are completely submerged. The ideal soil is one that can absorb abundant water in its organic substances, but also one in which the passages between the organic and mineral particles are filled with air.

Will you explain the terms "well-drained soil" and "waterlogged soil"?

A well-drained soil is one in which surplus water runs off quickly and which dries out readily after a rain or watering. A waterlogged soil is the opposite, containing too much water and little air. Soil can become waterlogged if it contains too much peat moss.

Stonecrops are among the plants that tolerate drought conditions.

Ann Reilly

Why would a loose, crumbly loam stay soggy?

Possibly there is a problem with drainage beneath the topsoil, in the subsoil layer. This can be corrected by having drainage tiles installed or by constructing raised beds.

What are some perennials that tolerate drought conditions?

Baby's-breath, basket-of-gold, bishop's hat, blanket flower, bleeding-heart, butterfly flower, campion, candytuft, catmint, foxglove, gayfeather, golden marguerite, hardy aster, hen-and-chickens, hollyhock mallow, lamb's ears, lily-of-the-valley, lily-turf, purple rockcress, rue, Russian sage, saxifrage, sea holly, Solomon's-seal, spotted dead nettle, spurge, stonecrop, sundrops, sunrose, tickseed, thrift, yarrow, yucca.

What are some perennials that tolerate wet soils?

Astilbe, avens, bee balm, daylily, forget-me-not, globeflower, goatsbeard, hardy aster, *Iris ensata*, lobelia, loosestrife, marsh marigold, plantain lily, primrose, purple loosestrife, queen-of-the-prairie, rose mallow, Siberian iris, snake grass, Virginia bluebells.

Light

How much sunlight do most perennials need?

Most common perennials do best in full sunlight, but there are many that can get by quite well if they receive only a half day of full sun. The shady period of the day should come from a vertical surface, such as a wall, hedge, or building, rather than from a tree, which offers root competition as well as shade.

How does exposure to sun affect blooming?

In various ways, depending on characteristics unique to certain plants. For example, a plant like chrysanthemum may bloom earlier if grown with afternoon shade because diminishing light conditions trigger its flowering mechanism. Conversely, other plants, such as peonies, grown with afternoon shade may bloom later in spring. Also, some flower colors, like the red or pink blooms of daylilies, are "washed out" in bright light.

Do light requirements differ for gardens farther north?

Most definitely. A plant that needs a location with full sun in the north may need light shade in order to grow well in southern climates. This is due both to the intensity of the light as well as to temperature. Also, midsummer days in the south are shorter than those in the north. Because they receive more light in the north, plants grow more quickly there.

What are some perennials that grow in the heaviest shade?

Bishop's hat, bleeding-heart, bugleweed, Christmas rose, foxglove, lily-of-the-valley, lily-turf, plantain lily, saxifrage, Siberian bugloss, Solomon's-seal, spotted dead nettle, violet.

What are some perennials that tolerate light shade?

Astilbe, bear's-breech, bee balm, bellflower, blue plumbago, bugbane, columbine, coralbells, creeping phlox, daylily, globeflower, goatsbeard, lady's-mantle, leopard's-bane, lobelia, loosestrife, lungwort, meadow rue, meadowsweet, primrose, Siberian iris, spurge, Virginia bluebells, windflower.

Temperature

What are hardiness zones?

The United States Department of Agriculture classifies regions of the country according to annual minimum temperatures and/or the length of growing seasons. These range from the near-tundra Zone 1 to the subtropical Zone 10, which seldom has frost. Rather than listing the hardiness zones with the plants in this book, the minimum winter temperature is given instead.

Do summer temperatures also affect plant growth and flowering?

Lupine, pink and red yarrow, and purple loosestrife all grow well in regions as far south as those with minimum winter temperatures of only 20° F.

Most definitely. Gardeners in the south face heat, humidity, and drought in the summer. In those conditions, plants may require frequent watering and light shade, as well as humus-rich

Maggie Oster

soils and a summer mulch to help them stay cooler. Windbreaks give valuable protection from hot, drying winds. Plants may go dormant in August, but then have a long fall season.

What are some perennials that grow best in areas that have cool summers?

Astilbe, beard-tongue, bleeding-heart, Christmas rose, columbine, delphinium, ferns, lupine, meadow rue, and primrose.

What are some perennials that will grow well as far south as areas with a minimum winter temperature of 20° F.?

Avens, balloon flower, beard-tongue, bear's-breech, bee balm, bellflower, blanket flower, bleeding-heart, blue plumbago, blue stars, bugbane, butterfly flower, campion, chrysanthemum, coneflower, coralbells, daylily, false indigo, foxglove, gay-feather, globe thistle, goatsbeard, golden marguerite, goldenrod, iris, lamb's-ears, meadowsweet, phlox, pincushion flower, plantain lily, purple coneflower, purple loosestrife, orange sunflower, ornamental grasses, rose mallow, sage, saxifrage, Siberian bugloss, snake grass, speedwell, spurge, Stokes' aster, stonecrop, sunrose, thrift, tickseed, torch lily, Virginia bluebells, wormwood, yarrow.

Why would a plant, supposedly hardy in a certain region, not live through winter?

There are several reasons, and soil temperature, rather than air temperature, is the more critical factor. Hardy perennials may die if there is no insulating snow cover or if alternate periods of freezing and thawing occur, causing plants to be heaved out of the ground. This can often be prevented by using a winter mulch.

What kinds of materials are good for mulching perennials in the winter?

Place leaves, straw, or wood chips around the plants, but not up against the crown (the point where stem and roots merge), to help to protect the roots. Place evergreen boughs over the crown of the plant.

When mulching with leaves or straw, leave a space around the crown of the plant, then cover the plant lightly with evergreen boughs.

Do late-blooming perennials present special problems?

Yes, because even if a plant is winter hardy, some, such as asters, chrysanthemums, gentians, rose mallow, and windflowers, may not bloom before the first autumn frosts.

What are some perennials that are the most tolerant of severe winter temperatures (-30° F. or below)?

Baby's-breath, balloon flower, basket-of-gold, bellflower (some species), blanket flower, bleeding-heart, blue stars, bugbane, bugleweed, bugloss, butterfly flower, Carolina lupine, catmint, coneflower, coralbells, gas plant, gay-feather, globe thistle, goatsbeard, golden marguerite, Greek valerian, leopard's-bane, lobelia, lungwort, mallow, Maltese cross, meadowsweet, mist flower, monkshood, Oriental poppy, ornamental onion, painted daisy, pearly everlasting, peony, perennial cornflower, phlox, pincushion flower, plantain lily, plume poppy, purple coneflower, purple loosestrife, Siberian iris, sneezeweed, snow-on-the-mountain, speedwell, stonecrop, tickseed, turtlehead, Virginia bluebells, wormwood, yarrow.

CONSIDERING THE PLANTS' CHARACTERISTICS

Once you have assessed your site for the factors of soil, moisture, light, and temperature, the next step is to consider the plants themselves. This, too, has several aspects, including height, bloom season, color, shape, texture, and growth habit (how much the plant spreads).

Height and Season of Bloom

How do I arrange plants in a new perennial border?

Essentially, you should think of a flower border as a group photo. The taller plants go in the back, midsize ones toward the center, and the shorter plants in the front, or foreground. In an island bed, the taller plants are toward the center, with medium and short plants on either side. However, for flower beds and borders to appear most natural and pleasing, there should be some overlap among the various heights.

Are there other factors with regard to height that I should think about?

Yes, consider that some perennials are cut back after flowering; so, a plant that is tall in bloom, such as delphinium, may be much shorter when the faded flowers are removed. Or, conversely, for most of the summer, plantain lilies are low, rounded plants, but in late summer they send up spikes of flowers. Complicating this whole process are the facts that some cultivars of one species grow taller than other cultivars of the same species and that mature height depends greatly on soil, light, moisture, and climate. (A *species* is the fundamental classification, including individuals that resemble one another and can breed together, but not usually with plants of other species. *Cultivars*—cultivated varieties, sometimes called varieties—are subdivisions of the species that have been bred together and maintain their characteristics under continued cultivation.)

The sequence of bloom is another major factor in the design of a perennial garden. Many gardeners like to design their flower gardens to have blossoms from early spring until fall frosts. This

Plan your flower beds so that tall plants are in the back, midsize ones toward the center, and short plants in the front, with some overlap among the various heights for the most pleasing effect.

Periods of Bloom and Relative Heights
of Selected Perennials

TALL (4 feet or more)	MEDIUM (1-4 feet)	SHORT (1 foot or less)
SPRING		
columbine	catmint	basket-of-gold
dame's-rocket	cranesbill	bleeding-heart
globeflower	early daylily	(Dicentra exima)
Japanese bleeding-heart	flax	candytuft
leopard's-bane	sweet William	creeping phlox
Maltese-cross	Virginia bluebells	dwarf iris
mountain bluet		primrose
painted daisy		purple rockcress
Siberian iris		rock cress
sneezeweed		violet
spurge		
EARLY SUMMER		
Carolina lupine	astilbe	Carpathian harebell
daylily	avens	coralbells
delphinium	beard-tongue	
false indigo	bellflower	
foxglove	butterfly flower	
gas plant	cranesbill	
German iris	daylily	
globe thistle	golden marguerite	
lupine	Oriental poppy	
mallow	painted daisy	
peony	perennial cornflower	
	speedwell	
MID- TO LATE SUMMER		
baby's-breath	astilbe	flax
bee balm	balloon flower	lamb's ears
bugbane	blanket flower	sea lavender
daylily	campion	Stokes' aster
false starwort	coneflower	
gay-feather	globe thistle	
monkshood	phlox	
phlox	plantain lily	
purple loosestrife	shasta daisy	
rose mallow	torch lily	
sneezeweed	turtlehead	
LATE SUMMER AND FALL		
bugbane	blanket flower	dwarf aster
false starwort	blue plumbago	dwarf chrysanthemum
hardy aster	chrysanthemum	dwarf stonecrop
lobelia	coneflower	
mist flower	mist flower	
monkshood	sage	
perennial sunflower	speedwell	
phlox	stonecrop	
rose mallow	turtlehead	
sneezeweed		
windflower		

is easier said than done, for plants and weather do not always cooperate. Still, it is possible to plan a garden around the approximate blooming period.

How can I organize the information about the plants that I want to grow in my own garden?

A perennial garden is continually evolving. Keep a notebook for recording blooming times, plant heights, and combinations that you observe in your area and garden. Then, you can move plants around in the garden, creating an ever more pleasurable garden.

Can you list some reliable perennials by the period of bloom and relative heights?

One can give only approximate ranges, because some plants bloom for long periods, spanning the seasons, and some have low, medium, or tall cultivars within the species. Also, what is tall in the spring may be medium the rest of the year. Refer to the chart on page 299 for guidance in planning the season of bloom and the height of the perennials you would like to grow.

Periods of Bloom of Selected Perennials

MARCH-APRIL	MAY	AUGUST-SEPTEMBER
basket-of-gold	basket-of-gold	balloon flower
bleeding-heart	bugleweed	bee balm
candytuft	cranesbill	blanket flower
catmint	dame's-rocket	bugbane
Christmas rose	flax	chrysanthemum
creeping phlox	globeflower	coneflower
iris	Greek valerian	false dragonhead
marsh marigold	hardy pinks	false starwort
mountain bluet	leopard's-bane	flax
primrose	lupin	gay-feather
purple rockcress	mallow	golden marguerite
rock cress	Maltese-cross	hardy aster
spurge	painted daisy	lobelia
sweet william	peony	mist flower
violet	primrose	orange sunflower
Virginia bluebells	sneezeweed	perennial sunflower
	snow-in-summer	perennial sweet pea
	speedwell	phlox
	stonecrop	pincushion flower
	thrift	plantain lily
		plume poppy
		purple coneflower
		rose mallow
		sage
		sneezeweed
		speedwell
		Stokes' aster
		stonecrop
		turtlehead
		windflower

My garden looks really wonderful during June and July, but is not very interesting in spring or fall. What do you suggest for those times of the year?

Although blooming time varies in different parts of the country, the times listed in the chart on pg. 300 are appropriate for much of those parts of the country with minimum winter temperatures of -10 to -20° F.

Color

Color in the garden has the same effect on feelings and moods as it does in your home or clothing. A vibrant color like red makes a flower bed seem larger and closer, while blues will make it appear smaller and more distant. The quantity and combinations of color used, as well as lighting, also affect our perceptions.

One of the greatest challenges of growing perennials is combining them not only according to height and period of bloom but also with regard to harmonious use of color.

The perennial borders I've tried before looked "blotchy." What was wrong?

Color makes a greater impact than any other aspect of garden design. If you mix many different colored flowers together, rather than carefully choose a color scheme, you will almost surely have the blotchy result you describe.

Is there some limit to the number of different colors I should use in a flower border?

The trend today, particularly in smaller gardens, is to choose one primary color, then add only about two more colors to the design.

What criteria should I use in choosing a color scheme?

It depends on your personal preferences, the color of your home, the climate, and the look you want to achieve. Reds, yellows, and oranges are warm colors, creating a feeling of activity, happiness, and cheerfulness. Cool tones—blues, purples, and pinks—are more relaxing.

Once I have chosen the main color I want to use, how do I select the others?

Using a color wheel, you can choose from several different color harmonies, or combinations. For example, if you select blue as your primary color, then orange is directly across the wheel from it. This is called *complementary* harmony. Another complementary harmony is yellow with purple. This is a strong combination and may be too overpowering in a small garden.

Pink combines well with purple and red-violet for an analogous color harmony.

Positive Images, Margaret Hensel

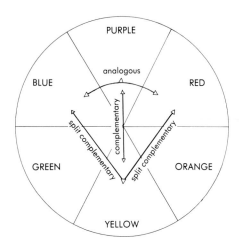

Use a color wheel to guide your choice of various color harmonies.

If you choose a primary color, say blue again, and work with one of the colors on either side of its opposite, this is called *split complementary harmony*. Examples of this are blue with yellow, or blue with red. You can also create complementary harmony using the intermediate colors, such as orange with violet.

A third type of harmony is *analogous harmony*, in which three colors in a row on the color wheel are used. Some examples of this are yellow-orange, orange, and red-orange, or blue-violet, blue, and blue-green.

What is monochromatic harmony?

A monochromatic harmony consists of only one color, such as all orange, all yellow, all pink, all blue. This can be monotonous unless you use different shades of the same color, as well as a wide variety of plants with a full range of heights and textures.

What about pink; where does it fit in?

Pink is actually a tone of red; mix red and white paint together and you have pink. In flower gardens, pink is often best combined with red-violet, violet, and blue flowers.

I like so many different kinds of flowers. Is there any way to combine many colors?

One way is to plant a border so that the colors flow along the color wheel. For example, start at one end with blue, purple, and red-violet flowers, then use pale shades of blue, followed by pale yellows, bright yellows, oranges, and end with red. The key to the success of this scheme is separating the primary colors with paler shades of the same color or with white flowers.

I have tried planting white flowers between colors but have not been satisfied. What makes it work?

You must plant a large enough area of white flowers in order to break up the colors.

Do I have to use the same color scheme in the back and sides of the garden that I've used in front?

No, you can use a different color scheme in each part of your yard. However, those areas that are relatively close together should be harmonious.

We have built a wonderful gazebo for our garden. What color flowers should we plant around it?

A focal point in the garden, such as a gazebo, should have bright flowers around it to draw the eye immediately to the brilliant reds, oranges, and yellows. If, on the other hand, you want to minimize an object in the garden, choose pastels, blues, and lavenders.

Is there some way to make my large property seem smaller?

Although there are ways in terms of overall design, such as dividing the property into smaller, roomlike areas, the colors you choose will also affect how large the space feels. For example, using the warmer tones of red, maroon, gold, orange, and yellow will make a garden look smaller than it is. Choosing plants with dark-colored foliage will also help.

Some favorite yellow perennials are basket-of-gold, Carolina lupine, cinquefoil, golden marguerite, goldenrod, leopard's-bane, orange and perennial sunflowers, sneezeweed, spurge, sundrops, tickseed, and yarrow. Red to orange standbys are avens, blackberry lily, blanket flower, butterfly flower, Maltese cross, Oriental poppy, and torch lily.

My townhouse garden is so small. Is there any way to make it look more expansive?

Choose colors that recede and calm, such as blue, lavender, purple, and white.

Some Examples of Color Harmonies

COMPLEMENTARY HARMONIES

YELLOW	WITH	PURPLE
basket-of-gold		bellflower
Carolina lupine		catmint
daylily		delphinium
goldenrod		false indigo
leopard's-bane		hardy aster
sundrops		iris
tickseed		monkshood
yarrow		sage
		speedwell

SPLIT COMPLEMENTARY HARMONIES

ORANGE	WITH	PURPLE
avens		bellflower
blackberry lily		catmint
butterfly flower		delphinium
Maltese-cross		false indigo
Oriental poppy		hardy aster
		iris
		monkshood
		sage
		speedwell

ANALOGOUS HARMONIES

YELLOW	WITH	ORANGE AND RED
daylily		avens
golden marguerite		blackberry lily
leopard's-bane		blanket flower
tickseed		butterfly flower
yarrow		Canadian columbine
		cardinal flower
		Oriental poppy
		torch lily

What are some easily grown blue-flowered perennials?

Speedwell (*Veronica* Crater Lake Blue, *V. longifolia subsessilis*), globe thistle, snake grass (*Tradescantia* James C. Weguelin), balloon flower (*Platycodon grandiflorus*), bellflower (*Campanula persicifolia*), blue plumbago, and blue stars.

Can you recommend some white flowers?

White windflower, rock cress, goatsbeard, false starwort, Shasta daisy, bugbane, gas plant, candytuft, gooseneck loosestrife, mallow (Alba), peony (Festiva Maxima), Oriental poppy (Field Marshall Vander Glotz), phlox (Miss Lingard and Mt. Fuji), and false dragonhead (Summer Snow).

I work at an office during the day and enjoy relaxing in the garden when I come home. What flowers look best at night?

White flowers as well as plants with silver or gray foliage show up very well at night. Some perennials to consider for their pale foliage include the various artemisias, rue, lavender cotton, Russian sage, and lamb's ears.

Combined astilbe, baby's-breath, daylilies, and peonies make an interesting study in textural contrasts.

Maggie Oster

My house is painted pale yellow, and my flower garden is on the south side. Should I use yellow, orange, and red to go with the house?

Although the colors are complementary, the warm colors of both the flowers and the house will make the area seem hotter than you'll probably like. Cool colors, like blues, lavenders, and purples, will be a much better choice.

Can I use perennials for their colored foliage alone in my perennial border, even if they have no, or insignificant, blooms?

Yes, plants with colored foliage can be part of the color design scheme, just like flowering plants.

What are some perennial plants grown mainly for foliage color?

Bugleweed, wormwood, rue, lamb's ears, and variegated cultivars of plantain lily, iris, and lily-turf.

Texture and shape

A balance of textures and shapes in the garden makes it more attractive and interesting. When planning the perennial garden, think about the shape, size, and texture of the individual leaves and flowers as well as the overall appearance of the plant.

What are the different types of texture?

Texture may be coarse, medium, or fine. Texture usually refers to the overall appearance of the plant, taking into consideration the plant's form as well as the denseness of the flowers and foliage. For example, leaves may be long and thin, large and round, or some other combination. The actual texture of the foliage and flowers also contributes to its appearance.

What are some perennials with coarse texture?

Bear's-breech, globe thistle, leopard's-bane, perennial sunflower, plantain lily, plume poppy, rose mallow, and saxifrage.

What are some perennials with medium texture?

Bee balm, blue stars, bugloss, butterfly flower, campion, coneflower, lady's-mantle, loosestrife, lupine, pearly everlasting, peony, phlox, purple loosestrife, Solomon's-seal, spurge, stonecrop, and sundrops.

What are some perennials with fine texture?

Astilbe, baby's-breath, basket-of-gold, bleeding-heart, columbine, cranesbill, golden marguerite, hardy pinks, lily-turf, meadow rue, monkshood, ornamental onion, pincushion flower, rock cress, snake grass, thrift, tickseed, torch lily, windflower, wormwood, and yarrow.

What effect does texture have on how I use different perennials?

Texture affects space just as color does. For example, fine-textured plants have a receding effect and can make a shallow border appear deeper. Coarse-textured plants give a feeling of closeness and could be used at the far end of a long border to bring it in closer.

What are some perennials that create a feeling of mass due to their dense foliage, making them ideal as a backdrop to a border?

Carolina lupine, delphinium, false indigo, goatsbeard, meadow rue, perennial sunflower, and rose mallow.

What are the basic forms of flowering plants?

Ground-hugging, vertical, rounded, and open. A flower garden can be composed all of one form, but the most interesting gardens usually alternate and repeat forms.

What are some perennials with a smoothly rounded form, a bushy habit of growth, and dense foliage from top to bottom?

Baby's-breath, blanket flower, bleeding-heart, cranesbill, daylily, false indigo, gas plant, goatsbeard, mist flower, orange sunflower, painted daisy, peony, plantain lily, Shasta daisy, sneezeweed, stonecrop (Autumn Joy and *Sedum spectabile*), tickseed, wormwood.

lamb's ears

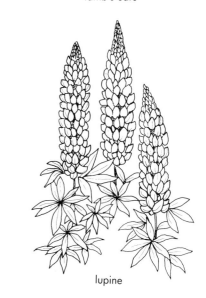

lupine

hosta

columbine

The basic forms of perennial plants are ground-hugging (lamb's ears), vertical (lupine), rounded (hosta), and open (columbine).

Maggie Oster

Ground-hugging lamb's ears make an excellent border plant in sun or very light shade.

What are some ground-hugging perennial plants that spread across the ground and grow less than eighteen inches tall?

Astilbe, baby's-breath, basket-of-gold, blue plumbago, coralbells, creeping phlox, dwarf bearded iris, hardy pinks, lady's-mantle, lamb's ears, lungwort, plantain lily, primrose, saxifrage, Siberian bugloss, thrift.

What are some perennials that have a vertical accent form?

Astilbe, beard-tongue, bear's-breech, betony, bugbane, Carolina lupine, delphinium, false indigo, foxglove, gay-feather, iris, lobelia, lupine, sage, speedwell, torch lily.

What are some perennials with open, loose form?

Columbine, globe thistle, meadow rue, Oriental poppy, pincushion flower, purple coneflower, rose campion, and snake grass.

Spread (Growth Habit)

More gardeners forget about this aspect of planning and planting a perennial garden than any other, and unfortunately, the mature spread of perennials can be the cause of some of the biggest problems as time goes on. It's hard to imagine that those little pots of flowers may become a four-foot-wide mass in a few short years.

When I got done planting my perennial border last year, it looked so bare that I added extra plants. Now it's a jungle. What do I do?

You'll have to remove some of the plants. Plants spaced too closely not only look jammed in, but they are more prone to diseases due to poor air circulation and must compete for light, water, and nutrients.

You will often have to thin plants fairly brutally as they naturally spread in future years. This often provides opportunities for sharing your garden surplus with friends. In some areas, yearly perennial plant sales afford a chance to exchange favorites, at the same time as to provide a fund-raising event for nonprofit organizations.

After you have considered your site, decided on a color scheme, and determined which plants you'd like to grow, it is time to draw up a garden plan. Although not absolutely necessary, a plan drawn on graph paper will help you to determine more accurately how many plants you need, see potential problems, and maximize the visual impact of the colors, shapes, and textures.

How do I go about creating a scale drawing of a perennial garden?

There is no one "right" way, but the following should get you started. First, make a list, by blooming season, of the perennials you are considering. Mark each one T, M, and S for tall, medium, and short. You might also want to include a code for texture. Some people like to make colored cut-outs of the different plants.

Choose graph paper with either four or eight squares to the inch and allow each square to represent a square foot of garden space. Using a sharp, fine-leaded pencil, first draw the shape of the bed or border you want to plant. Then begin drawing in areas for each of the plants.

How do I know what the garden will look like at different periods during the summer?

To get an idea of how the garden will look at different seasons, use sheets of tracing paper marked for each month or blooming period. Lay them over your main plan. Color in the appropriate areas for that season on each sheet of the tracing paper.

MAKING A GARDEN PLAN

— • —

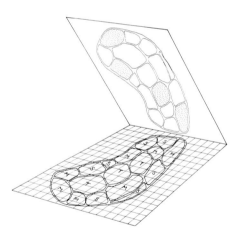

Make a garden plan on graph paper, indicating the heights of plant groupings by marking them T (tall), M (medium), and S (short). Overlay your plan with tracing paper and shade in various areas according to season of bloom and plant color.

13 *Perennials in the Landscape*

Creating perennial flower beds for specific purposes or to meet special needs or restrictions is both a challenge and a pleasure. The ideas that follow can serve to open limitless possibilities for the unique gardens you will want to design for your own home landscape.

What is a flower border?

Borders are at the edge of an area and are approached and viewed from only one side. Borders might be such plantings as sweet william along a fence, spurge in front of a hedge, asters along a driveway, or mixed perennials beside a foundation or shrub border.

How wide should a border be?

Most borders are three to five feet wide, to make maintenance as easy as possible. A rule of thumb is to make borders not wider than one-third their length so that surroundings and length are in good proportion to one another.

What are perennial beds?

Beds are irregularly shaped "island" gardens, perhaps including a few strategically placed large boulders or a small tree. Again, this garden is easy to work in, and different effects can be had from the various sides. In such a garden, it is possible to

◀ *A cheerful flower border of daisies, poppies, and dame's-rocket.*

accommodate both sun-loving and shade-loving plants as well as rock garden plants. Or, annuals and perennials can be mixed. If you wish to use only a few plants, apply an attractive mulch or perennial ground cover to fill the remaining spaces.

How large should a bed be?

This depends on the size of the surroundings, for as with borders, the bed should be in scale with the rest of the landscape. Usually any bed that takes up more than one-third of the area in which it is placed looks out of proportion.

Where can I locate perennial beds and borders?

Anywhere you'd like: along terraces, patios, decks, or driveways; in front of fences, walls, or shrubs; next to the foundation; along the walk to the front door. When planning a flower garden, always take into consideration the point from where it will be viewed.

What is the difference between a formal and a naturalistic garden?

Formal design uses straight lines and circular curves or arcs; informal design uses ovals, kidney shapes, or long, free-flowing curves. Formality emphasizes lines; informality emphasizes space, a concept necessary today in low-maintenance gardening. A formal garden need not, however, be large, elaborate, or filled with architectural embellishment.

Which is better suited to a small place, a formal or an informal garden?

Topography controls the type of design to a large extent. Where the ground near the house is flat, a rectangular (formal) type of design is easier to adapt. On rough land, particularly on slopes and in wooded areas, informality is desirable.

Can I use just one perennial as an accent?

The single-accent perennial is very effective, but it must be chosen with great care as it has to be decorative out of bloom as well as in bloom. A dramatic accent that works particularly well is a clump of peonies or daylilies by a garden gate, a grouping of Japanese iris by a small pool, or an ornamental grass against a fence.

Can I use perennials as ground covers?

Very definitely. Perennials should not be overlooked as ground covers for relief from high-maintenance grass. Such perennials as ajuga, lily-of-the-valley, sweet woodruff, and *Sedums* are all visually appealing and quite suitable in the right spot.

PERENNIALS IN THE LANDSCAPE

Is there really such a thing as a low-maintenance perennial garden?

The answer is a guarded "yes." The best way to achieve such a garden is to select only perennials that require the least amount of maintenance, although some care is always necessary. Particularly appropriate plants are those with the following characteristics:

- division needed no more frequently than every four years (see pages 325-26);
- hardy to -20° F. without winter protection;
- high degree of tolerance to pests, so that spraying is usually not necessary;
- stakes not necessary;
- wide range of soils tolerated;
- leaves either attractive throughout the growing season or die down quickly enough to be hidden by surrounding plants;
- no tendency either to self-sow or to spread by runners so vigorously as to become a nuisance.

What are some of the best perennials for a low-maintenance situation?

Astilbe, balloon flower, betony, blackberry lily, bleeding-heart, blue stars, bugbane, bugloss, butterfly flower, campion, candytuft, Carolina lupine, catmint, coneflower, coralbells, daylily, false indigo, gas plant, globe thistle, goatsbeard, goldenrod, hardy hibiscus, Jacob's-ladder, knapweed, lady's-mantle, lily-of-the-valley, loosestrife, lungwort, meadow rue, mugwort, Oriental poppy, ornamental grasses, Ozark sundrop, painted daisy, peach bells, peony, pincushion flower, plantain lily, purple loosestrife, sea holly, sea lavender, showy stonecrop, Siberian iris, snake grass, speedwell, Solomon's-seal, sunflower, tickseed, turtlehead, Virginia bluebells, yucca.

What perennials should I be cautious about introducing into my garden because of their tendency to take over?

Some varieties of yarrow (white, in particular), *Campanula persicifolia*, coreopsis, most *Sedums*.

Old-fashioned cutting gardens had the plants set in rows and were not very attractive. Do they have to be made that way?

No. By growing enough plants (a minimum of three) of each perennial in your garden, you should have plenty of flowers to cut for bouquets without destroying the effect of your garden.

What special care does a cutting garden need?

Since you want maximum flower production, regular feeding, watering, and deadheading (see pages 325-26) are especially important.

A LOW-MAINTENANCE PERENNIAL GARDEN

•

Maggie Oster

Easy-to-grow loosestrife, here shown in a purple variety, is also available with yellow or white flowers.

A PERENNIAL GARDEN FOR CUT FLOWERS

•

What is the best time and method to gather flowers?

Cut flowers early in the morning, using a sharp knife or scissors and making the stem as long as possible. Choose unblemished flowers that are in various stages of development. Immediately after cutting, plunge the flower stems into a container of tepid water. Put the flowers and container in a cool place for several hours before making your arrangements. Herbs and shrub foliage make fine filler material mixed in with your flowers.

What perennials are particularly nice for bouquets?

Aster, baby's-breath, beard-tongue, bellflower, blanket flower, chrysanthemum, coneflower, coreopsis, delphinium, false dragonhead, gay-feather, globeflower, globe thistle, iris, knapweed, leopard's-bane, lupine, meadow rue, mist flower, monkshood, mugwort, peony, sage, showy stonecrop, sneezeweed, speedwell, sunflower, torch lily, windflower, yarrow.

What are some perennials that produce flowers or seed pods especially adaptable to being dried for bouquets?

Baby's-breath, blackberry lily, Chinese-lantern plant, coralbells, delphinium, false indigo, globe thistle, pearly everlasting, sea holly, sea lavender, yarrow.

PERENNIALS FOR A ROCK GARDEN

— • —

I have a sloping area on my property, with a few rock outcroppings. Would such an area be suitable for a rock garden?

Yes, particularly if it is in sun and has well-drained, moderately fertile soil. Even those who enjoy rock gardens, but do not have a slope like yours, can create one by trucking in a few loads of topsoil and rocks.

What kinds of perennials can be planted in a rock garden?

Purists use only those plants found growing naturally on rocky slopes in poor soil, but there are many other low-growing perennials, as well as bulbs, annuals, and shrubs, suited for such a garden. Some of the readily available, easily grown perennials suited for a rock garden situation include basket-of-gold, betony, bishop's hat, blanket flower (Goblin), bugloss, bugleweed, campion, candytuft, Carpathian harebell, coralbells, cranesbill, creeping phlox, cupid's-dart, dwarf baby's-breath, dwarf columbine, dwarf iris, fernleaf bleeding-heart, flax, forget-me-not, hardy pinks, harebell, hen-and-chickens, Jacob's-ladder, lady's-mantle, meadowsweet (Flore Pleno), ornamental grass (blue fescue), plumbago, primrose, purple rockcress, rock cress, saxifrage, sea lavender, Silver Mound, snow-in-summer, speedwell, spurge, stonecrop, sunrose, violet, Virginia bluebells, wild ginger, woolly yarrow.

Are hummingbirds and butterflies attracted by color or scent?

Red, pink, and orange flowers will draw hummingbirds to the garden. Butterflies are attracted by the nectar, often recognized by its scent.

Will caterpillars destroy my garden?

Not necessarily, but if you want butterflies in your garden, you will also have to accept that there will be some foliage damage from their caterpillar stage. You should, of course, use only a minimum of pesticides in the garden if you wish to encourage insects.

What flowers attract hummingbirds?

Bee balm, beard-tongue, bellflower, betony, butterfly flower, campion, catmint, columbine, coralbells, daylily, delphinium, foxglove, globe thistle, hardy pinks, hollyhock, iris, loosestrife, lupine, Oriental poppy, phlox, sage, torch lily.

Maggie Oster

PERENNIALS TO ATTRACT BIRDS AND BUTTERFLIES

•

Many flowers, including this hardy aster, are especially beloved by hummingbirds and butterflies.

What are some perennials that will attract butterflies?

Bee balm, butterfly flower, coneflower, foxglove, gay-feather, globe thistle, hardy aster, hardy pinks, knapweed, lupine, mist flower, sunflower, sweet rocket.

PERENNIALS FOR A FRAGRANT GARDEN
·

I want to include as many fragrant-flowered plants as possible in my perennial border. What are some suggestions?

Bee balm, daylily (especially Bonanza, Catherine Woodberry, Earliana, Elizabeth, Holy Grail, Hyperion, Ice Carnival, Lexington, Little Wart, Rozavel, Seneca Moonlet), dropwort, evening primrose, forget-me-not, hardy pinks, lily-of-the-valley, peony (especially White Sands, Dutchess de Nemours, Festiva Maxima, Gardenia, Mary E. Nichols, Alexander Fleming, Edulis Superba, Sarah Bernhardt, Big Ben, Harry L. Richardson), phlox, plantain lily, primrose, sweet pea, sweet rocket, violet.

PERENNIALS FOR A CONTAINER GARDEN
·

Can perennials be grown in containers?

Yes. They can be grown in anything from ten-inch pots to large planters made of such materials as wood, concrete, clay, or fiberglass. Be sure that there are drainage holes in the bottom of the container, then add a layer of gravel and fill with a soilless potting mix. Feed during the summer with a liquid fertilizer and water frequently, especially in hot dry weather.

Will perennials overwinter in containers?

Possibly, especially in warm climates or regions with a great deal of snow cover. Elsewhere, the roots are likely to be damaged by frozen soil. If there is any doubt about their chances for survival, move container plantings into a cool greenhouse, garage, or cold frame, or group all of them together and cover them with foam insulating blankets and pine boughs.

What are some perennials that grow well in containers?

If a certain plant is particularly special to you, by all means try it in a container. Basically, however, consider those plants and varieties that are compact, form a clump, and bloom over a long period. Some possible perennials include balloon flower, beard-tongue, bellflower, betony, blanket flower, campion, catmint, cinquefoil, coneflower, coralbells, cranesbill, daylily, gas plant, hardy pinks, lady's-mantle, lavender cotton, loosestrife, mallow, painted daisy, phlox, sage, Shasta daisy, Solomon's-seal, speedwell, stonecrop, sundrop, torch lily, violet, yarrow.

Protect container-grown perennials over the winter by covering the pots lightly with foam insulating blankets.

What conditions will most ensure a successful flower garden near the seashore?

Choose a location protected from the wind and salt spray. Enrich the soil as much as possible with organic material such as compost, peat moss, or leaf mold. Seaweed can be used if it has been washed by rain for a season. Water plants frequently during the growing season; mulch and fertilize regularly.

What are some perennials that will do well in a seashore garden?

Baby's-breath, bee balm, betony, blanket flower, bugbane, bugleweed, bugloss, butterfly flower, campion, candytuft, coneflower, coralbells, cupid's-dart, daylily, false indigo, flea-bane, foxglove, globe thistle, hardy aster, hardy hibiscus, hardy pinks, hollyhock, leopard's-bane, loosestrife, marguerite, mugwort, ornamental grasses, rock cress, sea holly, sea lavender, spurge, stonecrop, thrift, tickseed, torch lily, yarrow, yucca.

PERENNIALS FOR A SEASHORE GARDEN

14 *Planting and Caring for Perennials*

Adequate soil preparation, the purchase of healthy plants, proper planting procedures, and regular care will go a long way toward ensuring that your perennial garden will be successful. Time and effort spent now will save having to correct mistakes later.

How shall I prepare new ground for perennials?

Every situation is different. For a precise recommendation for your own unique situation, have your soil tested by your County Extension Service (see p. 290). Generally speaking, you should mix in a three- to four-inch layer of well-rotted or dehydrated cow manure, leaf mold, peat moss, or compost, along with ten pounds of superphosphate to 100 square feet. Small gardens can be spaded, but you may wish to rent a rotary tiller for larger areas. You can also add a commercial flower garden fertilizer such as 5-10-10 at the rate recommended on the package.

Should I check and correct the pH of the soil?

A soil test conducted by an outside agency usually includes a pH test, but you can also check it yourself with a kit from the garden center. Most perennials grow best in a slightly acidic soil with a pH of 6 to 7. To raise the pH one point, you need to add ten pounds of lime per 100 square feet of soil. To lower the pH one point, work in three to four pounds of sulfur per 100 square feet.

◀ *Healthy plants, such as these white and purple bellflowers tumbling over the bench, and red, pink, and white sweet williams, will result if adequate care is provided.*

PREPARING THE SOIL
•

Should I remove all the weeds from the area that is going to be my new perennial bed?

If you are preparing the soil in the fall prior to planting the next spring, the weeds can be tilled in, and they will decompose over the winter. If you are preparing the bed in the spring for immediate planting, remove as many weeds as possible before adding organic matter and spading or tilling.

How deep should the soil be prepared for a new perennial garden?

For best results, the soil should be dug and prepared not less than twelve inches, but eighteen inches will give superior results.

In preparing a perennial garden, should I screen the soil to remove all stones?

No, do not screen the soil, but handpick out any stones larger than a lemon.

Is there any way to change the condition of a poor soil?

Unless the soil condition is extremely unfavorable, almost any soil can be improved with the addition of plenty of organic matter.

Is sand or clay better subsoil for a perennial garden?

Generally speaking, a sandy subsoil is preferable, but if the sand is too loose and porous, drainage will be excessive. If the subsoil is hard-packed clay, drainage will be stopped.

Our soil is sandy. How can we grow perennials?

Add plenty of organic matter, such as manure, compost, or peat moss. Keep the soil fertilized and water heavily when

A technique known as double digging entails removing a spade's depth and width of soil along one row, turning over a spade's depth of soil beneath the top layer, and then digging up the next spade's depth and width of soil and placing it into the first trench. Continue down the length of the bed in this manner and fill in the final row with soil removed from the first row.

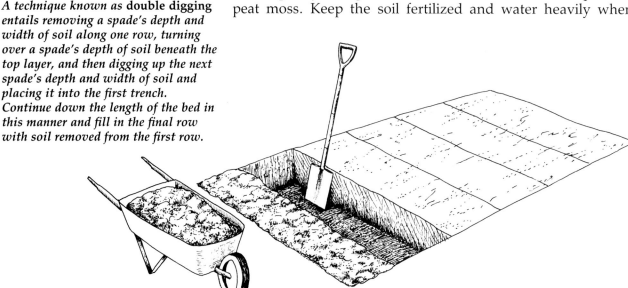

necessary. Plenty of organic matter will be needed for perennials to do best. Choose those perennials that do best in dry, sandy soil.

What makes clay soil so sticky?

Clay is composed of very minute particles, almost the whole surface of which absorbs water. It is this high water content that causes the stickiness. Never work clay when it is wet. It puddles and then hardens, making a poor environment for plant roots. If you dig too soon in the spring you may make your soil practically useless for the entire season.

The soil in my garden is mostly clay. Is there any way I can improve it so that I can grow perennials?

Spade in a three-inch layer of organic material, such as peat moss, compost, or manure, to a depth of six inches.

What is the best method of planting bare-root and container-grown perennials?

With a spade or trowel, make a hole of sufficient size to accommodate the roots without crowding. Remove the container-grown plant from its pot, and put the plant in the hole, placing it no deeper than it grew in the nursery. With your hands, push the soil back in the hole, working it between and over the roots and packing it firmly in. Soak with water.

Should I plant perennials when the soil is sopping wet?

No. Soil structure can be harmed as a result. Wait until the soil is crumbly but still moist.

Should perennials be planted in straight rows or staggered?

The effect is better in a staggered planting. It is also good practice to plant in groups of three.

When is the correct time to plant perennials in the spring? Will they bloom the same year?

Plant as early as the soil can be worked, as soon as possible after receiving them from the nursery. Plants, if large enough, will flower the same season.

I am new to gardening. Should I buy perennials from my local garden center or from mail-order catalogs?

As a new gardener, you may find it easier to select perennials in containers from a garden center. There are at least two advantages: The plants are usually in full growth, so that you can readily see what they look like, and you can set plants out

PLANTING BARE-ROOT AND CONTAINER-GROWN PERENNIALS

•

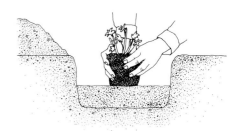

To set a container-grown perennial in place, make a hole large enough to accommodate the roots without crowding and deep enough so that the plant sits at the same height it grew in the pot.

any time during the growing season with the least disturbance of their root systems. However, mail-order nurseries are often less expensive and they are likely to offer more kinds of perennials and their varieties than a garden center can.

Container-grown perennials are available at my local garden center from spring until fall, and I am assured that they can be planted anytime during the growing season. Is this true?

Yes. More and more plants (including trees, shrubs, and roses) are being handled in this way. Because the roots of pot-grown plants suffer little disturbance when being transplanted, it is less critical to follow traditional rules to plant them only in the spring and fall.

Should I label my plants after they're planted?

Yes. Note the name of the plant and the planting date on an unobtrusive wood, plastic, or aluminum label to help you keep track of your gardening successes and failures. Such a marker can also keep you from digging into a dormant plant.

Label each new planting with the name of the plant and the date that it was planted.

CARING FOR THE PERENNIAL GARDEN

Can you give me an idea of how much time I'll need to spend taking care of a modestly sized perennial garden?

In general, a perennial garden needs at least some weekly care and maintenance during the summer, with extra hours necessary in spring and fall. Some plants, however, do require less water, fertilizer, pruning, dividing, and pest control than others. Fortunately, the beauty of the garden should make the time you spend caring for it pleasurable, and not particularly strenuous for the most part.

What constitutes good year-round care of a perennial border?

In the spring, when the frost has left the ground, remove the winter mulch. If rotted manure or partly rotted leaves were used, lightly fork the finer portions into the soil, along with a topdressing of complete fertilizer. Reset any plants that were heaved out of the ground by frost. More mulch can be applied to suppress weeds and keep the soil moist and cool, and to keep a crust from forming. Provide support for those plants that need it. Water thoroughly when necessary. Put on more mulch after the first severe frost.

Why do some hardy perennials die off after one or two luxuriant seasons?

There are several possible reasons: most perennials need to be divided and transplanted after two or three years; many are short lived; some do not do very well during the winter; still others succumb to diseases or insects.

Watering

How often should a perennial garden be watered?

Most perennials growing in an "average," humus-rich garden loam need the equivalent of one inch of water each week. A garden in a windy location or one with very sandy soil will need extra water. No definite intervals for watering can be set; the kind of soil and the needs of the various plants, among other factors, have an influence. The soil should be kept moist at all times during the growing season.

How can I determine whether my soil is receiving one inch of water each week?

Use a rain gauge to track rainfall. To check the amount that you are watering, place an empty coffee can halfway between the sprinkler and the furthest point it reaches. Time how long it takes for one inch of water to accumulate in the can. Presuming the water pressure remains constant, run your sprinklers for the amount of time it took for one inch of water to collect in the can.

Why do I need to water my perennials only once a week? Couldn't I sprinkle them lightly every day?

This is the worst thing you could do. Light, frequent watering encourages shallow roots. When it becomes hot or if you go away for a few days, the plants will not be able to survive as well. Deep watering encourages the roots to grow down rather than along the soil surface.

Do you have to water perennial flowers in the winter?

No watering is needed since there is no growth.

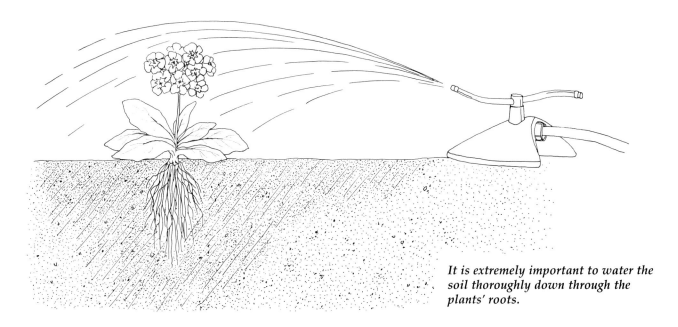

It is extremely important to water the soil thoroughly down through the plants' roots.

Is it true that water should not touch the leaves of perennials?

There is scant danger of water on the leaves doing any harm. Some gardeners believe that there is less risk of fungus growth if, when watering with an overhead sprinkler, you water in early morning so the leaves can dry quickly. On the other hand, if you water in the evening, the moisture has a chance to soak in and last longer without the drying effect of the sun.

Fertilizing

What is a basic fertilizing program for a perennial garden?

Perennials planted in a well-prepared soil should need only spring applications of an organic mulch and 10-10-10 fertilizer. If the fertilizer is dry, sprinkle it on the soil when the soil is moist and the plant's foliage is dry, and then water it into the soil immediately.

What do the numbers on a fertilizer label mean?

The combination 5-10-5, for example, means that the bag contains five-percent nitrogen, ten-percent phosphorus, and five-percent potash; the remainder is inert filler. These elements do not occur in pure form but as compounds with other materials.

Is there anything to be gained by fertilizing perennials during the growing season?

Some plants, such as phlox, delphinium, and chrysanthemums, are helped by supplementary feedings of liquid fertilizers applied when flowers are about to form. Whether or not this is necessary depends on the character of the soil, the initial preparation of the border, and annual routine practices to maintain its fertility.

Are organic fertilizers any better than inorganic ones?

Organic fertilizers can be highly complex, with the nutrients unavailable to plants until they have been digested or broken down into simpler forms by soil organisms. These organisms are partially dormant at temperatures below 60° F. and grow progressively more active up to about 90° F. Thus, organic fertilizers are not too effective in early spring. They have one quality that pure chemical or mineral fertilizers do not: They add organic matter to the soil.

Weeding and mulching

What is the best way to keep down weeds in a perennial border?

Make frequent use of a narrow scuffle hoe to chop off weeds before they attain much size. Run the hoe through the soil about

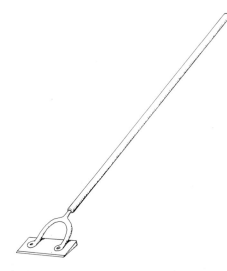

Use a scuffle hoe to chop out weeds before they grow too large.

an inch below the surface. Weeds among the flowers must be pulled out by hand. A mulch of organic materials also helps to keep weeds at a minimum.

How close to my plants should I work the soil, and how deeply can I cultivate it?

The depth depends on the type of plants: shallow-rooted plants need shallow cultivation; deep-rooted plants will take deeper cultivation. You can work close to them all, taking care not to cut their stems.

Will a mulch of organic material, such as straw, grass clippings, compost, cocoa bean hulls, or bark chips, help in weed control?

Yes. Applied in the spring, mulch will keep down weeds, and it will also hold moisture in the soil and help to keep the soil cool.

Are there any tips in applying such a mulch?

Yes, remove any weeds already growing. Spread the mulch two to three inches thick, leaving a small area unmulched around the base of the plant so that the crown is not smothered. Add a sprinkling of 10-10-10 fertilizer to compensate for the extra nitrogen needed for decomposition of the mulch.

Staking

How do I keep certain perennials from falling over, especially when they're in bloom?

The showy, heavy stems of delphinium may be loosely fastened to bamboo stakes.

Beginning in early spring, stake perennials to keep them from flopping over. A clever English tradition is to put twelve- to eighteen-inch-long (depending on the mature height of the perennial) brushy, woody stems around plants in the spring and allow the perennials to grow up through them. Commercially available, round wire forms on three legs are useful for bushy plants such as Shasta daisy, *Sedums* such as Autumn Joy, or balloon flower, as well as for plants with tall spiky flowers, like delphinium or monkshood. These tall, spiky plants may also be loosely tied to bamboo stakes.

Pinching and disbudding

Why do people pinch back their plants?

Sprawling, weak-stemmed plants such as balloon flower may be staked with brushy stems, put in place when plants are small.

Some plants are bushier and sturdier when mature if they are pinched back when they are young. Perennials that benefit from being pinched back are chrysanthemum, hardy aster, sneeze-weed, tall-growing speedwell, false dragonhead, and beard-tongue, as well as plants like summer phlox that tend to send shoots from the axils of the leaves. Poppies and lilies should not be pinched.

Maggie Oster

Wire forms support these veronicas.

Pinch out the growing tip of such perennials as chrysanthemums and sneezeweed in order to encourage sturdy, bushy growth.

How do I pinch back plants?

Using your thumb and forefinger, remove the top inch or so of growth just above a pair of leaves. This is usually done in April or May. Chrysanthemums need to be pinched several times, but other plants only once.

What is disbudding?

Disbudding involves pinching out some or all of the flower buds when they are about ⅛-inch in diameter, and leaving the main center one so as to have large flowers on a long stem. It is usually done only by people who exhibit such flowers as chrysanthemum.

Deadheading

What does the term deadheading mean?

The technique of removing faded flowers is known as dead-heading. Not only does it improve the appearance of many plants, but it also results in repeat bloom for some plants later in the season.

What are some perennials that do not need deadheading?

Bee balm, blackberry lily, blanket flower, butterfly flower, coreopsis, flax, purple loosestrife, the *Sedum* Autumn Joy, snake grass, and sundrops.

What is the best way to divide most perennials?

Dig up the plants and, with the help of two spading forks (or two hand forks if the plant is small), pry the rootstock apart into pieces of suitable size.

When should perennials be divided?

Fall is best, although early spring is a possibility for some plants. Divide early bloomers in early fall, late bloomers in the spring, and bearded iris and Oriental poppies in the summer. Some plants may even be moved about throughout the growing season if you are able to transplant them without greatly disturbing their root systems.

Is August a good month to revamp perennial borders?

Definitely not. It is the hottest and driest month as a rule, and newly transplanted stock (with the exceptions noted below) is likely to suffer.

Which perennials should be moved in midsummer or early fall?

Move bearded iris after it flowers; Oriental poppies in late summer; and bleeding-heart, Christmas rose, and peonies in late summer and early fall.

In northern Maine should perennials be divided and transplanted in fall or spring?

Either one is acceptable, though fall is best, at least four weeks before heavy freezing. In the spring it must be done as early as possible.

Should tall perennials be cut back when they are replanted or transplanted in the fall?

Tall perennials are better if cut back before being moved. Whatever foliage remains down near the soil matters little in the fall.

How do you suggest I rejuvenate my perennial garden?

First, dig up all your perennials in early fall. Obtain a supply of nursery flats or grocery cartons and fill them with the lifted perennials, taking care not to mix up varieties of the same plant. Then spread as much organic material, up to two to four inches

DIVIDING AND TRANSPLANTING PERENNIALS

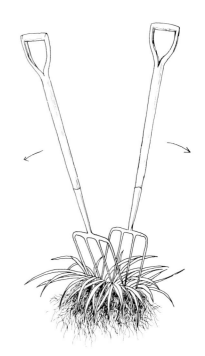

After digging up the plant, divide it by prying it apart with two spading forks.

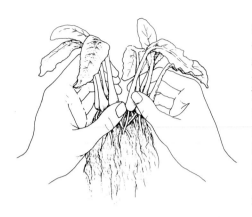

Some plants, such as primrose, need only to be gently pulled apart after being dug up.

deep, as you can afford. Use peat moss, your own garden compost if you have it, half-rotted leaves or leaf mold, rotted animal manures, or whatever is available. Also spread superphosphate, about three pounds per 100 square feet, or steamed bonemeal at the same rate. If your soil is very acid (you may wish to test it; see p. 290), spread ground limestone over the area at the rate of five pounds per 100 square feet, then use a rotary tiller to mix all these ingredients into the soil. (If you don't own a tiller, rent one from a garden or rental center.) Finally, rake over the area, allow the soil to settle for several weeks, and then replant. This is a good time to divide many of your plants.

How important is watering after planting or transplanting perennials?

Watering is crucial to success. Soak the soil well after planting. It's a good idea to add a special transplanting fertilizer or a bit of liquid seaweed or fish emulsion to the water. Continue to water every day for a week or two, unless it rains. After this initial period until winter sets in, water only when the soil is dry.

STARTING PERENNIALS FROM SEED

When is the best time to sow perennial seed either in a greenhouse or indoors under fluorescent lights or in a sunny window?

In late February or early March, using a sterile soilless mix specifically designed for starting seeds. Soon after germination, most kinds of seedlings will be large enough to be transplanted into small individual pots filled with soilless mix. From these small pots, the plants can be set outside directly into soil in a nursery bed (a bed set aside for young plants only) in May. Only the usual summer cultivation is required (see pgs. 320-23), and strong plants should be available for fall planting in the garden.

Which perennials are easiest to grow from seed?

Blanket flower, hardy pinks, columbine, coneflower, coralbells, coreopsis, delphinium, flax, fleabane, foxglove, lupine, orange sunflower, primrose, and some bellflowers.

Can perennials be raised successfully from fall-sown seed?

If your winters are severe and you have a cold frame, sow perennial seeds in the fall to give them an earlier start in spring. Be sure to plant them late enough in the season so that they do not germinate. If you try to carry small seedlings through the winter outdoors, losses will be great.

What is the advantage of sowing seed in August?

Some growers sow seed from their own or a neighbor's garden in August in order to secure the advantage of having fresh seed of the current season. However, spring sowing ensures huskier young plants that are better able to face their first winter.

Is it possible to sow seeds of perennials in the open ground?

Yes. Make a special seedbed by mixing fine leaf mold or peat moss and sand into the top three or four inches of soil. Sow as early in May as possible and keep the soil moist. Another good method is to sow into seed pans or flats that are buried to the rims in sand; cover with polyethylene until germination. With either method, transplant when the first true leaves develop. Provide light shade for a few days and water well.

Can any perennials be grown from seed simply by scattering the seeds where they are to bloom?

Success is hit-or-miss. The seeds of certain kinds of perennials, such as foxglove, coreopsis, and garlic chives, that naturally self-sow can be sown this way. These same types can even become a nuisance because of their prolificacy—one of the reasons to deadhead (see page 325).

Easy to grow from seed, masses of brilliant primroses provide welcome early spring color.

Maggie Oster

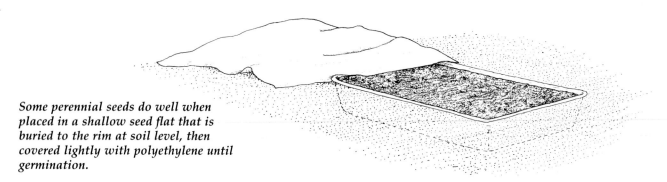

Some perennial seeds do well when placed in a shallow seed flat that is buried to the rim at soil level, then covered lightly with polyethylene until germination.

Can I count on seeds gathered from my own or a neighbor's perennials to produce plants that look like the parent?

It depends on the plant. Seedlings of hybrids and cultivars usually do not look like the parent and are inferior to it. To get an exact duplicate of the parent, these plants are usually propagated by division.

Why do the seeds I save come up so well, while the seeds (especially perennial seeds) I buy do so poorly?

Home-grown seed is usually fresher, and with some perennials this is crucial.

WINTER PREPARATION AND PROTECTION

I have heard that perennials should be cut back in the fall. When, and how much?

In late autumn, when the herbaceous stems have died down, cut the stems of most plants down to within an inch of the soil. Plants with a clump or rosette of green leaves should not be cut off; just cut the old flower stems. Some gardeners prefer to wait until spring before cutting off the tops of the perennials. Their argument is that there is less winter injury from snow and ice with the stems providing some natural protection.

Why are plants covered for the winter?

The rationale for covering plants with some kind of mulch is dependent upon the kind of plant and the climate. Nonhardy plants are covered *before* hard freezing to protect them from low temperatures, because once the plant cells are destroyed, these plants will die. Truly hardy plants are covered after the ground freezes, not to *protect* them from cold, but to *keep* them cold. Where fluctuation of ground temperature results in alternate freezing and thawing, hardy plants are susceptible to injury. Most winterkill occurs in late winter or early spring, for instance, when a mild spell in late winter is followed by a sudden hard freeze. In some cases, shading plants from the winter sun is sufficient. By waiting until after the ground is frozen before you mulch, you allow your plants a chance to harden somewhat, and, hopefully, by very late fall small rodents will have found winter quarters elsewhere.

Shall we let Mother Nature blanket our perennial garden with maple and locust leaves and, if so, when shall we remove the leaves?

Leaves are often used for winter protection, but because they tend to make a sodden mass, they may smother to death any but the most robust plants. Better protection is a loose, light material that does not compact, such as marsh hay, through which air can circulate. Remove the covering gradually when signs of growth are observed underneath. Choose a cloudy day to take off the final covering.

Which perennials need a winter mulch and which prefer none?

Most perennials—except those with heavy green tops, like torch lily—should be mulched, particularly in regions of alternate freezing and thawing. Leaf mold, marsh hay, pine needles, and evergreen boughs are some of the better materials. A covering of about three inches is sufficient for most perennials.

Is it necessary to protect newly planted perennials for the winter? What is the best method?

It is advisable in colder regions to protect all plants over their first winter. Use marsh hay, straw, or evergreen branches, laid on loosely, so as not to smother plants. Do not mulch until after the first hard freeze.

Perennial seeds that I planted in my cold frame in July have made good growth. Can I leave them in the frame until the spring, and if so, should I add a mulch after December?

A mulch will help, but you may want to cover them earlier than December, depending on when you get heavy freezing. Hardy perennials grown from seed sown in July ought to make strong enough plants by late fall not to require cold-frame protection, particularly if planted out in a bed.

15 Prevention and Control of Diseases and Pests

As a group, perennials are neither more nor less affected by diseases and pests than any other plants in the gardens. Although some perennials may be susceptible to a very specific disease or insect, generally those troubles that beset vegetables, herbs, trees, or shrubs are the same ones that affect perennials. It follows then, that control measures are similar. Keep in mind as you read this section that many of the questions and answers will never pertain to your garden, and certainly few of them will ever be a problem at any one time.

Are there ways to minimize disease and pests among perennials?

Yes. First, select those perennials and varieties that are most resistant to diseases and pests that are prevalent in your locality. Second, provide the best possible growing conditions for your perennials, including adequate water, fertilizer, and air circulation, plus proper soil drainage. Third, grow a variety of plants rather than just one type. A garden with variety is less likely to become severely infested, for what troubles one plant does not bother another. Fourth, immediately remove disease- or insect-infested plants or plant parts and destroy them; fall clean-up removes pests that may overwinter and multiply the following season. Finally, treat any problems as soon as they appear, rather than waiting until they become severe.

◀ *Pest- and disease-free gardens result when resistant varieties are planted, optimal growing conditions are provided, and problems are treated as soon as they appear.*

APPLYING PESTICIDES
•

Please remember these two important rules regarding the use of any pesticides you may be required to use: Always read the fine print on labels to determine what pesticide you are buying, and use them according to the manufacturer's directions.

What are the main spray materials to have on hand? I understand that identical sprays may be available under different names.

This is correct. Pesticides are sold under hundreds of different trade names, but basically the main controls for insects are malathion, carbaryl, *Bacillus thuringiensis*, pyrethrum, rotenone, and insecticidal soaps; and for fungi, they are sulfur, benomyl, and fenaminosulf. Copper sulfate is used mainly for fungi control, but it also kills flea beetles and leafhoppers. Karathane is the main miticide (formulation to kill mites), but insecticidal soaps will also work.

What is a garden duster?

A tool for applying insecticides or fungicides in dry dust form. For the small garden, choose a hand rotary duster or a dust gun, both of which range in size from one-pint to two-quart capacities. Choose one with an extension rod and a flange, which will allow you to stand up while using the duster and yet drive the dust from the bottom of the plant up through it so that the undersides of the leaves are coated. For the larger garden, a knapsack bellows or a rotary duster will save much energy in operation.

A hand rotary duster with an extension rod permits the operator to drive dust up under the plant.

For pesticides that come in powder form, how do you know how much to use? I tried a dust gun, but the leaves didn't seem sufficiently covered and it was a lot of work. Yet when I tossed the dust by hand it seemed too much.

You need to apply only a thin, even coating of dust, and this can be done only with some sort of duster, never by throwing it on. If yours is too hard to work, either it is of inadequate size and quality for the number of plants you need to treat, or else it needs adjusting. Coverage of the underside of the leaves is most important and can be done only with the right apparatus.

Do you dust plants when they are wet with dew or when they are dry?

There is disagreement over the answer to this question. If ornamental plants are dusted when they are wet, however, a conspicuous and unattractive residue remains.

What are garden sprayers?

Equipment to apply liquid pesticides in a fine mist. Sprayers vary from pint- or quart-size atomizers to huge power apparatus. For the average garden, a back-carried, cylindrical, com-

A back-carried, cylindrical, compressed-air sprayer.

pressed-air sprayer or a knapsack sprayer of one and one-half- to three-gallon capacity will be sufficient.

No sprayer is better than the care given it. Immediately after each use, rinse the sprayer thoroughly, and occasionally take it apart for cleaning. Extra parts can often be obtained from manufacturers or distributors to keep old sprayers in operation. It is a good policy to keep and label separate sprayers for each different product you use so as not to mix dangerous chemicals.

Is a hose proportioner type of sprayer sufficient for a home gardener?

Hose sprayers of the proportioner type are very convenient and easy to use. Solutions and emulsions are readily handled, but the undissolved particles in suspensions may cause clogging. Further, not all types give a suitable dispersion of the active chemical in the spray. Those with a shut-off near the nozzle are much preferable to those that have no shut-off, requiring you to place your finger over a hole to start the chemical mixing with the water spray.

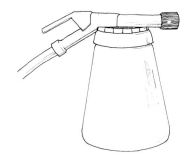

Hose proportioners add specified amounts of chemical pesticide to water as it flows from the hose.

What is an insecticide?

Chemical compounds that are used in the control of insects are generally called insecticides, which are grouped according to their main modes of action: a *stomach poison* attacks the internal organs after being swallowed; a *systemic insecticide* is a stomach poison that has been absorbed into the sap of plants; a *contact insecticide* kills upon contact with some external portion of the insect's body; a *residual-contact insecticide* kills insects by foot contact for long periods after application; a *fumigant* is a chemical that produces a killing vapor in the air; and a *repellent* is a substance that is distasteful or malodorous enough to keep insects away.

Of the various insecticides available, pyrethrum and insecticidal soaps are contact poisons. Rotenone kills both as a stomach and as a contact poison. Malathion and carbaryl, known commercially as Sevin, readily destroy many chewing and sucking insects.

INSECTS AND THEIR CONTROL
•

How are insects affected by insecticides?

Contact poisons usually work through their action on the spiracles (breathing apparatus) of insects. Chewing insects have jaws and bite holes in plant tissue; hence, they can be controlled by stomach poisons. Sucking insects obtain their food through a beak that pierces the plant to get at its sap, so therefore these insects can be killed only by systemic or contact poisons.

What are insecticidal soaps?

For many years, regular household soap was used as an insecticide. In recent years, this concept has been taken to a more refined level with the creation of specially prepared, pure soaps from natural fatty substances. These commercially available insecticidal soaps kill many insects on contact without damaging plants or harming people, animals, or beneficial insects such as honeybees and lady beetles; they are completely biodegradable and have no toxic aroma. Some insects that can be controlled with insecticidal soaps include aphids, mealybugs, whitefly, mites, earwigs, slugs, and scale.

What are biological insecticides?

They are naturally occurring insect diseases that can be produced commercially and formulated for application as sprays or dusts in the same manner that chemical insecticides are handled. They include two spore-forming bacteria, *Bacillus popillia* (milky spore disease) for Japanese beetle, and *Bacillus thuringiensis* (Dipel, Thuricide, Baktur), which is effective against various caterpillars, such as cabbage looper, gypsy moth, and bagworm. Their toxic specificity makes them safe to use around food, water, and animals. When the susceptible insects feed on the treated plant, the pests consume spores that inflict them with fatal disease.

I often see the name dicofol suggested for mites. What is it?

Dicofol is the accepted common name for Kelthane, a very effective and widely available miticide for spider mites on ornamental plants.

I have a cat and dog that roam around in my gardens. Will malathion sprays applied to the plants harm them?

Very unlikely. Malathion is one of the least toxic insecticides to warm-blooded animals. In addition, it loses its toxic properties rapidly upon exposure to air, so that in two days no toxic residue is left. Do keep pets and children away from freshly sprayed plants. Honeybees may be killed with malathion.

What is pyrethrum?

A contact insecticide obtained from the pyrethrum plant, which is a chrysanthemum, mostly grown in Africa. It is especially effective against aphids and soft-bodied insects, but it will kill whatever chewing insects it hits, including beetles, leafhoppers, whiteflies, caterpillars, and stinkbugs. It is useful for spraying flowers, because it leaves no stain.

What is rotenone?

The principal insecticidal constituent in the roots of such plants as *Derris* or *Lonchocarpus*. It acts as both a stomach and a contact poison for insects, and kills fish and other cold-blooded animals. It may be considered far less injurious to people than other pesticides, although it is often a throat irritant. It leaves no poisonous residue on the plant. Rotenone formerly was obtained from the Far East, but it is now produced in South America. Rotenone dust is available in a one-percent dilution.

Is Sevin safe to use?

Carbaryl, sold under the brand name of Sevin, is a very useful, broad-spectrum insecticide that is comparatively safe for both plants and the user. It suppresses or controls some rust and gall mites. It does kill bees and some other beneficial insects and can increase the spider mite problem, because it kills the mites' natural predators. Look for sprays that include a miticide.

What insects are harmless in the garden?

Of the harmless, or even helpful ones, lady beetles, ground beetles, and praying mantises are most often seen in the home garden. A sluglike creature, larva of the syrphid fly, also occasionally feasts upon aphids.

I have found several black, brown, and iridescent large beetles in the ground this fall. Are they harmful?

No, you probably found ground beetles, which have very prominent jaws and live in the earth or under stones. These are beneficial insects, feeding on cankerworms and other pests, and should not be disturbed.

I have often heard that praying mantises are helpful to have in the garden. Can you tell me something about them?

If praying mantises are not naturally present in your neighborhood—these ferocious-looking, but beneficial insects are not commonly found much north of 40° latitude—you may not be able to introduce them successfully. A member of the grasshopper family, the praying mantis is very long and thin, with prominent eyes and enormous front legs, often held up in a praying attitude and used for catching other insects, such as aphids, mites, and caterpillars.

Are ants harmful in the garden?

Ants are undesirable not because they afflict the plants themselves, but because they loosen the soil around the roots when they feed and thus cause the plants to wilt and die. In addition, they carry and nurse aphids and mealybugs for their honeydew. Apply either Sevin (carbaryl) or malathion to their nests to kill them.

What control program would you suggest for aphids?

Aphids are soft-bodied, sucking insects that often cluster at the tips of new growth, causing the leaves to curl. Their active

Lady beetle.

Praying mantis.

Aphids are extremely common sucking insects that often cluster at the tips of new growth.

time varies with the growth cycle of the host plant, so spraying is generally intermittent rather than regular. Use malathion, pyrethrum, rotenone, Sevin, or insecticidal soap as soon as you see the first few aphids.

Can anything be done to destroy the white aphids that feed on the roots of plants?

Pour a solution of malathion (one tablespoon to a gallon of water) into a depression around the plant's stem. Root aphids are usually tended by ants, so that ant control should also be started (see above).

What are the hard-shelled insects that are devouring my perennials?

These are probably some type of beetle, a large group of insects with chewing mouth parts and hardened front wings that form convex shields. Except for a few beneficial types, such as ground and lady beetles, they are injurious both in their grub, or larval, stage and as adults. Control them by stomach or contact poisons such as Sevin or rotenone used in the ground or on the foliage.

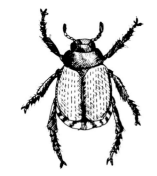

Japanese beetle.

What are effective ways to suppress Japanese beetles?

There are several techniques for fighting this one-half-inch-long, shiny metallic green beetle that is such a severe pest in some areas. First, from the end of June through the end of September, spray with carbaryl, rotenone, or pyrethrum to attack the adult beetles. The frequency and number of applications depends greatly on the amount of new growth, but weekly sprays are sometimes necessary. Another popular method is to handpick beetles and drop them into a jar or can of kerosene. Milky spore disease treatment on the lawn is an effective long-term control measure, but it takes several years for this to have a major effect on the beetle population. Finally, special traps may be placed at strategic locations around the property. As with the milky spore treatment, this technique may take several years before results are noticed.

Twelve-spotted beetle.

What can be done about twelve-spotted beetles? They ruin all the late blooms in my garden.

Twelve-spotted cucumber beetles are hard to kill, but dusting or spraying with carbaryl or rotenone is often helpful.

How can I combat flea beetles?

Flea beetles, which get their name from their habit of quickly springing several inches when disturbed, are small, black, oval beetles that chew tiny holes in the foliage of many garden plants. Dust or spray your plants with carbaryl or rotenone for control of these insects.

How can borers be prevented from doing their deadly work?

Borers are caterpillars or grubs, the larvae of moths or beetles, that work in woody or herbaceous stems. They are best prevented by burning old stalks of your plants at the end of the growing season. Destroy as many borers as possible by hand and use malathion at two-week intervals for control during the growing season.

The leaves of my plants have big holes, with a few worms, which I suspect did the damage. Do you agree?

The "worms," more properly called caterpillars, are the larvae of various butterflies, moths, and certain sawflies. Most insecticides will control them, but the safest method is to use *Bacillus thuringiensis.*

In July, when I approached some of my perennials, myriads of small insects came flying out. What were they?

They probably were leafhoppers, which can damage your plants. Green to yellow and only about one-eighth inch long, they are active fliers when disturbed. Control them with pyrethrum or malathion.

While digging in the ground recently, I saw quite a few slender, black insects about two inches long that looked like tiny, thousand-legged snakes. What could they be, and are they injurious to plants?

These are probably millipedes—meaning thousand-legged—although literally they have about fifteen pairs of legs. They are usually beneficial in the garden, preying on other insects, but they sometimes enlarge on damage begun by other insects.

Do earthworms (or angle worms) feed on and destroy peony, iris, and other tubers? I have dug them up and found worms embedded in the tubers, with nothing left but the outer shell.

Your peony probably succumbed to botrytis blight, and the iris, to borers and rot. Earthworms do not feed on living plant tissue, but are an important part of healthy, humus-rich soil.

Is there any way to exterminate earwigs?

There is little that can be done to exterminate earwigs, those beetlelike insects that may be scattered all around the yard. Trap them under boards, and then throw them into a can of kerosene, or spray them with insecticidal soap, pyrethrum, or malathion.

What are the fuzzy white bugs on my flowers?

They sound like mealybugs, which are sucking insects closely related to scale. Wash off your plants with a strong spray from the hose. Then, spray with insecticidal soap or malathion.

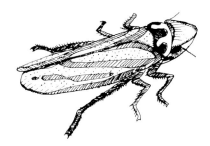

Leafhopper.

Millipede.

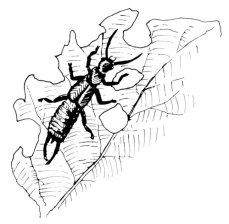

Earwig.

Mealybug.

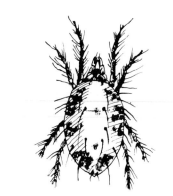

Spider mite.

Cyclamen mite.

What can be done to avoid or control mites?

Three kinds of mites are apt to be troublesome in the garden: spider mites, gall and rust mites, and cyclamen mites. Because they are microscopic in size, a hand magnifier is necessary to identify them as a problem. If you notice webbing on the undersides of leaves or between needles, or stippled or yellowed foliage, mites may be present. Spider mites are actually encouraged by the use of carbaryl (Sevin), because it kills many of the mites' natural predators as well as some of the mites. They can be partially checked by washing the foliage with strong jets of water and spraying with insecticidal soap or dicofol (Kelthane).

What are nematodes?

Nematodes are roundworms or eelworms, too small to see with the naked eye. They live in moist soil, in decaying organic matter, or as parasites in living plant tissues. They can travel only a short distance in the soil by themselves but are spread when surface water moves infested soil from place to place, and, very commonly, by local transfer and shipment of infested plants. Nematodes are particularly prevalent in sandy soils in southern states and in California. In the North, they may live during the winter in perennials and can also survive free in the soil.

How do you recognize the presence of nematodes?

Injury to plants is slow to show up and not at all dramatic. Usually, conspicuous above-ground symptoms do not appear until a heavy population of nematodes has built up. Nematodes should be suspected when plants show a slow decline in vigor and growth, when they become stunted and spare, when water does not help them much in drought, or when the foliage becomes discolored yellow or bronze. The plants' feeder roots may be lacking and the root system stunted and sparse or matted and shallow.

How are nematodes controlled?

Remove seriously infested plants. Cut off all plant tops after bloom. Make cuttings or divisions only from healthy plants, and either plant in a new location or sterilize the soil with a nematocide. The most effective nematocides, however, must be applied only by a certified applicator using specialized equipment. A good preventive against nematodes is to plant marigolds; their scent repels the insects.

Is there any way to rid my garden of slugs?

No, but they can be suppressed or minimized by a combination of good sanitation practices and the proper use of slug baits or traps. During the daytime, slugs and snails hide in the dark in

Slug.

very moist spots beneath stones, boards, and trash on the ground and in the soil. In a well-tilled garden, free of weeds and uncluttered by stones, stakes, and plant refuse, slugs will have few places to thrive.

Two slug baits sold under various trade names are metaldehyde and Mesurol. Mesurol should not be used around food plants (if you interplant flowers and vegetables), but metaldehyde may be. Be sure to follow label directions carefully when treating the soil, and do not treat plants directly.

Traps may be the best approach for small gardens. Place wooden boards in the garden to serve as hiding places. When you overturn them, you will find a multitude of slugs, which can then be eradicated. Alternatively, fill shallow dishes with beer and bury them to the rim at soil level, forming traps that slugs will crawl into and drown. Finally, sprinkle salt or lime directly onto slugs to kill them.

Thrip.

How can thrips be controlled?

Most thrips are small, slender insects, one-sixteenth inch long and only as wide as a small needle. They suck out the sap in leaves, causing a mottled appearance. Pyrethrum, rotenone, and carbaryl can be used as controls.

What is the black beetle that is so destructive to the petals of many of my perennials?

The black blister beetle is a common pest of hardy asters and chrysanthemums, particularly, as well as of other flowers. Unfortunately, it does prefer the petals to the leaves. Kill the beetles with stomach poisons or contact insecticides or by brushing them into cans of kerosene. Avoid touching the insects, as their secretions can cause a blister.

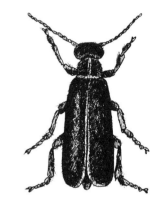

Blister beetle.

Can I recognize fungi on my plants by sight?

Fungi are members of the order of lowest plants, subsisting on both decaying and living tissue. Some fungi are readily recognized at a glance: mildew, with its white weft of threadlike fibers growing over a leaf; rust, which produces reddish dusty spore pustules; and smut, with its masses of black spores. Some can be differentiated only by microscopic examination.

FUNGI AND FUNGICIDES
•

What is a fungicide?

A material used to eradicate fungi in the soil or on seeds or plants. It is also used as a protectant to cover susceptible plant parts before the disease organisms appear. Some fungicides frequently used on perennials include benomyl (Benlate), copper sulfate-hydrated lime (bordeaux mixture), ferbam, folpet, and sulfur.

What is benomyl?

Benomyl is sold under the tradename Benlate. As a systemic fungicide, it is taken up into the vascular system of the plant and is excellent for control of powdery mildew and other fungi.

What is bordeaux mixture?

An old-fashioned fungicide still of value in the control of plant diseases. It is a mixture of copper sulfate and hydrated lime. Bordeaux mixture may be purchased in dry powder form to be mixed with water at the time of spraying or it may be made at home by thoroughly dissolving three ounces of copper sulfate (bluestone) in three gallons of water. Add five ounces of hydrated lime, and mix completely.

What amount of powdered bordeaux mixture should be mixed in per gallon of water?

The directions come on the package, but usually eight to twelve tablespoons of prepared, dry bordeaux powder to one gallon of water. For spraying of most ornamental plants, about half this amount is safer, less conspicuous, and equally effective.

Haven't ferbam and folpet been around a long time as fungicides?

Yes, these belong to a group of fungicides, all of which were first developed in the 1930s and 1940s. They control a broad range of fungus diseases and are very popular for home garden use. Ferbam is less toxic than folpet.

Is sulfur a fungicide?

Both elemental sulfur and lime-sulfur are effective in controlling many common fungal pests of plants, including powdery mildew and leaf spot. The lime-sulfur also helps to control spider mites, but it leaves a residue and stains painted objects, such as houses, fences, walls, and trellises. Neither product should be used when the air temperature is above 85° F. Sulfur is available as a dust, a ready-to-use spray, and as a concentrate for dilution as a spray.

What is the white powdery substance on the leaves of plants?

This is powdery mildew. It is most prevalent on phlox, delphinium, and chrysanthemum, but affects other perennials as well. Good air circulation around plants will help. Use benomyl or sulfur for control.

What will prevent crown rot?

Crown rot is a disease causing sudden wilting of plants from a rotting at the crown (the point where the plant stem and roots merge). A fungus called *Sclerotium rolfsii* is the cause, and the

Powdery mildew is common on such plants as delphinium, phlox, and chrysanthemum.

best prevention is to put healthy plants in a new location. The fungus may live for several years in the soil in the form of reddish-tan sclerotia, which resemble mustard seeds. Therefore, when the diseased plant is removed, it is important to take out all surrounding soil to a depth of one foot, and two feet or more wide, and replace it with fresh soil. If crown rot is a major problem, you should have the soil professionally sterilized.

What causes new growth to die back and spots with raised borders to appear on leaves?

You're describing anthracnose, or leaf spot. This is most likely to occur on chrysanthemum, columbine, daylily, hollyhock, delphinium, monkshood, violet, peony, and phlox. Remove and destroy diseased foliage. Chemical sprays are not always effective, but folpet sometimes works.

What is blight?

There are many different kinds of this plant disease, with a variety of appearances, but basically leaves become spotted or disfigured with lesions, a gray mold appears, and buds wither and do not open. Remove and destroy all diseased parts of the plants immediately. Benomyl and ferbam may be used as chemical controls.

The leaves of some of my plants are mottled and their growth is stunted. What might the reason be?

Very possibly some form of mosaic, caused by a virus. Perennials most often affected include chrysanthemum, dianthus, delphinium, iris, and primrose. There is no remedy. Plants should be destroyed. Virus diseases are sometimes spread by aphids, so controlling these will help. Also, select virus-free or virus-resistant varieties.

What is rust on plants?

True rust is a fungus that appears as reddish-brown or reddish-orange pustules of spores, or, in the case of red-cedar and apple rust, in long, gelatinous spore horns. Very often gardeners speak of rust when they merely mean a reddish discoloration of the tissue, which might be due to a variety of causes other than the true rust fungus.

Even after being watered, one of my perennials stayed wilted. Why was this?

The plant was affected by one of the two wilt diseases, fusarium or verticillium, where the water supply is cut off to either the entire plant or a part of it. The only solution is to remove the affected part or the entire plant. Do not try to grow the same kind of plant in the same place for two or three years.

ANIMALS

Do you have any advice on keeping dogs away from my perennial flower beds and borders?

Owners should be willing to keep their dogs restrained and, when walking them on a leash, should keep them curbed rather than allowing them to ruin plantings near a sidewalk. Moth balls and the various chemicals sold as dog repellents in garden centers may help.

What is the best way to control California pocket gophers?

There are many species of the pocket gophers (ground rats) found in California, Oregon, and Washington. There are special gopher traps on the market. Consult your County Extension Agent for regional restrictions and recommendations for available baits.

How do I get rid of moles?

It is unfortunate that moles, which really do a lot of good in the world by eating white grubs and other insects, should also have the bad habit of making unsightly ridges and mounds in gardens and disturbing the roots of flowers and vegetables by their tunnels. Feeding on the plants is actually done by mice that use the mole runs. There are not many nonpoison, nontrap options for control. A cat will discourage both moles and mice. Commercially available traps and poisons are effective control measures. Another method is get rid of the white grubs that attract the moles.

What is a good rabbit repellent?

The New Jersey Fish and Game Commission has listed nine repellents for harassed gardeners: (1) dust plants, when damp, with powdered lime; (2) dust liberally with dusting sulfur; (3) sprinkle plants with red pepper; (4) spray with a solution of three ounces of Epsom salts in one gallon of water; (5) spray with one teaspoon of Lysol in one gallon of water; (6) spray with two teaspoons of Black Leaf 40 in one gallon of soapy water; (7) spray with a solution of common brown laundry soap; (8) spray with one ounce of tartar emetic and three ounces of sugar in one gallon of water; (9) sprinkle naphthalene flakes between the plants. One of the easiest methods is the family's pet cat!

I want to attract birds to my garden, but squirrels always monopolize my feeding stations. Do you have any suggestions?

If the feeding station is hung from a horizontal wire, metal guards can be placed on either side; or if the feeding station is on top of a post, a guard can be placed underneath. If the feeder is anywhere within leaping distance of the ground, shrubbery, or trees, however, a guard is useless. You may simply have to put out enough food for the squirrels as well as for the birds.

How do I get rid of chipmunks?

These ground squirrels, which eat some slugs and insects, should not be destroyed without reason. To protect bulbs against chipmunks, plant your bulbs in wire baskets. Cats will also discourage chipmunks.

Is there any practical way to get rid of mice in the garden?

Not really, and what little can be done is only moderately helpful at best. Snap traps are the best and safest method. Cats that are good mousers help, but winter snows, as well as mulches, provide mice with protection. Consult your local extension agent for recommendations and currently available products.

Where can I turn for further help in diagnosing the pests and diseases that I suspect might be troubling my garden?

Your county Extension Service, often associated with a state land-grant university, is set up to give you exactly that advice. A wealth of valuable information is readily available through a visit or phone call to the local county agent of this educational arm of the U.S. Department of Agriculture. Phone and address listings for Extension Services can usually be found under county name in local phone directories.

How do I know that a pesticide is safe for home use?

Federal, state, and local laws regulate the sale and use of pesticides and at the same time help to protect both the public from dangerous residues and the environment from deleterious hazards. The Environmental Protection Agency approves specific pesticides, as well as their label directions, and any use inconsistent with these directions is then illegal under federal and state laws. Home gardeners often misuse pesticides by applying more, and more often, than the recommended rate, by treating when unnecessary, and by improperly disposing of toxic wastes in such places as sewage systems, storm drains, or sites where runoff ends up in streams or other bodies of water.

FURTHER HELP

•

16 Favorite Perennials

Adam's needle. See Yucca.

Amsonia. See Blue stars.

Astilbe *(Astilbe)*

Is the astilbe that flowers in the late spring and early summer related to spirea, the shrub?

No, but many nurseries and catalogs cause confusion by persistently labeling these herbaceous perennials—which are decidedly nonwoody—as "spirea." Like some spirea, the pink, rose, red, or white blossoms are fluffy. The common varieties grow eighteen inches to three feet tall and are hardy to -30° F.

I would like to grow astilbe plants in my flower garden, but I've been told that they require constantly wet soil. Is this true?

While the plants of astilbe revel in moist, rich soil, they also adapt to more average conditions. When planting, add good compost, leaf mold, or peat moss to the planting holes so that soil moisture will be retained. Astilbes usually do best in light shade, except in cool climates.

How do I propagate astilbes?

Large clumps may be propagated by division in the spring.

◀ *Bright-colored blanket flowers are easy to grow from seed, tolerate drought, and bloom almost continuously from late spring to fall.*

Astilbe: Grow astilbe in light shade unless your summers are rather cool.

Avens (*Geum*)

The avens I planted several years ago produced lovely orange-red flowers the first year or so, then they died out. What happened?

The most common varieties of avens are short lived. Try growing Borsii, Georgenberg, Heldreichii, and Starker's Magnificent.

Under what conditions will avens grow best?

They need rich, well-drained, moist soil, in partial shade. With winter mulch, most are hardy to -10° F. or slightly colder. Propagate by division.

Baby's-breath (*Gypsophila*)

Where should baby's-breath be planted in the garden?

It will grow in any reasonably good soil that is well drained, deeply cultivated, and not more than slightly acid. Plants need full sun and lots of space. Plant tall baby's-breath among spring bulbs or early-blooming perennials so that its lush growth hides the dying foliage of the spring plants.

Can baby's-breath be successfully transplanted?

Yes. Do so in the spring, and take care not to break the fleshy roots.

How is baby's-breath propagated?

Propagation is done by division, by cuttings, or by grafting on pieces of roots.

Does baby's-breath need to be staked?

Those kinds that grow over eighteen inches tall should be staked. Consider using one of the galvanized-wire rings made for this purpose, as they are sturdy and fairly unobtrusive.

Which baby's-breath is best for bouquets?

The double forms are the best for cutting and drying for use during winter months. Any of the varieties are excellent cut flowers. If the flowers are cut back before they go to seed, plants will usually bloom again.

Does baby's-breath have to be mulched in winter?

Baby's-breath is hardy to -40° F., but at these temperatures a loose winter mulch is recommended.

Balloon flower *(Platycodon)*

Does balloon flower need a rich soil?

No, any open, well-drained garden soil will suit it. Plant balloon flower in the spring, with the crown barely covered with soil.

Do balloon flowers need winter protection?

They are hardy to -40° F. and generally need no protection, although mice may eat their roots.

Are balloon flowers difficult to transplant?

Yes. They have long, fleshy roots, so you must take care when digging not to break them. The roots of old plants often go down eighteen inches or more; young plants are easier to move.

How is balloon flower propagated?

By careful division in the spring, or by seed sown in the fall or spring. Fortunately, balloon flower needs infrequent division, for it is not as simple as for most fibrous-rooted perennials. Cut off the outer sections of the thickened crown so that both buds and roots are present on each division. Dust cuts with fungicide to prevent infection.

I have been told that balloon flowers are slow to appear in the spring. Is this so?

Yes, they are one of the last perennials to appear above the ground. It's best, therefore, to mark their location in the fall so as to avoid injuring the plants in the spring before they emerge.

Basket-of-gold, Goldentuft *(Aurinia)*

What is the cascading plant with yellow flowers?

This is basket-of-gold. With its evergreen gray foliage and low growing habit, it is at its best planted in full sun, in very well-drained, neutral to alkaline soil. Use it at the top of a wall, at the front of a flower border, or along rocks. It is hardy to -40° F. After the plants flower, cut them back by a third. Propagate by dividing roots or from cuttings.

Why does basket-of-gold die?

Possibly because of "wet feet." Good soil drainage is necessary; the roots should never stand in water. This plant thrives on stone walls and in other dry locations. Because they are alpines, the plants are not long lived where summers are hot and humid.

Basket-of-gold: This low-growing plant thrives in dry locations.

Beard-tongue: Encourage neat growth by staking beard-tongue when it is about a foot tall.

Beard-tongue, Penstemon *(Penstemon)*

Is penstemon a hardy plant?

Hardy to -40° F., beard-tongue grows eighteen to thirty-six inches tall with spikes of scarlet, pink, or purple foxglovelike flowers in summer. Of the more than 250 different species of *Penstemon,* many remain green until long after frost appears. They need a very well-drained soil that is not particularly rich.

How do you trim and care for penstemons?

They need no trimming, but the wiry stems of the tall kinds need support, best supplied by twiggy brush inserted among the plants when they are about a foot tall. Tie loose stems to the brush and cut the tops of the brush away when flower buds form. Cut down the stems after bloom and top-dress with bone meal.

What is the best way to divide penstemon plants?

Remove the plants from the ground in early spring, pull them gently apart, and replant.

Bear's-breech *(Acanthus)*

My bear's-breech seldom bears the spikes of purple flowers it's supposed to. What can I do?

Bear's-breech prefers cool and dry, but sunny conditions. To survive in areas with hot summers, it must be grown in shady spots where it is cool and moist, but these conditions unfortunately keep it from blooming well.

Our winter temperatures go to -20° F. Will bear's-breech grow for me?

Bear's-breech is reliably hardy only to 10° F., but with well-drained soil and a heavy winter mulch, you may be successful.

How do I propagate bear's-breech?

Bear's-breech is easily increased by division of the roots. In fact, in California bear's-breech spreads so rapidly that the roots should be confined. Plants may also be started from seed.

Seemingly overnight there are slimy trails on the leaves of my bear's-breech and big portions have been bitten out of them. What is causing this?

Slugs and snails. Set out shallow pans of beer or use commercial slug bait.

Bee balm, Bergamot *(Monarda)*

I love the unusual flowers of bee balm, as do bees and hummingbirds, but I've had trouble keeping plants. What might be wrong?

Bee balm is easily grown if conditions are right. Hardy to -30° F., plants grow three feet tall in humus-rich, moist soil in full sun or light shade. Plants do not live long in areas with warm winters or dry soil. They should be divided every couple of years. To prevent pests from overwintering in the plants, cut them to the ground in fall and destroy the debris.

Bellflower, Canterbury-bells *(Campanula)*

What growing conditions do bellflowers require?

Provide them with fertile, humus-rich, and moist but well-drained soil. They prefer full sun except in hot climates, where they do better in light shade. A winter mulch may be necessary. In general, the bellflowers are relatively pest-free. Where slugs and snails may be a problem, put out shallow pans of beer or commercial bait. Divide plants every three or four years. Propagate by division or cuttings. Taller varieties may need staking.

I have problems with canterbury-bells rotting away, even in dry soil. What is the problem?

There are two soil fungi that may cause crown or stem rot under moist conditions, but your trouble may actually be due to insufficient water. Try another location in improved soil mixed with organic matter, such as leaf mold, compost, or peat moss.

Maggie Oster

Bellflower: Canterbury-bells (**Campanula Medium**) *are the showiest and best known of all bellflowers.*

SELECTED BELLFLOWERS

Carpathian harebell *(C. carpatica)* grows in twelve-inch mounds of crinkled, pointed, semievergreen leaves and bears blue or white upward-facing, open bell-shaped flowers in midsummer. Remove faded flowers for continuous bloom. Plant in cool, moist, well-drained soil, in the rock garden, in front of the flower border, or along paths.

Canterbury-bells *(C. Medium* and *C. Medium calycanthema),* the showiest and best known of the bellflowers, is a biennial. It bears two-inch white, pink, blue, or purple flowers on stalks two feet tall.

Peach-leaved bellflower *(C. persicifolia)* bears stately two- to three-foot spikes of blue or white, cup-shaped flowers throughout summer from a mound of long, narrow leaves. It can become very weedy in some areas, but the flowers are excellent for cutting. Carpathian harebell, danesblood, and peach-leaved bellflower are all hardy to -40° F.

Danesblood *(C. glomerata)* has upward-facing clusters of twelve to eighteen bell-shaped flowers on a one- to three-foot stem in midsummer.

Scotch harebell *(C. rotundifolia),* often found wild in parts of Europe, Asia, and North America, is a dainty plant about twelve inches tall with wiry branches of one-inch, deep blue bells during summer. It does best in cool climates.

Bergamot. See Bee balm.

Betony, Lamb's ears *(Stachys)*

Is betony really related to lamb's ears? They look so different.

They are indeed. Betony *(S. grandiflora)* has rippled, dark green leaves with scalloped edges; the rosy-mauve, eighteen-inch flower spikes develop in July. Lamb's ears *(S. byzantina)* is a wonderful edging plant, with soft, furry, silver-gray leaves; growth is ground-hugging, with spikes of small magenta flowers growing eighteen inches tall.

How hardy are lamb's ears and betony?

Lamb's ears is hardy to -30° F. and betony is hardy to -40° F.

What kind of soil and light does *Stachys* need?

Any good, well-drained garden soil and full sun or very light shade.

How is *Stachys* propagated?

By dividing in the fall or spring, or by seed.

Bishop's hat *(Epimedium)*

How is bishop's hat best used?

It makes an excellent ground cover and is fine for rock gardens, with its attractive foliage and tiny, unusual, pink, white, or yellow flowers in early spring. It is especially nice among the small spring-flowering bulbs, such as grape hyacinth, scilla, and aconite. Plant it where it is lightly shaded and has rich, moist soil. Most varieties grow one foot tall and are hardy to -30° F. Propagate by division.

Bishop's weed. See Snow-on-the-mountain.

Blackberry lily *(Belamcanda)*

I have a plant with an unusual seed pod that resembles a blackberry. Can you tell me what it is?

You're describing blackberry lily. Its long-lasting, six-petaled, star-shaped flowers may be orange, yellow, or apricot with darker speckles. The gray-green foliage resembles that of iris. Plants are hardy to -20° F. and grow one to three feet tall.

Is blackberry lily easy to grow?

Yes. It will grow in just about any soil, withstands drought, and does best in full sun, although it tolerates light shade. It is readily propagated from seed.

Blackberry lily: The star-shaped flowers of blackberry lily are quite long-lasting.

Maggie Oster

Bishop's hat: This plant makes an excellent ground cover or rock garden plant.

Blanket flower *(Gaillardia)*

Can you suggest a bright-colored plant that will bloom continuously from late spring until fall? It must also tolerate drought and be easy to grow.

Gaillardia will certainly meet your needs. With showy red or yellow, or combination red and yellow flowers, gaillardia is readily grown from seed. The two- to three-foot-tall plants are long lived in dry, sandy, infertile soils with hot summers and full sun. Dwarf varieties need more moisture and a soil rich in organic matter.

Do *Gaillardias* make good cut flowers?

They are indispensable for the person who enjoys bouquets indoors. Naturally long-lasting, they last even longer if picked when the flowers are still slightly cup-shaped rather than fully open. The globe-shaped seed heads are also useful in fresh and dried arrangements.

When should I divide my *Gaillardias*?

In early spring, break up the old plants into several pieces.

How can I keep grubs out of the stems of *Gaillardias*?

Your grubs may be larvae of the common stalk borer. The best control depends on cleaning up all weeds and woody stems in autumn. Serious infestations can be controlled with a spray of methoxychlor-Kelthane mixture in late June; repeat twice at ten-day intervals.

Bleeding-heart *(Dicentra)*

What are the cultural requirements of bleeding-hearts?

Most do best in light shade, although in cool climates they will grow in full sun. If planted in too deep shade, they will not bloom. Provide a rich, light, well-drained but moist soil. Propagate from seeds, plant division, or stem or root cuttings. Division should be made in September. Transplant in early autumn or early spring.

I mulched a large bleeding-heart with leaves last winter, and yet it died. What might have been the cause?

You may have used too many leaves and smothered the plant; or perhaps you covered it too early. Wait until the soil is frozen, then cover bleeding-heart plants lightly. Remove mulch gradually in the spring. It is also possible to lose bleeding-hearts because of mice eating the roots.

Blue plumbago, Bunge, Leadwort *(Ceratostigma)*

My flower border doesn't seem to have much color in late summer. Can you suggest a low-growing plant as an edging in the front of my sunny border?

Blue plumbago would be a good choice, with its cobalt-blue flowers from midsummer until frost. The foot-tall mass of dark green leaves turns reddish-bronze in autumn. With protection, it is hardy to -20° F. Plants grow in any good garden soil and can be propagated by dividing the roots in spring.

Blue stars, Amsonia *(Amsonia)*

Can you tell me the name of a lovely blue-flowered perennial in my neighbor's garden? It has willowlike foliage and bears clusters of clear blue, star-shaped flowers in midspring. Its height is about three feet.

You are probably describing blue stars or willow amsonia. It is native to much of the upper South and as far west as Texas, but it is also quite hardy in northern gardens. It does well in partial shade. Propagate by seeds or by division in spring or fall.

Boneset. See Mist flower.

SELECTED BLEEDING-HEART

Japanese bleeding-heart *(D. spectabilis)* grows two to four feet tall, with thin, blue-green, fernlike leaves. It blooms in spring with sprays of heart-shaped, rosy crimson or white flowers. It is hardy to -50° F.

Eastern bleeding-heart *(D. eximia)* grows twelve to eighteen inches tall, with handsome gray-green, finely divided leaves topped with sprays of small pink or white flowers in early spring and again in fall. In cool climates, flowering continues off and on all summer. Plants readily self-sow. It is hardy to -40° F.

Pacific bleeding-heart *(D. formosa)* grows to twelve inches tall, with small pink or white flowers. Plants may spread rapidly from root growth. It is hardy to -40° F.

Bugbane, Snakeroot (Cimicifuga)

Will bugbane naturalize in a moist, shaded area of my yard?

This is an ideal location, particularly if the soil is rich in organic matter. Propagate by division of the plant or by seeds sown as soon as they are ripe.

Will bugbane spread and become a pest if I plant it in my flower border?

No. Although it readily naturalizes, it will not get out of control. It is a very elegant plant for the back of the border. The blooms are lovely in bouquets, too.

Why might the bugbane that I planted last year not have bloomed?

Bugbanes need to be established for several years before giving the normal display of bloom.

Bugleweed (Ajuga)

What ground cover do you suggest for an area that has both sun and light shade?

Bugleweed (*A. reptans*) will quickly form a thick mat either in sun or shade in just about any soil, and it is hardy to -40° F. Its leaves are evergreen in mild climates. Space the ground-hugging plants six inches apart for quick cover. Propagate by division or from seed.

Bugloss (Anchusa)

Can you suggest a tall-growing, deep blue-flowered perennial for planting in masses in either full sun or partial shade?

Try perennial bugloss, which bears large, loose clusters of forget-me-not-like flowers in June and July. Extend the blooming season by removing the faded flower sprays.

Will you please give the cultural care of bugloss?

Good, moist but well-drained garden loam and division every three years. Bugloss also readily self-sows.

Bunge. See Blue plumbago.

Butterfly flower, Milkweed (Asclepias)

Butterfly flower is so beautiful in the fields and along roadsides. Can it also be grown in the garden?

Certainly. Even with dry soil and competition from grass, it produces masses of brilliant orange flowers on two- to three-foot

Maggie Oster

Bleeding-heart: This old-fashioned favorite does well in light shade in most areas.

stems during the hottest part of summer. Best of all, it attracts hordes of butterflies with its sweet nectar. Hardy to -40° F., it requires full sun and well-drained soil. Propagate by seed; division is possible but difficult due to deep roots.

Campion, Catchfly, Maltese cross (*Lychnis*)

How do I grow Maltese cross?

Lychnis chalcedonica grows two to three feet tall and bears clusters of brilliant orange-scarlet flowers in midsummer; it will continue to bloom if faded flowers are removed. Hardy to -40° F., it is long lived and easy to grow in either full sun or light shade, and well-drained soil. Propagate by seed or division.

Can you describe rose campion?

Rose campion has downy, silver-gray stems and leaves, and striking cerise, white, or cerise-eyed flowers on twenty-four- to thirty-inch plants. It self-sows readily and seedlings reach flowering size in a year, but plants are short lived. Provide full sun and well-drained soil. Cut off faded flowers.

How did catchfly get its name? How do I grow it?

The common name of *L. Viscaria* comes from the sticky stems just below the flowers. Tufts of grasslike foliage grow twelve inches tall and bear fragrant magenta flowers in midsummer. Hardy to -40° F., plants grow in full sun and well-drained soil. Propagate by division or seed.

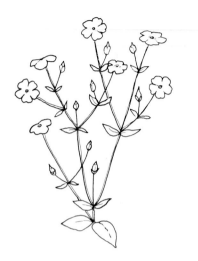

Rose campion: The self-sown seedlings of rose campion usually flower within a year.

Candytuft (*Iberis*)

Will you give me directions for the proper culture of candytuft?

Hardy to -40° F., candytuft, a tough little evergreen, usually grows satisfactorily in full sun or partial shade, in any well-drained garden soil that is not too acid. A good edging or rock garden plant, it should be cut back to within a couple of inches of the crown after it has flowered.

How can I propagate candytuft?

By seeds sown in the spring; by dividing the old plants in autumn or spring; or in the summer, by cuttings made of the young growth inserted in a cold frame.

Why does candytuft turn white and appear to die? It looks like mildew.

White rust is common on candytuft. It appears as white pustules on the underside of the leaves, which turn pale. Destroy diseased plants or plant parts, and dig out any cruciferous weeds, such as wild mustard. Spraying with bordeaux mixture may help.

Candytuft: A tough little evergreen, candytuft may be grown in either full sun or partial shade.

Canterbury-bells. See Bellflower.

Cardinal flower. See Lobelia.

Carnations, Hardy pinks, Sweet william *(Dianthus)*

Which of the hardy pinks do you recommend?

The most reliable of the garden pinks is cottage pink *(D. plumarius)*. Hardy to -40° F., this low-growing plant with gray-green, grasslike leaves has very fragrant, clove-scented flowers, in colors ranging from white to bright scarlet.

Is sweet william related to the hardy pinks? Is it a biennial or a perennial?

Yes, sweet william *(D. barbatus)* is one of the pinks and it is a biennial, but in cool climates it may live three or more years. It so readily self-sows, furthermore, that once it is established, you will seldom ever need to start new plants. In midsummer, the brilliant clustered blooms of sweet williams range in color from white to very dark red. Sweet william grows twelve to eighteen inches tall, although there are some very dwarf varieties.

Maggie Oster

Although technically a biennial, colorful sweet william readily self-sows and thus, once established, comes back year after year in many gardens.

What are some of the ways to use pinks in my garden?

Freely blooming pinks make good cut flowers, and are well suited for rock gardens, flower borders, or anywhere an edging is wanted.

After several years in my garden, my double pinks are all singles. What happened?

Pinks readily self-sow. Double types do not come true from seed, but the singles do.

How should I plant and care for hardy carnations?

Sow seeds indoors in March in a sterile, soilless mix. After seeds have germinated, transplant the seedlings into flats, 2 inches apart, or into peat pots. In May, prepare the outdoor bed, which should have well-drained soil and full sun. Fork in leaf mold or peat moss, and add about ten pounds of dehydrated cow or sheep manure per 100 square feet. Place plants about twelve inches apart. Water after planting. When seedlings are six to eight inches tall, pinch out the tips to induce branching. Cultivate the soil around the plants to keep it loose until the end of June, then mulch with old leaves or compost. Keep the plants watered. Disbud side shoots to encourage larger blooms on the main stem. Because carnations flower best in cool weather, keep buds removed until late summer.

The foliage of my pinks turns brown in the center of the clump and then spreads until the entire plant is dead. What is wrong?

It may be a fungus stem rot, which can be partially controlled by spraying with captan, or move healthy plants to a new location in very well-drained soil.

What is wrong with my hardy carnations? I get them started and they bloom until August, then droop and die.

Perhaps your carnations dry out. Try adding more organic matter to the soil to help retain the moisture. Or, the weather may be too hot and humid where you live.

Carolina lupine (*Thermopsis*)

What is the plant that looks like lupine, with its three- to five-foot-tall, bright yellow flowers in midsummer?

This is Carolina lupine, which is hardy to -40° F. It will grow in any deep, well-drained soil, is drought tolerant, and needs full sun. Divide the plants in spring or sow seed outdoors as soon as it ripens in the fall.

Catchfly. See Campion.

Catmint (*Nepeta*)

I recently visited a garden with a path edged in a plant labelled catmint. The bushy plants were about eighteen inches tall, with small, silver-gray leaves and sprays of tiny blue flowers. Can you tell me more about this plant?

Related to catnip, catmint is hardy to -40° F., and does well in sun in any well-drained soil. Blooming first in early summer, it will bloom again if the faded flowers are removed. Besides an edging to paths, catmint is also excellent in the front of the flower border, around beds of roses, or combined with pink flowers.

Chinese forget-me-not, Hound's-tongue (*Cynoglossum*)

I have average garden soil. Will Chinese forget-me-not grow successfully?

These two-foot plants do best in most soils, as long as they are well drained. Choose a site in full sun. Propagate by division in the spring or root cuttings in the fall. It is hardy to at least -20° F. Masses of rich, gentian-blue flowers, one-half inch across, are borne in July and August.

Chinese-lantern (*Physalis*)

The unusual, bright orange husks of Chinese-lantern are so wonderful for dried arrangements. Are the plants hard to grow?

Actually, Chinese-lantern is so easily grown in most soils that it can become a weed if the seeds are allowed to drop. It needs full sun. Plants grow thirty inches tall and are hardy to -40° F.

Cholla. See Prickly pear.

Christmas rose, Lenten rose (*Helleborus*)

Which of the hellebores is easiest to grow?

The Lenten rose. Growing eighteen inches tall, hybrid varieties provide a range of color from cream to pink, maroon, and green, with some spotted or streaked. Each stem bears several flowers that last up to three months. Plants self-sow and naturalize readily. It is hardy to -30° F.

How should I establish Christmas and Lenten roses?

Select a position in partial shade where the soil is rich and moist; add well-rotted manure, peat moss, compost, or leaf mold. Obtain young plants from local or mail-order sources and set them out in early spring. Do not allow plants to dry out during the summer.

Chinese-lantern: Bright orange Chinese-lantern plant readily self-sows.

*Lenten rose: Like Christmas roses,
Lenten roses do best in partial shade,
in rich, moist soil.*

What does the Christmas rose look like and when does it bloom?

The two-inch flowers have five white petals and golden stamens in the center; sometimes the petals are flushed with pink. Flowering occurs whenever temperatures are above 15° F. It is hardy to -40° F.

I have a Christmas rose that I have had for three or four years, and last year was the first it bloomed. Now I would like to move it. Will that set it back again three or four years?

Unfortunately, it may, for the Christmas rose does not like to be disturbed. Moving it carefully with a very large soil ball helps, but it is best to leave it in place.

Will you tell me how to divide hellebores? Mine are doing wonderfully well, but I would like to give some away.

It is best to divide them in late summer or autumn by taking a spading fork and lifting the side shoots without disturbing the main plant.

Chrysanthemum *(Chrysanthemum)*

I think of chrysanthemums as fall flowers. Is this so?

Chrysanthemums in the garden give a profusion of bloom in bright autumn colors as a grand finale to the gardening season.

Light frosts do little damage to either the flowers or foliage. If planted in protected spots, they will often remain attractive until mid-November in the latitude of New York state. Farther south, and in other milder climates, they are even better adapted, and a much larger selection of varieties can be used. Most will survive to -30° F. with some winter protection.

What are some tips to get chrysanthemums to bloom freely?

Choose a sunny location. Don't crowd them together or among other plants. Spade the soil deeply. Add a complete general-purpose garden fertilizer, plus a three- to four-inch layer of compost or other form of humus, to the soil under your plants. Cultivate frequently but lightly, and water copiously when needed. Divide plants every other year.

What type of soil is best for hardy chrysanthemums?

Any loose, crumbly soil is satisfactory. It should be well drained yet reasonably retentive of moisture. If the subsoil is heavy clay, improve its texture by adding manure, compost, leaf mold, or peat moss in the fall. Chrysanthemums will not succeed in waterlogged soil. They prefer soil with a pH 6 to 7, or slightly acidic.

Should hardy chrysanthemums be fed during the summer?

Apply a light dressing of a complete fertilizer, such as 5-10-10, into the soil around the plants when they are half grown. A liquid fertilizer applied in late summer or early fall works wonders, too.

When should one plant chrysanthemums?

Small plants are usually set out in the spring, but potted plants or plants with a large root ball can be set out any time during the growing season.

What is the best way to plant bare-root chrysanthemums?

With a trowel or spade, make a hole of ample size to accommodate roots. Set the plant in position so that the crown (the place where stem and roots merge) will be at soil level. Spread out the roots, and work the soil in among them, pressing the soil firmly with your fingers so that no air pockets remain. Do not plant chrysanthemums when the soil is wet and sticky. Water after planting.

How can I grow many-branched chrysanthemums?

Keep plants young by frequent division (see below), and pinch them back two or three times during the growing season—first when they are nine to twelve inches high, then when they are about fifteen inches high, and possibly a third time in late July. Cut back all strong shoots. A simpler way is to top the plants with a garden shears. Cushion-type varieties require no pinching. The shoots that you remove can be rooted.

What is the best way to care for chrysanthemums after they stop blooming in the fall?

Cut the stems back close to the ground. If brown foliage appeared during the summer, burn the stems and all dropped leaves—they may harbor insects or diseases. Cover plants lightly with evergreen branches and dry leaves when the soil is slightly frozen, after the first killing frost.

How should I care for hardy chrysanthemums in the spring?

Divide strong-growing kinds every year, and moderate-growing, every second year. When the shoots are three to four inches high, dig up the clump, and discard the old center portion. Separate the young offshoots, planting them singly, ten to twelve inches apart in well-prepared soil. If possible, give them a different location. Otherwise, fork some manure, compost, or fertilizer into the surface soil.

Can hardy chrysanthemums be moved when in bloom?

Yes. Be sure the soil is moist, then take up the clump of soil with a good root ball and replant immediately, firming the soil around the roots. Shade for two or three days, and don't neglect watering.

Why didn't my hardy chrysanthemums bloom this year? The leaves became gray.

Evidently the plants were badly mildewed. Do not crowd plants and be sure they have plenty of sun.

What causes the leaves of chrysanthemum to curl up and turn brown?

This is the most common problem of chrysanthemums. Verticillium or fusarium wilt, septoria leaf spot, or improper watering will all turn foliage brown, but in nine cases out of ten, leaf nematodes are to blame.

About July something attacked my chrysanthemums; they broke off about three inches from the ground, leaving piles of what looked like white ant eggs. What caused this?

The stalk borer was probably responsible, and what appeared to be ant eggs was excrement from the caterpillar inside the stem. When you see borer injury, it is usually too late to help the plant. Cleaning up weeds, especially in the fall, is the best prevention.

What insect causes chrysanthemums to open only partially?

This may be the gall midge, which lives in little conical projections of the leaves and flowers. Pick off and destroy infested plant parts. A fungus disease, ray blight, also deforms flowers.

What is the small insect similar to a ladybug, but green with black spots, that eats the flowers, particularly the centers, of chrysanthemums every fall?

It is the spotted cucumber beetle. Control is difficult because sprays discolor the flowers. Pyrethrum or rotenone would be best. As a last resort, spray or dust with carbaryl (Sevin).

Cinquefoil *(Potentilla)*

I planted several different kinds of the perennial cinquefoil as an edging to my flower border and in a rock garden, and they all died. What was wrong?

Perennial cinquefoils are excellent plants in the right climate, but they do not like extreme heat and need winter protection in areas with minimum winter temperatures of -30° F. Soil should be rich in humus but well drained. Cinquefoil tolerates both sun and light shade. Thin them annually for best growth.

How are cinquefoil propagated?

The trailing stems readily root. These new young plants can then be lifted and transplanted.

Columbine *(Aquilegia)*

My columbines never grow into healthy plants, although they have full sun and the other plants around them grow very well. Why?

Almost any location, except a hot, dry, windy one is suitable for columbine, although some light shade is beneficial. They need a well-drained, sandy loam that is neutral or slightly acid. Prepare the ground at least a foot deep and incorporate a two-inch layer of rotted manure, peat moss, or rich compost. Space the plants at least nine inches apart. Do not plant them too deep or the crown will rot.

How should I divide columbines?

Dig up the clumps, shake off the soil, and gently pull the plant apart, taking care to keep the roots from being broken.

What remedy will prevent crown rot?

Crown rot is caused by *Sclerotium rolfsii,* a fungus that is generally prevalent in the soil and attacks many different plants.

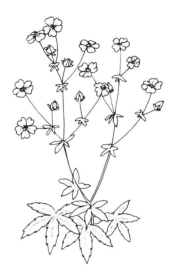

Cinquefoil: Provide winter protection for cinquefoil where winter temperatures drop to -30° F.

Columbine: Keep these graceful plants out of hot, windy, dry locations.

Maggie Oster

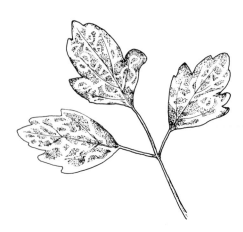

Leafminers make serpentine trails in the leaves of such plants as columbine.

Soil sterilization is difficult and not too satisfactory. The best treatment is to remove infected plants as soon as they are noticed.

The leaves of our columbine have little silvery-white lines all over them. Could you tell me the cause?

These are the serpentine tunnels of the columbine leaf miner. The larvae work inside the leaf and a small fly emerges to lay eggs for the next generation. Although this does not kill or even damage the plant, it is unsightly. There is no cure, but picking off and burning all infested leaves as soon as they are noticed, and cultivating the ground around the plants in the fall and early spring, will help prevent further infestations. Spraying with Orthene or malathion may help.

How can one keep the roots of columbine from becoming infested with worms?

The worms are probably millipedes, which usually swarm around when a plant is weakened or dead from other causes, either disease or unfavorable cultural conditions. They cause little injury, but can be controlled with either diazinon or malathion.

I lost hybrid columbines in a perennial bed where everything else thrived. What might have caused this?

Hybrid columbines, like hybrid delphiniums, are usually short lived. Your sudden loss, however, may be due to a fungus disease called crown rot, or to the columbine borer.

How can I fight columbine borer?

This is a salmon-colored caterpillar that works in the crown of the plant. All you can do is pull up and discard the infected plant, and in the fall destroy all weeds and other debris that might harbor borer eggs during the winter. Protect other columbines by spraying with Sevin.

What causes my columbine plants to turn brown?

This is probably due to spider mite, a tiny mite that makes webs on the underside of the leaves. Spray with Kelthane or insecticidal soap.

Coneflower, Gloriosa daisy *(Rudbeckia)*

What are the uses of coneflowers?

The bright yellow flowers of coneflowers in mid- to late summer are glorious—and they make lovely cut flowers. They are excellent for planting in large drifts (informally shaped groups) or meadow gardens. Most varieties survive minimum winter temperatures of -40° F.

What kinds of soil and light are best for coneflowers?

They will flourish in any reasonably fertile soil that is neither too wet nor too dry and receives full sun. Divide them every four years, or more frequently if plants are spreading quickly.

Coralbells *(Heuchera)*

Coralbells are so graceful. What are the growing requirements?

The low-growing clumps of leaves, marked by eighteen- to twenty-four-inch spikes of delicate coral-pink flowers in spring and summer, have made coralbells a favorite of gardeners and anyone who loves to bring bouquets of flowers indoors. They are easily grown in moist, rich, well-drained loam, in full sun or light shade. They are hardy to -40° F. The red-flowered types attract butterflies. Cutting off the spent stems of coralbells will cause flowers to be produced through summer, especially in areas with cool summer temperatures.

When and how do I divide coralbells?

Coralbells need division only about every three or four years, particularly if mulched. Take up clumps in early spring or fall, and break them into pieces with as much root attached as possible. Replant about twelve inches apart.

Cowslip. See Marsh marigold.

Cranesbill *(Geranium)*

I thought geraniums were houseplants, but I'm told there are perennial garden varieties. Can you explain?

The common houseplant geranium is really a *Pelargonium.* The true *Geranium* species has both frost-tender and hardy varieties that grow twelve to eighteen inches tall, with flowers ranging in color from lilac to rosy purple. They flourish in most well-drained soils in areas with cool summers; but with light shade and moist soil, they will grow in hot-summer regions.

How are geraniums propagated?

They seldom need dividing, but if you want additional plants, push your fingers into the soil at the base of a plant and take out a piece with some stem and root, and replant it.

Cupid's-dart *(Catananche)*

What growing conditions does cupid's-dart need?

These plants need sun and sandy garden soil. Hardy to -20° F., cupid's-dart grows eighteen to twenty-four inches tall. The small blue flowers are useful for cutting, are everlasting, and are

Maggie Oster

Coralbells: Although the foliage of coralbells is ground-hugging, the tall, graceful flower stalks are light and airy and do not interfere with this garden sun dial.

produced all summer long. Cupid's-dart can be started from seed or propagated by division.

Dame's-rocket, Sweet rocket (*Hesperis*)

There was a lovely, sweet-scented plant with clusters of magenta-colored flowers in our garden when I was growing up. The plants were bushy, about three feet tall, and bloomed during summer. What might it have been?

You're describing an old-fashioned flower that is lovely for bouquets—dame's-rocket. There is also a white-flowered variety. Plants thrive in full sun or light shade in any good garden soil. They are grown from seed and readily self-sow.

My dame's-rocket has cabbage worms. How do I control them?

Spray your plant with *Bacillus thuringiensis*.

Daylily (*Hemerocallis*)

What accounts for the popularity of daylily?

Today's daylily is perhaps the perfect summer perennial. It is difficult to think of another perennial that requires so little care. The ribbonlike foliage is superb, remaining in good condition throughout the growing season. Although each lily-shaped flower lasts only a day, each stalk is so abundantly budded that the actual flower display goes on for weeks. There are thousands of varieties, with colors ranging from pale cream to soft yellow, bright yellow and gold, as well as apricot, pink, maroon, and almost fiery red. The clumps are vigorous and can be divided every few years, or, if they do not outgrow their space, they can be left indefinitely without disturbance. Many are deliciously fragrant. They are especially useful in informal landscape schemes and look well in the foreground of shrub groupings as well as in the flower border.

When is the best time to plant daylilies, and how should I do this?

Plant them in either spring or summer. They can be lifted even when they are in full bloom if a good clump of soil is taken and care is used not to damage the roots. Plants must be watered deeply and kept well watered for a week or two. Dig the soil deeply, adding well-rotted manure, leaf mold, peat moss, or compost. When planting, make the holes deep enough so that the roots are not crowded, and set the plants with their crowns just level with the soil.

Do daylilies have to be planted in the shade?

No. Daylilies will grow in full sun if the soil is rich and moist, but the more pastel varieties do best in light or partial shade.

Maggie Oster

Daylily: Dependable, vigorous, and often sweet-scented, daylilies are one of the best perennials to grow.

Why might daylilies fail to blossom?

Most commonly this is due to too-dense shade or over-crowded plants and exhausted soil.

How shall I divide daylilies?

They are sometimes hard to divide, especially old clumps. The best method is first to dig up clumps, then push two spading forks through the clump, back to back, and pry the clump apart. (See pg. 325.) Do not make the divisions too small if you want flowers the next year.

What is the main blooming season for daylilies?

July and August, although some bloom in June and others in September and October. The variety Stella D'Oro has become very popular for its long period of bloom, from May until early fall; flowers are two-and-one-half inches across and plants grow two feet tall.

When should I fertilize daylilies?

Feed them in late winter or in very early spring, then again in early fall, using a low-nitrogen blend such as 5-10-10.

Is there a daylily that is particularly fragrant?

Although many hybrids have some scent, the sentimental favorite is canary-yellow Hyperion, which blooms from July into August. Lemon lily *(H. Lilioasphodelus* var. *flava)* is also quite popular.

Delphinium, Larkspur *(Delphinium)*

How are delphiniums best used in the garden?

One of the most spectacular of garden flowers, most delphiniums are tall-growing and thus best used toward the back of a mixed flower border where they create strong vertical lines and accent points. However, lower-growing strains have been developed, which let you add the beautiful colors of delphiniums to other parts of the flower border.

In what colors are delphiniums available?

While the clear blue colors of delphinium are the most highly prized, sparkling whites, rich violets, and soft, pleasing mauves are also available. Two new dwarf varieties are quite vigorous: Blue Fountain and Magic Fountain. An old favorite, developed by the noted photographer Edward Steichen, is the bush-type Connecticut Yankee.

What are the climatic requirements of delphinium?

They are grown successfully throughout the United States and Canada.

Should a beginner buy delphinium plants or start them from seeds?

Either is satisfactory, but for quick results, buy plants. If you do decide to begin with seeds, sow them in well-prepared soil in a cold frame in August, in rows spaced about two inches apart, with seeds spaced about one-quarter inch apart. Cover with soil just so that the seeds are barely out of sight. Leave the seedlings in the frame during the winter and transplant them to the garden in the spring. Seeds may also be sown in the open ground if special care is taken to protect the young seedlings. Shade both the seedbed and young seedlings until plants are well developed. Alternatively, sow seeds indoors any time between February 1 and May 1. If started early enough (before April 1), many of the plants will bloom the first year, in late August or early September. As soon as the plants are big enough to handle conveniently, transplant seedlings to flats or individual peat pots containing commercial soilless mixture. The flats must have drainage holes. Grow them under fluorescent lights.

Can manure be used on delphiniums? What about other fertilizers?

Manure, if well rotted, is excellent. Mix it in when you prepare the soil or add it later as a topdressing. Apply about five bushels per 100 square feet. Delphiniums have a higher nitrogen requirement than almost any other garden flower. Unless the soil is already very rich, they should be fertilized at least twice a year with a complete commercial fertilizer such as 5-10-5. Make the first application in the spring when the new shoots are about four inches tall. A second application can be made about five weeks later.

Maggie Oster

Do delphiniums require lime?

They do best in a slightly acid soil (pH 6.8). Use lime only when a pH test indicates a pH of 6.5 or lower. If the soil is rich in organic matter, they will tolerate a much wider range of pH values (pH 5.5 to 7.2). Spread the lime evenly over the soil surface and work it into the top three or four inches.

Is there a way one can tell by observing the plants whether the soil is too "sweet" (alkaline) for delphiniums?

The leaves appear mottled with yellow or, in severe cases, with white. The veins usually retain their dark-green color.

How far apart should delphiniums be planted?

In perennial borders, plant them two to three feet apart; in cutting gardens give them more room—three to four feet between rows and two feet between the plants in rows.

When should delphiniums be transplanted?

Very early spring is best, if possible before growth starts. They can also be transplanted with success in the fall or immediately after their first period of bloom. Move them with a large ball of soil in order to disturb their roots as little as possible.

Delphinium: This spectacular flower has a higher nitrogen requirement than most other plants, so fertilize it at least twice a year.

Can delphiniums be made to bloom in the fall as well as during their regular season?

Cut the flowering stems off as soon as possible after they have finished blooming. New shoots will then come up and flower in early fall.

How can a delphinium be staked?

When the plant is about three feet high, place three five-foot stakes in the form of a triangle around it. Tie a band of raffia or soft twine around the stakes about 1 foot above the ground. As the plant grows, tie additional bands around the stakes. If desired, individual stakes can be used for large-flowering spikes. This latter method is preferable in decorative plantings.

Do delphiniums need extra watering?

Delphiniums require large quantities of water, especially just prior to and during the flowering period. Water them thoroughly whenever the weather is dry as well.

Why have my delphiniums failed even though I moved them to a better spot and replanted them one foot from a hedge where they get southerly sun?

Probably the moving is responsible. They may do better as they become reestablished. However, you have set them too near the hedge. They should be at least two or three feet away. Keep them well fertilized and watered.

How can I prevent my delphiniums from growing tall and having brittle stems?

Vigorous delphiniums are likely to be brittle and break off during windstorms and rainstorms. Lack of nitrogen exacerbates the problem. Stake the plants adequately or buy lower-growing kinds.

Why do delphiniums freeze in the winter?

Delphiniums are really very hardy plants, seldom killed by low temperatures. They are more likely to be smothered by snow, ice, or poor drainage. Diseases, especially crown rot, can develop during the fall, winter, or early spring, and kill the plants. Heaving is another hazard. Freezing and thawing action can cause shallow-rooted delphiniums to be heaved out of the ground, exposing them to the air and cutting off their ability to absorb vitamins and moisture from the soil. Some leading growers consider the English strains hardier than the American strains, which were developed on the Pacific coast.

Should young, fall-planted delphiniums be mulched?

It is always a good idea to give seedlings transplanted in the fall protection from heaving by mulching them lightly with marsh hay or straw. In areas with very cold winters, give them extra protection by keeping them in a cold frame, covered by a window sash to keep out snow and rain.

Can delphiniums be grown in areas with warm climates, such as Florida?

Grow them as annuals by sowing seeds early each spring. The plants are not usually successfully carried over a second year. In fact, delphiniums live longer in regions where summers are fairly cool. Hot, muggy weather is not to their liking.

Is it wise to divide delphiniums that have grown to a large size?

Yes. Lift the plants, shake off the soil, and cut the clumps apart with a strong knife. Replant them immediately in well-prepared soil. Each division should contain three to five shoots.

Why do my delphiniums get a black rot after one period of bloom?

Rotting is usually worse in wet weather and with succulent tissue. Some growers feel that the act of cutting down the old stalks after they bloom actually spreads the rot organisms.

How do you control black spot on delphinium?

This bacterial disease appears as tarlike black spots on the leaves. It is not serious except in wet seasons, when it may be controlled by spraying with bordeaux mixture. In a normal season, picking off infected leaves and cleaning up old stalks in autumn should be sufficient.

Is there a remedy when leaves curl and the plants fail to bloom, or when they have green blossoms?

This is probably aster yellows, a virus disease carried by leafhoppers. There is no cure except taking out infected plants as soon as you notice them and spraying the plants with contact insecticides to control the leafhoppers. Such diseases are common in the Northwest.

Is mildew on delphiniums caused by the soil?

No. Mildew is a fungus disease that infects the leaves. It is seldom serious before late summer. It can be controlled by spraying the plants with Benlate or Karathane or by dusting with sulfur. Prevent mildew by giving plants adequate spacing, using mildew-resistant strains, and cleaning up old plant material.

What causes the yellowing of leaves on hybrids?

Your plants may need nutrients, especially nitrogen. Apply fertilizer every ten days, but be careful not to apply too much; getting too succulent a growth will mean more rot diseases. Yellowing might also be due to fusarium wilt, a fungus common in soils in the Middle West. In this case, there is usually a progressive yellowing of leaves from the base upward. The yellowing may also be due to crown rot, lack of water, or intense heat. Try a new location.

My delphiniums are deformed, stunted, and marked with black streaks and blotches. What is wrong?

Your plants are infested by an exceedingly minute, common, and serious pest—the cyclamen mite. This light-colored relative

Delphinium and desert-candle: The varying heights of tall desert-candle and delphinium contrasted with Oriental poppies make a striking display.

Maggie Oster

False dragonhead: Plant false dragonhead in a moist area, such as by a pond or stream.

of the spider mite is too small to see with the naked eye. It deforms the leaves, blackens the flower buds, usually preventing bloom, and stunts the plant. Cut off and destroy badly infested shoots. Spray every ten days from early spring to flowering time with Kelthane or insecticidal soap. Pick off any deformed plant parts, and discard severely infested plants. Avoid planting delphiniums near strawberries, which are also host to this mite.

What should be done for brown spots on the underside of delphinium leaves?

If these spots are rather glassy in appearance, they are due to the broad mite, which is not as harmful as the cyclamen mite and is more readily controlled with sulfur dust.

What causes blighted areas in the leaves?

The larvae of leafminers feed inside the leaves, which collapse and turn brown over rather large areas, usually near the points. Remove infested leaves. Spraying with malathion may help.

Desert-candle *(Eremurus)*

What is the name of the plant that produces four- to six-foot-tall spikes of bell-shaped white, pink, yellow, or orange flowers in midsummer?

These are desert-candles. The white-flowered form is hardy to -30° F., while the other species are hardy only to -10° F. Although the flower spikes are tall, the wide, straplike leaves form a rosette, similar to yucca, only a foot or so tall.

My desert-candle comes up early and is sometimes damaged by frost. What can I do?

This is often a problem with desert-candle. If frost is imminent, cover each plant with a box, bucket, or pine boughs in the evening and uncover them the following morning.

What growing conditions are necessary in order to grow desert-candle successfully?

Desert-candles need deep, well-drained soil, protection from summer winds and from full sun, and a winter mulch in northern areas. Work some superphosphate into the soil each fall. Usually plants younger than four years old bloom little, if at all.

When is the best time to plant desert-candle?

Plant in the fall, since top growth begins early in the spring. Spread the roots out flat or they will snap off when being planted. Plant so that the crown is about two inches below the soil surface. Too-deep planting is apt to cause the crown to rot, especially in a heavy soil.

Can desert-candles be divided, and when?

They can be divided only with difficulty, unless they send up offsets (young shoots around their edges). Early fall is the best time to divide them. Be sure each division has a bud, or eye.

Evening primrose. See Sundrops.

False dragonhead (*Physostegia*)

How is false dragonhead best treated?

In late summer, false dragonhead bears spikes of tiny, snapdragonlike flowers that make excellent cut flowers. It is hardy to -30° F. and grows twenty-four to thirty-six inches tall, with flowers in many shades of pink and white. It does best in rather moist soil, particularly near streams or pools, in either full sun or light shade. Dig up and divide plants every two or three years.

False indigo: This spiky flowering plant does best in full sun.

False indigo (*Baptisia*)

I have had little success growing lupines, but I like the flower spikes so much. Is there any other plant with similar flowers?

Yes; try false indigo. The three- to four-foot plants bear twelve-inch-long spikes of blue flowers in midsummer. The foliage is gray-green. After the flowers fade, there are attractive seed pods. Hardy to -40° F., false indigo prefers full sun but tolerates light shade. It withstands dry, sandy soil, but does best in average garden soil. Propagate from seed or by division.

False starwort (*Boltonia*)

Can you recommend a white fall flower?

A false starwort called Snowbank resembles a hardy aster and blooms at the same time. Hardy to -40° F., it grows four feet tall. Plants tolerate a wide range of soils, as well as heat and humidity. Plant in a sunny location. Propagate by division.

Ferns

What growing conditions do ferns require?

Most ferns need slightly acid (pH 6.0 to 6.5) soil, rich in organic matter. Before planting, work a three- or four-inch layer of compost, leaf mold, decayed manure, or peat moss into the soil. The most critical factors to success are adequate shade and

Maggie Oster

moist, but well-drained, soil. Propagate by division. All of the selected ferns (below) are readily available, easy to grow, and hardy to -40° F.

I have planted ferns under evergreens and they have not done well. Don't ferns need shade?

Sometimes the shade beneath evergreens is too dense even for ferns. Although it is possible to grow ferns under evergreens, the best location for them is beneath deciduous trees. Mass them along shady woodland paths, at the edges of pools and streams, or on the north side of the house.

What is wrong with a fern when it gets minute white and slightly larger brown specks all over it? The white ones can be moved, but the brown ones are tight.

This is a perfect description of fern scale. The white bodies are male; the brown, pear-shaped objects, female. A severe infestation ruins the fern. Remove badly infested fronds. Try spraying with malathion, using one-third the usual dosage; repeat three times at ten-day intervals and wash off with a pure water spray several hours later, as malathion injures ferns. Nicotine sulfate and soap will also clean up scale infestations.

SELECTED FERNS

The maidenhair fern (*Adiantum pedatum*) with beautiful, airy and graceful fronds, grows twelve to twenty-four inches tall and spreads slowly.

The lady fern (*Athyrium Filix-femina*) grows three feet tall with delicate, lacy fronds. With moist soil, it will tolerate full sun.

The Japanese painted fern (*Athyrium Goeringianum* Pictum) has two-foot, gray-green fronds marked with wine-red.

The hay-scented fern (*Dennstaedtia punctilobula*) is a rapidly growing variety that becomes invasive if planted in the wrong place, but given plenty of room, it is an excellent ground cover. Snails can mar the three-foot fronds; control them with slug bait.

The wood ferns (*Dryopteris* species) are excellent specimen plants, growing twenty-four to thirty inches tall with semi- to fully evergreen fronds, and are often used in flower arrangements.

The ostrich fern (*Matteuccia pensylvanica*) is one of the tallest of American ferns. Although they grow to ten feet in swampy areas, in most gardens four feet is the usual height. There are two types of fronds on the plants: the outer ones are lacy, while the stiff inner ones bear the spores. Plants spread by underground runners.

The sensitive fern (*Onoclea sensibilis*) is a rampant grower, whether in full sun or shade. The gray-green fronds are a markedly different color from that of most other ferns. Spore-bearing fronds are attractive in winter outdoors and provide fine material for dried-flower arrangements.

The cinnamon fern (*Osmunda cinnamomea*) is a bold plant with six-foot fronds. Although it needs constantly moist soil, it will tolerate full sun.

The royal fern (*Osmunda regalis* var. *spectabilis*) is another bold plant, also growing six feet tall. It requires very acid, moist soil. Both osmundas grow from a crown and spread slowly.

The common polypody fern (*Polypodium virginianum*) forms a low-growing, dense mat around rocks and fallen logs with moist soil and light shade. It is evergreen, even to -40° F.

The Christmas fern (*Polystichum acrostichoides*) resembles the Boston fern. Growing from crowns, the eighteen- to twenty-four-inch plants spread slowly. Fronds are semi- to fully evergreen.

What makes lacy holes in fern leaves? We can find no insect that causes it.

Possibly the Florida fern caterpillar, which feeds at night. It is about two inches long and varies from dark green to black. Spray plants and the soil surface with *Bacillus thuringiensis*.

Flax *(Linum)*

Are there any special requirements for growing perennial flax?

Perennial flax is a very undemanding plant, needing only full sun and well-drained soil. Plants may be propagated from seed or division, but, once established, they do not readily transplant. Winter protection may be needed at the northernmost limits of its hardiness.

Some days my flax does not bloom. Why is this?

Flax flowers will not open without sun. Also, flax has a tendency for the flowers to open only every other day.

Fleabane *(Erigeron)*

Does fleabane do well in most parts of the country?

In cool maritime climates, fleabane will flower all summer in full sun. In hotter climates, plants grow best in light shade and will flower for only a few weeks. Plant fleabane in a well-drained, sandy loam that is only moderately fertile. In the spring, propagate by division or sow seed. The pink to blue asterlike flowers are good for bouquets.

Foxglove *(Digitalis)*

Please describe foxglove and how to grow it.

Foxgloves bear spectacular, three- to six-foot-tall, white, lilac, purple, rose, and yellow flower spikes during midsummer. They do well in humus-rich, well-drained soil that is slightly acid. They grow in full sun if the ground is moist, and will readily naturalize in lightly shaded areas. Divide perennial foxglove in the spring.

Is there some way to get foxgloves to bloom a second time during the summer?

Yes. Cut off the main flower stem after it finishes blooming and other flowers will come up. Leave a few dead flowers on some of the plants to get them to self-sow and naturalize.

Should foxgloves be fertilized during the summer?

Yes. To get better blooms, feed them with a liquid fertilizer during flowering.

Maggie Oster

Lady fern: With its delicate, lacy fronds, lady fern tolerates full sun if the soil is moist.

Is a winter mulch necessary?

Most perennial varieties are hardy to -20° F., although in areas where temperatures typically drop that low, a light winter protection is beneficial. After a good freezing of the soil, apply a mulch of decayed leaves. Next, lay bare branches over the plants' crowns, and on top of this, spread an inch or two of marsh hay or straw. The branches serve to keep the covering from packing down on the crowns, thus causing rot. Evergreen boughs—not heavy ones—can also be used instead of the branch and straw combination.

What parts of foxglove are poisonous, if any?

Probably all parts. The drug digitalis (poisonous in overdoses) is obtained from the second year's young leaves.

Can you suggest some ways to use foxgloves in the landscape?

Plant them in masses among shrubs, in the flower border or along the edge of a woods or a brook. They are especially effective combined with pinks and sweet william.

Funkia. See Plantain lily.

Gas plant *(Dictamnus)*

How did gas plant get its name?

On hot, still summer days, a volatile oil builds up around the flower stalks. A lighted match placed near the flowers will give a flash of light from the gas as it actually ignites for an instant.

Is gas plant anything more than just a novelty?

Yes, it is actually a very beautiful, tough, long-lived perennial that is excellent both for the flower border and for cut flowers. The species has both white and pink forms, and blooms in early summer. Hardy to -40° F., the plants grow three feet tall. Leaves are a glossy, dark green with a faint lemony scent.

What are the growing requirements of gas plant?

They do best in a heavy, well-drained, rich soil in sun or partial shade. Once established, dry weather does not bother them. Plants do not respond well to transplanting, so let them stay where you plant them.

Gay-feather *(Liatris)*

What are the advantages of growing gay-feather?

These North American natives with grasslike leaves grow two to four feet tall, thrive in light soils, in sun or light shade, and are hardy to -40° F. Plants bear spikes of unusual, feathery purple or

Gas plant: A lighted match placed near gas plant flowers actually ignites the plant's volatile oil for an instant.

Maggie Oster

white flowers that are attractive to butterflies, excellent for cutting, and superb for drying. Propagate from seed sown in the fall, or by division of the tuberous roots.

Gentian *(Gentiana)*

No other flower color compares to the blue of gentian, but aren't they difficult to grow?

Try the less demanding crested gentian *(G. septemfida* var. *lagodechiana),* with deep-blue, bell-shaped flowers on plants six to twelve inches tall. Hardy to -40° F., it grows best in humus-rich, moist soil with light shade; it should be mulched. Divide in early spring.

Globeflower *(Trollius)*

The two-inch, buttercuplike blooms of globeflower are beautiful, but I've had difficulty growing the plants. Any suggestions?

The two-foot plants of globeflower *must* have humus-rich soil that is very moist but well drained, and light shade or full sun. They take several years to get established, but plants are hardy to -40° F. They may flower again after the main bloom of midsummer if faded flowers are removed.

How is globeflower propagated?

Because they are difficult to start from seed, globeflower plants should be divided. This is easily done, but it will be a while after division before they bloom again.

Globe thistle *(Echinops)*

A friend has an unusual plant that resembles a thistle, but I thought thistles were weeds. Can you tell me about this plant?

The globe thistle is neither a thistle nor a weed. It is a striking plant for the flower border, among shrubs, or as a bold specimen. About three feet tall, it has large, deeply cut, and very prickly leaves. Steel-blue, globe-shaped flowers, two inches across, bloom from June or July through September and attract bees.

Hardy to -40° F., globe thistle is very easy to grow, doing best in full sun and light soil. Plants seldom need dividing. They may be propagated from seed or by division.

How do I dry the flower heads of globe thistle?

Pick the flowers just before they open and hang them upside down in a cool, dry, dark, well-ventilated place to dry. The flowers may also be used in fresh arrangements.

Globeflower: Plant globeflower in humus-rich, very moist, but well-drained soil.

Globe thistle is a somewhat unusual and easy-to-grow blue-flowered perennial.

Maggie Oster

Goatsbeard: One of the best choices for wet spots, goatsbeard grows five to seven feet tall.

Goatsbeard *(Aruncus)*

What would you recommend for planting in a lightly shaded area along a small stream?

One of the best choices is goatsbeard. Hardy to -40° F., it grows five to seven feet tall. During summer, it produces spikes of feathery white flowers. If used in a perennial border, place it near the back and give it plenty of room. Clumps may be divided in spring, or start plants from seed.

Why is it that my goatsbeard never produces seed?

Goatsbeard has separate male and female plants. Yours must be a male plant, which does not produce seed.

Gloriosa daisy. See Coneflower.

Golden marguerite *(Anthemis)*

What is the plant with yellow, daisylike flowers and grayish, finely divided leaves that grows in poor, dry soil?

You're probably thinking of golden marguerite. The flowers, excellent for cutting, are two inches across, and plants grow two to three feet tall. They are hardy to -40° F. They flower best in full sun, but tolerate light shade. Plant them in masses; they grow and spread rapidly. Propagation is easy by seed or division.

Goldenrod *(Solidago)*

Won't goldenrod in the garden give me hayfever?

Contrary to popular belief, ragweed, which blooms at the same time, is the culprit, not goldenrod. Hybrids produce large sprays of golden yellow flowers in late summer. Easy to grow in any soil, they are a worthwhile addition to the garden. They do best in full sun, but tolerate light shade. They are hardy to -30° F.

How is goldenrod propagated?

Although goldenrod can be started from seed, cultivars should be propagated only by division.

Goldentuft. See Basket-of-gold.

Goutweed. See Snow-on-the-mountain.

Greek valerian, Jacob's-ladder *(Polemonium)*

What is the plant with fernlike foliage and blue or white flowers?

You are probably referring to the *Polemoniums*, Greek valerian or Jacob's-ladder. They prefer humus-rich, dry soil with light shade, and are hardy to -40° F. Sow seed in the fall or divide the plants in early spring.

Hardy aster, Michaelmas daisy *(Aster)*

What are the pink or purple, daisylike flowers growing along the roadside in the fall? Can they be grown in the garden?

These beautiful native plants are asters. Over the years, different ones of these have been selected and hybridized into some of our best garden plants. Most varieties grow three to six feet tall. New England asters *(A. novae-angliae)* and New York asters *(A. novi-belgii)* are both hardy to -30° F.

Are there any special tips for growing asters?

Asters tolerate a wide range of soils, though New England asters are more tolerant of wet soil. They do best with plenty of water during the growing season, but they must never have "wet feet" during the winter. Choose a site with full sun, and plant them in the spring, before they have more than an inch or two of growth. Pinch them back in early summer to encourage bushiness.

Greek valerian: Sometimes called Jacob's-ladder, this plant needs a relatively dry soil and light shade.

What are some ways to use asters in the landscape?

Plant them in large, informally shaped groups, called drifts. The taller types make a fine background for lower perennials, or use them in front of evergreens, along the edges of woodlands or roadsides, to soften a fence, and in the perennial border. They are excellent flowers for cutting.

How can I prevent my asters from getting a white powdery substance on the leaves?

This mildew can usually be prevented by keeping the soil moist during the growing season.

My asters bloom well, but the plants often "open up" in the middle. What should I do?

Asters have this tendency to open up as the plants age. Divide them at least every two years in the spring, thus maintaining only young plants in your garden. They multiply rapidly and there are always some to share.

Hardy begonia *(Begonia)*

Is there really a begonia that can be grown and overwintered outdoors in the north?

Begonia grandis (B. Evansiana), with red-veined, wing-shaped leaves and pink flowers, is hardy to -10° F., if it is mulched. It must have moist but well-drained, humus-rich soil and partial shade. Many gardeners in the South plant it among azaleas and camellias.

Hardy fuchsia (*Fuchsia*)

The unusual, pendulous flowers of fuchsia are my favorites. Is there a type that is hardy?

In areas with a winter minimum of 0° F., *Fuchsia magellanica* can be grown as a perennial. The three-foot-tall plant with dark green leaves bears red and violet flowers. It is often planted in rock gardens.

In what kind of light and soil should hardy fuchsia be planted?

Light shade and light, well-drained garden loam enriched with some leaf mold or other organic matter. Keep it out of exposed situations and try a light winter cover.

Hardy orchid (*Bletilla*)

Are there any orchids that can be grown outdoors but that do not require a lot of special care?

Bletilla striata is one of the easiest orchids to grow. Sprays of pink flowers appear in early summer. Lance-shaped leaves are a bright green. Provide moist, well-drained, humus-rich soil and partial shade. Plants grow twelve to eighteen inches tall. Propagate by division.

Hardy pinks. See Carnations.

Hen-and-chickens, Houseleek (*Sempervivum*)

How can I use ground-hugging hen-and-chickens in the garden?

Plant them among the paving stones of a terrace or path, in rock walls or gardens, or as an edging to a flower border. They like sandy, well-drained, fertile garden soil, with full sun, and are hardy to -30° F. To propagate, separate the offsets at any time of the year.

My hen-and-chickens died after it bloomed. What's wrong?

This usually happens, but because the plants produce so many offsets so quickly, it frequently goes unnoticed.

Offsets of hens-and-chickens may be dug up and replanted elsewhere.

Hollyhock (*Alcea*)

I thought hollyhocks were biennials, but my neighbor says she planted them only once and they bloom every year.

Although hollyhocks are officially biennials, they not only reseed readily but they also persist for a number of years. Hardy to -40° F., plants usually grow six to ten feet tall, though shorter varieties are available. There are both single- and double-flowering hollyhocks, in white, yellow, red, and pink. Plant them in full sun and deeply dug, humus-rich soil, and protect them from wind by planting them near a fence, wall, building, or hedge.

What causes the rusting, yellowing, and dropping of foliage of hollyhocks?

This is most likely fungus. Its spores are produced in little reddish pustules on the undersides of the leaves, while yellow areas appear on the upper surface. With a bad case of rust, the leaves turn yellow, wither, and fall off, and rust lesions can be seen on the stem as well as on the leaves. Remove infected leaves as soon as you see them. To prevent fungus, clean up all old stalks and leaves in the fall, and dust with sulfur and ferbam, starting in early spring. Be sure to coat the undersurface of the leaves.

Hound's-tongue. See Chinese forget-me-not.

Houseleek. See Hen-and-chickens.

Iris *(Iris)*

How are irises best used?

Iris comes in an array of sparkling hues and exquisite forms. Easy-care plants in a range of sizes and periods of bloom, irises

Iris reticulata: *This is one of the earliest irises to bloom, usually in March or April in a climate similar to that of New York City.*

Maggie Oster

are adaptable to many diverse uses in the landscape, such as in a mixed perennial border, but they are just as stunning when used as single accents by a wall or rock outcropping, for example. By themselves, they are not attractive during the greater part of the year. Clumps of one variety in front of evergreens are very effective. Many people interplant irises with daylilies. Irises are beautiful in bouquets, too.

How are irises classified?

There are both bulb and rhizome forms of iris. Among the bulbs are Dutch, Spanish, and English irises. Irises with rhizomes include both bearded and beardless irises, such as Siberian, Japanese, Louisiana, and crested.

Can you tell me the relative blooming times of the various irises?

Using the New York City area as a point of reference, you can anticipate blooms starting usually in March or April with *I. reticulata,* soon followed by the miniature, dwarf, and intermediate bearded irises in April and May. The tall-bearded and Siberian irises bloom in May and June, followed by Dutch, Louisiana, and Japanese in June and July. Some bearded irises bloom again in late July, August, and September.

Do irises grow better in sun or shade?

Most do best in full sun. Certain wild species, such as *I. cristata, I. gracilipes, I. verna,* and *I. foetidissima,* are satisfactory in partial shade.

Do irises grow better in low, moist ground or in dry soil?

Most irises need rich, well-drained loam. Bearded irises require sharp drainage. Beardless kinds, such as Japanese varieties, need plenty of moisture but not waterlogged soil; they should not be planted where water stands during winter. The yellow flag of Europe and our native *I. versicolor* and Louisiana irises succeed even in swamp conditions. Add bonemeal or superphosphate when making plant beds. If the soil is heavy, work in organic matter such as peat moss, leaf mold, or compost.

How should the soil be prepared for Japanese and Siberian irises?

These irises thrive in acid soil, or at least in soil that is not alkaline. Never apply lime, bonemeal, or wood ashes to Japanese irises. Siberian irises are more tolerant of alkaline soil, but prefer somewhat acid soil. Spade the bed deeply; incorporate plenty of humus—old rotted manure, leaf mold, peat moss, or compost. Also, if the soil is poor, spread on a thin layer of manure or general fertilizer.

What kind of soil is good for Dutch and other bulbous irises?

Any fertile, well-drained soil, other than heavy clay.

When, where, and how do you plant bearded irises?

The main planting period is in June or July after flowering to allow maximum time for recuperation before blooming the next year. They can also be planted in the spring and fall. Plant rhizomes level with the surface in well-drained, sunny beds in good garden soil. In light, sandy soil, the rhizomes can be covered an inch or so, but in heavy soils they should be left with the tops exposed.

When and how deep should Japanese irises be planted?

Plant them in early spring, before growth starts, or in late August. The crowns should be set two inches below the surface.

How should I plant Dutch, English, and Spanish irises?

Plant bulbs four to five inches deep, in October and November.

What distances should be allowed between irises when they are planted?

Tall-bearded, nine to eighteen inches; dwarf-bearded, six to nine inches; Japanese and Siberian, eighteen to twenty-four inches; bulbous, four to five inches. For the tall-bearded varieties, the shorter spacing will give a better effect the first year, but in the long run, the wider spacing is preferable.

Is manure good for irises?

Animal manure should not be used on bearded irises, but the beardless species (including the Japanese and Siberian irises) do better if well-rotted manure is applied. Dutch, English, and Spanish irises are heavy feeders and deplete the soil very quickly.

What fertilizer do you recommend for ordinary bearded irises?

When preparing the beds, mix into the soil a superphosphate fertilizer and unleached wood ashes (the nutrient value of wood ashes is quickly washed away by rain), together with a commercial fertilizer low in nitrogen. In subsequent springs, apply unleached wood ashes, which supply from five to twenty-five percent of iris's potash requirement, as well as thirty to thirty-five percent of the lime they need. Water the ashes in after applying about four to five ounces per square yard.

What is the best fertilizer to use on Japanese irises?

Apply rotted or dehydrated manure as a mulch in May or early June. If this is not available, use leaf mold or peat moss

Iris: These bearded irises are best transplanted in June or July after the blooming period.

fortified with a light dressing of complete fertilizer, such as one formulated for rhododendrons and azaleas (acid-loving plants). In fall, mulch with manure, leaves, or peat moss.

How much watering and cultivating do irises need?

Bearded irises ordinarily need no watering. Japanese, Siberian, and other beardless types need plenty of moisture until their flowering is through. Cultivate them shallowly and often enough to keep the surface loose and free of weeds.

How often should I transplant irises?

Overcrowding will lead to lack of bloom. Whenever irises become so crowded that the rhizomes are growing over one another (about every three years), lift them and replant. Avoid moving bearded irises until after the blooming season or they may not bloom that year. Japanese and Siberian irises usually bloom even after being moved.

When should Dutch, English, and Spanish irises be transplanted?

Let them remain in place for two years, then lift them and replant them in a new location.

How are bulbous irises handled in the South?

To keep stalks from developing after bloom, Dutch, English, and Spanish irises should be dug up after flowering and stored in a cool shed until late fall, when they are replanted. If not removed from the ground in this manner, they make fall growth, and flower stalks are then usually killed by a freeze in late winter.

Do Dutch irises have to be dug up each year?

Not unless they have suffered winter losses other years. In that case, try planting as late in autumn as the weather permits. In extreme climates, a winter mulch is beneficial.

What care should be given bearded iris rhizomes after the blooming season?

If they become overcrowded, divide them. Remove the flower stalks immediately after flowering and be on the alert for signs of borer pests or rots. Keep all dead foliage cleaned off.

How and when should Japanese irises be divided?

This is quite a job if the clumps are large. A heavy-bladed knife is the best tool. Cut the leaves halfway back and then chop the rootstock into pieces, each with three or four growths. Save only young, vigorous portions, and discard old, lifeless material. Do this work in the shade, in the autumn or just before growth

Beautifully intricate irises are adaptable to many diverse uses in the landscape.

starts in the spring. Keep the roots from drying out during the process.

How should I divide tall bearded irises?

After flowering, cut the leaves back halfway, lift the clumps, then with a sharp knife cut the rhizomes into pieces so that each has one strong fan of leaves (or, if preferred, two or three) attached. Be sure that divisions are disease free before replanting them. Divide again every three or four years.

Does it injure iris plants to take green foliage off in the late fall?

Leaves turning brown should always be removed promptly. Green foliage should not be removed or cut back in late fall because this may adversely affect next year's bloom.

What can be used as winter protection for irises?

Bearded irises need no protection, unless their rhizomes have been planted in late fall. Evergreen boughs then make the best protection. Marsh hay or excelsior can also be used. Dutch, English, and Spanish irises benefit from mulch where winters are severe.

Why won't Japanese irises bloom for me?

There are several possibilities, including too much shade, alkaline soil, dry soil, and water settling around the crowns during the winter.

My bearded irises grow and look well, but rarely bloom. What is the reason? They have been established more than two years, and get full sun at least half the day.

Most likely they are overcrowded and need to be divided. Some varieties of tall-bearded irises require dividing every year for good bloom. And the more sun, the better.

My early dwarf and Siberian irises bloomed the first year but not the following two years. What is wrong?

Perhaps they do not get enough sunshine, or they may be too crowded and need to be divided. Siberians are heavy feeders; add superphosphate and lime, if necessary, to the soil.

How do you destroy the borers that attack iris?

The iris borer, a fat, fleshy-colored caterpillar with a dark head, is the major pest of irises. Sanitary measures are most important in getting rid of iris borers. Sometime in October or November, after a killing frost, clean up and burn all old leaves and debris where the moth lays its eggs. Leave only fans of new leaves. In the spring, start spraying new growth with malathion, pyrethrum, or rotenone, and repeat every two weeks. Kill young borers already in the leaves by squeezing leaf sheaths between your thumb and forefinger.

What causes brown spots on iris leaves?

This is fungus leaf spot disease. Cut back diseased foliage and burn it, or the disease will spread through the garden. Be sure to pick off dead leaves and clean up old leaves in the fall, and in two years you will have eliminated the disease. Leaves may also be dusted or sprayed with two or three applications of maneb or bordeaux mixture during summer. Avoid splashing water on leaves as this spreads the disease.

Are irises subject to virus diseases?

Iris mosaic disease attacks both bearded and bulbous kinds, causing mottling or yellow striping of leaves and lack of vigor. Destroy all infected plants.

Some of my iris rhizomes are rotting. Although the shell seems dry, the inside, if opened before destruction is complete, is wet and slimy. There are also watery streaks on the leaves. What is the cause?

Bacterial soft rot. The rot may start in the leaves, following puncture by young borers; there is often a water-soaked appearance to the leaves. Roots are slimy and vile-smelling. To control, first take measures against the borer (see above). Next, remove and immediately destroy any rotting rhizomes. Dig them out along with surrounding soil, and disinfect your trowel with a solution of one-half cup bleach mixed with one-half cup water. Sterilize the soil, as well as your knives and other tools that might spread the disease, by soaking them with the same mixture. A 70-percent denatured alcohol solution can also be used. Clean off and burn dead leaves and rubbish in the fall. When planting new irises, select a different area, and avoid planting diseased rhizomes.

Why do my iris blooms last only one or two days and die?

The life span of a single iris flower is only a day or two. On the other hand, if after one or two flowers bloom, the whole stalk withers and dies, a fungus disease may be working at the crown; or there may possibly be a very serious infestation of thrips.

Why do iris leaves turn brown and dry during July and August?

Crown or rhizome rot fungi may be the cause, or perhaps merely overcrowding and lack of water. If there are any signs of gray mold or white fungus threads with seedlike bodies around the base of the plant, remove and destroy infected rhizomes and the surrounding six inches of soil. Plant your iris in a different location.

Do you know anything about a little round beetle that destroys iris?

A small, round, flat, dark weevil eats iris pods and sometimes the petals. Try spraying with methoxychlor.

My beautiful iris garden is being ruined by root knot nematodes. What can I do?

The root knot nematode is one of the worst problems to irises in the South, since it cannot be killed by winter cold; furthermore, it is not readily starved because it thrives on so many different kinds of garden plants. If you have any land that has not been growing nematode-susceptible plants, you can start a new iris garden there with new rhizomes. If you must use the same location, you can take out the iris and have the soil professionally sterilized. Or, leave the remaining healthy plants in place and apply Nemagon.

Jacob's-ladder. See Greek valerian.

Japanese anemone. See Windflower.

Joe-Pye weed. See Mist flower.

Jupiter's-beard, Red valerian *(Centranthus)*

How should I treat Jupiter's-beard in my garden?

The two- to three-foot plants have gray-green foliage and small clusters of tiny fragrant flowers, which may be bright crimson to light pink. Hardy to -30° F., they do best in climates with cool summers. Cut off dead flowers to get a second blooming. Plants readily self-sow, or they may be propagated by division in spring.

Knapweed. See Perennial cornflower.

Lady's-mantle *(Alchemilla)*

What is the plant with pleated, gray-green, round leaves that often are marked with dew drops?

This is lady's-mantle, an easily grown plant reaching only twelve to eighteen inches tall and hardy to -40° F. It bears a mass of tiny, chartreuse-colored flowers in early summer, but it is grown mainly for its foliage.

Will lady's-mantle do well in partial shade?

In hot, dry areas, light shade is essential, but in cool, moist climates, full sun is tolerated. In either climate, rich, moist soil is necessary for best growth. Propagate it by division or seed.

Lady's-mantle: Although lady's-mantle bears small, chartreuse-colored flowers, it is grown mainly for its ruffled foliage.

Cindy McFarland

Lamb's ears. See Betony.

Larkspur. See Delphinium.

Lavender cotton *(Santolina)*

Can lavender cotton be used as an edging?

Yes. The gray foliage of lavender cotton and its rounded growth habit create a lovely formal edging to beds, borders, or paths. Plants also can be used in rock gardens. Hardy to -20° F., plants grow twelve inches tall. A dwarf form is six to eight inches high. Provide light, sandy soil, and full sun.

Leadwort. See Blue plumbago.

Lenten rose. See Christmas rose.

Leopard's-bane *(Doronicum)*

Most yellow, daisylike flowers bloom in the summer or fall. Are there any that blossom in spring?

Leopard's-bane is the earliest daisylike flower. Hardy to -40° F., it grows twelve to eighteen inches tall, with coarsely toothed, heart-shaped leaves and single, two-inch flowers. The flowers are excellent for cutting, but they do close at night.

My leopard's-bane disappeared during the summer. Is something wrong with it?

No, leopard's-bane frequently is dormant in the summer in hot climates. It is important to keep the soil moist where it is growing, even when it is dormant.

What is the best way to use leopard's-bane in my garden?

In climates with hot summers, leopard's-bane does best in light shade, otherwise it tolerates full sun. Plant it among tulips, daffodils, and other spring-flowering bulbs, in front of shrubs, or in the rock garden.

What are the growing requirements of leopard's-bane?

The shallow roots need cool, rich soil. Before planting, incorporate plenty of organic matter. Put a mulch around the plants to keep the soil cool and moist. Divide about every two years after flowering. Plants may also be started from seed.

Lily-of-the-valley *(Convallaria)*

Can lilies-of-the-valley be grown in an absolutely shady place?

Yes. They will grow in dense shade if the soil is fairly good, but will probably not bloom as freely as those in partial shade.

Leopard's-bane: These plants often go dormant during hot summers.

What are the soil and other growing requirements of lily-of-the-valley?

Plant lily-of-the-valley in the spring in moist, but not wet soil containing generous amounts of humus. Improve the soil before planting by spading in rotted manure, leaf mold, and peat moss. Each year in early spring, top-dress the bed with rotted manure, leaf mold, or compost. Do not allow the plants to become overcrowded.

Although my giant lilies-of-the-valley have splendid foliage, they produce only a few stems that bloom, and the plants don't multiply. What could be the trouble?

In very rich soil, the foliage will be good, but flowers will be scarce. After the plants are firmly established and the excess nutrients are used up, they should begin to bear more flowers.

Are the roots of lily-of-the-valley poisonous?

Yes. The drug convallaria, used in the pharmaceutical manufacture of a heart tonic, is made from lily-of-the-valley roots. The red berries that appear in fall are toxic, too.

Lily-turf *(Liriope)*

I've heard that some kinds of lily-turf are pests. Which ones are the best to grow?

Big blue lily-turf *(L. Muscari)* is an indispensable perennial ground cover in areas with minimum winter temperatures of -10° F. or warmer. Growing twelve to eighteen inches tall, the

Lily-turf: The arching, evergreen leaves of lily-turf make the plant particularly suitable for edging borders.

Maggie Oster

plants have arching, grass-like, evergreen leaves and flowers that resemble grape hyacinths. Group lily-turf plants at the front of the perennial border, plant them under and between shrubs, or use them to edge paths or as a ground cover around trees.

Does lily-turf need any special care?

Plants grow well in shade, in most well-drained soils. If leaves look shabby in the early spring, cut them way back. Propagate plants by division in early spring. Slugs and snails are their only pests.

Lobelia, Cardinal flower *(Lobelia)*

I have repeatedly tried to grow cardinal flower. Do you have any suggestions?

No native flower is as striking as the three- to four-foot, brilliant red spikes of lobelia—nor as maddening for the gardener. These plants naturally grow in wet places, such as swamps and streamsides, and they need afternoon shade. Although theoretically hardy to -40° F., in areas colder than -10° F. a winter mulch is recommended, but too much mulch may smother plants. No matter what you do, lobelia is naturally short lived, so plan on renewing the plant by replanting the new basal rosettes each year or by letting plants self-sow. You may have somewhat better luck with blue cardinal flower, which is less dependent upon moist soil for success.

Loosestrife *(Lysimachia)*

I love the bent spikes of white flowers on gooseneck loosestrife in midsummer. What kind of light and soil does it require?

The three-foot-tall loosestrife needs bright sun, though it will tolerate light shade in very hot areas. Soil should be moist but well drained. Propagate by dividing the roots in spring or fall. Loosestrife is hardy to -40° F.

Will yellow loosestrife become a pest in my garden?

The yellow flowers on leafy three-foot stems of *L. punctata* make it a bright addition to the early summer garden. In moist to wet soil and full sun, it will grow vigorously, but it should not become a nuisance if given plenty of room. Plants are hardy to -20° F. and will tolerate moderately dry soil with light shade.

Lungwort *(Pulmonaria)*

Is lungwort a good choice for growing in rich, moist soil in full or partial shade?

The spreading clumps of hairy, often spotted, leaves of lung-wort grow twelve inches tall and are quite fine for the front of

Lungwort: These blue, pink or white blossoming plants are one of the first perennials to bloom in spring.

shady borders. Hardy to -30° F., they flower early in the spring with tiny, bell-shaped flowers of blue, pink, or white. Propagate by division in the fall.

Lupine *(Lupinus)*

Does lupine have any special soil requirements?

It needs a moist but well-drained loam. Incorporate leaf mold or peat moss when preparing the soil, and sprinkle well-rotted compost or a general garden fertilizer, such as 5-10-10, around established plants in early spring and again in summer. Most lupines do better in acid soil. Do not use lime around them.

Can lupines be transplanted?

Old plants do not readily survive being disturbed and are very hard to transplant. Young plants can be transplanted in very early spring if care is used to protect the roots. Lupines are short lived. For a constant supply, sow seed each year.

Mallow *(Malva)*

Are the mallows worth considering for the flower border?

These old-fashioned plants definitely add a lovely charm to the flower border. Easily grown, they do best with deep, moist, but well-drained, humus-rich soil, and full sun. For many weeks during midsummer they will bloom with white or variously shaded pink flowers that resemble single hollyhocks. Although short lived, they readily self-sow.

Maltese cross. See Campion.

Marsh marigold, Cowslip *(Caltha)*

What plant has bright golden, two-inch flowers and fresh green leaves in early spring, and grows along stream banks? Can it be grown in the garden?

Marsh marigold does best in very moist soil and shade, but adapts to average garden soil. Divide the plants in the spring.

Meadow rue *(Thalictrum)*

How can I use meadow rue in my garden?

The large, fluffy flower heads and columbinelike foliage of meadow rue add wonderful texture to the flower border. Provide a humus-rich, moist but well-drained soil. Plants need light shade in hot climates, but will take full sun in areas with cool summers. Propagate from seed or by division.

Ann Reilly

Lupine: Protect these showy plants against hot summer winds.

Meadowsweet, Queen-of-the-prairie *(Filipendula)*

Someone suggested a plant called queen-of-the-prairie for my garden. What is it like?

Queen-of-the-prairie, or meadowsweet, is a bold, dramatic plant that grows six feet tall, with feathery plumes of pink or white flowers from June to August. Hardy to -50° F., it is native to our meadows and prairies. To grow well, plants must have moist, humus-rich soil, and light shade. Some support may be necessary when plants are in bloom.

Michaelmas daisy. See Hardy aster.

Milkweed. See Butterfly flower.

Mist flower, Joe-Pye weed, Boneset *(Eupatorium)*

There is a beautiful flower similar to ageratum growing in fields near my house. What is it and would it be a weed in my garden?

The mist flower, or hardy ageratum *(E. coelestinum)*, is hardy to -10° F., and grows eighteen to twenty-four inches tall, with small, fluffy, azure-blue flowers in August and September. In sandy soils, it may spread too aggressively for a small garden, but in clay soils it makes a valuable addition to the flower garden. Plant it in full sun or light shade in moist but well-drained, average garden soil. Butterflies are attracted to the flowers, which are good for bouquets.

How deep should mist flower be planted?

The roots are stringy and shallow. Spread them out and cover them, about two inches deep, with soil. They are best moved in the spring before growth starts. Because they grow into quite a mat, which dies out in the center, they need to be lifted and transplanted every year or two.

One area of my garden has very wet soil. Is there a *Eupatorium* that will grow there?

Yes. The native plant known as Joe-Pye weed *(E. purpureum)* is excellent for naturalizing along woodland streams or in shady wet areas. Growing four to six feet tall, Joe-Pye weed has large, purple, showy heads of flowers in late summer and early autumn. Propagate from seed or division.

Monkshood *(Aconitum)*

Is it advisable to plant monkshood? I have heard that it is poisonous.

The roots of monkshood do contain poison. It is said to have been mistaken for horseradish on occasion and eaten with fatal

Maggie Oster

*Joe-Pye weed: A native plant, Joe-Pye weed (**Eupatorium purpureum**) is excellent for naturalizing in shady wet areas.*

results. With sensible precautions, there is no reason not to grow this stately plant with its spikes of blue, hoodlike flowers.

How can I best use monkshood in my garden?

Monkshood may be planted among shrubs or perennials in full sun to partial shade. It is especially effective with Madonna lilies, white phlox, and shasta daisies. The common monkshood (*A. Napellus*) has dark blue flowers in midsummer; azure monkshood (*A. Fischeri*) has lighter-colored flowers in late summer. Both grow three to five feet tall.

Does monkshood need winter protection?

It is hardy to -40° F., but it should be lightly mulched for the first and second winters after being planted.

How deep should I plant monkshood and in what kind of soil?

Plant it with the crown one inch under the surface, in rich, moist, well-drained, neutral to slightly acid soil. You can also sow fresh seed in late autumn.

How often should monkshood be divided?

These plants flower freely when they are in established clumps and can be left undisturbed for years.

Do you know why the glossy leaves of my monkshood might have turned black and diseased looking?

Hot, dry conditions can cause this. You may want to try moving it to partial shade. To do best, monkshood also needs plenty of moisture and a humus-rich soil.

Mountain bluet. See Perennial cornflower.

Mugwort. See Wormwood.

Orange sunflower *(Heliopsis)*

Where and in what type of soil should heliopsis be planted?

One of the best perennials for all-summer bloom, three- to four-foot-tall orange sunflower prefers full sun. Although it will grow in any garden soil, it will probably flower better in a fairly dry situation. It is hardy to -30° F.

Does orange sunflower require frequent division?

The plants are very vigorous, so they tend to become crowded after about three years, when they should be divided in early spring.

Maggie Oster

Monkshood: This old-fashioned, interesting flower can be left to flourish undisturbed for years.

Oriental poppy *(Papaver)*

Do poppies come in any color besides orange?

Yes. There are white, light and dark pink, deep red, and bi-color varieties. In addition, you can find a fine blood-red and a salmon-orange double.

Will you give full planting instructions and the care of Oriental poppies?

Plant poppies in August or September, or in early spring before growth starts. Oriental poppies dislike being moved, so be particularly careful to make the hole big enough so that the fleshy roots are not broken or twisted upward. Don't keep them out of the ground long. Water well if the weather is dry. A few weeks after being planted, a crown of leaves will appear. In relatively mild climates, these may remain green for part of the winter. To prevent crown rot, protect these plants in the winter with pine boughs or dry leaves.

Will Oriental poppies planted in the spring bloom the same year?

Yes, but only if you buy large, established plants. Plant them in March or early April, give them good care, and you are quite likely to get some flowers.

How shall I care for Oriental poppies?

They don't need much attention. Cut off the flowers as they wither. In the spring, work in a sidedressing of balanced fertilizer such as 5-10-5, but do not overfeed.

My Oriental poppies come up and grow well but never bloom. They get afternoon sun. Should they be in a different place?

Transplant in April or August into a sunnier spot.

After flowering, the leaves of my poppies start to turn yellow and then die. Is this normal?

Yes, poppies do lose their leaves, but new growth reappears in the fall. If you find them unsightly, plant something like daylilies nearby to hide them after they bloom.

Oriental poppy: These lovely flowers dislike being transplanted, but they grow well without much attention once established.

Ann Reilly

Ornamental Grasses

I'd like to learn more about ornamental grasses. Are they perennials or annuals and how can I use them in my garden?

There are both perennial and annual grasses for the garden. Most of the annuals are best grown for their flowers, which can be dried and used in arrangements. Perennial grasses can also be used this way, but they also add wonderful texture to the

Maggie Oster

Blue fescue: **Festuca ovina** *has stiff, silvery blue foliage that remains evergreen.*

SELECTED ORNAMENTAL GRASSES

The giant reed *(Arundo Donax)* grows six to twenty feet tall in moist, humus-rich deep soil. Hardy to 0° F., it bears leaves that are about two feet long and three inches wide. Red-brown flower plumes appear in late summer. Use among shrubs or as a specimen plant.

Feather reed grass *(Calamagrostis acutiflora* Stricta) produces a formal, vertical effect. Hardy to -20° F., it grows five to seven feet tall, with feathery blooms in midsummer.

Japanese sedge grass *(Carex Morrowii* var. *expallida)* has gracefully swirling variegated leaves that form clumps twelve to twenty-four inches tall. Use in the flower border or as an edging. It is hardy to -20° F.

Pampas grass *(Cortaderia Selloana)* is probably the best known of the ornamental grasses, but it, too, is hardy only to 0° F. It forms spectacular ten-foot mounds of thin foliage and long, silky white plumes, and thus is often grown as an specimen plant. A pink-flowered form is also available.

Ravenna grass *(Erianthus ravennae)* resembles pampas grass but is not as showy. It forms large five- to ten-foot-tall clumps, and has arching, silvery leaves that bear long, thin spikes of silver-purple flowers. Hardy to -10° F., it is tolerant of light shade.

Blue fescue *(Festuca ovina* var. *glauca)* grows only ten inches tall and has stiff, silvery blue foliage. Hardy to -30° F., these plants are evergreen, but old leaves should be trimmed off in early spring. Plant in the flower border, or use in masses or as an edging.

Eulalia *(Miscanthus sinensis)* is possibly the best all-round, large-growing grass. Hardy to -30° F. with protection, it has a variety of forms. Plants grow five to seven feet tall, and in late summer they bear plumelike flowers.

Variegated purple moor grass *(Molinia caerulea* Variegata) produces dense, two-foot clumps of narrow, arching leaves. Flower spikes persist well into the winter. It is hardy to -30° F.

Fountain grass *(Pennisetum alopecuroides)* is very showy with its bristly, silver-rose, wheatlike spikes of flowers produced from mid- to late summer. Leaves are very slender, dark green, and arching. Plants grow three to four feet tall and are hardy to -20° F.

Giant feather grass *(Stipa gigantea)* grows six feet tall, with huge flower heads that change from green-purple to yellow. It is hardy to -20° F.

Ribbon grass *(Phalaris arundinacea* var. *picta)* grows two feet tall with green-and-white striped leaves. Very vigorous, it needs plenty of room to spread. It is hardy to -40° F.

Fountain grass: **Pennisetum alopecuroides** *bears its showy, wheatlike spikes from mid- to late summer.*

landscape. Depending on the species, these grasses and grasslike plants range in height from ten inches to twenty feet.

What are the cultural requirements of ornamental grasses?

Most grow well in full sun and any moist but well-drained soil. Other than those you want for arrangements, leave the flowers on the plant during the winter, then cut back plants to the ground in the spring. The most reliable way to propagate plants is by division.

Ornamental onion *(Allium)*

I enjoy both regular and Chinese chives but I don't want a separate herb garden. Can I plant chives among my flowers?

Most assuredly. Both regular chives, which grow twelve inches tall with pink flowers, and Chinese chives, which grow two to three feet tall with white flowers, are very decorative plants that add immeasurably to any flower border. Both can be used as cut flowers, too. Clump-forming, they can be lifted and divided like other perennials.

Pearly everlasting *(Anaphalis)*

Is there a gray-foliaged plant that does well in very moist soil?

A good choice would be pearly everlasting. It grows twelve to eighteen inches tall and is hardy to -40° F. In addition to its silvery leaves, pearly everlasting has heads of tiny white blooms resembling strawflowers. Plants are propagated by division.

How do I dry the flowers of pearly everlasting?

Cut the flower stalks when the centers of the flowers begin to show. Put the stems in a container of water for several hours, then hang them upside down in a dark, dry, well-ventilated area.

Penstemon. See Beard-tongue.

Peony *(Paeonia)*

What makes the peony such a popular perennial?

Hardiness, permanence, ease of culture, and freedom from pests are but a few of its merits. Diversity in flower form, attractive colors, clean habit of growth, and deep green foliage combine to produce a plant of exceptional value for mass plantings or for the mixed border. Peonies rank high as cut flowers because of their extraordinary keeping qualities. They do best in the North, for they require the low temperatures of winter to break the dormancy of the buds before spring growth will take place.

I planted peonies the last of November; was it too late?

Planting can be done any time until the ground freezes, but the ideal months are September and October. This gives plants an opportunity to become partially established before winter. It is possible, however, to move them in the spring as soon as the ground has thawed and replant them immediately. If you move them early enough, they will bloom the same year. Keep the soil moist at all times.

What type of soil is best for peonies?

Any rich, friable garden soil is satisfactory. Heavy clay soil should be well drained and improved by additions of organic material, such as well-rotted manure, peat moss, or leaf mold, to make it more loose and crumbly. Sandy soil, too, needs additions of organic matter, such as well-rotted manure or rich compost, as well as commercial fertilizer. In either case, use about four bushels of organic material per 100 square feet.

What is the proper method of preparing the soil for peonies?

Spade it to a depth of twelve to eighteen inches. Thoroughly work in the organic material and incorporate three pounds of superphosphate to each 100 square feet.

Do peonies need lime?

Peonies grow best in a slightly acid soil (pH 5.5 to 6.5). If the soil is very acid (below pH 5), apply lime at the rate of five pounds per 100 square feet several weeks before planting.

What kind and how much fertilizer should I use once my peonies are established?

Apply a commercial fertilizer such as 4-12-4 or 5-10-5 at the rate of four pounds per 100 square feet. Well-rotted manure is also satisfactory, but avoid the use of fresh manure.

How deep do peonies need to be planted?

The crown, from which the buds arise, should be only one to two inches below the soil level. If planted too shallowly, there is danger of the roots being heaved out during the winter before they become established. If planted too deep, however, peonies won't bloom for many years.

Is it necessary to dig up peony roots every year and break them up to obtain more blossoms?

No. It is best not to divide and transplant peonies any more often than is necessary to maintain vigorous growth, ordinarily, every five to eight years. Better quality blooms can be had by fertilizing and making certain that the plants are well watered at the time they come into flower.

How are peony plants divided?

Dig the clumps carefully so as not to injure or bruise the roots. Wash off all the soil. With a heavy, sharp knife, cut each clump through the crown into several pieces. Each division should have several plump buds, which in the fall are approximately one-half inch long. Roots without such buds rarely produce plants.

Will peonies bloom the first summer after being transplanted?

Usually, if the plants are vigorous and were not divided into small pieces, but dividing is a severe operation, resulting in the loss of roots in which food is stored. Dividing at an improper time causes recovery to be especially slow. If the divisions are very small, it may take two to three years before the plants are vigorous enough to bloom, and the blooms may not be as large and perfect as those produced in succeeding years.

Why do peonies that are several years old fail to bloom?

The following conditions may prevent blooming: too deep planting; too much shade; poor drainage; need of dividing; root disease; botrytis blight disease; roots infested with nematodes; lack of fertilizer; lack of moisture; lack of sunlight; injury to buds due to late frosts.

How can you bring an old peony border back into bloom?

If the plants are very old, it is advisable to divide the clumps and replant them in well-prepared soil. Keep the bed free of weeds by maintaining a mulch and apply fertilizer in the spring to increase the quality and quantity of the flowers.

Should I disbud my peonies?

A peony stem usually has from three to seven buds. The main, or terminal, bud produces the largest and most perfect flower. If you wish this main bud to be particularly spectacular, pick off all other buds on that stem. Disbud when the plants are about eighteen inches tall, just as soon as the secondary buds become visible.

Do peonies need to be cultivated?

Very little cultivation is necessary, except to remove weeds. The best time to destroy weeds is very early in the spring before the plants have made much growth, or late in the fall after the tops have been cut off. A constant mulch will suppress most weeds.

Do peonies require much moisture?

A moderately moist soil is suitable. In the spring when the flowers are developing, if the natural rainfall is not abundant, thorough watering increases the size and quality of the flowers. It also tends to hasten flowering.

Is there any way to make the stems of peonies stronger?

Some otherwise fine varieties naturally have weak stems. There is little that can be done except to give them artificial support. It is also well to plant them in full sunlight (at least six hours a day), if possible, where they are protected from strong winds. They will also withstand light shade. Single-flowered varieties are more erect. Use special, circular wire plant supports, or tie individual stakes to each stem. Shake the water out of the peony heads after each rain. Planting in a location sheltered from the wind helps to prevent damage.

When should peony flowers be cut for use indoors?

Preferably in the early morning. For cutting, select buds that have just started to open. Do not take more stem than is actually required for the arrangement. It is advisable to leave at least two or three leaves below the point where the stem is cut.

Should the old flowers and seed pods of peonies be removed?

Yes, for two reasons. First, during the flowering season, old blossoms should be picked off before the petals fall, as this helps to control the botrytis blight disease. Second, seed pods compete with the roots for the food produced in the leaves.

The peony, with its variety of flower forms, attractive colors, clean habit of growth, and deep-green foliage, is an excellent choice for most gardens.

Maggie Oster

Should the foliage on peonies be cut back after the blooming season?

No. The foliage should not be cut until it has been killed by hard frosts. The food manufactured in the foliage is stored in the roots and thus helps produce flowers the following year. If the foliage is cut back shortly after blooming, the plants are deprived of their next year's food supply. An added advantage of leaving the foliage on is that the autumn coloring of peony leaves is usually quite attractive. Removing the *dead* leaves, however, helps to prevent the spread of disease, so it's an important task.

Should peonies be protected in the winter?

Peonies should be mulched the first year after planting so that they don't heave out of the ground. After plants are well established, no protection is necessary.

Are peonies hardy in cold climates?

They are among the hardiest of garden flowers, surviving winter minimum temperatures of -50° F.

What can I do to control ants that are eating the flower buds of my peonies?

Ants do not eat peony buds; they feed on the sweet, syrupy material secreted by the developing buds. They usually do not harm peonies although it's possible that they may spread botrytis blight disease.

Why do peony buds dry up without developing into blossoms? The plant seems disease free—the leaves are not dry and there is no sign of bud rot.

The problem is most likely botrytis blight, which can be prevented by carefully cleaning the peony bed in the fall and keeping it clean of dead leaves during all seasons. To control botrytis blight, spray the peonies with benomyl every fourteen days from the time the leaves show until the flowers open. Late frost in the spring can also kill buds, but disease is the more likely culprit.

Why do peony stalks wilt and fall over?

This is another symptom of botrytis blight. In wet weather, young shoots are often infected and become covered with gray mold, turn black, and rot at the base.

Why do peonies have brown spots on the petals?

This, too, is usually because of botrytis blight. Rain splashes spores from infected buds onto the opening blossoms, and everywhere a spore starts to germinate there is a brown spot on the petals. However, browning may also be due to thrips injury.

Why does foliage turn black after the blooming period?

It may, in a wet season, be due to botrytis blight. Blackening may also be due to stem rot, another fungus disease. Remove and destroy the infected shoots very carefully so as not to drop out any of the sclerotia, which are formed loosely in the pith (stem tissue) and fall out of the stalks.

What would cause roots to rot?

Possibly botrytis blight or stem rot, or sometimes a downy mildew that causes a wet rot of the crown. There is no chemical control. Peonies should not be planted in too wet soil; if you have heavy clay, lighten it with peat moss or other organic material. Never leave manure on as a mulch that shoots have to push up through.

How can I control rose chafers, the insects that have become troublesome around my peonies?

There is no very satisfactory answer to this universal question. Pick off as many as you can and spray your plants with Sevin or rotenone, repeating weekly as necessary. If it is any comfort to you, when the Japanese beetles get worse, the rose chafers diminish. (The same insecticides will somewhat control the beetles.)

Perennial cornflower: Shown here in front of pink Oriental poppies and lupine, blue cornflowers spread rapidly but not aggressively.

Perennial cornflower, Knapweed, Mountain bluet, Perennial bachelor's-button *(Centaurea)*

I'm developing a low-maintenance garden. Should I include the perennial cornflowers?

By all means. They tolerate a wide range of soils and full sun. Propagate by division.

Perennial forget-me-not *(Myosotis)*

Is there a perennial forget-me-not that will bloom all summer?

Myosotis scorpioides will bloom most of summer if located in shade beside a stream or pool. Plants grow about twelve inches tall, with both pink and blue flowers, and are hardy to -40° F. Divide in early spring, or sow seed directly where they will grow permanently.

Perennial sunflower *(Helianthus)*

Sunflowers are such cheerful plants, but the annual ones are too large for my garden. Is there something similar, but smaller, among perennial flowers?

Two types can be recommended for the home garden: the swamp sunflower *(H. angustifolius)* and *H. x multiflorus* varieties.

Cindy McFarland

What growing conditions do perennial sunflowers need?

Rich, deep, moist soil, and full sun to light shade. Fertilize each spring and divide every year.

Can you suggest some ways to use perennial sunflowers in the garden?

They are splendid at the back of the flower border, in clumps among shrubs, or naturalized along paths. They combine well with hardy asters and make good cut flowers.

Perennial sweet pea (Lathyrus)

Is it possible to grow perennial sweet pea from seed?

It is best started from seeds sown in autumn, preferably where they are to grow permanently, for the plant has long, fleshy roots and resents disturbance. Once established, it can be invasive, but by choosing a site carefully, you can readily enjoy its ten-foot, vinelike, gray-green foliage, and pink, rose, and white flowers. Try growing it on a lattice fence, as long as the slats are not too large for the tendrils to grasp. Special soil preparation or care is rarely needed. Hardy to -30° F., it requires only a sunny location and average garden soil.

I have a well-established perennial sweet pea that failed to bloom last year. How can I get it to produce blooms?

Try mixing superphosphate with the soil, six ounces per square yard.

Should hardy sweet peas be cut back in the fall?

They can be cut back to just above the ground level any time after the tops have dried up.

Phlox (Phlox)

Can you offer some tips on raising garden phlox?

Phlox grow best in a well-drained, humus-rich soil. They also need a fair amount of water. Cut off old flowers after they bloom. Lift, divide, and replant them about every three years, even more often for varieties that grow and spread rapidly. Phlox are subject to mildew; spray or dust regularly with an all-purpose insecticide-fungicide.

What are some of the ways to use the creeping phlox, moss pink? Do you have any tips for it?

The semievergreen, mat-forming moss pink (P. subulata) is covered with small flowers in April and May. It is hardy to -40° F. or lower. Because it grows only four to six inches tall, it is

Perennial sweet pea: The hardy, ten-foot vines of perennial sweet pea will readily cover a lattice fence in a sunny garden with average soil.

excellent for use on slopes or banks, along the tops of rock walls, in rock gardens, or as an edging. It tolerates hot, dry conditions, but it should have as good a soil as possible and full sun. Trim plants after blooming is finished. The bright pink type is common, but there are many varieties in other shades of pink, red, white, and blue.

What is the best exposure for phlox?

Although they will grow in partial shade, a minimum of three or four hours of sun is desirable, and they thrive in full sun.

When is the best time to plant phlox?

Either in early fall or early spring. Container-grown phlox can be planted in midsummer. If planted in the fall, phlox should be mulched with a three-inch layer of leaves or straw, to prevent possible heaving from the ground as a result of freezing and thawing.

How should soil be prepared for phlox?

The soil should be dug to a depth of twelve to eighteen inches and mixed with a three-inch layer of rotted manure, leaf mold, or a mixture of peat moss and compost.

How far apart should phlox be planted?

Set the tall-growing varieties fifteen to eighteen inches apart, and allow three or four shoots to grow from each plant. Shorter-growing types should be planted twelve to fifteen inches apart.

Do phlox require extra water and fertilizer?

If the bed was well prepared by deep digging and the incorporation of organic matter, extra watering may not be necessary. They do respond to sidedressings of fertilizer or to applications of liquid fertilizers when the flower buds are about to form.

How can I handle garden phlox to get perfectly shaped, rather than ill-shaped, heads of blossoms?

Probably your plants are old and need lifting, dividing, and replanting. Thin out the shoots that appear in the spring, leaving several inches between those that are left. Give liquid fertilizer weekly. It is also possible that your phlox are a poor variety, or they could be infested with mites or nematodes.

In transplanting phlox, how deeply should they be set?

Because phlox roots should be planted straight down, dig the holes deep and give them plenty of space, but the crown should be no more than one or two inches below soil level.

Maggie Oster

Moss pink: This creeping phlox is covered with small flowers in April and May and makes an excellent rock garden plant.

Phlox: Cut off the faded flowers of phlox after bloom.

How can I propagate perennial phlox?

Propagate phlox by lifting plants from the soil and dividing them in the fall. Choose the new divisions from the outer edge of the clump and discard the old center, which is too woody for good growth. Replant them as you would new plants.

Why did my phlox change color? Many plants that were white, salmon, or deep red are now a sickly magenta.

You probably allowed the seeds to ripen and self-sow. Unfortunately, self-seeded phlox tend to revert to their ancestral purplish color. As these natural forms are usually exceptionally vigorous, they crowd out the desirable but less sturdy varieties. Cut off faded flowers to prevent reseeding, and weed out any seedlings that do appear.

Why don't my phlox thrive? The foliage is sometimes whitish looking, then it turns to brown. The lower leaves drop off and the blooms are poor.

Garden phlox are subject to red spider mite infestations, which cause a whitish appearance at first, then the leaves turn brown. They are also subject to mildew and a disease that causes the lower leaves to drop. Deep, rich, moist but well-drained soil, and periodic dusting with sulfur or spraying with Karathane, will help.

What is the cause of every bit of phlox foliage drying up, from roots to flower?

This question is almost universal, and there is no real answer. Rather than being caused by a specific organism, it is evidently a physiological disease, possibly due to a blockage of food and water movement at the point of union of new and old growth. To prevent, cut old stalks back to ground level in the fall or early spring.

A small, soft-bodied insect, orange with black stripes, attacks my phlox. Nothing seems to control it, and I have never been able to find out what it is. Do you know?

This is probably the phlox bug, a sucking insect with reddish or orange margins on the wings and a black stripe on the back. Kill the nymphs by spraying with malathion, Sevin, or insecticidal soap.

Pincushion flower *(Scabiosa)*

How tall does pincushion flower grow and what color are the flowers?

Pincushion flower grows eighteen to thirty inches tall. The richly textured, three-inch flowers borne on long stems in midsummer are usually pale blue, but there is also a white form, as well as darker blue and violet hybrids. Plants are hardy to -40° F.

What can I do to get more flowers on my pincushion flower?

Plant them in a light soil. Temperatures above 80° F. inhibit flowering, so give them light shade in hot regions; elsewhere full sun is preferable. Remove faded flowers.

When and how do I divide my pincushion flower?

Plants two or three years old can be divided by cutting or pulling the plants apart in early spring and replanting them.

Pincushion flower: These unusual flowers need to be shaded in regions with hot summers.

Plantain lily, Funkia *(Hosta)*

How can *Hostas* be used in my landscape?

For partial to fully shaded conditions no plant can compete with the hostas. They are grown mainly for their foliage, which comes in various shades of green, edged or patterned with white or yellow, and strongly textured. Many varieties have lovely flowers, resembling small lilies, in shades of white, lavender, or purple; some are fragrant. They range in height from six inches to over three feet. They are easy to propagate by division. Use them as edging plants, as ground covers, as striking accents, grouped under trees and shrubs, in rock gardens, along streams or woodland paths—or even in the flower border.

How should I prepare the ground before planting *Hosta?*

Work the soil to a depth of twelve inches, incorporating plenty of organic matter such as compost, leaf mold, or peat moss. The soil should be moist but well drained.

How hardy are *Hostas?*

Most are hardy to -40° F., although not all new varieties are proven under these conditions. A late frost may nip the leaves of *Hosta*; plants should be covered if frost is imminent.

Plume poppy *(Macleaya)*

A friend of mine once grew plume poppy and it spread rapidly. Is there something similar that isn't so invasive?

Although *M. microcarpa* is excellent for naturalizing, the much more "sedate" *M. cordata* is recommended more frequently for garden use. Hardy to -40° F. and growing six to eight feet tall, it is a bold, dramatic plant. Although it produces plumes of white flowers in midsummer, the plant is mainly grown for the leaves, which are large, lobed, and blue-green with silvery undersides.

What are the growing conditions necessary for plume poppy and how should I use it in my landscape?

Plume poppies grow best in a moist but well-drained soil with full sun, except in very hot climates, where light shade is preferred. Propagate from seed or by division. Although it can be used in the back of the border, its striking effect is perhaps most appreciated when given a spot as a specimen plant.

Prickly pear, Cholla (*Opuntia*)

Cacti are some of my favorite houseplants. Are there any kinds that are hardy outdoors other than in the Southwest?

Prickly pear, the hardiest, will withstand temperatures to -10° F. It has flat pads that grow about six inches tall. In early summer, it produces bright yellow, two-inch flowers; these are followed by red-purple fruits that last several months. Prickly pears must have very well-drained, sandy soil to survive wet winters. Use them in a rock garden, seashore garden, or the front of a flower border composed of other drought-tolerant plants, such as butterfly weed and gaillardia. To propagate, break off a whole pad and stick several inches of it into the soil.

Prickly pear: This drought-tolerant plant flourishes in sandy soils and seashore gardens.

Maggie Oster

Primrose *(Primula)*

How is the primrose used in the garden?

Mass them for greatest effect from their brilliant colored flowers, of many varieties, in spring and sometimes in fall.

What kind of soil do primroses need?

A fairly moist, humus-rich soil with added leaf mold or peat moss mixed with rich compost. Primroses should be planted in partial shade.

Do primroses need fertilizer?

Yes, they need a fairly fertile soil. Use well-rotted or dehydrated animal manure, or an organic fertilizer recommended for camellias and rhododendrons.

What summer care and winter protection do primroses need?

They should be given shade and not allowed to dry out in the summer. Most primroses are hardy to -20° F.

What time of year is best for dividing primroses?

In late spring after they have finished flowering, or in late summer when they have started to go dormant.

Purple coneflower *(Echinacea)*

What is the plant with rosy purple flowers that resembles gloriosa daisy?

Purple coneflower, a native to our prairies and open woodlands, adapts well to our gardens. Hardy to -40° F., the stiff three- to four-foot plants bear their daisylike flowers with downward-bending petals from July until frost. Provide full sun and average garden soil. Propagate by division.

Purple loosestrife *(Lythrum)*

Purple loosestrife is such a charming wildflower growing in wet meadows and along streams and ponds. Does it adapt to the garden very well?

Native to Europe, purple loosestrife has made itself at home in North America in places like you describe. Growing four to six feet tall and hardy to -40° F., it can be used in naturalized plantings with moist soil, and full sun to light shade. As attractive as the blossoms are, however, purple loosestrife *(Lythrum salicaria)* is so aggressive that it can completely crowd out other plants. In fact, it has even been banned in some states because of its invasiveness.

Purple rockcress (*Aubrieta*)

Isn't there a purple-flowered, ground-hugging plant that blooms in early spring?

You're probably thinking of purple rockcress. It grows four to six inches tall and is covered with tiny leaves and brilliant purple, lavender, or rose flowers, depending on the variety.

How can purple rockcress be used in the garden?

Plant it as an edging to a perennial border, in the rock garden, at the top of a stone wall, or between stones of a path.

What are the growing requirements of purple rockcress?

Hardy to -30° F., it must have a sandy, well-drained soil, in sun or light shade. Transplant in fall or early spring. Immediately after plants flower, trim them back severely. Divide the plants in the fall or propagate from seed.

Queen-of-the-Prairie. See Meadowsweet.

Ragwort (*Ligularia*)

Where should I plant ragwort in my garden?

Ragwort must have very moist, humus-rich soil with light shade and plenty of space. Place plants two to three feet apart. Plant in the back of the flower border or at the edge of a pond or stream. They combine well with *Hostas*, Japanese iris, and royal fern. Propagate by division.

Red valerian. See Jupiter's-beard.

Rock cress (*Arabis*)

What is the creeping, white-flowered plant that blooms in the spring at the same time as basket-of-gold and purple rockcress?

This is rock cress. The variety of rock cress called Flore Pleno, a rock cress that grows six inches tall with dense gray foliage, bears fragrant flowers from early to late spring that are excellent for cutting. It is hardy to -40° F. Like other woolly-leaved plants, rock cress tends to rot in hot, humid climates.

How can I successfully grow rock cress?

Use rock cress along a rock wall or as an edging. Provide loose, well-drained soil. To encourage branching, cut plants back after flowering. Propagate by dividing the plants or by rooting cuttings in late spring.

Rock cress: An excellent rock garden plant, rock cress is also quite pleasantly fragrant.

Ann Reilly

Rose mallow *(Hibiscus)*

What is the plant with dinner-plate-size flowers?

The plant most likely to fit that description is rose mallow. The many hybrids of this plant are hardy to -20° F., grow three to eight feet tall, and have large gray-green leaves. The tropical-like flowers, which resemble a single hollyhock bloom, may measure from six to twelve inches across, and bloom from July to September. The colors range from white to shades of pink and red; often the flowers have an "eye" of a different color.

Where should I plant rose mallows?

They are easy to grow in moist, well-drained soil in full sun, although once established, they tolerate dry soil. Group them in masses, use them as specimen plants, or plant them among shrubs or at the back of large flower borders. Plant them at least two feet apart. In areas with winter minimum temperatures of 0 to -20° F., lightly mulch them before winter.

Rose mallow: These dramatic plants bloom from July through September.

How shall I treat rose mallow before and after flowering?

In the spring, dig in rotted leaf mold and bonemeal or superphosphate. After bloom, cut off faded flowers; prune plants back to the ground in the fall after frost.

How are rose mallows propagated?

Propagate by division, or sow seeds, two in a pot, and then plant established seedlings in the garden. They will take about three years to bloom.

Russian sage *(Perovskia)*

Russian sage's silver-gray foliage and spikes of tiny violet-blue flowers have such a delicate, airy effect in the flower border. What kind of soil and care does it need?

This perennial deserves to be much more widely planted. The three- to five-foot plants make a great addition to the back of the border. Semiwoody plants are hardy to -20° F. and need only sun and any well-drained soil.

Saxifrage *(Bergenia)*

On a trip to the south of France last spring I saw a low-growing plant with large, shiny, round leaves and spikes of pink flowers. Is it possible to grow it in the United States?

This is saxifrage, hardy to -50° F. Use it around shrubs or in the flower border. In many climates, the leaves of the twelve- to eighteen-inch-tall plants are evergreen.

Sea holly: Teasel-like sea holly is excellent for both fresh and dried arrangements.

I've not had much success growing saxifrage. What does it need to grow well?

Although it tolerates almost any soil, it does best in humus-rich, moist, well-drained soil with either full sun or light shade. To propagate, divide the clumps, cutting the thick stems apart with a sharp knife. Unfortunately, slugs favor the lush foliage.

Sea holly *(Eryngium)*

The photos of sea holly in catalogs look so interesting. Is it difficult to grow?

Sea holly's unusual flowers, with a prickly ruff surrounding a teasel-like center, make it an unusual addition to the garden as well as to fresh and dried bouquets. The plant's blue-gray color is also an asset in the garden.

It is actually quite easy to grow. Provide full sun, and sandy, only moderately fertile loam. Most species are hardy to -20° F. Plants may be started from seed or purchased; they do not divide readily and should not be moved once they are planted.

Sea lavender *(Limonium)*

How long will sea lavender stay in bloom?

Sea lavender bears twelve-inch-wide, eighteen-inch-tall sprays of tiny lilac flowers for eight weeks during summer. Use them fresh or dried in arrangements.

Is sea lavender difficult to grow?

No, it is very easy. Plants need only full sun and well-drained soil. Hardy to -40° F., the six- to nine-inch, low-growing, evergreen leaves form a rosette that is attractive in the front of the border or in the rock garden.

Can I start sea lavender from seed?

Yes, but it may be three years before plants flower. In the garden, plants sometimes self-sow. Once established, plants do not readily survive transplanting.

Sea pink. See Thrift.

Self-heal *(Prunella)*

Isn't self-heal a weed?

Most species can be pests, but *P. Webbiana* is a low-growing, nine- to twelve-inch plant that is useful in the shade garden or as a ground cover under trees and shrubs. It is easily grown, but does not readily get out of control. Plants bloom in midsummer with short, thick spikes of hooded flowers in shades of rose-purple, pink, lilac, and white. Plant in moist, humus-rich garden soil and propagate by division or from seeds.

Siberian bugloss *(Brunnera)*

Please describe Siberian bugloss.

Siberian bugloss is a lovely plant with blue flowers that complements daffodils and forsythias in the spring. Plants grow twelve to eighteen inches tall and are hardy to -40° F.

What are the best growing conditions for Siberian bugloss?

Let it naturalize among shrubs or trees. Plants tolerate dry to moist shade. Enrich the soil with organic matter, such as peat moss or compost.

Snake grass, Spiderwort, Widow's-tears *(Tradescantia)*

What growing conditions does snake grass require?

Plants are easily grown in humus-rich, moist but well-drained soil in light shade. They are hardy to -30° F. Propagate by division in spring or fall.

How big does snake grass get and when does it flower?

Most varieties grow eighteen to twenty-four inches tall. Plants bear three-petaled, one-inch flowers in early summer. If plants are cut back to the ground in midsummer, they will flower again in the fall. Flowers open in the morning and close by the afternoon.

Snakeroot. See Bugbane.

Sneezeweed *(Helenium)*

The bright yellow, daisylike flowers of sneezeweed, produced from summer into fall, are great in the garden, but the plants get so tall. Can I do anything about that?

Pinch out the growing tips in the spring to keep sneezeweed under three feet tall.

Where is the best place in the garden for sneezeweed?

It thrives in any soil in full sun. Consider using it in masses alone, or at the back of a large border or among shrubs. Excellent as cut flowers, sneezeweed also makes a good garden companion to Silver King artemisia, mist flower, butterfly bush, and rudbeckia. It is hardy to -40° F.

Maggie Oster

Snakegrass: Cut snakegrass back after the first midsummer bloom, and plants will flower again in fall.

What about the black bugs on sneezeweed?

Insects on sneezeweed are most often small black snout beetles, which start chewing the young shoots in early spring and often keep working until flowering. Spraying with a mixture of Sevin and Kelthane keeps them fairly well in check.

Snow-in-summer *(Cerastium)*

I need a low-growing plant as an edging. It must be able to survive dry, sunny conditions. What do you recommend?

Snow-in-summer is a popular plant for the conditions you describe. Growing about six inches high, it has white flowers and small, woolly, silver-colored leaves. Hardy to -30° F., it spreads rapidly. Plants are propagated by plant divisions made very early in the spring.

Snow-on-the-mountain, Gout weed, Bishop's weed *(Aegopodium)*

I need a vigorous ground cover that will succeed where nothing else seems to, in a narrow strip between the house and a concrete sidewalk. The plant does not have to be evergreen.

Snow-on-the-mountain will serve your needs very well. Hardy to -40° F., it grows twelve inches tall with white-edged green, three-parted leaves. You should be forewarned, however, that this plant spreads rapidly and aggressively and can become a real garden weed in some areas, particularly in the Northeast. Propagate by division.

Soapweed. See Yucca.

Solomon's-seal *(Polygonatum)*

What kind of soil and light does Solomon's-seal need?

Deep, moist but well-drained, humus-rich soil, and light shade. They survive minimum winter temperatures of -30° F. Propagate by division in early spring or fall. Solomon's-seal is a splendid plant to combine with rhododendrons and azaleas or with ferns, *Hostas*, and primroses.

Spanish bayonet. See Yucca.

Speedwell *(Veronica)*

There are so many different *Veronicas*. Can you sort them out for me?

This is a large group including both annuals and perennials. The perennial types all need moist but well-drained soil and full sun. They vary in height from ground hugging to two feet, but

Speedwell: This old-favorite perennial needs moist soil and full sun.

Maggie Oster

all are hardy to -40° F. and produce spiky flowers in shades of blue, pink, red, purple, and white. Two types are best for flower borders: Rosette-forming varieties, which form mats of toothed leaves with six- to eighteen-inch spikes of flowers in midsummer; and tall varieties, which grow to over fifteen inches in height, form vase-shaped clumps and flower in midsummer.

The crowns of my speedwells are rising above the surface of the ground. Can I remedy this?

Veronicas often do raise their crowns if left in the same spot for some time. Lift and replant them every two or three years.

My speedwells tend to sprawl. What can I do?

Some varieties do this more than others. To provide support, use commercially made round wire enclosures, or stick twigs in the soil around the plants when they are young.

How is speedwell propagated?

By division in the spring.

Spiderwort. See Snake grass.

Spotted dead nettle *(Lamium)*

Will spotted dead nettle become a terrible weed like some of its relatives?

L. maculatum seldom becomes a pest, but it is an excellent ground cover. It does best in partial shade, in any soil, and it tolerates drought well. Hardy to -40° F., plants grow about twelve inches tall. Flowers may be pink or white and resemble snapdragons, but spotted dead nettle is grown mainly for its foliage, which may be spotted with white or have other variegation. Divide plants in the spring.

Spurge *(Euphorbia)*

Someone told me that there are garden plants related to the Christmas poinsettia. What are they like?

Many *Euphorbias* do well in temperate perennial flower gardens. In climates with cool summers, cushion spurge forms a neat twelve- to eighteen-inch mound with chartreuse-yellow flowers in spring; it is hardy to -30° F. In climates with mild winters (minimum temperatures of 10° F.), *E. Characias Wulfenii* is a striking plant with its shrubby, evergreen, four-foot stems of tightly packed, blue-green leaves topped with chartreuse-yellow flowers.

What kind of soil does spurge need?

It does best in sandy, somewhat dry soils.

Spurge: The leaves of **Euphorbia Characias Wulfenii** *are evergreen.*

Maggie Oster

I've heard that spurge is poisonous. How toxic is it?

Euphorbia stems contain a milky sap that can cause skin irritation. Keep them away from the eyes, mouth, any cuts, and children.

Stokes' aster (*Stokesia*)

I'm fond of the lovely blue, two- to five-inch flowers of Stokes' aster for bouquets. Are the plants very hard to grow?

Stokes' aster is hardy to -20° F., but it must have well-drained soil to survive these winter temperatures. Otherwise, it is a relatively easy-to-grow plant. Provide sandy or light loam and full sun.

How long is the blooming period for Stokes' aster?

It depends on your location. In northern climates, it will bloom much of the summer; in the Southeast, during June; on the Gulf, through the winter; and in California, off and on all

Stokes' aster: In sandy soil and full sun, Stokes' aster will bloom off and on all summer in cool climates.

Maggie Oster

winter. Whatever the climate, faded flowers should be removed to extend the blooming period.

Are Stokes' aster blossoms ever any color other than blue?

Yes, there are white and purple forms, as well as less readily available pink and yellow forms. Plants grow twelve to twenty-four inches tall, with the most height coming in warmer climates.

How is Stokes' aster propagated?

Plants are easily raised from seed, but cultivars should be propagated by division.

Stonecrop *(Sedum)*

I've seen so many different looking plants labeled *Sedum*. What are the main ones to consider for my perennial garden?

Sedums are a large group of plants with fleshy, succulent leaves. They come in many different heights and flower colors, with various growth habits and hardiness tolerances. In general, *Sedums* are very easy to grow, thriving in full sun, and poor, dry soil. Most are hardy to -40° F. Autumn Joy is particularly popular. It has thick, bright green leaves on eighteen- to twenty-four-inch stems. In late summer, the large flower heads of pale pink gradually deepen to a rose-red. It is a favorite of bees and butterflies. The dried flower heads can be left on the plants for winter interest in the garden or cut for arrangements.

How should I use stonecrop in the landscape?

The low-growing forms are best used as an edging in the front of a flower border, cascading over stone walls, or planted in the rock garden. The taller kinds can be planted in masses alone or combined with other perennials.

How is stonecrop propagated?

From cuttings, divisions, layering, or seed.

Sundrops, Evening primrose *(Oenothera)*

Are sundrops, with their rich yellow flowers that bloom over so much of the summer, hard to grow?

About eighteen inches tall and hardy to -30° F., sundrops are easy to grow in any soil and full sun. Although they spread rapidly, they are easy to remove. The Ozark sundrop *(O. missourensis)* is a trailing plant with four-inch yellow flowers and attractive seed pods; grow these in dry soil only. Plants are propagated by seed or division in early spring.

Maggie Oster

Sundrops: This sunny, easy-to-grow flower spreads rapidly.

Someone told me there is an Oenothera that has flowers that change from white to pink. What is this?

The evening primrose *(O. speciosa)* has three-inch, white-to-pink flowers in late summer. Hardy to -20° F., this biennial readily self-sows and spreads rapidly by root runners as well. Choose a sunny location where it can grow unrestrained.

Sunrose *(Helianthemum)*

I have heard about a small plant, ideal for edging the flower border, that is evergreen and has pink, yellow, or red flowers. What is it?

You're referring to the various kinds of sunrose. Growing about ten inches tall and hardy to -20° F., they need full sun, and a light, heavily limed soil. Where temperatures normally go as low as -20° F., plants should be mulched before the winter. They bear one-inch, pink, yellow, copper-red, or white flowers, which open in the morning, from midsummer to fall.

What care does sunrose need?

Heavily prune back plants immediately after flowering or in early spring. They do not transplant well. Propagate from cuttings taken in spring or summer.

Sweet rocket. See Dame's-rocket.

Sweet william. See Carnations.

Sweet woodruff *(Asperula)*

I've had trouble getting anything to grow under some pine trees. Would sweet woodruff grow there?

Yes. It will quickly spread as a ground cover in shade with moist, humus-rich, acid soil. Contain the roots if you don't want them to spread. The whorled leaves of sweet woodruff grow six to twelve inches tall and are hardy to -40° F. Propagate by division.

Thrift, Sea pink *(Armeria)*

On a recent visit to Seattle, I saw plants that resembled chives. What might they have been?

The evergreen tufts of grasslike leaves with globe-shaped, early summer flowers in shades of pink, rose, and white are called thrift, or sea pink.

Will sea pinks grow near the seashore only?

No, but they do need very well-drained, sandy soil in full sun. The species may be propagated by seed, but cultivars should be divided in order to be certain of getting the desired strain.

Thrift: Evergreen thrift prefers well-drained, sandy soil in full sun.

Tickseed *(Coreopsis)*

I have heard that tickseed is one of the best perennials. Is this really so? Are some varieties better than others?

Tickseed is an excellent plant, producing bright yellow, daisylike flowers off and on all summer long, if the faded flowers are removed. It is not particular as to soil, but needs full sun. The best species to grow is *C. verticillata,* the threadleaf coreopsis, which is hardy to -40° F. Plants grow twelve to thirty-six inches tall. All the tickseeds make excellent cut flowers. In the flower garden, a favorite combination is tickseed planted with Shasta daisies in front of delphiniums.

Can tickseed be started from seed?

Yes. If seeds are sown in early spring indoors, the plants will bloom the first year. You can also plant it outdoors in summer for bloom next year. Plants may be propagated by division.

Toadflax *(Linaria)*

Is there a perennial that looks like a yellow snapdragon?

This sounds like toadflax, the cultivated relative of the wild-flower known as butter-and-eggs. Blooming from early to midsummer with lemon-yellow flowers, it grows thirty inches tall and has blue-green leaves. Plants are hardy to -40° F.

How do I grow toadflax?

Provide full sun and any well-drained soil. Propagate plants from seed or by division in early spring. Plants will self-sow but seldom become a weed. Consider combining it with blue-flowering plants like sage, globe thistle, and flax.

Turtlehead (Chelone)

I am trying to grow as many native plants as possible in my flower border. A neighbor told me of a plant called turtlehead. Can you tell me more about it?

Turtlehead deserves to be more widely grown. Three feet tall with glossy, dark green leaves, it is hardy to -40° F. The pink flowers, in clusters at the top of the stems, do indeed resemble a turtle with its mouth open.

I planted turtlehead in a sunny border and it died. What did I do wrong?

Chelones thrive best in moist, humus-rich soil in partial shade. Extra fertilizer, water, and mulch should be applied at blooming time. To get shorter plants, pinch out the growing tips when stems are six inches tall. Propagate from seeds, cuttings, or division of the roots in spring.

Violet (Viola)

Are violets just small versions of the familiar pansy?

For all practical purposes, yes. In general, violets have smaller flowers than pansies and are hardier, surviving minimum winter temperatures of -30° F., with a few exceptions.

What are the basic growing requirements of violets?

Most grow best under cool conditions in humus-rich, moist but well-drained soil in light shade. They are often used in rock and wildflower gardens as well as at the front of flower borders. Hot, exposed locations are not conducive to good results. Work in plenty of peat moss or leaf mold before planting violets.

Why do the plants grow up out of the soil instead of staying in it?

The plants root at the surface, with the crown above. As they develop, the crown rises still higher above the soil.

What is the proper time to plant violet seed for spring bloom?

Outdoors, in the latter part of summer; protect seedlings with a heavy mulch. Indoors, start them in late winter.

How may large blooms and long stems be produced?

Long stems and good flowers are produced on young, well-developed plants in a rich but well-drained soil. Thin out old plants in the spring.

Virginia bluebells *(Mertensia)*

Drifts of bluebells are so lovely in the spring. How can I best use them in my garden design?

The nodding flowers of Virginia bluebells are wonderful naturalized in woodland areas interplanted with daffodils and rhododendrons. These plants also combine well with hostas, which will fill in and be attractive after the bluebells go dormant.

What are the growing requirements of Virginia bluebells?

Hardy to -40° F., bluebells grow one to two feet tall and bloom in early spring. They need moist, humus-rich, deep soil, and naturalize well under deciduous trees and shrubs. To propagate, sow seeds immediately after they ripen or divide plants during their summer dormancy, marking them in spring so you can find them. Where slugs are a pest, they will find the bluebells.

Widow's-tears. See Snake grass.

Wild ginger *(Asarum)*

Will wild ginger grow as a ground cover in shade?

That is its best use. Hardy to -20° F., these six-inch, ground-hugging plants with glossy, kidney-shaped leaves are attractive and durable. Soil should be moist and humus-rich. Plants spread by rhizomes, and plantings can be increased easily in the spring by division.

Windflower, Japanese anemone *(Anemone)*

Are there any good fall-blooming perennials besides chrysanthemums and asters?

There are several that are very good, including the windflower, or Japanese anemone. Two to four feet tall, with white, pink, or red flowers, windflower has dark green foliage.

What kind of growing conditions do Japanese anemones need?

Plant them in a humus-rich, moist but well-drained soil. They seem to thrive best when planted in front of evergreen or deciduous shrubs or walls facing south. They need sun, but will tolerate afternoon shade. Water them during dry weather. Although they are hardy to -20° F., a light covering of leaves is often beneficial. Propagate by dividing the roots or sowing seed in spring.

Windflower: This is an excellent fall-blooming plant, available in white, pink, or red.

Maggie Oster

How can one protect windflowers from the blister beetle?

Only by constant vigilance when the beetles appear in mid-summer. Dust or spray with Sevin or insecticidal soap. Pyrethrum-rotenone sprays are also helpful, as is handpicking of the beetles.

Wormwood, Mugwort *(Artemisia)*

I recently saw a lovely perennial border with flowers in shades of pink, yellow, blue, and lavender. What really set the colors off were several different types of gray-leaved plants. What might some of these have been?

Some of the best gray-leaved plants belong to the genus *Artemisia*. Some favorites are southernwood *(A. Abrotanum)* and wormwood *(A. Absinthium),* both of which do best in full sun, in any well-drained soil. Propagate by division.

The local herb society sells wreaths made of Silver King artemisia. Is this hard to grow?

Silver King artemisia *(A. ludoviciana)* is very easy to grow. Hardy to -30° F., its branched stems grow about three feet tall with silver-gray leaves. Plant in full sun in any well-drained soil.

Yarrow: Excellent either as a fresh cut flower or for drying, yarrow is easy to grow and relatively pest free.

Maggie Oster

Yarrow (*Achillea*)

Can you recommend a plant with finely cut foliage and flowers that are excellent for cutting and drying?

Consider the many yarrows. These long-blooming plants are hardy to -40° F., grow two to five feet tall, tolerate dry soil, and do best in full sun. To dry them, cut the flower heads before the pollen forms.

Do yarrows need any special care?

Yarrows are relatively pest free, but the taller kinds may need a little support. This is easily provided by sticking a few twiggy branches into the soil around the plants in spring.

What is the best way to propagate yarrow?

The clumps of yarrow are easily divided, in either spring or fall. Plants may also be started from seeds, which, if sown early, will bloom the same year.

Yucca, Spanish bayonet, Adam's needle, Soapweed (*Yucca*)

How old (from seed) must a yucca plant be to blossom? Will it bloom frequently?

Yucca blooms when it is about four to five years old. After that the clump should bloom every year or at least every second year.

What kind of soil and light do yuccas need?

These stately perennials with evergreen, sword-shaped leaves and bold flower spikes of white bells need well-drained soil and full sun. They will tolerate very poor sandy soil and are almost indestructible once established. The clumps of leaves are usually two feet tall and the flower spike adds another two to four feet of height.

What is the preferred time for moving yuccas?

It is best done in early spring, when the plant is dormant, but even then it is not easy. Detach young suckers or divide old clumps.

I have several yucca plants that were on the property when we moved here five years ago. Why don't they bloom?

Perhaps they don't get enough sun or the soil is too heavy.

Maggie Oster

Yucca: Although yucca takes several years to bloom after being planted, it is almost indestructible once established.

Perennials Planting Guide

COMMON NAME	GENUS, SPECIES	ZONE	PLANT HEIGHT			CUT FLOWERS
			UNDER 2'	2-3'	OVER 3'	
Astilbe	Astilbe x Arendsii	4		x		
Avens	Geum species	6	x			
Baby's-breath	Gypsophila paniculata	3		x		x
Balloon flower	Platycodon grandiflorus	3	x			x
Basket-of-gold	Aurinia saxatilis	3	x			
Bear's-breech	Acanthus mollis	8			x	
Beard-tongue						
Common	Penstemon barbatus	3	x	x		x
Bedding	P. x gloxinioides	7	x			x
Bee balm	Monarda didyma	4			x	x
Bellflower						
Carpathian bellflower	Campanula carpatica	3	x			
Dane's-blood	C. glomerata	3		x		x
Canterbury-bells	C. Medium	3		x		
Peachleaf bells	C. persicifolia	3	x	x		x
Scotch harebell	C. rotundifolia	2	x			
Betony	Stachys grandiflora	3	x			x
Lamb's ears	S. byzantina	4	x			
Bishop's hat	Epimedium species	4	x			
Blackberry lily	Belamcanda chinensis	5		x		
Blanket flower	Gaillardia x grandiflora	3	x	x		x
Bleeding-heart						
	Dicentra eximia	3	x			x
	D. formosa	3	x			x
	D. spectabilis	2		x		x
Blue plumbago	Ceratostigma plumbaginoides	5-6	x			
Blue stars	Amsonia Tabernaemontana	3		x		x
Bugbane						
Cohosh bugbane	Cimicifuga racemosa	3			x	x
Kamchatka bugbane	C. simplex	3			x	x
Bugleweed	Ajuga reptans	3	x			
Bugloss	Anchusa azurea var.	3	x	x	x	x
Butterfly flower	Asclepias tuberosa	3		x		
Campion						
Maltese cross	Lychnis chalcedonica	3		x		x
Rose campion	L. Coronaria	3		x		
Catchfly	L. Viscaria	3	x			
Candytuft	Iberis sempervirens	3	x			
Carnation						
Allwood pinks	Dianthus x Allwoodii	4	x			x
Sweet william	D. barbatus	5	x			x
Maiden pinks	D. deltoides	4	x			x
Cottage pinks	D. plumarius	3	x			x
Carolina lupine	Thermopsis caroliniana	3			x	x
Catmint	Nepeta x Faassenii	3	x			
Chinese forget-me-not	Cynoglossum nervosum	5	x			
Chinese-lantern plant	Physalis Franchetii	3		x		x

FLOWER COLOR	FLOWER SEASON			LIGHT			SOIL		
	SPRING	SUMMER	FALL	SUN	PARTIAL SHADE	SHADE	DRY	MOIST, WELL-DRAINED	WET
white, pink, red		X			X			X	
orange, yellow	X	X		X	X			X	
white		X		X				X	
white, blue, pink		X		X	X			X	
yellow	X			X			X	X	
white, lilac, rose		X		X				X	
red, pink, purple		X		X			X	X	
red		X		X			X	X	
red, pink, white		X		X	X			X	
white, blue		X	X	X	X			X	
violet		X		X	X			X	
blue, white, rose		X		X	X			X	
white, blue		X		X	X			X	
blue		X		X	X			X	
pink		X		X				X	
pink		X		X			X	X	
red, yellow, white	X				X			X	
orange		X		X				X	
red, yellow		X	X	X			X	X	
pink		X	X	X	X			X	
pink		X	X	X	X			X	
pink, white	X			X	X			X	
blue		X	X	X	X			X	
blue	X			X	X			X	X
white		X			X	X		X	
white			X		X	X		X	
white, blue		X			X			X	
blue		X	X	X				X	
orange		X		X				X	
red		X		X	X			X	
magenta		X		X				X	
white, red		X		X				X	
white	X	X		X				X	
salmon	X	X		X				X	
white, pink, red	X	X		X				X	
pink	X	X		X				X	
white, pink, red	X	X		X				X	
yellow		X		X			X	X	
lavender		X		X				X	
blue		X		X				X	
orange			X	X	X			X	

Perennials Planting Guide

COMMON NAME	GENUS, SPECIES	ZONE	PLANT HEIGHT UNDER 2'	2-3'	OVER 3'	CUT FLOWERS
Christmas rose						
Stinking hellebore	*Helleborus foetidus*	6	x			
Corsican rose	*H. lividus corsicus*	8	x			
Christmas rose	*H. niger*	3	x			
Lenten rose	*H. orientalis*	4	x			
Chrysanthemum	*Chrysanthemum x morifolium*	4-5	x	x	x	x
Painted daisy	*C. coccineum*	3		x		x
Shasta daisy	*C. x superbum*	4		x		x
Cinquefoil	*Potentilla* species	4	x			
Columbine	*Aquilegia* hybrids	4		x		x
Coneflower	*Rudbeckia* species	3		x		x
Coralbells	*Heuchera* varieties	3	x			x
Cranesbill						
Spotted	*Geranium maculatum*	4	x			
Bloodred	*G. sanguineum*	3	x			
Cupid's-dart	*Catananche caerulea*	4	x			x
Dame's-rocket	*Hesperis matronalis*	3			x	x
Daylily	*Hemerocallis* species	3	x	x	x	
Delphinium						
	Delphinium x Belladonna	3		x	x	x
	D. elatum	2		x	x	x
	D. grandiflorum	3		x		x
Desert-candle	*Eremurus* species	4&6			x	x
False dragonhead	*Physostegia virginiana*	4		x		x
False indigo	*Baptisia australis*	3			x	x
False starwort	*Boltonia asteroides*	3			x	x
Ferns						
Maidenhair	*Adiantum pedatum*	3	x			
Lady	*Athyrium Filix-femina*	3		x		
Japanese painted	*A. Goeringianum* Pictum	3	x			
Hay-scented	*Dennstaedtia punctilobula*	3		x		
Wood	*Dryopteris* species	3		x		
Ostrich	*Matteuccia pensylvanica*	3			x	
Sensitive	*Onoclea sensibilis*	3		x		
Cinnamon	*Osmunda cinnamomea*	3			x	
Royal	*O. regalis* var. *spectabilis*	3			x	
Common	*Polypodium virginianum*	3	x			
Christmas	*Polystichum acrostichoides*	3	x			
Flax						
Golden	*Linum flavum*	5	x			
Blue	*L. perenne*	5	x			
Fleabane	*Erigeron* hybrids	5-6		x		x
Foxglove						
Yellow	*Digitalis grandiflora*	3			x	x
Merton's	*D. x mertonensis*	5			x	x
Common	*D. purpurea*	5			x	x
Gas plant	*Dictamnus albus*	3		x		x
Gay-feather	*Liatris* species	3		x	x	x
Gentian	*Gentiana* species	3	x			
Globeflower	*Trollius* species	3		x		x

FLOWER COLOR	FLOWER SEASON			SUN	LIGHT PARTIAL SHADE	SHADE	SOIL		WET
	SPRING	SUMMER	FALL				DRY	MOIST, WELL-DRAINED	
	x				x	x		x	
	x				x	x		x	
	x				x	x		x	
	x				x	x		x	
all but blue			x	x				x	
white, pink, red	x	x		x				x	
white		x		x				x	
pink, yellow, red		x	x	x	x			x	
red, blue, yellow, white, pink	x	x		x	x			x	
yellow		x	x	x				x	
red, pink				x	x			x	
pink		x		x				x	
pink		x		x				x	
blue		x		x			x		
purple, white		x		x	x			x	
yellow, orange, red		x	x	x	x			x	
blue		x		x	x				
blue, purple, pink, white		x		x	x				
white, blue		x		x	x				
white, pink, yellow		x		x				x	
white, pink		x	x	x	x			x	
blue		x		x			x	x	
white			x	x				x	
					x	x		x	
				x	x			x	
					x	x		x	
					x	x		x	
					x	x		x	
					x	x		x	
				x	x			x	
					x	x		x	x
					x	x		x	x
					x	x		x	x
					x	x		x	
yellow		x		x				x	
blue		x		x				x	
blue, pink		x		x			x	x	
yellow		x			x			x	
pink		x			x			x	
purple, pink		x			x			x	
pink, white		x		x				x	
white, pink		x	x	x				x	
blue		x			x			x	
yellow				x	x			x	x

Perennials Planting Guide

COMMON NAME	GENUS, SPECIES	ZONE	PLANT HEIGHT UNDER 2'	2-3'	OVER 3'	CUT FLOWERS
Globe thistle	*Echinops Ritro*	3			x	x
Goatsbeard	*Aruncus sylvester*	3			x	
Golden marguerite	*Anthemis tinctoria*	3		x		x
Goldenrod	*Solidago* hybrids	4		x		x
Greek valerian	*Polemonium caeruleum*	3		x		
Hardy aster	*Aster* varieties	4-5		x	x	x
Hardy begonia	*Begonia grandis*	6	x			
Hardy fuchsia	*Fuchsia magellanica*	7			x	
Hardy orchid	*Bletilla*	3	x			x
Hen-and-chickens	*Sempervivum tectorum*	4	x			
Hollyhock	*Alcea rosea*	3			x	
Iris	*Iris* species	3-4	x	x	x	x
Jupiter's-beard	*Centranthus ruber*	4		x		x
Lady's-mantle	*Alchemilla mollis*	3	x			x
Lavender cotton	*Santolina Chamaecyparissus*	5	x			
Leopard's-bane	*Doronicum caucasicum*	3	x			x
Lily-of-the-valley	*Convallaria majalis*	2	x			x
Lily-turf	*Liriope Muscari*	6	x			
Lobelia						
Cardinal flower	*Lobelia Cardinalis*	3			x	
Great blue lobelia	*L. siphilitica*	4		x		
Loosestrife gooseneck	*Lysimachia clethroides*	3		x		
Yellow	*L. punctata*	5		x		
Lungwort	*Pulmonaria* species	4	x			
Lupine	*Lupinus polyphyllus*	4			x	x
Mallow						
Hollyhock mallow	*Malva Alcea* var. *fastigiata*	4			x	
Musk mallow	*M. moschata*	3			x	
Marsh marigold	*Caltha palustris*	3	x			
Meadow rue	*Thalictrum aquilegifolium*	5		x		x
Yunnan	*T. Delavayi*	4			x	x
Lavender mist	*T. Rochebrunianum*	5			x	x
Meadowsweet	*F. vulgaris* Flore	3	x			
Queen-of-the-prairie	*Filipendula rubra* Venusta	2			x	
Queen-of-the-meadow	*F. Ulmaria* Flore Pleno	3			x	
Mist flower	*Eupatorium coelestinum*	6	x			x
Joe-Pye weed	*E. purpureum*				x	
Monkshood						
Azure	*Aconitum Fisheri*	3		x		
Common	*A. Napellus*	3		x		x
Orange sunflower	*Heliopsis scabra*	4			x	
Oriental poppy	*Papaver orientale*	3		x	x	x
Ornamental grasses						
Giant reed	*Arundo Donax*	7			x	
Feather Reed	*Calamagrostis acutiflora* Stricta	5			x	x

FLOWER COLOR	FLOWER SEASON			SUN	LIGHT PARTIAL SHADE	SHADE	DRY	SOIL MOIST, WELL-DRAINED	WET
	SPRING	SUMMER	FALL						
blue		X	X	X			X	X	
white		X			X				X
yellow		X		X	X		X		
yellow			X	X			X	X	
white, blue	X	X		X	X			X	
white, pink, purple, blue, red			X	X				X	
pink		X	X		X			X	
purple, red		X			X			X	
pink		X			X			X	
pink		X		X			X	X	
pink, red, yellow, white		X		X	X			X	
all colors	X	X		X	X			X	
white, red		X		X	X			X	
yellow-green		X			X		X	X	
yellow		X	X	X			X	X	
yellow	X			X	X			X	
pink, white	X				X	X		X	
lavender		X	X		X			X	
red		X	X	X	X			X	X
blue		X	X	X	X			X	
white		X		X	X			X	
yellow		X		X	X			X	
pink, white, blue, red	X				X	X		X	
blue, pink, red, white, yellow		X		X				X	
pink, white		X		X				X	
pink, white		X		X				X	
yellow	X				X	X			X
pink, white	X	X		X	X			X	
mauve		X	X	X	X			X	
mauve		X	X	X	X			X	
white		X		X	X				
white, pink		X		X	X			X	
white		X		X	X				
lavender			X	X	X			X	
purple			X		X	X			X
blue			X	X	X			X	
blue, white	X	X		X	X			X	
orange, yellow		X	X	X			X	X	
orange, red, pink, white		X		X				X	
red		X		X				X	
beige		X	X	X				X	

Perennials Planting Guide

COMMON NAME	GENUS, SPECIES	ZONE	PLANT HEIGHT UNDER 2'	2-3'	OVER 3'	CUT FLOWERS
Japanese sedge	Carex Morrowii var. expallida	5	x			
Pampas	Cortaderia Selloana	7			x	x
Ravenna	Erianthus ravennae	6			x	x
Blue fescue	Festuca ovina var. glauca	4	x			
Eulalia	Miscanthus sinensis	4			x	x
Variegated purple moor	Molinia caerulea	4		x		x
Fountain	Pennisetum alopecuroides	5			x	x
Giant feather	Stipa gigantea	5			x	x
Ribbon	Phalaris arundinacea var. picta	3	x			
Ornamental onion	Allium senescens	3	x			x
Chives	A. Schoenoprasum	4	x			x
Garlic chives	A. tuberosum	4	x			x
Pearly everlasting	Anaphalis margaritacea	3	x			x
Peony	Paenoia species	3		x		x
Perennial cornflower						
John Coutts	Centaurea hypoleuca	3		x		x
Knapweed	C. macrocephala	2-3			x	x
Mountain bluet	C. montana	2-3		x		x
Perennial forget-me-not	Myosotis scorpioides	3	x			
Perennial sunflower	Helianthus x multiflorus	4			x	x
Swamp sunflower	H. angustifolius	6			x	x
Perennial sweet pea	Lathyrus latifolius	4			x	x
Phlox						
Early	Phlox carolina	3		x		x
Wild blue	P. divaricata	3	x			x
Garden	P. paniculata	3		x	x	x
Creeping	P. stolonifera	3	x			
Moss pink	P. subulata	3	x			
Pincushion flower	Scabiosa caucasica	3		x		x
Plantain lily	Hosta species	3	x			
Plume poppy	Macleaya cordata	3			x	
Prickly pear	Opuntia humifusa	6	x			
Primrose	Primula species	5	x			
Purple coneflower	Echinacea purpurea	3			x	x
Purple loosestrife	Lythrum Salicaria	3			x	
Purple rockcress	Aubrieta deltoidea	4	x			
Ragwort	Ligularia species	4		x		
Rock cress	Arabis procurrens	4	x			
Double rock cress	A. caucasica Flore Pleno	3	x			x
Rose mallow	Hibiscus Moscheutos	5			x	
Rue	Ruta graveolens	4	x			
Russian sage	Perovskia atriplicifolia	5		x		x
Saxifrage	Bergenia cordifolia	2	x			
	B. crassifolia	2	x			
Sea holly	Eryngium hybrids	5		x		x
Sea lavender	Limonium latifolium	3	x			x
Self-heal	Prunella Webbiana	4	x			
Siberian bugloss	Brunnera macrophylla	3	x			

(continued)

FLOWER COLOR	FLOWER SEASON			SUN	LIGHT PARTIAL SHADE	SHADE	DRY	SOIL MOIST, WELL-DRAINED	WET
	SPRING	SUMMER	FALL						
white		x		x				x	
white		x	x	x				x	
silver, purple		x		x				x	
white		x		x				x	
beige		x	x	x				x	
beige		x	x	x				x	
silver-rose		x	x	x				x	
yellow		x	x	x				x	
white		x	x	x				x	
mauve		x		x				x	
pink		x		x				x	
white		x		x				x	
white		x	x		x		x		
white, red, pink	x	x		x				x	
mauve		x		x			x	x	
yellow		x		x			x	x	
blue		x		x			x	x	
blue, pink		x			x				x
yellow			x	x	x			x	
yellow			x	x	x			x	
pink		x	x	x				x	
white, pink, red		x		x	x			x	
blue	x	x		x	x			x	
pink, red, white		x	x	x	x			x	
pink, white, red, blue	x	x			x			x	
pink, white, red, blue	x	x		x				x	
blue, white, purple		x	x	x				x	
lavender, white		x			x	x		x	
white		x		x	x			x	
yellow		x		x			x		
white, red, blue, pink, yellow	x				x	x		x	
pink		x	x	x				x	
purple		x		x	x			x	
red, purple	x			x	x			x	
yellow		x		x	x			x	
white	x			x			x	x	
white	x			x			x	x	
pink, white, red		x	x	x	x			x	
yellow		x		x				x	
violet-blue		x		x			x	x	
pink	x			x	x			x	
pink	x			x	x			x	x
gray-blue		x	x	x			x	x	
lavender		x	x	x			x	x	
pink, white		x				x		x	
blue	x				x	x	x	x	

Perennials Planting Guide

COMMON NAME	GENUS, SPECIES	ZONE	PLANT HEIGHT UNDER 2'	2-3'	OVER 3'	CUT FLOWERS
Snake grass	*Tradescantia x Andersoniana*	4	x			
Sneezeweed	*Helenium autumnale*	3			x	x
Snow-in-summer	*Cerastium tomentosum*	4	x			
Snow-on-the-Mountain	*Aegopodium Podagraria Variegatum*	3	x			
Solomon's-seal	*Polygonatum* species	4		x	x	
Speedwell	*Veronica* species	3	x			x
Spotted dead nettle	*Lamium maculatum*	3	x			
Spurge	*Euphorbia Characias* Wulfenii	8			x	
Baby's breath	*E. corollata*	3		x		
Cushion	*E. epithymoides*	4	x			
Stokes' aster	*Stokesia laevis*	5	x			x
Stonecrop						
Aizoon	*Sedum Aizoon*	5	x			
Autum Joy	*Sedum* species	3		x		x
Kamtschat	*S. kamtschaticum*	3	x			
Ruby Glow	*Sedum* species	3	x			
Siebold	*S. Sieboldii*	3	x			
Showy	*S. spectabile*	3		x		x
Creeping	*S. spurium*	3	x			
Sundrops						
Ozark	*Oenothera missourensis*	4	x			
Evening primrose	*O. speciosa*	5	x			
Common	*O. tetragona*	4	x			
Sunrose	*Helianthemum nummularium*	5	x			
Sweet woodruff	*Asperula odorata*	3	x			
Thrift	*Armeria pseudarmeria*	6	x			
Sea pink	*A. maritima*	3	x			
Tickseed	*Coreopsis grandiflora/lanceolata*	5	x	x	x	x
Threadleaf	*C. verticillata*	3	x	x	x	x
Toadflax	*Linaria genistifolia*	3		x		x
Turtlehead	*Chelone Lyonii*	3			x	
Violet	*Viola* species	4	x			x
Virginia bluebells	*Mertensia virginica*	3	x			
Wild ginger	*Asarum europaeum*	5	x			
Windflower						
Japanese anemone	*Anemone x hybrida* var.	5		x	x	x
Pasque flower	*A. Pulsatilla*	5	x			x
Japanese anemone	*A. vitifolia* Robustissima	4		x		x
Wormwood	*Artemisia Absinthium*	3		x		
Southernwood	*A. Abrotanum*	5			x	
Silver King	*A. Ludoviciana*	4		x		
Silver Mound	*A. Schmidtiana*	3	x			
Yarrow	*Achillea*					
Fernleaf	*A. filipendulina*	3		x		x
Rosy	*A. Millefolium*	2	x			x
Sneezewort	*A. Ptarmica*	3		x		x
Woolly	*A. tomentosa*	3	x			
Yucca	*Yucca* species	3,5			x	

FLOWER COLOR	FLOWER SEASON			SUN	LIGHT PARTIAL SHADE	SHADE	DRY	SOIL MOIST, WELL-DRAINED	WET
	SPRING	SUMMER	FALL						
blue, white, pink, purple	x				x	x		x	
yellow, red			x	x				x	
white		x		x			x	x	
white		x			x			x	
white	x	x			x	x		x	
blue, pink, white, purple		x		x				x	
pink	x	x		x	x			x	
yellow	x			x				x	
white		x		x				x	
yellow	x			x				x	
blue, white		x	x	x			x	x	
yellow	x	x		x			x	x	
red			x	x			x	x	
yellow		x	x	x			x	x	
red			x	x			x	x	
pink			x	x			x	x	
pink, red, white		x	x	x			x	x	
red, pink		x		x			x	x	
yellow		x		x				x	
pink		x						x	
yellow		x		x				x	
pink, yellow, red		x		x				x	
white	x				x	x		x	
pink, white	x	x		x			x		
pink, white, red	x			x			x		
yellow		x		x			x	x	
yellow		x		x			x	x	
yellow		x		x				x	
pink		x	x	x	x			x	x
white, purple, pink, yellow	x				x			x	
blue	x				x			x	
maroon	x					x		x	
white, pink			x		x			x	
lilac	x				x			x	
pink			x		x			x	
yellow		x		x			x	x	
yellow		x		x			x	x	
yellow		x		x			x	x	
yellow		x		x			x	x	
yellow		x		x			x	x	
white, rose	x	x		x			x	x	
white		x		x			x	x	
yellow	x	x		x				x	
white		x		x			x	x	

PART V
HERBS

17 Gardening with Herbs

The subtle colors, pungent and heady fragrances, depend-ability, variety of usages, and legendry of herbs has, for centuries, made them endlessly fascinating to gardeners every-where. Any spot of sunshine can become home for an herb garden, whether that "garden" is a single flower pot or an intricately fashioned, Elizabethan-style knot garden.

Although botanists define herbs as plants that die down over winter rather than form woody stems, most gardeners and cooks recognize herbs for their medicinal, flavorful, or aromatic qualities. It is well known that a sprinkling of a few herbs magically and healthfully seasons and enhances cooked foods, but herbs are equally delicious in teas, butters, jellies, garnishes, and vinegars. Their uses extend beyond the kitchen to flower arrangements, sachets and potpourris, soaps and cosmetics, dyes, and insect repellents.

As the multifaceted world of herbs, and their culture, history, and usages open up to you in the chapters that follow, the pleasures of growing herbs will enrich your garden as well as your kitchen, and indeed your whole house.

What is the difference between an herb and a spice?

Because spices, like herbs, season or flavor food, it is clear that the differences between the two are subtle and overlapping. Some consider that herbs come from leaves and seeds, and spices come from fruit, roots, bark, and berries, but the roots of some herbs are useful, as are the leaves of some spices. Others classify temperate-climate plants as herbs and tropical plants as

◀ *Herb gardens, no matter how large or small, are endlessly fascinating to gardeners everywhere.*

spices. Yet others regard spices as more flavorful or hotter to the taste than herbs. At best, the definitions and differences are subtle.

What is the proper way to pronounce the word "herb"?

Either "urb" or "hurb" is correct. In the United States, the pronunciation is usually "urb"; in England, "hurb." American and British pronunciations of the word *basil* differ also, with Americans generally saying "bayzle," and British, "bazzle."

What is an "Herbal"?

Written as early as the fifteenth century, herbals were books that described the plants known in earlier times. This history, lore, and legend of plants that we still enjoy growing today continues to make fascinating reading.

Are herbs annuals, biennials, or perennials?

There are annual, biennial, and perennial herbs. An annual flowers, sets seed, and dies all in one year. A biennial flowers, sets seed, and dies over two years. A perennial lives from year to year, usually flowering and setting seed in spring and summer, dying to the ground in winter, and regrowing the following spring.

You list fennel, scented geranium, lemon grass, marjoram, and rosemary as perennials, but I thought they were annuals. Can you explain?

These herbs are not winter hardy in cold climates and are therefore grown in most parts of the country as annuals, although technically they are perennials.

Will you please explain the terms "winter hardy" and "hardiness zone"?

The U.S. Department of Agriculture has divided the United States and Canada into ten hardiness zones, based on the average minimum winter temperature in each area. Every perennial has been assigned a hardiness zone through which it will survive the winter outdoors. You should check the hardiness of each perennial herb you are planning to add to the garden to determine if it will grow in your area. When a plant is said to be not "winter hardy," it means it will not tolerate frost.

I have read that parsley is a biennial. Can't it be harvested the first year?

Actually, parsley is *best* harvested the first year. Although technically it is a biennial, because it does not flower until its second year, after it flowers it produces few—and bitter— leaves.

COMMON ANNUAL AND BIENNIAL HERBS

angelica
anise
basil
borage
calendula
caraway
chamomile (German)
chervil
clary
coriander
cumin
dill
fennel
garlic
lemon grass
lemon verbena
marjoram
oregano
parsley
pennyroyal (American)
perilla
rosemary
safflower
scented geraniums
sesame
summer savory
watercress

Parsley, a biennial, stays fresh and green even in very cold fall weather, but the leaves it produces the following spring are bitter.

Which other herbs are biennials? Can any be grown as annuals?

Angelica, caraway, clary, and watercress are biennials. If you are growing angelica and watercress for their leaves, which can be harvested at any time, they can be grown as annuals. Caraway is grown for its seeds, and it will not flower and set seeds until the second year. Clary, if grown for its foliage, can be grown as an annual, but it will not flower until the second year.

COMMON PERENNIAL HERBS

anise hyssop	horseradish	saffron
artemisia	hyssop	sage
bee balm	lavender	scented geraniums
burnet	lavender cotton	sweet cicely
catnip	lemon balm	sweet flag
chamomile (Roman)	lemon grass	sweet woodruff
chives	lovage	tansy
comfrey	marjoram	tarragon
costmary	mints	thyme
fennel	oregano	valerian
germander	pennyroyal (English)	winter savory
ginseng	rosemary	yarrow
horehound	rue	

What is meant by a hardy annual? What are some examples?

Hardy annuals are those annual herbs that are not damaged by frost and thus can be planted outdoors in early spring, or even in fall and overwintered. Some hardy annual herbs are anise, borage, calendula, German chamomile, chervil, coriander, dill, garlic (which is actually a bulb, but because the bulb itself is harvested, it is usually grown as an annual or biennial), American pennyroyal, and summer savory.

Why are some herbs called tender annuals?

These are annual herbs that are easily injured by frost and thus must be planted only after the ground has warmed up and all danger of frost is past in spring; they will be killed by the first frost of fall. Examples of these are basil, cumin, perilla, safflower, and sesame.

HERBS FOR SPECIAL PLACES AND PURPOSES

I don't have room for a large herb garden but would like to grow some herbs this year. How might I do this?

Herbs don't need to be grown in a garden by themselves (although they certainly can be if you have the room and the desire). You can mix herbs in flower beds and borders, integrate them in the vegetable garden, grow them in pots, or use them as edgings and borders, depending on their size and growth habits.

Why should I include herbs in my garden design?

The flavor of fresh herbs usually far surpasses that of dried herbs in foods and beverages, and some herbs have pretty flowers that can be enjoyed fresh or used dried, as well. Perhaps one of the greatest pleasures of growing herbs is learning about them, for they have more legend and lore attached to them than possibly any other group of plants.

Is it necessary to have full sun for growing herbs?

No. Many herbs need full sun, but others will grow in partial, or even complete, shade.

My garden is partially shaded, receiving sun for only a few hours in the morning. What herbs can I grow?

In partial shade such as you describe, try catnip, chervil, costmary, germander, horseradish, rosemary, sweet flag, sweet woodruff, or valerian. Mint does best in full sun but will survive (and not be as aggressive) in partial shade.

I'm confused about burnet. Is it a plant for sun or shade?

Burnet prefers full sun, but if it is very hot, it grows better in light shade.

My backyard has very light shade all day, as the sunlight is dappled by nearby trees. What can I plant there?

The herbs mentioned that grow in partial shade might do well in this situation. You could also add angelica, anise hyssop, bee balm, borage, calendula, chamomile, chives, hyssop, lemon balm, lovage, parsley, pennyroyal, perilla, saffron, sage, and tarragon.

Are there any herbs that will grow in a shaded, woodland garden?

Yes, chervil, ginseng, sweet cicely, and sweet woodruff will tolerate heavy shade. Watercress must also be grown in the shade if it is grown in the ground rather than in water.

I have read that herbs must have dry soil. Is this true?

Many herbs need dry soil to produce their most fragrant or flavorful foliage. The ones most demanding of this are anise, bee balm, borage, burnet, caraway, catnip, horehound, hyssop, lavender, lavender cotton, perilla, tarragon, thyme, and yarrow.

My Seattle garden is rarely dry during the summer. What can I grow in my herb garden, which has well-drained soil?

The list has many offerings. You could successfully grow angelica, calendula, chervil, chives, clary, coriander, dill, garlic, horseradish, lemon balm, lemon verbena, mint, pennyroyal, rue, saffron, savory, sweet flag, sweet woodruff, tansy, valerian, and watercress.

Like the gardener in Seattle, I also have moist soil, but my garden is much colder in the winter. Will the same herbs do well for me?

Yes, and you can add to your list ginseng and lovage plants that actually *require* cold winters, which would not occur in the Seattle area.

Are there any other herbs that must have cold winters to grow well?

Yes, besides ginseng and lovage, English lavender, hyssop, sweet cicely, silver artemisia, tarragon, and yarrow must have freezing temperatures during the winter or they will not grow well.

Chamomile did not grow well in my Nashville garden. What might be wrong?

It is most likely too hot during your summers for chamomile. For the same reason, you may not be able to grow calendula, chervil, parsley, pennyroyal, and watercress in your region. Try growing them in the spring or fall, or substitute other plants.

Maggie Oster

Sweet woodruff makes a lovely ground cover in partially shaded areas.

What herbs will tolerate the high heat of my Texas garden in summer?

The most heat-resistant herbs are angelica, cumin, germander, lemon grass, and sesame.

What does the term "kitchen garden" mean?

This descriptive phrase refers to a fairly small garden composed of edible plants, both vegetable and herb. If possible, it's nice to have such a garden close to the house, handy for last-minute additions to summer meals.

What annual herbs would you suggest for a beginner to grow in a kitchen garden?

The easiest herbs to grow from seed are basil, borage, chervil, chives, dill, parsley (really a biennial but grown as an annual), summer savory, and sweet marjoram.

Small kitchen gardens consist of edible plants, both vegetables and herbs.

Positive Images, Jerry Howard

I have never grown herbs before and would like to plant a few perennial herbs. What would you suggest I start with for a kitchen garden?

Try chives, French tarragon, peppermint, rosemary, sage, spearmint, and thyme. Rosemary will not survive outdoors where winters are below freezing, but it is easy to grow and such an important culinary herb that it should not be excluded from your garden (see pages 541-42). You will probably have greatest success if you purchase plants of all of these (except perhaps chives), rather than starting them from seed.

My mother does not see well, so I would like to plant a fragrant garden for her to enjoy. What should I include?

Many herbs fit this category. You can choose from angelica, catnip, costmary, horehound, hyssop, lavender, lavender cotton, lemon balm, lemon grass, lemon verbena, lovage, marjoram, the mints, rosemary, sage (especially pineapple sage), scented geraniums, southernwood, sweet flag, thyme, valerian, and wormwood.

Which herbs are grown for their seeds? I would like to use some herb seeds in baking bread and cookies.

The seeds of angelica, anise, caraway, coriander, cumin, fennel, lovage, and sesame are used in baking as well as for other purposes. Dill seed is well known as a seasoning for pickled cucumbers.

Which herb leaves are grown for culinary use?

The most common ones are basil, borage (young leaves only), burnet, chervil, chives, dill, fennel, lemon balm, marjoram, mints, oregano, parsley, sage, savory, tarragon, and thyme.

Culinary garden plan: (1) Basil, (2) chervil, (3) chives, (4) dill, (5) fennel, (6) lemon balm, (7) lovage, (8) marjoram, (9) oregano, (10) parsley, (11) sage, (12) spearmint, (13) summer savory, (14) tarragon, (15) thyme.

Maggie Oster

Lavender is among the many herbs attractive to bees, which are further welcomed into this garden by skeps (beehives made of twisted straw).

Which herbs are particularly attractive to bees?

Bee balm, borage, hyssop, lavender, lemon balm, lovage, marjoram, sweet cicely, and thyme.

What consideration should I give to the colored foliage of herbs when designing a garden?

Many herbs have gray foliage that blends well with other landscape plants and can be used as a buffer between plantings. Among these are the artemisias, borage, catnip, chamomile, dittany of Crete (see oregano), horehound, horsemint, lavender, lavender cotton, rue, sage, savory, sweet marjoram, and thyme. For a bright spot of color, plant the red-leafed perilla or purple-leafed basil as contrasts.

Other than color, how can the foliage of herbs enhance my garden?

A balance of foliage texture is also quite attractive. For example, use burnet, caraway, chervil, and dill, with their finely divided foliage, as a striking contrast to coarse-leafed angelica, bee balm, borage, and safflower.

Are there any herbs that make good ground covers?

Yes. Try dittany of Crete, mint, Roman chamomile, rosemary, sweet woodruff, or creeping thyme.

I want to grow herbs for fresh and dried flowers. What should I plant?

Many herbs, including bee balm, borage, calendula, lavender, rosemary, sage, tansy, thyme, valerian, and yarrow, have attractive flowers.

I would like to grow a theme garden of plants I can use to make herbal teas. What should I use?

Teas can be made from bee balm, calendula, chamomile, scented geraniums, ginseng, horehound, lemon balm, lemon grass, mints, sage, and sweet cicely.

What herbs would do well to edge a brick or stone wall?

Try basil, catmint, dwarf lavender, lavender cotton, sage, thyme, and winter savory.

What is a knot garden?

This traditional herb garden consists of low-growing plants or hedges planted in a formal, intricate design that resembles knotted ropes. First known in medieval times, knot gardens were very popular during the Elizabethan era. They require more time and work to plan, establish, and maintain than other herb gardens, but they are uniquely peaceful and serene.

What type of plants are commonly used in knot gardens?

The plants should be low-growing and capable of being closely clipped or sheared. Often, plants of contrasting foliage color are used to make the design more dramatic. You could use dwarf lavender, hyssop, lavender cotton, and rosemary. Germander is a traditional border plant for knot gardens.

I saw a knot garden in a local botanic garden and thought I'd try to duplicate it. Do you have any idea what material might have been sprinkled on the ground between the plants to make the design stand out?

It could have been any colorful material, such as marble chips, pea gravel, broken clay pots, sandstone chips, or redwood bark.

Knot gardens seem to take a lot of plants. What is the best way to plant a knot garden without having to buy a lot of plants in one year?

Start your own small nursery bed, increasing the plants every year by seeds, division, or cuttings. In a few years, you will have enough plants to design your knot garden.

PLANNING YOUR HERB GARDEN

—— • ——

▨ Germander (*Teucrium Chamaedrys*)

▦ Hyssop (*Hyssopus officinalis*)

▢ Blue Beauty rue (*Ruta Graveolens*)

▢ Munstead lavender (*Lavandula angustifolia*)

A traditional knot garden pattern constructed in a formal, intricate design that resembles knotted ropes.

Knot gardens are composed of low-growing plants of contrasting foliage color.

Which herbs would blend in best with annuals and perennials in flower beds and borders?

Many herbs mix quite nicely into the flower garden, including basil, borage, calendula, chamomile, chives, lavender, lemon balm, parsley, rosemary, rue, sage, and thyme. Some of these add their own blossoms to the flower garden; others contribute attractive contrasting foliage.

What is the difference between a bed and a border?

Beds are plantings that are accessible from all sides and intended to be viewed from all sides, such as a planting in the middle of your lawn. Borders are at the edge of an area, and are approached and viewed from only one side. Examples of borders are those plantings along a fence, driveway, foundation, shrub planting, or hedge.

How wide should I make an edging of thyme and rosemary along a walkway?

Edgings should be in proportion to their surroundings. A very wide edging would not look good along a very short walkway. A good rule of thumb is to make an edging no wider than one-third its length.

How large should beds be?

Again, this depends on the size of the surroundings. Keep herb beds in scale with the rest of the property. Any bed that takes up more than one-third of the area in which it is placed will look out of proportion. The size of the bed also depends on how much time you have to take care of it. If you're a beginner, start small; you can always add to it later. You can grow a lot of herbs in an area 3 to 4 feet square.

I'm planning an herb border against the fence in my backyard. How deep should it be?

Borders, too, should be in proportion to their length. Because they can be worked from one side only, however, they should be no deeper than 5 feet, no matter how long they are, so that maintenance will be possible.

What shape should beds be? Do I have to arrange my herbs in a formal bed?

Not at all. This depends on your taste and the style of your home. Formal beds are square, circular, rectangular, or some other regular shape, and they are usually symmetrical. Informal beds may be round, oval, kidney-shaped, or free-formed.

An herb border frames the edge of an area.

Maggie Oster

*This informal herb bed is enhanced by
a sundial placed on a short pedestal.*

What are the differences to be considered in designing a formal garden versus an informal one?

Formal gardens, most commonly consisting of straight lines in symmetrical arrangements, should be placed on a flat area with no large trees or shrubs. In contrast, where trees and shrubs are dominant features, it is best to plan an informal, curving garden around these permanent features. Consider both your personal preference and what blends with the style of your house and the rest of your garden.

On a trip to Europe, I saw some formal gardens with interesting designs and liked the effect. How could I recreate this?

Draw a plan to scale on graph paper and then transfer it to the garden bed, using strings or cord to lay it out before you plant. You can create your own original design in the same manner. Start with a square, and place squares, circles, triangles, or other symmetrical forms within it. Dissect the garden diagonally or from side to side with a path if you desire.

Should herb gardens have plants of the same height or varying heights?

That depends on the size of the garden and whether it is formal or informal. In small and formal gardens, low-growing

Formal gardens consist of symmetrically arranged patterns.

plants look best. In large, informal gardens, a variety of heights makes the planting more interesting. Place tall plants in the background, with intermediate-sized plants in front of them, and a low-growing herb as a border. Combine angelica, dill, fennel, lemon verbena, lovage, and southernwood, which are tall plants, with medium-sized anise, borage, oregano, rue, sage, or sweet cicely. Border the garden with basil, chamomile, parsley, or thyme.

Where can I locate herb beds and borders in my garden?

Anywhere where the light and soil conditions are right. Line your walkways or driveway, place a bed right outside the back door or in the middle of the backyard, or a border by the patio or along a fence. When deciding where to put your herb beds and borders, consider the points from which they will be viewed. If you want to see an herb bed from near the dining room, locate it near those windows. If you want to see it from the patio, that's where it should be. If the beds or borders contain mostly culinary herbs, place them near the vegetable garden or the kitchen.

Can I situate an herb garden on a slope?

Absolutely! Because water runs off them more quickly, slopes are often dry, and thus ideal for many herbs, especially those

Maggie Oster

Vegetables and herbs are natural companions.

Companion garden plan: (1) Summer savory, (2) asparagus, (3) tomatoes and basil, (4) peppers, (5) marigolds, (6) green beans, (7) summer squash and nasturtiums, (8) lettuce and onions, (9) chives.

that prefer dry soil. Choose low-growing herbs for the best visual effect.

I would like to put plants around the spokes of an old wagon wheel. How would you suggest doing this?

A wagon or oxcart wheel can be made the central feature of a small, formal herb garden. Select a level spot. Place the hub down into the ground and put a few plants of each variety between the spokes. Low-growing, compact plants, such as basil, chamomile, chervil, chives, coriander, hyssop, lemon balm, marjoram, parsley, and savory would be better than tall, scraggly ones.

Can I plant herbs among my vegetables?

Yes, in fact, many herbs, such as artemisia, chives, and thyme, are thought to repel insects that prey on certain vegetables. Be careful to choose herbs that tolerate fertilizer and water, since you will probably be feeding and watering your vegetable garden regularly. Chives and parsley can make decorative edgings in a vegetable garden. If your vegetable garden has raised beds with permanent paths, creeping thyme would make a lovely ground cover on the paths. Dill will grow and show off among squash, but is said to inhibit the growth of tomatoes. If you grow dill with cucumbers, the seeds will be at hand when it comes time for pickling. A few calendula plants add color and are said to repel asparagus beetles.

How can I extend the season for harvesting fresh herbs?

There are several ways. Perennial herbs are often harvestable before annual herbs. If you begin plants indoors by seed, you can set annual plants out earlier than normal in spring, and if

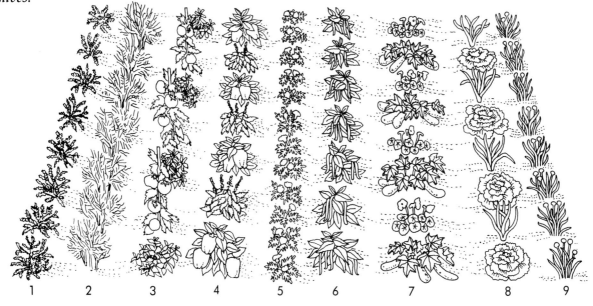

1   2   3   4   5   6   7   8   9

frost threatens, protect them with hot caps (plastic or paper tents made to protect young plants from wind and cold) or other covering. In fall, dig some herbs and move them into the cold frame for additional months of harvesting. The ultimate in extending the season, of course, is to grow herbs indoors.

I have a very small garden but I do want to grow a few herbs. What do you suggest?

If you have run out of space in the ground, try growing herbs in containers.

Which herbs grow best in containers?

Anise, basil, chervil, coriander, lavender, lavender cotton, lemon balm, parsley, rosemary, sage, scented geraniums, and summer savory. Edge containers with creeping varieties of chamomile or thyme, which will cascade over the sides.

Where can I place containers?

Containers can be used anywhere that the sun/shade conditions of the plants are met—on patios, porches, decks, balconies, along the walkway, at the front door. To take care of them most easily, be sure they are within reach of the garden hose.

Container-grown rosemary does well outdoors in hot, sunny weather, but must be wintered indoors in cold-weather regions.

What types of containers other than clay pots might be used for herbs set out on the terrace or sun deck?

Wooden tubs are ideal. Use an old butter tub if you can find one, or purchase redwood or pressure-treated pine planters. Plastic pots are durable and the soil in them stays moist longer than in clay pots. Avoid metal containers as these tend to get too hot.

Which herbs can I grow indoors? I'd like to have fresh herbs for cooking over the winter.

Basil, chives, marjoram, parsley, and rosemary are the best culinary herbs to grow indoors in the winter. Rosemary will need a cool (55° F.) spot in the house. Scented geraniums also do well inside if you want foliage for teas. For all these plants, provide a sunny window or gardening lights.

Is it better to buy seeds and plants from the local garden center or from mail-order catalogs?

Each has advantages. Mail-order catalogs usually have a larger selection and a more complete description of the individual varieties. Garden centers are good for last-minute purchases. Be sure to order or buy seeds early, especially herbs that need to be started indoors. If you order early you will also avoid the disappointment of finding an herb sold out.

Maggie Oster

18 *The Basics of Growing Herbs*

Herb seedlings can be purchased, of course, but for many reasons you may wish to start your own plants from seeds. Old favorites, less common herbs, and unusual varieties might not be available as plants. Growing plants from seed is also more economical, a serious consideration if you have a large garden. Plus, starting plants from seeds can be fun!

Why should I start seeds indoors rather than simply sowing seeds into the garden in spring?

Some herb seeds can be sown into the garden but others, because they have a long growing season, will not flower and produce seeds if you do not provide the extended season obtained by starting them indoors. Others may not need to be started indoors, but will flower or be ready for harvest much earlier if they are. Plants with fine seeds should be started indoors as they can easily wash away in the rain outside or they will have a difficult time competing with weeds when they are young.

What are the herbs that I should start inside?

You should start seeds of cumin, germander, lemon balm, rosemary, savory, sesame, valerian, wormwood, and yarrow indoors, or buy plants. Savory, wormwood, and yarrow have fine seeds; the others have such a long growing season that they need a head start indoors. Many others can be started indoors if you so desire.

◀ *Basil will be ready for harvest much earlier if seeds are begun indoors.*

INDOOR SEED PROPAGATION
•

449

Madelaine Gray

Because the seeds of winter savory are so fine, it is best to sow them indoors.

Are there any herbs that should *not* be started indoors?

Borage, caraway, and horehound should not be started indoors, because they do not transplant well.

Are there any herbs that cannot be grown from seeds?

Yes, usually because they don't set seeds and thus must be propagated from cuttings or division. These include costmary, horseradish, lemon grass, lemon verbena, saffron, French tarragon, and English thyme, a variety of culinary thyme.

Are there examples of herbs that can be grown from seed, but would be better propagated by another method?

Yes, some are difficult to germinate or take a long time to become established from seed, and others do not come true (are not exactly like the parent plant) or are not flavorful from seed. Herbs that are better propagated by division or cuttings include scented geraniums, germander, ginseng, lavender, most mints, oregano, pennyroyal, rosemary, some sages, sweet woodruff, and valerian.

When should I start seeds of annual herbs indoors?

That depends on several factors. The first thing to determine is whether the herb is a hardy annual or a tender annual (see chart on pages 562-63). Hardy annual plants can be set into the garden in mid-spring, while tender annual herbs must not go outdoors until all danger of frost has passed. Once the planting date has been determined, back up six to eight weeks for most herbs, and start the seeds then.

When should I start seeds of biennial herbs indoors?

Since many biennial herbs are grown as annuals, the seeds are usually started indoors in late winter and the plants moved outside in mid-spring, so the plants can be harvested the same year. As an alternative, seeds can be sown either indoors or outdoors over the summer, and seedlings moved to their permanent place in the garden in early fall for harvesting the second year.

When should I start seeds of perennial herbs indoors?

Perennials are treated in much the same way as biennials (see previous questions). They can be started indoors any time from spring through summer and transplanted into the garden at least six weeks before the first fall frost.

What are the basic requirements for starting seeds indoors?

You will need a sterile sowing medium (page 452), steady moisture (page 456), adequate sunlight or fluorescent lights (page 456), suitable temperature (page 457).

Containers and Soil for Indoor Propagation

What kind of container should I use to start seeds indoors?

Traditionally, seeds are started in flats or pots. However, many other specially designed units, modifications of the traditional system, are sold today for the purpose of helping to simplify the process, especially for beginners. Look for trays containing six or more compressed blocks of a special peat-based growing mixture into which you sow one or two seeds per block. Another popular variant is the Jiffy-7—a flat, peat-moss wafer when dry; when moistened, it expands to form a small, filled pot into which a seed or seeds are sown. The wafers are usually placed side by side in a flat or other container. Large seeds can be sown one to a wafer and the plants that result are left to grow until ready to be transplanted outdoors. Small seeds are usually sown several to a pot and transplanted once before being set outdoors.

Commercial growers sometimes now use special flats formed into cone-shaped compartments that are filled with germinating medium. One or two seeds are placed in each compartment, so that after germination the seedlings can become well established in their growing "plug." The advantage of this method is that transplanting shock is minimized; the disadvantage is that you have wasted space if all the seeds do not germinate.

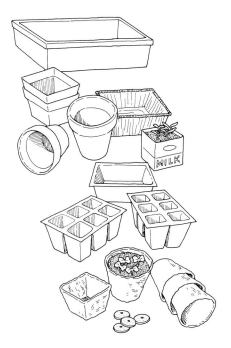

Purchased flats and peat pots, as well as a variety of other containers, are suitable for beginning seedlings indoors.

What is a flat?

It is a shallow, topless box, usually about 3 inches deep, with slits or holes in the bottom to allow for drainage of water from the sowing medium. It can be used for seed germination, as well as for propagating by cuttings. Shallow flats without drainage holes should be avoided because the sowing medium can too easily become waterlogged, or equally bad, dry out too quickly. Use aluminum foil pans, cut-down milk cartons, or other discarded kitchen containers as flats, and punch drainage holes in the bottoms.

Is there any rule about the dimensions of flats?

A great variety of flat sizes is acceptable, as long as the flat is not less than 2½ inches, or more than 4 inches deep. If the dimensions are greater than 14 x 20 inches, the flat is likely to be too heavy to carry comfortably.

Are there advantages to using flats made of compressed fiber?

Yes, but disadvantages too. Compressed fiber flats are very porous, which ensures good aeration and lessens the chance of overwatering. However, they dry out very quickly and must thus be constantly watched. Do not reuse these flats as they are not sterile after their first use.

Are there any special techniques necessary when using fiber or peat flats or pots?

Yes, make sure these containers are completely soaked in water before you fill them with medium and sow your seeds or the container will act as a wick and pull moisture from the medium.

Are individual pots or Jiffy-7s ever particularly advantageous for sowing seeds?

Some seedlings, such as anise, dill, fennel, lovage, parsley, perilla, safflower, savory, sesame, and sweet cicely, do not transplant well. If you plant them in individual pots you will not disturb their roots when you move them into the garden.

How many flats should I plan on? I have never started seeds indoors before.

You can safely estimate that a flat 5 ½ x 7 ½ inches will hold 100 seedlings of large seeds, 200 seedlings of medium seeds, and 300 seedlings of fine seeds.

Should I sow more seeds than I need?

Definitely! Not all of the seeds will germinate, and some will be lost in transplanting. If you have extra plants, you can share them with your neighbors and friends.

What sowing medium is preferable for seeds sown indoors?

It is best to use a soilless mix such as half sand, perlite, or vermiculite and half peat moss. The most convenient material is a prepared, sterile mix sold for this purpose and containing sufficient nutrients to carry seedlings through until transplanting time. If grown indoors in garden soil, seeds do not germinate well, and a fungus disease called damping off (see page 485) is common.

I have never started seeds indoors before. How much sowing medium will I need?

You can estimate that 4 cups of medium will be needed for each 5½ x 7½-inch flat.

I filled my flats with sowing medium and then watered the medium prior to sowing. But all the perlite floated to the top, and the medium didn't moisten evenly. What went wrong?

The medium must be moistened before it is placed into the flats. Put it in a large bowl or plastic bag to moisten it. Use about 1½ cups of water for every 4 cups of medium.

How should I go about sowing seeds of herbs indoors in a flat?

Cover the drainage holes in containers with moss or pieces of broken flower pot; follow with an inch of flaky leafmold or peat moss; fill with moistened sowing medium to within ¼ inch of the top of the flat; press down level and sow the seeds.

How deep should seeds be planted in flats and pots indoors?

Indoors, very small seeds are firmly pressed into the soil with a tamper or covered with a dusting of fine soil, sand, or vermiculite; medium-sized seeds are covered ⅛ to ¼ inch deep; large seeds, about two to three times their diameter.

What is a tamper?

Used for tamping soil firmly in flats, a tamper is an oblong piece of board with a handle attached (similar to a mason's float). If you don't have one, the base of a tumbler or small flowerpot can be used.

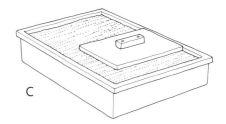

I sowed seeds of wormwood indoors last year and did not cover them with medium because they were very fine. However, germination was poor. What did I do wrong?

Fine seeds must be in contact with the moistened medium to germinate. It is possible that you were unsuccessful because the seeds were caught in a small air pocket when they were sown. After sowing fine seeds, gently press them into the medium, or water them with a very fine spray of water to ensure that they are touching the medium. A rubber bulb sprinkler is the best way to do this, as the spray of water is very fine and will not dislodge the seedlings.

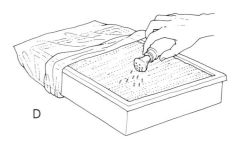

(A) Layer broken pottery, peat moss, and moistened sowing medium in flat before sowing seeds; (B) mix very fine seeds with a bit of sand to ensure more even broadcasting; (C) press seeds into soil with a tamper; (D) gently moisten seed bed with a rubber bulb sprinkler and cover flat with plastic.

Can seed flats be reused from year to year?

Yes, plastic or foil flats can be reused because they can be thoroughly cleaned to prevent transmission of disease. Those made of compressed peat or fiber should not be reused, however, as they cannot be cleaned properly.

How should I clean flats before reusing them?

To prevent damping off and other diseases, disinfect flats by washing them thoroughly with soap and water and rinsing them in a 10-percent solution of bleach in water.

Can I reuse sowing medium?

No, you should not reuse sowing medium for germinating seeds, as it may not be sterile. You can use it, however, for transplants, container plants, and houseplants.

Valerian seeds are short lived and must be used only when fresh.

Maggie Oster

Are there any rules about which types of seeds to sow together? I want to grow several types of seedlings in the same flat.

Yes, combine those seeds that need the same temperature and light conditions to germinate, and that will germinate in the same length of time.

Is it better to scatter the seeds or to sow them in rows?

When flats are used, it is preferable to sow them in rows. You can judge germination better, cultivate lightly without danger of harming seedlings, and transplant with more ease. To sow seeds, hold the seed packet between your thumb and third finger and tap gently with your forefinger to distribute the seed.

How can very small seeds be sown evenly?

You may find it easier to broadcast very fine seeds, as they are often difficult to sow in rows. Mix them thoroughly with sand before sowing.

Is it a good idea to sow all of my seeds?

No, save a few, just in case something goes wrong and you have to start over.

What other accessories will I need to get seeds to germinate indoors?

So you don't need to rely on your memory, use labels to record the type of plant and the sowing date. Also keep a record book to help you next year in deciding which herb seeds to buy, how long it took for the seeds to germinate, whether you started them too early or too late, and whether you grew too few or too many of a particular plant.

I saved seeds from last year. Is there any way to tell if they are still good before I sow them?

Yes, take ten seeds and place them in a moist paper towel. Place the paper towel in a plastic bag. Set it in a warm spot (unless it is an herb that likes cool temperatures to germinate). Check the chart on pages 564-65 to see how many days are normally required for germination. After that time, start looking at the seeds. If eight or more have germinated, the seeds are fine. If five to eight have germinated, sow more heavily than usual. If fewer than five have germinated, you won't have good results. Fewer than two, don't use them at all.

Are there any herbs whose seeds can't be saved from year to year?

Yes, some have short-lived seeds that must be used only when they are fresh. These include angelica, anise, lovage, and valerian.

Caring for Herb Seedlings Indoors

After I sow my seeds, how should I treat the flats?

It is important to keep humidity high around a seed flat so seeds will germinate properly. Slip your flats into a clear plastic bag or cover them with a pane of glass until germination occurs to keep humidity at its proper level. Once seeds have germinated, remove the plastic or glass. This technique will also eliminate the need for watering, which may dislodge the seeds during the germination period.

I placed my flats in plastic bags and then noticed a great deal of condensation inside. Was I right to remove the flats from the bag for a few hours to let the medium dry out?

Probably, although condensation can be caused by a change in room temperature and does not necessarily mean the flats are too wet. If the medium appears quite wet, however, allow the flat to dry out a little before placing it in the plastic bag.

How much light is needed during germination?

That depends on the type of seed you are sowing. Since more seeds must be completely covered with sowing medium because they require darkness to germinate, they do not need to receive any special light until after they have germinated, when they must be moved onto a sunny windowsill or under fluorescent lights. Other seeds *require* light to germinate. These seeds should not be covered with medium and must be placed in good light.

Which herb seeds need darkness to germinate?

The list includes borage, calendula, coriander, fennel, and parsley.

When starting seeds in the house in the winter, how do you keep plants short and stocky, not tall and spindly?

A combination of good light, moderate temperature, and avoidance of overcrowding will encourage short, stocky growth. Turn the pots daily to keep the plants from "drawing" to the light. If your windows supply insufficient light, use fluorescent lights.

When should herb seeds be planted in seed flats under fluorescent lights?

Most seedlings require six to eight weeks of growth time indoors before being transplanted into the garden. The timing is the same whether the seedlings are grown under fluorescent light or on a windowsill, provided the window supplies enough light.

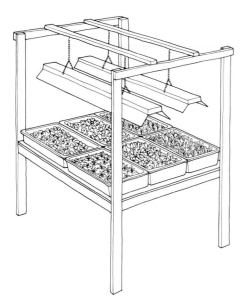

An adjustable fluorescent light unit can be raised as the plants grow.

Do any seedlings require more than six to eight weeks indoors?

Germander, lemon balm, and valerian will require ten to twelve weeks of growing time indoors before they can be transplanted.

What fluorescent unit is best for starting seeds under lights?

The most commonly sold unit consists of two 20-watt fluorescent tubes 2 feet long. This is enough light for most seedlings until they reach a sufficient size for planting outdoors. However, for superior results and to get flowering of many herbs (as well as houseplants) indoors, use a larger unit. The most popular setup is a unit consisting of four 40-watt fluorescent tubes 4 feet long. The light unit should be adjustable so that it can be raised or lowered according to the needs of the plants. When the plants are small, set the lights about 3 inches above them, and then gradually raise the unit as the plants grow.

How can I tell if my seedlings are receiving the proper amount of light?

If the plants show signs of burning, the lights should be raised. If seedlings are growing tall and spindly, they are not receiving enough light, and the lights should be lowered.

Should I leave fluorescent lights on constantly or should plants have a dark period?

For growing seedlings, the lights are generally left on for twenty-four hours until the seeds germinate. After that, leave them on during the day from fourteen to sixteen hours. A time clock is a great convenience in turning the lights on and off.

What are the advantages of growing seedlings under fluorescent light as compared to growing them in a sunny window?

Fluorescent units give a steady supply of light at all times. Because of cloudy days and the low intensity and short duration of winter light, natural light from a window is often inadequate.

To water seed flats without risk of washing away soil, place flat in a larger container of water, filled to a depth of about 1 inch.

How should seed flats be watered after the seed is sown?

Water thoroughly after seeding with a fine overhead spray from a watering can or a bulb-type or mist sprinkler until the soil is saturated. Subsequently, water when the surface soil shows signs of dryness. The medium should be constantly moist but never soggy. It is important not to overwater, but also not to permit the flat to dry out.

Many growers prefer to put the entire flat in a larger pan containing about 1 inch of water, as there is less danger of washing out fine seeds. Do not leave the flat in water any longer than necessary for moisture to show on the surface, and do not submerge the flat so water washes in and displaces the seeds.

When should I start to fertilize my seedlings?

Start fertilizing once the first set of true leaves has developed (the first leafy growth you will see are *cotyledons*, which are food storage cells, and not true leaves). Use a soluble plant food at one-quarter label strength at first, gradually increasing to full strength as the plants mature.

Why do seedlings begun in the house grow to about an inch, bend over, and die?

This is due to damping off, a fungus disease. Prevent it by germinating seeds in sterile medium only, thinning seedlings properly, not overwatering, and giving seedlings fresh air without drafts.

I have heard that parsley seeds should be soaked before being sown. Why is this?

Parsley seeds are very slow to germinate. Soaking them in warm water before sowing them speeds up the time for germination. Cover the seeds two to three times their depth in water. Soak them for twenty-four hours, changing the water several times. When the soaking period is over, sow the seeds immediately and do not allow them to dry out.

I have had problems germinating angelica and anise seeds indoors. What might be the cause?

Seeds of some herbs, including angelica, ginseng, lavender, and sweet cicely, require a chilling before they are sown. This process is known as *stratification*. Seeds must also be moist during the chilling, so do not chill them in the seed packet. Mix the seeds with moistened sowing medium, using about two to three times as much medium as you have seeds, and place them in the refrigerator for the necessary time period. (See the specific plant listings in Chapter 21.)

Can seeds be stratified outdoors?

Yes, you can prechill your seeds outdoors, provided the temperature is constantly below 40° F. for at least the necessary chilling period. Seeds can be presown in flats and placed outdoors for the necessary time, or sown directly into the ground in fall for germination the following spring.

What temperatures do seeds need to germinate properly indoors?

Most seeds require a temperature of 70° F. within the medium. (See next questions.)

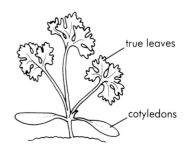

The lower leaves are called seed leaves or cotyledons.

*Watercress seeds require a cool room
for germination.*

What seeds require a cool room for germination?

Bee balm, chamomile, coriander, rosemary, thyme, and watercress require a cool room, about 55° to 60° F. An unheated sun room, attic, or basement might be the perfect place.

I keep my house very cool in winter. What can I do to give my seeds the warmth they need to germinate?

Apply bottom heat to the seedling flats during the germination period. Your garden center should supply heating cables or heating trays, which you place under the flats to keep them warm. Some have a thermostat that automatically keeps the flats at the proper temperature. If the heating cable doesn't have a thermostat, use a soil thermometer to make sure the temperature is right.

Instead of heating cables, it is usually warm enough on the top of the refrigerator to germinate seeds. Once the seeds have germinated, move them from this spot into good light so they will grow properly.

Will heating cables be needed during the summer to germinate seeds?

No, probably not, unless your house is air conditioned.

Is there any way I can prevent seedlings begun indoors from too-rapid growth and decline?

Too-high temperatures and too early a start often account for the conditions described.

What is the proper method of transplanting seedlings indoors?

First, water the seedlings well. Next, prepare the cells or pots and fill them with moistened medium, making a hole in the center into which the seedlings will be placed. Gently lift the seedling from the flat using a spoon handle or similar tool. To eliminate the possibility of breaking the stem, always handle the seedlings by their leaves, never by the stems. Lower the seedling into the hole and gently press the medium around the roots.

After I transplanted my seedlings, they wilted. What should I have done?

Wilting is normal after transplanting. Place the newly transplanted seedlings in good light, but not full sun, for a few days before returning them to full light. If transplants are severely wilted, place them in a plastic bag or mist them regularly until they recover.

Do seedlings need to be pinched back after being transplanted?

Some, especially angelica, basil, borage, mint, perilla, and scented geraniums, benefit from pinching at this point. Any other seedlings that are growing too tall can be pinched to keep them from becoming too leggy. Simply reach into the center of the plant with your fingers and pinch out the growing tip. Removing the growing shoot in this manner encourages branching.

How do you make new plants blossom earlier in the season?

There is not much that can be done to make herbs bloom early unless they are forced in a greenhouse. Most plants have to reach a certain age before they will flower.

Can I transfer my seedlings directly to the garden from the flat in which they were sown?

This is generally not a good practice unless the seeds were sown in individual pots or cells. Once two sets of true leaves have developed, it is best to transplant seedlings into individual cells or pots so their roots can develop properly and not be subject to transplanting shock later on.

What is the best mixture for transplanting seedlings from flats into pots?

You can use a mixture of 50-percent good garden soil, 25-percent organic matter, and 25-percent perlite, vermiculite, or sharp sand, or a potting mixture, which can be purchased at local garden centers.

THE FIRST TRANSPLANTING OF HERB SEEDLINGS

•

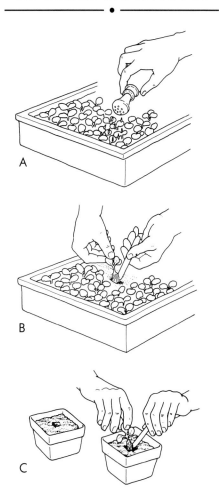

To transplant young seedlings, (A) water well; (B) lift seedling with a spoon handle; and, (C) holding leaves, lower seedling into the hole and firm soil well.

Pinch the growing tip to encourage branching.

OUTDOOR SEED PROPAGATION

If you have little room in your house to start seedlings indoors, most herbs that can be grown from seed can be started right in the garden. The exceptions are cumin, lemon balm, germander, rosemary, sesame, valerian, wormwood, and yarrow. On the other hand, borage, caraway, and horehound *must* be started in the garden. Others that do well started outside include anise, dill, fennel, lovage, parsley, perilla, safflower, sesame, and sweet cicely.

What should the temperature be before herbs are planted in the garden?

There is no set temperature. Most perennial, biennial, and hardy annual herb seeds can be sown as soon as the ground is ready to work, and tender annuals can be started when all danger of frost is past for the region.

Can I start seeds of biennial and perennial herbs outdoors during the summer?

Yes, as long as they are started early enough to germinate and grow large enough by the first fall frost to carry them over the winter.

Which herbs can I sow outdoors in early spring?

Borage (upper left) can be sown in the fall to germinate the following spring; chamomile (right) should be sown outdoors in early spring as soon as the soil can be worked.

As soon as your soil can be worked, sow anise, bee balm, calendula, chamomile, dill, horehound, rosemary, rue, summer savory, tansy, and thyme.

Madelaine Gray

Are there herb seeds that I can plant outdoors in the fall?

Yes. Angelica, borage, hyssop, lavender, lemon balm, lovage, and sweet cicely can be sown in the fall to germinate the following spring. Caraway can be sown early in the fall so it will germinate in the fall and be ready for harvest the following season. Parsley can be sown and germinated in the fall and harvested in the spring in mild-winter areas.

How can I tell when my soil is ready to be worked?

To test the soil for readiness, take a handful and squeeze it. If it stays together in a ball, it is too wet and should not be worked. When you work in too wet soil, you push the air out of it, compacting it so that when it dries it is rock hard and ruined for planting purposes until it is retilled. Wait a few days and try again. When the soil crumbles, it is ready.

I have purchased a self-ventilating cold frame. When can I sow herb seeds in it?

These solar-powered frames usually open automatically when the temperature reaches around 70° F. and close when it drops to 68° F. In most northern areas, perennials, biennials, and hardy annuals can be sown into them in March or early April, and tender annuals a few weeks later.

What does this mean: "Sow seeds when the maple leaves are expanding?"

The unfolding of the maple leaves in the spring indicates that the season has sufficiently advanced to sow perennial, biennial, and hardy annual seeds outdoors.

Preparing the Outdoor Seedbed

How should I prepare my outdoor seedbeds? I am putting in an herb garden for the first time.

Remove the grass and any stones or debris that are in the soil. With a spade or fork, turn the soil over to a depth of 12 inches. Many herbs, such as anise, burnet, caraway, dill, fennel, lovage, parsley, and sweet cicely, have a deep tap root, and the soil should be prepared as deep as the roots will grow. Perennial beds should be well prepared so the plants do not need to be disturbed unless they are divided or transplanted. If you have a tiller, this will make the job easier.

Can I plant my herb garden in the same spot every year?

As long as the soil is well prepared each year and organic matter and fertilizer are added when it is necessary, there is nothing wrong with the practice. However, those herbs that are prone to root rot, such as anise, dill, fennel, sage, and thyme, and aster yellows, such as caraway, chamomile, dill, parsley, and sage, should be rotated each year to avoid these soil-borne disease problems.

What type of soil and what fertilizing programs are best for herbs?

That varies with the herb: Some like soil that is rich in organic matter, such as compost or peat moss; others have the best fragrance and flavor if little organic matter is present. Likewise, some herbs do better if the soil is not fertilized. See the following questions for general advice or refer to Chapt. 21 for information about specific herbs. Most herbs will thrive in average garden soil that is well-drained and rather light rather than claylike.

Which herbs grow best in soil that has little organic matter?

Anise hyssop, bee balm, borage, burnet, catmint, catnip, chamomile, costmary, horehound, lavender cotton, lemon balm, oregano, rue, savory, sweet woodruff, thyme, and yarrow should receive no organic matter when preparing the soil.

Which herbs should be grown in soil to which organic matter has been added?

Calendula, chervil, chives, clary, ginseng, horseradish, lemon verbena, lovage, mint, parsley, pennyroyal, perilla, saffron, sweet cicely, sweet flag, sweet woodruff, tansy, tarragon, and valerian like generous amounts of organic matter (at least 25 percent of the soil volume), such as compost, peat moss, or leaf mold, when preparing the soil. For other herbs, add moderate amounts of organic matter (about 10 to 15 percent of the final soil volume).

Should I incorporate fertilizer into the soil before planting?

Except for those herbs that should not be fertilized, add a small amount of complete fertilizer, such as 4-12-4 or 5-10-5, before planting, or in the spring when growth starts. Further fertilizing during the year will rarely be necessary. Tarragon should receive no chemical fertilizer, but likes to be fed with fish emulsion. Fresh animal manures will cause rust on mints and oregano.

How much fertilizer should I use?

That depends on the type of fertilizer and the herb. As a general rule, for those herbs that require fertilizer, you can estimate using 1 pound of 5-10-5 fertilizer per 100 square feet on a new bed and ½ pound per 100 square feet on an established bed. Read the fertilizer label for detailed instructions.

Maggie Oster

Lavender cotton and thyme grow best in soil that has little organic matter.

What do the numbers 5-10-5 mean?

The numbers refer to the percentages of nitrogen, phosphorus, and potassium (NPK) present in the fertilizer. A bag of 5-10-5 contains 5-percent nitrogen, 10-percent phosphorus, and 5-percent potassium; the remaining 80 percent is inert filler. Nitrogen is necessary for foliage and stem growth; phosphorus, for root development and flower production; potassium, for plant metabolism and the production of food.

What is slow-release fertilizer? Can it be used on herbs?

Slow-release fertilizer is a special type of fertilizer that is inactive until released by water or temperature. The three- or six-month formulation works very well on herbs. Apply in early to mid-spring; no additional feedings will be necessary.

I like to apply liquid fertilizer to my flower and vegetable garden during the summer. Should I feed my herbs at the same time?

With the possible exception of scented geraniums and those herbs that are grown for their flowers, application of liquid fertilizer during the summer would provide too rich an environment for herbs.

What sort of amendments should I add to the soil to improve its texture?

If drainage is poor, add perlite, vermiculite, gypsum, or coarse sand. The addition of organic matter such as peat moss, leaf mold, or compost depends on the type of herb you will be growing. These materials enrich as well as improve the texture of soil, and as has been noted, some herbs do better in soil that has no added organic matter.

I hear a lot about soil pH. What is it, and need I be concerned about it when I grow herbs?

The pH is a measurement of the relative acidity and alkalinity of soil on a scale of 1 to 14. Most herbs like a pH of 6.0 to 7.0, which is slightly acid to neutral. You can test your garden soil with a soil test kit available at your local garden center, or have it tested by your county extension service agent. If the pH needs to be raised, use lime; if it needs to be lowered, use sulfur. Do not add fertilizer to the bed for two weeks after any such adjustment.

Which herbs will tolerate a soil that is more acidic than 6.0?

Dill, lemon verbena, lovage, pennyroyal, perilla, rue, scented geraniums, and thyme will grow well when the pH is 5.5. Angelica, basil, borage, calendula, catnip, lemon balm, rosemary, sage, sweet flag, and tansy will tolerate a pH as low as 5.0. Horehound, wintergreen, and yarrow will take a pH as low as 4.5. Sweet woodruff must be grown where the pH is 4.5 to 5.5.

Which herbs will tolerate an alkaline soil?

Basil, borage, burnet, calendula, caraway, chervil, coriander, cumin, fennel, horehound, horseradish, hyssop, lavender cotton, lemon balm, lovage, marjoram, mint, parsley, pennyroyal, rosemary, rue, sage, savory, sweet cicely, tarragon, watercress, and wormwood will grow in a pH up to 8.0. Lavender will grow in a pH up to 8.5. There are no herbs that will tolerate a pH higher than 8.5.

I have heard that there are different types of lime. Which is best for the garden?

If you use hydrated lime, which is quick acting, it should be applied several weeks prior to planting and watered in well to avoid any likelihood of its burning plants. Crushed limestone is much slower acting and longer lasting. Although it requires a heavier application, it can be used with less chance of burning. Dolomitic limestone is particularly good as it contains the essential trace element magnesium.

Planting and Nurturing the Seed Outdoors

I planned my herb garden on graph paper. What is the best way to transfer the design to the ground?

Using clothesline or lime, outline the design on the herb bed. The markings can be removed after the seeds have germinated or have been thinned.

Maggie Oster

Borage should be sown where it is to grow, as it is difficult to transplant.

Should the seedbed be wet or dry when I sow the seeds?

It is important to water the beds first to ensure that they are evenly moist before sowing. After sowing, water again. Seeds will not germinate unless they are in contact with moist soil.

How deep should I plant my seeds?

Instructions are usually given on seed packets, but a good rule of thumb is to plant them to a depth equal to their thickness.

I have trouble planting my seeds at the proper depth. Any ideas?

Make a furrow in the soil at the proper depth with the side of a trowel or a yardstick. After sowing, pinch the soil together with your fingers and firm it well to assure good contact between seeds and soil.

How close together should I plant my seeds?

Instructions will be given on the seed packet, but generally you should sow them twice as close together as the final recommended planting distance (see pages 564-65).

How often should I water my seedbeds?

The bed should never be allowed to dry out, so until the seeds germinate, water every day unless it rains. When seeds first germinate, they will continue to need daily watering. After a week, reduce the watering gradually until you are watering thoroughly just once a week. Deep watering encourages deep roots, and thus plants that will be better able to withstand heat and drought when summer comes.

What other care do I need to give my herb beds at this time?

Keep the beds well weeded, as weeds compete with herbs for light, water, and nutrients. Weeds also cause crowding and increased possibility of insects and disease. Remove weeds carefully so that the herbs are not disturbed, and water after weeding. Watch for signs of insects and disease. Slugs and snails, in particular, may damage young seedlings. Place bait after every watering or rain.

When should I thin my seedlings?

After seedlings are 2 to 3 inches high, or have developed two or three sets of true leaves, it is time to thin them.

What is the best way to thin seedlings?

On a cloudy day, if possible, water the ground first to make it easier to remove unwanted seedlings. Pull up the weakest before they crowd each other, leaving 2 to 6 inches between those remaining, according to their ultimate size. When those left begin to touch, again remove the weakest, leaving the remainder standing at the required distance apart. Pull seedlings carefully so the ones to remain are not disturbed. You can use the seedlings in another part of the garden, or share them with neighbors, friends, or family. Spread the operation over two to three weeks or as necessary as the plants develop.

What is meant by succession planting?

This entails planting seeds of an individual herb every one to two weeks, from spring planting time through early summer to midsummer, in order to have a continual supply of herbs. Succession planting is desirable for annual herbs that mature rapidly, especially when the entire plant is harvested by cutting it to the ground, or for herbs like dill and coriander that go to seed quickly in hot weather and stop producing foliage. In addition to dill and coriander, anise, chervil, and summer savory benefit most from succession planting, but it is an effective technique for any herb that is harvested continually or that matures quickly.

Which herb seeds should be sown where they are to grow because they are difficult to transplant?

Anise, borage, caraway, dill, fennel, horehound, lovage, parsley, perilla, safflower, savory, sesame, and sweet cicely.

OTHER FORMS OF HERB PROPAGATION

You may find it convenient to start herbs by methods other than seed. Cuttings taken from abundantly growing herbs allow you to carry young plants over the winter indoors; plants that are growing too densely can be divided; and new plants can be started from parent plants by a technique called layering.

Cuttings

Which herbs can I grow from stem cuttings?

Many herbs, especially perennials, can be grown from stem cuttings. These include anise hyssop, bee balm, Roman chamomile, costmary, germander, ginseng, horehound, hyssop, lavender, lemon balm, lemon verbena, marjoram, mint, oregano, pennyroyal, rosemary, rue, sage, scented geraniums, southernwood, sweet woodruff, tarragon, thyme, winter savory, and wormwood. Horseradish is increased by root cuttings.

What is the benefit of growing oregano, tarragon, and mint from cuttings?

True culinary (French) tarragon, as well as the artemisias, costmary, horseradish, lemon grass, and lemon verbena, cannot be grown from seeds and must be propagated by rooting cuttings or by division. Oregano and most mints are often not flavorful when grown from seeds, and cuttings are therefore better. Seeds sold as oregano may even sometimes be marjoram or savory seeds (see page 537). Another group of herbs, while they can be grown from seed, are often more successfully propagated from cuttings or division. These include English thyme (a named variety of common thyme), germander, ginseng, lavender, pennyroyal, rosemary, sage, scented geraniums, sweet woodruff, valerian, and winter savory.

When should cuttings be taken?

Because new growth does not root as successfully as established growth, cuttings should be taken after the new growth has become tougher, less tender and succulent. With most herbs, this will be in midsummer.

Can you please explain the correct procedure for taking and preparing a cutting?

Make the cut just above a leaf. Carefully remove the bottom two to three leaves to expose the leaf nodes, which are the points where the new roots will grow. If there are any flowers or flower buds on the cutting, they must be removed. Most perennial herbs root easily and need no rooting hormone. Ginseng and other woody perennials benefit from dipping the end of the cutting in a hormone such as Rootone.

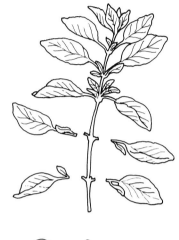

How long should cuttings be?

That depends to some extent on the plant. A cutting should have about four to six leaves above the cut.

What type of medium should I use to root cuttings?

Use the same medium as for sowing seeds, which is half peat moss and half perlite, vermiculite, or coarse sand. Cuttings may also be rooted in clean, sharp sand—a coarser sand than beach sand, which is available at building supply stores and garden centers.

To take cuttings, cut just above a leaf, remove lower leaves on cutting, to expose leaf nodes.

How deeply should the cutting be planted in the medium?

Fill the container to within ¼ inch of the top with moist medium. Make a hole with a dibble (a small tool used for making planting holes) or a pencil, and insert the cutting so that the leaf nodes you have exposed are completely covered with medium. Press the medium gently around the cutting.

Why do my cuttings wilt when I first place them in rooting medium?

Cuttings wilt because they have lost moisture and do not have roots yet to replenish the lost moisture. To ease this problem, place the container with the cuttings inside a clear plastic bag, or place a large glass jar over the container and the cuttings. When roots have developed, the bag or jar may be removed.

How can I tell when cuttings are rooted?

After about three weeks, gently tug on a leaf. If the cutting has rooted, it will offer resistance. If it can be removed from the medium easily, return it to the container and test it again in several more weeks.

In what type of light should cuttings be placed while they are rooting?

Indoors, keep cuttings in bright light, but not full sun, until they have rooted. Then move them into full sun.

Can I root cuttings outdoors?

Yes, cuttings can be rooted outdoors during the summer. Place them either in containers or in well-prepared soil, in a spot in partial shade, and cover them with plastic or a glass jar just as for indoor cuttings. Start them early enough so that they will be rooted at least six weeks before the first fall frost. Cuttings can be rooted late in the season in a cold frame.

I forgot to take cuttings during the summer. Is it too late to do it in the fall?

If you don't have a cold frame and expect frost soon, take cuttings and root them indoors. Transplant them outside early the next spring.

Division

Which herbs are usually increased by division?

Most perennial herbs, except those that have deep tap roots, can be divided. These include angelica, anise hyssop, bee balm, catnip, chives, costmary, germander, horehound, hyssop, lavender cotton, lemon balm, lemon grass, lovage, mint, oregano, pennyroyal, rosemary, rue, sage, sweet woodruff, tansy, tarragon, thyme, valerian, watercress, winter savory, wormwood, and yarrow.

When is the best time to divide herbs?

Herbs may be divided either in early to mid-spring when growth starts, or in early fall about six weeks before the first fall frost.

How are herbs divided?

Carefully dig up the plant, damaging as little of the root system as possible. If necessary, wash soil from the roots so you

Many herbs can be divided by gently pulling them apart with your fingers.

can better see what you're doing. Carefully pull the roots apart with your fingers. If they are too strong to pull apart by hand, use a trowel or knife to divide them. Replant before the roots dry out.

Should I cut the tops back after I divide herbs?

If you divide in early spring when top growth is small, it will not be necessary to cut the tops back. If you divide herbs in the fall, cut the tops back by about a half when dividing.

What care should I give plants after they are divided?

Treat them as you would a new seedling. Water the soil right after the plants are transplanted, and again daily for about a week. After that, water as necessary. If the tops wilt, resume watering or place plastic or a glass jar over the divisions until they are no longer wilting and have started to grow.

I would like to get a half dozen or so mint plants to give away to friends. Do I have to dig up my whole clump of mint?

No. You can simply dig into the clump with a sharp shovel and chop out pieces for re-planting. Rugged plants, such as mint or horseradish, can be handled quite roughly and still survive and spread.

Layering

What does layering plants mean?

This is a method of propagation that is accomplished by taking a long, flexible stem of a perennial (or other woody plant) and securing it to, or slightly under, the ground. Sometimes a slight cut is made at the point where the stem touches the ground. Where the stem contacts the ground, it will root, and in time can be cut from the mother plant and transplanted.

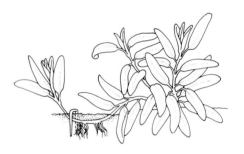

To layer perennial herbs, fasten down a long, flexible stem using a large hairpin.

How should I secure the plant to the ground?

You can weight it down with a rock, or pin it down with a piece of metal, such as a large hairpin.

When should I layer my plants?

Plants are layered during the summer and will usually be rooted by fall. If roots are still small, wait until the following spring to move the new plant.

Which plants in my herb garden can I layer?

The plants most commonly layered are lavender, lavender cotton, rosemary, sage, thyme, and winter savory.

PURCHASED SEEDLINGS

•

TRANSPLANTING INTO THE GARDEN

•

When should I go shopping for my herb plants?

Purchase plants as close to the time that you are going to plant them as possible. If you buy them too early, you will have to water them every day to keep them from drying out, or you may even be faced with the possibility of a late frost.

What should I look for when buying plants?

Look for healthy, dark green plants that show no sign of insects or disease, are not too tall or spindly, and show signs of new growth. If you are buying herbs whose leaves you will be using in cooking, smell them or take a tiny taste of a leaf to make sure you like the flavor.

I ordered herbs from a mail-order firm, and when they arrived, they were dried out. What should I do?

Water the plants right away and keep them in a cool area out of direct sun until they revive. Then plant them. If they do not make it, write to the company and ask for a replacement.

Whether you begin your own herb plants by seed or other methods of propagation, or purchase plants at a reliable nursery, the techniques for getting them off to a healthy start in the ground outdoors are the same.

When should seedlings that were raised in flats be transplanted? How many times?

The first transplanting should be done indoors when the seedlings form their first true leaves (see pg. 457). Many plants, when they are 2 or 3 inches high, benefit from a second transplant to individual pots before they are moved outdoors. However, seedlings grown in flats can be thinned and the remaining plants allowed to grow in the original tray or flat until they are ready to go outdoors. They may need a light feeding before being set in the garden. Move plants to the garden according to their hardiness. Plant hardy annuals, perennials, and biennials in the garden any time after the soil can be worked in mid-spring; transplant tender herbs when all danger of frost has passed.

Is there anything I need to do to get my herbs ready to be moved into the garden?

Yes. They must be put through a process called *hardening off*. One week before you transplant them into the garden, move the plants outdoors and place them in a shady spot. Bring them back inside at night. Each day, move them into greater light, and toward the end of the week, leave the plants out all night.

How can I remove small plants from their containers at transplanting time without damaging the roots?

Most purchased plants today are grown in individual cells or pots. Removal is easy; if the plants don't fall out easily, they can be pushed up from the bottom. Water thoroughly a few hours before transplanting.

If your plants are not in individual cells, with an old knife or a small mason's trowel, cut the soil into squares, each with a plant in the center. This should leave the plant root systems almost intact.

Herbs that have been grown individually in peat pots need not be removed from their pots when they are planted. It is advisable, however, to break or peel the pot in a few places to help the roots penetrate into the soil more readily. Be sure to set the top edge of the pot *below* the soil level, or it will act as a wick or sponge, drawing water from the soil. Because the water then quickly evaporates, instead of nourishing the plant, the plant can suffer. Water thoroughly after planting and as necessary thereafter until the plant roots have penetrated through the pot into the soil and the plant has started to grow.

Peat pots should be broken somewhat before planting, and rims should be set below soil level.

What is the right technique for setting out (planting) herb plants?

Water both the ground and the transplants first. Remove the plants from the flats or the pots with as little root disturbance as possible. Stab the trowel in the soil, pull toward you, set the plant in the hole, remove the trowel, push the soil around the roots, press the soil firmly, and leave a slight depression around the stem to trap water.

How far apart should I space herbs when thinning them or planting them out?

The distance varies according to the type of herb and its habit of growth. A rough rule is a distance equal to one half of its mature height. Look for directions on the seed packet or plant label, or follow the guidelines for individual herbs in Chapt. 21.

What is the best time of day to transplant?

Move plants late in the afternoon, or on a cloudy day, to help reduce transplanting shock.

How should I care for my transplants?

Water them well after transplanting and again daily for about a week until the transplants are well established and show signs of growth. Gradually reduce watering until about once per week, which should be sufficient for the remainder of the summer unless it becomes quite hot and dry. Keep the beds well weeded and watch for signs of insects and diseases, especially slugs and snails (see pgs. 481-87). Some transplants may wilt at first, but daily misting and/or shading will help them to revive quickly.

Use hot caps to protect tender herbs from late spring and early fall frosts.

After I transplanted my basil seedlings, we had an unexpected late frost, and I lost them all. Is there anything I could have done?

Yes. Basil is particularly susceptible to frost, but other tender herbs can be damaged by frost as well. If frost is predicted, place hot caps or styrofoam cups over the seedlings in the evening, and remove them in the morning. Watering the seedlings can also help, since when the water on the leaves freezes, the layer of ice insulates the plant cells and keeps them from freezing.

NURTURING HERBS IN THEIR PERMANENT BEDS
•

How often should I water my herb garden?

Under normal circumstances, herbs should receive a thorough (1 inch) watering once a week. If it becomes very hot during the summer, or if your garden is in a windy spot, or if your soil is very sandy, it may need watering more often. Overwatering an herb garden causes most plants to lose their flavor or fragrance—or it may even kill the plants.

How can I determine that my soil is receiving 1 inch of water?

To check the amount that you are watering, place an empty coffee can halfway between the sprinkler and the farthest point it reaches. Time how long it takes for 1 inch of water to accumulate in the can. Presuming the water pressure remains constant, run your sprinklers for the amount of time it took for 1 inch of water to collect in the can. You can also place a rain gauge in the herb bed to measure the amount of water.

Why do I need to water my herb garden only once a week? Couldn't I sprinkle it lightly every day?

This is the worst thing you could do. Light, frequent watering encourages shallow roots; then if it becomes hot or if you go away for a few days, the herbs will not be able to survive as well. Deep watering encourages the roots to grow down. Some herbs must have dry soil, and watering daily would kill them (see page 465).

Is it a good idea to water my herb garden with an overhead sprinkler? If not, what other method could I use?

Overhead watering is perfectly acceptable in many instances, and actually cools the plants and washes dirt off the foliage. Where leaf spot or mildew disease is a problem, water in the morning so the foliage is not wet during the night. You could also use soaker hoses to alleviate this problem, as well as to avoid damaging tall or weak-stemmed plants with overhead watering.

Because we get very little rain in the summer, we have watering restrictions. Can I still have an herb garden?

Many herbs actually like dry soil. For those herbs that prefer moist soil, mix a quantity of organic matter into the soil when preparing beds and mulch with additional organic matter, which will retain water.

Which herbs should be pinched back and at what stage?

To keep them compact and bushy, plants of angelica, basil, borage, geraniums, mint, pennyroyal, and perilla should be pinched back (see pg. 459) when they are 2 to 4 inches high. Herbs that are not being grown for their flowers or seed can be cut back during midsummer if they get too tall or spindly.

Why is the recommendation given to remove the flowers of some herbs before they develop?

The leaves of herbs grown for their foliage, such as basil, are generally more flavorful or more highly scented before flowers form. Also, because many plants stop growing once flowers form, you will receive a more abundant harvest of leaves if you remove flowers.

Should herbs that are grown for their flowers be treated in any special way?

Removing flowers as soon as they are ready for harvest will encourage more flowers to form.

I never grew herbs because I had heard that so many of them needed staking. Is this true?

A few, such as angelica, anise, and valerian, need to be staked. Bee balm and dill also tend to flop over, but if they are grown close together, they will prop each other up. In addition, look for shorter varieties of dill that do not need staking.

What type of material can I use as a stake?

Try bamboo sticks, metal poles, or most anything that will hold the plants up. With a twist tie or a string, tie the plants loosely to the stakes so that the stems will not be pinched or damaged. For large plants, set two to four stakes around the plant and tie string in a circle around the stakes and the plant. Large herbs can also be grown in wire tomato or peony cages.

Can I clip the plants in my knot garden at any time during the summer?

Clip plants as needed to keep them neat and trim. Woody plants such as lavender cotton, lavender, and germander should not be clipped after midsummer. A late pruning would force out new growth that would not harden off (see pg. 470) before freezing temperatures.

Make a figure eight tie when staking tall, heavy herbs.

Isn't it true that some herbs can spread throughout my garden and choke out other plants?

Yes. Plants that do this are said by gardeners to be "invasive." Some of the worst culprits among herbs are angelica, bee balm, burnet, catnip, chamomile, chervil, costmary, dill, horseradish, mint, pennyroyal, tansy, white yarrow, and wormwood.

Other than to avoid growing those herbs that become invasive, what can I do to control this problem?

Some herbs are invasive because they drop seeds (see the next question). For these herbs, do not allow flowers to form, or cut the flowers off before they drop seeds to the ground. Others are invasive because of a vigorous root system. These can be kept in control by inserting metal or plastic edging down into the ground at the border of the herb beds or around the individual plants. Such plants can also be grown in cinder blocks, PVC drainage pipe, or containers plunged into the ground to keep them in bounds. Horseradish grows freely from pieces of the roots that remain in the ground after harvesting. This is difficult to control, so delegate a section of the garden for horseradish only.

Insert metal or plastic edging down into the ground to control such herbs as bee balm, the roots of which spread rapidly.

I have noticed that plants of angelica, anise hyssop, burnet, chamomile, chervil, dill, and lemon balm come up each year. Are these plants perennials?

Some are, and some are not. If the plants are small, what you are seeing are seedlings that grew from seeds that dropped the previous season.

Can I leave the self-sown seedlings growing in the garden, or should I pull them up?

You can leave them as long as they don't make the planting overcrowded. You will probably need to thin some of them out. In a formal garden, you will want to remove all of them or they will upset the balance and symmetry. If self-sown "volunteers" become a nuisance, be sure to remove all flowers before seeds form and drop.

Can I save seeds from my herb plants for use next year?

Most herbs are not hybrids, therefore seeds can be saved and grown the following year and come true to type. Seeds of angelica, anise, lovage, and valerian must be sown right after they are harvested or they will not germinate. Seeds of mint and oregano may produce plants that have little flavor.

Is weeding really that important?

We wish we could say no, but actually weeds harbor insects and disease, and compete with the herbs for light, water, and nutrients.

Do you have any suggestions to lighten the chore of weeding?

Since many weeds are spread by seeds, it is important to pull weeds before they flower and the seeds fall and sprout. There are several methods of keeping weeds down. Besides hand-pulling, you can weed mature plantings with a hoe, and keep plants well mulched.

Can I apply liquid weedkiller to the herbs in my garden?

This would be unwise, for it would probably do as much harm to the herbs as to the weeds. Weedkiller might also be unsafe for use near plants that are raised for culinary purposes.

I have read about using black plastic as a mulch. Does this prevent weeds?

Yes, it does, and quite well. Be sure to punch holes in the plastic, though, so water can penetrate to the plants' roots. If you don't like the appearance of black plastic, cover it with a mulch of leaf mold, bark chips, pine needles, or other attractive material.

What are the other advantages of mulch in addition to controlling weeds?

Mulch keeps the soil cool and moist, reducing the need for watering. It also adds a decorative finish to the herb garden.

What materials make good mulches?

Use an organic material, such as shredded leaves, bark chips, pine needles (unless the herbs require alkaline soils; see pages 31-32), or hulls of some kind. Each spring, unless you are growing herbs that do better without added organic matter, mix the mulch in with the soil to enrich it, and add new mulch.

Can I use grass clippings as mulch?

Yes, provided you dry them first, and there are no weed seeds in the grass. As they decompose, grass clippings give off a great deal of heat, which could damage the roots of herbs.

Will I need to provide winter mulch to my perennial herbs?

That depends on where you live and how hardy your herbs are. If you live near the edge of an herb's hardiness zone (see pages 434, 711), winter protection will be helpful.

What should I use for winter protection?

Try oak leaves, pine needles (although these will make the soil more acidic), evergreen boughs, soil, or even shredded newspaper.

Maggie Oster

Heavy mulching is one of the best ways to prevent the spread of weeds.

When should winter protection be applied?

To allow the base of the plants to harden off sufficiently, put protection on *after* the ground has frozen. Placing winter protection on too early will also encourage rodents to make their winter homes there.

I have had problems keeping lavender alive over the winter in my Ohio garden. I protect it, but it usually dies. What should I do?

Check to be certain that the lavender you are growing is winter hardy; several varieties of lavender will not survive the cold winters of the north. Lavender, as well as tarragon, sage, and thyme, is damaged more by wet soil and poor drainage over the winter than it is by cold. Make sure your soil has excellent drainage. Do not place these plants in low areas of the garden where water may collect. Where severe problems exist, place a small wooden or rigid foam box over the plants to keep rain and snow off them during the winter.

When should winter protection be removed?

Remove it gradually in the spring as soon as plants start growing.

CONTAINER-GROWN HERBS

Which herbs can I plant into containers on my patio?

Almost any low-growing herb will grow well in a container. Select one that is in proportion to the container. Try basil, calendula, chamomile, chives, lavender, lavender cotton, parsley, sage, scented geraniums, or thyme, among others.

What type of soil should I use in containers? Is it all right to dig soil from the garden?

No, garden soil by itself should not be used. Root growth will not be good because the soil is too heavy, and, in addition, it can introduce insects and diseases. For most herbs, use a soilless mix of peat moss with perlite and/or vermiculite. Those that like infertile soil can be grown in garden soil combined with a small amount of soilless mix to lighten it.

Can I grow herbs in a large ceramic urn?

So that roots don't become waterlogged, containers should have drainage holes. If your urn does not have them and you don't want to punch holes in the bottom, add a thick layer of gravel to the bottom.

How often should my containers be watered?

That depends on the size of the container and the moisture requirements of the herb you are growing. If you are growing an

Maggie Oster

An awkward corner can be made more interesting by an attractive arrangement of container-grown herbs.

herb that likes dry soil, allow the top inch of the container to dry out before watering. If you are growing an herb that likes average to moist growing conditions, water the container as soon as the medium starts to dry out. Small containers will naturally need to be watered more often than large ones. Check every day to be sure; when it is very hot or if it is windy, you may need to water daily or even twice a day. It will be convenient to have a water source nearby if you have a large number of containers.

How should I fertilize container-grown herbs?

Because containers are watered more frequently, the fertilizer washes out through the soil very quickly. Therefore, feed lightly but more often than you would fertilize the same herbs in the ground. Too much fertilizer usually does more harm than good when growing herbs.

Last year the herbs in my containers did not grow evenly. What should I do to get even growth this summer?

They probably were growing towards the light. Rotate containers regularly so this does not happen. If the container is large and heavy, place it on a dolly so it can be turned more easily.

Place large pots on dollies so that they can be moved more easily.

Can I leave my potted herbs out on the terrace in New York during the winter?

No, they will not survive. If possible, replant perennial or biennial herbs in open ground for the winter, or dig a hole and place the entire pot in the ground until spring.

Can I bring my containers inside for the winter?

Yes, if they are small enough, if the herb is a type that will grow well indoors, and if you have a room with enough sun or can provide plant lights. Otherwise, take cuttings and start new plants, and then replant the containers next spring.

Which herbs will do well if I move them inside?

If grown outdoors all summer in pots, not in the ground, basil, chives, scented geraniums, lemon verbena, marjoram, parsley, thyme, summer savory, and rosemary may be brought indoors for the winter. Either move the potted plants indoors, or start new plants from seed, division, or cuttings (see pgs. 449-69).

Container-grown herbs can be placed near the doorway for last-minute additions to summer meals.

Derek Fell

How should I care for mature herbs indoors?

Herbs should be grown indoors on a sunny windowsill or under fluorescent lights. Water them when the top of the soil surface has dried out. Most will be happy at normal room temperature, except rosemary, which likes a cool (55° F.) room. Do not fertilize from mid-fall through mid-spring. At other times, feed lightly.

If I grow herbs indoors under fluorescent lights, how many hours each day should the lights be on?

Keep the lights on for fourteen to sixteen hours each day. Plants should be about 12 to 18 inches below the lights.

I've tried to grow herbs indoors during the winter, but they don't do well. The leaves yellow and dry out.

Perhaps the humidity is too low. Grow the herbs on pebble trays that can be kept filled with water; run a humidifier in the room; or put a bowl of water or a wet towel on the heat source. As the water evaporates, the moisture in the air will increase.

19 *Herb Problems and How to Solve Them*

One of the nicest things about herb gardening is that herbs are seldom troubled by diseases or insect pests. In fact, many herbs make excellent companion plants to *repel* harmful insects in vegetable and flower gardens. For example, chives, peppermint, and tansy are said to repel aphids; basil, the asparagus beetle; catnip and tansy, the Japanese beetle; coriander, the spider mite; thyme and wormwood, the whitefly. Some herbs, such as wormwood, pennyroyal, sage, and tansy, can serve as the basis of repellent sprays against insect pests, and pennyroyal is thought to repel mosquitos. Hung in closets or laid in drawers, lavender and wormwood are old, and effective, guards against moths.

If herbs—particularly those raised indoors, which may be more susceptible to attack by the common pests of houseplants—are bothered by insects, try using nonchemical control, rotenone, or pyrethrum. (See Herbs, as repellents, in the Index.) If all else fails and you feel you must resort to chemical control, be sure to use products formulated for vegetables, and follow carefully the label instructions regarding the waiting period before harvest and consumption.

INSECT PESTS

What are the tiny green, semi-transparent insects that appear along stems and flower buds? The plants are distorted and withered and the leaves have curled. There is also a black, sooty substance on the leaves.

Aphids, or plant lice, may be green, as you describe, as well as yellow, brown, black, or red. Not only do they suck juices from

◆ Most herbs are remarkably free of pest and disease problems, particularly if good cultural practices are followed.

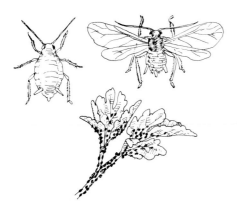

Aphid. These insects spread disease from plant to plant as they suck juices from stems, leaves, buds, and flowers.

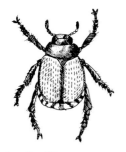

Japanese beetle. These common garden pests can be controlled biologically with milky spore disease.

Spider mite. Mites are especially prevalent during very hot, dry weather.

plants, but they also can carry many diseases. Wash them off with a stream of water, use insecticidal soap, or spray with rotenone or pyrethrum.

Which herbs are most likely to be bothered by aphids?

Aphids can be troublesome to a large number of herbs, but those most severely affected are angelica, calendula, caraway, costmary, cumin, dill, horseradish, mint, parsley, tansy, valerian, wormwood, and yarrow.

What is the black sooty substance that appears on the leaves of herbs when aphids are present?

Aphids secrete a sticky substance called honeydew, on which black, powdery mold often grows. This can be washed off with water after the aphids are controlled.

Holes are being chewed in the leaves and flowers of some of my herbs, probably by the small, hard-shelled insects on the plants. What do you suggest?

There are a number of beetles that attack herbs, although they are not usually a serious problem in the herb garden. If they are few in number, hand-pick them off. Traps sometimes work, but can often attract beetles from a neighbor's garden as well. If the infestation is severe, release beneficial nematodes (available through suppliers of beneficial insects; see Appendix). Use milky spore disease (*Bacillus popilliae*) to control Japanese beetles.

Which herbs are most likely to be attacked by beetles?

Borage, calendula, horseradish, mint, and wormwood are their favorite host plants.

The leaves of my herbs have turned a dull color, with black specks on their undersides and webbing between them. What can I do?

You have spider mites, and if you can see webbing, the infestation is very advanced. Mites do not like water, so keep the plants well watered, and syringe the undersides of the leaves with clear water. Try spraying with pyrethrum. If the problem continues, it may be best to remove the plant and dispose of it, rather than risk the pests spreading to other plants.

Mites were more of a problem last summer than they had been in the past. Why was this?

Perhaps it was hotter and drier than usual. Mites are most prevalent under these conditions. When it is very hot and dry, spray the undersides of the leaves with water every day to help prevent mite infestations.

I have a heavy infestation of mites on my mint plants this summer. Will they spread to other plants?

They may. Mites like scented geraniums, lemon verbena, parsley, valerian, and wormwood, in particular.

How can I control the plant bugs I see on my lavender plants?

These small sucking insects are hard to control. They are very active, produce several generations of new insects a season, and occur on many kinds of plants, stinging the flower buds and spotting the leaves. Dust or spray with rotenone. Clean up all trash and weeds to remove the bug's favorite places for hibernation.

Plant bug. A small, sucking insect, the plant bug is sometimes hard to control.

Will the plant bug infest plants other than lavender in my herb garden?

In addition to lavender, plant bugs like calendula, mint, and valerian.

When I brush against the valerian in the garden, a cloud of tiny white insects appears. Are they doing damage?

Yes. These are whiteflies, which suck juices from the plants. They can be controlled with insecticidal soap, pyrethrum, or commercially available, sticky, yellow traps, the color of which attracts them.

Groups of whiteflies are often well hidden on the underside of such leaves as this mint.

Ron West

Some of my plants wilted and lost their color. When I dug them up, I noticed swellings on the roots. Is this related to their demise?

Yes, this was most likely nematode damage, but you'd have to have your soil tested to be sure. Minimize risk by not planting the same kind of plant in the same space for three to four years. Plant the marigolds *Tagetes erecta* or *T. patula* in affected spots to kill the nematodes. These insects can be serious pests in the herb garden, their favorite plants being basil, caraway, chamomile, coriander, fennel, ginseng, horehound, horseradish, hyssop, mint, parsley, sage, and tansy.

After I planted my young herb seedlings in the garden, something ate them at night. What might it have been?

If the plants were cut off at the soil surface and left lying on the ground, cutworms were at work. Prevent them from doing damage by inserting a plastic or cardboard collar around the stems when you plant them. If the foliage was eaten and you see silvery streaks nearby, slugs or snails are present. Trap these in shallow saucers of stale beer.

Place a 2-inch wide cardboard collar around herb stems to protect against cutworm damage.

What can one do to get rid of the soft, white, fungus scale on mint? Scraping it off doesn't do much good.

Neither a fungus nor a scale, mealybugs are your culprits. These soft, white, sucking insects resemble tiny balls of cotton. Mealybugs, like most sucking insects, thrive in a dry atmosphere, but too little water cannot "cause" them. Also, if the plants are unhealthy from a waterlogged soil, they may succumb more readily to mealybug injury. Wash, or if possible actually scrub, the plant with insecticidal soap. Individual adults can be killed by swabbing them with rubbing alcohol.

Slug. Chewed foliage and evidence of silvery streaks suggest the presence of slugs and snails.

What other herbs are likely to be bothered by mealybugs?

Mealybugs attack calendula, thyme, valerian, and wormwood as well as mint.

How can I control the caterpillars that appear in the garden in spring?

If experience has shown caterpillars to be a problem in the past, spray in advance of an infestation with the biological control *Bacillus thuringiensis*, commonly called Bt.

Mealybug. If you see soft, fuzzy, white spots on the underside of leaves, you may have an infestation of mealybugs.

Are all plants susceptible to caterpillars?

No, those most likely to be bothered are calendula, caraway, dill, horseradish, lavender, and parsley. Plants that are situated near trees may be attacked more than those that are not.

My hyssop plants are covered with small, oval, hard, crusty growths. What are these?

These are scale insects, which suck the plant juices from the stems and eventually weaken and kill the plants. Wash the plant with insecticidal soap.

I sowed herb seeds this spring. The seedlings germinated and started to grow, then suddenly fell over and died. What did I do wrong?

This sounds like damping-off fungus, which can be lethal to seedlings. Use only sterile medium that has not been used before. Do not overwater, and provide good air circulation.

Some of my herbs lost their color and stopped growing, and I removed them from the ground. The roots were dark in color and appeared slimy. What caused this?

The plants had root rot, which can be caused by a number of fungi. Avoid this problem by providing good drainage and by not overwatering your herb garden.

Which herbs are most susceptible to root rot?

Root rot can theoretically occur anytime the ground has poor drainage and is constantly wet. However, the most susceptible herbs are angelica, anise, catnip, chamomile, dill, fennel, ginseng, horseradish, lavender, parsley, rosemary, safflower, sage, thyme, and valerian.

Spots have developed on the foliage of some of my herbs. What should I do?

Leaf spot disease is best treated by removing the spotted leaves from the plant and the ground. Water plants only in the morning, and, if possible, do not let the foliage get wet.

On what herbs might leaf spot disease occur?

Leaf spot disease attacks a number of herbs, including angelica, anise, bee balm, borage, burnet, catnip, cumin, dill, ginseng, horehound, horseradish, lavender, lemon balm, lemon grass, mint, parsley, pennyroyal, sesame, and tansy.

What is the white powder that develops on foliage in early fall?

Powdery mildew is a fungus disease that is most prevalent when days are warm and nights are cool. Cut off infected plant parts and water only in the morning. If possible, do not water from overhead. Improve air circulation by not crowding plants.

HERB PLANT DISEASES

•

Which herbs are most likely to be affected by mildew?

Mildew is not a serious problem for herbs, but may be seen on burnet, horseradish, mint, pennyroyal, safflower, sage, tansy, and wormwood.

Leaves of my mint plants have developed an orange powder on the undersides. What is this?

This is rust, a fungus disease. Remove and destroy all infected leaves, and water only in the morning.

I never had rust in my Pennsylvania garden, but I have moved to Oregon where it often occurs. What might be the problem?

Rust is a particular problem in the Pacific Northwest because it occurs most frequently when the weather is cool and damp.

Is rust a problem only on mint?

Rust is more serious on mint than on other herbs, but it also affects angelica, anise, bee balm, burnet, chives, ginseng, sage, tansy, and valerian.

There is a grayish brown powder on the flowers and flower buds of my scented geraniums. How can I get rid of this?

Botrytis blight usually occurs when it is cool or cloudy. Cut off infected plant parts. Do not overwater. It is primarily a problem of scented geraniums but may also affect catnip, lemon balm, and thyme.

After reaching full growth and flowering size, my caraway dried up and died. What was the cause?

It may have been aster yellows, a virus disease transmitted from diseased to healthy plants by leafhoppers. When the plant loses its chlorophyll, the leaves turn yellow and the blossoms turn green. Plants are usually stunted and will eventually die.

About a third of my scented geranium cuttings have shrivelled at the ground, turned black, and died. What is the cause?

Either a fungal or a bacterial stem rot. Take cuttings from healthy plants and place them in clean, fresh sand or a mixture of peat moss and perlite that has not been used before. Keep them on the dry side, as the disease is most prevalent when the medium is overwatered. Drainage must be excellent.

My scented geraniums have leaves with small, water-soaked blisters. What should I do about this?

They suffer from oedema, a common problem of all geraniums. Once infected, the plant can't be cured, but good cultural practices such as providing excellent drainage and taking care not to overwater will prevent this disease.

Will other herbs be affected by aster yellows?

Yes, chamomile, dill, parsley, and sage are also prone to aster yellows.

How can I prevent aster yellows?

Only by getting rid of the insects, often leafhoppers, that transmit the disease. Remove affected plants immediately, so there will be no source of infection. Spray frequently with pyrethrum to kill the leafhoppers.

Last year the leaves of my safflower plants developed small holes in them and the plant became weakened. Is this an insect problem? I saw no signs of insects.

It could be an insect, but it is likely that it is spot anthracnose, a fungus disease. As small areas of leaf tissue die, they lose their color and fall out of the leaf, leaving small spots behind. Remove infected leaves and don't let the plants become overcrowded.

20 *Enjoying the Herb Garden*

Both fresh and dried herbs are perfect no-salt seasonings for all kinds of dishes, from appetizers right through desserts, as well as for butters, vinegars, jellies, and teas. Whether you choose classic combinations, such as a sauce seasoned with *fines herbes*, or enjoy a non-traditional experiment featuring fennel and fish, or tomatoes and tarragon, herbs will enliven your cooking and give pleasure to those you cook for. Equally satisfying are the non-culinary uses of herbs, particularly for dried flower arrangements and scented soaps and potpourri. A few simple principles followed at harvest will ensure maximum success.

HARVESTING AND STORING HERB LEAVES AND SEEDS

When can I harvest leaves for fresh use?

The leaves of most culinary herbs have enough flavor throughout the season that you can harvest them at any time. Pick healthy, green leaves as you need them, being careful not to injure the stem when you remove the leaves. If plants are small, do not remove too many leaves from one stem.

My plants have become a good size by midsummer. Can I cut them back and use the leaves?

Yes, and not only will you enjoy the harvest but you will encourage the plant to become bushier. You can either cut them back with hedge shears or pinch out the growing tips.

◀ *Artemisia, lavender, tansy, and a variety of other herbs and flowers decorate this handsome wreath.*

What do I need to do to leaves before using them fresh?

Nothing, except to wash and dry them quickly by blotting them with a paper towel.

When should I cut leaves for drying?

Most herbs are at the height of their flavor when the flowers are just starting to bloom.

Are there exceptions to this rule?

A few. Read the individual descriptions in Chapt. 21 to be sure. Lavender contains the most fragrant oil just before the flowers open, and sage, too, should be picked as soon as flower buds appear. Hyssop is best when its flowers are in full bloom. Thyme and sage, on the other hand, are flavorful throughout the season.

Does it matter what time of day I cut herbs?

Yes, cut them on a dry, sunny morning after the dew has dried, but before the sun is hot.

How far back should I cut the stems to harvest leaves for drying?

That depends on the time of year and whether the plants are annuals or perennials. Established perennial plants such as oregano, thyme, mint, and sage can usually be harvested two or three times during the summer if you cut just one-third of their height. The last harvest should be light and completed in early fall. Annual herbs may be cut to the ground in the fall.

What is the best way to dry herb leaves?

There are two basic methods of drying herbs: drying them on screens, or hanging them upside down (see questions following). Check the individual plant entries in Chapt. 21 to see which method is best for the herb you are growing. Both methods require a dry spot with good air circulation so that the air will absorb the moisture without destroying the flavorful oils. Herb leaves should also be dried in the dark, or at least out of direct sunlight.

I'd like to hang my herbs to dry them. Could you describe the proper procedure?

Cut the stems as long as possible and pick off any yellow, damaged, or dead foliage. Wash the herbs in cool water, and blot them dry with a paper towel. Tie the ends together in small bunches of about a dozen stems and hang the herbs upside down from the ceiling, rafters, or from an old-fashioned clothes-drying rack. Choose a place out of direct light, with good air circulation. After a week or two, they should be dry and crisp. Remove the leaves carefully and store them in an airtight container.

Cut long stems and tie bundles of about a dozen together to hang upside down in an airy place until dry and crisp.

Fifteen Popular Herbs and Their Usage

HERB	INTERPLANT IDEAS	CULINARY SUGGESTIONS	GIFTS
Angelica		Natural sweetener for tart fruits; candied stems	Fancy pastries decorated with candied stems
Basil	Companion to tomatoes; dislikes rue	Tomatoes and tomato dishes, minestrone soup, pesto sauce for pasta, eggs, fish, lamb, zucchini casseroles	Pesto sauce in decorative jars, purple basil vinegar, container-grown basil, dried herb
Catnip	Deters flea beetles		Handmade catnip toys, fresh cuttings, tea leaves
Chives	Companion to carrots	Omelettes, cold soups, green salads, cheese, fish, dips, vegetable dishes	Fresh cream cheese and chive spread, container-grown chives
Dill	Companion to *Brassicas*; dislikes carrots	Leaves: cucumbers, salads, fish (especially salmon), potatoes, vegetables, sour cream and yogurt, egg dishes. Seeds: pickles, salad dressings, meats, breads	Jars of homemade dill pickles, dill vinegar, fresh dill weed
Fennel	Plant alone	Salmon and oily fish, salad dressings, breads and rolls, apple pie	Freshly baked seeded rolls and breads, fennel-flavored oil
Marjoram	Throughout garden	Poultry seasoning, meats and game, sauces and marinades, soups, egg dishes	Bouquet garni, sachets, tea, herb butter
Mint	Companion to cabbage and tomatoes	Summertime beverages, cold soups (especially fruit soups), fruits, minted peas, salads, lamb, teas, candies	Mint jelly, mint tea, candies, sachets, root divisions
Oregano	Throughout garden	Pizza, pasta, Mexican and Italian dishes, tomatoes and tomato dishes, soups, eggs, ground beef, vegetable casseroles	Dried Italian seasoning mix, container-grown plant, flavored oil
Parsley	Tomatoes	Soups, stews, salads, all vegetables, fish, steaks, garnish	Bouquet garni, tea, fresh sprigs, container-grown plant
Rosemary	Sage, beans, broccoli, cabbage, carrots	Meats (especially lamb and pork), poultry, game, marinades and sauces, carrots, breads	Meat marinade mix, sachet, tea, hair rinse, container-grown plant
Sage	Rosemary, carrots, cabbage; dislikes cucumber	Poultry stuffing, pork, cheeses, breads	Sage cheese, stuffing mix, tea, hair rinse
Savory	Beans, onions	All bean dishes, stuffings, fish, soups, vegetable dishes and juices	Bouquet garni, tea, container-grown herb, sachets
Tarragon	Throughout garden	Sauce béarnaise, fish, chicken, eggs, cold summer salads, salad dressings, vinegar, soups, vegetable juices	Flavored vinegar, tarragon jelly, fines herbes mix
Thyme	Cabbage	Meat, chicken, fish, soups and stocks, stews, vegetables, sauces, salads, clam chowder, poultry stuffing	Bouquet garni, tea, sachets, cuttings

Herbs may be dried and stored in a cool, dark place, waiting for use in the kitchen or in potpourris or winter decorations.

I have heard that herbs being dried should have a paper bag placed over them. Why is this necessary (other than to collect seed)?

The paper bag is not necessary, but it does have advantages. Herbs retain more flavor when dried in the dark, and the bag will also keep dust off the leaves and catch any leaves that drop.

Which herbs should be dried upside down?

This method will work well with most herbs, providing the stems are long enough. Marjoram, mint, rosemary, sage, savory, and thyme are often dried this way. If the stems are short or you are drying individual leaves, drying on a screen is the only practical method.

How are herb leaves dried on a screen?

There are commercially made driers, or you can make your own from old window screening. The screen must be elevated by wood, bricks, books, or something of the sort, so air will circulate under the screen as well as over it. Wash the leaves, blot them dry with a paper towel, and carefully remove them from the stems. Place them on the screen to dry, and turn the leaves once or twice to make sure they dry evenly.

Can I dry herbs in the microwave?

Yes. Put a single layer of herbs between two paper towels and dry for two minutes. If they are not yet dry, continue to microwave them for thirty-second intervals until they are brittle. For future reference, keep records of how long each variety of herb takes. Time varies with the type of herb and the microwave.

Can all herb leaves be air dried?

No, a few lose their color or flavor when air dried. The flavors of chervil and chives are best preserved by freezing. Fennel and burnet have no flavor when dried, and thus must be frozen. Parsley and dill can be stored for a short time wrapped in a moist paper towel and placed in the refrigerator.

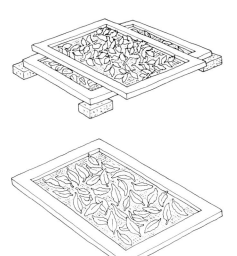

Place herb leaves on old window screens, elevated to ensure good air circulation.

Which herbs freeze best, and what is the procedure?

Basil, burnet, chervil, chives, dill, fennel, parsley, and tarragon can be frozen. Burnet, chervil, fennel, parsley, and tarragon benefit from being blanched in boiling water for one minute and then cooled in ice water before being wrapped and frozen. Others need only be washed. Remove the leaves from the stems, wrap them in aluminum foil or place them in plastic bags, and put them in the freezer. It is more convenient if you package them in amounts you are likely to use at one time.

I have a friend who stores herbs in the freezer in ice cube trays. How is this done?

Place 2 cups of the herb in a blender with 1 cup of water and blend well. Pour the mixture into ice cube trays and freeze. The cubes can be removed from the trays and stored in the freezer in plastic bags for quick and fresh seasoning for soups and stews.

I love pesto but have eaten it only when fresh basil is abundant. Can it be frozen?

Pesto freezes very well. A very special seasoning for pasta, soup, or potatoes, pesto must be made from fresh basil. A typical recipe is 1 ½ cups fresh, crushed basil combined thoroughly with ¾ cup grated parmesan cheese, 2 crushed cloves of garlic, and ¾ cup of olive oil. Many pesto recipes also call for ½ cup of pine nuts, pecans, walnuts, almonds, or cashews.

When should herb seeds be harvested?

The seeds are usually mature enough for harvest several weeks after the plants have flowered. Check them frequently to be sure you get them before they fall to the ground. Often their color changes to tan or gray. Choose a dry day, and cut the stem as long as possible.

How are seeds cured and dried?

In a dry spot with good air circulation, hang or place the stems upside down in a paper bag. As the seeds mature and fall from the plant, they will fall into the bag. Be sure the seeds are dry before you store them. To complete their drying, if necessary, spread them out on a fine screen or piece of cheesecloth.

What is the best method of storing dried herb leaves and seeds?

Leaves and seeds must be stored away from light and heat, in airtight containers so they do not absorb moisture. Placing them in clear glass jars on a spice rack over the stove is the worst thing you can do to them. Herbs can be stored for a week or so in the refrigerator if you wish.

Should leaves be stored whole, or can I chop them up first?

Leaves will retain more flavor if they are stored whole and broken up or ground when needed.

A few weeks after I stored my herbs, I noticed condensation on the inside of the container. Could this have been avoided?

The herbs were not dry enough when you bottled them. Take them out of the container and dry them again for another day or two or they will deteriorate.

How long will dried herbs keep?

That depends on the herb and how it is stored. If it has no scent, crush some of the leaves together, and if it still has no scent, it will have no flavor and should be discarded.

DRYING HERB FLOWERS

•

I would like herb flowers for dried flower arrangements and potpourris. When should I cut flowers for drying?

Most flowers dry best if they are cut when they are about one-third open. Check the listings in Chapt. 21 for specific advice about individual flowers. Do not cut flowers that are wet from rain or dew.

How are flowers best dried?

Dry them by hanging them upside down or placing them on screens, in the same manner you would dry herb leaves. Some flowers, particularly calendula, can be dried with a desiccant, such as silica gel.

How can I dry flowers with silica gel?

Place 2 inches of silica gel (sold at craft shops) in a cookie or cake tin or other sealable, airtight container. Lay the flowers on the silica gel, sideways or face up, depending on their shape. Sprinkle more silica gel over the flowers until they are completely covered. Cover tightly and dry for two days to a week. When the flowers are dry, gently pour off the silica gel and lift the flowers out, blowing or brushing away any particles that stick to the petals.

Are there desiccants other than silica gel?

Yes, you can use sand or borax, but the container should not be sealed and the process will take longer.

Which herb flowers may be dried?

The herbs most commonly grown for dried flowers are calendula, chamomile, chives, clary, horehound, hyssop, lavender, lavender cotton, safflower, tansy, and yarrow.

Lay flowers on silica gel, pour more silica gel over them until they are covered, then cover the container tightly.

COOKING WITH HERBS
•

When recipes call for dried herbs, how much fresh herb should I use?

Because dried herbs have lost their moisture, their essential oils are more concentrated than in a comparable amount of fresh herbs. Therefore, if you wish to use fresh herbs in a recipe that calls for dry herbs, double or triple the amount listed.

At what point in the preparation should herbs be added?

Herbs release their oil quickly when they are heated. If you are cooking a dish, such as a stew, that takes several hours, add the herbs during the last half hour. When preparing foods that cook quickly, put the herbs in at the beginning, or sprinkle them on top of the dish when it is completed.

I often see the expression *"fines herbes"* in cookbooks. What does this mean?

A traditional French herb mixture, *fines herbes*—chives, chervil, parsley, and tarragon (and sometimes other herbs)—are used to season sauces, soups, and cheese and egg dishes. Gourmet cooks believe the flavor of these herbs is enhanced in combination, more than if any of them were used alone.

Can you give me a recipe for herb butter?

Mix ¼ cup of minced fresh herb or 2 tablespoons of the dried herb of your choice with one ¼-pound stick (½ cup) of softened butter. Combine well, using a blender or electric mixer if you wish. Let the mixture stand at room temperature for a few hours, then refrigerate it overnight.

Is there any way to "hurry up" herb butter for a last-minute dinner?

Soaking dried herbs in hot water for a few minutes before mixing them with the butter will release their oils, and therefore flavor the butter more quickly.

Can I use herbs in cold spreads other than butter?

Yes, use herbs to pick up the taste of margarine, cream cheese, sour cream, cottage cheese, or mayonnaise.

I grew bee balm, calendula, chamomile, hyssop, lemon balm, and sage so I could make teas. What is the best way to proceed?

Teas can be made from fresh or dried herbs. You can use one herb or a mixture of several different flavors—experiment to find a taste you like! Preheat a teapot, place a teaspoon of dried herbs or a tablespoon of fresh herbs, into it, and add boiling water. Steep for about ten minutes, strain, and serve.

I made some herbal tea, but the flavor wasn't strong enough. Should I steep it longer?

It would be better to add more herbs—steeping it longer will probably result in a bitter taste.

I didn't steep my herbal tea too long, but it still was bitter. What was wrong?

Did you use a metal tea pot? Metal pots, even those made from stainless steel, will make the tea bitter. Always use china or glass containers for tea making.

Herbal vinegars and teas and home-made jellies are only a few of the culinary uses of herbs.

What are the best herbs to use to flavor cold drinks?

Use the same herbs in the same proportion as for hot teas. Since it takes longer to get flavor out of an herb in cold liquid, prepare the cold drink twelve to twenty-four hours in advance, or to speed things up, steep the tea in boiling water and then chill it in the refrigerator, or faster still, the freezer.

I usually make apple jelly every fall. Is there any herb I could combine with it to make it special?

Make the jelly the way you normally do, but place two or three leaves of basil, lemon balm, mint, rose geranium, rosemary, sage, or thyme in the jars before you pour the jelly into them.

What is herbal vinegar, and how can I make it?

Herbal vinegar can be made with white, cider, or wine vinegar, flavored with the herb of your choice. Use white vinegar if you want to show off the color of herbs, such as chive blossoms or purple basil. Mix 1 tablespoon of dried herbs or ½ cup of fresh herbs with 2 cups of vinegar. Allow this mixture to stand in a covered glass jar in a warm, dimly lit place for four to six weeks. Strain out the herbs, and store the vinegar in a labelled glass jar or bottle.

What herbs can be used to make vinegar?

You can use one or a combination of the following herbs: basil, burnet, caraway, chive flowers, dill, fennel, garlic, lavender, lovage, marjoram, mint, oregano, parsley, rosemary, sage, savory, scented geraniums, tarragon, and thyme.

How is herbal vinegar used?

Use herbal vinegar in any recipe calling for vinegar: sauce, marinade, salad dressing, stew, or vegetable.

I understand borage flowers can be candied and used as decorations on cakes. How is this done?

There are several ways to candy flowers. One of the easiest is to brush beaten egg white on the flowers, and then lay them on wax paper and sprinkle them with powdered sugar. Dry in a sunny window (it will take two to three days), or in a 200° F. oven for half an hour. Flowers can also be candied by dipping them in a sugar solution, and then sprinkling them with granulated sugar.

Candy borage flowers by brushing them with beaten egg white and sprinkling them with powdered sugar.

Is it possible to make homemade candied angelica for Christmas baking?

Yes, it's quite simple if you use a candy thermometer. Cut the stems into small pieces, and simmer them in a solution of 2 cups of sugar in 2 cups of water for twenty minutes. Drain the pieces, saving the sugar solution, and put them in the refrigerator, covered, for several days. Put the angelica back into the sugar syrup and heat it again for twenty minutes at 238° F., using a candy thermometer to check the temperature. Drain and dry. Store in airtight containers. Licorice-flavored candied angelica is an old-fashioned Christmas treat.

Herb-scented soap is delightful. Can you describe how to make some with homegrown herbs?

The easiest way is to make a semi-liquid gel by first grating any pure, mild, unscented soap. Next, boil 1½ cups of the desired herb, such as ground chamomile or lavender flowers, or the whole leaves of lemon grass or mint, in 6 cups of water for ½ hour. Cool and strain. To 3 cups of the scented water, add 2 cups of the grated soap and ½ cup of borax. Boil for 3 minutes and cool.

SCENTED CRAFTS FROM THE HERB GARDEN

•

To make a hard soap, grate a bar of unscented, pure soap. Add to it ¼ to ½ cup of water in which you have steeped 2 tablespoons of your favorite herbs. Mix well until it takes on the texture of molasses. Place it into molds or roll it into a ball with your wet fingers. Allow it to dry for several days. If you formed it into balls, turn them often so that they stay evenly round.

To make the soap smoother, you can heat the mixture in a double boiler over water.

What is potpourri?

Literally, potpourri means "rotten pot." Such an unpromising name, however, is actually a lovely mixture of dried flowers, leaves, essential oils, and spices, combined with a fixative, that retains its fragrance for many years.

What are essential oils?

These are the result of a distillation process that extracts an oil containing the distinctive aroma—the essence—of the plant. The distillation process is complex, so these oils are usually purchased from stores or mail-order companies that offer potpourri supplies (see Appendix). There are also essential animal oils such as ambergris, civet, and musk, used in making perfumes, but these are no longer available to the public, except in synthetic form.

What is a fixative?

A fixative aids in both preserving the leaves and petals, and retaining their natural scent. Angelica root, benzoin and gum storax, calamus root, orrisroot, and sandalwood are common fixatives. Orrisroot also seems to have a color-fixing effect, but you should be aware that some people are allergic to it. Fixatives, too, may be purchased where potpourri and dried flower supplies are sold.

What leaves and petals can be used for making potpourri?

The nicest thing about potpourri is that you can invent your own recipe by using any leaves or petals that have a pleasing fragrance. Some of the best, traditionally used ingredients are from the shrubs rose and jasmine; the annual and perennial flowers heliotrope, marigold, mignonette, stock, and wallflower; and the herbs geranium, lavender, lemon balm, lemon verbena, mint, rosemary, santolina, southernwood, thyme, and violet.

I want to make a potpourri of rose petals and herbs from my garden. How can I do this?

Pick fragrant rose petals (red holds its color best) when the flowers are in full bloom but not completely blown. Spread them carefully on sheets of paper, a screen, or strips of cheesecloth in a dry, airy room, away from the sun. Turn them daily. Let them dry completely—they should be crisp. This will take from a few days to a week, depending on the heat and the humidity. To each quart of petals, add 1 ounce of orrisroot as a fixative. Such herbs as lavender, lemon verbena, peppermint, rosemary, and thyme make wonderful additions to a rose potpourri, and you may also add, if you wish, one-half teaspoon each of such spices as cloves, cinnamon, coriander, and mace, along with a few drops of essential oil. Keep in an airtight earthen jar.

What is "wet potpourri," and how is it made?

Like the dry potpourri described in the previous question, wet potpourri contains rose petals, as well as petals of any other fragrant flowers that are available. First, partially dry the petals on fabric or paper, then pack them in layers in an earthenware jar, with a sprinkling of table salt or coarse salt over each layer, until the jar is filled. Add 1 ounce of orrisroot, an essential oil, and, if desired, some cloves, allspice, and cinnamon. Put a weight (such as a stone) on the petals and let them stand in the jar, covered, for several weeks before mixing. In addition to rose petals, scented geranium and lemon verbena leaves and lavender flowers and leaves are the most commonly used ingredients. Wet potpourri keeps its scent longer than dry potpourri.

I have heard that it is possible to make a potpourri that will repel moths. What is the recipe?

The basic, moth-repelling components can be lavender, lavender cotton, mint, pennyroyal, southernwood, or tansy. To make the scents pleasant to us, but not to moths, add cloves, lemon verbena, rosemary, or thyme. Use 1 ounce of chipped orrisroot per quart of petals as a fixative, and twice the amount of essential oil that you would add to other potpourris.

What herbs can I use to make holiday wreaths?

Silver King artemisia is the most commonly used base for a wreath, and lavender cotton is also good. Fresh southernwood makes excellent wreaths, which can be allowed to dry after they are fashioned. To the herbal wreath, add dried flowers of any kind for decoration. You can also make living wreaths of rosemary, sage, or thyme by filling a circular wire frame with sphagnum moss and inserting small plants into the moss. Place the live wreaths on a shallow tray in bright sun, and remember to water them regularly. These can be dried after the holiday season, if desired.

What is a tussie mussie?

A tussie mussie, or nosegay, dates back to the seventeenth century, when this tight bouquet of herbs and flowers was first used to deliver a message through the language of flowers. For

The silvery gray leaves of the artemisias are particularly fine in dried arrangements and wreaths.

Traditionally, tussie mussies were used to deliver messages through the symbolic language of flowers.

example, basil meant good wishes; borage, courage; burnet, merriment; rose geranium, preference; marjoram, joy; rosemary, remembrance; sage, good health; thyme, happiness; valerian, pleasure.

Make your own tussie mussie by arranging fresh herbs and flowers in a small bouquet and tying the stems together. Place scented geranium, lavender cotton, or tansy foliage around the flowers—and a paper doily under the flowers. Add colored ribbons for decoration. You may air dry it or dry it in silica gel.

Is there a way to scent our bathwater with herbs?

Scented bathwater is an old, and lovely, custom. Some nice herbs for this use include angelica, mints, rosemary, and thyme. You can simply add the fresh herbs to the bathwater or chop them and place them on a small piece of cheesecloth, which you can then gather into a bundle and tie with a ribbon. When they have "steeped" in the hot water for a few minutes, they will release a gentle, heady aroma for a delightfully relaxing bath.

What herbs are good for sachets?

Use dried mints, thyme, rosemary, sage, dill, lavender, sweet woodruff, or savory. You may wish to experiment with various combinations of these herbs. Let them sit in a closed container for the scents to marry, then grind them to a powder before filling your sachets.

Do you have any suggestions for how to cover sachets?

The coverings for sachets can be as simple as a pretty piece of calico sewn pillowcase fashion and gathered at the neck with a pretty ribbon. If you enjoy handcrafts, knit, crochet, or hand-weave your own fabric or use old table or bed linens, quilts, or old laces. If the fabric you choose has a loose weave or knit, make a muslin inner bag to hold the herbs so that they can't leak out.

How can I fix catnip for my cat to enjoy?

Follow the instructions on pg. 490 for harvesting and drying catnip. You can stuff the dried catnip into something as simple as a small fabric pillow, tightly machine-stitched closed, or use a purchased pattern for a small stuffed toy—mouse-shaped, if you wish.

What are lavender bottles, and how are they made?

An old English invention, lavender bottles are formed by bending fresh, blooming lavender stems back upon themselves, weaving the stems with ribbon to shape the "bottle," and then allowing it to dry. Lavender bottles may then be placed in drawers or hung in closets as moth repellents. To shape bottle, be sure to use only freshly picked lavender so that stems don't

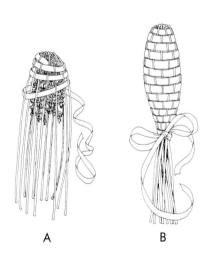

A   B

To make a lavender bottle (A) tie a thread around a bundle of stems just below the flower heads and gently bend stems down over the flowers; (B) weave ribbon through stems until flower heads are covered and fasten at the bottom with a bow.

break. Gather about fifteen stems and tie them tightly together with string just below the flowerheads. Holding the bundle with the flowerheads down, carefully bend each stem back down over the flowers. When all stems are down, weave 1/4-inch wide, velvet or satin ribbon between the stems until you have covered all of the flowers, tightening and smoothing the ribbon as you weave. You will need about 3 yards of ribbon. Tie a string around the stems at the base of the weaving and hang the bottle in an airy place until the lavender has dried thoroughly. You may need to tighten and smooth the ribbon, as the stems will shrink somewhat when they are dry. Wrap ribbon around the stems to hide the string. Decorate with bows.

21 *Favorite Herbs to Grow*

E ach herb has its own legend and lore, as well as specific characteristics and cultural needs. In this chapter, you will find descriptions, background information, and complete growing instructions for about sixty favorite herbs to enjoy in your garden. For further advice about the hardiness, height, uses, propagation, and light and soil needs of herbs, see the chart on pages 562-63. Hardiness zones (see p. 434) are given for most herbs, and a zone map is included on page 564 for your reference.

Angelica *(Angelica Archangelica)*

Angelica sounds "heavenly." How did it get its name?

Angelica has been called "the herb of angels" because it was said to have been a gift from the angels to protect mankind from the plague.

What is angelica, and how is it used?

Angelica is a biennial that grows 5 feet tall and has large, aromatic, 2- to 3-foot, three-part leaves. It looks and smells a bit like celery. The leaves are used fresh or dry as seasonings, especially in drinks. The stems and leafstalks may be served in salads or as a vegetable, or they may be candied to decorate confections (see pg. 497). The seeds are used for flavoring and for oil, and the roots are sometimes dried and ground for use in baking.

◀ *The bright red blossoms of bee balm attract bees and hummingbirds to the garden.*

Angelica: The large leaves of this herb may be used fresh or dried to flavor beverages.

Can I grow angelica in my southern Vermont garden?

Yes, you live on the northern boundary of angelica's hardiness range, which is Zone 4. Angelica is fairly resistant to heat and will grow anywhere through Zone 10. It should be given winter protection at the edge of its hardiness zone.

I planted angelica for the first time last year, and it did not flower. Did I do something wrong?

No, but because angelica is a biennial, it will not form the large, flat or round clusters of greenish white flowers until early in its second summer.

How should I grow angelica?

Angelica prefers full sun or light shade, and fertile, moist, cool, well-drained soil, rich in organic matter. Feed plants with all-purpose plant food in early spring when growth starts. Mulch around the plants in mid- to late spring to keep the soil moist and cool. When plants are 1 foot high, pinch them back to keep them bushy (see pg. 459). Where winters are windy, stake or protect the tops of the plants to avoid damage.

Can I propagate angelica from seeds?

Yes, you can. Sow seeds indoors in early spring after storing them in moist sphagnum peat moss in the refrigerator for six to eight weeks. Germination will take twenty-one to twenty-five days. Move plants outdoors in mid-spring after the soil has warmed up, setting them 3 feet apart. You can also plant angelica seeds outdoors in fall, at a depth of ¼ to ½ inch, for germination the following spring. If you do not harvest angelica, the seeds will drop and readily self-sow. Angelica can also be propagated by root division in early spring.

This spring I tried to sow some angelica seeds that a friend gave me two years ago, but they did not germinate. What went wrong?

Angelica seeds are very short-lived and must be sown as soon as possible after they are harvested. The seeds you used were too old to germinate.

How should I harvest angelica?

Being careful not to damage the stem, pick the leaves in the fall of the first year or in the spring of the second year before the plant flowers. The leaves can be used fresh, or they can be dried in a cool, dark, dry, well-ventilated place. To harvest seeds and roots, you will have to forsake harvesting leaves and stems. Cut off the flower heads as the seeds start to turn light beige, and hang the flower clusters upside down in a paper bag in a dark, cool, dry area. Roots can be dug as soon as the seed heads are removed.

Anise *(Pimpinella Anisum)*

I have heard that anise has an ancient history. Is this true?

Yes, it was one of the herbs used for payment of taxes by the Romans, who brought it from Egypt to Europe. Anise, with its licoricelike flavor, soon became popular for use in bread, cookies, cake, and candy. Now, both leaves and seeds are used not only in baking but also as a flavoring in soups, salads, and Italian sausage. If anise is chewed after a meal, it is said to aid digestion and to sweeten one's breath.

What does anise look like?

With small, lacy leaves and flat clusters of yellowish white flowers, anise is a dainty, spreading plant that grows 18 to 24 inches high and blooms in early summer.

When can I plant anise into the garden?

Anise is a hardy annual that can be moved into the garden in early to mid-spring, as soon as the soil can be worked. Plants should be spaced 6 to 9 inches apart.

I would like to try propagating my own anise plants instead of buying them this year. Is that possible?

Anise is easily propagated from seeds. You can either start them indoors in late winter or sow them outside, ⅛ inch deep, as soon as the soil can be worked in spring. They will germinate in twenty to twenty-eight days. Anise does not like to be transplanted, so if you start seeds indoors, sow them into individual peat pots that can be planted directly into the ground without disturbing the roots. Seeds are short-lived and should not be saved from one year to another.

What care should I give to anise in the garden?

Anise should be grown in full sun in a dry, light, sandy soil. This herb should not be overwatered, so water only when the ground starts to become dry. Incorporate fertilizer into the soil before planting, and no other seeding will be necessary. Because stems are weak and may become leggy, stake them or mound soil around the base of the plants to give support.

How should I harvest anise?

Anise leaves can be picked from the plant at any time and used fresh or dried. To dry them, lay them on a screen in a dark, dry, cool, well-ventilated area. Harvest seeds after they mature, which is two to three weeks after flowering has ceased, when they are grayish brown. Cut off the flowering stem, tie stems in bunches, and hang them in a cool, dark place inside a paper bag. Be sure seeds are dry before storing them in an airtight container.

Anise: The licoricelike flavor of anise is popular in breads, cookies, cakes, and candies.

Maggie Oster

Ann Reilly

Anise hyssop: The leaves of anise hyssop make a nice addition to potpourri.

Anise hyssop *(Agastache Foeniculum)*

Is anise hyssop a cross between anise and hyssop?

No, it isn't, and it does not look like either plant, although its flavor is similar to anise and it is in the same botanical family as hyssop. It is a perennial, hardy to Zone 3, and grows 3 to 4 feet tall. Stems are square; leaves are oval, pointed, and sharply toothed; and flowers, which bloom in summer, are purplish blue.

How has anise hyssop been used?

The Plains Indians used anise hyssop leaves as a tea, sweetener, and medicine; the roots were used for coughs and colds, although it is no longer considered safe for culinary use. The leaves make a nice addition to potpourri.

Is anise hyssop easy to grow?

Yes, it is very easy to grow. In fact, it can become somewhat weedy because its roots spread quickly, and it self-sows easily. Grow it in full sun or light shade in sandy, well-drained soil. If the soil is rich in organic matter, growth will be even more rampant. It needs little fertilizer, but if you must apply some, do so in early spring.

How is anise hyssop propagated?

Anise hyssop can be grown from seeds sown at a depth of ½ inch either indoors or in the garden. Seeds germinate in seven to ten days. Propagation may also be accomplished in spring or fall by division, or by cuttings taken and rooted in summer. Space plants 18 inches apart.

How is anise hyssop dried?

Cut individual leaves or entire stems before the flowers appear. Dry them on a screen, or hang the stems upside down in a cool, dark, dry area.

Artemisia *(Artemisia* species)

How should I treat artemisia in the garden?

Grow it in full sun in well-drained soil. Although it does best in a good garden soil, it will tolerate soil with little organic matter, and either wet or dry soil conditions. Fertilize with bonemeal each year when growth starts.

Can the artemisias be grown from seeds?

They can, but the seeds are very fine and should therefore be sown indoors, not outdoors. They need light to germinate, so should not be covered. Germination will occur in seven to ten days. Move the plants into the garden four weeks before the last spring frost, and set them 18 inches apart.

What other method of propagation can I use besides seeding?

Divide artemisia plants in spring or fall, or take stem cuttings during summer.

I have seen reference to Silver King and Silver Queen artemisias in catalogues. Could you describe them please?

These are cultivars of *A. ludoviciana*, which is sometimes called Western sage. Plants are perennial and grow 2 to 3 feet high. The aromatic leaves of Silver King are narrow and silvery, while those of Silver Queen are wider, grayer, and downier. They are both very drought resistant.

How are these artemisias used?

Besides being very attractive mounded garden plants, these artemisias are used for wreaths and other handicrafts. Both the foliage and the yellow flowers, which are cut for drying just as the flowers start to open, will last for many years.

Silver King artemisia: This popular artemisia is excellent when dried for use in wreaths and arrangements.

Is Sweet Annie another cultivar of that species?

No, Sweet Annie is a tender annual artemisia, *A. annua*. It grows 6 feet or more high and has highly fragrant, green foliage that turns red in the fall. It is also used in wreaths, dried arrangements, and sachets.

What does wormwood look like?

A perennial hardy through Zone 2, wormwood (*A. Absinthium*) grows 3 feet tall and has gray, hairy, deeply divided leaves and inconspicuous yellow flowers in late summer.

Is wormwood the same plant that was used to flavor absinthe?

Yes, it is, but because of its harmful effect on the nervous system, this drink is illegal throughout the world. While wormwood should not be ingested, its dried leaves are one of the most effective moth repellents for stored clothing.

Wormwood: The dried leaves of wormwood make a very effective moth repellent.

Is southernwood related to wormwood?

Yes, southernwood (*A. abrotanum*) is a closely related species, with the same cultural requirements. However, whereas wormwood is a gray, sprawling plant, southernwood is bushy, green, and lush. Wormwood spreads rapidly underground, while southernwood does not. Southernwood is available in a variety of lovely fragrances—lemon, tangerine, and camphor.

How should I harvest wormwood?

Cut the stems in late summer, leaving a few inches of stem for winter protection. Remove the woody portion of the stem and dry only the green, upper portion by hanging the stems upside down in a dry, cool, well-ventilated spot.

Basil *(Ocimum Basilicum)*

I have always liked the taste of fresh basil in pesto and other Italian dishes, as well as in a variety of sauces and soups, but is it attractive enough to use in the garden as an ornamental?

Yes, both green- and purple-leaved varieties are lovely in the flower garden, and they bloom all summer until frost, with white to purplish flower spikes on 18- to 24-inch stems. The purple-leaved variety blends well with yellow-flowered annuals. A variety called Spicy Globe forms perfectly round, neat, 12-inch mounds of tiny foliage and flowers late in the season, if at all, making it an excellent border plant in both herb and ornamental gardens.

Basil: Spicy Globe basil makes an excellent border plant, with its round, neat, 12-inch mounds of tiny foliage.

Ann Reilly

How can I propagate my own basil plants?

Basil is a tender annual, propagated from seeds. It can be started indoors in spring, six to eight weeks before the last frost. The seeds will germinate in seven to ten days. Transplant the young plants outdoors after all danger of frost has passed. Seeds can also be sown outdoors, ¼ to ½ inch deep, after the danger of frost is over. Space plants 10 to 12 inches apart in the garden.

Is basil easy to care for in the garden?

Relatively easy. Grow it in full sun in a light-textured, well-drained soil, with a moderate amount of organic matter. Water it when the soil starts to dry out, and keep it evenly moist but not overly wet. To avoid leaf spotting, apply water to the ground and do not wet the leaves. If fertilizer is mixed into the soil before planting, no other feeding will be necessary. When plants are 4 to 6 inches tall, pinch them to encourage bushiness (see pg. 459). Basil likes warm soil, so apply a mulch in early summer.

I grew basil last year, but the plants were killed by an early frost before I got a chance to harvest the leaves. Is there anything I might have done to save them—other than harvesting early?

Yes. Basil is one of the first plants in the garden to be affected by frost. If an unexpected early frost is predicted, cover the plants at night with a clear plastic container or hot cap (see page 44). Plants can be treated in the same way if a late frost threatens to damage the plants in spring.

I picked my basil after the plants had started to flower and they didn't seem to have much flavor. Was it the variety?

Leaves harvested after the plants flower are not as flavorful. If you pinch out the flowers as soon as they appear, you will extend your period of harvest, allowing you to pick leaves throughout the summer. Be careful when you pick basil leaves, as they bruise easily, another cause of flavor loss.

What is the best way to dry basil leaves?

If you want to dry basil leaves for use in the winter, place them on a screen in a warm, dry, dark, airy place, freeze them (see pg. 693), or steep them in oil or vinegar.

Can basil be grown indoors?

Yes, it can. It is best to start new plants from seeds for the indoor kitchen garden, and grow them under lights or in a sunny window.

Basil: This standby of Italian dishes thrives in full sun in well-drained, moderately rich soil.

Are there any legends connected with basil?

Even though to many Westerners basil is synonymous with pasta and Italian cooking, some Hindus consider it sacred, believing that it makes the passage to heaven easier.

Bee balm, Bergamot (*Monarda didyma*)

I have heard that there is some association between bee balm and the American Revolution, but I can't recall the details. Can you tell me about this?

When colonists protested the use of the English tea tax by instigating the infamous Boston Tea Party and foreswearing the use of English tea, they satisfied their craving for tea by brewing bee balm leaves. Because this beverage was introduced to them by New York Oswego Indians, it was called Oswego Tea.

I am looking for an herb that will add some color to my garden. Can you suggest one?

Bee balm is an excellent choice, for not only does it have interesting and colorful red, pink, purple, salmon, or white flowers in early summer, but it also attracts bees and humming-birds. This 2- to 4-foot perennial is hardy through Zone 4. Its hairy, somewhat coarse leaves have a minty fragrance.

My garden is lightly shaded. Can I grow bee balm?

Yes, it will grow well in full sun or light shade.

How can I start bee balm plants?

Bee balm can be grown from seeds or from cuttings. Start seeds indoors, as long as you can provide a temperature of no more than 55° F. for germination. Seeds will sprout in fifteen to twenty days. It may be easier to start seeds outdoors, sown ¼ to ½ inch deep, as soon as the soil can be worked in spring. Plants can also be divided in early spring or early fall and replanted 12 inches apart.

I grew bee balm last year, but it soon grew into the lawn and became a nuisance. What can I do?

The roots of bee balm, being related to mint, travel rapidly underground and can be invasive. Install a metal or brick edging to help control its growth. Plants tend to die out in the center, as the strong, young growth travels out from the original plant, so lift plants each year and replant the newer, outside pieces where you want them.

How are bee balm leaves dried?

Leaves can be dried on a screen, but they lose a lot of their flavor when dried and are therefore better used fresh.

Beefsteak plant. See Perilla

Bergamot. See Bee balm

Borage *(Borago officinalis)*

Is borage an annual or a perennial?

Borage is a hardy annual, which readily self-sows. It is easily grown from seed planted outdoors in fall or very early spring. Seeds sown in fall will germinate the following spring; seeds sown in spring will sprout in seven to ten days. Because borage is very difficult to transplant, starting it indoors is not recommended. Outside, sow it where it will grow, in full sun or light shade, ½ inch deep, and thin it to 12 inches between plants. Plants grow 2 to 3 feet tall and bloom all summer.

What are the uses of borage?

Young leaves may be used in salads, but mature leaves are coarse and hairy, and may be toxic if ingested often, in large quantities. The blue or purple, star-shaped flowers are pretty floated in drinks and punch bowls, or candied for use on cake, ice cream, and other desserts (see pg. 497). Both the leaves and the flowers have a cucumber flavor.

What is the history of borage?

Known from Roman times as a symbol of courage, Christian Crusaders were often toasted farewell with a borage-garnished drink.

I have fertile soil, rich in organic matter, but my borage doesn't grow well. What might be wrong?

Borage, like some other herbs, prefers dry, infertile soil, with no added organic matter.

My borage plants look unattractive by midsummer. What can I do?

To keep borage attractive, pinch plants back when they are 6 inches tall to encourage bushiness (see pg. 459). In midsummer, prune them back by one-half. They will produce a new crop of tender leaves that can be harvested in late summer.

Burnet (*Poterium Sanguisorba*)

I find raw cucumbers hard to digest, but I love the flavor of cucumbers. Are there any herbal substitutes?

Yes, the leaves of burnet taste very much like cucumbers, and should cause no digestive problems. They can be picked at any time throughout the season, and are particularly nice in salads and iced drinks. The leaves have no flavor when dry, but keep both their color and flavor when stored in vinegar. They may also be frozen.

What does burnet look like?

Burnet is a pretty plant, with finely cut leaves that are bunched in a 6-inch clump at the base of the plant. Gracefully arching, 18- to 24-inch stems are covered with small, toothed leaves. Dense tufts of white or rose-pink flowers bloom in early summer to midsummer. Burnet is a very hardy perennial, withstanding temperatures as cold as Zone 3. Its leaves stay green and flavorful even when covered with snow.

What growing conditions does burnet need?

Burnet likes full sun, but in hot climates it will need light shade. Soil should be alkaline, infertile, sandy, and well-drained, with no additional organic matter. Keep the ground dry.

I have had problems dividing burnet. Any suggestions?

Burnet has a long tap root and is thus very difficult to divide. If you want to try it, do so either in early to mid-spring or early fall. You will have better success if you propagate by seed. Start seeds indoors any time from early spring through early summer, and move plants into the garden up to six weeks before the first fall frost. Alternatively, sow seeds directly outdoors, any time from mid-spring up to two months before the first fall frost. Plant seeds ¼ to ½ inch deep. They will germinate in eight to ten days. Final spacing for plants should be 15 inches.

Burnet: The leaves of burnet taste very much like cucumber.

Maggie Oster

I like burnet, but it becomes weedy in my garden. What can I do?

Burnet easily reseeds and does in fact become weedy. Remove flowers as they start to fade to prevent seeds from dropping and sprouting.

Calendula, Pot marigold *(Calendula officinalis)*

I know that calendula is often called pot marigold. Is it a form of marigold?

Marigolds are distant relatives of calendula, but although gardeners in Shakespeare's time thought they were the same plant, they are not. Sixteenth-century gardeners grew them in pots, which is how they got their name.

Can I plant calendula in my flower garden?

Absolutely! Their pretty, daisylike flowers of orange, yellow, apricot, off-white, or gold are double, and the petals are crisp. Plants grow 6 to 24 inches high.

How is calendula used?

Calendula flower petals may be used for garnishes in soups and on hors d'oeuvres, in rice as a substitute for saffron, in butter for coloration, and in herbal teas, as well as in potpourri. Petals lose their slightly bitter flavor quickly, but retain their color.

I tried to grow calendula last summer in my Virginia garden, but it did not do well. Can you suggest why not?

This hardy annual likes cool climates but does not tolerate heat. Because Virginia summers are too hot for it, try growing it in the spring or fall. Be sure your soil is fertile, well-drained, and rich in organic matter, and keep it well watered. You should be able to grow it in either full sun or light shade. Fertilize prior to planting and again when flower buds start to form. A mulch applied in early spring will help to keep the soil cool and moist, and thus help prolong the life of calendula.

How should I propagate calendula?

Calendula can be propagated by seed, either indoors or directly in the garden. Germination will take ten to fourteen days. Indoors, start seeds six to eight weeks before you wish to plant them outdoors, whether you are planting in spring or fall. Cover the seeds completely, as they need darkness to germinate. Outdoors, sow seeds ¼ to ½ inch deep, in early spring, as soon as the soil can be worked. In mild areas, sow seeds in late summer for fall and winter bloom. Space plants 12 to 15 inches apart.

Maggie Oster

Calendula: The flower petals of calendula, or pot marigold, may be used as a soup or salad garnish.

Should I remove the petals from the flower heads of calendula before I dry them, or should I dry the flowers whole?

It doesn't matter—either method works equally well. Pick flowers as soon as they are fully open and dry the petals or the entire flower on a screen in a warm, dry, well-ventilated place. Petals may also be used fresh.

Caraway (*Carum Carvi*)

I'm familiar with the thin, crescent-shaped seeds of caraway in breads, rolls, cakes, and cookies, but what are the other uses of caraway?

The finely cut, dark green leaves may be used fresh in salads. The tap root, which looks like a white carrot, is edible and very nutritious. In ancient times, caraway was used as a medicine.

I planted caraway last spring, but the plant never developed flowers or seeds. What happened?

Caraway is a very hardy biennial (Zone 3), which, when sown in the spring, does not flower and set seed until the second summer. If sown and germinated in the fall, it will flower and set seed the following summer.

Does caraway fit well into the flower border or knot garden?

Caraway grows 2 to 2½ feet tall and can be rangy in growth, so it is not an appropriate plant for knot gardens or formal flower gardens. Its flat clusters of white flowers are lovely, however, in informal herb or flower gardens. It blooms in summer.

How is caraway grown?

Sow caraway seeds outdoors, ⅛ inch deep, in early fall to have flowers and seeds by the following summer. Thin the plants so that they are 6 to 9 inches apart. Caraway is very difficult to transplant; thus, sowing seeds indoors is not recommended. You will have greatest success if the soil does not have much organic matter. Also, do not water much, as this tends to keep the stems soft and causes the blossoms to fall before setting seed. Dry, sunny weather favors this crop, as does a light fertilizing prior to planting and again when growth starts in spring.

Can I harvest leaves, seeds, and roots from the same plant?

Yes. Leaves can be harvested at any time but are best when young and tender, and used fresh. After the flowers bloom and the seeds have turned brown, cut off the seed heads and hang them upside down in a plastic bag in a cool, dark, dry place. Then, dig up the plant for its roots. Roots can be harvested earlier in the year, but at the expense of the seed crop.

Ann Reilly

Caraway: A hardy biennial, caraway grows about 2 feet tall, with clusters of flat, white flowers.

My caraway seeds are covered in a fluffy chaff. How can I remove it?

You can either sift seeds through a ¼-inch mesh screen, or drop them, in a thin stream, into a bowl outdoors on a breezy day so that the chaff blows away.

Catmint. See Catnip

Catnip (*Nepeta Cataria*)

I would like to try growing catnip to make toys for my cats, but how can I keep the cats out of the garden while the catnip is growing?

Grow plants from seeds planted directly in the garden so that the fuzzy, gray-green foliage—which contains the oil that attracts the cats—is not bruised during transplanting. Bruising the leaves releases the scent, and once cats find this treat, you won't convince them to keep away from it. They are likely to trample neighboring plants as well as the catnip when they revel and roll in it.

I would like to grow catnip from seeds. What are the best procedures?

Start your seeds indoors any time in early spring through early summer, and transplant them into the garden in spring through late summer, up to six weeks before the first fall frost. Choose a soil that is dry, with little organic matter, in full sun or partial shade, and space plants 18 to 24 inches apart. If it's more convenient, you can also sow seeds directly into the garden during spring or summer, up to two months before the first fall frost. Plant them ¼ inch deep. Germination takes seven to ten days.

Will catnip return year after year?

Yes, catnip is a very hardy perennial (Zone 3) if the stalks are left on the plant and the plant is mulched. It is a very rapid grower and may need dividing every year to keep it within bounds. A metal edging around the plant will also help to contain it. Every year in the spring cut off the old, dead growth to improve its appearance. Fertilize little, if any, so that you don't encourage even heavier growth than normal.

Will catnip bloom more than once a year?

As soon as the first flowers fade, cut the plants back by half to encourage catnip to rebloom. The first blooming of the white to light purple, spiked flowers appears on 2- to 4-foot stems in early summer.

Positive Images, Jerry Howard

Catnip: Cut back plants after they flower to encourage a second period of bloom later in the summer.

When should catnip leaves be picked?

For the heaviest aroma, pick leaves before the flowers bloom. After drying them on a screen in a cool, dry, well-ventilated place, chop the leaves or rub them with your fingers to release more scent.

What is the difference between catnip and catmint?

Catmint *(Nepeta mussini)* is a different species of the same genus and thus closely related to catnip. Catmint has the same cultural requirements as catnip, and it also attracts cats, although it does not make them act as outlandishly.

Chamomile *(Chamaemelum nobile; Matricaria recutita)*

What is the difference between the two chamomiles?

They share many characteristics, although one is an annual and one is a perennial. Roman chamomile *(C. nobile)* is a perennial, hardy through Zone 4. A creeping, 6-inch plant that has lacy, gray-green foliage, it makes a fine ground cover. The tiny, strongly scented, daisylike flowers, which bloom in late summer, have yellow centers and white petals, although the petals are often missing. German chamomile *(M. recutita)* is an annual. The foliage and flowers are similar to Roman chamomile in appearance, but German chamomile grows 2 to 2½ feet tall, and blooms all summer if it is not too hot. Unlike Roman chamomile, the foliage of the annual carries an apple scent and makes a better-tasting tea.

Is there any difference in the uses of the two chamomiles?

The flowers of both chamomiles are used in making teas. The flowers of perennial chamomile are sometimes used as a hair rinse by blondes.

Are the two chamomiles grown in the same way?

Both prefer full sun or light shade and sandy, well-drained soil, with little organic matter. If the soil is too rich, few flowers will form. Once plants are established, both tolerate drought and excessive moisture, and neither likes hot summers. Both self-sow readily if flowers are not removed. The one area of difference is spacing: Perennial chamomile should be spaced 3 to 4 inches apart; annual chamomile, 8 inches apart. Perennial chamomile used as a ground cover can be cut with a lawn mower in early spring to encourage fuller growth.

Are both types of chamomile propagated the same way?

Both chamomiles can be propagated from seed. If sowing is done indoors, a temperature of 55° F. must be maintained. Seeds germinate in seven to ten days. Move plants into the garden

Positive Images, Jerry Howard

Chamomile: Pick flowers when they are in full bloom, but before they start to fade.

when they are young, because the long roots that older plants develop make transplanting difficult. Seeds may also be sown outdoors in spring as soon as the soil can be worked. Sow them ¼ to ½ inch deep. Perennial chamomile can also be propagated from cuttings.

How are the flowers harvested and treated?

Pick the flowers of both chamomiles when they are in full bloom, but before they start to fade. Dry them on a screen placed in the sun. Watch out for insects that hide in the flowers, and if you see any, pour hot water over them and start the drying procedure again.

Chervil (*Anthriscus Cerefolium*)

What is the flavor of chervil?

Chervil has a slight anise, or licorice, flavor. It is rarely used alone, but is an ingredient of *fines herbes*, a French culinary staple. It can be used in place of parsley in soups, stews, sauces, and salads.

Is there any use for chervil's flowers and seeds?

Chervil has flat clusters of white flowers that bloom on 24-inch stems in early summer, but only the finely divided, light green leaves are used as seasonings. Once the flowers bloom, the plants usually die back.

How is chervil grown?

Chervil is a hardy annual that is propagated from seeds, with germination taking seven to fourteen days. Seeds may be started indoors in winter, but because chervil does not like to be transplanted and may bloom prematurely if disturbed too much during transplanting, sow seeds into individual pots. Move plants outside as early in spring as the soil can be worked, setting them 6 to 8 inches apart. Seeds may also be sown outdoors in early spring or early fall, ¼ inch deep.

How should I treat chervil in the garden?

Light to full shade is beneficial. Soil should be sandy, well-drained, and evenly moist, with a lot of organic matter. Chervil grows well only when the night temperature is below 55° F., so it is often grown as a spring or fall plant, or as a winter plant in the south. Mulch the soil to keep it cool. Chervil self-sows readily if the flowers are not removed.

Does chervil need a lot of fertilizer?

If all-purpose fertilizer is incorporated into the soil before planting, no further fertilizing will be needed.

Chervil: The delicate leaves of chervil have a mild licorice flavor.

Is it true that chervil leaves can be frozen?

Yes, chervil leaves can be used fresh or frozen.

Chives (*Allium Schoenoprasum*)

Can chives be grown from seeds or must I buy plants?

They can be grown from seeds, but buying plants is much easier. Outdoors, sow seeds ¼ inch deep early in the spring through midsummer; indoors, sow them from late winter until early summer. Germination will take ten to fourteen days. Move plants outside any time after the soil is workable in spring, and space plants 6 to 8 inches apart. Chives can also be divided in early spring or early fall.

Are chives interchangeable with onions?

This onion relative can be used in any recipe that calls for raw green onions, though the chive flavor is more delicate. They are also well-loved mixed with sour cream, chopped into soups, and used with eggs and fresh tomatoes. Even the onion-flavored, pinkish purple flowers can be used in salads and omelettes. Chive flowers steeped in white vinegar will impart their rose color and oniony flavor to the vinegar.

I'm looking for a plant for the perennial border that doubles as an herb. Any suggestions?

Chives are one of the leading contenders. Hardy to Zone 3, these plants grow only 8 to 12 inches tall and have globe-shaped clusters of flowers, surrounded by grassy foliage, in late spring.

Do chives need moist or dry soil?

Plant chives in moist soil, rich in organic matter, in full sun to light shade.

Can chives be grown indoors?

Yes, they can. Grow them on a sunny windowsill, and for best results, place them in the refrigerator for four weeks during the winter to simulate dormancy.

How can I dry chives successfully? Mine shrivel up and lose their flavor.

Chives do not dry well. Try freezing them instead (see page 61).

What are garlic chives?

Also known as Chinese chives, garlic chives (*A. tuberosum*) have a delicious, subtle garlic flavor, making them an excellent salt substitute for chicken, pork, and lamb dishes, as well as a variety of soups and stews. They are also used raw in salads.

Chives: The striking pinkish purple flowers of chives make them an ideal plant for the late spring perennial border.

Madelaine Gray

Their leaves are flat in contrast to the round leaves of regular chives, and their flowers are white and fall-blooming. They freeze well. Planted near roses, they are said to enhance the rose scent.

Cilantro. See Coriander

Clary sage *(Salvia Sclarea)*

Is clary sage related to the perennial flower salvia? They are similar in appearance.

Both annual and biennial clary sages are members of this family. Biennial clary sage forms a rosette of foliage in the first year, and 3-foot spikes of white or purple flowers in the second year.

How do I use clary?

The flowers can be dried and used in arrangements. The essential oil, similar in taste to culinary sage, is commercially extracted from clary.

How is clary grown?

Clary is propagated from seeds. Sow them indoors in late winter and transfer them into the garden in mid-spring. Set plants 12 inches apart. Seeds can also be sown outside in early spring or early fall, ¼ to ½ inch deep. Plants like full sun and a moist soil, rich in organic matter.

Comfrey *(Symphytum officinale)*

Why is comfrey known by such common names as boneset, bruisewort, knitbone, and healing herb?

In the past, comfrey had many medicinal uses: It was believed to heal broken bones, sprains, and bruises when applied to the body in a paste form; and it was used as a gargle, as a cure for bleeding gums, and in teas to relieve digestive problems. Currently, there is a great deal of controversy about the safety of comfrey. Some herbalists contend it has been safely used for centuries; others claim it is carcinogenic. Comfrey is a good addition to the compost pile, as it is thought to activate bacteria and be a good soil conditioner.

Is comfrey a perennial? What does it look like?

Comfrey is a coarse, hairy perennial, hardy through Zone 2. Plants grow 3 feet tall and have hollow, angular, hairy stems. There are leaves all along the main stem, with those that spring from the base of the plant growing up to 10 inches long and looking like donkey's ears; the upper leaves are smaller. The

Madelaine Gray

Clary sage: This plant likes full sun and a moist soil, rich in organic matter.

Maggie Oster

Comfrey: Because of its invasive nature, comfrey is best grown in a bed by itself.

white, pink, or pale purple flowers are bell-shaped and nodding, and bloom in clusters in mid-spring; they often continue to flower throughout the summer. The roots are juicy—black on the outside and white on the inside—and grow 1 to 6 feet in length and 1 inch in diameter.

How should I grow comfrey?

Comfrey likes full sun to partial shade and average to rich garden soil that is kept evenly moist. Plants will grow in dry soil, but they will not be as vigorous. To start your own plants, grow them from seeds sown outdoors in fall or early spring, or from purchased or divided roots planted in early spring and spaced 3 feet apart.

I understand that comfrey can become quite invasive. Is this true?

Yes, and because of this it is best to grow it in a bed by itself. Any piece of root left in the ground will grow into a new plant. The plant also freely self-sows, which can be controlled by removing the flowers as soon as they start to fade.

How is comfrey harvested?

Pick the mature leaves as the flowers start to open and dry them on a rack or a screen. Roots can be dug in the spring or the fall.

Coriander (*Coriandrum sativum*)

Is it easy to grow coriander seed?

Yes, but because coriander does not like to be transplanted, you must start the seeds outdoors in early spring where plants are to grow, ¼ to ½ inch deep. Seeds will germinate in ten to fourteen days. Thin them to 8 to 10 inches apart.

I have been told that coriander has an unpleasant scent. Why grow it?

Although the scent of the fresh leaves and seeds can be unpleasant, when they ripen and are dried, they become very fragrant. The lemon-scented seeds look like white peppercorns, and are the featured flavor in dishes from a variety of nations, including Indian curries, Oriental stir-fry dishes, and Scandinavian breads and cookies. The leaves have a flavor not unlike a combination of sage and citrus, and are sometimes called cilantro.

Will coriander grow in my partially shaded garden?

No, coriander needs full sun. It also needs moist soil, and should be fertilized at planting time.

When can I harvest coriander leaves and seeds?

Harvest their leaves throughout the summer and dry them on a screen in a dark, cool, well-ventilated place. The white or pale pink flowers bloom in late summer on 30-inch stems; seeds form about three weeks later. Cut stems off in early morning and hang them upside down in a paper bag to collect the seeds.

Costmary *(Chrysanthemum Balsamita)*

Can I grow costmary from seeds? I have never seen them in catalogues.

No, costmary cannot be grown from seeds, for it seldom blooms, and when it does, seeds usually do not form. Costmary is a perennial, hardy through Zone 4, and must be grown from root divisions or cuttings in early spring.

What does costmary look like?

Similar in appearance to some chrysanthemums, costmary grows 2 to 3 feet tall, with aromatic, oblong foliage. When flowers do appear, they are daisylike, with yellow centers and white petals, and bloom in late summer.

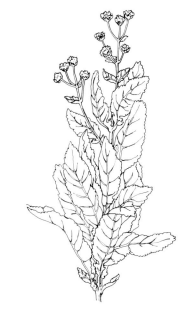

Costmary: A hardy, fast-growing perennial, costmary imparts a spearmint flavor to salads, soups, and stew.

Is costmary easy to grow?

Some gardeners would say it is *too* easy to grow, in fact, it can be weedy. It likes full sun, but will grow less vigorously in partial shade. It grows quickly, so space plants 3 feet apart and fertilize little, if any.

How is costmary used?

In the Middle Ages, before brewers started using hops, costmary was used in beer. It was once called "Bibleleaf" because early settlers used it as a bookmark in their Bibles and nibbled on it to keep awake during church sermons. Leaves have a spearmint flavor and can be used fresh or dried in salads, soups, and stews.

Cumin *(Cuminum Cyminum)*

I tried to grow cumin last year in my northern Wisconsin garden, but the plants never flowered. Can you suggest why?

Cumin must have at least three months of hot summer weather to flower and set seeds. In areas with short growing seasons, such as northern Wisconsin, seeds must be started indoors before the last spring frost. Since cumin is a tender annual, set plants into the garden in full sun after all frost danger has passed. Where the growing season is long, sow seeds in the garden where they are to grow, ¼ inch deep. The plants need not be thinned too radically; if you space them about 6 inches apart, the weak 6-inch stems can support each other.

How long does it take for cumin seeds to germinate?

Seeds will sprout in ten to fourteen days.

Can cumin be grown in average garden soil?

Yes, average is fine, if it is well drained. Water when the soil starts to dry out. Incorporate fertilizer at planting time; no further feeding is necessary.

Can the leaves of cumin be used?

The threadlike *leaves* of cumin are not used in cooking, but the pungent *seeds* were used in Biblical times, and still continue to be used in Mexican, North African, Indian, and Portuguese dishes, in chili, curry, cheese, and sausages.

How should I harvest cumin seeds?

The seeds will mature about three weeks after the flat clusters of white or rose flowers appear. Cut the stems and hang them upside down in a paper bag to collect the seeds.

Dill (*Anethum graveolens*)

I often use dill seeds for pickles and dill leaves on fish. Did dill ever have any other uses?

Dill is taken from an Old English word that means "to lull" because it was once used to soothe cranky babies to sleep. Ancient superstition held that dill could be used to cast a spell to keep witches away.

I grew dill last summer, but the plant was unattractive and the stems fell over. What can I do?

The 2- to 3-foot tall stems of dill are naturally weak, and they get especially top-heavy when the flat clusters of yellow flowers appear in midsummer. Stake them or grow them close together (4 to 8 inches) so that they will support each other.

Is dill an annual?

Yes, it is a hardy annual, which means that it can be planted in the garden in early spring as soon as the soil can be worked.

I have not had success growing dill from seed. Any suggestions?

Indoors, dill seeds must not be covered when sown, as they need light to germinate. You can start them indoors in late winter, in individual pots because they resent being transplanted. They take twenty-one to twenty-five days to germinate.

Dill: Grow dill plants rather close together (4 to 8 inches) so that they will support each other.

Madelaine Gray

Move plants to the garden as soon as the soil can be worked in spring. Seeds can also be sown outdoors in early spring, ¼ inch deep.

What parts of the dill plant can be used in cooking?

The finely divided, light green leaves may be used fresh or dry to season eggs, vegetables, fish, and sauces. Use the seeds for flavoring, especially for pickles. Seeds form following bloom in midsummer.

What care does dill need in the garden?

Provide dill with full sun and a well-drained, moist soil, with a moderate amount of organic matter. Fertilize prior to planting only. Dill self-sows easily and can become weedy unless seed heads are removed before the seeds drop. Do not plant it near fennel, as the two will cross-pollinate and the seeds will not be usable.

I am not interested in dill seeds, only the foliage. How can I increase my harvest?

Do not allow flowers to form. You can continue to pick the leaves at any time and use them fresh or dried. Leaves do not have much flavor if air dried. To store them for short periods, wrap them in a paper towel and place them in a paper bag in the refrigerator.

Are there any special techniques in drying dill seeds?

Cut the stems and hang them upside down in a paper bag. Unlike many other herbs, dill must be dried in a hot (90° F.) area.

Dittany of Crete. See Oregano

Fennel (*Foeniculum vulgare*)

Fennel's licorice-like flavor reminds me of anise. Are they related?

No. Actually, fennel looks much like a large dill plant, with threadlike, bright green foliage and flat clusters of yellow flowers in summer. It grows 4 to 5 feet tall.

How is fennel used?

Fennel leaves are used in soup, salad, and fish dishes. They do not retain their flavor when dried, so must be used fresh, or if desired, they can be frozen. Fennel seeds are used in bread, cookies, sauces, and sausages. Fennel stalks, eaten raw like celery, are said to reduce the appetite. They can also be placed on the barbecue to flavor fish when grilling it.

Fennel: This herb will continue to develop if you keep flowers from forming.

Is fennel an annual or a perennial?

Fennel is a tender perennial, but it is best grown as an annual for it is only slightly frost tolerant.

I have heard that there are some special considerations to be alert to when planting fennel in the garden. Can you explain?

If fennel is planted near dill, the two will cross-pollinate, and the seeds will be unusable. It will not grow well when planted near either coriander or wormwood, and it harms the growth of bush beans, caraway, tomatoes, and kohlrabi.

Do you have any historical information about fennel?

The ancient Battle of Marathon, which gave its name to the long-distance run, was fought in a field of fennel.

How is fennel grown from seed?

Because fennel does not transplant well, start seeds indoors in individual pots, six to eight weeks before the last spring frost. Seeds will germinate in ten to fourteen days. Move them into full sun in the garden after the last frost. After frost danger is past, seeds may also be sown outdoors, ⅛ inch deep, where they are to grow. Final spacing for plants should be 8 to 12 inches.

Is fennel fussy about soil?

Not really. It likes moderately fertile, alkaline soil, and tolerates a wide range of moisture levels.

How can I increase the harvest of fresh leaves of fennel?

Leaves will continue to develop, increasing your harvest, if you don't let flowers form. This, of course, means that there will be no seeds to harvest.

Are fennel seeds difficult to harvest?

They are a little more time-consuming to harvest than other herb seeds because all the seeds on a single stem do not ripen at the same time. One way to harvest them is to hold each flower head over a paper bag and knock seeds off gently every day or two. If this seems too time-consuming, wait until seeds start to fall, and then cut the stem and hang it upside down in a paper bag.

Garlic *(Allium sativum)*

Can garlic be grown from seeds?

Yes, but it is usually grown from the small bulblets called "cloves" that grow around the base of the main bulb. You can buy cloves in a garden center or just use garlic from the supermarket. Plant the cloves outdoors in mid-spring, just below the soil surface, 3 to 4 inches apart, and harvest them the following fall.

Garlic: Full sun and moist, sandy, fertile soil are preferred by this popular herb.

Can garlic be grown in Florida or other areas where summers are hot?

Yes, it can, but because it doesn't like excessive heat, it will grow better if it is planted in the fall and harvested in the spring.

I see that garlic is a member of the onion family. Does it resemble onions in its growth habits?

It looks a lot like other *Alliums*. The leaves are long, narrow, and flat, and the white flowers bloom in globular clusters on 3-foot stems in midsummer. Small bulblets may be found within the flowers. Unlike some *Alliums*, it will not withstand freezing weather.

Is garlic of any use in the vegetable garden?

Interplanting garlic between other plants is an excellent way to conserve space, and garlic also helps to deter cabbage moths, Japanese beetles, and aphids.

Are the care requirements of garlic the same as for vegetables?

Yes, garlic likes full sun and moist, sandy, fertile soil, with moderate amounts of organic material.

How do I know when garlic is ready to be harvested?

When the foliage starts to turn yellow at the end of the season, bend the tops over (without breaking them off) to speed up ripening and drying. Leave the bulbs in the soil for two to three days, then dig them up and let them dry in the sun. Braid the tops together and hang them in a cool, dry, well-ventilated spot. Save several bulbs for cloves for next year's crop.

Garlic chives. See Chives

Geraniums. See Scented geraniums

Germander *(Teucrium Chamaedrys)*

How is germander used in the garden?

Because it is an evergreen shrub only 10 to 12 inches high and can be kept closely clipped, germander is used primarily as a decorative edging in herb gardens, especially knot gardens. It has small glossy leaves, and flowers in late summer with loose spikes of purple or rose-colored flowers, which are often removed to maintain the neat shape of the plant and keep the pattern of the planting intact. This herb was once thought useful to alleviate gout.

What are the cultural requirements of germander?

Although it tolerates partial shade, heat, and poor, rocky soil, germander will be best and densest in full sun and well-drained soil, rich in organic matter. It is hardy through Zone 5, but will need winter protection in Zones 5 and 6 to keep the tops evergreen and alive.

Can I grow germander from seeds?

Yes, seeds can be sown indoors or outdoors, planted ¼ inch deep. They take twenty-five to thirty days to germinate. Germander seedlings grow very slowly, however, so if you propagate by division or take stem cuttings you will have plants more quickly. Set plants 12 inches apart in the garden.

Ginseng (*Panax Quinquefolius*)

I have always thought of ginseng as an exotic herb. Can I grow it in my New Jersey garden?

Ginseng has centuries of mystery surrounding it, perhaps more than any other herb. It has been used and esteemed by the Chinese for its perceived medicinal, restorative, and aphrodisiac qualities. The roots are used to make a tea with a strong, bitter flavor. Ginseng is a woodland plant hardy through Zone 3, but it will not grow in areas that do not have freezing weather during the winter.

Can you describe ginseng to me?

It is a perennial, growing 15 to 18 inches tall, with whorls of five-part leaves and small clusters of greenish white flowers. Early summer-blooming flowers are followed by red berries.

Is ginseng easy to grow?

Growing ginseng is a challenge as its growing requirements are very stringent. It must have light, fertile, well-drained soil that is slightly acidic and rich in organic matter. Keep the soil constantly moist; enrich it with woodland material such as leaf mold; and use a low-nitrogen, slow-acting fertilizer such as bonemeal. A summer mulch will help keep soil moist as well as cool. Grow in full shade, preferably in deep woods where it will be cool and moist. Apply a protective mulch in winter.

I saw ginseng seeds listed in a seed swap. Is it easy to grow from seed?

No, growing plants from seed is as challenging (if not more so) as growing the plants themselves. Seeds cannot be started indoors. Rinse seeds in a 10-percent bleach solution before sowing them outdoors in the fall, ½ inch deep. They may germinate the following spring, although sometimes not until

Ginseng: Long recognized as a Chinese tea, ginseng must be grown in a woodland setting.

the second spring. It is easier to root plants from cuttings in spring, planting them 1 inch deep. After rooting occurs, space plants 15 inches apart.

How should I harvest ginseng?

In the fourth or fifth year, dig up the roots carefully. Wash them with water and dry them on a rack or screen in a warm, well-ventilated spot. It may take four weeks for them to dry completely.

Heliotrope. See Valerian

Horehound *(Marrubium vulgare)*

How did horehound get its name?

Horehound was used years ago as a remedy for dog bites. Today, the flowers and leaves are used to brew a tea said to relieve coughs, and it is the major ingredient in an old-fashioned candy; it is also one of the bitter herbs used in the Passover seder.

I planted horehound for the first time last summer, but it did not bloom. Is this normal?

Yes, it is. When grown from seeds, this perennial, hardy to Zone 3, often does not produce its whorls of tubular, white flowers until the second summer.

Will you describe the appearance of horehound?

Horehound is a spreading plant that grows 18 to 24 inches high. Square, gray, downy stems are covered with deeply veined, woolly, aromatic leaves.

How is horehound propagated?

Horehound can be grown from seeds sown outdoors from as early in spring as the soil can be worked until two months before the first fall frost. Plant seeds ½ inch deep; they will germinate in ten to fourteen days. Thin the plants to stand 8 to 10 inches apart. Because horehound is difficult to transplant, starting seeds indoors is not recommended. Division, too, although possible in mid-spring or early fall, can also be difficult. Rooting cuttings in spring or summer works well.

How can I keep horehound from becoming rangy and spindly?

Plant horehound close together to help the weak stems support each other. Every few years, divide and replant, or take cuttings and discard the original plant. For strongest growth, plant horehound in full sun.

Maggie Oster

Horehound: A spreading plant, horehound does best in full sun.

What type of soil does horehound require?

Horehound prefers average, sandy, well-drained soil, but tolerates poor soil and dry conditions, as well as a wide range of soil acidity. Fertilize plants each year when growth starts.

When should I harvest horehound?

Pick flowers and leaves when the plants are in full bloom. Dry them on a screen in a cool, dry, well-ventilated spot. The flowers are very sticky to handle.

Horseradish (*Armoracia rusticana*)

Is horseradish a more potent form of radish?

No. Although they are in the same plant family, they are not of the same genus (the next biological grouping under family).

What does horseradish look like?

Horseradish is a large, coarse plant with leaves sometimes 2 feet long and tiny, white flowers that appear in June. The plant is grown for its pungent roots, which may be as long as 2 feet.

Will horseradish grow in my Missouri garden?

Yes, it is a perennial, hardy through Zone 4.

How do I propagate horseradish?

In spring or fall, cut pieces of the root into 2- to 8-inch long sections, and plant them 1 foot apart and 6 to 12 inches below the soil surface. Horseradish rarely sets seed, and even when it does, the seed is hard to find.

Can horseradish become invasive?

Yes, it can. Confine it to a section of the garden where you want to grow nothing else. No matter how hard you try, it is impossible to remove all pieces of root from the soil, and even the smallest part of a root will grow into a new plant.

What type of growing conditions should I give to horseradish?

Horseradish likes full sun or partial shade and a deep, rich, moist, loose soil, rich in organic matter.

When should I harvest the roots of horseradish?

Dig up the roots in the fall of the second year; after that, they may become bitter and grainy. If you store the roots whole and grate them as you need to use them, you will get a stronger flavor. Beware, however—fresh, homegrown horseradish can be very "hot" indeed!

Ann Reilly

Horseradish: The pungent roots of horseradish may be as long as 2 feet.

Hyssop (*Hyssopus officinalis*)

Is the hyssop we grow today the same kind of plant that was mentioned in the Bible?

No one knows for sure, but it's possible. We know that in the Middle Ages it was strewn on floors to give the house a fresh, clean smell. Today, it is used as a flavoring in liqueurs, in a tea thought to relieve sore throats and coughs, and as a border or hedge plant in formal herb and knot gardens.

Is hyssop a perennial?

Yes. Hardy through Zone 3, hyssop grows 18 to 24 inches tall and has aromatic, dark green leaves and spikes of blue-violet flowers in summer.

Does hyssop require special care?

Hyssop likes dry, well-drained, alkaline soil. It grows well in full sun or light shade, but not where winters are warm. For best results when fertilizing it, use fish emulsion. With these conditions supplied, it is easy to grow.

How is hyssop propagated?

Hyssop may be propagated from seeds, by division of the roots, or by stem cuttings. Sow seeds ¼ inch deep indoors in early spring or outdoors in early spring or fall. Germination will occur in seven to ten days. Divide plants in spring or fall, and take cuttings in summer.

How far apart should hyssop be spaced?

In the garden, space plants 18 inches apart; as a hedge or in a knot garden, 12 inches apart.

When should I harvest hyssop?

Pick leaves and flowers when the plant is in full bloom, and dry them on a screen in a dry, well-ventilated place.

Hyssop: This herb is equally fine in the garden as a neat border plant and for culinary use as a flavoring or a tea.

Lavender (*Lavandula angustifolia*)

What is the care and use of lavender?

Lavender grows well in a dry, sunny place, in any light, well-drained soil that is not too acid. Cut dead branches back in the spring after new growth near the base is fairly strong. Lavender is grown for both ornament and fragrance. The blue-violet flowers that bloom on 18- to 24-inch spikes in early summer are used in perfumes, potpourri, soaps, aromatic vinegars, and sachets. The aromatic, gray-green, needlelike leaves are attractive in the garden.

Ann Reilly

Lavender: Grown for both ornament and fragrance, lavender does best in a dry, sunny place, in any light, well-drained, non-acid soil.

How can I make lavender plants produce more bloom?

Lavender gives much more prolific bloom, and better fragrance, if grown in a light, well-drained soil, high in lime content. Heavy soils or soils too rich in organic matter encourage foliage growth rather than bloom, and fertile soils produce flowers that are not fragrant.

When should lavender flowers be harvested?

Pick flowers when they are about to open, and dry them on a screen or upright in a vase in a dark, airy place.

Can lavender grow and live over winter as far north as Boston?

It should, if it is given good winter protection, such as marsh hay or evergreen boughs. The soil must be well-drained, for excessive moisture in the soil in winter kills lavender more than the cold does. Even with protection, plants three years old or more have a way of dying back in winter.

How can I start lavender from seed?

Seeds germinate rather slowly, and the tiny plants grow slowly. Start seeds indoors in early spring after refrigerating them for four to six weeks. Set out the new plants after all danger of frost is past. As soon as buds appear the first year, cut them off to prevent them from blooming. Outdoors, sow seeds in fall, ½ inch deep; they will germinate the following spring.

Can I propagate lavender from cuttings?

Yes. In either late fall or early spring, cut 2-inch shoots, taking a little piece of the main stem—a "heel," or portion of older wood—attached to the base of the shoot. Remove lower leaves from cuttings for about 1 inch, and insert the cuttings in well-packed sand. Keep the sand moist. Slight bottom heat will encourage rooting. When roots are not more than ½ inch long, put cuttings in small pots in a mixture of half sand and half soil.

Lavender cotton (*Santolina Chamaecyparissus*)

Is lavender cotton related to lavender?

No, the two plants are not related. Lavender cotton forms a shrubby mound of aromatic, woolly, silver, fernlike foliage. Because it is easy to trim, it is often used in hedges and knot gardens. In summer, it has golden yellow, buttonlike flowers that are clipped off if the gardener wishes to control the plant's shape closely. Insects dislike the scent of lavender cotton, so it makes a good moth-repellent.

Is lavender cotton a perennial?

Yes, but it is hardy only through Zone 6. In cold areas, you can grow it as an annual.

What growing requirements does lavender cotton have?

Grow it in full sun. Although it prefers average, dry, well-drained soil, it is very tolerant of poor, sandy soil. It is also a good seashore plant as it tolerates salt spray. In regions where it would be only marginally hardy, protect it in winter with evergreen boughs or salt hay. To encourage new growth, cut plants back to 4 to 6 inches in spring.

What is the best way to propagate lavender cotton?

Plants are easy to grow from seeds sown either indoors or outdoors from early spring through midsummer. Sow seeds ¼ inch deep; they will germinate in fifteen to twenty days. Plants will flower the first year, if started early enough. Set plants into the garden 18 to 20 inches apart. Lavender cotton can also be propagated by division in early spring, by rooting stem cuttings in summer (though cuttings are slow to root), or by layering.

When should I harvest lavender cotton?

Pick leaves and flowers when the plant starts to bloom, and dry them on a screen in a warm, dry, well-ventilated spot.

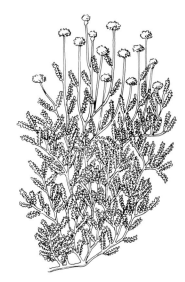

Lavender cotton: In the garden, lavender cotton forms a shrubby mound of aromatic, silvery foliage; dried, it serves as an excellent moth repellent.

Lemon balm (*Melissa officinalis*)

What are the uses of lemon balm?

Refreshing, lemony, hot and cold drinks can be brewed from lemon balm. In fact, in early England, longevity was credited to drinking lemon balm tea. It can also be used in jelly and fruit salad. The crisp leaves have more flavor when used fresh, although they can be dried. Lemon balm oil is used as furniture polish, but fresh leaves rubbed on wooden furniture also make a fine polish.

Can I grow lemon balm in my southern Florida garden?

Probably not. Lemon balm does not like hot, humid climates, although it will tolerate dry heat. It is a perennial, hardy to Zone 4.

Can lemon balm be grown from seeds?

Yes, it can. Start indoors in early spring, at least ten weeks before the last spring frost. Seedlings germinate in fourteen days, but they need a long time to become established. Do not cover the seeds, as they require light to germinate. Alternatively, you can sow seeds outdoors in early spring or early fall. Thin plants to 18 inches apart. Lemon balm can also be propagated by division or stem cuttings.

Will lemon balm grow in light shade?

Yes, it actually does best in light shade. It also likes light, sandy, moderately fertile, well-drained soil. Although it prefers moist soil, once established it tolerates drought.

Maggie Oster

Lemon balm: Brew refreshing, lemony, hot or cold drinks from lemon balm.

What other care requirements does lemon balm have?

After the white flowers bloom in summer, shear the plants back by half to stand about 12 inches high; this will keep them compact.

How should I dry lemon balm leaves?

Before the plants bloom, cut stems off at ground level and hang them upside down in loosely tied bunches in a dark, dry, airy space. Handle the leaves as little as possible during harvesting or drying as they bruise easily. In order for leaves to retain their green color, they must be dried at 90° to 110° F.

Lemon grass *(Cymbopogon citratus)*

What is lemon grass?

The blades of lemon grass, which can grow to 6 feet tall, are used commercially to distill a lemon-scented oil that is used in perfumes and artificial flavorings. Use fresh leaves in cooking or in tea, and dried leaves in potpourri. Cut leaves at any time for fresh use, or spread them on a screen to dry.

Can I grow lemon grass in my South Carolina garden?

Lemon grass is a tropical plant that will survive outdoors year-round only in the warmest parts of Zone 10. However, it can be grown as an annual in the ground or in containers, provided the summer is long and hot.

How should I grow lemon grass?

Give lemon grass a spot in full sun with sandy, well-drained soil. Keep it well watered. If container-grown, apply liquid fertilizer every two weeks. If planted in the ground, feed it once every two months during the growing season.

How can I propagate lemon grass?

Lemon grass rarely flowers and sets seed, so plants are propagated by division. Since it is seldom grown as a perennial in the United States, you will probably have to buy new plants each year.

Lemon verbena (*Aloysia triphylla*)

Is lemon verbena a perennial?

This open-growing shrub is hardy only in Zones 9 and 10. However, it may be possible to grow it in other areas of the country if you dig up the plant with its roots in fall, store it indoors over the winter, and replant it in spring after frost danger has passed. It must be confessed, however, that your chances for success with this procedure are limited.

How is lemon verbena used?

When dried, the lance-shaped, lemon-scented leaves retain their fragrance for many years in potpourris and sachets. In fact, their lemon scent lasts longer than that of any other lemony herb.

Can lemon verbena be grown from seeds?

No, it can't. Propagate it by rooting stem cuttings in summer.

Can lemon verbena be added to the flower garden?

Its lovely green foliage makes a fine accent plant in the June garden, but the spikes of white to lavender flowers that bloom in late summer are rather insignificant.

How is lemon verbena grown?

Plant it in full sun in sandy, moist, well-drained soil, rich in organic matter. Fertilize at planting time.

Can lemon verbena be grown indoors over the winter?

Some gardeners have luck growing lemon verbena indoors, particularly on an enclosed porch or in a plant window where the temperature is cool (55° F.). If you bring it inside and the leaves fall off, place the roots in a cool place and then move the plant outdoors in spring.

Ann Reilly

Lemon grass: The leaves of lemon grass retain their lemon scent unusually long in potpourris and sachets.

When should the leaves of lemon verbena be harvested?

Any time throughout the summer. Dry them on a screen in a cool, dark, well-ventilated spot.

Lovage (*Levisticum officinale*)

I understand lovage can be used as a celery substitute. Is this true?

Yes, lovage looks like celery, although it grows much larger—up to 3 feet high when it is not blooming and 6 feet high in bloom. Lovage and celery have many similar uses. The hollow stems may be used as a substitute for celery in soups; leaves, which, like seeds, are celery flavored, may be used fresh or dried in salads, soups, and stews; whole seeds, in baking; and crushed seeds, like celery powder.

Can I grow lovage in San Diego?

No. Lovage is a perennial that must have winter temperatures of at least as low as 20° F. (though no lower than 0° F.).

How is lovage grown from seeds?

Start seeds indoors in early spring in individual pots, as lovage does not like to be transplanted. Germination takes ten to fourteen days. You can also sow outdoors, ½ inch deep, in fall or spring. Be sure seeds are fresh, as they do not live long. Alternatively, you can divide plants in early spring or late fall, setting plants 12 to 15 inches apart, in full sun or light shade.

Should I add peat moss when improving the soil to grow lovage?

Yes, lovage likes a moist, well-drained soil, rich in organic matter. Fertilize yearly when growth starts and again in summer if leaves turn light green.

How should I harvest the various parts of the lovage plant?

For fresh leaves, cut off the outside leaf stalks. For dried leaves, cut the stem before the greenish yellow flowers bloom in summer. If you cut down the stems, there will, of course, be no seeds to harvest. Dry leaves on a screen in a warm, dry area or in a warm oven. As soon as seeds start to turn tan, harvest them by placing the seed heads upside down in a paper bag.

Marjoram, Sweet marjoram (*Origanum Majorana*)

Is marjoram a perennial or an annual? I have seen it listed both ways in books.

A member of the Mint family, marjoram is a perennial, but it is hardy only to Zone 9, so it is usually grown as an annual. It has

Maggie Oster

Lovage: A celery look-alike, lovage may often be used as a celery substitute.

Maggie Oster

Marjoram: Usually grown as an annual, marjoram is hardy as a perennial only to Zone 9.

oval, velvety, aromatic leaves and inconspicuous clusters of pinkish white flowers in summer. Plants grow 8 to 10 inches high.

How is marjoram propagated?

Marjoram is grown from seeds, preferably indoors because the seeds are very small. Sow seeds in late winter (germination takes eight to fourteen days), and move the plants outdoors in mid-spring, setting them 6 to 8 inches apart. You can take cuttings in fall and grow plants indoors over the winter.

What growing conditions does sweet marjoram need?

Give marjoram a light, well-drained, neutral soil, with a moderate amount of organic matter, and full sun. Fertilize lightly at planting time.

How is marjoram used?

The leaves of marjoram are used fresh or dry in egg or tomato dishes and to flavor meat, vegetables, and salads.

How should I harvest marjoram?

Pick the leaves any time before the flowers bloom. You can extend the harvest period, in fact, by removing the flower buds as they form. Dry leaves on a screen in a warm, dry place, or hang stems upside down to dry.

Mint (*Mentha* species)

How is mint grown?

Mint grows best in deep, moist soil, rich in organic matter, in an open, well-drained spot, in either full sun or light shade. Fertilize lightly after plants are harvested. Mint can be invasive, so control it by thinning yearly or by inserting an underground barrier such as metal edging. Pinch off growing stems regularly to prevent the plants from becoming leggy.

Can mint be grown from seed?

Yes, it can, but plants, especially peppermints, do not come true from seeds and may vary in flavor from the parent. The best way to grow mint is from cuttings or divisions of a variety whose flavor you like. Take cuttings in summer or divide roots in early spring. Plants grow quickly and can be set 12 to 24 inches apart.

How is mint dried?

Peppermint is best for drying, although the fragrances and flavors of spearmint, orange mint, and apple mint also will last

Selected Culinary Mints

COMMON NAME	BOTANICAL NAME	CHARACTERISTICS
Apple	*M. suaveolens*	Hairy foliage; an especially decorative variety is pineapple mint (*Variegata*); pineapple mint loses its flavor when dried, but apple mint actually improves
Corsican	*M. Requienii*	Creeping, tiny-leaved mint; strong flavor used for the liqueur *crème de menthe*; not winter hardy in most Northern regions
Horsemint	*M. longifolia*	Flavor resembles spearmint; tall perennial with long, gray, hairy leaves
Peppermint, or woolly	*M. x piperita*	Refreshingly flavorful; best mint for drying
Spearmint	*M. spicata*	Most common culinary mint; an attractive variety of *M. spicata* is curly mint

for years. Cut stems before the plant flowers and hang them upside down in a cool, dry, well-ventilated place. All mints may be used fresh in hot and cold drinks, salads, and jellies, or as a garnish.

Oregano (*Origanum vulgare*)

How can I determine what oregano is best to buy?

Dried oregano packaged to season Italian dishes does not come from one plant but is a mixture of dried herbs blended for their flavor. To further confuse things, there is some disagreement among botanists and herb experts as to what species is considered "garden oregano." Some common oreganos are *Origanum vulgare*, *O. virens*, and *O. dictamnus*. When you are selecting plants, to be sure you are getting the flavor you want, taste a tiny bit of the leaf or rub a leaf to see if it emits a strong, pleasant fragrance. Tasty oregano usually has clusters of white flowers, while less interesting ones have purple or pink flowers.

Can oregano be grown from seeds?

Yes, it can, but although some varieties may be to your liking, many of the plants lack flavor. Taste-test to find your preference, then take divisions or cuttings from your favorite plants. If you do start from seed, sow seeds indoors in late winter. Germination takes ten to fifteen days. Sowing seeds outdoors is not recommended. Move the plants to the garden after frost danger has passed, setting them in full sun, 12 inches apart.

What type of soil does oregano like?

Oregano likes a light, well-drained soil, with no added organic matter. Fertilize very lightly, if at all.

Is oregano a perennial?

Some species are. If you are uncertain, protect your plants over winter with a heavy mulch of leaves, evergreen boughs, or straw.

How should I harvest my oregano?

Cut the stems when they start to bloom, and hang them upside down to dry in a cool, well-ventilated, dry room.

What is dittany of Crete and how is it grown in the herb garden?

Dittany of Crete (*O. Dictamnus*) is an ornamental oregano with round, gray leaves. It may be started from seeds or by taking cuttings. Not hardy where winters are cold, it must be wintered indoors in pots. Provide it with sandy soil, perfect drainage, and full sun.

Maggie Oster

Oregano: For the best oregano, begin new plants from cuttings or division from taste-tested specimens.

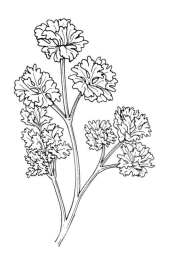

Curly-leaf parsley: This popular herb makes an especially attractive garnish.

Italian parsley: Known also as flat-leaf parsley, Italian parsley is considered by many to have a better flavor than the more familiar curly-leaf variety.

Parsley (*Petroselinum crispum*)

Is parsley a biennial or an annual?

Parsley is technically a hardy biennial, but it is usually grown as an annual because the foliage becomes tough and bitter the second year. If you grow it as a biennial, it will form flat clusters of yellowish green flowers late in spring of its second year.

I have read that parsley seed is difficult to germinate. Are there any tips you can give me?

Parsley is *slow* to germinate. In fact, a traditional saying maintains that it goes to the Devil and back nine times before it germinates. You can speed up germination, however, by soaking seeds in warm water for twenty-four hours before sowing; if this is done, seeds should germinate within twenty-one days. Another way to speed germination is to freeze seeds in ice cubes for three weeks before sowing.

Can I start parsley seeds indoors?

Yes, but because parsley does not like to be transplanted, sow seeds into individual pots. You may also sow seeds outdoors, ¼ inch deep, two to four weeks before the last spring frost. Thin plants to stand 6 to 8 inches apart. In mild areas, sow seeds outdoors in fall for harvest the following spring. Cover the seeds completely as they need darkness to germinate.

What type of soil does parsley need?

Parsley likes a deeply prepared, well-drained soil. Add generous amounts of organic matter to the soil when planting. Fertilize plants when they are 4 inches tall and again one month later.

Does parsley need full sun?

Parsley will grow in full sun or light shade.

How is parsley used?

Use parsley fresh or dried in almost any meat, fish, egg, or vegetable dish, or as a garnish. If used with garlic, it will cut the garlic aftertaste. Parsley is one of the ingredients of *fines herbes*.

How should parsley be dried? On my first attempt at drying it, the leaves lost their color.

Drying parsley on a screen usually results in loss of color. Try drying it on paper towels in a microwave oven (you will have to experiment cautiously for the required time, as that depends upon the size and power of individual ovens). You can also dry parsley in a slow-cooker set on low for overnight. It can be stored for a short time wrapped in paper towels and placed in the refrigerator.

Parsley did not do well in my summer herb garden in Phoenix last year. Can you suggest why?

Parsley does not like summer heat. If you garden where summers are hot, grow it in fall, winter, and spring.

Can parsley be dug in the fall and potted for winter use in the home?

Yes, it can, but because the roots are very long and deep, be careful when digging and plant it in a large pot. Better yet, sow new seeds or use very young plants for your windowsill garden.

Pennyroyal *(Mentha Pulegium)*

What is the difference between American and English pennyroyal?

English pennyroyal *(M. Pulegium)* is a perennial, hardy through Zone 3. A spreading plant with dark green leaves, it grows 6 inches tall. American pennyroyal *(Hedeoma pulegioides)* is an upright, annual plant with light green leaves; it grows 12 inches tall. Both American and English pennyroyal have pungent, citronella-like leaves and spikes of lavender-blue flowers in summer. Their growth needs and uses are identical.

How is pennyroyal used?

Pennyroyal got its name from one of its bygone uses—a body lice deterrent for British royalty. Although it is no longer used medicinally as it was in the past, it is one of the best herbs for repelling insects. It is also used in potpourri and tussie mussies.

Can pennyroyal be grown anywhere in the United States?

English pennyroyal can be grown as far north as Zone 3, although it will need winter protection in the northern limits of its hardiness. Neither the English nor the American pennyroyal likes extremely hot weather.

How is pennyroyal propagated?

Annual pennyroyal is propagated from seeds started indoors or in the garden, sown ¼ to ½ inch deep. It germinates in fifteen days. Because perennial pennyroyal is slow to germinate, it may be better to propagate it from division in either spring or early fall, or by rooting cuttings in summer. Space plants 12 to 24 inches apart.

Does pennyroyal need full sun?

Pennyroyal grows equally well in full sun or light shade.

Ann Reilly

Pennyroyal: Use pennyroyal as an insect repellent, or in potpourris and tussie mussies.

What type of soil does pennyroyal need?

Pennyroyal likes sandy, well-drained soil, kept constantly moist and rich in organic matter. Fertilize around it in early spring when growth starts and again after harvesting.

When should pennyroyal be picked?

Harvest pennyroyal before the plant flowers by cutting the stems to the ground. Hang the stems upside down in a dry, cool, well-ventilated place.

Perilla, Beefsteak plant (*Perilla frutescens*)

I have admired perilla growing in the Bahamas. Can I grow it in my New York garden?

If you grow it as a tender annual, you can. This very pretty plant has crisp, deeply cut, green or reddish purple foliage with a metallic sheen. Plants grow 18 to 36 inches high. You can grow it as a bedding plant for its foliage color or in the herb garden. It makes a colorful and striking addition when the fresh leaves are used in salads and with fruit. The fresh flowers are eye-catching added to fish or used in soup, stir-fry cooking, and meat and vegetable dishes.

What are the flowers of perilla like?

The lavender, pink, or white flowers bloom on spikes in early fall. Where growing seasons are short, the plants may not bloom.

I tried to grow perilla from seed last year, but did not have success. What happened?

Perilla has several specific growing requirements that you must meet. Do not cover the seeds in the sowing flat, for they must have light in order to germinate. Sow it in individual pots, because it is one of the herbs that does not like to be transplanted. Be sure to wait until all danger of frost has passed before sowing the seeds outside. Seeds germinate in fifteen to twenty days.

What kind of soil does perilla need, and how far apart should it be planted?

Soil should be dry and moderately rich in organic matter, with fertilizer added at planting time. Space plants 12 to 15 inches apart, in full sun or light shade. When the plants are 6 inches high, pinch the growing tips to encourage bushiness.

When can I harvest perilla?

Pick leaves and flowers at any time and use them fresh.

Ann Reilly

Perilla: The crisp green or reddish purple foliage of perilla makes a striking addition to the flower or herb border.

Pot marigold. See Calendula

Rosemary *(Rosmarinus officinalis)*

Are there any legends connected with rosemary?

Rosemary, a native of the Mediterranean region, is said to have gotten its name because the Virgin Mary hung her cloak on it when the Holy Family fled from Herod's soldiers to the safety of Egypt. Because of its associations with constancy and remembrance, its leaves have long been used in bridal bouquets and crowns. It is said to be a good hair rinse for brunettes. Legend aside, it is excellent with lamb and other meat dishes, as well as with poultry.

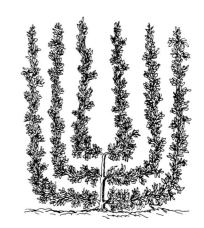

Rosemary: Whether grown in containers or directly in the ground, shrubby rosemary can be trained into various espalier forms.

Is rosemary a perennial? I have noticed it blooming in California in late winter.

A member of the Mint family, rosemary is a perennial shrub only in Zones 8 through 10. In colder areas, grow it as an annual, although if the growing season is not long enough, it may not bloom. Where it is hardy, it blooms with short spikes of pale blue flowers in late winter or early spring and grows as tall as 5 feet.

What is the best way to grow rosemary?

Grow it in light, well-drained, slightly moist soil, in full sun or partial shade. Space plants 12 to 18 inches apart. When rosemary is grown as an annual, fertilize it at planting time; when grown as a perennial, fertilize when growth starts in spring. Mist the foliage daily during hot weather, but be careful not to overwater this plant.

Can I grow rosemary from seeds in my Pennsylvania garden?

In your hardiness zone you would be better off buying plants or propagating rosemary from cuttings. Because it develops slowly from seeds, rosemary is best seeded only in warmer areas. If you start seeds indoors, provide a cool room (55° F.) for germination, which will take eighteen to twenty-one days. Plants can be set outside two to four weeks before the last spring frost. Outdoors, sow seed ¼ to ½ inch deep as early in spring as the soil can be worked.

When should I undertake the various methods of propagating rosemary if I don't start it from seed?

Divide established plants in spring of their second or third year, root stem cuttings in summer, or layer the branches by weighting an outside branch to the ground until roots form, also in summer.

Can I keep rosemary plants in a garden in Illinois from one year to another if I give them heavy winter protection?

No amount of winter protection will keep rosemary alive outdoors during an Illinois winter. You can try growing it in containers and bringing the containers indoors for the winter if you have a cool (55° F.) room or greenhouse. If you don't have space for large plants in the house, take cuttings and grow small plants indoors during the winter.

When can I harvest rosemary?

For fresh or dry use, cut stems back any time before the plant flowers. Dry leaves on a screen in a cool, dry, well-ventilated area, or hang stems upside down to dry.

Rue *(Ruta graveolens)*

Can I use rue in cooking?

Definitely not. Although rue is found in some old recipes, it is potentially harmful. It is a good insect repellent, but it is grown primarily for its decorative foliage, which is deeply cut, lacy, fernlike, and blue-green. It grows 1½ to 3 feet tall, and has buttonlike flowers that bloom in clusters in early summer to midsummer. Rue has a very strong aroma. The fresh foliage often causes dermatitis, so wear gloves when handling it.

Rue: Grown primarily for its blue-green, fernlike foliage, rue prefers full sun and a heavy, but well-drained, soil.

Maggie Oster

Is rue hardy in northern gardens?

Rue is hardy to southern New England, but in very severe climates it should be kept indoors during the winter or grown as an annual.

What are the cultural requirements of rue?

It prefers full sun, and heavy but well-drained soil, with little organic matter. Keep the soil evenly moist. Fertilize in early spring.

How can I propagate rue?

Sow rue seeds ½ inch deep, indoors in late winter or outdoors in early spring as soon as the soil can be worked. Germination will take ten to fourteen days. Move plants outside in early spring, setting them 6 to 12 inches apart. Plants can be divided in summer. Stem cuttings can be rooted, but this is the least successful means of propagation.

How should I harvest rue?

Because rue sometimes causes an allergic rash, wear gloves when picking the leaves. Spread the herb on a screen in a cool, dry, well-ventilated place. Once leaves are dry, they will no longer cause skin irritation.

Safflower *(Carthamus tinctorius)*

Why is safflower called "false saffron"?

True saffron, valued for both its subtle flavor and the golden color it lends to foods, is produced from a corm and it takes a large number of corms to produce a small amount of the herb. Safflower's thistlelike, deep yellow to orange, summer-blooming flowers can be dried, crushed into a powder, and used as a substitute for the rarer, and thus expensive saffron. Safflower may also be used as a dye for wool and, especially, silk, and its dried flowers are attractive in everlasting bouquets and in potpourris.

Safflower: The thistlelike, deep yellow blossoms of safflower may be dried and used as a substitute for the more expensive saffron.

Can I grow safflower in my sunny annual flower garden?

You can, but keep in mind that it has a coarse texture, with large, toothed, and hairy leaves. The plants grow 3 feet tall, so should be placed at the back of the border and spaced 12 inches apart. Grow safflower in average, well-drained soil; be careful not to overwater it.

Can safflower be grown from seeds?

As a matter of fact, this is the only way to propagate safflower. Sow seeds indoors 8 weeks before the last spring frost, sowing in individual pots since safflower is very difficult to transplant. You can also wait until after all frost danger has passed, and sow seeds outdoors where plants are to grow, planting them ¼ inch deep. Seeds germinate in ten days.

When should I pick flowers for drying?

Pick flowers as soon as they are open and before they start to fade. Dry them on a screen in a warm, dry, well-ventilated place, or, if you plan to use them only for ornamental purposes (not culinary), in silica gel. Store flowers, either whole or ground, in an airtight container.

Saffron (*Crocus sativus*)

Saffron is so expensive at the market. Is it possible to grow my own?

Yes, you can grow saffron, but it will be difficult to grow enough plants to produce any sizable amount for the kitchen. Saffron is produced from a corm (a modified stem filled with food storage tissue; similar to a bulb), related to spring-flowering crocus and very similar to it in appearance. The three central orange or red stigmas (part of the flower's female reproductive system) are harvested, ground into a powder, and used to color and flavor such foods as bread and rice. Because it takes several hundred plants to produce enough saffron to fill a tiny container, you might want to consider growing safflower (see entry above).

Saffron: Produced from a corm, saffron resembles spring-flowering crocus.

Is saffron grown the same way as crocus?

It is similar, except that saffron flowers in the fall. Plant saffron corms in early fall, 3 to 4 inches deep and 3 to 4 inches apart, in full sun or light shade and well-drained, moist soil, rich in organic matter. Plants will bloom the same fall they are planted and every fall thereafter in Zones 6 through 10. Do not remove the foliage, which lasts all winter, until it turns completely brown in the spring. Fertilize plants when the foliage turns brown or when growth restarts in fall. At the edge of its hardiness limit, apply a heavy winter protection.

Can saffron be grown from seeds?

No. Instead, in fall or early spring, when plantings become crowded, or if flowers diminish in number, dig up the saffron and divide it by pulling off the cormels (tiny new corms) that form around the base of the original corm. Replant the new cormels immediately, but discard the mother corm, as it will not grow again.

How can I produce powdered saffron?

Pick the flowers in the early morning as they start to open. Remove the orange or red stigmas from the center of the flower and dry them in a warm, dry, well-ventilated location. When they are dry, grind the stigmas, and store the powder in an airtight container.

Sage *(Salvia officinalis)*

Which kind of sage should I grow for culinary use?

The sage used in poultry stuffing, sausage, Italian veal dishes, cheese, and tea, is *S. officinalis*. Tricolor is an attractive cultivar of *S. officinalis*, with variegated leaves of green, white, and purple. Pineapple sage *(S. elegans)* has pineapple-scented foliage and red flowers. Although it is not winter hardy, it can be grown as an annual. A closely related herb is clary (see pg. 519). Both are members of the Mint family.

I have been unsuccessful in growing sage. What are its needs?

Sage enjoys a well-drained, light, sandy soil. It prefers average to moist growing conditions, but must have dry soil during the winter. Plant it in full sun or light shade. Fertilize plants each spring as growth starts, and at the same time, prune plants

Sage: Leaves may be harvested several times over the course of the summer.

Maggie Oster

back to encourage bushiness. It is quite hardy, through Zone 3, and should not need winter protection unless winters are very harsh.

What are the best propagation methods for sage?

Start plants from seeds sown either indoors in late winter or outdoors in early spring, ½ inch deep. Germination takes fourteen to twenty-one days. Because plants are slow to develop, however, propagation is usually done by division in spring when growth starts. You can also root stem cuttings in late spring, or layer them in early fall by weighting down an outer branch with a rock until the branch takes root; transplant the new plant the following spring. Space plants 12 to 18 inches apart.

My sage plants are quite large. Can I cut them back severely when harvesting leaves this fall?

Not unless you live in a warm climate. If you cut off more than ⅓ of the plant in the fall, sage may be susceptible to winter damage. Wait until spring to cut it back heavily.

When can I pick leaves for drying?

Pick leaves before the plant blooms in late spring and early summer, and again in late summer. Tie the stems into bundles and hang them upside down to dry, or strip leaves from the stems and dry them on a screen in a warm, well-ventilated, dry place.

Scented geraniums (*Pelargonium* species)

My scented geraniums do not have the blooms that my garden geraniums do.

Both are of the genus *Pelargonium*, but they are different species, or subgroups, of that genus. Scented geraniums are

Selected Scented Geraniums

COMMON NAME	BOTANICAL NAME	HEIGHT	DESCRIPTION
Finger bowl	*P. crispum*	3 feet	Pink flowers; small, lemon-scented leaves
Fragrant	*P. x fragrans*	12 inches	Trailing plant; white flowers; nutmeg-scented leaves
Lemon	*P. x limoneum*	2 feet	Purple and lavender flowers; lemon-scented foliage
Nutmeg	*P. odoratissimum*	18 inches	Trailing plant; white flowers; apple-scented foliage
Oakleaf	*P. quercifolium*	4 feet	Rose-purple flowers; almond-scented leaves
Peppermint, or wooly	*P. tomentosum*	3 feet	White flowers splotched in red; velvety, mint-scented foliage
Rose	*P. graveolens*	3 feet	Rose-colored flowers; rose-scented foliage

Madelaine Gray

Scented geraniums: Rose and other scented geraniums make good garnishes for drinks, jellies, and fruits.

characterized by fragrant foliage, and their loose clusters of small flowers are secondary, although they do bloom lightly during summer. Their delicious scent is released in the hot sun and by rubbing the leaves. Fresh leaves may be used in baked goods, cold drinks, and jellies, as well as to garnish fruit; dried leaves may be used in teas and potpourris.

Are scented geraniums annuals?

Technically, they are perennials, but they are hardy only in Zones 9 and 10, so plants are usually grown as annuals.

Can I propagate scented geraniums from seeds?

Yes, you can, but sowing seeds is often not as successful as rooting cuttings. Seeds must be started indoors twelve weeks before the last spring frost, and germination is slow—up to fifty days. Move plants to the garden after the last frost. Starting seeds outdoors is rarely successful.

How can I root scented geraniums from cuttings?

Take stem cuttings from new growth in summer and root them in peat moss and perlite or sand (see pgs. 466-67). Pinch them when they are young, to encourage compactness.

What type of soil do scented geraniums prefer?

Rich, light, well-drained soil. Water plants when the soil starts to dry out, but be careful not to overwater. When the plants are growing or flowering, fertilize monthly with houseplant fertilizer.

When can scented geranium leaves be picked for drying?

Pick them at any time to use fresh, or dry them on a screen in a dark, cool, well-ventilated place.

Can I grow scented geraniums indoors over the winter?

Yes. You can either bring entire plants indoors, or root cuttings in late summer and grow them indoors over the winter. Rooting new cuttings each year will give more satisfactory results, as old plants tend to get woody and do not grow well. Grow scented geraniums in full sun or under lights, fertilize monthly, and water when the soil dries out.

Sesame (*Sesamum indicum*)

Does the command "open sesame" from the Arabian Nights have anything to do with the herb sesame?

Yes, it probably was inspired by the fact that the ripened pods of sesame burst suddenly to expel the seeds. Egyptians and Persians were familiar with the plant and ground its seeds for flour. Ground sesame seeds are still used in Near East cooking. The nutty seeds are often found in a variety of cakes, cookies, breads, and bagels, and they are the main ingredient of benne wafers, a Charleston, South Carolina favorite.

Can I grow sesame in my Alabama garden?

Yes, your climate would be ideal. Sesame is a tender annual and needs a long, hot growing season of at least 120 days to flower and set seeds. Sesame would probably not grow well in regions colder than Zone 7.

Does sesame make a good garden ornamental?

Yes, it does. Plants, which grow 2 to 3 feet tall, have long, pointed, dark green, slightly hairy leaves and spikes of bell-shaped flowers in summer.

How can I grow sesame from seeds?

Sesame seeds can be started indoors or outdoors, but where hot summer weather lasts less than four months, seeds must be started indoors. Sesame does not like to be transplanted, so seeds must be started in individual pots. Germination takes five to seven days. Move plants outdoors after frost danger has passed, setting them 6 inches apart. Where seeds can be sown outdoors, sow them ¼ inch deep after frost danger has passed and nights are above 60° F.

Does sesame require any special care?

No, give it full sun and average soil. Fertilize at planting time, and water when the ground starts to dry out.

Sesame: A warm-climate plant that requires a long, hot growing season, sesame thrives in full sun and average soil.

How do I harvest seeds without losing them?

Cut the mature pods *before* they burst open by cutting the stems off at ground level and placing them upside down in a paper bag.

Southernwood. See Artemisia

Summer savory *(Satureja hortensis)*

What is the difference between summer savory and winter savory?

Summer savory is a hardy annual, while winter savory (see page 559) is a perennial. Both, however, have linear, gray-green leaves and loose spikes of white, pink, or pale lavender flowers in summer. Summer savory is bushy, growing 12 to 18 inches high, and winter savory is spreading, growing 6 to 12 inches high. Both have a peppery flavor, but the flavor of summer savory is more delicate and is an excellent substitute for sage in poultry stuffing. Use either summer or winter savory fresh or dry to flavor meat, beans, and other vegetables. If you put summer savory in the cooking water, it will cut the odors of cabbage, turnip, and other strong-smelling vegetables.

What kind of soil culture does summer savory need?

Summer savory grows best in a moist but light, sandy soil, with little organic matter. Choose an exposed sunny site. Never allow the soil to dry out. Fertilize at planting time; no further feeding is necessary.

I started seeds of summer savory indoors last year, but they did not do well when I transplanted them. What was wrong?

Summer savory does not like to be transplanted, so use individual pots when sowing seeds indoors. Because the very small seeds need light to germinate, do not cover them with planting medium. Seeds germinate in ten to fifteen days. Move plants to the garden, placing them 4 to 6 inches apart, four weeks before the last spring frost. You can also sow seed outdoors in early spring as soon as the soil can be worked. Make a succession of plantings for a continuous harvest.

Why should I make successive plantings of summer savory?

Because summer savory must be harvested by cutting the entire stem back just before the plants bloom, planting summer savory every two weeks (known as succession planting) will ensure a continuous supply all summer and fall. After you have cut the stems, tie them in bunches and hang them upside down to dry in a warm, dry, well-ventilated place.

My plants of summer savory were quite spindly last year. Will fertilizing them more help?

Feeding may actually make them *more* spindly, because it encourages stem and leaf growth. Because "leggy" growth is normal for summer savory, you may wish to set plants close together so that they will support each other.

Sweet Annie. See Artemisia

Sweet cicely *(Myrrhis odorata)*

Can I grow sweet cicely in my North Dakota garden?

Yes, sweet cicely, a perennial herb hardy to Zone 3, would survive North Dakota winters. In fact, it prefers northern climates, especially if you can provide it a shaded, woodland garden with soil rich in organic matter.

What does sweet cicely look and taste like?

With its soft, fernlike foliage and small, white flowers, it looks much like a large version of chervil. It grows quickly, reaching a height of 2 feet in May. The leaves, stems, and seed pods, which taste like anise, may all be eaten.

I tried to grow sweet cicely from seed last year, but it didn't germinate. What did I do wrong?

Sweet cicely seed needs stratification, or cold treatments (see pg. 457), before it will germinate. If you want to start this plant indoors, place seeds in moistened peat moss in a covered container in the refrigerator for two to three months before sowing. After sowing, germination will take thirty days or more. To begin sweet cicely outdoors, sow *fresh* seeds ½ inch deep, as soon as they form in the fall: they will germinate the next spring.

I understand sweet cicely is difficult to transplant. Is this true?

Yes, it is. Because sweet cicely has a long tap root, it does not like to be moved. When growing seedlings, sow them into individual pots or transplant them when they are very small. Mature plants are difficult to divide, and are best propagated by cuttings.

How is sweet cicely used?

Eat the licorice candylike seed pods of sweet cicely fresh. Use leaves fresh or dried in teas, with vegetables, or as a substitute for anise or fennel. Place stems of sweet cicely on the barbecue coals when grilling fish.

Maggie Oster

Sweet cicely: This perennial herb prefers northern climates and shaded, woodland gardens.

Sweet flag *(Acorus Calamus)*

What is sweet flag?

A perennial, hardy through Zone 3, sweet flag is a waterside plant that looks like grass or cattails, with its fragrant, sword-shaped leaves growing 1½ to 6 feet tall. It is grown for its rhizomes (underground, horizontal root stocks).

How is sweet flag used?

Its dried root, also called calamus root, is used as a fixative in potpourri (see pgs. 498-99). Some American Indians used sweet flag for fever, coughs, colds, and toothaches; others believed it brought courage when rubbed on the skin. During the Depression, it was used as a substitute for chewing tobacco, but it is now considered carcinogenic.

I want to grow sweet flag in my herb garden. Does it need full sun?

Full sun is not necessary for sweet flag, although it will grow in full sun. If it is not grown by the water, it must have moist soil, rich in organic matter.

How is sweet flag propagated?

Increase sweet flag by dividing the rhizomes (see pg. 468).

How do you recommend harvesting and drying sweet flag?

Sweet flag rhizomes should be dug in early fall. Dry them in the sun, preferably at 85° or 90° F., for several days.

Sweet flag: This grasslike perennial must be grown by water, or in very moist soil.

Sweet woodruff *(Galium odoratum; formerly Asperula odorata)*

How is sweet woodruff used?

A traditional beverage known as May wine is flavored with the leaves of sweet woodruff. To make May wine, fill a quart jar with fresh sweet woodruff leaves and pour enough Rhine wine over the leaves to fill the jar. Cover, refrigerate, and allow the mixture to steep for four weeks.

Although the fresh leaves are odorless, when dried they take on the scent of clover or new-mown hay and so are popular in sachets.

What garden conditions should I provide for sweet woodruff?

With its loose clusters of star-shaped, white flowers in late spring, this 6- to 8-inch plant makes a fine perennial ground cover, hardy through Zone 4. Give it an open, acid, rather moist soil, rich in organic matter. It must have good drainage, but it thrives in either shade or partial shade. It should not be fertilized.

Can I propagate sweet woodruff from seeds?

Germination is often poor, so it would be better to propagate by dividing plants in early to mid-spring when growth starts, or by rooting stem cuttings from new growth in late spring and summer.

When should sweet woodruff leaves be harvested?

The best time is in the spring before the plants flower. Dry them on a screen in a cool, dry, well-ventilated area.

Tansy (*Tanacetum vulgare*)

Is it true that tansy is a good insect repellent?

Yes. Strew fresh leaves on doorsteps to keep ants away, hang dried leaves and flowers in doorways to repel moths, and set live plants around the outside of the house to discourage a variety of insects from entering.

Does tansy have other uses?

Because it contains a poisonous drug, tansy may not be used for food or drink. With its fernlike foliage and clusters of buttonlike, bright yellow flowers on 4-foot stems, it is an attractive addition to the perennial flower or herb garden. It blooms in late summer and is hardy to Zone 3. The flowers are excellent in dried arrangements, and both flowers and leaves can be used in sachets and potpourri. The dried leaves and stems also make a natural dye.

What type of soil does tansy like?

Grow tansy in moist, well-drained soil, rich in organic matter. Fertilize each year in spring when growth starts.

I grew tansy last year, but it got very weedy. I wondered if it was in too sunny a spot?

Tansy spreads naturally and rapidly, and giving it less sun will only make it more leggy. Set new plants 12 to 18 inches apart, and insert an underground metal barrier around them to help keep them within bounds. You can also grow tansy in a container. Thin or cut tansy back every year.

How should I propagate tansy?

Divide tansy in either spring or fall—you'll find that any piece of root that has a bud eye will grow into a new plant. You can also grow tansy from seed. Start seeds indoors in mid-spring, or

Ann Reilly

outside in early spring as soon as the soil can be worked, sowing seeds ½ inch deep. Germination will take ten to fourteen days.

When should I pick tansy?

Cut the stems at ground level just before the flowers have fully opened. Hang the stems upside down and dry them in a dark, dry, well-ventilated place.

Tarragon (*Artemisia Dracunculus* var. *sativa*)

I have come across both tarragon and French tarragon in recipes. Are they the same thing?

The tarragon referred to in recipes is French tarragon. Russian or Siberian tarragon, for which you may find seeds, is a tasteless, invasive weed. French tarragon rarely flowers, and when it does produce an occasional yellow bloom, it does not set seed.

How can I recognize French tarragon when I buy plants?

Taste a little piece of a leaf. If it has a delicate licorice flavor, it is French tarragon. Tarragon is a woody perennial with dark green, linear leaves, and with the potential for growing 3 feet high.

How is tarragon used in cooking?

Tarragon is particularly nice with fish and chicken and in bearnaise sauce. Along with parsley, chives, and chervil, it is

Tarragon: The delicate, licoricelike flavor of tarragon is particularly suited to fish and chicken dishes.

one of the *fines herbes* used in French cooking. Like many culinary herbs, tarragon may be used dried but is much better fresh.

What kind of soil does tarragon need?

Almost any well-drained garden soil, rich in organic matter. Water when the soil starts to dry out. Roots must be dry during the winter or the plants will not survive. Fertilize with fish emulsion in early spring when growth starts and again in early summer, but do not use chemical fertilizer to force growth, as the quality of the leaves is adversely affected by a too-fertile diet.

Does tarragon need full sun?

It prefers full sun, but will endure light shade.

I tried to grow tarragon in Monterey, California, last year, but it did not do well. What is the problem?

It may not be cold enough during the winter. A true perennial, tarragon must have temperatures between 32° and -10° F. (Zones 5 to 8) during the winter. If you wish to grow tarragon where winters are mild, you can dig up plants and refrigerate them over the winter: Wash soil off the roots; prune the roots back so that they are about 2 inches long; place the entire plant in a plastic bag, fastened closed; and store in the hydrator for about six weeks.

Can tarragon be grown from seed?

As explained above, the culinary herb French tarragon does not set seed. To propagate, therefore, you must divide plants in early spring or take cuttings in summer. Space new plants 12 to 24 inches apart.

When should I pick tarragon leaves?

To use leaves fresh, pick them at any time. To dry them, pick leaves in the early fall and dry them on a screen or in a paper bag in a warm, dry, well-ventilated area. Handle the leaves carefully during picking and drying as they bruise easily and bruising causes them to lose their essential oil and flavor.

Thyme (*Thymus vulgaris*)

I have seen many different kinds of thyme. Which is the one used in cooking?

The best and most commonly used thyme for cooking is *T. vulgaris*. A spreading perennial, 6 to 12 inches tall with small, aromatic, gray-green leaves and clusters of lavender-blue flowers in spring and summer, thyme delicately flavors poultry stuffing, soups, egg, meat, and vegetable dishes. Bees that feed on its nectar produce a distinctive honey. Legend holds that thyme was one of the herbs used in Christ's manger.

What are some other thymes that I could use in my herb garden?

Two other popular culinary thymes are lemon thyme *(T. x citriodorus)*, which has round, deliciously flavored leaves, and caraway thyme *(T. Herba-barona)*, which has small leaves with a flavor similar to caraway. The ornamental or creeping thymes, such as mother-of-thyme *(T. praecox)*, are aromatic and can be used in cooking, but they are not as tasty as *T. vulgaris*. All thymes are members of the Mint family.

I would like to grow thyme for seasoning. Will it stand our severe western New York winters?

In western New York, you are on the edge of thyme's winter hardiness limit, which is Zone 5. Protect it during the winter with a mulch of evergreen boughs or straw. The greatest menace to thyme during winter, however, is not so much the cold as it is the wetness caused by snow and poor drainage, which is apt to cause winterkill. One means of preventing this is to grow thyme on rather poor or sandy soil, containing gravel or screened cinders. Do not feed thyme in summer to force growth, and do not cut its tops after September 1. Try these ways of keeping plants dry during winter: Place them in a cold frame, cover them with boxes to help keep the snow off, and be certain that their position is well drained.

Thyme: Lemon thyme is a particularly popular culinary thyme.

Madelaine Gray

What are the best growing conditions for thyme?

Full sun in light, sandy, dry, well-drained soil. Fertilize very lightly in early spring with bonemeal or cottonseed meal. Prune back plants in spring or summer to encourage bushiness.

How can I increase my thyme plants?

The best culinary thymes are not easily propagated from seeds, so we recommend making divisions, taking cuttings, or layering. Other thymes may be started from seeds indoors in late winter through late spring; seeds will sprout in twenty-one to thirty days. Sow seeds outdoors in early spring as soon as the soil can be worked, ¼ to ½ inch deep. Divide established plants in early spring; take stem cuttings in summer. Set new plants 10 inches apart.

If I begin new plants by layering this summer, can I move them this fall?

To be certain that the roots are well developed, wait until the following spring.

When can thyme be harvested?

Whenever the plant is large enough to pick the leaves, up until the time the plant is in full bloom.

Valerian, Heliotrope (*Valeriana officinalis*)

Is valerian still used medicinally?

Although its roots were once used in medicines, valerian is now grown principally for its clusters of fragrant flowers in a perennial border. In addition, its roots, which have an unpleasant odor when fresh, seem to attract earthworms to the garden. Legend holds that because the roots were also thought to attract rats, the Pied Piper of Hamlin carried valerian. When dry, the roots lose their unpleasant odor and are used as a fixative in potpourri (see page 498).

Is valerian a perennial?

Yes, but when it is being grown for its roots, it is dug up in its second year. If you wish to grow some as perennials, harvest only what you need and save the rest for propagation for following years. Valerian is hardy through Zone 3.

I tried valerian two years ago for the first time. It was a pretty background for the rest of the garden, but it needed staking. Would fertilizer strengthen its stems?

Valerian grows 3 to 5 feet tall and normally needs to be supported in some way. Set plants 12 inches apart so that they can help to support each other. Fertilize in spring when growth starts but additional fertilizing will not help strengthen the stems.

What kind of soil does valerian need?

Valerian likes well-drained soil, rich in organic matter and constantly moist.

Will valerian grow in partial shade?

Yes, it does equally well in full sun or partial shade.

When does valerian bloom?

The flat to round clusters of white, pink, lavender, or blue flowers fill the garden with bloom from late spring to late summer.

I have not had luck growing valerian from seeds. Am I doing something wrong?

If your seeds are not fresh they will not germinate. Further, do not cover seeds, as they need light to germinate. Start seeds indoors except in the longest of growing seasons, because it takes twenty-one to twenty-five days for the seeds to germinate and ten to twelve weeks for a seedling to reach transplanting size. Move plants outdoors four weeks before the last spring frost, and set them 12 inches apart. Less time-consuming, divide plants in spring or fall.

When should valerian be harvested?

The flowers do not dry well, but they can be cut for fresh bouquets at any time. Dig roots in the fall of their second year before the first frost, wash all soil from them, split any that are larger than ¾ inch, and dry them in an oven at 120° F.

Watercress (*Nasturtium officinale*)

Does the botanical name of watercress, *Nasturtium officinale*, mean it is related to garden nasturtium?

No, they are not even in the same plant family, but they both have a pungent, peppery flavor and a somewhat similar appearance. Watercress is a biennial aquatic plant with thin, divided, round leaves and four-petaled flowers. It grows best in cold, running water at the edge of a clear, fresh stream.

Can I grow watercress in a garden without running water?

Yes, plants will last for a time in a moist, shady spot in the garden, but they will not live through the winter unless covered with water. They can also be grown in tubs, whiskey barrels, or other watertight containers. They become true perennials only when grown in running water that has an alkaline pH.

As an alternative, you can grow annual garden cress (*Lepidium sativum*), which will furnish salad greens in three to four weeks, or annual garden nasturtium, the leaves, flowers, or seeds of which may be used in salads. (Do *not* eat packaged nasturtium seeds, which may have been chemically treated.)

What are the uses of fresh watercress?

Use watercress in salads, in sandwiches, and as a garnish, or cook it with vegetables for a peppery flavor.

How should I grow watercress from seed?

Sow seeds in water or in a constantly wet medium that has a temperature of 55° F., and do not cover them. Germination will take seven to ten days. You can also divide watercress in spring or fall.

When should I harvest watercress?

If you allow some plants to flower, they will drop their seeds in late summer, giving you new plants to begin harvesting by late fall.

Wintergreen *(Gaultheria procumbens)*

How is wintergreen used?

Wintergreen is a 3-inch evergreen shrub, commonly seen as a ground cover in North American woods. It is a well-known flavor of commercial candy and chewing gum. The fresh-picked leaves lend a refreshing mint flavor to tea.

What soil does wintergreen require?

Wintergreen needs the soil typically found in the woods—rich, moist, acidic, and well drained. Fertilize plants in spring when growth starts, and keep them mulched with 2 to 4 inches of pine needles during the summer.

Can I grow wintergreen on a sunny slope?

No, wintergreen needs a site in partial to full shade.

Does wintergreen flower?

Yes. Small, white, bell-shaped, spring flowers are followed by red berries in fall.

Can I grow wintergreen from seeds?

Cuttings or layering are easier methods of propagation, but if you want to grow wintergreen from seeds, either sow the seeds outdoors in fall for germination the following spring, or place them in moistened peat moss in the refrigerator for three months. Germination may be slow.

Maggie Oster

Wintergreen: A true woodland plant, wintergreen requires a rich, moist, acidic, well-drained spot.

Can I dig a plant of wintergreen from the wild and move it into my garden?

You can, but small plants transplant most successfully. It is probably better to take cuttings or buy a plant at a nursery.

When should I root cuttings of wintergreen?

Root cuttings in early summer, using new growth. You can also propagate wintergreen by pinning outside branches to the ground. The newly rooted plants can be dug the following spring. Set plants 12 inches apart.

When can the leaves of wintergreen be harvested?

Harvest leaves at any time for fresh or dry use. Keep plants compact and shapely by pruning them in spring, and use the prunings fresh, or dry them on a screen in a cool, dry, airy place.

Winter savory (*Satureja montana*)

How do winter and summer savory differ?

Actually, they are quite similar, except that winter savory is a perennial, hardy through Zone 5, and summer savory is an annual. Both have the same uses and are grown in the same

Winter savory: Perennial winter savory should be pruned severely in early spring to encourage compact growth.

manner. To encourage compactness, severely prune winter savory in early spring when growth starts. It may need winter protection in cold climates. (See also summer savory, page 549.)

Are winter and summer savory propagated the same way?

Each can be propagated by seed and has the same germinating requirements, although winter savory may take a little longer to sprout. Winter savory can also be propagated by division in early spring or by layering during the summer. Plants will be rooted and ready to transplant the following spring. Set plants 12 to 15 inches apart.

Wormwood. See Artemisia

Yarrow (*Achillea Millefolium*)

Can you tell me about the history of yarrow?

The Latin name for yarrow, *Achillea*, stems from Achilles, who is said to have recognized its healing properties. Even during the

Yarrow: Formerly valued for its healing properties, yarrow is now used primarily in dried flower arrangements and in herbal bath products.

Ann Reilly

Elizabethan era soldiers carried it as a first-aid treatment for wounds. Today its primary use is for dried flower arrangements and herbal bath products.

Can I grow yarrow in a sunny flower garden?

With its fernlike foliage and clusters of pink, magenta, or white flowers, yarrow is an extremely attractive plant, which blossoms in early summer and again in fall if it is cut back after the first bloom. Flowering stems grow 2 to 3 feet tall over a clump of foliage at their base. It can be invasive, however, so grow it in a container or with an underground barrier around it, or be prepared to thin it out each year.

I have seen yarrow with yellow flowers. What is this plant?

Yellow yarrow (*A. filipendulina*) is a closely related species. Grown in the same manner as *A. millefolium*, it is a slightly taller plant, with slightly larger flower heads.

Can I grow yarrow in my south Florida garden?

Probably not. Yarrow is a perennial best grown in Zones 3 to 8, because it needs freezing temperatures during the winter.

What type of soil does yarrow prefer?

Yarrow likes a dry, acidic, well-drained soil with little organic matter. It needs little or no fertilizer, but it benefits from a light application of bonemeal in spring when growth starts.

If I start plants from seed, will they bloom the first year?

When started from seed, plants usually will not bloom until the second year, unless given a very early start indoors. Be sure not to cover the seed as it is very fine and needs light to germinate. Seeds will sprout in ten days. Outdoors, sow seeds from mid-spring to midsummer, and space seedlings to stand 8 to 12 inches apart.

When can I divide plants of yarrow?

Divide the plants in either early spring or early fall. Since yarrow will need thinning almost every year, the plants that are removed can be given to friends and neighbors or transplanted to another part of the garden.

When should I cut yarrow for drying?

Cut the flowering stems off at the base just before the plants are in full bloom. Hang the stems upside down in a warm, dark, dry place.

Characteristics of Favorite Herbs

NAME	ANNUAL/ PERENNIAL	HEIGHT	PLANT PART USED	BASIC USES	PROPAGATION	EXPOSURE	SOIL
Angelica	B	5'	L,St,Se,R	Cu,D	S	S,LtSh	M
Anise	HA	18"-2'	L,Se	Cu	S	S	D
Anise hyssop	P	3'-4'	L	P	S,D,C	S,LtSh	D,A
Artemisia	P	2'-3'	L,F	F,I	S,D,C	S	D,A,M
Basil	TA	18"-2'	L	Cu	S	S	D
Bee balm	P	2'-4'	L	D	S,D,C	S,LtSh	D,A
Borage	HA	2'-3'	L,F	Cu,G	S	S,LtSh	D
Burnet	P	18"-2'	L	Cu,D	S,D	S	D
Calendula	HA	6"-2'	F	F,G,Cu,D,P	S	S,LtSh	M
Caraway	B	2'-30"	L,Se,R	Cu	S	S	D
Catnip	P	2'-4'	L	(see page 491)	S,D	S,PtSh	D
Chamomile (Roman)	P	6"	F	D,Co	S,C	S,LtSh	D,A,M
Chamomile (German)	HA	24"-30"	F	D	S	S,LtSh	D,A,M
Chervil	HA	2'	L	Cu	S	LtS,PtSh,Sh	M
Chives	P	8"-24"	L,F	Cu	S,D	S,LtSh	M
Clary sage	B	3'	F	F	S	S	M
Comfrey	P	2'-3'	R,L	(see page 519)	S,D	S,PtSh	A,M
Coriander	HA	30"	L,Se	Cu	S	S	M
Costmary	P	2'-3'	L	Cu	D,C	S,PtSh	D,A
Cumin	TA	6"	S	Cu	S	S	A
Dill	HA	2'-3'	L,Se	Cu	S	S	M
Fennel	P(A)	4'-5'	L,Se,St	Cu	S	S	D,A,M
Garlic	HA	3'	R	Cu	S,Cl	S	M
Germander	P	10"-12"	-	H	S,D,C	S,PtSh	D,A
Ginseng	P	15"-18"	R	D	S,C	Sh	M
Horehound	P	18"-24"	L,F	Cu,D	S,D,C	S	D,A
Horseradish	P	2'	R	Cu	C	S,PtSh	M
Hyssop	P	18"-24"	L,F	D,H	S,D,C	S,LtSh	D
Lavender	P	18"-24"	F	Cu,P,Co,I	S,C	S	D
Lavender cotton	P	18"-24"	L,F	P,H,I	S,D,C	S	D
Lemon balm	P	2'	L	D,Cu	S,D,C	LtSh	D,A,M
Lemon grass	P(A)	6'	L	Cu,D,P	D	S	M
Lemon verbena	P(A)	3'	L	P	C	S	M
Lovage	P	3'	L,Se,St	Cu	S,D	S,LtSh	M
Marjoram	P(A)	8"-10"	L	Cu	S,C	S	A
Mint	P	12"-18"	L	Cu,D	S,D,C	S,LtSh	A,M
Oregano	P,A	18"-24"	L	Cu	S,D,C	S	A
Parsley	B(A)	8"-12"	L	Cu,G	S	S,LtSh	A
Pennyroyal (American)	HA	1'	L	P,I	S	S,LtSh	M
Pennyroyal (English)	P	6"	L	P,I	D,C	S,LtSh	M
Perilla	P(A)	18"-36"	L,F	Cu	S	S,LtSh	D
Rosemary	P(A)	1'-5'	L	Cu,Co	S,D,C,L	S,PtSh	A

Characteristics of Favorite Herbs

NAME	ANNUAL/ PERENNIAL	HEIGHT	PLANT PART USED	BASIC USES	PROPAGATION	EXPOSURE	SOIL
Rue	P	18″-36″	L	H,I	S,D,C	S	M
Safflower	TA	3′	F	Cu,P,F	S	S	A
Saffron	P	6″-8″	F	Cu	Co	S,LtSh	M
Sage	P	18″-24″	L	Cu,D	S,D,C	S,LtSh	A,M
Scented geraniums	P(A)	1′-4′	L	Cu,D,P	S,C	S	A
Sesame	TA	2′-3′	S	Cu	S	S	A
Summer savory	HA	12″-18″	L	Cu	S	S	M
Sweet cicely	P	2′	L,Se,St	Cu,D	S,C	Sh	M
Sweet flag	P	18″-6′	R	P	D	S,PtSh	M
Sweet woodruff	P	6″-8″	L	D,P	D,C	PtSh,Sh	M
Tansy	P	4′	L,F	F,I,P	S,D	S	M
Tarragon	P	3′	L	Cu	D,C	S,LtSh	A
Thyme	P	6″-12″	L	Cu	S,D,C,L	S	D
Valerian	P	3′-5′	R,F	P	S,D	S,PtSh	M
Watercress	B	3′	L	Cu,G	S,D	Sh	M
Wintergreen	P	3″	L	D	S,C,L	PtSh, Sh	M
Winter savory	P	6″-12″	L	Cu	S,D,L	S	M
Yarrow	P	2′-3′	F	F,Co	S,D	S	D

Plant Type: P = Perennial
          P(A) = Perennial grown as an annual
          B = Biennial
          B(A) = Biennial grown as an annual
          HA = Hardy Annual
          TA = Tender Annual

Plant Part Used: L = Leaves
          F = Flowers
          R = Roots
          Se = Seeds
          St = Stem

Basic Uses: Co = Cosmetic
          Cu = Culinary
          D = Drinks, hot or cold
          F = Dried flower
          G = Garnish
          H = Hedge
          I = Insect Repellent
          P = Potpourri

Method of Propagation: S = Seeds
          C = Cuttings
          Cl = Clove
          Co = Corm
          D = Division
          L = Layering

Exposure: S = Sun
          LtSh = Light Shade
          PtSh = Part Shade
          Sh = Shade

Soil: D = Dry
    A = Average
    M = Moist

Germination Time and Plant Spacing

HERB	GERMINATION TIME (in days)	PLANT SPACING
Angelica	21-25*	3 feet
Anise	20-28	6-9 inches
Anise hyssop	7-10	1½ feet
Artemisia	7-10	2-4 feet
Basil	7-10	1 foot
Bee balm	15-20	1 foot
Borage	7-10*	1 foot
Burnet	8-10	15 inches
Calendula	10-14	12-15 inches
Caraway	10-14*	6-9 inches
Catnip	7-10	1½-2 feet
Chamomile (Roman)	7-10	3-4 inches
Chamomile (German)	7-10	8 inches
Chervil	7-14*	6-8 inches
Chives	10-14	6-8 inches
Clary	14-21*	1 foot
Comfrey	7-10*	3 feet
Coriander	10-14	8-10 inches
Costmary	not grown from seed	3 feet
Cumin	10-14	6 inches
Dill	21-25	4-8 inches
Fennel	10-14	8-12 inches
Garlic	10-14	3-4 inches
Germander	25-30	1 foot
Ginseng	*	15 inches
Horehound	10-14	8-10 inches
Horseradish	not grown from seed	1 foot
Hyssop	7-10*	12-18 inches
Lavender	20-40*	1 foot
Lavender cotton	15-20	1½ feet
Lemon balm	14	1½ feet

Germination Time and Plant Spacing

HERB	GERMINATION TIME (in days)	PLANT SPACING
Lemon grass	not grown from seed	3 feet
Lemon verbena	not grown from seed	2-5 feet
Lovage	10-14	12-15 inches
Marjoram	8-14	6-8 inches
Mint	12-16	1-2 feet
Oregano	10-15	1 foot
Parsley	14-21	6-8 inches
Pennyroyal (American)	15	1-2 feet
Pennyroyal (English)	not grown from seed	1-2 feet
Perilla	15-20	1-1½ feet
Rosemary	18-21	1-1½ feet
Rue	10-14	6-12 inches
Safflower	10	1 foot
Saffron	not grown from seed	3-4 inches
Sage	14-21	1-1½ feet
Scented geranium	20-50	1-2 feet
Sesame	5-7	6 inches
Summer savory	10-15	4-6 inches
Sweet cicely	30 +*	2 feet
Sweet flag	not grown from seed	1-3 feet
Sweet woodruff	not grown from seed	1-1½ feet
Tansy	10-14	1-1½ feet
Tarragon	not grown from seed	1-2 feet
Thyme	21-30	10 inches
Valerian	21-25	1 foot
Watercress	7-10	12-15 inches
Wintergreen	30 +	1 foot
Winter savory	15-20	12-15 inches
Yarrow	10	8-12 inches

*Sow in the fall for spring germination

•

PART VI
FRUITS

22 *Your Home Fruit Orchard*

A bundant, fresh fruit for baking, jams and jellies, or simply eating fresh from the harvest is surprisingly easy for home gardeners to grow. Even for those with limited space, container-grown dwarf trees or hanging strawberry baskets will provide an impressive amount of fruit with relatively little care. And fruit trees and bushes are often extremely ornamental additions to the home landscape throughout the season. The brilliant pink spring blossoms of a peach or the fall-ripened orange fruits of a leafless persimmon make a stunning addition to a front yard or back patio. If you have room for a garden of any size, you have room to grow fruit.

Knowing certain details about the climate where you live is even more important when you are planning to grow fruit than it is for vegetables or flowers. Not only do temperate climate fruits need a certain amount of warm weather, but they also require a certain amount of cold weather—called the *chilling requirement* (see p. 570). To determine which fruits you can grow where you live, study the descriptions of individual plants on pp. 591-619 ask your county Extension Service agent for advice about what varieties are suited to your region, and search for a dependable local or mail-order nursery that carries the full range of fruit-bearing plants that grow well in your area.

What are hardiness zones?

These zones (see map, page 711), established by the United States Department of Agriculture, are numbered 1 through 10:

◆ *The brilliant pink blossoms of a peach tree make a stunning addition to the spring landscape.*

CLIMATE CONSIDERATIONS
•

Zone 1 receives the lowest average annual minimum temperature; Zone 10 receives the highest. The zones don't necessarily separate the best from the worst gardening places. Furthermore, even if your area has temperatures that dip very low in winter, it may have a greater number of frost-free days or the sun may shine more often than in areas with milder winter temperatures.

Is it true that some varieties of peaches, apricots, and blueberries will grow in much colder regions than commonly considered possible for these fruits?

Yes. By hybridizing, plant breeders have developed strains of fruits that can withstand colder than usual climates. You should, however, approach such varieties with caution, planting only one or two, until you are sure they will stand up to conditions in your yard. The *length* of your area's growing season is just as critical as its annual minimum temperature. A number of other climatic factors should be considered as well: Extremes of wind, rain, snow, or ice can be even more devastating than very cold winters. Early spring thaws in cold-weather regions can bring on early blossoming in apricots; subsequent cold snaps will kill the blossoms and ruin the crop. Wet springs harm peaches by spreading leaf curl.

Is there any reason why I shouldn't plant all extra-hardy varieties, just in case a rare cold winter comes along?

Before you do that, consider the fact that extra hardiness often comes at the sacrifice of flavor, disease resistance, and other virtues. Decide whether this trade-off is worthwhile to you, as well as whether these extra-hardy varieties will grow in your climate at all.

Exactly what is a chilling requirement?

The fruiting period must be followed by a dormant period during which the plant rests and regains strength for another fruit set the following year. The length of this dormant period is measured in hours between 32° and 45° F. Varieties with low winter chilling requirements need from 300 to 400 hours below 45° F.; medium chilling needs are 400 to 700 hours; high chilling needs are 700 to 1,000 hours.

Can I extend the warm season for growing fruits?

Yes, but with difficulty. You can sometimes find a microclimate within the boundaries of your own land where, because of the amount of available sun or the slope of the land, you can grow plants that would find a spot just a few feet away inhospitable. You can grow trees against walls, under plastic tunnels, or in greenhouses, and you can even cover dwarf trees with cloth draped over a wooden frame and warm them from below with light bulbs or candles. This sort of troublesome protection is not practical year after year with a number of plantings. It's better to plant the proper varieties for your region.

Can I extend the winter chill in my area?

Aside from planting in the coldest section of your yard—for example, at the bottom of a slope where cold air runs at night—there is nothing practical you can do.

Will fruits and berries grow in the shade?

All fruits must have full exposure to the sun for most of the day. Although they will grow in partial shade, the harvest will be light and the fruit not as sweet. Sour cherries need less sun than other tree fruits.

How important to fruits, berries, and grapes is soil drainage?

A well-drained site is very important. Peach and cherry trees are less tolerant of soggy soils than are apples and pears, but no fruit tree will grow in soil that is always wet.

Stark Brothers Nurseries and Orchards

EVALUATING YOUR SITE

•

Most fruit trees have a chilling requirement—a dormant period measured in hours when temperatures range between 32° and 45°F. The chilling requirement for this Rainier cherry tree is 700 hours.

I would like to plant a peach tree in the center of my vegetable garden. Is this a wise thing to do?

If the tree will need to be sprayed for pest and disease control (see pp. 586–88), this may not be the best place for it, as you must never allow fruit tree sprays to drift onto vegetables or fruits. Fig and persimmon trees, which need no spraying, might be appropriate for such settings. If your garden space is limited, however, even small trees may take up more room and cast more shade than would be desirable for the vegetables you are trying to grow.

Can I plant grapevines, berry bushes, and fruit trees on sloping ground?

Midway down gentle slopes is ideal, because cold air will drain away from plantings on frosty nights. Low spots surrounded by higher land are the least desirable, because cold air drains into them.

What sort of soil is best for fruits?

Most fruits grow best in the same sort of soil that is good for growing vegetables (see pages 630-31).

Are there any kinds of fruits that will grow on land that is too poor for garden vegetables?

Figs do best without supplemental nitrogen and prefer heavy clay soil, so you might consider them if your climate is suitable. Grapes will thrive on soils containing clay, slate, gravel, and sand, although the better choice for them is a well-drained, deep, fertile loam. In general, it is best to improve a poor soil before planting fruit in it. (See pgs. 631-37 for methods of improving soil.)

Will fruit trees grow in thin soil over a layer of rock?

If you have less covering than 12 inches, no fruit trees will survive, and you should consider planting genetic dwarf fruit trees in large tubs instead.

We live on the seacoast and get steady winds during most of the year. Will fruits grow well here?

Wind is a problem for most plants, because it dries out plant tissue and physically damages limbs and branches. Build or plant windbreaks, behind which you can plant dwarf trees. Consult your local Extension Service agent, who will give you advice about windbreaks based on the experience of others in your area.

There is no plant nursery in my area. Where can I get good planting stock?

Choose a respectable, well-established mail-order nursery, such as the ones listed at the back of this book. Be sure to plant stock promptly upon its arrival.

How reliable are the berry bushes and fruit trees I see for sale at grocery and drug stores?

Too often such places sell plants that are not suited to the local climate. If you see a healthy-looking specimen of a variety you know will grow well under local conditions (see Chapt. 24 for specific varieties), you might try it, but check closely for damage, pests, and disease before you buy. Remember, too, that the sellers may not be able to answer the questions that arise as the specimen grows.

Does it matter where the stock I buy was grown?

No. Named varieties are genetically identical and will perform identically in your garden no matter where they were produced.

I have heard that I must plant two of each kind of fruit tree I grow. Is that true?

Sometimes, but not always. Before you purchase a fruit tree, you will need to know whether it will produce fruit on its own, or whether it needs to grow near a pollinator tree of a different variety. Trees that pollinate themselves are called *self-fruitful*; trees that cannot pollinate themselves—which include most fruit trees—are called *self-sterile*. The descriptions of individual fruits in Chapt. 24 tell which ones need a pollinator and which can stand alone. Self-sterile trees not only need a pollinator tree within 100 feet of them, but that pollinator tree must blossom at approximately the same time or it will not fertilize its neighbor. Because bees carry the pollen from one tree to another, it is important to avoid the use of any substance on your property that might kill bees.

Could you please explain the difference between container-grown, balled-and-burlapped, and bare-rooted plants?

Container-grown plants have been grown in some kind of pot—usually peat, plastic, or clay—for most or all of their lives. They should be kept moist, in a semishaded spot, until you are ready to plant them. Balled-and-burlapped plants have been dug up with the soil carefully maintained around their roots and wrapped in burlap (or plastic-backed burlap). Bare-rooted plants, too, have been dug from their growing place, but without retaining the root ball. If you get your plants from a mail-order nursery, they will most likely come bare-rooted, with their roots protected with something like damp sphagnum moss. Bare-rooted plants are the most susceptible to damage.

PURCHASING BERRY BUSHES AND FRUIT TREES

•

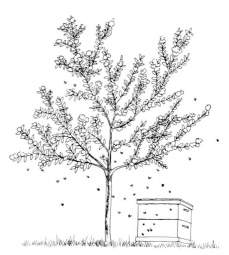

Bees, which carry pollen from one flowering fruit tree to another, are valuable assets to fruit growers.

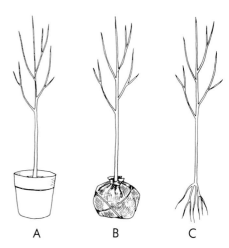

A   B   C

(A) Container-grown. (B) Balled-and-burlapped. (C) Bare-rooted.

The roots of bare-rooted trees should be submerged in water for from 3 to 24 hours before planting.

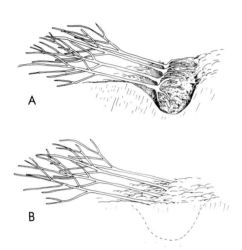

If it will be more than 24 hours before you can plant a tree in its permanent location, heel it in by (A) laying it on its side in a shallow trench and (B) covering the roots with at least 6 inches of soil. Water the trees lightly and keep them shaded.

Are there any advantages to planting bare-rooted plants?

Bare-rooted plants are almost always considerably cheaper than potted or balled-and-burlapped plants, and your first harvest is not likely to come any later. In cold-winter areas, bare-rooted plants should be planted in the spring, so if you live up north and want to put in fruit during the summer, you should buy potted or balled plants.

What should I do with my plants when I get them home?

Immediately remove bare-rooted plants from the protective material in which they are enclosed. Submerge the roots in water. You can leave them in water for up to twenty-four hours in a garage or shaded, protected place. Plant them as soon as weather permits. A good nursery won't ship your plants to you until the proper planting time where you live. Wrap the roots of balled plants in plastic and keep them, too, in a sheltered location. If you must hold either bare-rooted or balled-and-burlapped stock for more than twenty-four hours, plant them temporarily using a technique known as *heeling in* (see illustration).

What size fruit tree should I buy?

Buy trees on the small side, but not tiny little whips. Small trees will establish themselves sooner than larger, older trees with larger root systems. Whether the tree you plant is simply one long stem or is lightly branched does not make a great amount of difference.

What other things should I consider when choosing among varieties?

Be practical and take into account your desires and needs. What kind of fruit do you like to eat? How much space do you have? What is your climate like? Do you can, freeze, or dry fruits? Choose varieties suited to your purposes.

Do dwarf fruit trees have any special advantages?

Full-sized fruit can be produced on the diminutive, attractive dwarf fruit trees that are now widely available in increasingly many different varieties. These trees produce roughly the same amount of fruit—or sometimes more—for the amount of space they take up as standard-sized trees, and usually at a younger age. Pruning, spraying, and harvesting dwarf trees is easier, too, as you need have no tall ladders or special equipment. In fact, they need less pruning because they are not as vigorous growers.

What are the disadvantages of dwarf trees?

They require more frequent irrigating in dry climates than do standard trees. Some are not as sturdy in high winds and need

Positive Images, Jerry Howard

These dwarf apple trees are easier to prune, spray, and harvest than standard-size apple trees—and they bear a surprising amount of fruit.

more support when their limbs are heavy with fruit. They usually don't live as long as standard trees, nor are they as hardy against cold. Deep, icy snow may break off low-growing branches, and herbivorous animals can easily reach foliage.

What are genetic dwarfs?

Genetic dwarfs are the smallest fruit trees of all. Though they grow well in large tubs, they can also be planted in the ground, where they will reach a larger size—some of them up to 8 or 9 feet. If you live in the North, you can grow genetic dwarfs in tubs. Take them into an unheated shelter (*not* the heated house) during the winter months. Genetic dwarfs bear fruit of medium size that, while generally not of as high a quality as the larger trees, is still tasty. They usually come into bearing the second year after being planted.

What are five-in-one trees, and are they worth considering?

These curious trees consist of a rootstock with five different varieties of the same fruit—usually apples—grafted to it. These trees are rather expensive, and not as easy to grow as one might think. Often one or two of the grafted varieties will grow much more vigorously than the others, and need more pruning. In addition, very careful attention must be taken to avoid entirely cutting off one of the varieties during the dormant pruning season, when it is hardest to distinguish one variety from another. On the other hand, the trees can be quite beautiful if they bloom in multicolor, and their novelty appeals to many.

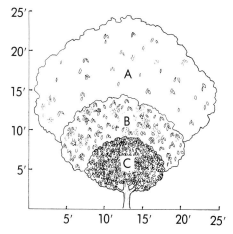

(A) Standard. (B) Semi-dwarf. (C) Dwarf.

575

23 Planting and Growing Fruits and Berries

Growing fruits is surprisingly easy—aside from annual pruning and an intelligent program of pest and disease control, there is little of the day-to-day care required by some vegetables and flowers. In addition, many fruits are little affected by moderate fluctuations in weather. If you follow the given here on planting, fertilizing, watering, and pruning your trees and bushes, you will soon be harvesting succulent fruits for your table and pantry. Be sure to prepare your soil, assemble the planting and staking materials that you will need, and even dig your holes before your planting stock arrives.

How should I prepare the soil before planting fruits and berries?

Incorporate about ½ bushel of compost or aged manure per planting hole to lighten a heavy soil or improve the water-holding ability of a sandy soil. This is best done in the fall for a spring planting, but always *before* your stock arrives. A green manure crop (see pg. 631) will also improve the soil before planting. Refer to pgs. 630-37 for other ways to improve your soil.

Rather than trying to improve all the soil in the area, can't I improve just the spots where my fruit trees will be?

Although your trees, properly spaced, will use all the soil in the area when they are mature, you can start out by preparing the soil just in a 5-foot circle around the planting holes. You can then continue to improve the surrounding soil as your trees

◀ *If espaliered, apples are among the many fruits that can be grown in limited space.*

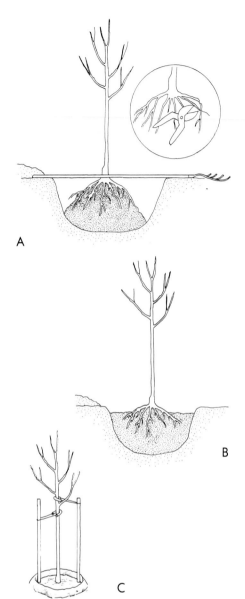

To plant a bare-rooted tree, (A) in a hole twice the width of the plant's root spread, mound up soil at the bottom, dampen it, and set the tree roots on it so that the graft union lines up at 3 or 4 inches above ground level; cut off any withered or broken roots. (B) Fill the hole, gently pressing down on the soil with your hands as you go and taking care to leave no air pockets around roots; mound soil around the tree about 3 inches above ground level, leaving the graft union 1 inch above ground level; water well. (C) Create a shallow, doughnut-shaped dish in the soil around the tree; drive two stakes into the ground on either side of the tree and stretch wires from the stakes to the tree, covering the wires with hose where they touch the tree.

grow by planting green manure crops and adding manure and compost as necessary. (See page 61 and information on specific trees.)

How early in the spring should fruit trees and grapes be planted?

Plant just as early as the soil can be worked. As long as the trees or vines are dormant, there is no danger of planting too early, provided the soil has dried out enough to be worked. Avoid working clay soils that are wet enough to be squeezed into a tight, elastic mass (see page 631). In warm-winter areas, bare-rooted plants can be planted in autumn, when leaves have just begun to fall.

How far apart should I space fruit trees?

That depends entirely on the mature size of the trees you are planting. Fruit trees usually grow about as wide as they do tall, so determine the mature height of the varieties you are planting, and space the young trees so that at full size their outer branches will come just short of touching the branches of the next tree over.

How can I know whether my trees need to be staked when I plant them, and how should I go about staking them?

Stake dwarf trees, trees liable to encounter high winds or physical abuse from animals or passersby, or trees 4 feet or taller. Sink two stakes into the ground, one on each side of the tree, just outside of where the roots are, and *loosely* tie the tree to them with rags, rubber strips, old nylon stockings, or nonsticky plastic tape—don't use strong, thin string, or anything that might cut into the bark. If your tree is quite small at planting time, but you expect to stake it as it grows, put the stakes in now, when there is less risk of damaging the roots.

Should I prune my trees at planting time?

Container-grown trees that have been in their pots for some time should be pruned only very lightly by removing just broken or poorly placed growth. To encourage strong root growth, cut back the tops of bare-rooted or balled-and-burlapped trees by about one half, or slightly more if the trees are especially tall and skinny. You can either remove all the side (scaffold) branches or cut them back by half.

How should balled-and-burlapped trees be planted?

Follow the procedure used for bare-rooted trees (see illustration). When you lower the root ball onto the mound of soil in your hole, pull the burlap covering away from the tops and sides (but not from the bottom) before filling the hole with soil. If the covering is plastic, remove it from the hole. Remember to apply plenty of water as you go, as well as when you're finished.

How should I plant container-grown trees?

Plant them as you would bare-rooted trees, but don't attempt to break the roots free from the tight ball of soil they hold. Loosen the outer roots from the soil ball by rubbing them with your fingers, roughing them up with a stick, or spraying them with a stream of water. If, on the other hand, the tree hasn't been growing in the container long and the soil falls away when you lift the plant from the container, shake the dirt free and treat as a bare-rooted tree.

When should I begin fertilizing newly planted fruit trees?

There are no hard and fast rules about fertilizing. If a young tree is growing well, looking healthy, and producing good crops, the only fertilizer it may need is a nitrogen supplement. Large, mature trees usually need 1 pound of nitrogen per year; smaller, immature trees, from ¼ to ⅓ of a pound per year. Keep the ground around the trees mulched with an organic material that will decompose into the soil. Leave a ring of exposed soil 8 inches around the trunk, to discourage rodents and insects. In addition to contributing nutrients to the soil, mulch will keep down weeds, prevent water evaporation during dry weather, prevent erosion, and ameliorate soil temperature fluctuations.

Should I add phosphorus and potassium to the soil, too?

Most soils contain enough of these nutrients for growing fruit trees. If a soil test shows otherwise, or your local Extension Service advises you to, add them before planting, and subsequently as further tests dictate.

At what time of year should I fertilize?

Early spring, after the trees have leafed out, is best. In general, the least desirable time to fertilize is just before, or during, fruit growth. Fast-acting, commercial fertilizers should go down in early spring. Bulky organic fertilizers, because they release nutrients slowly, can be added later in the season (though not just before winter), and pose a lesser risk of overfertilization. In colder areas, do not fertilize after the first half of summer, because this encourages late, tender new growth that would be susceptible to winter damage. To fertilize, pull back the mulch and give a light application of a high-nitrogen fertilizer, or a 2- to 3-inch layer of steer manure, dusted around the drip line (corresponding to the outermost branches) and then turned into the top few inches of soil. Water thoroughly. Don't cultivate too deeply or you might injure the roots.

Will a cover crop help my fruits and berries?

A cover crop of clover or some other legume will provide a living mulch and contribute nitrogen to the soil as well. Flower-

FERTILIZING FRUIT TREES

•

ing cover crops such as mustard, clover, buckwheat, and sweet alyssum attract bees and other beneficial insects. Cover crops should be mowed occasionally, and their clippings left to decompose into the soil.

What sort of pH do fruit trees need?

A slightly acid soil is ideal, but not absolutely necessary. Severely imbalanced soils should be corrected.

WATERING FRUIT TREES

A drip watering system takes water to the exact spot where it is needed.

How much water does a newly planted fruit tree need?

Keep a watch on your tree for the entire first year, and water heavily once a week when it doesn't rain. In a heavy soil, too much water will flood the soil, robbing plants of oxygen, and in a sandy soil too much water will wash away valuable nutrients. Mulch the soil to conserve moisture.

How can I know when my fruit trees need to be watered?

Water mature trees when the soil is dry 4 to 6 inches below the surface. If the leaves are wilted early in the day, you've allowed them to get too dry. Water deeply and not often, adjusting your watering schedule to the weather rather than the calendar. If the ground beneath your trees is always moist, you're watering too often. Keep the root crown dry.

What is the best way to water?

Although it involves a substantial initial investment, a drip watering system will later save you money on water, for it puts water only where your trees need it. On dry, sloping ground it is almost a must because water loss from runoff is eliminated. Disadvantages include not being able to grow green manure or cover crops and the trouble of working around drip lines when adding bulky soil amendments. Drip watering is probably not worth the expense with standard trees that need little irrigation, but for dwarf trees it is superior. Try to keep the ground adjacent to the trunks dry.

Do I need to water a fruit tree growing in a lawn that gets watered twice a week?

Yes, because the relatively shallow watering most lawns receive is not adequate for fruit trees. Use a deep root irrigator to water trees growing in lawns. This tool, available at any garden center or nursery, is a long, hollow needle that attaches to your garden hose and applies water slowly to the soil down where a tree's roots are.

Is pruning fruit trees and berries really essential?

Yes, and proper pruning is quickly learned and easy to do. Fruit trees need pruning into a shape that will invite sunlight into their interior branches, that will allow good air circulation and ease of spraying and harvesting, and that will create sturdy limbs that can support a heavy load of ripening fruit. The trees also need to be pruned to remove dead and diseased wood. For information on how to prune grapes and berries, see individual entries in Chapter 24.

Is there one principle to keep in mind that will help me as I get started pruning?

Err on the side of pruning too little: No serious harm will come to your trees if you leave a little too much wood on them. You can always remove it later when you are more sure of what you are doing.

At what time of year should I prune?

Prune during the dormant season, before buds have begun to swell. As the tree puts out new growth in the spring, you can pinch off long or unwanted shoots, but it's best to refrain from major pruning during the time when a tree is actively growing.

In what shape should I train my trees to grow?

Refer to the individual fruit tree descriptions in Chapt. 24 for the shape best suited to the trees you are growing. Fruit trees are most often pruned in one of three configurations—open-center (also called vase training), modified leader, or central leader.

Open-center training does not create as strong a limb structure as other methods, a potentially serious problem if the tree will carry heavy weights of fruit, as well as of ice and snow. It also needs more lateral space than trees pruned in other ways. It has the advantage, however, of letting sunlight into a tree's center, where the light and warmth ripen the fruit and dry up moist, potentially disease-causing conditions. Open-center-trained trees are easiest to keep from growing too tall.

Modified-leader-trained trees are sturdier than open-center-trained trees, because they don't carry their load of fruit (or snow or ice) so far away from their trunk. Modified-leader-trained trees have a single trunk that runs a few feet higher than the trunk of an open-center-trained tree, and then branches out. Trees grow to a moderate height this way.

Central-leader-trained trees are the strongest and tallest of the three configurations. A single trunk continues up the center of the tree, with all scaffold branches emanating from it. Trees trained in this way are difficult to prune, spray, thin, and harvest, and are hard to drape with protective netting if birds are

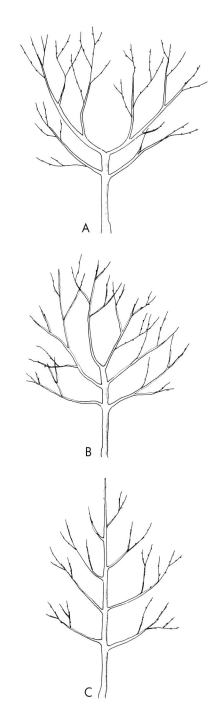

PRUNING FRUIT TREES

(A) *Open-center- or vase-trained.*
(B) *Modified-leader-trained.*
(C) *Central-leader-trained.*

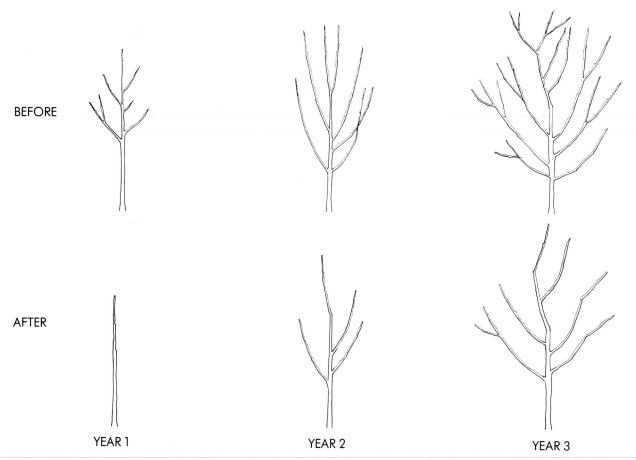

BEFORE

AFTER

YEAR 1   YEAR 2   YEAR 3

Characteristic pruning during the first three years of a tree's growth.

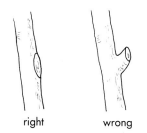

right   wrong

When pruning side branches, leave no stub.

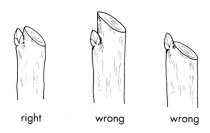

right   wrong   wrong

Avoid making pruning cuts too close or too far from a bud.

a problem. On the other hand, they serve as windbreaks, offer privacy and shade, and are quite stately and lovely.

How often should I prune?

Prune your trees when you plant them, and then yearly thereafter.

How should I prune for the sake of maintenance?

Remove any diseased, broken, or dead wood, and cover the cuts with tree-patching compound if they are 2 inches or more across. Prune off lateral branches that extend so far horizontally that they are likely to break under heavy loads. Remove tangled wood and excessive growth that blocks sunlight.

How can I prune to bring an old neglected tree back into shape?

Go easy on the old-timers. Take away a small amount of wood each season until, within three to five years, the tree has the amount of wood you want on it. You can't very well train an old tree into a new shape, but you can prune it to take advantage of the shape in which it has been growing over the years.

Are there any advantages to espaliering, or is it done solely for ornamental purposes?

To espalier fruit trees means to train them to grow flat. Their great advantage is that they can be grown in a quite small place up against a wall, and they will thrive even if their roots are underneath paved walks or driveways. Since many fruit trees need to be planted in pairs (see p. 573), two single-stem cordon espaliers (see illustration) can be planted two feet apart, providing pollen for each other, yet taking up little space. If you plant an espalier against a white-painted, south-facing wall, you may be able to grow a variety that normally needs warmer climates. And they are easy to access for care and harvest.

What are the disadvantages of growing espaliers?

If you buy them already trained, they are expensive. Although it is not hard to train them yourself, you must prune them continuously throughout the growing season or they will lose their shape. Preventive spraying can stain the structure against which the espalier is grown, and painting the structure is difficult.

Do espaliers encounter any problems that other fruit trees do not?

Since their trunks are not shaded by their leaves, they can get burned by the sun. To counter this, paint the trunks white. In warmer climates, espaliers planted against a wall can get too hot: Temperatures above 90° F. will damage the leaves and fruit. If this might be a problem where you live, plant them against an east wall, along a free-standing wire system stretched between posts, or in some other place that does not receive direct sun in the heat of the day.

What fruit trees are best for espaliering?

Any tree that you can get on dwarf rootstock will work. Apples, cherries, peaches, pears, and figs are among the best for espalier.

ESPALIERS

•

A single-stem cordon espalier.

To train a single-stem cordon espalier, (A) plant tree midway between concrete-based posts in front of tautly stretched wires. (B) With strips of cloth, tie two side shoots to the lowest wire, leaving a third shoot to grow as the trunk. (C) During the second spring of growth, train two more side shoots to the second wire; leave a shoot to continue trunk growth.

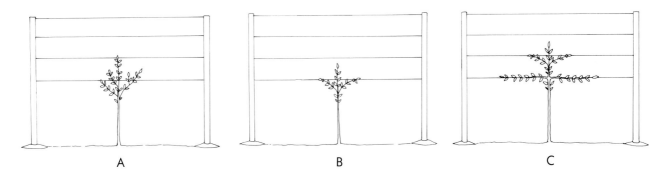

A   B   C

How should I feed and water espaliers?

Apply a small handful of a high-nitrogen fertilizer to espaliers in the spring, and then prune them back heavily in the summer. Water thoroughly after fertilizing.

GROWING FRUIT TREES IN CONTAINERS
•

To repot a container-grown tree, gently remove the plant from the pot (soil should be damp, but not wet); cut away an inch of soil and roots around the circumference of the root ball; wash the container with soap and hot water; spread new soil on the bottom of the pot; center the plant in the pot, packing new soil around the sides; water thoroughly; prune lightly, if necessary.

Can I grow all kinds of fruit trees in containers?

Yes, though all but fig trees must be dwarfs.

What sort of container should I use?

Anything that is well drained and large enough to hold the tree's roots. Make sure that your containers are not treated with any toxic chemical. (For further information about container plants, see pages 653-55.)

What are your suggestions for watering container-grown fruits?

Water often, especially during dry weather. Water in such a way that you don't disturb the soil with a hard stream. Drip systems work well with container-grown fruit trees. Mulch to conserve water.

What is the best way to fertilize container-grown fruits?

Liquid fertilizers, such as fish emulsion, are ideal. Fertilize more often than you would in-ground plants—about once a month—but with about one-half the strength recommended for in-ground plants. Fertilizer is quickly washed out of container-grown plants because of frequent watering, but they can't withstand heavy doses or they'll get burned.

How often should I repot container-grown fruit trees?

If after a few years in the same pot, a plant starts sending roots up to the soil surface, seems to need watering too often, or simply lacks vigor, the tree is giving signals that it needs repotting.

Can I grow fruit trees completely indoors?

This is possible, but most need full sun to produce good fruit. Try growing trees outdoors and bringing them inside for brief spells when they are at their most beautiful.

Where should I store a plant while it is being protected from winter cold?

An unheated garage is a good place to keep a tree during its dormancy. The temperature must stay above 15° F.

Is it okay to shake fruit out of a tree onto a blanket?

You're likely to bruise your fruit this way. Often bruises don't show up until later, when they turn to soft, mushy spots. Eat bruised fruit first.

What kind of weather is best for harvesting fruits?

Dry, cool weather is best. Avoid picking wet fruits, and if you must pick on hot days, move harvested fruits to a cool place without delay.

Do you have any other advice about harvesting?

Please remember your own safety. Ladders set on moist ground topple easily, so have someone hold the ladder for you as you climb it. Remember that tree limbs laden with fruit may be just short of their breaking point and should not be burdened with your body's weight, too. It's better to let those last few, out-of-reach apples fall to the ground on the next windy day than to risk your limbs for them. Apple-picking tools allow you to pick high-growing fruits from the ground.

THE FRUIT HARVEST
— • —

Dry, cool weather is best for harvesting fruits; if you must pick on hot days, move harvested fruit to a cool place as soon as possible.

Positive Images, Jerry Howard

INSECT PESTS AND DISEASES OF FRUITS AND BERRIES

Ron West

Flathead borers burrow beneath the bark of trees, especially those that are unhealthy or stressed.

Ron West

Finely stippled leaves covered with fine webbing are the calling card of spider mites.

If you take measures to remove all insect pests from your garden, you will remove all of the pests' natural enemies as well. Although the chances are that the pests will one day return, their predators may not. It is best, therefore, to maintain a balance you can live with. Paying attention to the soil, water, fertilizer, and pruning needs of your trees and berries, taking adequate garden sanitation measures, and choosing varieties that are suited to your area's growing conditions will go a long way toward avoiding most problems. In addition, learn to recognize whatever is bothering your trees and plants, so that you can choose an effective course of action in defense, and to take into account local conditions, so that you can anticipate the pests and diseases your plants are most likely to encounter and take preventive measures against them before any damage occurs.

Can you tell me which chemicals should be applied to stop the various pest and disease outbreaks?

Your county Extension Service agent can tell you precisely what works best in your area, and your local nursery, garden center, or hardware store will offer a large selection of pesticides and disease-fighting substances under many different brand names. A number of new natural pesticides on the market are less harmful to people, pets, beneficial animals, and the environment than some chemical pesticides, but even natural pesticides must be used with care (see also pages 658-61).

What is dormant oil?

Applied when the buds have begun to swell, but before any leaf or flower tissue has emerged, dormant oil is a refined petroleum product especially marketed for use on plants. Most dormant oils are sold as spray oils, listed as "60" or "70 sec." The numbers refer to a viscosity rating. The lower the number, the less viscous (the thinner) the oil.

Protecting Your Fruit from Animals

ANIMAL PEST	DETERRENT
Gophers	Traps
Deer	Surround young trees with a circle of woven wire. Erect double fences, each 4 feet high, placed 5 feet apart, or a 5-foot-high fence with an angled-out section on top.
Rabbits and rodents	Encircle the base of trunks with hardware cloth. Keep mulches from pressing against the tree.
Birds	Drape trees with bird netting.

Insect Pests of Fruits and Their Controls

INSECT PEST	CONTROL
Aphids	Spray with dormant oil to kill eggs during winter. (See also page 656.)
Apple maggots	Promptly gather and destroy infested fruit. Hang commercially available red spheres coated with sticky lure as traps. Spray with wettable rotenone (5-percent) at petal fall and then every two weeks through October.
Black cherry aphids	Spray with dormant oil in early spring. Spray aphids with a strong jet of water combined with 2 or 3 tablespoons of soap per gallon.
Cane borers	Prune off and burn infested portion.
Cherry slugs (pear slugs)	Same control as for black cherry aphid. Hand-pick. Dust with wood ashes, then rinse three days later. Spray with dormant oil or rotenone.
Codling moths	To destroy eggs, spray with dormant oil before buds open. Destroy fruit that falls from trees. Thin infested fruit at ping-pong-ball size. Scrape loose bark from trunk. Remove large weeds and debris from below tree. Hang codling moth pheromone traps: two per large tree, one per small tree. Spray just-hatched larvae with *Bacillus thuringiensis* (Bt). Release trichogramma wasps, beneficial insects that are their natural predators. Plant flowering cover crops such as clover, mustard, sweet alyssum, buckwheat, or daisies.
Flathead borers	Protect trunks and bark from damage by coating trunks of young trees with thinned, white latex paint. Dig out borers from trunk and seal scar with tree-patching compound. Destroy infested wood.
Japanese beetles	Hand-pick. Milky spore disease. Pheromone traps.
Leaf rollers and tiers	Hand-pick.
Mites	Spray with dormant oil when buds are just opening (in summer for pears).
Peach tree borers	Dig cautiously into bark and destroy the larva. Spread mothballs around the trunk and cover them with 3 to 4 inches of soil to kill borers in the trunk. (Remove mothballs before irrigation or winter rains begin, and don't apply in summer.)
Peach twig borers	Dormant oil spray.
Pear psyllas	Dormant oil spray. Summer infestations can be controlled with 2 to 3 sprays applied one week apart.
Pear sawfly	Spray for codling moth in the spring to control sawfly as well.
Plum curculios	Gather fallen fruit daily. Promptly gather and destroy infested fruit. Lay a tarp under the tree and shake the tree branches; collect and destroy fallen curculios. Keep trees well pruned. Apply Imidan (considered by some to be less harmful to people and the environment than rotenone and other botanical pesticides) according to label instructions as soon as insects appear, and again one week later.
Rose chafers	Hand-pick. Place a jar of decomposing rose chafers under the vine.
Scales	Dormant oil spray.
Shothole borers	Prevent sunburn on young trees by coating trunks with thinned, white latex paint. Avoid damage to bark.
Tent caterpillars	Use *Bacillus thuringiensis*.

apple maggot

codling moth

leaf tier

rose chafer

Japanese beetle   peach tree borer   plum curculio   shothole borer   scale

Diseases of Fruits and Their Controls

DISEASE	CONTROL
Apple and pear scab	Remove and burn fallen leaves. Spray with micronized sulphur when buds begin to swell in spring, at petal fall, and twelve days after petal fall. Spray sulphur every week during warm, wet, or damp weather.
Bacterial leaf spot	Remove and burn infected and fallen leaves. Prune for good ventilation. Avoid overfertilization.
Bitter rot (apples)	Remove infected fruit and fruit mummies. Scrape off loose bark. Prune away dead and damaged limbs.
Black knot (plums and prunes)	Plant new trees away from infected trees. Prune away infected growth 4 inches below the infection.
Black and white rot	Prune out diseased branches. Remove fruit mummies. Prune for good ventilation.
Brown rot (stone fruit)	Pick all fruits from trees at harvest. Remove infected fruit, fruit mummies, dead and diseased wood, fallen leaves and fruits. Apply dormant spray. Spray blossoms with bordeaux mixture, fixed copper, or sulphur.
Cedar apple rust	Don't plant near juniper or red cedar (or at least remove galls from nearby junipers).
Crown gall	Avoid injuring trees at planting time and while cultivating. Plant disease-free trees in uninfected soil. Remove galls with disinfected knife and cover wound with tree-patching compound. Remove and burn heavily infected trees.
Crown rot	Supply good soil drainage, and keep trunk dry while watering.
Eutypa dieback (*Cytosporina* canker)	Rough, dark cankers appear on pruning wounds, from which gum may ooze. Sterilize your pruning shears between cuts (use 10-percent bleach and 90-percent water), and paint pruning wounds with pruning compound. Keep the area around the tree clean of dead branches and rotted fruit.
Fireblight	Cut back infected growth 12 inches below diseased portion, sterilizing cutting tool between each cut (use 10-percent bleach and 90-percent water). Apply bordeaux mixture (4 tablespoons per gallon of water) three times weekly during bloom. Control sucking insects, which spread the disease. Prune trees yearly. Avoid overfertilization with nitrogen. Use a sod mulch rather than a cover crop.
Gummosis (or bacterial canker)	Prune for strong branch structure. Avoid injury to bark. Inspect tree for borers and control them (see p. 587). Remove badly injured wood.
Peach leaf curl	Spray thoroughly with bordeaux mixture or lime sulphur when leaves drop in fall, and again in spring when the buds have begun to swell, but before they color. Reapply if rain washes away application within 24 hours. Remove and destroy infected leaves.
Powdery mildew (apples)	Prune for good ventilation. Remove mildewed twigs. Spray with sulphur before bloom and biweekly thereafter through spring, especially when days are warm and nights damp.

Photos by Ron West

Bacterial leaf spot.

Peach leaf curl.

Powdery mildew.

How long does it take a fruit tree to bear after it's been planted?

That depends upon the fruit and its variety, whether it is a dwarf or a standard, local climate conditions, and cultivation factors. Some apples and pears require several years to reach bearing age, although many dwarf apple trees bloom after two or three years. Peaches usually bear at three years, as do sour cherry trees. Sweet cherries begin at five to seven years, and plums at six to seven years. Highly vigorous trees are slower to come into bearing than trees that grow at a normal pace. Trees low in vigor because of poor drainage, lack of nitrogen, and injury to the leaves from insect or disease can be slow to begin fruiting.

What are the reasons that fruit trees may fail to bear?

Low winter temperatures, or spring frosts when the trees—especially early-blooming trees such as apricots, peaches, and sweet cherries—are in bloom, may kill the flowers. If prolonged cold, wet weather occurs during fruit bloom, bees will not fly and cross-pollinate. If only one self-sterile tree is planted, flowers will fail to set fruit. Over-fertilization can induce a tree to grow a lot of foliage at the expense of fruit bearing. Trees in shady locations won't set fruit, or will bear only lightly.

Our apple tree produces a lot of fruit, but the fruit is always very small. Is there something wrong with the tree?

No. It is simply setting more fruit than it can grow to maturity. When the fruit is about the size of a ping pong ball, thin it, leaving one apple every 6 to 8 inches. Other types of fruit can be thinned in this way, leaving enough space between fruits to accommodate their size.

Our apple tree sets a lot of fruit, but then much of it falls off while it's still green. What's the matter with it?

The tree is simply thinning its own fruit. As long as enough remains, consider the job well done.

WHY FRUIT TREES FAIL TO BEAR

•

24 *The Fruits We Grow*

Apples; Crabapples *(Malus pumila)*

How large do apple trees grow?

Apple trees come in the widest variety of sizes of any fruit tree, ranging from dwarfs that grow to only 4 feet, to standards that can reach 30 feet. Standard crabapples, smaller than apples, usually grow to about 15 feet. Semidwarf apples are usually about 13 feet.

Should I plant more than one apple tree for adequate pollination?

Most apple varieties are self-fruitful, but they will bear more heavily and dependably if another variety that blooms at about the same time is planted close by. Check with your nursery to make sure that trees you use for pollinators are reliable for that purpose. Mutsu, Gravenstein, Jonagold, Winesap, and certain other varieties, for example, will not pollinate other varieties.

Aren't there a lot of potential pest and disease problems for apple trees?

The codling moth is a significant pest, as is plum curculio. Apple maggot, fireblight, and San Jose scale can also be problems. Apple trees need to be sprayed with dormant oil, insecticides, and disease-controlling substances at the correct times, according to local conditions. See pages 586-88.

◀ *Harvest apples for storage when they are a bit underripe.*

591

Selected Apple Varieties

NAME	FRUIT DESCRIPTION	USES	TREE CHARACTERISTICS
Akane	Bright red, small fruit with crisp, juicy, white flesh	Cider, drying, eating	Early-bearing; scab- and mildew-resistant
Cortland	Large, round fruit; skin red with blue blush; pure white, crunchy, sweet flesh that resists discoloration after slicing	Cider, cooking, eating, storing	Mid- to late-season; Zones 4-8
Dolgo Crab	Bright red, olive-shaped, ½-inch fruits	Canning, jelly	Self-fruitful; very hardy and disease-resistant; abundant white flowers in spring; slender spreading branches; abundant, glossy, reddish green foliage; needs 400 hours of chilling; Zone 2
Empire	Solid red skin; creamy white, crisp, juicy, flavorful flesh	Cider, eating, storing	Self-fruitful; needs thinning; heavy bearer; Zones 4-7
Golden Delicious	Large fruit with yellow skin and crisp, juicy flesh	Cooking, eating	Self-fruitful; early bearing; skin bruises easily; Zones 5-9
Granny Smith	Large, green fruits; crisp, tart, very juicy, white flesh	Cooking, eating, storing	Needs 500-600 hours of chilling; vigorous; early bearing; heavy producing; needs long growth season (170-190 days from bloom to harvest)
Gravenstein	Highly fragrant; thin skin is light green or orange-yellow with red stripes; yellow-white flesh is crisp and juicy	Cider, cooking, eating	Vigorous; bears in summer; fares best in areas with cool summers; Zones 5-8
Grimes Golden	Yellow, lightly russeted skin; sweet, yellow aromatic flesh	Cider, eating, storing	Moderately resistant to cedar-apple rust and fireblight; Zones 6-8
Jonagold	Large fruits; skin yellow with red strips; crisp, juicy, tart flesh	Cooking, eating, storing	Vigorous; self-sterile; susceptible to mildew and scab; Zones 5-8
Jonathan	Round, red fruits with thin, tough skin; juicy flesh	Cooking, eating, storing	Heavy bearer; disease-resistant; self-fruitful but improves with cross-pollination; needs 700-800 hours of chilling; Zones 5-8
Liberty	Shiny, red fruits with crisp, juicy, yellow flesh	Cooking, eating, storing	Extremely disease-resistant; hardy; vigorous; productive; needs thinning; needs 800 hours of chilling; Zones 4-8
Lodi	Light green to yellow fruits with crisp, juicy flesh	Cooking	Heavy and early bearer; requires pollinator; resists apple scab; Zones 4-8
Macoun	Red skin with a blue blush; firm, juicy, white flesh	Eating	Disease-resistant; popular in the Northeast; needs thinning; tends to bear every other year; resists fireblight; needs 600 hours of chilling; Zones 3-4
McIntosh	Red-striped fruits; white, crisp, aromatic flesh	Cider, cooking, eating, storing	Hardy; heavy bearer; needs thinning; fruits ripen simultaneously; popular in Northeast; resists cedar-apple rust; Zones 4-8 and mild parts of Zone 3
Mutsu (Crispin)	Large, yellow fruits; firm, juicy, spicy flesh	Cider, cooking, eating, storing	Vigorous; heavy and early bearer; self-sterile; resists powdery mildew but susceptible to scab; needs 500-600 hours of chilling; Zones 4-8
Newtown Pippin	Yellow fruits with crisp, aromatic, yellow flesh	Cider, cooking, eating, storing	Large and vigorous; early bearing; self-fruitful; Zones 5-8

Selected Apple Varieties

NAME	FRUIT DESCRIPTION	USES	TREE CHARACTERISTICS
Northern Spy	Skin light green with red stripes; flesh firm, crisp, juicy, and yellow	Cooking, eating, storing	Slow to bear fruit (up to 15 years); heavy bearer; hardy; good in northern states; needs 800 hours of chilling; Zones 4-8
Red Delicious	Dark red, shiny skin; five lobes on the blossom end; tall, tapered shape; crisp, tender, mild, juicy flesh	Eating	Many Delicious varieties; productive and fast growing; self-sterile (needs a pollinator within 100 feet); resists fireblight and cedar-apple rust; Zones 5-8
Rome Beauty (Red)	Large, round, red fruit; white, tart, crunchy flesh	Cider, cooking, eating	Vigorous; early bearing; self-pollinating; Zones 5-8
Spartan	Deep red fruits; aromatic, firm, white flesh	Eating	Early and heavy bearer; self-fruitful (yields increase if planted with Lodi); resists scab, mildew, and fireblight; good in Midwest
Stayman Winesap	Deep red color; tender, juicy, tart, yellow flesh	Cider, cooking, eating	Resists fireblight; needs 600-800 hours of chilling; needs pollinator; Zones 5-8
Winter Banana	Large, pale yellow fruits with a light red to pink blush; crisp, tender, coarse-grained, flavorful flesh	Cider, eating, storing	Bears at a very young age; needs pollinator; needs 100-400 hours of chilling; good in mild-winter West Coast areas; Zones 4-6

A mature standard apple tree is one of the stateliest of trees.

Positive Images, Jerry Howard

Apple-picking tool.

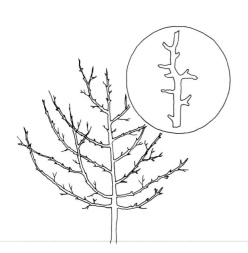

SPUR-TYPE APPLE TREE

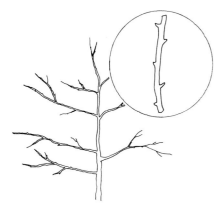

REGULAR APPLE TREE

Spur-type trees have more fruit spurs on each limb and bear from the trunk out.

How are apple trees pruned?

Apples produce fruit on terminal spurs (short, stiff, thin, fruit-bearing branches) on two- to eight-year-old wood. Thin out weak, unproductive, and tangled branches to allow sunlight to penetrate to the center of the tree. Remove old spurs by cutting back the branches they are on. To regulate your tree's height, cut back upper branches to short lateral branches. (See also pages 581-82.)

Should I thin the fruit from my apple tree?

Standard apple trees should be thinned (see pg. 589), but crabapples need not be.

When should I start harvesting apples?

Harvest apples when the skins change from a dull to a bright color. The seeds of ripe apples are a solid, dark brown. Harvest apples for storage while they're a bit underripe. Don't let ripe fruit hang on the tree.

What are spur-type apple trees?

Spur-type apple trees are extremely productive semidwarfs (12 to 15 feet tall and equally wide), which bear fruiting spurs all along their branches, rather than mostly toward the ends.

I have just moved to Mississippi from New England, where I had several apple trees. Can I grow apple trees in the South?

The only places where apples usually aren't grown is where there are very warm winters (as in southern Florida), extremely dry heat (as in the Nevada desert), or uncommonly fierce weather combined with short growing seasons (as in Montana). Yet there are apple trees even in these places, grown by folks who tend their trees carefully and who have done a little research into unusual and hard-to-find varieties (such as Tropical Beauty and Beverly Hills, both of which are adapted to warm climates, and Honeygold, a very cold-hardy variety).

Apricots (*Prunus armeniaca*)

How can I incorporate apricot trees into my garden design?

Apricots are as ornamental as they are productive, with their soft green, heart-shaped leaves and brilliant white blossoms. Their gnarled trunks and branches lend beauty and interest to a landscape at any time of year. Because the dwarf varieties grow well in containers, gardeners living in climates too cold for apricots can grow dwarfs in tubs set on dollies, and bring them under cover during the winter months.

How big do apricot trees get?

Dwarfs are 8 feet or smaller; semidwarfs, 12 to 15 feet; standards, 15 to 20 feet. All types are usually about as wide as they are tall, depending upon how you prune them.

Can apricot trees be grown outside only in very warm climates?

Apricot trees will grow surprisingly far north, but they won't set fruit, because they have the maddening habit of blossoming so early that subsequent late frosts ruin the fruit. Though it is true that apricot trees will grow in Zones 5 through 9, it is more accurate to say that they will produce fruit where there are *not* heavy, late spring frosts. Even in marginal areas, however, if you choose the proper variety for your locality, and plant an apricot tree in a spot that is neither a frost pocket nor the first place in your yard to receive spring heat (which will cause too-early blossoming), it may bear fruit, if not every year, at least in some years. One of the hardier varieties, such as Moongold, may even thrive in a protected area in Zone 4.

Selected Apricot Varieties

NAME	FRUIT DESCRIPTION	USES	TREE CHARACTERISTICS
Chinese (Mormon Chinese)	Yellow to orange fruits with good flavor	Eating	Late-flowering habit protects it from spring frosts; trees bear at young age; heavy producer; needs 700 hours of chilling
Early Golden	Large, sweet, succulent fruits with smooth, orange-gold skin	Canning, cooking, drying, eating	Self-fruitful, but improved with pollinator; needs 450 hours of chilling; good in South and Southwest; Zones 5-8
Goldcot	Firm, golden yellow skin; tangy, juicy, freestone flesh	Canning, freezing, eating	Late-flowering habit protects it from spring frosts; needs thinning; very hardy; vigorous; heavy-bearing; self-fruitful; good in Northwest; Zones 5-8
Moongold	Soft, golden fruit with firm, sweet, freestone flesh	Canning, eating, preserves	Very hardy (to -25° F.); disease-free; needs Sungold as a pollinator; Zones 4-9
Moorpark	Large, orange fruits with a red blush; juicy, highly aromatic flesh	Canning, drying, eating	Vigorous dwarf; beautiful pinkish white blossoms; good in the Southeast and the West Coast; needs 600 hours of chilling; self-pollinating, but better in pairs; Zones 5-8
Sungold	Gold skin with orange blush; sweet, juicy, freestone flesh	Canning, eating, preserves	Heavy bearer; pink blossoms; pollinate with Moongold; the two are the hardiest of all apricots; Zones 4-9

What is the best place to grow an apricot tree?

Plant apricot trees in well-drained, fertile soil, in a spot that is cool in spring and warm in summer.

Do apricot trees need to be planted in pairs for pollination?

Most varieties are self-fertile, but planting two or more trees assures a maximum harvest, especially in cooler climates.

Do apricot trees need a lot of pruning?

Fruit is borne on one- to four-year-old spurs. Each year, prune heavily to remove old, spent spurs, cutting the old wood right back to the larger branches. If for some reason you cannot prune, make sure to thin the fruit, soon after it sets, to 3- to 4-inch spacings (see page 589).

When should I harvest apricots?

Most varieties ripen all their fruit within a one-week period, and it must be harvested as soon as it begins to soften slightly. Fruit for canning and processing may be picked while it is still slightly hard, but tree-ripened fruit is best for eating fresh or drying. A mature tree can produce as much as 100 pounds of fruit.

How are apricots dried?

Split the apricots open at the seam, remove the pit, and lay the halves open-side-up on a tray. Place them in an oven with a pilot light or dry them outdoors, bringing them under cover at night, until they are shriveled and slightly leathery.

Cherries (Prunus cerasus; P. avium)

In what kind of climate must cherry trees be grown?

Although generally cherry trees can be grown in Zones 4 through 9, sweet cherries are more demanding than sour cherries. Depending upon the variety, sweet cherries need at least 800 hours of winter chill and cannot withstand high summer temperatures. Significant rainfall in the weeks before the harvest can make the fruit split. Humid climates are not favorable to sweet cherries, nor is foggy weather. Sour cherries are easier to grow, so if you have hot summers where you live, or humidity, fog, or a short chilling season, start with the sours. Sour cherries make better preserves and pies, and when tree-ripened they can be delicious eaten fresh, with a taste more tart and sweet than sour.

Should I plant more than one cherry tree for cross-pollination?

Sour cherries are self-pollinating. Two, and sometimes three, sweet cherry trees must be planted within pollinating distance of each other.

Do cherry trees require a lot of watering?

The ground beneath cherry trees should be kept moist, because the trees have shallow root systems that can easily dry out. Use organic mulches. Water newly planted trees every week; older, established trees may be watered less often. Sour cherries tolerate drought better than sweets. Water the trees after the harvest, and every three to four weeks thereafter if there are no summer rains.

Selected Cherry Varieties

NAME	FRUIT DESCRIPTION	TREE CHARACTERISTICS	POLLINATOR
Bing (sweet)	Large, firm, aromatic, sweet fruits; dark red skin	Grows best in dry, warm summers; good in the West; does not do well in hot, humid weather; fruit ripens all at once; needs 700 hours of chilling; Zones 5-8	Black Tartarian or Van
Black Tartarian (sweet)	Dark, heart-shaped, soft fruits with sweet, rich flavor	Early-blooming and -ripening tree; heavy bearing; good pollinator; grows 30 feet tall; needs 700 hours of chilling; Zones 5-7	Most other varieties (Lambert not recommended)
Lambert (sweet)	Large, sweet, firm fruit with dark skin and very dark red flesh	Late blooming and bearing; not resistant to splitting; needs 800 hours of chilling; Zones 5-7	Black Tartarian, Rainier, Stella, or Van
Montmorency (sour)	Bright red fruit with firm, yellow flesh	The classic tart cherry; heavy bearing; needs 700 hours of chilling; Zones 5-7	Self-fruitful
Napoleon, or Royal Ann (sweet)	Yellow skin with red blush; sweet, juicy flesh	Ripens midseason; tree grows 20-25 feet tall; heavy bearer; needs 700 hours of chilling; Zones 5-7	Black Tartarian, Stella, or Van
North Star (sour)	Large, light red fruits with red flesh and juice	Naturally dwarf tree, grows 6-12 feet tall; heavy and early bearing; disease-resistant; very hardy; needs 1000 hours of chilling; Zones 4-8	Self-fruitful
Rainier (sweet)	Yellow fruit with a red blush; firm, fine-textured flesh	Early and heavy bearing; split-resistant; very hardy; tolerates hot summers; need 700 hours of chilling	Bing, Black Tartarian, Lambert, Napoleon, Stella, or Van
Stella (sweet)	Heart-shaped, dark red fruit with sweet, juicy flesh	Vigorous and hardy trees; grows 25-30 feet tall; good pollinator; bears early and abundantly; resistant to splitting; needs 700 hours of chilling; Zones 5-8	Self-fruitful
Van (sweet)	Large, dark, firm fruit	Split-resistant fruit; hardy; excellent pollinator; needs 700 hours of chilling; Zones 5-7	Bing, Lambert, Napoleon, Rainier, or Stella

How much pruning and thinning should I give my cherry trees?

Sweet cherries are best trained to a vase shape (see pg. 581) to allow light to penetrate into the center of the tree and to make picking easier. Prune bare-rooted trees down to 24 to 36 inches when you plant them. You needn't thin the fruit of cherry trees.

How can I tell when it's time to harvest cherries?

Harvest Bing and other dark-skinned cherries when the fruit has turned thoroughly dark. Don't be too anxious to get them off the tree—the longer they stay on, the sweeter they'll be. When you pick, leave the stems on the cherries, and take care not to damage the fruiting spurs that the cherries are attached to. Store cherries in the vegetable crisper of your refrigerator until you are ready to use them. Under storage, they need cool, humid air.

How can I keep birds from harvesting all my cherries before I get to them?

The only sure way is to cover your trees with protective netting. It is much easier to accomplish this on dwarf and semidwarf trees. Some people believe birds are less attracted to yellow or golden cherries, such as Golden Sweet.

Sweet Van cherries are hardy and resistant to splitting.

Stark Brothers Nurseries and Orchards

What insects cause problems for cherry trees?

The principal insect pests include black cherry aphids, eye-spotted bud moths, and pear slugs (cherry slugs). The cherry fruit fly (apple maggot) can be a problem in the Northwest. See pages 586-87 for controls.

Are there any diseases that attack cherry trees?

Bacterial canker is one of the most serious, because it can kill young cherry trees. Also known as gummosis, the disease manifests itself by large gobs of amber-colored gum oozing from the branches. Cherry trees growing in areas of high rainfall may experience brown rot. See page 588 for controls.

Our summers are very hot. What can I do to prevent sunscald?

Paint the trunks with a white latex paint to prevent sunscald (extensive cell damage to the bark, caused by the dark trunk getting hotter than the air).

Figs *(Ficus carica)*

May figs be grown only in warm climates?

Although the fig tree and its soft fruit look tropical, and figs are most commonly grown in areas with a Mediterranean climate, they are actually hardy down to 15° F. and can be grown as container plants almost anywhere, so long as they are moved under cover during winter. The plants grow as shrubs in colder areas. Young trees may be damaged by 25° to 27° F. temperatures, and killed by cold at 22° F. In the West and the South, figs can stay in the ground all year, as they are best suited to Zones 8 through 10. In Zone 7, figs may survive in a warm garden location, especially if the trunk is wrapped with an insulating material such as fiberglass insulation or burlap stuffed with dried leaves or straw during the winter. Cover the insulation with waterproof plastic, tied closed at the top, and mulch the root zone deeply. Unprotected fig bushes that die back to the ground will grow up again when the warm weather resumes. Wherever you plant a fig tree, it must receive full sun.

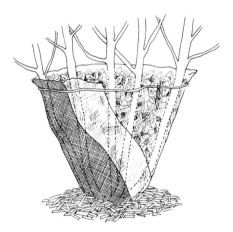

Fig trees may be protected over winter in cool climates by wrapping the trunks with burlap stuffed with dried leaves or straw.

What kind of soil do fig trees need?

Fig trees do best in heavy clay soil that is poor in nutrients, but they must have good drainage. The soil should not be acid, nor should it contain excessive boron, sodium, or herbicides. Too much nitrogen encourages lush foliage at the expense of a heavy fruit crop.

Must I plant more than one fig tree for cross-pollination?

No. Almost all figs are self-fertile.

Is it difficult to espalier fig trees?

Fig trees are quite amenable to training, and make excellent espaliers. They are usually trained with three to five principal branches. The tree can be kept quite low and wide by yearly pruning of the top growth during the dormant season. (See pages 581-82.)

Should I thin the fruit on my fig tree?

Though fig trees often set very heavy crops, their fruit does not need thinning. In the West most figs bear two crops. The first, or *breba*, crop comes in early summer, and the second in fall.

Should I fertilize my fig tree?

Do not fertilize fig trees unless they are growing in extremely poor soil and are putting out less than 1 foot of new growth a year. If so, and you know that the cause is poor soil rather than unsuitable weather, add small amounts of nitrogen—about 1 pound for a mature tree—in winter. The best soil amendment for figs is bulky organic matter, which will provide the water retention and drainage that the trees need.

Will fig trees tolerate drought?

Yes, but for the best crop, water trees deeply whenever the soil dries out 3 to 4 inches below the surface. Stop watering as soon as the fruit begins to swell.

How will I know when it's time to harvest my figs?

In general, figs are ripe and ready to be harvested when they are heavy enough to weigh their stems down. The easiest way to tell is simply to pick a few (with their stems attached) and bite into them to see if they taste ripe.

Selected Fig Varieties

NAME	DESCRIPTION	USES	CHARACTERISTICS
Brown Turkey	Purplish green to mahogany-brown skin; sweet, juicy, strawberry-colored flesh	Canning, drying, eating, jam	Hardiest of all figs; bushy plant grows to 10 feet; self-pollinating; winter hardy; needs 100 hours of chilling; Zone 5 with protection
Celeste	Violet-brown skin; light pink, firm, sweet flesh	Eating	Hardy; self-pollinating; popular in Southeast; Zones 7-10
Conadria	Large fruits with light green skin; whitish pink flesh	Drying, eating	Very productive; good in very hot-summer areas (West Coast); needs 100 hours of chilling
Texas Everbearing	Fruit dark brown with green cast; amber flesh	Preserves	Bears fruit from late summer to late fall; small tree, good for container growing; self-pollinating; good in Southwest; Zones 7-10

How are figs stored?

Don't store them stacked up or they may ferment. If you plan on canning them, harvest figs just before they are ripe. If you plan on drying them, leave them on the tree until they begin to shrivel and drop off; then pick them, arrange them on trays, and dry them in the sun or a slow oven.

Do figs have many pest and disease problems?

Figs are virtually pest- and disease-free, and do not need to be sprayed.

Peaches; Nectarines *(Prunus persica; P. persica var. nuciperica)*

What is the difference between peaches and nectarines?

Only the smooth, fuzzless skin of the nectarine.

In what regions will peach trees survive?

The hardier cultivars will survive temperatures of -10° F. once they're well established. Generally speaking, peaches and nectarines can be grown in Zones 6 through 9. The crucial factors are the depth of winter temperatures and the lateness of spring frosts. Cold, damp spring weather is not suitable to peaches, nor are cool or humid summers. Varieties with low chill requirements (see p. 570) will bear in Zones 9 and 10; most varieties need 600 to 900 hours of chilling. The ideal peach-growing climate is found in the inland valleys of California, where spring comes early, and summers are entirely without rain and of low humidity.

I live near Boston. Is there any chance I could grow peaches?

Contact your local Extension Service agent and ask for a list of varieties best suited to your area. There may be a warm location on your property where a peach tree will grow, or you could use a genetic dwarf peach or nectarine in a container, which could be brought under cover during sub-zero weather. These miniature trees are charming and much easier to manage than large, in-ground peach trees. Give peaches and nectarines full sun, and avoid frost pockets.

What kind of soil do peach trees need?

A well-drained, rich, sandy loam is best for peaches. Heavy clay soils should be modified with large amounts of bulky organic material prior to planting. Continue adding more organic matter throughout the lifetime of the tree.

Is it necessary to plant pairs of peach trees for pollination?

Most varieties are self-fertile.

Are there any advantages to growing dwarf peach or nectarine trees?

There are some excellent genetic dwarf varieties (see p. 575). If you plant them in tubs, you can move them out of the rain and thus avoid peach leaf curl without spraying. In addition, it takes only a small amount of netting to protect the fruit from birds.

Selected Peach Varieties

NAME	FRUIT DESCRIPTION	USES	TREE CHARACTERISTICS
Belle of Georgia	Soft, aromatic fruit with white flesh; freestone flesh tinged with red	Canning, desserts, eating	Hardy; vigorous; self-fruitful; disease-resistant; needs 800-850 hours of chilling; Zones 5-8
Bonanza	Yellow flesh with red blush; freestone	Eating	Genetic dwarf, grows 4-5 feet tall; masses of large, pink, self-fruitful blossoms; very productive; needs 250-500 hours of chilling; good for South and West
Early Elberta	Large, yellow-fleshed, freestone fruits with sweet, rich flavor	Canning, eating, freezing	Hardy, productive, and reliable; self-fruitful; best for warm climates; needs 500 hours of chilling; Zones 5-8
Elberta	Skin yellow with a pink blush; juicy, yellow, freestone flesh; peels easily	Canning, eating, freezing, jam	Disease-resistant; productive, though tends to drop mature fruits; self-fruitful; needs 800-950 hours of chilling; Zones 5-8
Hale Haven	Large, oval-shaped, yellow fruit with red blush, tough skin; firm, sweet, juicy flesh	Canning, freezing	Abundant producer; vigorous; hardy; needs 850 hours of chilling; Zones 5-8
Honey Babe	Yellow skin with deep red blush; sweet, freestone, red-speckled, orange fruit	Eating	Genetic dwarf, grows 3-5 feet tall; good in West; dense foliage; self-fertile; needs 500-600 hours of chilling; Zones 6-9
Indian Blood Cling	Crimson red skin and flesh; clingstone; tart flavor	Baking, eating, preserves	Resistant to bacterial leaf spot and brown rot; dependable; heavy bearing; needs 750-900 hours of chilling
J.H. Hale	Large, round, uniform, firm fruits with yellow flesh; skin deep crimson and almost fuzzless	Canning, eating	Must have a pollinator; excellent keeper; needs 850-900 hours of chilling; Zones 5-8
Red Haven	Red, nearly fuzzless fruit; firm, yellow, freestone flesh	Canning, eating, freezing	Hardy; self-fruitful; tolerant of cold and leaf spot; heavy yielding and reliable; needs thinning; good in lower Midwest; needs 800-950 hours of chilling; Zones 5-8
Redskin	Large fruit with yellow, freestone, non-browning flesh beneath a red skin	Canning, eating, freezing	Vigorous and productive; resistant to bacterial spot; needs 750 hours of chilling; Zones 5-8
Reliance	Medium-sized fruit with yellow skin, blushed red; bright yellow, juicy, sweet flesh; freestone	Canning, freezing	Self-fruitful; best choice for cold winter areas (to -25° F.); needs 1,000 hours of chilling; Zones 5-8
Rio Oso Gem	Large, yellow fruit with red blush; firm, freestone flesh; excellent flavor	Eating, freezing	Short-lived, not vigorous; self-fertile; needs 800-850 hours of chilling

Selected Nectarine Varieties

NAME	FRUIT DESCRIPTION	TREE CHARACTERISTICS
Fantasia	Skin yellow with red blush; smooth, firm, freestone flesh	Heavy bearing; self-fruitful; susceptible to bacterial leaf spot; needs 500-600 hours of chilling
Flavortop	Large, red-over-yellow fruits; juicy, sweet, fine-textured, freestone flesh	Self-fruitful; vigorous; heavy-bearing; large, showy blossoms; good in both East and West; needs 650 hours of chilling
Garden Beauty	Yellow, clingstone flesh; usually sweet	Genetic dwarf, grows 4-5½ feet tall; large, double, dark pink blossoms; self-fruitful; needs 500-600 hours of chilling
Mericrest	Smooth, dark red fruit with sweet, juicy, yellow, freestone flesh and tangy flavor	Self-fruitful; resists brown rot and bacterial leaf spot; needs 800 hours of chilling; hardiest nectarine; Zones 5-8
Nectar Babe	Large red fruits with sweet, yellow, freestone flesh	Genetic dwarf, growing no more than 6 feet tall; quite productive; needs pollinator (Honey Babe); needs 500-600 hours of chilling; Zone 9
Red Gold	Skin mostly red, with some yellow; deep golden, firm, juicy, freestone flesh; outstanding flavor	Winter hardy; extremely productive and vigorous; self-fruitful; susceptible to bacterial spot and mildew; needs 850 hours of chilling; Zones 5-8

Will I have to give my peach trees much pruning?

Heavy annual pruning is necessary for good crops, because peaches and nectarines bear fruit only on *new* wood. Train young trees to a vase shape (see pg. 581), keeping in mind that good light penetration is vital. When the trees are mature, begin removing one half of the new wood late in the dormant season. Prune the tops of peach and nectarine trees annually to maintain a workable height.

Check with your local Extension Service to determine the best method of pruning for your area. Each climate dictates certain pruning programs that may not apply to other climates.

Should I fertilize my peach trees?

Advice for fertilizing varies from one area to another, so it is best to contact your local Extension Service agent on this matter. Here are a few rules of thumb. Peaches and nectarines are heavy feeders, and should be fertilized at least once a year, preferably in late spring just as the new growth gets going. Fertilizing a peach or nectarine after the harvest can be risky business, because ensuing cold weather could damage the new, lush growth that results from fertilization and thus weaken the tree. During the growing season, mulch with compost or manure around mature trees to add some nitrogen and other plant nutrients and increase the content of organic matter in the soil.

Is it true that peaches and nectarines are prone to many pests and diseases?

Leaf curl and brown rot are the foremost diseases. Powdery mildew must be contended with in humid climates. Peach tree

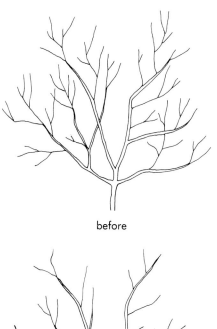

before

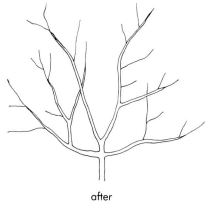

after

Peach trees should be heavily pruned to a vase shape.

Before peaches are the size of ping pong balls, thin fruits, leaving about 6 inches between each one.

borer is the major insect pest, though plum curculio, San Jose scale, and aphids can also be problems. See pages 586-88 for controls, and contact your local Extension Service for the spraying program that has been developed specifically for your area.

Should I thin peach fruit?

Thin the fruit before it reaches ping-pong-ball size, leaving 6 to 8 inches between fruits of early ripening varieties, and 4 to 6 inches between late ripeners. Leaving too many fruits on the branches weakens the tree considerably.

When can I harvest my peaches?

A ripe peach or nectarine should come free with just a gentle tug. Keep fresh-picked fruit in a cool place, and eat it as soon as possible.

Pears *(Pyrus communis; P. pyrifolia)*

What is the difference between European and Asian varieties of pears?

The most common European varieties of pears grown in North America include Bartlett, Bosc, Anjou, Seckel, and Comice. They range in color from brown, green, and red to many shades of yellow, and in form from almost oval to bell-shaped. Asian pears, on the other hand, look much like apples, with very juicy and crisp, mild-flavored, somewhat coarse-textured flesh. They are grown much like European pears, though they are slightly hardier; they need cross-pollination from European or other Asian pears.

What kind of climate do pears need?

Depending on the variety, pears may be grown in Zones 3 through 9. All pears need a certain amount of winter chill, which makes them difficult to grow in frost-free areas, and yet any pear will suffer blossom damage from spring frosts. Give all pear trees a sunny, low-frost location.

Are pear trees particular about the soil they grow in?

Pear trees prefer deep, somewhat heavy soils containing good amounts of organic matter. They tolerate wet soils better than do apples and peaches.

Should I plant more than one pear tree for cross-pollination?

Yes, they should be planted in pairs or larger groupings. Although some varieties are self-fertile, they will produce better crops if another variety of a similar bloom period is growing nearby.

Selected Pear Varieties

NAME	FRUIT DESCRIPTION	USES	TREE CHARACTERISTICS
Anjou (Beurre D'Anjou)	Large, light green fruit; mild, aromatic, somewhat dry flesh	Canning, drying, eating, storing	European; large; vigorous; hardy; needs pollinator (Bosc or Bartlett); somewhat blight-resistant; needs 800 hours of chilling
Bartlett	Large, golden fruit blushed with red; sweet, juicy, white flesh	Canning, eating, preserves	European; vigorous; highly productive; long-lived; partially self-fruitful in arid or warm climates, but needs pollinator elsewhere (Anjou or Bosc); needs 800 hours of chilling; Zones 5-7
Bosc (Beurre Bosc)	Long, thin-necked, tapered fruits; heavily russeted skin; firm, rich, sweet, aromatic flesh	Baking, drying, eating	European; slow-growing but productive; needs pollinator; susceptible to fireblight in warm, moist areas; needs 800-900 hours of chilling; Zones 5-8
Chojuro (Old World)	Skin thick, brown, russetted; flesh firm, highly flavored	Storing	Asian; needs thinning; needs pollinator (Shinseiki, Hosui, Bartlett); needs 450-500 hours of chilling
Clapp's Favorite	Large, elongated, lemon-yellow fruit with russet flecks; fine-grained, sweet, white flesh	Canning, eating	European; strong, hardy, vigorous tree; susceptible to fireblight
Comice	Very large, thick-skinned, yellow fruits with red blush; juicy, firm, sweet flesh	Eating	European; very late ripening; large; somewhat fireblight-resistant; does well in Oregon and California; needs 600 hours of chilling
Hosui	Brownish orange skin; juicy, sweet flesh similar to a melon	Storing	Asian; needs pollinator (Chojuro, Bartlett, Shinseiki); popular in California and the Northwest; needs 450-500 hours of chilling
Kieffer	Large, yellow fruits with red blush; crisp, juicy white flesh	Baking, canning, preserves, storing	European; hardy; vigorous; dependable; tolerates hot weather, but grows well in most areas; highly resistant to fireblight; needs 350 hours of chilling; Zones 4-9
Moonglow	Large fruit is dull yellow with red blush; soft, white flesh	Canning, eating, storing	European; developed by USDA for blight resistance; bears heavily while still young; needs pollinator; excellent pollinator for other varieties; needs 700 hours of chilling; Zones 5-8
Seckel (Sugar Pear)	Small, yellow-green skin with red blush; extremely sweet, very juicy flesh	Canning, eating, pickling and spicing	European; bears abundantly; some blight resistance; self-fruitful but better with cross-pollination; grows only 15-20 feet tall; needs 500-800 hours of chilling; Zones 5-8
Shinseiki	Large, round, yellow fruit; mild, sweet, crisp, creamy white flesh	Eating, storing	Asian; heavy-bearing; needs pollinator (Bartlett, Chojuro, Hosui); moderate resistance to fireblight; needs 450 hours of chilling; Zones 6-9
20th Century (Nijiseiki)	Medium-sized, yellow fruit with green mottle; quite juicy, mild, crisp flesh	Eating, storing	Asian; ornamental tree with large, glossy leaves; productive; tolerates drought and heat, but not disease resistant; needs 450-500 hours of chilling; Zones 6-9

Do pear trees need much pruning?

Pears have an upright growth habit that is conducive to training for a vase shape (see pg. 581), but like apples, they produce on long-lived spurs and need little pruning. Remove tangled, weak, and diseased limbs, and cut away wood that does not conform to the shape you desire for the tree. Young trees can be trained to three or four scaffold branches emanating from the trunk.

Should I thin pear fruit after it sets?

Both European and Asian varieties should be thinned to stand 4 to 6 inches apart if the tree sets a heavy crop. Often they don't need thinning at all.

How much fertilizing do pear trees need?

Excess nitrogen encourages lush stem growth that is highly susceptible to fireblight. Do not fertilize a pear tree that is putting out at least 12 inches of new growth a year and setting a good amount of fruit. If you do fertilize, do so sparingly. A thick mulch of organic matter is highly beneficial, and will usually provide an adequate supply of nutrients.

When should I harvest my pears?

Asian varieties should be left on the tree to ripen. After you pick them they will keep in the refrigerator for months. European pears must be picked at full size but while still green and quite unripe. The seeds of a harvest-ready pear will be light brown to brown. To ripen the harvested fruit, keep it in a cool (50°-70° F.), dark place until the blossom end turns slightly soft. Placing several pears together in a paper bag hastens the process. Check the fruits often for ripeness. Winter varieties, such as Anjou and Bosc, should be held at cool (32° to 34° F.) temperatures from one to four months. Take these pears out of the refrigerator a week before you plan to eat them.

What can I do to combat pear fireblight?

Fireblight is the great enemy of pears, so much so that in some areas pears are impossible to grow because the disease is so widespread. Ask your local Extension Service agent if you aren't sure about your area. Plant resistant varieties, and check your trees closely in the spring for any shriveled, darkened growth (a burned appearance). Cut it off immediately, taking with it 9 inches of undiseased wood as well. After each cut, sterilize your cutting shears (use 10-percent bleach and 90-percent water). Bordeaux mixture applied at a solution of 1 tablespoon per quart of water when 20 percent of the blossoms have opened, and again when 70 percent of them have opened, and once more at full blossom, will help control the problem. (See also pg. 588.)

Both Asian and European pears should be picked when they are still unripe; the seeds of a harvest-ready pear are light brown to brown.

Aphids and other sucking insects spread the disease, so control them as described on pages 587 and 656.

Are there other pests or diseases that afflict pears?

Pear psylla, pear slug, codling moth, and most other insects that bother apples. For controls, see page 587.

Persimmons *(Diospyros virginiana* and *D. Kaki)*

Are persimmons hard to grow?

Perhaps there is no fruit tree so beautiful and easy to care for as the persimmon. It needs no spraying or pruning (except perhaps for shaping or removing dead or tangled limbs), little or no fertilizing, and, once established, no irrigation in most regions. It can withstand damper soil than most trees.

What do persimmon trees look like?

They are medium to large sized and well shaped, with large, pointed, oval leaves, and serve as excellent shade givers. The foliage, which turns yellow, orange, and red in autumn, drops from the trees to leave a colorful display of ripened fruit hanging on the branches until winter.

What do persimmons taste like?

The fruits are delicious, whether eaten fresh, sliced in sweet salads, baked in persimmon puddings, breads, and cookies, made into wine, or dried—they taste something like dates and are a great delicacy in Asia.

What is the difference between American and Oriental persimmons?

The American variety *(Diospyros virginiana)*, grows in the wild from Connecticut south, and west from Kansas to Texas. It is hardy to -25° F. Its fruits are small (from 1 to 2 inches in diameter), with seeds that Native Americans used for making bread. Notably, the fruit must be fully ripe before it can be eaten; it is otherwise unbearably astringent. Oriental persimmons *(Diospyros Kaki)* are larger and often seedless. The trees are less hardy than the trees of the American species, but will withstand winter temperatures down to 0° F. once established. The non-astringent types may be eaten while still firm, while the astringent varieties, such as Hachiya, must be fully ripe to be eaten fresh.

How large do persimmon trees grow?

American persimmons grow to 40 feet; Oriental types, to 30 feet. You can easily prune either type down to smaller sizes, including espaliered configurations, although you need only remove damaged, dead, or crossed limbs. Fruit thinning is unnecessary.

Where will persimmons grow?

American persimmons will grow in Zones 4 through 8; Oriental persimmons, in Zones 7 through 10.

Are persimmons fussy about their soil needs?

Though persimmons prefer a loamy, well-drained soil, they tolerate wet soils fairly well. Plant in a sunny location so the fruit will ripen.

Do persimmons need to be planted in groups?

With the exception of Meader, American persimmons need a pollinator nearby. Oriental persimmons produce seedless fruit without a pollinator.

When are persimmons harvested?

American persimmons ripen in the fall, about a month earlier than Oriental types. Harvest them before the first frost, when the fruit has colored but is still firm. If you pick them before they are fully ripe, set them stem-end-down at room temperature until soft. Nonastringent oriental types can be eaten right away; place astringent types stem down at room temperature until they are very soft and sweet.

Selected Persimmon Varieties

NAME	FRUIT DESCRIPTION	USES	TREE CHARACTERISTICS
Early Golden	Large, sweet fruits; good flavor	Canning, eating	American; somewhat self-pollinating, but better with a pollinator; hardy
Fuyu	Round and flat-shaped, shiny, orange-red fruit; nonastringent; delicious, mild, sweet flesh	Drying, eating (peeled), freezing	Oriental; self-fruitful; hardy; needs 200 hours of chilling
Hachiya	Large, acorn-shaped fruits; deep orange skins; very sweet when soft and ripe; astringent	Cooking, drying	Oriental; extremely ornamental tree, especially with bright fall foliage; self-fruitful; needs 200 hours of chilling; Zones 7-9
Meader	Orange skin with red blush; sweet, high-quality fruit	Canning, eating	American; hardy; productive; self-fruitful, very ornamental tree with large, dark green foliage; bears early; good in colder areas (to -35° F.); ripens in October
Tanenashi	Astringent until fully ripe; seedless; large orange-red fruits with excellent flavor	Eating	Oriental; grows to 40 feet; self-pollinating; heavy bearing

Plums and Prunes *(Prunus* spp.)

Are plums difficult to grow?

Plums are one of the easiest fruits to grow. They come in the widest variety of colors, shapes, flavors, and sizes of all fruits. There is at least one plum variety that will grow in any of Zones 3 through 10. You haven't tasted a good plum until you've had one sun-ripened on the tree!

What is the difference between a plum and a prune?

Prunes are made from plums that, because they are small and not too juicy, dry easily. Prunes are usually made from the European-type plums.

What are the differences between European, Japanese, and American plums?

The fruit of European plums is usually small and egg-shaped, with dry, very sweet flesh (although some varieties are juicy and unsuitable for drying); the trees are upright and need little

Underwood plums, a Japanese-American cross with yellow flesh and a mild flavor.

thinning or pruning. European plum trees are hardier (Zones 5-8), later blooming, and later ripening than Japanese types.

The large, soft, juicy fruits of the Japanese plums are usually born on branches that tend to hang, or "weep." Their flesh ranges from sweet to tart, some types having sweet outer flesh and tart flesh close to the pit. The trees are less hardy than European types (Zones 5-9). They blossom very early in spring, and their foliage is lighter green than that of European plums.

American plum trees, usually called bush or cherry plums, are by far the hardiest of the three types (Zones 3-7). Native American plums are tart and tough-skinned, good for jellies and sauces. American hybrid plums will thrive where weather conditions are too harsh for other fruits. You can also choose from hybrid crosses of American and Japanese plums, or the native bush or tree forms. Check with your local Extension Service for the best varieties for your area.

Selected Plum Varieties

NAME	FRUIT DESCRIPTION	USES	TREE CHARACTERISTICS
Burbank	Large, purple fruits with firm, juicy flesh; semifreestone; excellent, sweet flavor	Canning, eating	Japanese; naturally small tree (12-15 feet); needs 400 hours of chilling; Zones 5-9
Green Gage	Yellow-green skin; sweet, amber flesh	Canning, cooking, eating, preserving	European; hardy; productive; self-fruitful; needs 500 hours of chilling
Methley	Skin purple with red blush; red, sweet, juicy flesh; distinctive, good flavor	Eating, jelly	Japanese; bears abundantly and consistently; self-fertile; needs 150-250 hours of chilling; Zones 5-9
Ozark Premier	Very large fruits; red skin; yellow, firm, juicy, clingstone flesh; sweet, tangy flavor		Japanese; good in South and Midwest; best with pollinator (other Japanese); Zones 5-9
Santa Rosa	Large, purple-red fruit; purple flesh	Canning, eating	Japanese; vigorous; productive; self-fruitful, but better near other Japanese varieties; very popular in the West; needs 300 hours of chilling; Zones 5-9
Shiro	Large, yellow fruits; yellow, clingstone flesh; sweet, well-flavored, extra juicy	Canning, cooking, eating, preserving	Japanese; reliable; prolific; needs pollinator (Methley, Ozark Premier); needs 150-500 hours of chilling; Zones 5-9
Stanley Prune	Large, dark blue fruits with yellow-green, freestone flesh; highly sweet	Canning, cooking, drying, eating, preserving	European; heavy- and early-bearing; self-pollinating, but better planted with other variety; good for North and Midwest; needs 900 hours of chilling; Zones 5-8
Underwood	Dark red skin; yellow flesh; mild flavor		Japanese-American cross; needs pollinator; recommended for North (hardy to -50° F.), but grows in Zone 8 as well

How big do plum trees get?

Depending on the rootstock on which they are grown, plum trees usually range from 10 to 15 feet in height. European types can be espaliered; bush types can be grown as hedges.

Where should I plant plum trees?

Give plums full sun and well-drained soil. European plums prefer heavy soils, while the Japanese varieties prefer light, loamy soils.

Do plums need pollinator trees nearby?

American plums are self-fertile; European plums, too, are self-fertile, but produce more heavily with a nearby pollinator; Japanese plums must have a pollinator either nearby or grafted onto the same tree.

Do plum trees require a lot of pruning?

American varieties grown as bushes should have their shoots thinned out every two or three years. European plums don't need much pruning other than the removal of unwanted, dead, or tangled limbs, although young trees should be trained to a modified leader or vase shape. Japanese plums need heavy pruning to remove rampant, bushy growth; they are best trained to a vase shape. The fruit of all varieties is borne on both new and old wood; fruit should be thinned to 4- to 5-inch spacings.

How much fertilizer should I give my plum trees?

Plums are smallish trees that bear extremely heavy crops. A thick organic mulch will add nitrogen to the soil. This may be all the tree needs, but many gardeners provide yearly applications of compost and manure.

Can plum trees survive drought?

Yes, once established. Trees growing in areas with dry summers need to be watered deeply whenever the soil dries out 3 to 4 inches beneath the surface.

How ripe should plums be for harvesting if I plan to cook them?

Fruits intended for cooking should be harvested while slightly underripe. Store the fruit in the refrigerator or other cool place, and cook it soon. Plums that will be dried to make prunes should be gathered from the ground promptly after they've fallen from the tree.

Ron West

Plum trees should be grown in full sun, in well-drained soil.

BERRIES AND GRAPES

•

Maggie Oster

A plastic snake draped in a blueberry bush will frighten away birds that compete for the harvest.

Blueberries *(Vaccinium* spp.)

What are the climate needs of blueberries?

Highbush blueberries can be grown in most areas of the United States, but they are best suited to regions that don't often get temperatures below -20° F. and where there are at least 800 hours of chilling (see page 570).

What kind of soil do blueberries require?

Fertile, acid soil (pH of 4.5 to 5), with a lot of organic material and good drainage.

What guidelines can you suggest for helping me determine how many blueberry bushes I should plant?

A healthy, six- to eight-year-old plant can produce up to 10 quarts of fruit per bush. Each mature plant takes up about 4 to 5 feet; the bushes should be planted about 6 feet apart in rows, with about 8 to 10 feet between rows.

How should I plant blueberry bushes?

If possible, plant on a cloudy afternoon as soon as the ground can be worked in the spring. Although blueberries can be planted in the fall, spring planting is safer and is recommended in most areas. Prune off any damaged or excessively long roots, any weak or broken wood, and all flower buds. Plant bushes 1 to 2 inches deeper than the plants grew in the nursery.

Do blueberries need to be planted in pairs for pollination?

Although they are generally self-fruitful, interplanting cultivars will improve yields.

What kind of care must I give blueberries?

Fertilize them two or three times a year, prune once a year, and make sure they have enough water—they need a constant moisture supply for best growth. Use soaker hoses to avoid getting ripening berries wet or they may split. Apply about an inch of water during each watering.

How should I fertilize blueberries?

The first application should be made about one month after planting. Apply about ½ cup of 5-10-10 or 10-10-10 fertilizer per bush in a broad band at least 6 inches, but not more than 12 inches, from the base. Repeat in early July, and, if plants are not vigorous, again in fall after the leaves drop. Mature plants will need about twice this amount of fertilizer each year, two-thirds at the beginning of bloom and the remainder about five or six months later. Do not apply fertilizer too early in the autumn or you may encourage late growth that can winterkill. Because blueberries prefer acid soil, do not use bonemeal or wood ashes around your plants.

What other care do blueberries need?

Cultivate them frequently, but shallowly, and mulch with an organic material to a depth of about 6 inches. Prune to remove diseased or broken wood and to encourage new wood for future seasons' fruits (see illustration).

What are some good blueberry varieties?

Try Flordablue in the South. A good early variety is Collins; midseason, Patriot, Bluecrop, Berkeley, and Blueray; late season, Elliott's Blueberry and Herbert. Be sure to choose a variety suited to your geographic area.

Grapes (*Vitus* spp.)

Are grapes restricted to certain geographic areas?

With literally thousands of different grape varieties suited to a wide range of climates and soils, there is some variety of grape that will flourish in all parts of the United States and in several Canadian provinces. The best grape climates are regions where the growing season is 150 to 180 days, where relative humidity is low, and where summer rains are sparse rather than frequent. Choose the most suitable varieties for your area and plant them in the most sunny, sheltered, well-drained place you can find on your property.

Do I have to provide support for my grape vines?

Although grapes can be grown ornamentally along fences, for best harvest results train vines to grow on a trellis system (see illustration). Be sure to set end posts securely, 3 feet deep and

before pruning

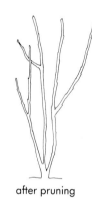

after pruning

Thin young blueberry bushes (2 to 5 years old) by removing all dead and diseased wood, and about one-fourth of their main branches.

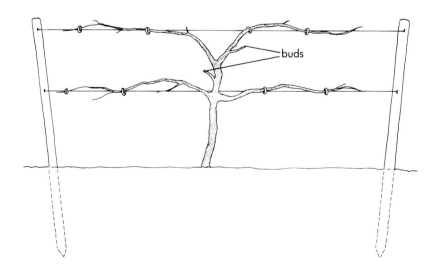

buds

To prune grapevines, during the dormant period following the second or third growing season, choose four of the strongest canes for arms and prune back the rest, leaving two or three buds for renewal spurs; tie each arm along a horizontal wire.

Harvest grapes after their seeds turn brown.

angled outward. Staple no. 9 wire to posts. Most grapes should be planted 8 to 10 feet apart in the row, with rows 10 to 11 feet apart. Plant the vine at the same depth it grew in the nursery, and prune it back to a single stem, three buds tall.

When should I harvest my grapes?

Color is a poor indicator of grape ripeness. Some people judge simply by taste, but the seeds are also good measures: Green seeds mean unripe grapes; brown seeds show maturity. Always use shears to snip off fruit, rather than pulling it off the vines.

Can you suggest some grape varieties to try?

Good early varieties are Himrod and Interlaken Seedless; midseason varieties are Catawba, Concord, Fredonia, and Niagara; a popular late-season variety is Delaware.

Raspberries and Blackberries *(Rubus)*

What is the difference between raspberries and blackberries?

There are red, yellow, purple, and black raspberries and three types of blackberries, recognizable by growing habits. Cultivated blackberries tend to be less hardy than raspberries. Raspberries do best in the North and East, while blackberries are fine in more temperate climates. Raspberries tend to be more delicate and less seedy than blackberries. Some excellent red raspberries include the everbearers Fallred, September, and Southland; the midseason Newburgh; the early Sunrise; and the late Taylor. A good variety for the North is New Heritage. Some popular varieties of black raspberries are the early Allen and New Logan, the midseason Bristol and Cumberland, and the late Blackhawk and Morrison. An excellent blackberry variety is Darrow.

Do raspberries and blackberries need a lot of care?

They are among the easiest plants to grow. If plantings are well cared for, they may produce good crops for ten years or more. Most are seldom bothered by pests or diseases.

What kind of soil do raspberries and blackberries need?

Red raspberries prefer a neutral to alkaline soil of no lower pH than 6.0. Blackberries tolerate a more acid soil, between pH 5.0 and 6.0. Blackberries need a large supply of moisture as they grow and ripen, but the area must also be well drained. The fall before you plan to plant raspberries, prepare the area by digging in lime, compost, and commercial dried sheep manure and plant a cover crop of rye. The following spring, as soon as the soil can be worked, turn under the rye; do not fertilize at this time. Do not plant if the soil is excessively wet. If winters are not too severe in your region, red raspberries may be planted in the fall.

How do I plant raspberries and blackberries?

Cut back the tops of blackberries to about 2 inches. Set plants about 2 feet apart. Cut a slit in the soil with the blade of the shovel, then put the plant roots in the hole, setting the plant so that it is about the same depth as it was in the nursery. Firm soil around the root with your heel. Water heavily immediately after planting and every two days for the following two weeks. Mulch heavily.

How are raspberries and blackberries pruned?

After harvest cut down all canes that bore fruit that year; remove and burn these canes. Cut new canes to stand 4 feet tall. Wear thick gloves for this chore. In the spring you may wish to do further thinning to remove weak canes and to allow better air circulation and ease of picking.

How should I harvest raspberries and blackberries?

Reds are best when they are a deep garnet and begin to push away from the stem. Pick blackberries as soon as they become sweet, not necessarily when they first turn black; fruit should be fully ripened but firm. Pick both varieties often. Blackberries do not spoil as quickly if picked in the morning as when picked in the afternoon. Both are delicate and perishable; place them in small baskets so that they aren't crushed, and never press them down. Keep picked berries in the shade, and move them in to cool storage as soon as possible.

Harvest red raspberries when the fruit begins to push away from the stem, and move the picked fruit into a cool place as soon as possible.

Ron West

Strawberries (*Fragaria* spp.)

What is the difference between June-bearing and everbearing strawberries?

June-bearing strawberries produce one crop per year, in June. Everbearing types produce in spring, and then again in late-summer. A third type, called day-neutral, produces a heavy June crop, and then continues to produce smaller amounts of berries throughout the summer. The June-bearing types are a good choice for those who want a large crop all at once for canning, freezing, or preserving, while the everbearers and day-neutrals are good for those who don't want a big rush of strawberries all at once. The day-neutrals make wonderful hanging-basket plants, because they produce berries on the ends of their runners. Most strawberry lovers plant at least two kinds.

Can I grow strawberries in North Dakota?

You should be able to. Strawberries grow in Zones 3 through 10, though winter protection (mulching) is needed in colder climates. Selection of a suitable variety for your climate is of great importance, and not difficult since there are so many varieties available, both at garden centers and by mail.

What kind of soil should I provide for strawberries?

Strawberries grow best in fairly rich, slightly acid soil (pH 5 to 6) that is high in organic matter and well drained. Raised beds (see pg. 629) are a good idea where the soil is too heavy to drain well. Give strawberries full sun, and avoid planting them in low spots where frost collects. Prepare your soil by incorporating into it well-rotted, or dry, manure and great amounts of organic material at least a season ahead of planting time (preferably in the spring, although fall is acceptable).

What is the technique for planting strawberries?

Container-grown plants can go directly into planting holes with their root balls intact. If you are planting bare-rooted plants, soak them in water as you lay out the planting bed, then arrange them in any configuration, so long as the plants are 12 inches apart. Rows are usually 18 inches apart. Water the bed immediately after planting.

Will I be able to harvest strawberries the first year they are planted?

Not June-bearing varieties. Pinch off the first blossoms on both June-bearing and everbearing varieties. The everbearers will produce blossoms again for a late summer crop, but you will

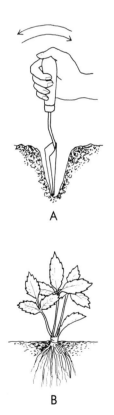

To plant strawberries, (A) make a hole by inserting the blade of a trowel straight into the soil, then pressing it back and forth and tipping it to both sides. Next, (B) set plant so that the base of the crown is at the level of the soil surface; spread out the roots; carefully firm the soil around them, leaving no air pockets in the soil; water well.

The second year after planting, remove enough of the new plants that have formed on runners, leaving 6 to 8 inches between remaining plants.

have to wait for the second year for June-bearers. Also pinch off runners from both types the first year. These practices help the plants establish themselves for better crops in later seasons. The second year after planting, leave enough runners on the plants to allow them to reproduce themselves without overcrowding the bed. Once the plants are 6 to 8 inches apart in the beds, pinch off all runners.

Should I fertilize my strawberry bed?

A constant mulch of compost or well-rotted manure will probably provide adequate fertilization. Add a modest amount of nitrogen if, after the plants have been bearing for a while, the leaves are pale.

Should I water my strawberry bed?

Strawberries need to be kept moist in a well-drained soil. Compost, straw, or manure mulch will help. For best results in dry climates, use soaker hose or a drip-irrigation system.

In order to encourage vigorous plant growth, remove blossom stems on first-year plants as soon as they appear.

How are strawberries harvested?

Once the plants begin to produce, pick the ripe berries every day, stems intact. Refrigerate them until you eat them, and do eat them soon—strawberries don't keep well.

Birds have been the greatest pests of my berries. How can I keep them away?

Plastic netting suspended over supports will keep them from damaging your crop.

Are there many insect pests of strawberries?

Earwigs, slugs, and snails are big problems in some areas. You may also be bothered by Japanese beetles, aphids, thrips, weevils, nematodes, and mites. See pp. 587 and 655-60 for controls.

Pick ripe strawberries daily, keeping their stems intact.

Selected Varieties of Strawberries

NAME	FRUIT DESCRIPTION	PLANT CHARACTERISTICS
Allstar	Large, firm, light red fruits with mild, sweet flesh	June-bearing; productive; disease-resistant
Cardinal	Very large, bright red, firm, sweet fruits	June-bearing; bears abundantly; vigorous; disease-resistant except for verticillium wilt; good for the North, but will do well in Zone 8 also
Earliglow	Large, deep red, glossy, sweet berries	June-bearing; vigorous and productive; resistant to verticillium wilt, leaf spot, and leaf scorch; good in mid-Atlantic, Northeast, and North Central regions; Zones 4-8
Guardian	Very large, glossy, light red, firm berries	June-bearing; later than Surecrop, but more resistant to disease; ripens midseason; Zones 4-8
Ozark Beauty	Large, bright red, long-necked, firm fruits	Everbearing; highly productive; hardy; bears from late spring through September; adaptable to variety of soils; good in the North and Southern mountains; Zones 4-8
Red Chief	Medium to large, glossy, red berries	June-bearing; resistant to root rot; productive; good in Northeast to North Carolina and Illinois
Sparkle	Dark red berries	June-bearing; vigorous; hardy; disease-resistant except for verticillium wilt; good in Northeast to Maryland and Illinois
Surecrop	Large, deep red, glossy, slightly tart berries	June-bearing; productive; disease-resistant; good choice for beginners; good for North and Central United States; Zones 4-8
Tristar	Medium-sized, glossy, deep red, sweet fruits	Day-neutral; highly disease-resistant; runners set fruit even before they take root; good in hanging basket; Zones 5-8

What are the diseases of strawberries?

Verticillium wilt is the principal disease problem. It is best controlled by purchasing certified disease-free plants and rotating crops every three to four years. Root rot is preventable with proper planting depth and well-drained beds. Leaf spot, a fungus disease, can be prevented by providing good air circulation and by planting resistant varieties.

I don't have much room, but I would love to grow strawberries. Is it possible to grow them in containers?

A very attractive way of raising strawberries is to grow them in a barrel. Cut four 1-inch drainage holes in the bottom of a barrel. Cut additional 2-inch holes in the sides of the barrel, spaced about 1 foot apart horizontally and 8 inches apart vertically. Fill the bottom of the barrel with 6 inches of gravel, for drainage. Form a chicken-wire cylinder, 4 inches wide and as long as the barrel is high. Place the cylinder in the center of the barrel and fill it with gravel. For your soil mixture, use equal parts of rich garden loam, compost, and vermiculite or sand.

To set the plants, pour in enough soil mixture on top of the gravel to reach the bottom of the first row of planting holes. Carefully push the strawberry roots through the hole from the outside in, and, making sure that the roots point downward rather than sideward, push them into the soil. Add more soil and gently firm the plants into place. Fill all of the bottom row of holes, before adding more soil to bring the soil level up to the next row of holes. Continue planting in this manner until all holes are filled. When the barrel is filled, add three or four plants to the top. Water thoroughly. See pgs. 653-55 for directions on the care of container plants.

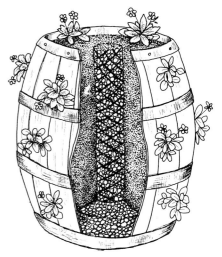

A barrel makes a convenient and attractive planter for growing an abundance of strawberries in a small space.

PART VII
VEGETABLES

25 *Your Home Vegetable Garden*

Raising vegetables can be one of the most satisfying kinds of gardening. Nothing purchased at the store can ever quite match the tender, crisp, sweet freshness of vegetables rushed from the garden to the table. Of all the plants one can grow, vegetables are among the easiest to nurture and the quickest to reach maturity. And, as if these were not assets enough, vegetable plants are often quite beautiful: Witness the ruffles and frills of lettuces and kale, the hearty gleam of tomatoes and peppers, the feathery grace of carrots and asparagus. Well-tended beds filled with the many textures and hues of vegetables and framed by neatly mulched straw paths earn a place of pride in any landscape. To achieve such a goal, all that is needed is thoughtful planning and careful nurture of the soil and the young plants growing in it.

What climatic factors should I consider when planning my vegetable garden?

Begin by determining whether the hardiness zone where you live (pgs. 569-70) is suitable for the vegetable variety you wish to grow. Next, ask yourself some questions about your own location within the general hardiness zone: Do you live at the top or the bottom of a hill? Frost comes earlier to valleys than to high places, because cold air runs downhill at night and collects in "pools," just like water does. Is there a lot of wind where you live? Wind lowers ambient temperatures, creating the "chill factor" that makes you pull your coat tightly around you on

SELECTING THE SITE
— • —

♦ *Nothing purchased at the supermarket can ever quite match the crisp, sweet freshness of vegetables straight from the garden.*

623

blustery days. Do you live in a deep, narrow valley, where the summer sun can be very intense? The direct rays of the sun can burn tender plant leaves, as well as heat the soil to harmfully high temperatures. All these factors contribute to micro-climates—the combined effects of weather and geographical conditions from acre to acre and plot to plot. Because of micro-climates where you garden, you may be able to grow a wider variety of vegetables and fruits than you might have first imagined.

What is the best climate for growing vegetables?

Fortunately for gardeners spread out across the continent, there is no single area in which one must live to enjoy great vegetable gardening success. Some vegetables, such as *Brassicas* (cabbage, broccoli, and Brussels sprouts, for example) prefer cool weather without intense sunlight, while others, such as tomatoes, peppers, eggplants, and melons, require hot, sunny weather. With care, you can grow vegetables for which your climate seems unsuitable. No matter where you live, however, you will find that there are certain vegetables that thrive in your particular climate.

How much sunlight does a vegetable garden need?

Your garden needs full sunlight at least five or six hours a day. If you have no sunny spot, you could create one by pruning back or removing a tree or hedge. Grow vegetables in your front yard, if necessary; a well-kept vegetable garden can only enhance the beauty of a front landscape.

Are there any vegetables that I can grow in the shade?

Lettuce needs at least a half day of full, though not intense, sunlight, but it actually benefits from midday shade. Asparagus and rhubarb will tolerate shade after their growth in early spring. Cucumbers do well in partial shade. Vegetables that survive with minimal sunlight (five to six hours per day) are beets, carrots, cauliflower, radishes, spinach, and Swiss chard.

How close to a large maple tree can I plant my vegetable garden?

Plant it no closer than the outer reaches of the tree's branches, and preferably a few feet farther away than that. Trees too close to a garden will rob the plants of nutrients and water, as well as sunlight.

I have no flat areas in my yard. Is there any way I can have a vegetable garden?

Terrace otherwise-useless slopes with heavy timber or stone walls, filled in with topsoil. Plant vegetables that need the warmest, sunniest conditions on the highest terraces, with more cold-tolerant varieties toward the bottom, where chill temperatures or even late spring or early frosts may settle.

If I don't have a southern exposure for my garden bed, am I at a real disadvantage?

Although southern exposures warm up fastest in the spring, northern exposures are good for growing cool-weather crops such as lettuce and peas. There is no one perfect exposure.

On my small lot, I have little choice about where my vegetable garden will be. Is there any way that I can modify the climate where my garden must be placed?

Yes. Even if an ideal site is unavailable, you can improve weather conditions with the addition of windbreaks, shade-giving structures or plants, mulches (pgs. 647-48), and irrigation practices (pgs. 648-50).

What size garden should I start out with?

This depends on how much space you have available, how much produce you want from your garden, and how much work you are willing to put into it. A modest-sized, 10-by-20-foot plot is quite manageable in terms of weeding, cultivating, planting, harvesting, and, in dry climates, irrigating. Even a 10-by-10-foot plot will give you plenty of room for a salad, or "kitchen," garden, which will supply you with greens and herbs for salads

A 10-by-20-foot garden is easy to manage and produces a great variety and quantity of food for a family.

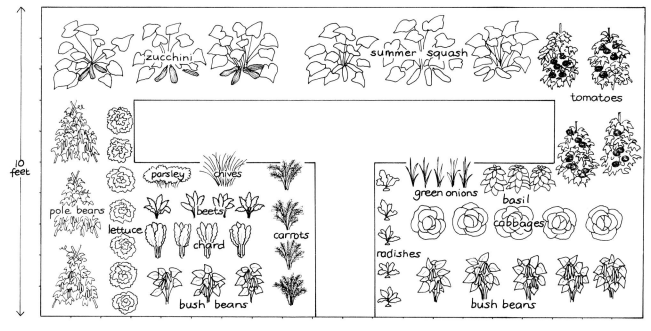

and seasonings on a daily basis. Kitchen gardens traditionally feature lettuce, radishes, tomatoes, peppers, scallions, and herbs. If you want to start more slowly or if you have very limited space, plant vegetables in containers (see pp. 653-55).

WHAT SHALL I GROW?

SHORT-SEASON CROPS

Arugula
Beans (bush)
Beets
Cabbage, early (including Chinese)
Carrots
Lettuce
Mustard greens
Onions (from sets)
Peas
Radishes
Scallions
Turnips

LONG-SEASON CROPS

Artichokes
Asparagus
Beans (dry, lima, and soy)
Celery
Eggplant
Kale
Leeks
Onions
Peppers
Potatoes
Rhubarb
Tomatoes

How can I know which vegetables will do best in my area?

Begin by asking your gardening neighbors and friends, as well as local gardening clubs and your county Extension Service agent, who is intimately acquainted with local growing conditions and is thus an extremely valuable source of information and encouragement. (County Extension Services are branches of the U.S. Department of Agriculture, and often associated with the state university.) Many catalogues provide detailed planting instructions for each variety listed, and seed houses often offer free advice over the telephone to anyone with a question.

What vegetables shall I grow in my small garden?

Here are three good guidelines to follow: Plant the vegetables you and your family like to eat; plant crops that do well in your area; and decide whether you wish to grow crops for fresh use only, or also for freezing, storing, drying, and canning. To get the most out of limited space, plant short-season crops (those that mature rapidly) and follow them in the same spot by another crop of the same or a different vegetable. See the chart on this page for suggestions.

What are the most productive crops?

In space, as well as the time it takes to grow them, the most productive vegetables are tomatoes, followed in order by bush beans, broccoli, onions (from sets; see page 689), beets, carrots, Swiss chard, Chinese cabbage, New Zealand spinach, mustard greens, lettuce, turnips, cabbage, radishes, spinach, and bush (summer) squash.

What are the easiest crops to grow?

Try tomatoes, beans (green and dry), beets, lettuce, potatoes, radishes, most root crops, salad greens, squash (summer and winter), sunflowers, and Swiss chard.

What are the more challenging crops to grow?

In most areas, that list includes cantaloupe, cauliflower, celery, Chinese cabbage, corn, leeks, parsnips, peas, and watermelon.

CROPS THAT GROW BEST IN COOL WEATHER

Artichokes, Jerusalem
Arugula
Asparagus
Beans, broad (fava)
Beets
Broccoli
Brussels sprouts
Cabbage (including Chinese)
Carrots
Cauliflower

Celery
Chicory
Collards*
Endive
Kale
Kohlrabi
Leeks
Lettuce
Mustard greens
Onions

Parsnips
Peas
Potatoes
Radicchio
Radishes
Rhubarb
Rutabagas
Swiss chard*
Shallots
Spinach
Turnips

* Will also grow well in hot weather

CROPS THAT GROW BEST IN WARM WEATHER

Artichokes, globe
Beans (except fava)
Corn
Cowpeas (blackeyed peas)
Cucumbers

Eggplant
Lima beans
Melons
Okra
Peppers

Pumpkins
Soybeans
Spinach, New Zealand
Squash, summer and winter
Sweet potatoes
Tomatoes

What is the purpose of a garden journal?

This can be as fancy or as simple as you like. It should include a map of your garden and a record of what you have planted where, and the date. You may wish to record your impressions of how well or how poorly certain varieties have fared from one year to the next, your smashing successes and regrettable failures—and the way you'll do things next time, now that you know better.

Should my planting rows run north and south or east and west?

More important than compass orientation, a garden's rows (or rectangular planting beds) should run *along* a slope rather than up and down it, and tall-growing plants should not shade other plants.

What other things should I consider when laying out my garden plan?

Be sure to leave room to move around and to bring in equipment, such as a wheelbarrow or garden hose. It's nice, if possible, to have the garden close enough to the kitchen so that you won't hesitate to run out and pluck a few leaves of this or that while the pots boil.

DECIDING ON A GARDEN PLAN

SPACE REQUIREMENTS OF VEGETABLES

Least Space-Consuming

Beans (bush and pole)
Beets
Carrots
Chinese cabbage
Eggplant
Leeks
Lettuce
Mustard greens
Onions
Parsnips
Peppers
Radishes
Sunflowers
Swiss chard
Tomatoes
Turnips

Most Space-Consuming

Artichoke (globe)
Broccoli
Cauliflower
Corn
Cucumbers
Melons
Peas
Potatoes
Sweet potatoes
Winter squash

What are the advantages of growing vegetables in beds rather than in rows?

If you plant in single rows, a path will run between each row and most of your garden will be devoted to paths rather than vegetables. When vegetables are planted in beds (wide rows), they benefit from the warm, moist microclimate created by the beds and their roots are removed from the dry, compacted soil of the paths. If you plant in permanent beds year after year, you never fertilize ground that will in the future be walked upon, and

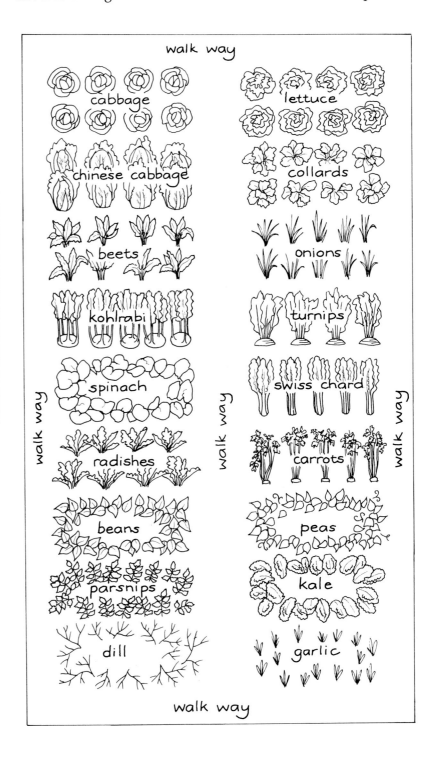

Vegetables planted in wide rows, as shown here, benefit from the warm, moist microclimate created by the beds.

you never walk upon and compress soil that will in the future support plants. Furthermore, if you make each of your permanent beds equal to 100 square feet (5 by 20 feet, or 4 by 25, for example), you will be able to compute fertilizer needs quite simply. Permanent beds tend to turn into raised beds as you add soil amendments over the seasons.

How are raised beds made?

Remove the topsoil from the areas where the paths between the beds will be, and add it to the beds. Or, bring in enough soil-building material to bring up the beds to their proper height—4 to 12 inches higher than the surrounding soil.

Mark the site of the bed by hammering in stakes at the corners and connecting the stakes with string to define the sides. The bed should be no wider than 40 to 48 inches, so that you can easily reach the center from either side. Make the paths about 16 to 24 inches wide. Dig the soil to a depth of about 10 inches, working from the center of the bed out to the sides. Add topsoil from the paths to the bed and work that in as you dig. This is the time, too, to incorporate compost or other organic material, if you wish. Allow the freshly dug bed to settle and dry in the sun for a few days, and then lightly rake soil up from the edges of the bed to the center and flatten the bed with the back of the rake to level it. Some gardeners build wooden frames around their raised beds to hold the soil in place, but this isn't usually necessary, and may, in fact, encourage insect pests such as slugs to take up residence in your garden. The best material for framing is cedar or redwood, both of which resist rot.

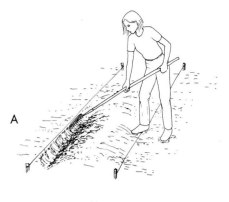

A

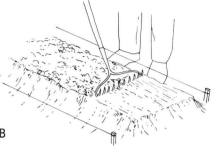

B

Form raised beds by (A) raking about 4 to 6 inches of topsoil from the path onto the bed and (B) smoothing the top of the bed with the back of the rake.

In an established raised-bed garden, you never fertilize ground that will in the future be walked upon, and you never walk upon and compress soil that will in the future support plants.

Martha Storey

PREPARING THE SOIL
•

What do gardeners mean when they say, "Plants don't like to have wet feet"?

Ideally, water should drain gradually through the topsoil, into the subsoil, and then into the water table, without staying in one place for a long time and causing waterlogged roots. If puddles stay on the ground several hours after a hard rain, the ground is poorly drained. Heavy clay soils can hold water for so long that the roots of plants growing in it become deprived of oxygen, and the plants actually drown. Extremely sandy or gravelly soils, on the other hand, don't hold water long enough. The water passes by the roots so quickly that the plants are not able to take in enough moisture, and they die of thirst.

What can I do about a soil that holds water for too long?

The first step is to add plenty of organic matter, such as manure or compost, which will help loosen and aerate the soil. You can also plant a green manure crop (see pg. 631) and then till it in. Gypsum, available at nurseries, will help break up a heavy clay soil. Make certain never to work a heavy clay soil when it is wet, or you will break down the soil structure and cause it to dry in cementlike clods that will be almost impossible to break up. If the water problem is severe, build raised beds on top of the ground and fill them with a 50/50 blend of topsoil and peat moss.

What should I do about sandy soil that won't hold water?

Mix great amounts of organic material into the soil each fall, and again in the spring. Peat moss is especially good for sandy or gravelly soils, because it holds many times its weight in water. Begin by mixing it into the top 4 inches of soil; each year, as you add more, you can dig it in a little deeper. If your soil is little more than sand, you might consider purchasing good-quality topsoil from a reputable nursery. Be sure to add organic matter even to purchased topsoil.

Is a soil test necessary?

Not always. Your Extension Service agent or a knowledgeable nursery person can tell you much about the soil in your region, and what the gardeners in your area add to their soil for optimum growing conditions.

Should I add lime to my soil?

Lime needs vary greatly throughout North America. In some areas the soil is alkaline rather than acid, in which case lime would only make conditions worse. Contact your Extension Service agent, who will know whether lime is needed in your area.

What is green manure?

Green manure is a cover crop, such as buckwheat, grown to be dug back into the soil to increase soil fertility and improve soil texture. Green manure crops are beneficial even on gardens as small as 10 by 25 feet. Check with your Extension Service agent for suggestions of what are the best crops to use in your area.

Won't a green manure crop turn into a weed problem?

Not if you turn it under *before* it produces mature seeds. Green manure can actually be used as an aid *against* weed problems (see pages 646-47).

What is humus?

Humus is decomposed animal or vegetable matter, available from such sources as well-rotted manure, peat moss, seaweed, leaf mold, and compost. It acts as a sponge, holding water and oxygen in the soil; protects soil from erosion by water and wind; improves the texture of hard clay soil by separating it into smaller clumps; stabilizes the soil chemically, buffering your plants against fertilizer burn; and makes nutrients more available to plants. Some gardeners say that the difference between "dirt" and "soil" is humus.

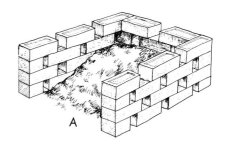

Compost

How can I make my own compost?

Simply combine rough organic matter, soil, and moisture with a high-nitrogen substance, such as fertilizer, blood meal, fresh manure, or cottonseed meal. As the compost pile decomposes, it heats up and changes in character from a mixture of, for example, manure, kitchen scraps, garden soil, leaves, grass clippings, and blood meal into the light, sweet-smelling, almost fluffy material known as compost.

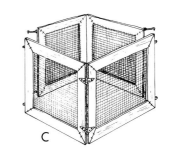

How big can my compost heap be?

A good workable size is 4 feet by 4 feet, and no more than 4 feet high. You can buy a ready-made unit or make your own.

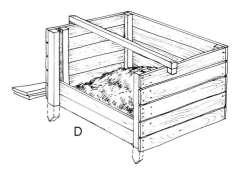

Can composting be done in a trash barrel?

Yes—or even in plastic trash bags. Mix your materials well, moisten them, and fill your barrel or bags and seal them. They may be ready in three weeks in warm weather or two months in cool weather.

Compost bins can be simply made with (A) concrete blocks, (B) fencing, (C) a frame made of 1x6s and 1-inch wire mesh, or (D) a sturdy box with a removable front and a bar across the top to prevent spreading.

How can I make sure my compost pile heats up?

Add plenty of nitrogen, stir the heap every week or so to incorporate oxygen (by sinking pipes into the compost and rocking them in a circular motion), and make sure the heap never dries out—it should be moist but not soggy.

Can I compost in the winter?

Where the ground freezes, no composting action will occur until there is a thaw, and even in milder areas, very little composting will take place during the winter. If you continue to add kitchen scraps, leaves, lawn clippings, and soil, however, as soon as the weather warms up, your pile will begin to "work," or heat up.

How hot will a compost heap get? Is there danger of fire?

The more nitrogen you add, the faster your compost heap will heat up and, to a point, the hotter it will become. It should reach 150° F. Piles do occasionally smolder, so don't put yours next to a house, tree, or anything that could catch fire.

How do I keep the pile from smelling unpleasant?

If you add fresh manure or kitchen scraps, cover it with dirt or dried clippings to keep odors and flies at bay.

Can I add tree and bush prunings to my compost heap?

Thick, unshredded, woody material takes longer to break down, and is therefore best not added. As a rule of thumb, don't add anything that you can't easily break up with the edge of a shovel.

Will seeds from grass clippings and weeds stay in my compost and later sprout in my garden?

If your compost pile heats up to 150° F. (you can check it with an oven thermometer), all weed seeds will be destroyed. Turning your pile occasionally ensures that everything in it gets heated up.

Is there anything I shouldn't add to my compost heap?

In addition to woody material such as branches and thick twigs, avoid magnolia leaves, which don't break down easily; eucalyptus, which contains an oil that is detrimental to plant growth; and any plants that are noxious weeds or implacable spreaders (morning glory, English ivy, Bermuda grass, and nut grass are examples). Also avoid meat scraps. Anything that might attract animals to an unenclosed compost heap should be buried deeply in the heap.

Digging the Garden

When is the best time to work the soil?

Dig in the fall, and leave the ground rough. Freezing and thawing during winter breaks up clods and aerates the soil, insect enemies that might otherwise have overwintered in the soil will be turned out, and settling will lessen the likelihood of air pockets in the soil when planting. One exception: Light, sandy soils, which can suffer from erosion by winter rains, are usually best tilled in the spring.

Must I use a power tiller, or will a spade do?

If you have a large garden—particularly if it is presently in sod—you will find a rotary power tiller immensely helpful. You can usually hire someone to come and do this for you or you can rent equipment if you don't wish to purchase it. On the other hand, some people enjoy turning over established gardens with a spade, and raised beds (see pg. 629) must be done this way. Work on a cool day, and take your time so that you don't strain unused muscles.

What if I didn't dig in the fall—can I dig in the spring?

Yes, but before you begin, make this simple test: Pick up a handful of soil and squeeze it into a ball. If the ball breaks up easily, the soil is ready to be dug. If the ball is sticky and elastic, and retains its shape under pressure, the soil is still too moist to be dug.

Is there more I should do in the spring if I have tilled and fertilized and added compost to the soil in the fall?

For best results, add more organic matter to the soil in the spring a week or two before planting. Spread compost, aged manure, or other bulky, organic, soil-building material 2 to 4 inches deep on top of the soil, and dig it in to a depth of 12 inches.

Is it enough to turn over the soil at spade depth, or do I need to dig down really deeply?

Some gardeners favor the double-digging method devised by French intensive gardeners (see illustration). In deeply dug gardens, plant roots find it easier to reach down in search of water and nutrients. The result is plants that are healthier, better able to ward off insects, compete with weeds, and withstand dry spells, and thus a garden that does not need as much attention as a shallowly dug one. In most dry locations (except for some sandy soils) it is especially necessary to encourage roots to strike deeply in search of moisture.

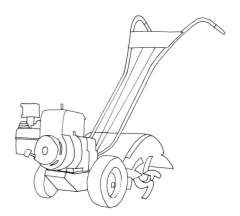

A rotary power tiller is helpful if you have a large garden to cultivate.

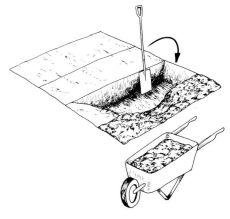

To double-dig a garden, remove one row of soil (a shovel's width and depth) from one end of the garden and place it in a wheelbarrow. Loosen the exposed subsoil a shovel's depth. Cover the exposed subsoil with the top layer of the next row of soil (as shown by arrow), and loosen the newly exposed subsoil a shovel's depth. Continue down the bed in this manner, using the reserved soil from the wheelbarrow to fill the final trench.

Fertilizing

What is the difference between organic and inorganic fertilizers?

The former are made from animal, vegetable, or mineral sources, such as bonemeal, blood meal, or cottonseed meal, and rock phosphates; the latter are made from treated minerals (such as superphosphate, nitrate salts, or potash salts) or extracted from the air (ammonium forms of nitrogen).

What are the advantages of natural fertilizers?

Perhaps the greatest advantage is that they encourage beneficial life forms in the soil rather than harming them, as some commercial dry fertilizers can. Many of the natural fertilizers build soil structure by adding valuable bulky organic matter that increases the humus content of the soil. Natural fertilizers also add minor nutrients, which are less well understood than N, P, and K (see pg. 636), but vital to the health of all plants. Furthermore, they release their nutrients slowly, which is the safest way to fertilize.

What are the disadvantages of natural fertilizers?

Some people object to the odor of manures and fish emulsions, though some dry commercial brands are deodorized. Because many natural fertilizers contain a great deal of soil-building organic material, they can be difficult to transport, and more time-consuming to apply. The nutrient content of most natural fertilizers is not as easy to determine as it is for commercial fertilizers.

What are the advantages of commercial fertilizers?

They contain nutrients in precise amounts, so that you know exactly what you're applying. In addition, they are less bulky than natural fertilizers such as manure or compost, they act quickly, and they are usually less expensive than store-bought natural fertilizers in terms of the amount of N, P, and K that they provide per dollar.

What are the disadvantages of commercial dry fertilizers?

They add no soil-building organic matter to the soil. Soils supplemented with commercial dry fertilizers and nothing else tend actually to die—that is, earthworms disappear, soil microbes and enzymes die or stop working, and the soil breaks down and loses its structure, with erosion the result. Fast-acting synthetic fertilizers have some other risks. If you add too much at once, your plants will be burned by salts in the fertilizer, and soils enriched with these fertilizers must be fertilized more often than soils enriched with slow-releasing natural fertilizers.

Percentage Composition
of Common Organic Materials

	NITROGEN	PHOSPHORUS	POTASSIUM
Activated sludge	5.00	3.00	
Alfalfa hay	2.45	.50	2.10
Animal tankage	8.00	20.00	
Apple leaves	1.00	.15	.35
Basic slag	.80		
Blood meal	15.00	1.30	.70
Bonemeal	4.00	21.00	.20
Brewer's grains (wet)	.90	.50	.05
Castor pomace	5.50	1.50	1.25
Cattle manure (fresh)	.29	.17	.35
Cocoa shell dust	1.04	1.49	2.71
Coffee grounds (dried)	1.99	.36	.67
Colloidal phosphate		18-24	
Cornstalks	.75	.40	.90
Cottonseed	3.15	1.25	1.15
Cottonseed hull ash		8.70	24.00
Cottonseed meal	7.00	2.50	1.50
Dried blood	12-15	3.00	
Feather meal	12.00		
Fish scrap (red snapper)	7.76	13.00	3.80
Granite dust			5.00
Greensand		1.50	5.00
Guano	12.00	8.00	3.00
Hoof meal and horn dust	12.50	1.75	
Horse manure (fresh)	.44	.17	.35
Incinerator ash	.24	5.15	2.33
Leather dust	5.5-12		
Oak leaves	.80	.35	.15
Peach leaves	.90	.15	.60
Phosphate rock		30-32	
Poultry manure (fresh)	2.00	1.88	1.85
Rabbit manure (fresh)	2.40	.62	.05
Red clover	.55	.13	.50
Seaweed	1.68	.75	5.00
Sheep manure (fresh)	.55	.31	.15
Swine manure (fresh)	.60	.41	.13
Tankage	6.00	8.00	
Tobacco stems	2.00		7.00
Wood ashes		1.50	7.00

What do the numbers on the fertilizer bags mean?

They give the percentages of the most important plant nutrients: nitrogen (N), phosphorus (P), and potassium (K), always in that order. A bag of fertilizer with the formula 5-10-5 contains by volume 5-percent nitrogen, 10-percent phosphorus, and 5-percent potassium. The remaining 80 percent is some kind of filler—usually organic matter that will increase the humus content of your soil.

What is "organic gardening"?

In general, to garden organically is to add only mineral-, plant-, and animal-derived materials to the soil and plants, and to refrain from using chemical pesticides or herbicides. Both aspects—adding nutrients *and* avoiding chemicals—are crucial to the success of this method.

Should I use both commercial dry fertilizers and manure?

If you garden organically, aged and composted manure, followed by sidedressings of compost and cottonseed or blood meal, once your plants get going, should be enough. The commercial fertilizer equivalent of this would be a 5-10-5 mixture.

What does the term "complete fertilizer" mean?

This term is misleading, for such a product sometimes contains only the three major nutrients (N, P, and K), and these three are far from a complete list of plant nutrients. The closest thing to a truly complete fertilizer is compost, which you can make yourself (see pages 631-32).

What is "plant food"?

The primary "food" for plants is sunlight. It is better to think in terms of feeding the *soil* rather than feeding the *plants* growing in it. Healthy soil contains not only nitrogen, phosphorus, and potassium, but microbiotic life forms, oxygen, earthworms, enzymes, trace elements, and many other things that contribute to the health of plants.

When should I add commercial fertilizer to the soil?

Spread it over the soil before you begin digging so that you can work it into the soil as you dig.

What is a "starter" or "transplanting" fertilizer?

This consists of a small amount of a powerful fertilizer, high in phosphorus (such as bonemeal, phosphate rock, or superphosphate), dissolved in water. Pour a cupful around the plants when they are transplanted, or pour a cupful directly on the seed for every 3 feet of row. An ounce of 13-26-13 fertilizer, or 3 ounces of a 5-10-5 fertilizer dissolved in a gallon of water, are typical starter solutions.

What is a "sidedressing" fertilizer?

A sidedressing is applied to a plant once it is growing. Heavy feeders such as corn and cabbage family crops benefit in particular from additional small applications of fertilizers between the time they are planted and the harvest. Leaves streaked with yellow are a signal that a sidedressing may be needed.

What should I use for a sidedressing?

Compost or dried manure spread 1 inch deep around each plant, or to either side of a row of plants, and then raked in, makes a good sidedressing. Manure or compost "tea" (made by soaking the material overnight in a bucket of water) is also effective. Or you can use 1 tablespoon of dry commercial fertilizer per plant or two or three parts fertilizer to one part water. Water the fertilizer in immediately. Plants with high nitrogen needs, such as corn, should be sidedressed with a high-nitrogen fertilizer.

Is there much difference in various animal manures?

Poultry manure, much higher in nitrogen than steer or horse manure, should be aged at least nine months and used in smaller quantities. Aged horse manure is an excellent soil builder and conditioner: Spread about 3 inches of it across the top of the soil before you dig. Nitrogen content is sometimes written on the package label of commercial dry manures. Refer to the chart on pg. 635 if you have a local source of animal manures.

Is it necessary to age fresh manure before using it?

Yes, both to keep it from burning plants and to kill the weed seeds in it.

Do some types of vegetables have special fertilizer needs?

Leafy vegetables, such as lettuce, Swiss chard, and cabbage, use large amounts of nitrogen. Seed- or fruit-producing vegetables, such as beans and tomatoes, use much potassium. See Chapter 27 for more information on individual crop needs.

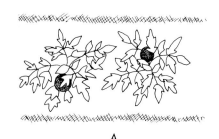

Sidedressing fertilizers may be applied (A) along both sides of a row of plants or (B) in a circle around plants.

26 *Planting and Growing Vegetables*

I t seems a shame to let those first spring days of warmth and sunshine pass by without starting something growing, yet if seeds are planted outdoors too soon, a late frost can put your work to waste. That's why it's a good idea to start seeds in containers, flats, or cold frames before dependable gardening weather arrives. This way you not only have something to relieve that persistent gardening itch, but you will reap your rewards much sooner in the form of early crops.

How soon should I start seeds indoors?

As a rule, start seeds eight weeks before you would plant them outside. See the entries for individual vegetables in Chapter 6 for more precise guidelines.

What are seed flats?

Traditional seed flats are simply small, open, well-drained wooden boxes, easily built out of redwood or cedar scraps. A good size is 12 by 24 inches and no less than 3 inches deep. If you plan to keep seedlings in the flats for six weeks or longer, make the flats 6 inches deep so that roots have more room. Leave ⅛-inch spaces between the slats on the bottom so that the soil can drain easily.

You can also start seeds in cottage cheese containers, cut-off milk cartons, margarine tubs, foam or paper cups, or yogurt containers, with several holes poked in the bottoms of them for

STARTING SEEDS
IN FLATS
—— • ——

◀ *Seeds started indoors in flats or other containers will give you a head start on the gardening season.*

drainage. (Arrange them on a tray so that when the seedlings must be moved, the containers' shapes are not distorted and the root systems thus disturbed.) Seed catalogues and garden centers sell plastic trays with many individual cells, which make removal for transplanting easy. Some have plastic domes that fit snugly over them to create a warm, humid, greenhouselike atmosphere, especially conducive to germination.

Can I use garden soil in my starter flats?

Garden soil is too dense for optimum seed sprouting in flats. The best choice for indoor sprouting is a potting soil, available wherever garden supplies are sold. If you use sterilized soil, your plants will be less likely to suffer damping-off disease, which frequently causes young seedlings to die.

How much light should I give indoor-planted seeds?

Most seeds will sprout in the dark if they are warm enough, but once they're up they need a lot of light. Place them in a sunny window, but don't let intense sunlight dry out or overheat newly sprouted plants.

Will vegetable seedlings grow well under artificial light?

Yes. Fluorescent tubes, turned on fourteen hours a day, will provide plenty of light. You can supplement weak natural light by turning fluorescent lights on at 4 p.m. and off at 9 p.m. Suspend them 4 inches above the growing surface, and move them up as the plants grow so that they are always about 4 inches above the tops of the plants.

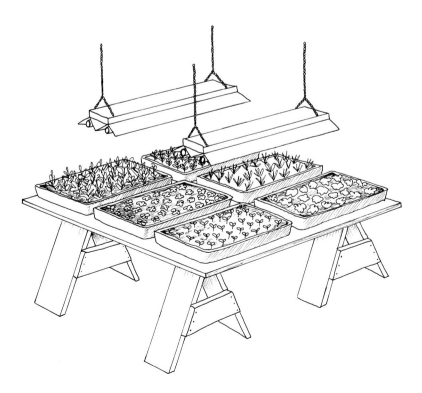

Fluorescent lights should be suspended about 4 inches above the growing surface of the plants and raised as the plants grow.

Should I thin vegetable seedlings in flats before transplanting them?

If you sow the seeds far enough apart in the flats, you won't have to do much thinning. If the little plants are crowded, however, thin them when they put out their first set of true leaves (the set of leaves that appears after the first leaves).

How deeply should I plant seeds in flats, trays, or containers?

As a general rule, plant them four times as deep as their diameter—the same depth at which you would plant them in the garden. Don't forget to label them!

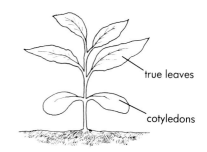

True leaves appear after the first seed leaves, or cotyledons.

How warm should the potting soil be?

For germination, provide 60° F. for hardy plants and 70° F. for tender ones. If you place heat cables or mats beneath seed flats or trays, remove them as soon as the seedlings are well up. Soil temperatures above 90° F. are harmful. After they are growing, hardy plants, such as members of the cabbage family, can withstand night temperatures of 40° to 50° F., though 60° F. would be better.

How should I water seeds sprouting in containers?

Use a plant mister or a watering can with a very fine-holed nozzle. Indoors, flats or containers can be watered from beneath by setting them in leakproof trays. This method assures that the seeds won't be uncovered and washed away. Sufficient, uninterrupted moisture is essential.

Since starting seeds in flats means that I will have to move plants into the garden, what are the best vegetables for transplanting?

All members of the cabbage family transplant well, as do tomatoes, eggplants, peppers, onions, leeks, lettuce, and celery. Melons and squashes should not remain in containers more than two or three weeks.

Which vegetables don't transplant well?

Parsnips, carrots, and other root crops don't respond well to transplanting, though beets are an exception if handled carefully. Beans and corn are best started in the ground because you need so many of them.

What is "hardening off"?

It is the process of acclimating indoor-grown seedlings to outdoor weather conditions so that they won't suffer transplant shock. Starting two weeks before transplanting, set your flats or containers outside during the daylight hours in a well-protected, partially shaded area. After three or four days, leave them out at night if you can be sure that it will not get too cold.

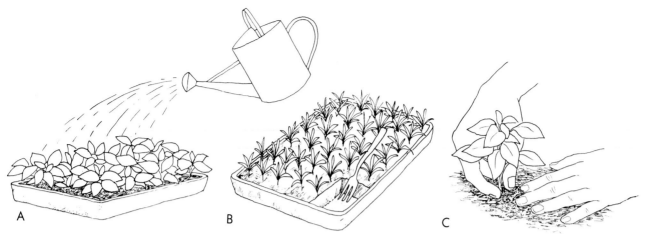

To transplant seedlings into the garden, (A) moisten plants before beginning. (B) Remove seedlings from flats by cutting out the block of soil on which they are growing. (C) Gently lower seedling into a prepared hole, watering the plant immediately and firming soil to settle soil around roots.

TRANSPLANTING SEEDLINGS INTO THE GARDEN
·

How should I go about transplanting?

Have your garden beds well prepared (see pgs. 630-37) before you do anything to your seedlings. Water the containers in which they are growing so that the soil is well moistened, but not soggy. If the seedlings are growing in a molded plastic "plug" tray, lift them out gently by the two strongest leaves, place them immediately in the furrow or holes you have dug, and firm the soil around them. Plants growing in individual containers can be removed by inverting the container into the palm of your hand. A rap on the bottom of the container is sometimes necessary to free the root ball. Seedlings growing in a flat need to be separated from each other before being removed from the flat. Use a hand fork, an old kitchen spatula, or a putty knife to cut the soil into blocks. When the roots of the individual seedlings are well separated in this fashion, lift them from the flat and plant them.

Should I water the plants after transplanting them?

Light watering immediately after transplanting is helpful. It is the gentlest way to settle soil around the roots. Do not tightly compress wet soil around the roots of transplanted seedlings.

DIRECT SEEDING
·

Direct seeding is the most common method of planting most vegetables. After you have prepared the soil thoroughly (see pgs. 630-37), rake it smooth and remove large stones, as you would before transplanting.

How should I direct-seed in rows?

Create shallow furrows with the edge of a hoe, drop in the seeds, cover them over with compost, leaf mold, or potting soil, tamp down the covering with the flat end of the hoe, and label what you've planted.

Is it always best to plant in furrows?

Not necessarily. You can plant in any pattern you like, as long as you provide adequate spacing for mature plants and leave yourself access to what you plant. Small kitchen gardens often feature curved rows, accent plantings of only two or three plants of one kind in one place, and geometrically shaped blocks of colorful vegetables (such as red- and green-leafed lettuces) interposed against each other.

Can you explain the meaning of a hill planting?

A hill is a cluster of plants as opposed to a row—it is not necessarily raised higher than the surrounding ground. Cucumbers, melons, pole beans, and squash are all often planted in hills.

What is a drill?

A drill is a very shallow seeding hole, such as you would poke with a finger or small stick.

Should I remove stones of all sizes from the planting bed before seeding?

No. The soil should be made up of many different-sized particles of dirt and stone, rather than fine as dust. Remove only stones that are large enough to prevent the emergence of a seedling or that occupy too much space in the garden bed.

If you are planting seeds in rows, make a straight furrow by dragging the corner of a hoe along the row.

When is the right time to plant seeds outdoors?

This depends on local conditions and on what you are planting. Check with your local Extension Service to find out the date of the last expected frost in your area. The lists on pg. 627 will help you determine which vegetables can go in the ground first, and which should be planted once the soil has warmed up.

How deeply should I plant seeds outdoors?

The same depth as indoors—roughly four times the diameter of the seed. Follow seed packet instructions for planting depth and spacing.

What is pelleted seed?

Some seed companies coat very small seeds with a nutrient substance to make them larger for easier planting and better germination. Pelleted seeds are always more expensive than uncoated seeds, and are sometimes available only in large quantities.

How does one broadcast seeds?

Gardeners with raised beds often broadcast their seeds. Toss the seeds as evenly as you can and then rake them shallowly into

Wide-row plantings should be kept thinned so that plants just touch their neighbors. Floating row covers (top, left) protect plants against insect damage and cold weather.

the soil. Broadcast plantings usually need a great deal of thinning, but the closely spaced plants they give rise to shade out weeds and retard water evaporation from the soil.

What is seed innoculant, and how should I use it?

Many gardeners coat seeds of the legume family (beans and peas) with innoculant before planting. Innoculant is a powder that encourages increased numbers of nitrogen-fixing bacteria around the plant roots. Just before planting, moisten the seeds with water, sprinkle the innoculant powder over them in the amount called for on the package, and mix well. Store unused innoculant in the refrigerator, and discard it after the date on the package. Be sure to buy an innoculant powder that is specified for the legume you are planting.

Is there any harm in planting seeds closer together than package advice?

Many gardeners deliberately space plants very close together because they plan to eat the thinnings as their first harvest of the season. Beets, lettuce, radishes (leaves and all), and chard all taste wonderful in the immature stage. Just don't let your vegetables crowd each other as they mature, or your crops will be small and malformed. Another advantage to planting closely is that all those extra seedlings will compete with weeds. Furthermore, a tight row of vegetables with very tender sprouts, such as carrots, seems to have an easier time breaking through heavy soil than do solitary, well-spaced seedlings.

Should I water at seeding time?

If there has not been rain for some time and the soil is dry, water deeply and slowly two days *before* planting. This will give the water time to seep down into the subsoil, yet the topsoil will have time to dry enough so that it won't be muddy when you plant. It's important to get water into the lower layers of the soil, because although you can water the topsoil right after you plant the seeds if you use a fine spray of water so as not to disturb the seeds, it's much harder to get water to the subsoil after seeding. If you water *after* seeding, clay soils can compact and form a crust difficult for new sprouts to push through.

How often should I water after seeding?

Water just as often as it takes to keep the soil moist—in some areas of the country this may be several times daily. Do not let heavy soils crust over from lack of water, or plants may never sprout.

CARING FOR YOUR GROWING PLANTS

I hate to uproot a healthy little plant. Is thinning really necessary?

It certainly is. Although most plants seem to benefit from being sown rather closely together, once they come up they should not have to compete for root space, water, and sunlight. For recommended final spacing, refer to the seed packet or to our advice for specific varieties in Chapter 27.

Should I thin to the proper spacing all at once or in stages?

In stages is best, if you have the time to return to the garden two or three times as the plants grow larger. Let them stand far enough apart so that their leaves are just touching. The shade these leaves cast will keep the soil from drying out quickly, and will also shade out competing weeds.

Do the plants need to be spaced evenly after thinning?

Don't worry about perfect spacing. While a certain degree of regularity is more apt to result in plants of consistent size, the plants seem to make up for uneven spacing as they grow. Root crops such as carrots and beets will push each other to the side as they grow, so that two perfectly shaped, large roots can grow right next to each other if there is adequate space on their free sides.

Controlling Weeds

I've sometimes thought I would never plant vegetables again because weeds give me so many problems. Do I always have to fight a losing battle against weeds?

By developing a weed control program of *prevention*, you can be a gardener of vegetables and not weeds. Remember this cardinal rule: get them while they're young. Plan to put in most of your weeding time in the spring, and after that you probably won't need to weed more than once every two weeks. Avoid introducing into your garden anything—especially uncomposted manure—that may contain weed seeds. Buy weed-free manure, or thoroughly compost fresh manure in a well-heated compost heap. In the fall, plant a cover crop that you can turn under in the spring. Annual ryegrass will crowd out many weeds, and once turned under (before it forms seeds) it will not become a weed problem itself (see pg. 631). Apply a mulch (see pages 647-48).

A cover crop of winter rye can be planted even on small beds to control weeds and improve the nutrient content of the soil.

Positive Images, Jerry Howard

What is the best way to weed?

Hand-pulling is effective in most cases, and must be used for established perennial weeds. Large gardens should be cultivated by hoeing or tilling. Early in the season, cultivate 3 inches deep around newly sprouted or transplanted vegetable plants and then apply a mulch. Cultivate more shallowly among mature plants to avoid disturbing roots near the surface. Compost the weeds to conserve their valuable nutrients and bulky fiber.

What about controlling weeds with herbicides?

For home vegetable gardening, avoid chemical herbicides. The risk of damaging your plants is too great and some herbicides will ruin the soil for vegetable culture for several seasons. They may also eventually prove to be dangerous to your own health as well as to the health of the ecosystem.

I have a terrible problem with Bermuda grass. No matter how much I pull, it seems to increase its domain over my garden. What should I do?

The best way is to start a year before you plant a garden in that spot. Till the garden in the summer and seed buckwheat at a rate of 6 ounces per 100 square feet. As soon as it starts to blossom, turn it under and plant another crop of buckwheat at the same rate. Again turn it under when it begins to flower. If the Bermuda grass is still around after that, it will be very weak, and you may be able to pull it all out. If you want to be extra safe, plant one more cover crop, such as winter rye. (Ask your local Extension Service agent to recommend a winter cover crop that does well in your area.) By spring you should have a garden with very few weeds. Buckwheat has a tremendous ability to crowd out troublesome weeds, so this method works not only for Bermuda grass, but for other perennial weeds and rapidly spreading grasses as well. It also vastly improves the texture and nutrient content of a soil.

How can I keep out the perennial weeds and grasses surrounding my garden?

Maintain a swath of bare ground around the perimeter of your garden by turning the soil under with a power tiller; plant a vigorous cover crop such as vetch or clover around the garden; or sink a plastic or metal weed barrier 4 to 6 inches into the ground as an edging.

Are there any crops that don't need much weeding?

Crops that grow tall quickly, such as corn and pole beans, and crops that grow large leaves, such as squash, require less weeding than others because they shade out weeds before they have a chance to take over.

What crops require the most weeding?

Lettuce, carrots, and onions cannot compete with weeds, and need more attention from you and your hoe than most vegetables. In general, the more slowly a crop grows and the less shade it casts, the more weeding you will have to do to grow it.

Mulching

What are the advantages of mulching?

Mulches hold water in the soil, keep down weeds, add bulky organic matter and nutrients to the soil, and keep the soil cool.

What are the best mulching materials?

Among organic materials, dried leaves, buckwheat hulls, ground corn cobs, peat moss, shredded sugarcane (called bagasse and sold as chicken litter), salt-meadow or marsh hay, grass clippings, sawdust, cocoa hulls, wood chips, bark, and straw. Plastic sheeting, usually black, is also popular.

Why do so many gardeners use straw or hay for mulch?

Probably because it is cheap and plentiful. You can buy large bales of it for a few dollars—cheaper if you can find a farmer with spoiled hay he wants to get rid of (hay is not technically straw, but it works well if you apply it thickly). Weed-free organic mulches are usually more desirable, but if you mulch straw deeply enough—up to 1 foot when the plants are reaching maturity—the weeds won't get the sunlight they need to germinate and grow.

How should I go about mulching with hay?

Cut the wire or string from a bale of hay and separate 2- to 3-inch thick pieces from it. Lay these on the soil wherever you don't want anything to grow. This is best done in late spring, or whenever the ground has thoroughly warmed up. If you cover low-growing weeds completely this way, you won't have to bother pulling them up, unless they are right next to your vegetable plants. If your plants aren't sprouted yet, mark the planting locations and lay the mulch around but not over them.

Are plastic mulches good to use?

Plastic mulches, available at nearly all garden centers, are easy to use. You must use black or some other weed-preventing plastic if you want to arrest weeds. Simply roll it out, anchor it with dirt, rocks, wire, or pegs, and poke holes where your plants will be. Used in conjunction with drip emitters, plastic mulches have the added advantage of saving water. On the negative side, the plastic is unattractive, adds no nutrients to the soil, and is at present not a recyclable substance.

Watering

What is the most effective way to save water?

Build good soil that is full of humus.

At what time of day should I water?

Early morning watering is best, although evening watering is good too, provided there is enough time for leaves to dry before nightfall. Although midday watering is not harmful to plants, it is wasteful, since much water evaporates in the heat and sun.

How can I know when to water?

Observe your plants: If they are wilted in the morning or the ground is dry 2 to 4 inches deep, it is time to water. (A dry top inch will do no harm, and is actually desirable for older plants.) Don't hose down the garden because you see your plantings wilting in the heat of day. By sprinkling instead of deep watering, you will encourage plants to develop weak, surface root systems that need constant watering. These plants will suffer badly should even one of these waterings be missed on a hot day. A good rule of thumb is that vegetables should get the equivalent of 1 inch of water each week.

For how long should I water?

Avoid depending on hand watering with the faucet turned up all the way. The top inch or so of soil will get well saturated, but much water will run off the surface to the edges of the beds

Positive Images, Jerry Howard

Because deep watering is crucial to a healthy garden, set up a sprinkler in the garden and leave the water running slowly for a long time, so that you are watering to a depth of about 1 inch per week.

instead of deep into the soil where it belongs. It is much better to use a soaker or sprinkler hose, sprinklers, or a drip irrigation system, and to leave the water running slowly for a long time, moistening the soil thoroughly 4 to 6 inches down. After watering, keep the moisture in by laying down as heavy a mulch as possible without smothering plants. If you use a sprinkler, set an empty can in the path of its spray to determine how long it takes for an inch of water to accumulate.

Are some garden layouts better than others for conserving water?

Yes. Long, single rows of plants leave much ground exposed, which results in rapid evaporation. Raised beds, advantageous where poor drainage is a problem, hold the plants up higher than ground level and expose them to moisture-robbing wind. Ground-level, closely planted beds offer plants protection from the wind, and offer the soil protection from the sun. Whatever plan you use, mulch your paths, which can act as wicks that draw moisture from the beds and give it up to the sun.

Any other suggestions for saving water?

Put water only where it's needed. Sprinklers that spread water beyond your garden are great water wasters, as are sprinklers that throw water up into the air on windy days. Soaker hose (which is inexpensive), sprinkler hose turned face down, or drip irrigators under mulch put water exactly where it's needed.

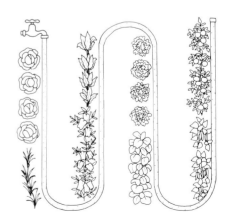

A drip irrigation system such as this, covered with mulch, is an excellent water saver.

649

Is it possible to water too much?

Yes. If the soil becomes soggy, plants don't get enough oxygen and become subject to root rot and other problems.

Are there any crops I should think twice about planting in very dry areas?

The big water-users include corn, cucumbers, lettuce, celery, and leaf and root crops. Tomatoes and peppers, and seed crops, such as beans and sunflowers, can get by with less water. In areas with long growing seasons, plant moisture-loving plants during the months when rainfall will supply your water. Look for drought-tolerant varieties in the seed catalogues.

We live in the high desert of New Mexico, and our water is very alkaline. Will this harm our crops?

Alkaline water creates alkaline soil, which most vegetables do not favor. Dig plenty of compost and organic matter into your soil as often as possible, and plant varieties that tolerate alkaline soils. Consult your Extension Service agent to determine whether you should add sulphur or some other acidifying substance to your soil.

HARVESTING VEGETABLES

How often should I pick my beans?

Beans, as well as many other crops, such as cucumbers, peas, and summer squashes, should be picked often and continuously. Because its life purpose is to reproduce itself, once one of these plants has produced enough seeds, it will stop producing and die. When you pick continuously, you prevent seeds from maturing, and thus the plant continues to produce. If you can't eat everything you pick, preserve, give away, or sell the excess. Harvest vegetables immediately before cooking them; they will be sweeter, more tender, and more nutritious.

I have heard that it is best, from a nutritional standpoint, to harvest early in the day. Is this so?

In fact, it is usually better to harvest late in the day, when vitamin C content, proteins, and carbohydrates are at their highest points, especially if the sun has been shining hard. On the other hand, crispy crops, such as lettuce and cucumbers, are best picked in the morning. Generally, pick vegetables as close to the time you eat them as possible.

Is it true that beans should not be picked after a rain?

Yes; this promotes the spread of disease. Don't touch your bean plants in the early morning when they are wet with dew or after a rain or a watering.

What is succession planting?

This is a technique whereby a second (or even a third) crop is planted in a bed as soon as possible after a harvest. With good planning, in some areas it may be possible to get three crops by beginning the season with a cool-weather crop, following it with a warm-weather crop, and succeeding that one with another cool-weather crop. Even very small gardens can produce impressively large amounts of food with this method.

How much fertilizer, and of what type, should I add when planting a succession crop?

Use a little less than 1 pound of horse or cow manure per 10 square feet of soil, or a commercial, balanced fertilizer for vegetable crops. In addition, add compost and some bonemeal, as well as a sprinkling of lime if your soil is very acid.

How can I tell whether a succession crop will make it to maturity before the cold weather comes on?

Determine the date of the first fall frost. If there remains sufficient time for the new crop's days to maturity, as indicated on the seed packet, you are on safe ground.

Can a succession crop be planted in the same bed as an established one before the older one is harvested?

That would be risky because you are likely to damage the new crop when you remove the old one. Further, while the old one is still in the ground, it is competing with the new one—probably successfully—for water, light, and nutrients. It is far better to start your second crops in containers and then transplant them, at the seedling stage, after you remove the first crop.

How can I be assured of a continuous supply of lettuce throughout the season?

Succession planting is not confined to following one crop with a different crop. Lettuce and other crops that must be harvested over a short period of time (such as bush beans) will probably give you too big a harvest all at once unless you plant them in stages. Sow such crops at one- to two-week intervals for a continuous harvest of vegetables—and one that you can savor rather than feel overwhelmed by.

Are certain crops best succeeded by certain other ones?

It is best to follow crops such as corn or *Brassicas*, which take a lot of nutrients from the soil (known as "heavy feeders"), with crops such as radishes, which need little fertilizing, or those such as beans or other legumes, which actually contribute rather than remove nutrients. It is especially important not to grow heavy feeders in the same bed year after year.

SUCCESSION PLANTING

•

VEGETABLES TO CONSIDER FOR SUCCESSION PLANTING

Heavy Feeders

Artichokes
Broccoli
Brussels sprouts
Cabbage
Cauliflower
Celery
Collards
Corn
Cucumbers
Eggplant
Kale
Lettuce
Melons (including watermelon)
Mustard
Okra
Peppers
Parsley
Pumpkins
Rhubarb
Spinach
Squash
Sunflowers
Swiss chard
Tomatoes

Light Feeders

Beans
Beets
Carrots
Chicory
Endive
Leeks
Parsnips
Peas
Potatoes
Radishes
Rutabagas
Shallots
Sweet potatoes
Turnips

•

CROPS THAT WITHSTAND EARLY FALL FROSTS

Beets	Endive	Peas
Brussels sprouts	Jerusalem artichokes	Radishes
Cabbages	Lettuce	Rutabagas
Carrots	Mustard	Spinach
Cauliflower	Parsley	Swiss chard
Collards		

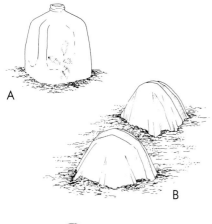

Protect tender plants against late spring and early fall frosts by covering them with (A) cut off plastic milk bottles, (B) hot caps, or (C) floating row covers.

Are there any varieties that are particularly good for cold weather growing?

Plant extra-hardy varieties for your fall garden. They will have to be able to germinate in warm weather and produce in cool weather, which is the opposite of the normal cycle for many varieties. Scan the catalogues, and consult your county Extension Service agent for the late-crop varieties best suited to your area.

What can I use to protect plants against fall frosts?

Cloches, mini-greenhouses, and floating row covers will protect against light frosts. With a 1 ½- to 2-foot mulch of straw or dried leaves and snow cover, plants such as kale and other members of the cabbage family, as well as many root vegetables, should survive well into winter. Be sure to mark the location of root vegetables so that you can find them under the snow. In some cases, you may wish to invert bushel baskets over your plants and then cover them with mulch.

FALL CLEANUP

Is there anything I should do to ready the garden for winter after I have taken the last crop of the season from it?

Remove any tough, thick, fibrous plant material, chop it up, and throw it on the compost heap. Turn all remaining crop residue into the soil, spread a layer of manure on the soil, and sow a cover crop of winter rye (see page 61), or apply a 1-foot deep mulch of straw or leaves. If you leave the ground bare through the winter, heavy rains may erode the soil; a cover crop or mulch will add valuable organic matter and nutrients to your soil, improving both its texture and its fertility.

Won't crop residues that are turned into the soil harbor pests and diseases?

No. When you turn them under the soil, they decompose, destroying the pests that were on them, and many kinds of diseases as well. Exceptions are eggplant and tomatoes—burn or dispose of any diseased stems and leaves of these plants.

We live in California, where winter rains bring us our green season in November through April. Should I mulch during the winter, till the ground, and plant a cover crop, or just let the weeds grow?

If weeds grow in abundance in your garden during the winter, you can keep them down either with a thick mulch or a cover crop. Don't let weeds go to seed, or you will have years of constant weeding ahead of you.

Why should I consider container gardening?

People grow vegetables in containers for a variety of reasons: Some have no room for a garden; others are faced with extremely poor soil; some gardeners in the West have a tremendous gopher problem in their in-ground gardens; elderly and handicapped gardeners may choose container gardens for their ease of access; still others grow vegetables in containers because of the highly ornamental nature of many of them. In its most basic form, container gardening requires only a container with sides and a hole in the bottom, soil, seeds, sun, and water. You will find many gardening chores much easier with container gardening: Protective devices against cold snaps or insect pests are simpler to put in place; succession crops are easier to manage by adding or moving containers around; plants are likely to be closer at

CONTAINER VEGETABLE GARDENING

For would-be gardeners with no in-ground space, robust, colorful vegetables can be grown in containers.

Positive Images, Jerry Howard

hand for tending and harvesting, as well as enjoying visually; and, of course, their relatively small size makes them less time-consuming.

How large a container do I need for growing vegetables?

The larger and, especially, the deeper the container the better; plants like plenty of root space. Make 8 inches your minimum, but try to find containers 1 to 2 feet deep.

What sort of container is best?

Plastic is fine, as long as there is a hole or holes in the bottom for drainage. The only material that is not suitable for container-grown vegetables is wood that has been chemically treated to prevent rot.

What kind of soils should I use for container-grown vegetables?

Any one of the following: premixed potting soil, available from garden centers (specify that you will be using it for vegetables); a homemade mixture of equal proportions of compost, coarse sand, and garden loam (light, rich soil, not heavy clay or poor, infertile soil); well-aged compost of neutral to slightly acid pH; a mixture of 1 part peat moss to 1 part sharp sand to 2 parts garden loan, plus fertilizer. Add perlite or vermiculite to your potting mixture if you think it needs extra water- and air-holding capacity.

How often do container-grown plants need to be watered?

Quite often, especially if they receive full sunlight. There is no deep water reserve for container plants, and the combined evaporation of water from the soil and dehydration of leaves and stems from the wind and sun tax the plants' strength. Water at least once a day during hot weather, and check the plants every day whether you water or not. Poke your finger down into the soil an inch or two (1 inch only for very young or small plants); if you feel no moisture down there, it's time to water. When in doubt, water. You will know you've applied enough water when it starts running out of the drain holes. The bigger the pot, the less often you will need to water. Pots with porous sides need more frequent watering. Set containers in water-catching saucers to conserve water.

How should I fertilize container-grown plants? And what kind of fertilizer should I use?

Since container-grown plants need more frequent watering than in-ground plants, the nutrients they need tend to get washed out of the soil. It's best, therefore, to apply a complete fertilizer (such as 5-10-5, depending on the crop) every fifteen to twenty days. Liquid fertilizers, such as fish emulsion, seem to

---

WAYS TO CONSERVE WATER WHEN CONTAINER GARDENING

- Plant in containers with non-porous sides; less water will be lost by evaporation.
- Apply mulch.
- Arrange your container-grown plants close to each other. They will shade each other's soil, create a humid microclimate, offer each other wind protection, and cut down on the amount of reflected heat from the cement, asphalt, or ground they are standing on.
- Set the containers out of the wind.
- Unless they need the extra heat, set container-grown plants away from walls that reflect the sun.
- Root and leaf crops will grow with as little as 4 to 6 hours of direct sunlight a day. Shaded plants use much less water than plants in full sunlight.

work especially well for container-grown vegetables. If you use a granulated fertilizer, make sure it is suitable for vegetables, and water heavily immediately after applying it. Time-release fertilizers are also available at garden centers and through catalogues. Apply all fertilizers according to package instructions, but use less fertilizer than recommended on a more frequent schedule than recommended.

Are there any vegetables that can't be grown in containers?

Asparagus, corn, summer and winter squashes, and melons are not commonly grown in containers, yet all but asparagus among these vegetables have been grown successfully in containers by determined patio gardeners.

What is vertical gardening?

This is a way of arranging low-growing, shade-tolerant plants beneath tall or vining plants. For example, try growing pole beans in containers along a fence or trellis they can climb, with carrots planted in the same containers beneath them. Or let peas climb a net or string trellis placed against a fence or a wall, and sow radishes in the same containers with the peas. The radishes will be ready to harvest before the peas make enough headway to shade them out.

Can I use a container more than once without changing the soil?

Yes, if you improve the soil each year in the same way that you would build soil in the garden (see pgs. 630-37). Rotate crops of the same plant family from container to container on a four-year schedule to minimize the danger of soil-borne diseases.

Is it all right to move containers once the plants are growing in them?

This is an advantage of container growing: You can move your garden to suit both its needs and your preferences. Set larger tubs and pots on platforms with casters so that they will be easy to move.

Is it possible to have a pest- and disease-free garden?

Like the completely weed-free garden, the completely insect- and disease-free garden is an ideal seldom attained. Your best approach is preventive gardening: Build a healthy soil so that the healthy plants growing in it will be more resistant to disease and insect attack. Plant disease-resistant varieties, give your plants good care (weeding, thinning, and watering), and learn to recognize signs that they are in need of moisture or fertilizer. If insect or disease problems do arise, be prepared to deal with them as soon as possible.

INSECT PESTS AND DISEASES OF VEGETABLES

Insect Pests and Their Controls

INSECT	TYPE OF DAMAGE	CROPS AFFECTED	CONTROL
Aphids	Suck sap from buds, leaves, and stems	Beans, celery, okra, peas, peppers, potatoes	Apply a strong spray of water. Spray with soap and water solution (1 teaspoon mild dishwashing soap to 1 quart water), followed by thorough rinsing later that day. Dust wet plants with wood ashes or diatomaceous earth. Sprinkle bonemeal around plants. Plantings of tansy or pennyroyal may discourage ants.
Asparagus beetles	Eat tips and foliage	Asparagus	Do a thorough fall clean-up (but don't remove dead ferns until spring in cold-winter areas). Use pyrethrum or rotenone to kill larval stage. Shake beetles from plants into a can of soapy water.
Cabbage loopers and cabbage worms	Leaves chewed, sometimes to the extent that plants starve and die	All *Brassicas*, potatoes, radishes	*Bacillus thuringiensis* (Bt). Garden clean-up. Rotation of *Brassicas* and root crops with other plant families on a three-year schedule. Wood ashes spread on soil after each rain or watering.
Cabbage root maggots		*Brassicas*, parsnips, radishes, turnips	Apply lime or wood ashes to soil.
Colorado potato beetles	Defoliation	Nightshade family (potatoes, tomatoes, peppers, eggplants)	Daily hand-pick both adults and eggs, which hide on the undersides of leaves. Rotate Nightshade crops with other plant families. Alternate rows of potatoes and bush beans. Time planting to avoid these, if possible. Turn over the soil in late fall.
Corn borers	Feed inside stalks	Corn	Dust once a week with rotenone or other approved insecticide. Cut a slit in the stalks of infested corn plants and remove worm. Turn under or burn infested stalks in the fall.
Corn earworms	Feed on foliage and kernels. Opens plants to disease and other insect pests	Corn	Just after silk has browned, apply 10 to 20 drops of mineral oil containing rotenone with an eyedropper to the silk tassles or spray mineral oil on tassles. Apply *Bacillus thuringiensis* (Bt) formulated for this purpose. Grow varieties with close-tipped husks. In the fall, turn old broken cornstalks under and thoroughly cultivate soil.
Cutworms	Plants cut off at ground level and left	*Brassicas*, peppers, tomatoes	Place cardboard collars around young seedlings.
Flea beetles	Tiny holes in leaves	*Brassicas*, eggplant, radishes	Sprinkle rotenone or wood ashes on the plants. Observe clean garden practices. Rotate plant families.
Harlequin bugs	Kill young plants by sucking out juices	Cabbage	Rotenone or pyrethrum kills the nymph stage.
Japanese beetles	Chew holes in leaves	Beans	Pheromone traps. Attract birds, which will eat Japanese beetles. Hand-pick small infestations.
Leaf hoppers	Suck plant juices, and in the process introduce disease	Beans, lettuce, Nightshade family	Drape or suspend cheesecloth over plants. Apply pyrethrum or rotenone.
Leaf miners	Wavy, silverish lines through leaves	Beets, spinach, Swiss chard	Pull off all affected leaves and burn them. Drape plants with cheesecloth.

aphid

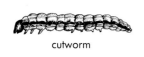

cutworm

flea beetle

harlequin bug

leafhopper

Insect Pests and Their Controls

INSECT	TYPE OF DAMAGE	CROPS AFFECTED	CONTROL
Mexican bean beetles	Feed on foliage, leaving only leaf skeleton	Beans	Apply rotenone. Set out pheromone traps. Hand-pick. Release predatory worms. Clean up spent bean plants after harvest.
Onion maggots	Tunnel into onion bulbs	Onions	Pull up and destroy plants with infested, softened bulbs. Spread onions throughout the garden rather than in one bed.
Rust fly	Maggot stage feeds on root system	Carrots	Sprinkle wood ashes around the base of plants.
Slugs and snails	Eat entire young plants or leave gaping holes in more mature plants; leave silver trails along ground.	Globe artichokes, lettuce, peppers	After dark, use a flashlight to find slugs. Hand-pick them, and put them in soapy water (wear cotton gloves to avoid getting sticky excretion on your fingers). Trap them under boards and then destroy them. Circle beds with a band of thin copper or a gritty material such as sand, lime, or wood ashes. Trap them in small saucers filled with beer sunk into the ground.
Squash bugs	Cause leaves to wilt and vines to blacken	Squashes	Remove leaves with eggs on them and burn them. Hand-pick. Maintain a clean, neat garden. Throw away old vines after harvest. Rotenone will kill nymph stage. Trap bugs at night by laying a shingle on the ground near plants; overturn shingle and destroy bugs in the morning. Dust with a mixture of wood ashes and slaked lime.
Squash vine borers	Holes in stems; wilted leaves	Cantaloupe, cucumber, squash	Cut borers out of stems. Use rotenone at larval stage. Clean up vines right after harvest. Till soil after harvest to expose cocoons to foraging birds and the elements.
Striped and spotted cucumber beetles	Spread garden disease, such as verticillium wilt	Beans, corn, cucumbers, melons, squash	Use floating row covers over plants to prevent new eggs from being laid. Clean up the garden well after harvest. Mulch with a dry material such as straw. Cultivate in spring and fall to help break the insect's life cycle. Dust with wood ashes, rock phosphate, rotenone, or pyrethrum. Grow plants on trellises.
Thrips	Dark specks on foliage, followed by large, white blotches; drooping shoots; suck plant juices	Onions	Weeds attract thrips. Burn onion tops after harvest. Insecticidal soap or rotenone. Rotate crops.
Tomato horn worms	Defoliation	Tomatoes	Hand-pick. Use *Bacillus thuringiensis* (Bt). (Small white sacks attached to worms are the cocoons of a parasitic wasp that effectively destroys horn worms: Do not kill worms that carry these sacks.)
Weevils	Long snout punctures leaves, stems, and fruits	Peppers, sweet potatoes	Time planting to avoid infestation, if possible. Hill up soil around stems of sweet potato vines. On peppers, hand-pick or control with rotenone. Rotate crops.
Wireworms	Feed on roots and underground stems	Beets, carrots	Choose a new location next year. Avoid planting in places that have recently been converted from sod.

Mexican bean beetle

slug

onion maggot

squash bug

striped cucumber beetle

wireworm

thrip

When seed catalogues offer several different varieties, each of which is resistant to a different disease, how can I know which one would be best for me to grow?

Your Extension Service agent will advise you on which diseases are likely to be common in your area. You can then choose the seed variety that is resistant to those diseases.

What vegetables are most susceptible to disease?

This depends on where you live. In general, cabbage crops, melons, tomatoes, and cucumbers are more susceptible to disease than most others.

I know that farmers rotate their crops. Is this something I should do to combat pests and disease?

By all means. If you keep a garden journal (see pg. 627) you'll be able to see what you planted where last year, and the year before that. Try not to grow the same kind of crop in the same bed more than once every three years. In fact, avoid growing successive crops from the same plant families: tomatoes, peppers, eggplants, and potatoes belong to the Nightshade family; broccoli, cabbages, kale, collards, and Brussels sprouts are all *Brassicas*; beans and peas are legumes. The time-honored practice of rotating crops not only breaks the life cycles of insects and diseases that feed or live on particular plants, but helps prevent depletion of soil nutrients by such heavy feeders as corn and cabbages.

Insect Pests

What are botanical poisons?

They are plant-derived substances that are poisonous to insects and have little residual effect. They include rotenone, pyrethrum, nicotine solutions, and ryania. Though they are less dangerous than synthetic compounds, they should still be used with caution and a good knowledge of their effects. Like synthetic compounds, botanical poisons are toxic, and may be harmful to beneficial insects as well as insect pests. Rotenone, for example, although harmless to warm-blooded animals, kills bees, which are crucial for plant pollination; to minimize this risk, apply rotenone in the evening when bees aren't flying.

How are botanical poisons applied?

Rotenone and pyrethrum are both applied as a dust or a wetted powder. If they are washed away by rain or overhead watering, they must be reapplied. Pyrethrum, which is made from pyrethrum flowers, must be freshly ground before use. Because it sometimes stuns insects rather than killing them, the insects must be collected and destroyed before they wake up.

Ron West

The cabbage looper moves about with a characteristic looping motion, similar to an inchworm.

Ron West

The Colorado potato beetle is the major pest of potato foliage east of the Rocky Mountains.

Some people are very allergic to pyrethrum, so it should be used with caution. Ryania, effective against aphids, corn borers, Japanese beetles, and codling moths, comes from a Carribean shrub. Like rotenone and pyrethrum, it must be applied frequently.

What are the advantages and disadvantages of commercial insecticides and disease controls?

If you closely follow the label instructions, commercial products work quickly and easily. The products available to home gardeners have been thoroughly tested for effectiveness, and if you are using the right one for the problem you have, they will probably rid your garden temporarily of that insect. Once you start using these chemicals, however, your garden can become dependent upon them because they kill beneficial as well as harmful insects. In addition, used on vegetable gardens, commercial chemicals introduce into your food substances whose long-term effects may not be known. If you do use commercial garden chemicals, carefully follow the label instructions, paying particular attention to the advice on how close to harvest you can safely apply the product.

Helpful Insects and Animals

What are beneficial insects?

A great number of insects further your gardening efforts by feeding on harmful insects. Some of the most common are praying mantises, ladybugs, and lacewing flies (aphid lions). Both ladybugs and lacewing flies prey on aphids. Lacewing flies construct funnel-shaped pits in which to trap aphids, which they then snatch with their long, curved jaws. You may be able to obtain any of these insects from mail-order seed companies or garden centers.

Ladybug.

How can I encourage beneficial insects to live in my garden?

The key is not to *dis*courage them. If you spray to get rid of insect pests, you will unfortunately kill beneficial ones as well. Grow flowering plants among the vegetables to provide pollen and nectar for adult beneficial insects. Dill is very attractive to beneficial worms.

Besides beneficial insects, are there other living things that could help my garden?

Two of the very best are earthworms and birds. Earthworms loosen and aerate the soil, fertilize it with their castings, and help create humus. Yet strong commercial fertilizers, insecticides, and herbicides can kill earthworms. Find out which birds in your area can be most helpful in controlling insect pests, and invite

Beneficial insects, such as this praying mantis, feed on harmful insects in the garden.

them into your yard by providing the kind of houses or trees and shrubbery that they nest in, and providing water and, if necessary, food.

Won't these beneficial birds also eat seedlings in my garden?

Some of them will—if you let them. Protect seedlings with wire enclosures. Narrow lengths of chicken wire folded into long tents work wonderfully on long rows (be sure to enclose the ends of these tents). For wide beds, arch chicken wire over from side to side. Or you can construct movable boxes with scrap wood. Covered with plastic, these can double as mini-greenhouses during early spring.

Are there any other non-chemical controls for areas with great numbers of insect pests?

Cover your seedbeds with floating row covers, available in garden centers or by mail, until plants are fully established.

Plant Diseases

How will I know which diseases my garden might be susceptible to?

Regional seed catalogues usually specify which varieties resist the diseases that most commonly attack in a given area. If you know which diseases you are likely to encounter in your region, you can make wise purchases from any good seed catalogue. For disease problems common to specific plant species, see Chapt. 27.

What are the best ways to keep my plants from contracting diseases?

Plant resistant varieties; rotate crops; keep garden free of rotting plant material; promptly discard or burn diseased plants; provide good ventilation around plants; and build healthy soil on an ongoing basis.

Are plant diseases a big problem in home gardens?

They are not usually as much of a problem as for farmers growing large crops of a single kind. A home garden is more varied, with a greater number of checks and balances to control an outbreak of disease or an insect infestation.

Can humans spread disease from plant to plant in a garden?

Yes, this can happen with some vegetables. For example, if you cultivate beans while the leaves are wet, you may spread disease. Or if you smoke cigarettes near members of the Nightshade family, the plants may contract tobacco mosaic.

27 Favorite Vegetables to Grow

Artichoke, Globe *(Cynara)*

Where are artichokes best grown?

This perennial vegetable is grown as a winter crop in California, between San Francisco and Los Angeles along the coast, where it gets the mild winters and cool, moist summers in which it thrives. It also finds favorable weather conditions on the Gulf Coast, and in the South Atlantic states. In the eastern states (as far north as Massachusetts), artichokes are a summer crop; and their root crowns are mulched during the winter or dug up and brought indoors.

How can I get artichokes started?

It is best to purchase root divisions. Plant them 6 inches deep, spaced 6 feet apart, as soon as the ground warms in the spring. Alternatively, you can start seeds indoors, planting them ½ inch deep in containers four to six weeks before the last spring frost. Set the seedlings out after all danger of frost is past.

What kind of soil do artichokes need?

Dig plenty of rotted manure or compost into the soil before planting, and give plants a sidedressing of nitrogen halfway through the season. Artichokes need rich, well-drained soil. Mulch with organic materials. If you live in a place that gets hot summer sun, provide your artichokes with partial shade and frequent watering.

◄ *Ruby cabbage and vinca co-exist in serendipitous color harmony.*

Maggie Oster

Globe artichoke: Harvest these intricately formed vegetables when the buds are still firm and tightly compacted.

Jerusalem artichoke tuber.

How should I harvest artichokes?

Cut buds off while they are still firm and tightly compacted. The younger the bud, the tenderer the leaves—but the smaller the heart.

Artichoke, Jerusalem *(Helianthus)*

Are Jerusalem artichokes perennial also?

They are, and the name of one popular variety—Stampede—gives you an idea of what these plants will do in your garden if you don't take measures to keep them from spreading.

How should I plant Jerusalem artichokes?

As soon as you can work in the ground in the spring, take small pieces of the tubers with eyes and plant them about 6 inches deep and 18 inches apart. You'll get a big harvest from just a few plants, so unless you have an enormous appetite for them, it is best to plant just a few.

Are Jerusalem artichokes fussy in their needs?

Not at all. You needn't bother with fertilizer, and watering is necessary only in very dry areas. They are troubled by few diseases or pests, except perhaps gophers.

When should I harvest Jerusalem artichokes?

Dig up the tubers in autumn after the tops have died, and store them in plastic bags in the refrigerator until you use them. You can also leave tubers in the ground to harvest as you need them. If you do this in a cold-winter climate, mulch the ground enough to keep them from freezing.

Where can I get planting stock?

You can cut up and plant the Jerusalem artichokes sold in the grocery store as a vegetable. Many seed catalogues sell them, too.

Arugula; Roquette *(Eruca)*

Would you please describe the taste and origins of arugula?

Peppery arugula belongs to the mustard family and adds a nice zip to a tossed salad. Arugula is a long-time standard in Italy and is now popular in nouvelle cuisine.

Can I grow arugula in my garden in New Hampshire?

It should do quite well there, for it prefers chilly, wet weather and cold soil. Early spring, late summer, and fall are best for growing arugula, though in more southern areas where temperatures don't fall below freezing, you can grow it during the winter in a cold frame. It is seldom bothered by either pests or disease.

What are arugula's growing requirements?

Sow a small planting every week or two for a continuous crop; arugula is a very fast-growing and fast-bolting crop. Scatter the seeds across a wide bed and sift ¼ inch of light soil over them. Fertile, well-drained soil is ideal.

What is the best way to harvest arugula?

Pick the leaves off as you need them, or cut the entire plant off a few inches above its base and it will come back again. The plants come to full maturity in forty days, but you can eat thinnings and young tender leaves well before that.

Asparagus *(Asparagus)*

Where will asparagus grow?

Perennial asparagus takes well to all areas of the U.S. except the very coldest North, the Deep South, and Southern California. It actually needs cold winters, and will withstand winter temperatures of -40° F. A well-tended bed will last at least twenty years.

How should I go about starting an asparagus bed?

Prepare a planting bed in late fall or as early in the spring as the ground can be worked. Spread lime if your soil is acid, then dig lots of compost and well-rotted manure 2 feet into the ground. In early spring spade an 8- to 10-inch deep trench in this bed and set in the root crowns, 12 inches apart. Gradually fill in the trench once the plants are actively growing, taking care not to cover the growing tips.

How must I care for my asparagus bed?

Mulch with an organic material, such as compost, that will feed the soil and keep the weeds down. If you don't mulch, weed regularly. If you have acidic soil, spread lime generously on either side of the bed a few days before fertilizing in the spring. Fertilize again after the harvest period. If you live in a cold-winter area, mulch thickly before winter sets in, but pull the mulch aside in early spring so the ground can warm up faster.

I've heard there is a limit to how much asparagus you should harvest. Is this so?

Don't harvest any spears the first year of growth from root crowns (or the first two years of growth from seed). Harvest

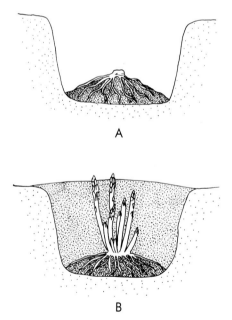

A

B

(A) Set asparagus root crowns in a prepared 8- to 10-inch deep trench, and (B) gradually fill in the trench once the plants are actively growing, taking care not to cover the growing tips.

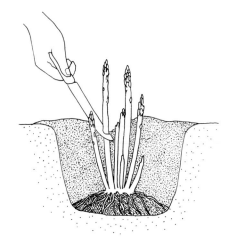

Harvest asparagus by cutting the spear just below ground level when it is about a finger's thickness.

Scarlet runner beans: Often grown as ornamentals, these beans may be used as snap beans or shelled for use in casseroles, soups, or salads.

lightly from root-crown plantings the second spring. If the spears are skinny, don't harvest them at all. Start picking in earnest the third year, and never miss that spring fertilizing. Cut the spears just below ground level when they are about a finger's thickness, and leave enough skinny ones to grow into ferns that will nourish the plant. Don't harvest at all after midsummer.

What are some good rust-resistant varieties of asparagus?

If asparagus rust is a problem in your area, plant Mary Washington or Waltham Washington.

How can I grow white asparagus?

Blanch emerging spears by covering them with airy heaps of a light, organic mulch.

Beans, bush and pole (Legumes)

Which is better to plant—pole beans or bush beans?

Bush beans bear earlier, but over a shorter season. Pole beans produce more abundantly, over a greater length of time (if they are picked regularly), and they have a fuller flavor. Most bean varieties available today are stringless.

Are beans difficult to grow?

Beans grow well in any garden soil. Plant bean seed directly in the ground after all danger of frost is past, two or three weeks after the date of the average last killing frost. The seeds need a soil temperature of at least 60° F. to germinate. Sow bush types 1 inch deep and 2 inches apart, and plant in succession (see page 81) until 50 to 60 days before the first fall frost. Leave 2 or 3 feet of space between rows so you will have room to pick. Wide beds can be planted intensively (see page 58). Beans tend to thin themselves, so plant them close together and let the leaves shade out weeds. Sow pole beans 1 inch deep and 3 inches apart, with 7 seeds around the base of each pole and with 4 feet between rows.

Should beans be fertilized?

If you use commercial fertilizer, apply 2 ½ pounds of a 5-10-10 formula per 100 square feet of row or wide bed. If they are pale, or seem to be growing poorly, apply a sidedressing 3 inches from the plants once they've leafed out and are growing strongly. Beans usually do quite well without very much fertilizer.

Should I water bean plants?

Water them infrequently but deeply, and water at the base of the plants rather than on the leaves, to prevent disease from spreading.

How can I prevent downy mildew or other disease?

Avoid going into your bean patch in the early morning dew, after a rainfall, or at any time when the leaves are wet. Rotate your bean crops.

I've heard that beans are good vegetables to plant in rotation with other crops. Why is this?

Beans are the perfect crop to plant following a crop of heavy feeders, such as corn, because beans take nitrogen from the air and fix it into the soil.

Selected Beans

COMMON NAME	BOTANICAL NAME	EDIBLE FORM	USES	DESCRIPTION	GROWING INFORMATION
Azuki (or Adzuki)	*Vigna angularis*	Immature pods, shelled, or dried	In Japan, dried azuki beans are used for desserts as well as in hearty vegetable stews	Small, brick-colored beans; bushy, delicate plant	Best started indoors in peat pots, as they take 120 days to mature
Chickpeas; garbanzos	*Cicer arietinum*	Dried	Use in Middle Eastern dishes, salads, and soups	Lacey, unusual plants; one or two peas to a pod	Require over 100 days to mature, and prefer a warm, dry climate
Fava; broad; horse	*Vicia faba*	Immature pods (2 to 3 inches long) or shelled	Eat young beans like snap beans (some people of Mediterranean descent are allergic to fava beans)	Large, shiny, plump pods, each with five to seven fat, green beans; sweet-smelling flowers are white with black centers	Semi-hardy—in warm climates, plant them in late fall; in the North and East, plant them in the spring as soon as the soil can be worked
Lima	*Phaseolus limensis*	Fresh	Alone or in casseroles and soups	Both bush and pole varieties; heavy producers	Prefer cool summers (in hot climates grow the more heat-tolerant butterbeans, such as Henderson's Bush)
Mung	*Vigna radiata*	Sprouts	Chinese dishes such as stir-frys and chop suey	Small, green bean	Need a long, hot, preferably humid, summer
Runner	*Phaseolus coccineus*	As snap bean, or shelled	Alone or in casseroles, soups, or salads	Beautiful, profuse red or white flowers; large, shiny, handsome beans; often grown as an ornamental; perennial in warm-weather areas	Same as string beans
Soybeans	*Glycine max*	Shelled or dried	Tofu, soy milk, tempeh, salad oil, cattle feed; boil green soybeans in their pods for 5 minutes, shell them, and then cook for 15 minutes more; use dried beans in casseroles	Round, almost white bean	Drought-tolerant, easy-to-grow; green varieties mature in 75 days; dried beans mature in 105 to 120 days

When should I begin harvesting my beans?

To keep beans producing, start picking them (including their stems) as soon as you see the first edible bean—that is, as soon as their seeds begin to show through their skin, or even earlier if you like them extra tender. If you have more beans than you can harvest and eat, let some plants go completely to seed, and concentrate on harvesting a few plants thoroughly. Shell these "seedy" beans and eat the seeds fresh, as you would limas. If they're not hybrids, dry them and use them as seed next year.

Dried beans are so inexpensive. Are they really worth growing for drying and shelling?

Most drying beans are good to eat at the immature green bean stage and good also shelled and eaten green. This makes them multipurpose plants in every way. Furthermore, there are a good many wonderful drying beans for sale in catalogues that simply can't be purchased in most stores. Many of them, such as Jacob's Cattle, Soldier, Yellow Eye, and Swedish Brown beans, are stunning in their beauty as well as their flavor when you bake or boil them.

When should I pick beans for shelling and eating fresh?

Shelling beans are eaten in the stage between green and dried. If you plant them once a week over the first month of the growing season, you can have fresh shelling beans all season long.

Pole beans readily climb twine provided for them and produce more abundantly and for a longer time than bush beans.

Martha Storey

Beets *(Beta)*

Why are beets so popular with vegetable gardeners?

Beets are one of the most versatile vegetables you can grow. They are hardy—you can start them early or late—and if you mulch them well, you can harvest them even after unmulched ground has frozen. Their leaves have an exquisite, sweet, yet mildly acid flavor, and their roots lend themselves well to pickles, soups, and salads, or simply serve boiled beets whole or sliced with butter. Look for cylindrical slicing beets, golden or white salad beets, and varieties developed for leaf flavor.

How should I plant beet seeds?

Spread lime if your soil is acid. Sow beet seeds when the ground has begun to warm up in the spring. Beet seeds come in clusters, so sow thinly, about 10 seeds per foot, ½ inch deep in rows 12 inches apart. You can keep planting every two weeks until midsummer, and again six to eight weeks before the first frost. Don't plant beets during the hot months. Although they will grow in clay soil, beets prefer light, sandy soil and steady moisture. Mulch after sowing.

When should I begin harvesting beets?

Thin beets when the greens and young roots are the size of a quarter, and eat the thinnings. A few leaves may be picked as the beets mature. In warm climates, beets can be left in the ground in the fall, and harvested through the winter as needed.

Ann Reilly

Beet: Both tops and roots of Burpee's Golden beets are tender and sweet.

Broccoli *(Brassica)*

Should I sow broccoli seeds directly in the ground or buy seedlings?

Broccoli is usually transplanted using purchased seedlings or seedlings begun indoors, rather than directly seeded in the ground. Early plantings should go in during March and April; later plantings, if you have sustained cool weather, can go in during May. For a fall harvest, plant in late summer. Broccoli can take light frosts in the fall.

How should I plant broccoli?

Make sure your soil is rich in nutrients—especially calcium—and well drained. Space transplants 18 to 24 inches apart in rows 2 to 3 feet apart. Plant seeds ½ inch deep, twelve seeds to a foot, and thin to the same spacing as for transplants. These thinnings, if handled carefully, can be used to start another row.

Maggie Oster

Broccoli: Purple-headed broccoli turns emerald green when cooked.

Do broccoli plants require watering and fertilizing?

Provide continuous soil moisture, but don't flood the roots. Mulching helps. Apply a nitrogen fertilizer as a sidedressing to established plants every month or so to keep them growing fast.

When should broccoli be harvested?

Cut off the heads a few inches down the stem when the flowers have formed but are still tight. If you leave a good amount of stem, side shoots will form, which may be cut and used later. Some varieties are known for producing lots of side shoots over a long period. Don't let any buds go to flower.

Brussels sprouts *(Brassica)*

When can I plant Brussels sprouts?

Brussels sprouts need cool weather. Although they will withstand a certain amount of summer warmth, they won't thrive in hot summers. The cool, damp climate of the central coast of California is ideal for Brussels sprouts. Set out transplants (after broccoli) in mid-May through mid-June for a fall harvest. If you sow seed outdoors (you need a long growing season to do so), plant it the same way as you would broccoli seed.

What kind of soil and fertilizer needs do Brussels sprouts have?

Give them rich, well-drained soil, steady water, and side-dressings of nitrogen-rich fertilizer.

How can I know when to harvest Brussels sprouts?

The sprouts, or buds, mature from the bottom of the stalk up. Remove leaves as they turn yellow; the leaves will usually snap off easily as far up the stem as the sprouts are ready to cut. Twist-snap the sprouts off when they're firm. Very small Brussels sprouts make fine baby vegetables. Leave Brussels sprouts in the garden for the first light frosts, which improve this vegetable's flavor. Before the first hard freeze, cut entire stalks, remove the leaves and the crown, and hang them upside down in a cool, dark, dry place. They'll keep for many weeks this way.

Cabbage *(Brassica)*

Can I grow cabbage in the South?

Cabbage is a cool-weather crop, needing from 60 to 125 days to mature, depending on the variety. In the South, you'll need to plant cabbage in fall to mature in winter. Plant short-season, early cabbage in mid- to late winter, so that it will mature before extreme heat sets in.

How should I prepare for planting cabbage?

See to it in the fall that your cabbage bed is well limed so that it has sufficient calcium content and pH balance. Dig in fresh, uncomposted manure during the fall so that it will decompose sufficiently by spring.

Should I begin seeds indoors or can I plant cabbage directly into the garden?

You can start seeds indoors for transplanting four to six weeks before the last frost. Set the seedlings outdoors after the last frost, spacing them 12 to 18 inches apart in rows 2 to 3 feet apart. Alternatively, you can direct-seed, but wait until the soil is at least 50° F. and then sow four seeds per foot, ½ inch deep, in rows 2 to 3 feet apart. Thin to 12- to 18-inch spacings in the rows. In general, those varieties that take the longest to mature also keep the longest. If you're planting late varieties, which mature just in time for winter storage, get them started as soon as possible in the spring.

Does cabbage require fertilizer and extra watering?

Cabbages are heavy feeders, and should be planted in well-fertilized, rich soil. Fertilize a week before planting, and in addition, apply one or two sidedressings of fertilizer during the growing season. Since cabbage roots are shallow, the plants need frequent watering during dry weather. If the heads crack, the cabbages are growing too fast. This can come from too much fertilizer at once, or from a sudden burst of growth when rains fall after a long dry spell. To prevent further cracking, clutch the heads in your hands and give them a half-turn twist. This will break some of the roots and slow the plants' growth.

How should I harvest cabbages?

Pull up the plants, roots and all, when the heads are mature. Cut off the root and compost it after chopping it into pieces with your spade.

What is Chinese cabbage?

This large group of cabbages is divided into two categories: heading and nonheading. The heading types *(Brassica pekinensis)* include the Napas (also called Michili, celery cabbage, and Pe Tsai), which are often found in grocery stores. The most common of the nonheading Chinese types *(Brassica chinensis)* is Bok Choy (also called Pac Choi). Most all Chinese cabbages, and in particular the heading types, require cool growing conditions. Like all cabbages, they should grow fast and steadily for the best flavor and health. You can transplant or direct-seed. An excellent nonheading variety is Mei Qing Choi, also known as Baby Bok Choy.

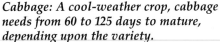

Cabbage: A cool-weather crop, cabbage needs from 60 to 125 days to mature, depending upon the variety.

Maggie Oster

Carrots *(Daucus)*

When can I begin planting carrots?

Beginning two weeks before the last spring frost, plant carrots in succession (see pg. 651) throughout the season until sixty days before the first killing frost. Although germination takes longer in cold soils, in mild-winter areas you can sow carrot seed all year round, as long as rains don't wash seeds away before they have time to sprout. Sow seeds ¼ inch deep in rows 1 to 2 feet apart. Give this tiny, shallow-planted seed some special attention, for it germinates slowly (one to three weeks). If you have heavy soil, water it well the day before planting; cover the seed with peat moss after planting. Water with a very fine mist. Sow radish seeds among the carrot seeds, at a ratio of about one radish seed to nine carrot seeds. The radish seeds will take only a few days to germinate, so they'll come up and mark your carrot rows for you while also gently loosening the soil around the carrots to give them a good start. Pull the radishes as soon as they are mature.

I have tried growing carrots, but my soil is heavy and my carrots are always crooked. Any suggestions?

Try growing the short, stubby, or even round varieties that are widely available today. Since these carrots don't extend deeply into the soil, they are less likely to twist or fork, and they are easy to harvest. You can also dig a trench and fill it with lighter soil, or build up a raised bed of lighter soil.

Do carrots need watering and fertilizing?

Keep carrot seeds moist until they sprout, and then water infrequently but deeply, so that the roots will reach down for moisture. Avoid using fresh manure; it causes the roots to be hairy and to fork. Too much nitrogen will produce wonderful foliage but not very good roots. Carrots are not heavy feeders and shouldn't be overfertilized. Weed carrots faithfully.

When can I start harvesting carrots?

Eat baby carrots from your thinnings, usually within forty days of planting. When they reach about finger thickness they will be extremely sweet. Thin carrots to stand 2 inches apart. If your soil gets really hard, soak it well before attempting to pull your carrots. If they break, you'll have to dig them out.

How should I store carrots for the winter?

The best way is to layer them in damp sand or sawdust, but they keep a long time in a ventilated plastic bag or in burlap if you put them in a dark, cool place. Or mulch the ground with hay bales or plastic bags of leaves to keep the ground from freezing, so that you can dig them up through the winter.

Carrots: For the best carrots, weed faithfully and thin so that plants stand 2 inches apart.

Cauliflower *(Brassica)*

Our summers are hot. Is it possible for me to grow cauliflower?

Start cauliflower indoors in the spring eight to ten weeks before the last spring frost or in the late summer, 80 to 100 days before the first killing frost. Cauliflower seedlings can go in the ground in the spring two weeks before the last expected frost.

How big should my seedlings be before I put them in the garden?

Seedlings should be four to five weeks old (and no older) when you set them out. Be sure to harden them off first (see page 641. Space the plants 18 to 24 inches apart in rows 2 to 3 feet apart.

How much water and what kind of soil should I give cauliflower?

The most important thing you can do for your cauliflower is to give it a regular supply of moisture so that it grows fast. Never let the soil dry out, but don't flood it, either. Cauliflower is best when the weather is cool. Sprinkle the plants with water during hot spells to keep them cool, and to maintain a humid atmosphere around them. Cauliflower prefers "sweet" soil—that is, soil with a pH a little on the alkaline side (between 6 and 7).

How can I be assured of white, sweet-tasting heads?

You must blanch the stalks by bending the outer leaves together over the curds (center) and tying them in place once the curds reach about 3 inches in diameter. Leave them this way until the head matures. Make sure the head is dry when you tie it up, and arrange the leaves in such a way that water can't trickle through to the curds and rot them. Untie the leaves of a few plants now and then to see how the heads are forming and whether any water is getting in.

When should I harvest cauliflower?

Cut the heads from the stalks when the curds are still tight, usually one or two weeks after tying them up. If the weather is getting hot, check them often, or they'll get away from you and begin to swell and form flowers.

I've seen self-blanching varieties advertised in many catalogues. What does this mean?

The leaves of these types grow over the curds, saving you the trouble of tying them up. Romanesco cauliflower (sometimes called Romanesco broccoli) has beautiful, pointed, green curds that look like little towers. Purple cauliflower, which turns green when cooked, is also available.

To be assured of white, sweet-tasting cauliflower, blanch stalks by bending the outer leaves together over the curds and tying them in place until the head matures.

Celery *(Apium)*

Isn't celery difficult to grow?

If you have a soil that holds water well, and a three-month cool-weather season, you can grow celery. If you have only two months of weather that is cool but not freezing, you can still give celery a try if you plant it in a spot where you can supply a little shade during hot spells.

How are celery seeds begun indoors?

In the spring, sow seeds in a light potting soil in flats, ten to twelve weeks before the soil warms up. Sow the seeds thinly and very shallowly (about ⅛ inch deep), and keep the soil in the flat warm and moist (up to 75° F.) until the seedlings emerge after two to three weeks. Once they're up you can let the soil get cooler—down to 60° F. When the plants are about 2 inches tall, transplant them into individual containers. Two or three weeks after the last expected frost, set the plants out in the garden, 6 inches apart in rows 2 to 3 feet apart.

In warm-summer areas, sow celery seeds in a well-prepared outdoor seed bed, about thirteen to fifteen weeks before the first expected frost. The plants will withstand light frost but not hard freezing in the fall. To transplant from seed beds into the garden,

A frame of boards and burlap around this row of celery blanches the plants, creating more tender hearts and stalks.

Maggie Oster

dig the seedlings carefully to avoid breaking the fine root system. Avoid doubling up or bunching the roots when you set them in their garden bed; pack the soil firmly around the plants, at the same level as it was in the seed bed.

Do celery plants need to be watered frequently?

Celery requires abundant and very consistent moisture, which means that soils with poor water-holding ability should be improved with plenty of organic matter.

Should I fertilize celery heavily?

Sidedressings of fairly rich fertilizer two or three times during the growing season will keep the plants strong and fast growing. But don't use too much fertilizer. Look closely at the plants as they grow and base your fertilizer applications on what you see rather than on any formula. Phosphorus (see pg. 634) promotes strong stalks. Make sure that your soil has adequate calcium in it by adding lime (if your soil is acid), gypsum, crushed eggshells, or phosphate rock.

Must celery be blanched?

Blanching creates paler, more tender hearts and stalks. One traditional blanching method involves planting celery in shallow trenches and then filling in the trenches with soil as the plants grow tall. The disadvantage of doing it this way is obvious to anyone who has ever spent a lot of time cleaning dirt from celery hearts and stalks before cooking them. Better methods of blanching are to pile straw around your celery plants, lean boards up against them, or tie shopping bags around the stalks with string—anything that blocks the sun but allows the circulation of air. Make sure plants are dry before you cover them, and leave the tops uncovered.

Celery may be blanched by wrapping stalks with paper and piling soil against them.

How should I store celery after harvest?

Pull up the entire plant once the stalks are blanched. To store celery, leave the roots on, spray the stalks and foliage with cool water, and then shake the water off. Let the stalks dry but keep the roots moist. Now plant them again in a shallow trench, in boxes in a cool cellar or in a cold frame, with the temperature just above freezing. You can keep celery fresh for many weeks this way.

Is celery troubled by diseases?

Celery blight is sometimes a problem. Rotate your crops to avoid it. If it occurs, dust or spray with bordeaux mixture every week or ten days, taking special pains to coat the lower leaves, especially the undersides. If very dry weather occurs, the disease may abate and you can stop treatment.

Chicory; Escarole; Radicchio *(Cichorium)*

When should I plant radicchio, or red-headed chicory?

In mild-winter areas, sow seeds in the fall. The plants will mature by spring, and fall frosts will give the plants the lovely red color they are known for. Where winter temperatures drop below 10° F., sow seeds in late May to early June. Cover the seeds with a very thin, ¼-inch layer of soil. Space them rather closely, but thin later to 8 to 12 inches apart. If you are growing a variety that needs cutting back, shear it back to a stub in early September. Within 4 to 6 weeks you'll be harvesting mature plants.

How are escarole and chicory grown?

Treat them like lettuce, and harvest before the first hard frost. Because they mature more slowly than lettuce, allow ninety days from sowing to grow large heads.

Collards *(Brassica)*

I don't know much about collards. Are they a good vegetable to grow?

Collards are non-heading cabbages that have much to recommend them. They are high in calcium, iron, and vitamins A and C. They don't mind frost, but can take considerable summer heat, which is perhaps one of the reasons why they are so widely grown in the South. Collards are also especially delicious after they have been touched by frost in the fall.

When should I plant collards?

Sow seeds in the ground at any time in the growing season, giving them eighty to ninety days to mature. Hot-area plantings are often made in the summer, so that the plants will mature in time to be touched by frost and thereby sweetened. In cold climates, seedlings are set out in the spring. Early spring to mid-spring plantings yield summer crops. Sow twelve seeds to the foot, ¼ to ½ inch deep in rows 2 feet apart. Thin the plants as they grow (and eat the thinnings) until they are growing one plant per foot.

What growing conditions should I provide for collards?

Collards are grown in the same way as other *Brassicas*. Supply calcium in the form of lime (in acid soils), gypsum, crushed eggshells, or phosphate rock for good harvests of nutrient-rich greens. You may need to stake the plants once they get leggy and top-heavy.

How are collards harvested?

Pull or cut off the lower leaves as you need them. Or cut out the tender, central loose head. Their preparation and uses are much like spinach or any other cooking greens.

Corn (*Zea*)

What are the various types of sweet corn?

Standard is the traditional variety. It has a crisp, crunchy texture but once picked, it loses its sweetness. SE (Everlasting Heritage, EV, or Sugar Enhanced) varieties are sweeter and more tender than standard varieties for a longer period after harvest. These varieties may be planted within 25 feet of standard sweet corn without risk of cross-pollination. SH_2 (Supersweet, Extra Sweet, or Xtra Sweet) varieties are very sweet and remain sweet long after harvest, because their sugar turns to sucrose rather than starch as in standard sweet corn. Their seed is shriveled and smaller than other corns. SH_2 varieties must be isolated at least 100 feet (or planted at different times) from both standard and SE varieties or both crops will produce tough, starchy kernels.

When can I plant corn?

The soil at planting time should be at least 70° F. for SE or SH_2 varieties and 65° F. for standard sweet corn. Particularly for SE and SH_2 varieties the soil should stay quite moist until the seedlings appear. As a rule, the newer corn types are not as hardy as standard hybrid varieties, and must be fertilized and watered with extra care.

What can I do to get my first corn extra early?

Plant an early variety such as Early Sunglow or Earlivee in a warm, sunny location. If the soil is still cold, use seed that has been treated with a fungicide; soak it for twenty-four hours in warm water. Plant it a little deep, and don't fertilize at all until the danger of frost is past. Black plastic mulch will help warm the soil, and a polyethylene tunnel placed over the rows will warm the air temperatures around the plants. You can also start corn in flats and transplant it, providing the seedlings are not kept too warm and then set out in cold ground too early. Peat pots or homemade tubes of newspaper work best as starter containers, because you don't disturb the roots when you transplant.

How is corn normally planted?

Sow seeds 1 to 1½ inches deep at 4-inch intervals, thinning the seedlings to 8- to 12-inch spacings. Space corn rows 2 to 3 feet apart so that you don't get scratched when harvesting. Corn needs steady moisture to germinate, so water your corn patch if

When the corn tassles, as shown here, apply a sidedressing of fertilizer and water it in well.

Maggie Oster

the weather is dry. During hot weather, when the soil is already warm, you can mulch a newly planted bed with a thin layer of organic material to keep the soil from drying out in the hot sun.

The row of corn I planted last year never bore for me. What was wrong?

If you planted one long row, chances are it was poorly pollinated. In order to ensure pollination, corn must be planted in blocks of at least four rows. Different varieties should go in different blocks rather than every other row. Don't plant sweet corn near field corn, or the field corn will pollinate your sweet corn and give it tough kernels.

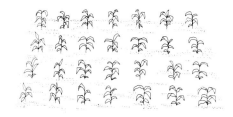

Corn must be planted in blocks of at least four rows to assure good pollination.

Does corn need much care?

Cultivate your corn bed to kill weeds until the plants reach a foot high. After that, cultivate very shallowly. Hill up dirt against the corn stalks so that you don't have to cultivate too close to them. Better yet, apply a mulch to keep weeds down and retain moisture in the soil. Corn is a very heavy feeder, and should be planted in soil that has been fertilized with a complete, nitrogen-rich fertilizer. Follow this with a sidedressing of high-nitrogen fertilizer when the corn is almost a foot high. When the corn tassles, give yet another sidedressing of fertilizer, along with extra water, and continue to water steadily until the ears ripen.

Should I remove suckers (side shoots) from corn stalks?

No, this old practice has no apparent benefits.

How can I tell whether my corn is ready to harvest?

Corn is ready to harvest when the silks have turned brown and dry. Squeeze the tops of the ears to see if they are filled out. If they seem to be, peel back the husks and have a look. If the kernels are full and round and ooze milk when you poke them with a fingernail, they are ready to pick. Don't peel back any more husks than necessary, for this exposes the ears to insect attack.

Is it true that you should put the water on to boil before you go out to harvest the corn?

To assure the freshest tasting corn with the old standard varieties, the faster you can get it from the garden to the table, the better. The new supersweets have so much sugar that an hour or so wait will cause no discernible loss in sweetness. If you refrigerate them promptly, they will still taste wonderful even a day later.

How can I avoid having the wind blow over stalks?

This problem is called "lodging." Plant resistant varieties, and protect planting with windbreaks. If the stalks fall over, though there has been little wind, look for European corn borer damage.

A white gall that later turned black appeared on my corn last year. What was it?

It was corn smut, a fungus growth that comes through the stem into the ear or tassle. It is one of the most disturbing-looking corn diseases, but usually causes no serious problems. Cut out these galls, and either burn them or wrap them in plastic and dispose of them—but *not* in your compost heap. Also destroy smutty ears as soon as you find them. Plant a smut-resistant variety next time.

Crows got in and pulled up all my corn seedlings to eat the plump kernels at their bases. How can I keep them away?

The best method to combat birds is to protect newly planted rows with long, narrow tents of 18-inch chicken wire. Be sure to close the tents on either end, or the birds will simply hop inside one end of the tent and eat their way to the other. Some gardeners report success with deep mulches, though these aren't recommended for cold soils.

The worst problem I've had in raising corn is raccoons. Is there any defense against them?

Raccoons seem to be better than people are at calculating the ripeness of corn. 'Coons will climb almost anything but an electrified fence—which they may dig their way under. You could try one of the traps that captures animals without harming them, but if you don't have experience with releasing raccoons from a live trap, seek advice from your local animal shelter or from the trap's manufacturer. Raccoons can be as vicious as they are cute, and they can transmit rabies.

I grew wonderful corn one year, but the next year when I grew it in the same place, my harvest wasn't nearly as good. Was it the weather?

Weather might have had something to do with it, but it is more likely that the soil was exhausted of nutrients. It is best not to grow corn twice in the same place until three or four years pass. Follow heavy-feeding corn crops with heavy-giving crops of peas or beans (see page 651).

My cornstalks grew tall and heavy, but bore no ears. What might the problem have been?

They could have been spaced too close or been given too much nitrogen. This happens, too, if plants are not sown in 4-row blocks.

What causes stalks to tassle when they are only 2 or 3 feet tall?

Stress caused by acid soil, dry weather, dark days, or a lack of fertilizer.

After pollination has taken place, spray mineral oil on browning corn silk to deter corn earworms.

What would cause corn ears to fail to fill out?

It could be nutrient-poor soil, plants that are spaced too closely, cross-pollination with field corn, or corn borers in the stalk just below the ear.

Cucumbers (*Cucumis*)

Where should I plant cucumbers in my garden?

Cucumbers need partial shade and something to climb on. They look delightful growing rampantly on a fence or porch railing, and the fruit will be easier to harvest. Simply plant them under a fence, or against a wall onto which you can hang strings and tie the vines to the strings or fence with strips of cloth where necessary. Plant bush varieties in containers.

Should I start cucumber plants indoors?

Cucumbers are warm-weather plants, and many gardeners thus start them indoors so that they can have seedlings heading skyward in the garden just as soon as the warm weather begins in earnest. Indoors, plant cucumbers in soil that is about 70° F. during the day and 60° F. at night. Start them four weeks before setting them outside. Transplant the seedlings with great care after all danger of frost is past. If the weather is still cool, set them under hot caps. Space them 6 inches apart in rows 4 to 5 feet apart.

What kind of soil do cucumbers need?

Good quality garden loam that is fairly high in nutrients will support cucumbers. The soil should not be acid, and it should be well drained. Keep the ground moist at all times, especially during hot spells, or the fruit will turn bitter.

How should I care for cucumbers?

Weed faithfully until the plants are large enough to shade the ground. Mulch once the soil is warm, not only to keep down weeds and hold moisture in the soil, but also to keep mud from splashing onto the leaves and spreading disease. When the plants are knee high, sidedress them with bloodmeal, cotton-seed or soy meal, or some other nitrogen-rich fertilizer.

How can I get my cucumber plants to keep producing?

Check the plants every day during peak production and harvest often, for once a cucumber plant satisfies itself with a few mature fruits, it stops producing and dies. Young cucumbers taste better than aged ones, so pick them smaller than the ones you see in the store. Avoid touching the plants when they're wet, so that you won't spread disease.

Positive Images, Jerry Howard

Cucumber: Give cucumber vines partial shade and something to climb on.

Eggplant (*Solanum*)

Is it true that eggplant makes a good ornamental plant?

Long grown as an ornamental as well as a food plant, eggplant comes in white, green, yellow, and pink, as well as the familiar purple varieties. Specialty vegetable catalogues carry seed for Thai, Japanese, Chinese, Indian, Persian, Italian, and other varieties.

Should I begin eggplant indoors?

Yes. Start seeds indoors eight to ten weeks before warm weather has arrived for good. The seeds need warm (at least 70° F.) soil in order to germinate. When you transplant them into the garden, space them 18 to 24 inches apart in rows 24 to 36 inches apart. Protect seedlings from cold snaps with hot caps.

Eggplant: An ornamental as well as a food plant, eggplant is available in white, green, yellow, and pink, as well as the familiar purple varieties.

Ann Reilly

What care should I give eggplant?

Sidedress the plants with a balanced fertilizer three weeks after transplanting them, and again when the fruits are just beginning to emerge from the blossoms. Water regularly and deeply. Mulches are valuable once the soil has warmed thoroughly. Stake the plants if they begin to be pulled down by heavy fruits.

How can I tell when eggplant is ready to be harvested?

Harvest the fruits while the skin is still tight, when the flesh gives a little to finger pressure. The seeds should not yet be brown. For an extended harvest, keep picking the plants as the fruits mature.

How can I protect eggplants against verticillium wilt?

Grow eggplants in containers of commercial, sterilized potting soil. Apply a soluble fertilizer to container-grown eggplants once a week.

Last year we had an unusually cool season after I planted my eggplant and all the new blossoms fell off. How could I have helped?

Temperatures below 50° F. or above 90° F. stress eggplant and cause blossoms to drop. Plenty of compost worked into the soil before planting and a thick mulch of organic material will help the plants withstand temperature extremes.

Escarole. See Chicory

Leeks *(Allium)*

Are leeks complicated to grow?

Although they take a very long time to reach maturity, leeks are a simple and satisfying crop to grow. Their culture takes more attention than skill.

Will leeks reach maturity in my New England garden?

You should be able to grow hardy early varieties such as King Richard and Blue Solaise with fine success.

Should I begin leeks indoors?

If you have a short growing season, it is crucial. Start leeks from seed sown ¼ inch deep in flats, twelve weeks before the last frost. Thin the sprouts so that each plant has 1 inch of space. When the leeks are pencil thick, transplant them into the garden 4 to 6 inches apart in rows 8 to 12 inches apart. In more southern areas with 140 days of growing season, gardeners can start leeks outdoors in mid-January to mid-February, or plant seeds in August through November for harvest the next spring.

How can I blanch leeks?

The traditional way to plant leeks is to set them in 6-inch furrows, and then gradually fill them in to blanch the stalks as the plants grow. This technique has two disadvantages: It requires a lot of work, and it gets grit into the folds of the stalks. To save work in both garden and kitchen, try wrapping the leeks with brown paper, or slipping 6-inch tubes of cardboard or plastic (such as thin-walled, 2-inch, PVC pipe) over the stalks when they're almost an inch thick. Even if you don't get around to blanching your leeks, they will be fine in soup.

When should I harvest leeks?

Leek varieties vary in maturity dates from 70 to 140 days. Harvest your leeks close to their maturity date, if they have reached 1 to 2 inches in diameter. Don't let them send up flower stalks, for they will be too tough to be of value in the kitchen.

Lettuce *(Lactuca)*

How can I choose among the many lettuce varieties available?

Advances in breeding, coupled with recent importations of English, French, Italian, other European, and Scandinavian varieties, have brought what seems to be a boundless choice of lettuce varieties to today's gardener. Some of the most beautiful

Ann Reilly

Leeks: Blanch leeks as shown here by planting them in 6-inch furrows and gradually filling in the furrows with soil as the plants grow.

Maggie Oster

Lettuce: If you begin lettuce indoors, be sure to harden it off before setting it into the outdoor garden.

are the frilly red and green, and the cream-colored, looseleaf lettuces, such as Lollo Rosa. Pirat is a butterhead type with bronze-mottled leaves known in Switzerland as Sprenkel lettuce. Choose lettuces according to the temperatures you are likely to have at different times of the season. Winter varieties respond to short days. Fall-planted lettuces are especially cold-hardy. Spring- and summer-sown varieties are less likely to become bitter or bolt to seed (mature too rapidly to seed).

How can I be assured of fresh, tender lettuce all season?

Sow small amounts of seed every seven to ten days so that new plants are continually coming along.

Should I start lettuce plants indoors?

Lettuce is a prime candidate for starting indoors in flats or pots and transplanting into the garden as early as the ground can be worked. Harden it off first (see pg. 641), and water after transplanting. Outdoors, sow seeds ¼ inch deep, and thin so that each plant has 8 inches of space—12 inches for heading and Romaine types. Be sure not to plant seed too deep, because it needs light to germinate.

Can I grow lettuce where summers get quite hot?

In such areas, you'll have best success growing lettuce in the spring and fall. Midsummer plantings in hot areas may work if you can find a partially shaded area or provide shade with a 50-percent shade cloth screen from 10 a.m. to 4 p.m. Bolt-resistant varieties are your best bet, though even they are cool-weather plants (60° to 65° F. is ideal), developed to stand up to hot spells, not continuous hot weather.

Can I start heading lettuce or Romaine directly in the vegetable garden?

These varieties take longer to mature and must thus be started indoors in short-season areas. Unseasonal light frosts won't damage most varieties at the seedling stage.

Does lettuce need to be watered?

A constant supply of water is perhaps the most important requirement of lettuce, especially during weather above 65° F. Otherwise, your plants will produce bitter greens and be more likely to attract pests. Fertilize the ground before planting with compost, manure, or a complete fertilizer, and then moisten it well whenever it is the slightest bit dry.

How is lettuce harvested?

If some lettuces, such as Curly Oakleaf, Salad Bowl, Matchless and other looseleaf types, are cut back to their roots, they will grow another, smaller crop of leaves. This is called "cut-and-come-again" culture, and is best done when the plants are 4 to 6 inches high. The standard way to harvest lettuce is to cut off heading types, including Bibb, just below the head, and to pull leaves a few at a time from looseleaf types.

Melons *(Cucumis)*

Are melons related to cucumbers?

Two kinds of common melons are related to cucumbers: *Reticulatus* or netted melons, including muskmelons (sometimes called cantaloupes, though true cantaloupes are rarely seen) and Persian melons; and *Inodorus* or winter melons, including casabas, crenshaws, and honeydews. Watermelons belong to a different genus *(Citrullus)*. All three groups are hot weather plants, but you can grow them in less than ideal weather conditions if you give them special attention and don't mind taking a few risks.

We have dependable warm weather in April where we live. Must I start melons indoors?

Even if you live in a warm-climate area, you might want to start your melon vines indoors three to four weeks before the average date for the last frost. Plant seeds in peat pots, or other containers that can be set directly in the ground, for melons don't take well to having their roots disturbed at transplanting time.

When can melons be planted outdoors?

Transfer them to the garden once daytime temperatures regularly reach at least 60° F. You can set them out a little earlier if you put them under hot caps or cloches. Plastic milk jugs with their lids off and their bottoms cut out work well—but remember to remove them during the day if the sun shines hard or the plants might get burned.

How should I plant melon seeds?

Sow seeds 1 inch deep in hills (see pg. 643), two to four seeds per hill, 4 to 6 feet apart. Some bush varieties can be spaced closer together. If you plant melons in rows, space them according to package directions.

I don't have much space left in my garden. Can I train melons to climb a trellis?

Yes, and they look quite attractive grown this way. To be certain the fruits don't break off, or pull the vines from their supports, you may wish to create little "hammocks" for them with pieces of cloth or nylon stockings.

Ann Reilly

Muskmelons: When muskmelons are ripe, the stems will easily break away from the vines.

Can I grow melons in dry areas?

In dry areas, plant the seeds in depressions 3 to 5 inches deep. If you're transplanting seedlings, set them halfway up the sides of the depressions and train the plants away from the depressions so that they won't get muddy.

Can I grow watermelon in my area, where summers are cool?

If you live in a cooler climate, grow the smaller, "ice-box" watermelons. Search seed catalogues for varieties that can be grown in your area or seek advice from your Extension Service agent. Always reserve the warmest spot in your garden for melons. All melons, but particularly watermelons, need not only warm air both day and night, but warm soil as well. Keep down weeds that shade the soil and compete with the melons for water and nutrients. Use black plastic mulch to trap heat in the soil.

How much fertilizer do melons need?

Fertilize at planting or transplanting time (and water thoroughly without delay), again when the plants are well established and about to send out runners, and once again when the runners are 2 feet long. The best way to fertilize melons is to work the fertilizer into circular furrows 8 inches all the way around the plants.

Will I have to give melons extra water?

Melons need plenty of water, but they must also have good drainage. This is why they are usually planted in raised mounds. However, if water is in short supply where you live, planting them on the "walls" of a depression accomplishes the same effect. Drip irrigation systems under mulch are especially suited to melon culture.

How can I know when melons are ready to harvest?

For muskmelons, record your planting date, so that you know when to expect them to mature. When the melons look ripe, with your thumb apply a little pressure where the stem meets the fruit. If the stem easily breaks away, it is at the "full slip" stage and is ripe. If merely lifting up the melon separates it from the vine, it is "vine ripe," or even overripe. If the fruits smell melony, chances are they are ripe.

For watermelons, snap your fingertip or rap with your knuckle against the melon: If the sound is sharp and high, the melon is immature; if dull and hollow, it may be ripe. When the tendril, or curlicue, closest to the melon is alive and green, it is almost certainly immature. When it dies, the melon is ripe. Don't leave the melon on the vine longer than two weeks after the tendril dies. Another test is to watch for a yellowing of the spot where the melon rests on the ground. A ripe melon, when pressed with a bit of weight, will usually "crackle," but if you plan to store the melon, it is better not to push on it in this manner.

Mustard *(Brassica)*

What are mustard greens like?

Mustard greens are very easy to grow, and quite tender and flavorful when they are young. Chinese or Japanese mustard greens are much more subtle, extremely delicious, and less bitter than common mustard greens. Oftentimes they appear in catalogues simply as "greens" or "Oriental greens." Look for Tatsoi, Mizuna (delicious raw in salads), Purple Mustard, and Gai Choy.

How is mustard grown?

The seeds of this cool-weather *Brassica* should be thinly sown as early in the spring as the ground can be worked—¼ inch deep and ¾ inch apart in rows 12 to 14 inches apart. Thin the seedlings (and eat the thinnings) to whatever spacings are recommended for the variety you are growing. Mustard makes a good container plant because its roots are not extensive.

Are there any special tricks to keeping mustard from getting too bitter?

Keep mustard growing fast in good garden soil and it will develop its mildest, most subtle flavor. Hot spells may encourage it to bolt, so you probably won't have much luck starting succession crops after late May. It would be better to wait and plant in late summer for a fall harvest. Fertilize as you would for cabbage.

How is mustard harvested for greens?

Some varieties, such as Tatsoi, form a rather tight rosette, and are best harvested in their entirety. Others, such as Osaka Purple, may be picked a leaf at a time, which is all you need to spice up a salad. As long as you leave a few leaves on a mustard plant, it will keep growing for you as long as the weather stays cool and the ground stays moist. If you let mustard bolt to seed, it will produce a lovely show of yellow, sweet-smelling flowers. Don't let the seed pods mature, however, or you may have a weed problem in future years.

Are only the leaves and seeds of mustard edible?

All parts of Chinese mustard, including the root, are edible. The flowers make lovely additions to salads. Mustards are highly nutritious, abounding in calcium, vitamins C and A, and iron, as well as fiber.

Okra *(Abelmoschus)*

What is okra like?

This vegetable is unusual for its ability to thicken soups and stews, and it is also a favorite for pickling. Many East Indian curries call for okra. It has large, yellow flowers with red centers, borne on 4- to 5-foot-tall leafy bushes. Dwarf varieties grow 2 to 3 feet tall.

Can I grow okra in New England?

Yes, but the harvest will be brief. Okra loves hot weather and sunshine, and will not do well without them. If you live in a cool or cloudy area of the country, you may be able to grow okra by starting the seed indoors a month before setting it out. When there is no danger of frost, bring the plants outdoors to harden off (see pg. 641), and transplant seedlings to the warmest spot in your garden, away from any cool breezes.

How should I plant okra seed outdoors?

Soak the seed in water for twenty-four hours, and then plant it in good garden soil that has not been heavily fertilized, setting the seed ¼ inch deep in rows 24 to 30 inches apart. Later thin seedlings to stand 12 to 18 inches apart. You can also grow it three plants to a hill 3 feet across.

What are okra's water and fertilizer needs?

Okra stands up to droughty conditions, but don't let it get completely thirsty. Occasional deep waterings are best. Too much nitrogen makes the plants grow large and leafy without setting many pods. Make sure your soil contains plenty of phosphorus (found abundantly in bonemeal and rock phosphate).

How should I harvest okra?

Okra, like green beans, needs to be harvested at the immature stage. Continual picking of the pods when they are 3 inches long and not too thick across the middle will keep the plants producing. Large pods are pithy and tough.

Onions; Scallions; Shallots *(Allium)*

Are onions difficult to grow?

No matter where you live, there is at least one variety of onion that will thrive there. But because this vegetable is particular about the number of hours of light and darkness it gets as it grows, you must not only plant the appropriate variety for your area, but the right one for the time of year in which you grow it. It is particularly important to plant short-day types, such as Yellow Bermuda or Crystal Wax, if you live in the South and long-day types, such as Early Yellow Globe or Southport White Globe, if you live in the North.

How should I prepare the soil for onions?

Onions are heavy feeders and need well-limed, well-fertilized, heavy (but not sticky and wet) soil. Whether the soil is claylike or sandy, onions do best when lots of organic matter has been added to the soil. Work plenty of manure into the soil before you plant, and add a balanced fertilizer at the same time. Wood ashes are excellent for onions; sidedress liberally when the plants have put out a number of shoots.

Should I plant seeds or sets?

Grow onions from sets for summer use, or from seed for winter storage. Onions are also commonly transplanted from seedlings. Many gardeners feel that seed-grown onions are better than those grown from sets.

How are sets planted?

As soon as the soil can be made ready in the spring, push sets into prepared soil, so that their tops are about ½ inch below the surface. If you want to grow large onions, space the sets 3 to 4 inches apart; for scallions or bunching onions, space sets about 1 inch apart. Don't plan to thin out and use alternate onions for scallions, because this disturbs the roots of those left to form large bulbs.

How are onion seeds planted?

Indoors, sow seeds five to six weeks before planting time in the garden (a few days after the average last frost date), and transplant seedlings into the garden, spaced 4 inches apart in rows 12 to 15 inches apart. Snip just a little off the tops of the greens and the bottoms of the roots at transplanting time to encourage rapid growth. To begin seeds outdoors, as early in the spring as the ground can be worked, plant seed in rows 12 to 15 inches apart, with one to three seeds per inch, and cover them with ¼ inch of soil. Thin so that seedlings are 3 to 4 inches apart for large onions.

Why is it important to plant onions early in spring?

Onions need to grow big tops before the lengthening day triggers bulb formation. If the tops are still small when bulbs begin to form, the bulbs will be small. By getting onions into the soil as early in the spring as possible, you give them plenty of time to grow food-producing leaves that will feed the bulbs so they can grow big.

Ann Reilly

Onions: These heavy feeders need well-limed, well-fertilized soil.

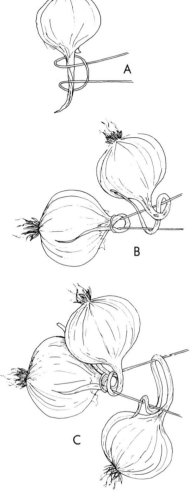

To braid onions, (A) loop string around onion top as shown, (B) braid in second onion, and (C) repeat with third onion and others.

What care should I give the growing plants?

Weed thoroughly early in the season, then mulch to thwart weeds. Onions are shallow rooted, and frequent hoeing would damage roots. Make sure to water during dry weather. The ground should never dry out below the surface. If flowers begin to form, break the flowering stalks so that they hang bent over. Don't break them all the way off, as they may collect water, which could rot the bulb.

When should onions be harvested?

Wait until the tops have fallen over and begun to brown, then pull up the onions and leave them to dry outside in the sun for a week or more. Be sure they have plenty of warmth and ventilation so that they dry completely. Remove the tops, and store the onions in a dry, dark, cool place. To make onion braids, leave the tops on some onions, and after they have dried, braid the tops together with a length of cord and hang them in a cool, dark place. Plant good storing onions if you intend to keep them for a long time. Spartan Sleeper, for example, will keep for up to six months at room temperature, but Walla Walla, a wonderfully sweet and juicy onion, should not be stored for any length of time.

Is it true that onions repel insects from other plants?

This seems to be the case, but keep onions away from your peas and beans, for these are not good onion companions.

What are scallions?

Several kinds of onions with long straight bulbs are used for scallions. You can harvest immature, seed-grown onions before they form bulbs and call them scallions, or you can grow perennial bunching onions, most commonly White Lisbon, although yellow and red varieties are also available. These form many small narrow bulbs, or stalks, rather than one fat one, as typical onions do. Once bunching onions are sown they will continue to divide on their own, dying back in cold winters and reappearing in spring, when they are best and mildest. You can also harvest immature shallots as scallions. When harvesting scallions from bunching onions, leave some behind so that they will continue to grow and divide.

Could you please describe shallots?

Shallots are as easy to grow as onions, especially when planted from sets. Each shallot plant separates into a number of bulbs, and the smaller ones are used as sets to grow new clusters of bulbs. Place them 1 inch deep, 6 inches apart, in rows 8 inches apart. Shallots are so hardy that you can plant sets in September for scallions during the winter.

How should I treat shallots when they are growing?

Tend to your shallot bed as you do your onion bed. Harvest them after their tops die down in the summer. Dry them in the sun for a few days, and then store them in a cool, dark, dry place.

Parsnips *(Pastinaca)*

When and how should I plant parsnip seeds?

Sow parsnips when you sow carrots. To hasten germination, soak seed overnight before planting. The seed takes two to three weeks to germinate under ideal conditions; keep the soil well moistened during this period. A thin mulch of organic material will help immensely. Set the seed ¼ inch deep, twelve seeds per foot, and cover it with sifted compost or leaf mold. Leave 18 to 24 inches between rows. Thin seedlings to stand 3 to 4 inches apart.

What kind of soil do parsnips need?

Since parsnip roots can easily reach 12 inches in length, they need deep, loose, well-drained soil, free from large rocks and chunks. Parsnips take up to four months to grow, and sometimes more. Don't give them too much nitrogen or they'll put their energy into growing lush tops rather than tasty roots. Phosphorus, responsible for strong stem and root development in plants, must be in good supply for parsnip crops. If the tops start to flower, break off the flower stalks.

When should I harvest parsnips?

The roots taste sweetest after the tops have been touched by a few fall frosts. Dig them up in the fall, or, if you live in a cold-winter area, leave them in the ground and dig them up in March—few things are more satisfying to a northern gardener than harvesting sweet parsnips from the soil at that bleak time of year. Store parsnips as you would carrots. In the refrigerator, they keep best in a plastic bag.

Peas *(Legumes)*

What are the differences between garden, snap, and snow peas?

Garden peas—or English peas as they are sometimes called—are available in both bush and climbing varieties. Although bush peas bear for a shorter period than pole beans, they don't require support. Unlike garden peas, both snap and snow peas have edible pods. Snap pea pods are sweet and crunchy; some varieties may also be shelled. Snow peas, common to Oriental cuisine, are harvested when still flat-podded.

A permanent trellis for peas (or beans) can be constructed A-frame fashion, using 2x2s for uprights and top horizontal, and rebars for the bottom horizontals. String twine between top and bottom horizontals to support vines.

Climbing peas will readily climb a wire fence, netting, or trellis.

What is the best way to support peas?

You can buy netting made expressly for this purpose. Or use chicken wire stapled to stakes or twine strung between horizontal poles.

Can I grow peas in Louisiana?

You will have most success if you grow them as a fall crop. Peas are a cool-weather crop that can be grown just about anywhere, so long as you plant them at a time of year when sixty to seventy days of mild, cool weather are ahead.

How can I tell when peas are ready to harvest?

Garden peas are ready to pick when the pods are swollen and still shiny. Pick sugar pod peas once the pods have filled out but before the individual peas begin to show through in bumps. Snow peas taste best when they are about 3 inches long. While bush varieties of garden peas tend to ripen all at once, pole and snow peas produce over a longer period of time, and should be kept picked so that they will continue to produce. When you are done harvesting for the season, till the vines back into the soil for their value as a green manure.

Positive Images, Jerry Howard

Are peas prone to diseases?

In damp climates, mildew can be a problem if peas are planted so tightly that they lack ventilation. Dust with sulphur, and next time space your rows more generously. Crop rotation and the planting of resistant varieties are your best controls against disease.

Peppers *(Capsicum)*

Will peppers grow in cooler climates?

Both sweet and hot pepper varieties have been developed for cooler climates.

Should I start peppers indoors?

Yes. Start them eight to ten weeks before it will be safe to transplant them outdoors. Keep them in the warmest spot in your house (80° F. if possible) until they germinate; then move them to a sunny windowsill. Move them away from the window to a warmer spot at night if the weather outside is icy. Pepper seedlings are not as hardy as tomato seedlings. If you plant the seeds outdoors, it is essential to wait until the soil is warm. Sow four seeds per foot and thin to 12 to 18 inches apart in rows 2 to 3 feet apart.

How can I keep pepper seedlings from getting tall and spindly?

Move them to larger pots as they grow. When you set them out in the open, they should be bushy and compact. They may have some flower buds on them, but it is best if the buds are not yet open. Protect the seedlings from chilly winds with hot caps (see page 652).

Can I grow peppers in containers?

These plants thrive in containers and are one of the most ornamental annual vegetables you can grow. Given plenty of light in a sunny (but not intensely hot) window, they can even be grown indoors. If you grow them indoors, hand-pollinate them by moving from one flower to the next, gently brushing them with a soft-bristled brush, such as a makeup or artist's brush.

Last year I had beautiful foliage on my pepper plants, but the blossoms dropped before fruiting. What went wrong?

The ideal outdoor temperatures for peppers are between 70° and 80° F. during the day, and no lower than 60° F. at night. Smaller-fruited varieties withstand more variation in temperature than the larger-fruited. Some experts believe too much nitrogen causes blossom drop, but all experts agree that temperatures above 90° F. cause blossom drop, and insufficient calcium causes nutrient deficiency. To keep peppers cool, spray

Ann Reilly

Peppers: These Sweet Banana peppers have thick, sweet, mild flesh.

Ron West

*Peppers: String bumper crops of hot
peppers and hang them to ripen and
dry in a warm, airy place.*

them with water in the middle of a hot day. Keep them supplied
with calcium by adding gypsum or lime to the soil before
planting, and give sidedressings of chicken manure and dolomitic limestone right after blossom set, and every three weeks
thereafter. Don't dig these materials in, because peppers have
shallow, easily damaged roots. Hand-weed for the same reason.
The first blossoms are likely to drop no matter what you do—
don't worry about that.

When can I start picking peppers?

Pick the first peppers while they are green and rather small, to
give the plants opportunity to set a good main crop. In long-
season areas, peppers can be left on the bush to ripen to their
expected color—dark green, yellow, orange, purple, chocolate,
or red. String bumper crops of peppers and hang them to ripen
and dry in a warm, airy place.

How can I avoid blossom-end rot?

Be sure plants are receiving adequate moisture and calcium.

Potatoes *(Solanum)*

Can you suggest some new varieties of potatoes to grow?

The selection of potato varieties now available is delightful—finger potatoes, yellow, red, and blue potatoes, enormous bakers, and diminutive salad potatoes. Look for yellow-fleshed Bintje and Yellow Finn potatoes and Ruby Crescent, a deep pink, fingerling type with yellow flesh.

Is it necessary to start potatoes from seed?

Though potatoes can be grown from seed, it is easier to purchase certified disease-free seed potatoes. Keep them in a cold place until you are ready to plant them.

What kind of soil and climate do potatoes need?

Potatoes prefer a sandy or clay loam, and do not do well in heavy clays. Acid soils are best, though not a must. Plant potatoes four to six weeks before the last frost date in your area. Potatoes need three to four months to mature. Potatoes can be grown in any region of the United States and Canada where other vegetables are grown. They are warm-weather plants but prefer fairly cool summers.

How do you prepare the seed potatoes for planting?

Cut 1½- to 2-inch chunks, each containing at least one eye, from the seed potatoes. Larger chunks are better than smaller, and small potatoes need not be cut at all. Let the chunks air-dry in a cool, dark, indoor spot for three to five days before planting.

To prepare seed potatoes for planting, cut them into 1 1/2- to 2-inch chunks, each containing at least one eye.

We have clay soil. We're working on improving it, but it is still very heavy. Is there any way we can grow potatoes?

Plant your potatoes on top of the soil if it's claylike or alkaline. Work the soil loose a foot or so down, and cover it with a 4-inch layer of straw or dry leaves. Lay pieces of seed potato on top of the mulch, and then cover them with another foot of straw or leaves. The potatoes will send roots into the soil and stems and leaves up through the mulch and into the air. New tubers will form in the mulch itself; they'll be easy to harvest and easy to clean. Potatoes grown this way rarely contract diseases. But the crop yield isn't as large as with in-ground potatoes.

How should I plant potatoes in the ground?

Three to five days before planting, dig a trench 1 foot wide and 6 inches deep, and work in some fertilizer and compost. Compost is particularly important because it helps the soil drain—if potatoes sit in water they are likely to rot. Don't use fresh

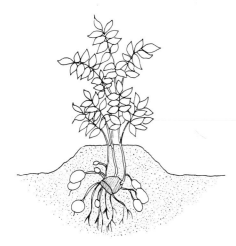

Hoe up soil around potato vines as they grow taller; potatoes grow underground on roots sent out from the seed potatoes.

manure, and do *not* lime the soil—potatoes prefer an acid pH. Set the potato chunks in furrows 3 inches deep, spacing them 6 to 12 inches apart. Closer spacings provide more, but smaller, potatoes. Water after planting.

How should I care for the potatoes while they are growing?

Hoe soil up around the vines as they grow taller, so that the tubers won't be exposed to light (which makes them turn green). This procedure also provides support to the vines and increases yields. A mulch of straw or dry leaves will help keep the ground cool and moist. Because potatoes have shallow roots, they need *regular* watering (about once a week) during dry weather. Alternate drought and wet causes potatoes to be rough and knobby.

How many potatoes will I get from a 50-foot row?

With a lot of compost and acid soil, you should be able to harvest about one bushel for every 50-feet.

When can I start harvesting potatoes?

Early potatoes—what a treat!—are ready to eat when they reach about golf-ball size. Let them sit in the refrigerator for a day before you eat them. To harvest full-grown tubers for storing, wait until the tops die down and then dig the entire crop. A potato fork is the best tool for this job. Dry your potato harvest in a dark, airy place for a few days before moving the tubers to a dark, quite cool place for long keeping.

Are potatoes likely to be attacked by disease?

Avoid diseases such as scab and late blight (the blight that caused the great Irish potato famine) by planting only certified seed potatoes, caring for your planting as described above, and rotating your crops on a three- to four-year basis.

I have heard that potatoes can be grown in containers. How is it done?

Simply plant them the same way you would in-ground potatoes, providing them with a deep container in which you can start the plants low and add a loose potting mix as the vines grow up. A trash can with drainage holes is not especially attractive, but will produce a surprisingly great number of potatoes. Keep the plants cool and moist.

Pumpkins. See Squash

Radicchio. See Chicory

Radishes *(Raphanus)*

When can I put radishes in?

Sow radish seeds as soon as the ground can be worked in the spring, and thereafter in succession until warm weather. Sow late crops in early fall.

How should I plant radishes?

Loosen the soil a foot down, work in plenty of compost, rake it smooth, and run a line of seed ½ inch deep and ½ to 1 inch apart in rows 8 to 12 inches apart. Or you can broadcast the seeds onto a seed bed before it is completely smooth, and then rake it flat. Tamp down the soil and water immediately. Thin radishes to stand 1 to 2 inches apart once the seedlings are an inch or so high. You can also mix radish seeds thinly with other vegetable seeds; the quick-sprouting radishes will break the soil for their tenderer companions and mark the rows for you.

Do radishes need any special care?

Water and weed regularly. Though radishes will grow no matter what, they must grow as quickly as possible in order to be sweet and tenderly crisp.

What is the Japanese Daikon radish like?

From 8 inches to 3 feet long, the Japanese Daikon tastes wonderful raw. It can also be pickled—it's beautiful in a tall jar with a small red pepper or two.

Rhubarb *(Rheum)*

Can I grow rhubarb in the South?

This hardy perennial is a cool-weather plant and most varieties need to be in frozen ground two months a year. If you live in a warm climate, be sure to buy a variety developed for warm weather.

How is rhubarb planted?

As early in the spring as you can work the ground, prepare the planting bed by digging in a good amount of compost. Soak rhubarb crowns in a bucket of water while you prepare the planting bed. Plant three or four crowns 2 inches below the surface of the soil, and space the groups 2 to 3 feet apart. Water immediately.

How much fertilizer and water should I give rhubarb?

Mulch with manure once a year to provide the modest amount of nitrogen that rhubarb needs. Keep rhubarb watered but not overly wet, and give it sun but not intense heat.

When can I begin harvesting rhubarb?

Harvest no stalks the first year. You can snap off a few stalks at the base the second year, but go lightly. Starting the third year you should be able to harvest all you need from the three or four crowns you planted. Do not eat the leaves—they contain oxalic acid in poisonous amounts.

Can I divide rhubarb?

Mature crowns can be dug up and separated to create new plants. Try growing some rhubarb in containers. It makes a handsome plant, with its thick, green leaves and lipstick-red stalks.

Roquette. See Arugula

Rutabaga. See Turnips

Scallions. See Onions

Shallots. See Onions

Spinach (*Spinacia*)

Every time I try to grow spinach it bolts. Why is this?

Spinach requires the hard-to-find weather combination of bright sun and cool air. Faced with any sort of stress, be it warm weather, inadequate moisture, or rapid temperature changes, it bolts to seed, turning bitter in the process. In spite of this, spinach is worth growing because of its nutritional value and exquisite flavor, both raw in salads and cooked as a pot herb. It needs rich soil and steady moisture in a sunny, weed-free bed.

If I get my seeds in early enough, will the spinach be less likely to bolt?

Get your spinach seeds in the ground just as early in the spring as you can, so that they will have time to grow up before warm spring weather causes them to bolt. In mild-winter areas, plant spinach from mid-January to March 1, and then again from August 1 to mid-November. In colder areas, plant it six to eight weeks before the last expected frost, and again four to six weeks before the first expected fall frost. Sow seeds ½ inch deep, 2 inches apart, in rows 12 to 18 inches apart; thin to 4 inches in the rows. Plant in succession every seven to ten days for a large, prolonged harvest.

How is spinach harvested?

You can begin harvesting outer leaves when they are egg-sized. If you wait until the plants are more mature, be sure to catch them before they bolt. Cut plants all the way down to an inch above the soil; they will come up again for a second shearing.

Will spinach be likely to have many pest and disease problems?

Spinach, fast grower that it is, is not terribly bothered by insects. Leaf miner is the worst pest: Destroy damaged plant leaves. Grow varieties that are tolerant to mosiac virus and downy mildew (blue mold).

I have seen New Zealand spinach advertised as being able to tolerate heat. Is that true?

New Zealand spinach, sometimes called summer spinach, is not spinach at all, but resembles it when cooked. Unlike true spinach, it loves heat and is very easy to grow, but it makes a slow start. Soak seed two or three days before planting; sow eight to ten seeds per foot in rows at least 2 feet apart; thin plants to about 8 inches. Although New Zealand spinach grows best in hot weather, it will sprout only in cool soil, so plant it early. This plant is a tremendous yielder, and an average family needs only a few feet of row.

Squash, summer and winter (*Cucurbita*)

When should I start squash seeds if I plant them indoors?

Three to four weeks before all danger of frost is past. When you transplant them into the garden, be especially careful not to disturb the roots. You can also sow seed directly into the soil, when all frost danger is past. You can plant summer squash in rows 4 to 5 feet apart, with seedlings 3 feet apart; or you can plant them in hills 4 to 6 feet apart, with each hill containing three plants, 6 inches apart. To accommodate sprawling vines, place winter squash hills farther apart, up to 8 feet. You can pinch off the growing tips of vines where you want them to stop. The soil must be at least 60° F. at planting time, but 70° F. is much better. Squash seed simply won't germinate in cold soil. If you dig in great quantities of manure and compost before planting, you'll get bigger fruits.

What kind of care does squash require while it is growing?

Keep down weeds until the plants' leaves are big enough to shade them out. Water very deeply once a week if there is no rain, but avoid watering from above, as this invites disease. Stop watering winter squash once the vines start to die. Don't worry

If you are planting in hills, smooth a flat, 1-foot in diameter circle on the prepared soil and evenly space six to nine seeds around the circle, gently pressing them into the soil with your fingertip to the required planting depth. Firm soil by tamping with your hand or a flat-bottomed tool such as a hoe.

Ann Reilly

Summer squash: Once plants begin to put out flowers, they produce fruit that ripens very rapidly, and plants should be harvested frequently to keep squashes from getting too large.

when the leaves of many squashes droop most forlornly in the midday sun—they will perk up later in the day. Provide a trellis for climbers such as tromboncino. Sidedress with a complete fertilizer before the plants get big.

When should I start harvesting summer squash?

Keep a close eye on the plants once they begin putting out flowers. Many of the flowers will probably be male flowers, so they won't all set fruit, but those that do will ripen very quickly. All summer squashes are far superior when they are quite small—six inches or less is the rule for zucchini. Harvest tromboncino at 8 to 18 inches. Those oversized specimens that hide behind leaves until they reach baseball bat size can be stuffed, or grated for zucchini bread.

Can you suggest some good summer squashes to try?

The fairly new Sunburst patty pan, an All-America winner, is as prolific as zucchini, and like the other patty pans is delicious. Scallopini, crookneck, Goldrush zucchini, and the tremendous Italian tromboncino, which puts out a 30- to 40-foot vine in one season, are all excellent summer squashes.

When should I harvest winter squash?

Leave winter squashes on their spent vines right up until just before the first hard frost. Avoid scratching or bruising the skin and leave a length of thoroughly dried stem on each squash to keep rot from entering at the scar while they are stored.

How should I store winter squash?

Store winter squash in a cool (45° to 50° F.), quite dry place. Some gardeners wipe the fruits with a light bleach and water solution before putting them away, to kill bacteria and fungi on the surface. Squashes keep best if they are set, with their sides not touching, on shelves. Check them regularly, and eat the ones that first show damage to their skins. Stored properly, the squashes may last you well into February or even longer.

Can you suggest a good variety of winter squash?

Perhaps the most delicious of all are the Japanese kabocha, or butterball, types. These smallish (3 to 4 pounds), light or dark green to flashy orange squashes taste as sweet as pumpkin pie when cut in half and baked face-down in a 350° F. oven until soft. They are prolific and about as easy to grow as anything you can plant.

Winter squash: Buttercup squashes like this Sweet Mama are sweet, easy to grow, and good storers.

Ann Reilly

Pumpkins: Miniature pumpkins make perfect fall decorations.

Is it true that squash flowers are edible?

Squash blossoms are a table delicacy that is often difficult to find in a market. Some varieties, such as Butterblossom, have been bred to put out great numbers of male blossoms. Costata Romanesco and Florina produce small fruits with the flowers still attached. Squash blossoms can be sautéed, deep-fried, stir-fried, stuffed with ricotta cheese and chives, and used in many other delicious ways. Picking the male flowers only does not hurt production.

What are some good pie pumpkins?

Select one of the smaller, "sugar pumpkin" varieties. Any sweet, orange-fleshed winter squash can be used for good pumpkin pie.

How can I grow extra large Jack-o-lanterns?

Plant three seeds to a hill, but thin to the one healthiest seedling. As soon as the fruits appear, remove all but two or three, or even one, of the young fruits, and pinch off extra vines. If you do this, all the plants' energy will be concentrated on these few pumpkins, which will grow quite large. In addition, side-dress the plants by putting fertilizer in circular trenches several feet out from the stem, two or three times during the season.

Can squashes be planted in containers?

Almost any bush variety of summer squash does splendidly in large patio containers, and varieties of acorn squashes that grow on compact bushes, such as Table King, can be grown in containers.

Sunflowers *(Helianthus)*

Why grow sunflowers in the garden?

The seeds of these enormous flowers are easy to harvest, they make fine snacks for humans, small animals, and birds; and, not least important, there is something spirit-lifting about a line of sunflowers at the edge of a garden.

How are sunflower seeds planted?

Sow sunflower seeds ½ inch deep and 6 inches apart after all danger of frost is past. When they are 3 inches high, thin them to 2-foot spacings.

Are sunflowers particular about where they grow?

Sunflowers thrive in the worst soil, and they don't need a lot of water. If your soil is good and nutrient-rich, you may have to stake the 12- to 14-foot sunflowers that spring out of it. Sunflower

Photo/Nats, Dorothy S. Long

Sunflowers: Seeds from a row of cheery sunflowers are excellent snacks for both people and birds.

stalks, cured in the sun and stored in a cool, dry place, make good bean poles. You can even grow some kinds of pole beans on live sunflower stalks, if you strip enough of the flowers' lower leaves to let the sun get to the beans.

How should I harvest sunflowers?

Cut the heads from the stalks when the seeds are fully mature. Rub two heads together or, better still, rub the heads on a piece of ½-inch hardware cloth stretched over a wooden frame. Cure the seeds in a very dry and airy place for a week, and then store them in sealed jars or other airtight containers. For next year's planting, save some seed in a cool, dry place.

Are sunflowers hard to grow?

Birds may harvest your sunflower seeds before you do. If you don't want them to, tie nylon screen or netting over the heads before the seeds mature. Insects and disease don't bother sunflowers.

Sweet potatoes *(Ipomoea)*

Is it possible to grow sweet potatoes only in the South? I'd love to be able to grow them here in Vermont.

Although sweet potatoes, which are also called yams, are grown commercially only in the hottest states, home gardeners grow them in much cooler places—even in Vermont. The secret is to plant slips (small plants sprouted from slices of sweet potatoes) at the correct time, and to protect the young plants on cold nights.

When should I get sweet potatoes in the ground?

Sweet potatoes go in the ground in late spring, when the soil has thoroughly warmed. Order certified disease-free slips from a mail-order house (be sure they will arrive as close to planting time as possible), and plant them 3 inches deep, 10 to 12 inches apart, in raised beds 3 to 4 feet apart.

What kind of soil should sweet potatoes be planted in?

Enrich your soil with compost, well-aged manure, or other organic matter two weeks before you plant. Sweet potatoes do not fare well in heavy clay soil. They need nitrogen, but not too much. If you buy a commercial preparation, use 5-10-10.

Do sweet potatoes need much care?

Weed regularly until the vines have grown big enough to take care of themselves. While the plants are still young, protect them during cold nights with a thick straw mulch. A sidedressing of 5-10-10—about 2 teaspoons per plant—is helpful once the plants have established themselves, but don't use too much. The vines will ramble, but don't injure them by pruning. Instead, loosen the soil where the stems are rooting at the joints.

How will I know when my sweet potatoes are ready for harvest?

Get your sweet potatoes out of the ground before the first fall frost—don't wait until the tops die down, as you would for Irish potatoes. If a light frost is possible, mulch the tops at night with a thick layer of straw or dried leaves. The potatoes should be mature four to five months after setting them out. If the first frost comes along before that and you have to dig up your crop early, the potatoes won't be "unripe," just a bit smaller than average. Sweet potatoes spread out farther from the parent plant than do Irish potatoes. Because they break easily, dig them up carefully, starting from a few feet to the outside of the plants, rather than right on top of them. Leave the potatoes on a dry patch of ground for just a few hours to dry in the sun, then keep them in a humid spot with a temperature of 70° to 80° F. to cure for two to three weeks. Long-time storage should be at 50° to 60° F. Avoid handling them while in storage, and eat bruised ones first. Don't wash sweet potatoes until you are ready to cook them.

Do sweet potatoes have any potential problems?

To avoid root-knot nematode infestations, do not plant sweet potatoes in a bed recently converted from sod. Sweet potatoes are robust growers, not affected greatly by insects or disease.

Swiss chard *(Beta)*

Is Swiss chard related to beets? The leaves look and taste somewhat alike.

Swiss chard (or just "chard") is a bulbless beet grown for its leaves and stems. Apart from being delicious, especially when steamed and eaten with butter and lemon juice, chard is a garden favorite because it is so easy to grow. The green and red leaf varieties are equally tasty.

Does Swiss chard have to be started indoors?

No. Sow seeds directly in the ground as early as the soil can be worked in the spring. In warmer climates, chard is also sown in the fall for harvests all winter long. You don't have to succession-crop chard because one patch, picked leaf by leaf, will keep you in greens indefinitely.

How far apart should chard seed be planted?

Sow the seed, which is grouped in clumps like beet seed, ½ inch deep, 4 inches apart, in rows 2 feet apart. Thin to 8-inch spacings in the rows.

Does chard need special care?

Chard will flourish in any good garden soil. If you let it reseed itself from year to year, the patch will have to be fertilized now and then with plenty of compost, manure, or a balanced commercial fertilizer. Chard will continue to produce, even during a drought. It is troubled by few pests and diseases.

Is it better to pull up whole plants, or harvest chard leaf by leaf?

Cut the outer leaves at the base, rather than pulling up the plant by the roots. You can cut the inner leaves, too, if you like the small, tender ones. The plants will take longer to come back this way, but come back they will.

Ann Reilly

Swiss chard: Easy-to-grow Swiss chard is prolific and delicious.

Tomatoes *(Lycopersicon)*

Is it true that tomatoes were once considered poisonous?

It is true, but they are now the most commonly grown home-garden vegetable. Seed catalogues offer innumerable varieties of tomatoes adapted to many climates and cultural conditions. The tomato is ideally suited to container growing, too, and can be trained to grow up, down, and around almost any trellis you provide it with.

FRUITS AND VEGETABLES

I have seen tomatoes designated determinate and indeterminate. What do these terms mean?

Catalogue and seed-packet descriptions usually note whether a tomato variety is determinate or indeterminate. The vines of determinate types do not grow endlessly, but confine themselves to a fairly compact bush shape. Some gardeners stake them for extra support. They make good container and small-garden plants. The vines of indeterminate varieties continue to grow at their tips, and most gardeners provide support for them. They produce larger fruits over a longer period of time, but come into production later than determinate types.

Should I start my own seedlings or purchase nursery-grown ones?

Growing your own seedlings allows for a much wider choice of varieties. With care, you should be able to grow better plants at home than you sometimes find for sale—and they are on hand when planting conditions are just right. It is easier to buy plants, but if you need more than a few, the cost becomes significant. If you buy seedlings, choose those that are short and stout, and without fruit or, if possible, without flowers. Check to be sure that they are free of insects.

Tomatoes: Sun-ripened tomatoes have no match among the greenhouse varieties, and are the top favorite vegetable for gardeners to grow.

Positive Images, Jerry Howard

Can you please describe how to start seeds indoors?

Plant seeds in pots, peat pellets, or divided flats six weeks before the date of your last expected spring frost. Keep the soil warm, from 75° to 89° F., with the heat preferably coming from below. A heat mat is ideal, but the top of a radiator, water heater, or even the refrigerator will do the trick. Transplant the seedlings to 4-inch pots when the second set of leaves appears. Use potting soil when you transplant. If the leaves discolor, fertilize with fish emulsion or a diluted, liquid, complete fertilizer (according to label instructions). When you are sure there will be no more frosts, and nighttime temperatures go no lower than 45° F. (or better yet, 50° F.), take the plants outdoors to harden off for about a week before they are transplanted into the ground (see page 641).

How should I transplant tomatoes?

After hardening off, plant tomatoes as shown in the illustration on this page. For each plant, add 1 teaspoon of rock phosphate or 2 teaspoons of bonemeal at transplanting time, to supply the extra phosphorus tomatoes need. Or mix 2 teaspoons of 5-10-10 fertilizer in each planting hole, cover it with an inch of soil or compost, and plant the seedlings on top of that. Protect each plant with a cutworm collar (see pg. 656). Water thoroughly, and continue to water every two or three days, or every day in hot weather, for a week. It is best to transplant in the evening or on a cloudy day. If it is windy or cold, protect the seedlings with some kind of enclosure.

If you set tomato cages (see next question) in place at transplanting time, they can serve as frames to wrap plastic sheeting around. Cover the tops at night with paper, cardboard, or cloth (never plastic). Once the weather has fully warmed, the plants will outgrow their protective devices and do quite well on their own.

Should I use stakes or wire cages to support my tomatoes?

Wire cages have advantages over stakes: The cages reduce the risk of sunscald, which can be caused when fruits are totally exposed to the sun's rays without sufficient leaf covering; and the plants' side branches grow through the wire mesh and become self-supporting. In drought years, plants will lose less moisture to the wind if they are allowed to sprawl over a hay mulch, but generally, unsupported fruit is subject to rotting and greater insect damage. Tomatoes may also be trained up a trellis.

Will I have to give tomatoes a lot of extra water?

During dry weather, water occasionally but deeply, from below rather than above, if possible. Mulch heavily with straw, shredded leaves, or some other dry organic material to retain moisture, but don't apply this mulch until the weather is warm, or you will cause the soil to be too cool.

Maggie Oster

Tomato cages reduce the risk of sunscald, provide carefree support for fast-growing plants, and lessen the incidence of pest and disease problems.

Do I have to prune tomatoes?

Pruning is not necessary except in short-season areas, where indeterminate types may not bear soon enough before the fall frosts. To prune, remove suckers from the vine crotches about once a week, when the plants are past the seedling stage. One or two suckers left low on the main stem of each plant will produce alternate main stems, making the plant fuller and reducing the likelihood of split fruits.

Do tomatoes need much fertilizing?

Once the fruit appears, sidedress with a complete fertilizer, following package instructions. A number of reliable fertilizers especially formulated for tomatoes are available through catalogues or in nurseries and garden centers. Avoid applying too much nitrogen, or the tomatoes may grow a lot of foliage at the expense of abundant fruit.

Why are my tomatoes producing flowers that drop off instead of developing fruits?

Blossom drop is caused most often by night temperatures below 55° or above 75° F. Perhaps you are growing a variety not well suited to your climate.

My tomatoes were high in quality but stopped fruiting by late July. What did I do wrong?

You planted a determinate variety, which sends up a limited number of growing stems, then stops growing vegetatively (stems and leaves) and produces fruits. While determinate varieties are early and heavy fruiting, their period of production is usually short.

My tomatoes went all to foliage. Why?

This may be due to too much shade (perhaps from spacing the plants too closely), or too much nitrogen in the soil. A fertilizer high in phosphorus, especially when applied at the time of flowering, will encourage heavier fruit yields and early ripening.

Why do tomatoes get black spots at the blossom end?

Blossom end rot comes from inadequate or irregularly supplied water. Regular irrigation will solve the problem. Also, add calcium, in the form of rock powders, to your soil.

Our summers are not cold, but the skies are overcast almost every day. Can we still grow tomatoes?

You will have difficulty ripening them, because tomatoes need at least six hours of sunlight each day. Grow a northern variety such as Sub-Arctic Maxi, Rocket, or Scotia, and bring the fruits indoors to ripen in a cool, dark place. Experiment with plantings

Ann Reilly

One or two cherry tomato plants produce a great quantity of fruit over a long period of time, and they provide a cheery decorative accent as well.

of several varieties recommended for areas with low amounts of sunshine (ask your county Extension Service agent).

Our tomatoes got big this year, but they never turned dark red. What happened?

Perhaps they suffered from sunscald, which happens when temperatures reach the nineties, or when intense sunlight shines directly on the fruit. Varieties resistant to sunscald bear large leaves that hide the fruit. Use tomato cages.

During the season pick your tomatoes as they ripen. If a fall frost is approaching, pull up the entire plants and hang them upside-down in a sheltered place, such as a garage, where they'll ripen in time. You can also ripen green tomatoes by putting them in a paper bag with an apple.

What pests and diseases bother tomatoes?

The most common tomato pests are aphids, flea beetles, Colorado potato beetles, hornworms, cutworms, and whiteflies. See pgs. 656-57 for controls. Of diseases, early blight is one of the most common, especially among early, determinate varieties. It appears as brown spots ringed by an expanding circle, which spreads from the lower to the upper leaves. To avoid it, lay an organic mulch around your plants, and water from below rather than above. Practice clean garden sanitation, including the removal of weeds and fall crop residues. Leaf spot can be controlled by crop rotation. If fusarium and verticillium wilts are a problem in your area, plant resistant varieties. Nematode deterrence is also bred into some plants. Tobacco mosaic can be prevented by never smoking near tomato plants, never handling tomato plants with unwashed hands after you have smoked, and never planting tobacco nearby.

Turnips; Rutabagas *(Brassica)*

What is the difference between turnips and rutabagas?

Turnips are a hardy root crop with tasty and highly nutritious greens; rutabagas (also called Swedes) are their cousins, and are more reliable keepers than turnips for winter storage. Although turnips are usually white-fleshed and rutabagas yellow-fleshed, there are yellow turnips and white rutabagas. Turnips bear the more tender greens of the two. The roots of raw turnips and rutabagas make crisp, flavorful additions to salads, both contribute a full, sweet flavor to soups and stews, and both are also delicious boiled or steamed, mashed, and served with butter.

When should I plant turnips?

Turnips grow faster than rutabagas, and can be seeded in early spring to mid-spring and again in late summer and early fall.

Frost doesn't bother them. Rutabagas take from ninety to over one hundred days to mature, depending on the variety and cultural conditions, and in colder regions they are usually planted in late spring to midsummer for a fall harvest and winter storage. In warmer areas they are planted in early spring and in early to late fall. Sow the seeds of each directly in the ground, ½ inch deep and 1 inch apart in rows 1 foot apart. Thin so that plants stand 4 to 6 inches apart. The thinnings are tasty eaten raw or steamed.

What can I do to provide the best growing environment for turnips?

Try to keep both turnips and rutabagas growing steadily, but not fast. They will do best in slightly alkaline soil (add lime if your soil is at all acid). The soil should be moist and low in nitrogen but enriched with potassium—apply 2 pounds of wood ashes, greensand, or granite dust per 100 feet of row to alleviate excess nitrogen.

How will I know when turnips are ready to be harvested?

Harvest both turnips and rutabagas on or before their maturity dates, as roots that grow too big will become tough. This is especially true for turnips. Harvest rutabagas for storage after they have been hit by a few frosts. Store them as you would carrots, in very cold, wet sand or sawdust (see page 673).

Zone Map

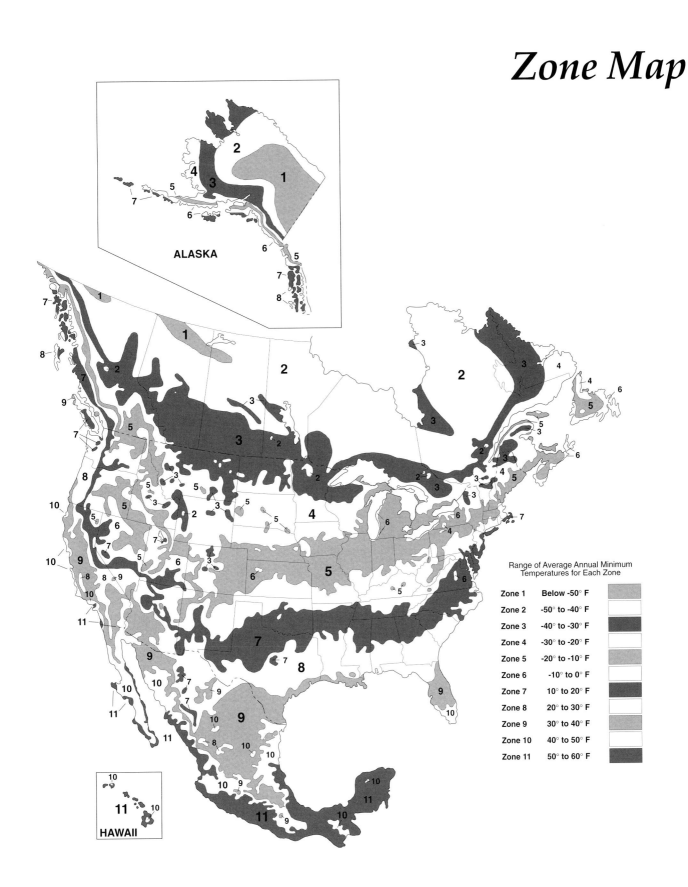

ALASKA

HAWAII

Range of Average Annual Minimum
Temperatures for Each Zone

Zone 1	Below -50° F
Zone 2	-50° to -40° F
Zone 3	-40° to -30° F
Zone 4	-30° to -20° F
Zone 5	-20° to -10° F
Zone 6	-10° to 0° F
Zone 7	10° to 20° F
Zone 8	20° to 30° F
Zone 9	30° to 40° F
Zone 10	40° to 50° F
Zone 11	50° to 60° F

Index